SPECIAL
TOPICS
IN

POLICING

SECOND EDITION

Harry W. More

anderson publishing co.
2035 Reading Rd.
Cincinnati, OH 45202
(800) 582-7295

Special Topics in Policing, Second Edition

Copyright © 1992, 1998
Anderson Publishing Co.
2035 Reading Rd.
Cincinnati, OH 45202

Phone 800.582.7295 or 513.421.4142
Web Site www.andersonpublishing.com

Library of Congress Cataloging-in-Publication Data

More, Harry W.
    Special topics in policing / Harry W. More -- 2nd ed.
        p.   cm.
    Includes bibliographical references and index.
    ISBN 0-87084-839-9 (pbk.)
    1. Police--United States.   I. Title.
HV8141.M66   1998
363.2'0973--dc21

                                98-11109
                                CIP

Cover design by Edward Smith Design/New York, NY

EDITOR Elisabeth Roszmann Ebben
ASSISTANT EDITOR Elizabeth A. Shipp
ACQUISITIONS EDITOR Michael C. Braswell

Preface

The police are one of the few parts of the criminal justice system that have constant and continuing daily contact both with crime and the public. The entire system—courts and corrections as well as the police—is charged with enforcing the law and maintaining order, but it must be remembered that the police funnel miscreants and alleged violators of the law into the system. For the most part, the police perform this function with limited scrutiny on the part of other elements of the justice system. The distinctive feature concerning the police responsibility is their charge of performing these functions where all eyes are upon them and where the going is roughest—on the street. The police are arbiters of personal conduct on the part of citizens, and in many instances the actions they take offend victims as well as violators. The police see the raw side of life, ranging from automobile accidents to murders, and must intercede as agents of the law. Because this is a time of increasing violence, social unrest, and increasing public sensitivity to both, it is a time when police work is particularly significant, complicated, conspicuous, and delicate. In fact, it has never been more demanding of the individual officer and the police organization. The police are at a critical point of change. It presents them with a challenge that must be confronted with initiative and innovation.

Over the years, the police have assumed primary responsibility for dealing daily with crime—where, when, and as it occurs. This concept is changing slowly as community policing begins to dominate the way the police deal with the crime problem. The fact is, of course, even under the most favorable conditions, the ability of the police to act against crime is limited. The police did not create, and cannot resolve, the social conditions that stimulate crime. They did not start, and cannot stop, the convulsive social changes taking place in America. They do not enact the laws they enforce, nor do they dispose of the criminals they arrest. The police are only one part of the criminal justice system; the criminal justice system is only one part of the government; and the government is only one part of society.

The police encounter a broad spectrum of critical issues such as policing in a free society, the use of deadly force by officers, and the murder of police officers. Unionization is included because of the continuing conflict between unions and management. Stress remains a perennial problem as policing becomes more complex and dangerous. Other significant issues include corruption, the increasing use of female officers, and the implications of equality. For the first time since the initial publication of this text in 1972, a chapter is included that discusses crime and the political process. The politics of justice has been honed to a fine cutting edge as used by President Bill Clinton at the national level, and numerous politicians at state and local levels.

Not to be overlooked, this edition includes a discussion of the importance of roles and values to the policing process as a foundation for current policing patterns. Finally, consideration is given to internal as well as external review of police conduct, and the reality of enforcing the law. These topics are selected for inclusion in this text because they represent perennial problems. Students of criminal justice must give serious consideration to these issues if law enforcement is to function adequately in today's changing society.

Harry W. More

ACKNOWLEDGMENTS

Many individuals contributed to the completion of this work by either providing material or granting permission to reproduce material appearing in other publications. William Nay, U.S. Department of Energy, Washington, DC assisted in the research for material on affirmative action. I would like to thank the following individuals who provided information utilized in the preparation of the text: Sam H. Killman, Chief (ret.), Charlotte, North Carolina Police Department; William A. Geller, Associate Director, Police Executive Research Forum, Washington, DC; Captain Tom Nishisaka, Milpitas, CA Police Department; Don Burr, Acting Chief, Milpitas, CA Police Department; Richard P. Emerson, Chief, Chula Vista, CA Police Department; Terry More, Sergeant (ret.), Palo Alto, CA Police Department; James D. Sewell, Director, Criminal Justice Information Systems, Florida, Department of Public Safety, Tallahassee, FL; Louise A. Cobarruviaz, Chief, San Jose, CA Police Department; Suzie Sawyer, Executive Director, COPS, Camdenton, MO; William F. Powers, Director, Public Safety Officers' Benefits Program, Department of Justice, Washington, DC; Michael J. Farrell, Deputy Commissioner, Policy and Planning, Police Department, City of New York; Mark Fazzini, Olympia Fields, IL Police Department; Louis Freeh, Director, Federal Bureau of Investigation, Washington, DC; Philip Wilcox, Office of the Coordinator for Counterintelligence, U.S. Department of State, Washington, DC; Claire Gonzales, U.S. Equal Employment Opportunity Commission, Washington, DC; Willie Williams, former Chief, Los Angeles, CA Police Department; Katherine Mader, Inspector General, Los Angeles, CA Police Department; Penny E. Harrington, Director, National Center for Women and Policing; Douglas F. Smith, Chief of Police, Tucson, AZ Police Department; Mary C. Dunlap. Director, Office of Citizens Complaints, Police Commission, City and County of San Francisco, San Francisco, CA; Loren Siegel, Director, Public Education Department, American Civil Liberties Union; Ida L. Castro, Director-designate, Women's Bureau, U.S. Department of Labor.

Additional thanks are extended to the following organizations: Charles C Thomas, Publisher; Association for the Sexually Abused; American Bar Association; Commission on Accreditation for Law Enforcement Agencies; Law Enforcement News; San Jose Mercury News; Arizona Daily Star; Law and Order; and the International Association of Chiefs of Police. Additionally, The American Federation of State, County and Municipal Employees; the Southern

Poverty Law Center; Center for Democratic Renewal; International Association for Civilian Oversight of Law Enforcement; National Institute Against Prejudice and Violence; Municipal Reference and Research Library, City of New York; and Office of NYC Criminal Justice Coordinator, City of New York.

Special thanks must be given to my wife, Ginger, for her support during the development of this manuscript, resulting in the success of this text since its initial publication almost 30 years ago. I would like to commend the editor of this text, Elisabeth Roszmann Ebben, for her support and outstanding expertise.

1998

TABLE OF CONTENTS

CRIME: ITS NATURE AND EXTENT IN A POLITICAL ENVIRONMENT

1

The study of this chapter will enable you to:

1. Describe the importance of crime as a community problem.

2. Compare crimes reported to the police to crime rates identified in victimization studies.

3. Identify the types of crimes that are viewed as real neighborhood problems.

4. List five reasons that cause individuals to report personal crimes.

5. Write an essay describing the arming of America.

6. Describe the implementation of the "Brady Bill."

7. Discuss handgun victimization.

8. Compare the presidential campaigns of 1988 and 1992.

9. Compare the 1996 presidential campaigns of Clinton and Dole.

10. Describe the way local politicians use the crime issue to their advantage.

11. Discuss the impact on a community when crime statistics are altered.

12. Specify the extent of the police role in the political process.

13. Describe the impact of the Law Enforcement Steering Committee on legislation that affects the police process.

14. Discuss the duties performed by the legislative counsel of the International Association of Chiefs of Police.

There are no greater immediate needs in this free society than the control and reduction of crime. It is paramount in the minds of most Americans who change their lifestyle, turn homes into fortresses and, in increasing numbers, arm themselves. In one study, a majority of the respondents indicated that they were afraid to walk alone at night and many felt unsafe at home. When queried about the threat of crime, only a little more than one-quarter felt they were safe in their community (Maguire and Pastore, 1996: 148).

Regarding self-protective measures to combat crime, respondents stated that they: installed special locks (43%); had a dog for protection (38%); bought a gun (30%); carried a weapon (27%); installed a burglar alarm (18%), and 10 percent carried a whistle. (Maguire and Pastore, 1993: 187 and 193). All of these measures serve to alter the lifestyle of citizens and indicate the great concern they have about crime. In some instances, particularly for the elderly, it has made people prisoners in their own homes. The key variable in this instance is the fear of crime. It is amazing that each day we move closer to the type of society described in the President's Crime Commission of the 1960s. It viewed our cities as armed enclaves where people moved from one secure place to another secure place on freeways fully aware that between home and a place of work they were living in an asphalt jungle. As one reads the newspaper, listens to the radio, or watches television, crime news plays a very important part in the total presentation. It is a key element in news reporting and ratings are paramount in the topics selected for presentation. Bad news dominates good news.

Drive-by shootings, carjackings, home invasions, serial killers, and the abduction of children all reinforce the belief that crime is rampant. To this has been added bike-jackings as another crime that affects many in our nation. It is no wonder that an increasing number of Americans have developed a siege mentality. The Center for Media and Public Affairs monitored the three major television networks and found that the number of crime stories on the evening news in 1995 had quadrupled since 1991. This can only be described as a television crime wave (Whitman, Ito, and Kost, 1996: 54-62). Stories about crime took up twice as much time on local news as reports on other events such as politics or education (Burchell, 1996: 8A). When the public was asked if there was too much violence on television, 80 percent responded there was too much (Maguire and Pastore, 1994: 236). In another survey, 74 percent of the respondents felt that television programs contributed to violence (Maguire and Pastore, 1996: 222).

There is clear-cut evidence that television is one factor that causes violence in our nation. Violence on television is more than a reflection of its occurrence in our society—it is a reality and it is difficult to refute. Some claim that a cause and effect relationship between media violence and the acts of violence that have become a part of our daily life cannot be shown. But some 3,000 studies of this critical issue refute that argument.

There have been 84 major studies that have demonstrated a causal relationship between media violence and societal violence. In one other major study, paid for by NBC, the causal relationship was refuted, but an ensuing review of the study by three experts concluded that the evidence did show a causal relationship (Cannon, 1995: 17-24). Even those who do not support this position admit that there is probably too much violence on television. Anecdotal evidence, time and again, demonstrates that offenders imitate violence that they have seen on television.

There is no question that the presentation of negative news influences the attitudes of many toward the extent and nature of our crime problem. If a large segment of the population thinks that crime is rampant, then it is rampant, and an effort should be made to deal with the fear generated by this belief. This problem is exemplified by a nationwide survey. Participants responded to the question, "Is there more crime in your area than there was a year ago, or less?" Forty-six percent felt that there was more crime, and 20 percent responded that there was less crime. Approximately 25 percent believed the crime level was the same (Maguire and Pastore, 1996: 134).

This raises a number of questions. What governmental agencies other than the police should be responsible for dealing with crime? Specifically, for what can the police be held accountable when performing their duties? Do citizens have some responsibility in providing for their own safety and welfare? Can we ever return to a society where one would feel free to leave doors unlocked or windows open? Must one limit activities because of crime? These are perennial questions and in some instances, with all of our knowledge about crime, we are still in the dark when it comes to much, other than descriptive rhetoric. The real cause of crime still eludes us and the best way to deal with crime is still a challenge. We must continue to deliberate about this complex problem and hopefully, over time, we will be up to the challenge.

Crime as a Community Problem

Americans rate the crime rate as a significant problem in their community. When asked the question "What do you think is the most important problem facing this country today?" respondents stated that crime (23 percent) was an important problem, followed by health care and unemployment (Maguire and Pastore, 1996: 114). Over the years, during periods when the economy is relatively good and unemployment is low, people have the tendency to identify other problems that are of importance to them such as crime. This does not minimize its importance, but places the crime problem in proper perspective. The sheer volume of crime overwhelms the criminal justice system.

The subtitle of a book by Judge Harold J. Rothwax best describes the current system as *collapsing*. He describes the system as following an arcane process that ignores the truth and protects the defendant at all costs (Rothwax, 1996: 232-238). The statistics in Table 1-1 reflect the number and rate (per 100,000 population) of offenses known to the police and illustrate the enormity of the problem. These statistics show that from 1967 to 1996 the number of reported index crimes increased per 100,000 population from 2,989.7 to 5,078.9. What is most disturbing is that during those years, the police reported an increase of 34 percent in violent crimes (murder, non-negligent manslaughter, forcible rape, robbery, and aggravated assault) and a 58 percent increase in property crimes (burglary, larceny-theft, motor vehicle theft, and arson). What is more shocking is that in 1994 there were 544,880 offenses in which victims were murdered, robbed, or assaulted with some type of firearm (Federal Bureau of Investigation, 1996: 85-94). No matter how one looks at it, our society is violent.

At the same time, there has been a reduction in crime index offenses over the last five years, but this has not altered the public perception that crime is rampant. The deeply held public fear of crime that developed over decades may be slow to dissipate even in the best of circumstances (Johnson, 1997: 9-14). In 1996, violent and property crimes dropped. The most dramatic decline was in murder, which was considerably below the peak of 24,700 murders in 1991. Additionally, there was a six and one-half percent decline in violent crimes during 1996 compared to the previous year, but this was 13 percent above the 1987 level. Why the decline? Some argue that it is because of improvements in policing (Karmen, 1996: 8-10); others attribute the decline to the maturation of the drug market (Montgomery, 1996: 1 & 8A).

Credit is also given to technological innovations, such as mapping software. Another view is that demographics are quite favorable at this time. The number of people in their late teens are at a very low point and this is the group that commits a large number of crimes. Others take the position that the reduction in crime has been caused by the greater involvement of numerous people in the lives of teenagers rather than letting them grow up by themselves. Additionally, some point out that anti-crime efforts by neighborhood groups has reduced crime.

Pessimists point out that the number of teenagers will rise sharply during the first decade of the twenty-first century. Other possible factors include what appears to be the reaction to the extensive negative publicity generated by the Rodney King incident. For example, in Los Angeles in the five years since the videotaped beating, arrests dropped by more than 100,000 in a five-year period. It seems that officers do not want to be identified as a problem officer so they make fewer arrests and as a consequence receive fewer complaints (*Law Enforcement News*, 1996a: 1).

It should also be noted that approximately one-fourth of arrests, in many departments, do not result in further processing through the criminal justice system because of lack of evidence. This time-honored technique of order maintenance has resulted in artificially inflated crime statistics. It is a process sanctioned by police administrators to the detriment of those arrested. There is not a clear-cut reason as to why the crime rate is falling, but someone will always take credit for such an event. Politicians and police administrators have no qualms about taking credit for the reduction of crime even though it is largely beyond their control. We live in a time when crime is clearly excessive, but its solution continues to be evasive.

Table 1-1
Offenses Known to the Police

Year	Total Crime Index	Violent Crime	Property Crime
1967	5,903,400	499,930	5,403,500
1977	10,984,500	1,029,580	9,955,000
1987	13,508,700	1,484,000	12,024,700
1992	14,438,191	1,932,274	12,505,917
1993	14,140,952	1,924,188	12,218,777
1994	13,989,543	1,857,670	12,127,507
1995	13,867,143	1,798,785	12,068,358
1996	13,437,614	1,682,278	12,063,935
Rate per 100,000 Population			
1967	2,989.7	253.2	2,736.5
1977	5,077.6	475.9	4,601.7
1987	5,550.0	609.7	4,940.3
1992	5,660.2	757.5	4,902.7
1993	5,484.4	746.8	4,737.6
1994	5,373.5	713.6	4,660.0
1995	5,277.6	684.6	4,593.0
1996	5,078.9	634.1	4,444.8

Source: Federal Bureau of Investigation (1976, 1986, 1988, 1993, 1994, 1995, 1996, 1997). *Crime in the United States, 1975,1985,1987,1994,1995,1996*. Washington, DC: U.S. Department of Justice, USGPO.

The above table reflects crimes reported to the police that diverge markedly from victimization studies. Table 1-2 compares the victimization rate and the crime index for selected years. The percentage difference between the sources is significant. It is clear that statistics reported to the FBI clearly underestimate crime. In 1995 there was a 35 percent difference between the two rates. The victimization survey for 1995 reflected a drop of 6.6 percent in the total number of crimes committed when compared to the previous year. If the police are to deal realistically with the crime problem, they should use victimization statistics because they more closely represent the reality of what has happened to people, and use the UCR measures as an indication of crime reported to the police.

The specific types of crimes that citizens view as problems in their neighborhoods are set forth in Table 1-3.

From these statistics it is apparent that citizens do not even feel safe in their homes. Slightly more than one-third had their home invaded, which leaves one feeling helpless against the world. Crime strips one of dignity and when this is coupled with the sale or use of drugs (34 percent), as a real neighborhood problem, it is easy seen why so many are *afraid* of crime and suffer from it as well as the deterioration that occurs in crime-infested neighborhoods.

Table 1-2
Comparing Crimes Reported to the Police to Vicitimization Studies

Year	Crime Index	Victimizations	Difference
1977	10,980,500	40,314,380	29,329,880
1987	13,508,700	35,336,440	21,827,740
1992	14,438,191	33,649,000	19,210,809
1993	13,140,952	43,547,000	30,407,048
1994	13,989,543	42,362,840	28,373,297
1995	13,867,143	38,446,000	24,578,857
1996	13,473,614	N/A	N/A

Source: Federal Bureau of Investigation (1977, 1987, 1988, 1993, 1994, 1995, 1996, 1997). *Crime in the United States, 1978, 1988, 1994, 1995,* Washington, DC: USGPO; Department of Justice, *Criminal Victimization in the United States: 1973-1990, 1992,* Washington, DC: USGPO; Lisa Bas (1995). *Criminal Victimization 1994,* Washington, DC: U.S. Department of Justice; Bruce Taylor (April 1997). *Changes in Criminal Victimization, 1994-1995,* Washington, DC: Bureau of Justice Statistics.

Table 1-3
Types of Crimes that are Viewed as Real Neighborhood Problems

Crime	Percentage
Breaking into Houses	35
Sale or Use of Drugs	34
Attacks on People on the Street	13
Attacks on Older People	11
Prostitution	6
Gambling	6
Drunkenness	24
Auto Thefts	25
Knifings and Shootings	12
Rape	9

Source: Kathleen Maguire and Ann L. Pastore (eds.) (1994). *Sourcebook of Criminal Justice Statistics 1993.* Washington, DC: U.S. Department of Justice, Bureau of Justice Statistics.

It is interesting to review the reasons individuals report personal and household victimizations to the police. Table 1-4 lists these reasons, which range from stopping or preventing the incident to punishing an offender. Noteworthy is that 5.2 percent of the respondents felt it was their duty to report an offense. Approximately 23.9 percent reported it because it was a crime. In addition, 5.0 percent reported an offense because they wanted to recover their personal property and 8.7 percent wanted to prevent crimes by the offender against anyone. Altogether, the reasons for reporting crime can serve as a base for the police working with members of the community in an effort at resolving personal crimes.

Table 1-4
Distribution of Reasons for Reporting Personal Crimes

Reason	Percentage
To Stop or Prevent This Incident	14.5
Needed Help Due to Injury	2.1
In Order to Collect Insurance	0.3
To Recover Property	5.0
Prevent Further Crime	17.1
Prevent Crimes by Offender Against Anyone	8.7
To Punish Offender	7.3
To Catch or Find Offender	5.6
To Improve Police Surveillance	2.0
Duty to Notify Police	5.2
Because it Was a Crime	23.9
Some Other Reason	7.1
Not Available	1.2
	100.0

Source: U.S. Department of Justice (1997). *Criminal Victimization 1994.* Washington, DC: Department of Justice.

Whatever one's perspective of crime and its causation, it remains a vexing problem, but one must realize that historically violent crime rates have been much higher. In medieval times, Europe had approximately 10 times the murder rate that we have today. Furthermore, during the Great Depression, the murder rate was about the same as it is today. Violent crime is not a new phenomenon and it is not endemic to America, but at the same time it must be dealt with. It is not just a police problem, but something that our society must actively confront. We should accept the fact that crime is eclectic in origin. We must give up looking for scapegoats and work diligently to reduce crime and make our cities and towns better places in which to live. If there is any potential for the reduction of violence, it is to start thinking about ways to strengthen the family and foster individual responsibility (Kopel, 1995: 273).

responsibility

The Arming of America

At the same time that we have become totally frustrated by the ever-flourishing crime rate and intensifying violence, the arming of America has become a reality (Kleck, 1995: 12-47; Spitzer, 1995: 6-17). The U.S. Bureau of Alcohol, Tobacco and Firearms (BATF) estimated that in 1991 Americans owned 230 million firearms. This means that there are eight firearms for every 10 Americans or 2.1 weapons per household (Reynolds and Caruth, 1992: 14). In effect, it is the highest rate of private gun ownership in the world. Data from one survey found that 50 percent of those questioned reported having a gun in their home or garage. (Witkin, 1996: 32). Only one-third of the guns known to be in circulation are handguns, and when owners of these weapons were asked why they owned a handgun, about 40 percent responded that they owned the gun for sport and recreational activities, 40 percent owned a handgun for self-defense, and the remainder indicated that their occupation required ownership of a weapon (Wright, 1995: 65).

In the National Survey of Private Ownership of Firearms (NSPOF) it was found that 14 million adults (approximately one-third of gun owners) carried firearms for protection at least once during the previous 12 months. Four million of them indicated that they carried guns for protection "in connection with work." Two-thirds who carried guns kept them in their vehicles, while the others sometimes carried them on their person. Respondents who owned at least one gun stated they purchased a weapon to defend themselves against criminals. Slightly more than one-half of the gun owners said that their firearms (handgun and long guns) were stored unlocked, and one-fifth had an unlocked loaded weapon in their home. Overall, the proportion of American households that keep firearms appears to be declining (Cook and Ludwig, 1997: 1-12).

Survey data for the period between 1987 and 1992 estimated that guns were used for self-defense 82,000 times annually out of 1.5 million instances of criminal violence involving firearms. Estimates of defensive gun use (DGUs) vary. For example, the 1994 NSPOF estimated 23 million DGUs. When the estimate met the criteria of Kleck and Gertz, however, the number dropped to 4.7 million. Regardless which estimate one believes, only a small fraction of adults used guns defensively in 1994. One problem is that the DGU data are open to debate as to whether the ownership of firearms deters crime or makes it more deadly (Kleck and Gertz, 1995: 150-187; Cook and Ludwig, 1997: 1-12). Another problem is that the term *self-defense* is a vague term. Among a sample of prisoners, 48 percent of those who fired their guns while committing crimes claimed that they did so in self-defense (Roth, 1994: 4). Notwithstanding this problem, guns probably are used infrequently in self-defense because the criminals often rely on stealth, suprise, or sudden force to achieve their goal. Few victims have sufficient time to secure a weapon. Although many gun owners keep a gun in their home at least in part for self-protection, studies conducted over the past decade suggest that the risks of keeping a gun in the home outweigh the potential benefits (Kellerman, 1996: 1).

Males are more apt to own guns than females, as are whites than African-Americans, older than middle-aged or young, and rural than urban individuals (Maguire and Pastore, 1994: 203). This means that the person who is most apt to own a weapon is a white male who is beyond middle age and lives in a rural area.

The arming of Americans has taken another twist as indicated by a dramatic increase in the number of states that have adopted laws allowing citizens to carry a concealed weapon. Florida passed such a law on October 1, 1987 (Reynolds and Caruth, 1992: 14-16). Since the passage of the Florida law, a total of 266,710 permits have been issued, and of that number 470 permits were revoked at a later date. Of those revoked, 242 occurred because the permit holder committed a crime, and of that number only 19 involved the use of a weapon (Lee, 1995: 16). On May 22, 1995, the state of Oklahoma passed a concealed weapons act. This was followed by Idaho, which passed legislation enhancing an existing law that required sheriffs to issue a permit within 60 days after an eligible person filed an application.

In Texas, on May 26, 1995, the governor signed a bill allowing responsible citizens to carry a concealed handgun. Eligible Texans who are 21 years of age or older are issued a concealed weapons permit after completion of a 15-hour training course and successfully passing a weapons proficiency test (Lee, 1995: 15-16). Since November 1995, Texans received 98,148 licenses to carry concealed weapons. Applicants must pay $140 for a four-year permit, and upon renewal permit holders must complete a four-hour refresher handgun course. Since the enactment of this law, there have been 23 reported incidents involving those who have a license. Of these, there were two shooting deaths and two suicides (*Law Enforcement News*, 1996c: 23). Permit holders are not allowed to carry a concealed firearm in city buildings in 14 of the largest cities in Texas. The attorney general has issued several legal opinions upholding the right of local government, businesses, and transit systems to ban concealed weapons in specific instances when signs are posted (*Law Enforcement News*, 1996d: 1).

During the same year, three other states passed concealed weapons legislation—Utah, Arkansas, and Virginia—bringing the total to 31 states that have concealed weapons legislation. With the emphasis on local or state control in this nation it can readily be seen that where one lives has a decided impact on the ease with which one can obtain a concealed weapons permit or be denied one. It is interesting to note that, historically, the sheriff or the chief of police has had unilateral power, in many instances, to deny or restrict the issuance of licenses. As new state laws have been passed, the power to issue concealed weapons permits has been taken away from the police, who have been accused of favoring friends when issuing permits (Witkin, 1996: 32).

Typical of concealed weapons laws is the one passed in Arizona where 33,000 individuals received concealed weapons permits as of the beginning of 1996. The Department of Public Safety issues permits based on the following applicant criteria (Arizona Department of Public Safety, 1994: 1-9):

- A resident of the state.

- Twenty-one years of age or older.

- Not under indictment for and has not been convicted in any jurisdiction of a felony.

- Does not suffer from mental illness and has not been adjudicated mentally incompetent or committed to a mental institution.

- Is not unlawfully present in the United States.

- Satisfactorily completes a firearms safety training course.

If an applicant is cleared after the background check and completion of a two-day firearms safety training course, a permit is issued for four years. The class emphasizes the awesome responsibility that goes with carrying a concealed weapon for lawful self-defense. Stress is placed on the fact that if one finds it necessary to use the weapon, the law will only protect the carrier of the concealed weapon if every action has been within the law. In fact, the majority of the classroom time is spent on the importance of using the firearm as a last resort and within legal requirements.

Feature

Concealed Weapons Permits for Sale

In one small town in California the chief of police issued concealed weapons permits to more than one-half of the residents. The fee was $500.00 and as a result of this the town made $50,000.00, clearly a tidy sum for a small town with 833 residents. The licensing process was extended to non-residents and it was anticipated that the concealed weapons fees would bring in $176,000, increasing the police department's budget by 80 percent. The Attorney General of the State of California froze the town's licensing process and took the official position that the town could only charge $3.00 for a permit unless the voters approved a higher fee.

Source: *Law Enforcement News*, John Jay College of Criminal Justice (1996). "Fighting Gun Battles on Several Fronts." Vol. XXII, No. 458, December 31: 23.

Other states are very restrictive in the issuance of concealed weapons permits. In San Mateo County, California, guidelines for determining eligibility require residents to prove that they have a high exposure to attack, that a death threat has been received, or that their life is at stake. If one meets the criteria and a background investigation is successfully completed, a license for one year is issued. The application fee is $85.00 and the annual renewal fee is $21.00. In the County of San Mateo, approximately 200 individuals are authorized to carry a concealed weapon and between 20 and 30 applicants are rejected annually (Mena, 1996: 5B). The restriction for issuance of a concealed weapons permit in San Mateo County is such that the vast majority of citizens are not eligible for a permit. It would seem that if one lived in a high-crime area of the county or was genuinely afraid that these factors would be sufficient grounds for obtaining a permit, but such is not the case.

In a 1996 study, John Lott of the University of Chicago Law School took the position that research indicated that concealed-handgun laws deter violent crime. This study showed that legally concealed weapons, during 1992, would have prevented 1,570 murders and 4,177 rapes. In addition, the study found that accidental deaths did not increase as a consequence of carrying legally concealed weapons. Other researchers have attacked this study, stating that there is no credible evidence to support such a conclusion (*Arizona Daily Star*, 1996, January 3: A3). The debate is likely to continue for some time to come.

The Brady Handgun Violence Prevention Act

Enacted after years of extensive debate, the Brady Bill is a highly volatile issue subject to a great deal of debate. Opponents of gun control note that criminals can easily circumvent the law by purchasing handguns on the secondary market or by having friends or spouses without a criminal record purchase a weapon from a gun dealer. More recently, some gun ranges have began to rent weapons, which is another means of circumventing the Brady Bill. Proponents acknowledge that criminal record checks alone will not prevent felons from obtaining firearms, but take the position that checks can reduce dealer sales to disqualified persons and complement other crime-control measures, such as stiffer mandatory sentences for firearms offenses (Rabkin, 1996: 4).

Since 1968, convicted felons, illegal drug users, and fugitives from justice have been barred by federal law from purchasing guns from federally licensed firearms dealers. Under the Brady Bill, other ineligible categories include fugitives from justice, unlawful drug users or addicts, and individuals adjudicated mentally defective or committed to a mental institution. It also includes persons dishonorably discharged from the armed forces, illegal aliens, and individuals who have renounced their U.S. citizenship. With the enactment of the Brady Bill, national procedures were established for dealers to verify whether customers were ineligible purchasers.

In 1994, a U.S. General Accounting Office study of 20 law enforcement jurisdictions found that of the 457,020 applications processed during the first year, 19,740 applicants were denied (4.3 percent). Almost one-half of these denials (48.7 percent) were because the prospective handgun purchasers had felony or misdemeanor criminal histories, 4.1 percent were based on other Brady ineligible categories, 0.8 percent involved restraining orders, 7.6 involved traffic offenses, and the remaining were based on administrative or other reasons.

Nearly all of the denials based on criminal histories were for felony-related reasons. Other denials based on criminal history records involved prospective handgun purchasers with outstanding misdemeanor warrants. As of July 1995, a total of seven persons had been prosecuted for making false statements on the Brady handgun purchase form. Three of these cases involved drug-related convictions, and these individuals received prison sentences of 12 to 24 months. During the first one-half of 1996, about 34,000 ineligible customers were identified and three-fourths of these rejections were based on the finding of a felony conviction or indictment (Manson and Lauver, 1997: 2). It was estimated that during 1997, 6,600 prospective handgun applicants were being rejected monthly. Since the enactment of the law, more than 86,000 sales have not occurred because background investigations indicated that the potential purchaser had a criminal record. The five-day waiting period will be eliminated in 1998 (or later) when the National Instant Criminal Background Check System goes online (Manson and Lauver, 1997: 1-5).

Nationally, the law enforcement community supported the Brady Bill. One of the leading proponents was the International Association of Chiefs of Police, which strongly expressed the need for a five-day waiting period. Other law enforcement organizations supporting the bill included:

- Major Cities Chiefs of Police

- National Association of Police Organizations

- Fraternal Order of Police

- Police Foundation

- Federal Law Enforcement Officers Association

- Police Executive Research Forum

- National Troopers Coalition

- National Organization of Black Law Enforcement Executives

- International Brotherhood of Police Organizations

Notwithstanding the support of the organizations listed above, law enforcement was not totally in accord with the Brady Bill. Eight sheriffs and one sheriff's association (Wyoming) initiated court cases challenging the constitutionality of the bill. As of July 1995, of the cases decided by district courts, all but one found that phase I of the Brady background provision was unconstitutional. The courts found that the remainder of the bill was severable and therefore operative. This was a defeat for the U.S. Department of Justice and they appealed the decisions. In September of 1995, the U.S. Court of Appeals for the Ninth Circuit upheld the constitutionality of Brady cases (Rabkin, 1996: 9-49; Kirby, 1996: 15). These cases challenge the authority of the federal government to order local and state agencies to conduct background investigations on prospective handgun purchasers. In 1997, the U.S. Supreme Court ruled that the federal government was not empowered to require state and local law enforcement agencies to conduct background checks on prospective gun buyers (Nolan, 1997: 20-24).

Study of Handgun Victimization

Another dimension of violence in America is handgun victimization. In 1992, handgun crimes accounted for about 13 percent of all violent crimes (Greenfeld, 1994: 2). On average, per year during the period 1987-1992, approximately 62,200 victims of violent crime, about one percent of all victims of violence, used a firearm to defend themselves (Kleck, 1995: 12-47). Another 20,300 used a firearm to defend their property during a theft, household burglary, or motor vehicle theft. Table 1-5 sets forth details regarding victims who used firearms for self-defense during a crime of violence.

Table 1-5
**Victims Who Used Firearms for Self-Defense
During a Crime of Violence: 1987-1992**

	Average annual number of victimizations in which victims used firearms to defend themselves or their property		
	Total	**Attacked Offender With Handgun**	**Threatened Offender With Other Gun**
All Crimes	82,500	30,600	51,900
Total Violent Crimes	62,200	25,500	36,700
With Injury	12,100	7,300	4,900
Without Injury	50,000	18,220	31,800
Theft, Burglary, Motor Vehicle Theft	20,300	5,100	15,200

Source: Michael R. Rand (April 1994). "Guns and Crime." *Crime Data Brief,* Washington, DC: U.S. Department of Justice.

Approximately 37 percent of the victims who defended themselves with a firearm attacked the offender, and the others threatened the offender with the weapon. One-fifth of the victims who defended themselves with a firearm suffered an injury, compared to almost one-half of those who defended themselves with weapons other than a firearm or who had no weapon. On average, between 1987 and 1992, about 35 percent (or 22,000 per year) of the violent crime victims defending themselves with a firearm faced an offender who also had a firearm. Males were twice as likely as females to be victims of handgun crimes, and African-Americans three times as likely as whites. Of all the groups, young African-American males continued to be the population subgroup most vulnerable to handgun crime victimization. For males age 16-19, the rate for African-Americans (40 per 1,000) was four times that of whites (10 per 1,000). For males age 20-24, the rate for African-Americans (29 per 1,000) was more than three times that of whites (9 per 1,000). Until recently, firearms injury data were not readily available. A recent study by the Centers for Disease Control and Prevention (CDC) found that about 17 percent of the victims of nonfatal gun crimes were injured and almost one-half of these victims were shot in an arm, hand, leg, or foot. Nine of 10 victims of gunshot wounds were male and about six of 10 were African-American. About one-half of the victims were between 15 and 24 years of age (Zawitz, 1996: 1-3).

Offenders, more than ever, are armed. Since 1965, the arrest rate for weapons offenses has more than doubled. Juveniles accounted for 16 percent of those arrested for weapons offenses in 1974 and 23 percent in 1993. Between 1985 and 1993, the number of juvenile arrests for weapons offenses increased by more than 100 percent, from just under 30,000 to more than 61,000. Eighteen-year-old males have the highest per capita arrest rate (1,007 per 100,000 population). Most arrests for weapons violations occur in cities (81%), then in the suburbs (14%), followed by rural areas (5%). The following table lists weapons offense arrests by race and age.

Table 1-6
Weapons Offense Arrests by Race and Age: 1993

	Weapons offense arrests per 100,000 population		
Race	Total	Age 18 or Over	Under Age 18
Total	105	109	94
White	70	69	73
Black	362	430	221
Other	40	41	37

Source: Lawrence A. Greenfeld and Marianne W. Zawitz, November 1995, *Weapons Offenses and Offenders,* Washington, DC: U.S. Department of Justice, Bureau of Justice Statistics, 3.

Young African-Americans are doubly exposed to weapons. Not only are they more apt to be a victim of a weapons offense, but they are five times more likely to be arrested for a weapons violation than whites. Weapons offenders in state prisons were more likely to be African-American (56%), and in federal prisons 35 percent of those convicted of weapons violations were African-American.

While juvenile weapons violations are of increasing concern, other offenders still dominate in this area. In 1993, state and local law enforcement agencies made 262,300 arrests in which a weapons offense was the most serious charge. Since 1974, the arrest rates have remained fairly constant for weapons offenses, while the number of violent offenses committed with a firearm increased 78 percent. What happens to weapons offenders is especially interesting. In state courts, two-thirds of the offenders convicted of felony weapons offenses were sentenced to incarceration. The average sentence length was approximately four years for those sentenced to prison and six months for those sentenced to jail. This compares to 1984 felony offenders, who spent 11 fewer months in prison (Greenfeld and Zawitz, 1995: 3-5). This is a significant increase in the amount of time spent in prison and reflects increasing concern about weapons violations.

Unfortunately, firearms are plentiful, easily obtained, and regularly used by offenders in major urban areas. As might be expected, the illegal firearms market has played a large role in providing arrestees with access to weapons. In one study, the majority of those interviewed reported that it was easy to obtain firearms illegally, and one-third of the arrestees said they could obtain a gun in less than a week. Arrestees' beliefs about firearms suggest a set of norms that support and encourage the use of guns to settle disputes (Travis, 1995: 1-2).

Violent crime in America is not a new phenomenon. It has been with us since the inception of our nation, and although there has been a slight reduction during the last three years, it is anticipated by some that violent crime will grow more rapidly as we come into an era in which there will be an increasing number of people between the ages of 14 and 24. It is best to put such predictions in perspective. In 1993, there were approximately 21 million teenagers and seven percent were convicted of violent crimes, and many of these were repeat offenders. As dark as some may paint youth crime in America, it is best to keep in mind that 99 percent of our youth are not violent criminals (Valenti, 1996: 43).

Political Elections and Crime

Crime has become one of the focal points of every political election at almost every level of government since the end of World War II. In some instances, an election is won or lost based upon a candidate's position on crime. If the public perceives crime as a problem, politicians respond accordingly in the struggle for votes. Promises made during campaigns are, in many instances, ignored or are found to lack support as verbosity exceeds the actual implementation of policy. A campaign promise seldom has any relationship to reality. It is a means to an end. Candidates in many instances will say whatever is necessary. The following Feature illustrates the importance of the crime issue in a presidential campaign.

Feature

Bush and Dukakis on Crime

A television commercial that aired extensively after Labor Day during the 1988 presidential campaign emphasized that George Bush supported the death penalty for first-degree murderers and Michael Dukakis not only opposed the death penalty, but allowed the release of first-degree murderers from prison. The commercial then showed a mug shot of William Horton, accompanied by the statement that Horton murdered a boy, stabbing him 19 times. The commercial then pointed out that Horton, who received a life sentence, received 10 weekend passes from prison. The commercial then shifted to a news photograph showing Horton being escorted by police after being arrested for kidnapping, rape, and stabbing a man. The commercial ended with the statement, "Weekend prison passes—Dukakis on Crime."

Source: From *Crime and Politics of Hysteria* by David C. Anderson. Copyright © 1995 by David C. Anderson. Reprinted by permission of Times Books, a division of Random House, Inc.

Presidential Election of 1996

Presidential candidate Bill Clinton presented a crime control program focused on placing additional police officers on the streets of America. He reintroduced the concept of a national *police corps*, and continued his emphasis on community-based policing. Part of his 1992 campaign proposals had not been funded by

Congress, so he included these as part of his crime fighting platform. He postured himself in such a way as to emphasize a real law and order approach as crime came to be of increasing concern to the public. Such items as more funds for metal detectors in schools and encouraging states to increase the authority of school officials to search automobiles and lockers, implementation of teen curfews, and dress codes for schools that require students to wear uniforms are the antithesis of traditional Democratic approaches to crime. There has been a clear distinction between what he has done compared to his sensitivity to political winds (Kramer and Michalowski, 1995: 99). Political expediency constantly governed his position on crime.

Feature

Crime Control: America's Political Football

The public has a legitimate concern regarding the extent of crime in this nation, particularly violent crime, and the apparent inability of our justice system to deal effectively with this problem. It is a dilemma that is exploited by candidates of both political parties.

It was unprecedented, in our history, for so many police executives to appear at the White House to witness the signing and announcement of a crime-control initiative. Not to be outdone, political opponents responded by holding press conferences that focused on their own tough stance on crime.

Without question, much can be done to improve crime prevention techniques, and the processing of lawbreakers through the justice system. Unfortunately, a great many of the proposals to improve the justice system are political "feel good" measures to assuage a public victimized by crime and endangered in their pursuit of daily activities.

Source: John Warner (1996). "Crime Control: America's Political Football." *Law Enforcement News*, Vol. XXII, No. 451:12.

In his 1996 State of the Union message, President Clinton called for a crackdown on drugs and gangs in the nation's inner cities. Additionally, he urged the media to be more responsible in depicting violence that could affect children. A summary of his position is set forth in Figure 1-1.

President Clinton's crime control policies can best be described as eclectic in nature, ranging from prosecution to incarceration. Oddly enough, his overall solution to the crime problem supports the basic conservative crime control policies espoused by the Republicans, rather than the more historically Democratic approach of crime prevention and rehabilitation.

Bob Dole, throughout the 1996 presidential campaign, took the position that he was tough on crime. One of his major goals was to reduce the teen use of drugs by 50 percent within four years. He set forth an anti-drug slogan—"Just Don't Do It." Dole proposed the creation of 1,000 community-based anti-drug coalitions, no-frills prisons, limits on parole, exclusionary rule reform, and tougher penalties for child pornographers. Dole felt that Clinton's drug policy during his time in office was clearly subject to criticism. He attacked Clinton on what were perceived as inadequacies of the presidential law enforcement program, but most of his criticism seemed to fall on deaf ears.

Figure 1-1
Bill Clinton's Solution to Crime During the 1996 Presidential Campaign

1. Continued support of placing 100,000 new police officers on the streets of America.
2. Expansion of community-based policing.
3. Reiterated his desire to create a national "police corps."
4. Banning of cop-killer bullets.
5. Testing more prisoners for drugs.
6. Passage of a victim's rights constitutional amendment.
7. Addition of chemical tracers to explosives.
8. Continued support of the five-day waiting period for handgun purchases and the ban on certain assault weapons.
9. Proposed the loss of a driver's license as a tool to curb teenage drug use and drinking.
10. Tougher penalties for youth violence.
11. Tougher measures to deal with gangs and drugs.
12. Institution of a national system to track sexual offenders.
13. Support for a national community policing telephone number for non-emergency calls to authorities.
14. Increased funding for drug interdiction along the Southwest border.
15. Continuation of the Council on Crime Prevention.

Politicians' records seem to catch up with them during a political campaign. Dole criticized Clinton for cutting the drug czar's office by 25 percent even though he had voted against the creation of such an office. Additionally, Dole conveniently ignored the fact that Clinton restored the budgetary cuts. Dole attacked Clinton for a significant rise in the use of marijuana by teenagers, during the previous four years, but in actuality the increase began prior to Clinton's presidency. On the other hand, Clinton took credit for putting 100,000 new police officers on the streets of America, but as of November 1996, only 21,000 were on the streets and only 40,000 positions were funded, and these officers were distributed throughout the nation—not in the cities and communities with the greatest crime problems.

Research has demonstrated that 10 percent of all places in the United States are where approximately 60 percent of all crimes occur. However, it is more politically acceptable to distribute funds to as many communities as possible rather than fund a few communities. In fact, some towns that received funding for police officers were so small that they had never reported crime data to the FBI. Clinton continually stressed that the violent crime rate had dropped, ignoring the fact that there had been a dramatic increase in juvenile crime. These are only a few examples of the distortion and exaggeration of statistical data that have become part of presidential campaigning.

Figure 1-2
Bob Dole's Solution to Crime During the 1996 Presidential Campaign

 1. Creation of 1,000 community-based anti-drug coalitions.
 2. No-frills prisons.
 3. Specific limits on those eligible for parole.
 4. Reform of the exclusionary rule.
 5. Tougher penalties for child pornography.
 6. Appointment of tough, no-nonsense conservative judges.
 7. Victims' rights amendment to the U.S. Constitution.
 8. Crackdown on juvenile crime.
 9. Those accused of sexual assault automatically tested for HIV.
10. Mandatory drug testing of federal inmates.
11. Expansion of "Megan's Law."
12. Abandoned his pledge to repeal the assault weapons law.

Just prior to the Congressional recess for the election, the White House persuaded the Republicans to drop funding for a special commission to investigate federal law enforcement agencies. At the same time, Clinton was successful in funding a council on crime prevention. Police unions also played a part in the presidential election—the fact that Clinton received the endorsement of the 270,000 member Fraternal Order of Police was a reversal of their position because in 1992 the police union supported George Bush. Additionally Clinton won the support of the National Association of Police Organizations. Presidential candidate Dole was not without police support inasmuch as he received the endorsement of the 35,000-member New York City Patrolmen's Benevolent Association.

Local Politics and the Issue of Crime

In a study of five major cities for a period of 31 years, politics and crime were found to be almost inseparable. In fact, our history of local politics can only be described as one involving the study of corruption and the resultant calls for reform. Almost every major city has seen incumbent politicians indicted for corrupt activities and other politicians ride into office on an anti-corruption platform. Politicians have attacked opponents as being soft on crime from the podium, but when it has come to policy implementation, the actual reduction of crime has proven to be highly elusive.

Prior to the 1970s, the police, because of the large number of employees compared to other municipal entities, became pawns in the patronage game, and police officials and officers came and went as political winds shifted. The story is circulated that an incumbent mayor saw his brother-in-law working on a dump truck and called him over and appointed him to the position of chief of police. Reform movements and civil service have lessened political influence on the appointment and retention of officers, but it is still common practice for police chief executive officers to serve at the pleasure of the mayor. Overall, reform movements aroused public opinion with their exposure of graft and corruption and their general opposition to political machines (Morgan, 1989: 42).

A Philadelphia police commissioner was the arbiter of power that exceeded that found in other large cities. Typical of this is the power exercised by Commissioner Frank Rizzo. After assuming the "top cop" position in 1967, Rizzo stressed that he would respond immediately to any disturbance. In his view, he was a vigorous disciplinarian and he would not tolerate outside agitators disrupting the community. He promised to make the outside agitators who came to Philadelphia sorry and he intended to deal with them swiftly. Rizzo's position was that he wanted to avoid the civil disobedience that had occurred in Newark and Detroit (Ruchelman, 1974: 51-52).

In a few police departments, the chief's position is subject to the voting process. For example, in Santa Clara, California, the chief runs for election every four years, so without question the chief is a political actor and exerts needed effort to gain political power. Elected chiefs take the position that they are more responsive to public needs, which is similar to the opinion of sheriffs who run for office. There seems to be some truth to this assertion based on the activities of some chiefs who isolate themselves from the community they serve. An elected police executive must interact with the community on a continuing basis if he or she is to remain in office.

In some instances, cities have seen the manipulation of crime statistics as city elections approached. In Philadelphia, the larceny rate increased dramatically during the time when the police commissioner was running for mayor. During a subsequent campaign there was another increase in the larceny rate. This strongly suggests that the crime rate was manipulated (Heinz, Jacob, and Lineberry, 1983: 3-17). A strong law enforcement candidate can then actually reduce an artificially high crime after being elected. This is a key issue. When is a crime really a crime? Is it a crime or an infraction? What is the cost of a bicycle? Is it the purchase price or what someone will currently pay for it? How is that computed? Computed one way it becomes a lesser offense representing a differential crime rate. Computed another way, it becomes a felony. Crime statistics do not always reflect the reality of the situation. All one has to do is to compare the Uniform Crime Report statistics to those provided by victimization studies. Obviously, there is more crime than what is reported.

During the 1996 campaign, George Cunningham, running for state senator as a Democrat in Arizona, dealt with the crime issue by expressing his support of the death penalty, a juvenile crime bill, an adult omnibus crime bill, and a drive-by shooting bill. In newspaper advertisements, he acknowledged the support of a local sheriff, the state Fraternal Order of Police, and the Associated Highway Patrolmen. Additionally, he affirmed his support for Mothers Against

Drunk Driving. His Republican opponent, David Turner, expressed the need to be aggressive against crime and the need to break the cycle of crime through such programs as Peace Builders, support for the Family Stability Act, and neighborhood intervention. In previous elections, Republican candidates had expressed a stronger law enforcement orientation, but such was not the case during the 1996 political campaign. Democrat George Cunningham was the clear-cut winner with a solid "law and order" platform.

In one California district, the National Rifle Association was a central issue in the Senate campaign. The California Democratic Party released a brochure that criticized Bruce McPherson as a Republican candidate without mentioning his opponent. This brochure pointed out that McPherson voted no on an assault weapon ban, supported mass legalization of concealed weapons, voted to allow convicted drunk drivers to carry concealed weapons, as well as voting to allow concealed weapons to be carried in public buildings and parks.

In 1997, Mayor of New York City, Rudy Giuliani was re-elected for an additional four-year term after campaigning on a crime agenda that demonstrated a falling crime rate. Over the last three decades, crime has come to be of increasing concern to local politicians, particularly when the overall crime rate placed the community in an unfavorable light, and as can be seen in the case of New York City as dropping crime rate can be used to political advantage. As crime rates increased, it became more politically significant. Through the years, public safety has had to compete with other community problems such as transportation, unemployment, education, the quality of services, race relations, and school desegregation (Jacob, 1984: 22-24). When crime became less of a salient issue, it still remained a priority in the political agenda because it allowed many politicians to posture against crime.

Altering the Crime Rate

Tucson, Arizona, has found one means of significantly reducing the crime rate, hence statistically making the community safer. In 1996, the city council unanimously approved a plan to cut the crime rate by decriminalizing the stealing of fuel from gas stations. Thus, larceny-theft legally became a breach of contract (a civil matter) rather than a Part I uniform crime offense. With the policy change, in reporting of offenses, more than 10,000 gas theft complaints were eliminated from the crime docket and this was anticipated to move Tucson from the third highest crime rate in the United States to a position out of the top 20 (Burchell, 1996: 1-8A).

In another community, the position has been taken that credit card fraud is a penny-ante crime that that takes more time and funds to prosecute than it is worth. In one instance, a citizen was the victim of a credit card identity fraud and her credit was ruined when the suspect ran up charges of $15,000 (Kristof, 1996: 2). In other cities, the police do not investigate cases when someone writes a check involving a bank account in which there are insufficient funds. Other communities refuse to investigate forged checks under a specified amount, such as $200.

During 1996, two police commanders in New York City were alleged to have "cooked the books" in order to show a reduction in the crime rate. In one precinct, the overall crime rate decreased 40 percent over a 10-month period. An audit reflected the fact that crimes were misclassified, in some cases, felonies were classified as misdemeanors. Another commander was accused of reducing the number of assault cases by charging offenders with harassment (a lesser offense). It is alleged that the police officials were under tremendous pressure to reduce crime (*Law Enforcement News*, 1996b: 9).

The politicizing of crime has always been with us and it will continue in the future. While the increase in the crime rate has lessened slightly in the last few years, it will continue to be a major issue for the police, politicians, and many citizens. Politicians have claimed credit for the reduction of crime by citing the passage of crime bills, "three strikes and you're out" laws, sex offender registration laws, longer sentences for violent offenders and, to say the least, the recent introduction of chain-gangs (Rosen, 1995/1996: 1). To declare a continuing war on crime is like supporting apple pie and ice cream—who can be against it? The politics of crime continues.

The Police Role in the Political Process

Increasingly, police departments are becoming involved in the political process as either supporters or opponents of specific legislation, or supporters of candidates. This is a departure from the traditional posture of benign neglect, with the exception of police executive officers who attend city council meetings and respond to inquiries from council members. In the past, law enforcement agencies took the position that involvement in the legislative process was not compatible with the professional model of law enforcement. A proactive response was unacceptable. The only proper thing to do was to respond to the legislation produced by the political process. When legislation was under consideration and then eventually enacted, police agencies were forced to react, in many instances, to legislation that was difficult to enforce or actually was a detriment to the agency (Whitehead, 1993: 5-10).

Active involvement in the legislative process allows law enforcement agencies to voice needs and concerns regarding pending legislation. The police should take a position on pending bills and make every effort to influence legislation that affects the agency.

Legislative Liaison Units

Frustrated by the reality of street law enforcement and the contradictions that occur as officers enforce the law, the police have felt the need to become involved in the political process. The taboo of non-involvement in politics has gone by the wayside. Of special concern to the police are criminal laws and judicial procedures that impinge on police activities. This includes such volatile issues as the assault weapons ban, the "cop killer" bullet, concealed weapons permits, and gun registration.

Some agencies have either assigned officers to serve in a legislative liaison capacity or have created specific units to perform such functions. In Maryland, officers from local police departments and the state police serve as full-time legislative monitors. The New York City Police Department has a Legislative Affairs Unit that works with the mayor's staff, and the Denver, Colorado Police Department has a Legislative Unit within its Public Information Office. These units are proving to be highly successful, and it is anticipated that numerous law enforcement agencies will become more active in the political process.

Law Enforcement Steering Committee

In 1985, five national law enforcement associations united to oppose firearms legislation pending in the U.S. Senate. This new working group was called the Law Enforcement Steering Committee (LESC). Its first task was to modify the proposed McClure-Volkmer Act (Senate Bill 49) by drafting amendments to the bill that minimized its negative impact on law enforcement. LESC was also instrumental in influencing the manufacture and sale of armor-piercing ammunition.

Since its inception, the LESC has expanded its representation to include police research organizations, police management groups, and labor groups. Representing more than 400,000 officers, the LESC has dealt with such legislative issues as asset forfeiture, body armor, firearms, funding of state and local police agencies, terrorism, tow truck deregulation, police officers' bill of rights, and environmental crimes training (Whitehead, 1993: 5-10; Kime, 1996: 8).

International Association of Chiefs of Police

The legislative counsel of the International Association of Chiefs of Police (IACP) reviews pending legislation and court cases. For example, in a 1995 survey, it was determined that more than one-half of the state legislatures had considered amending their juvenile justice system. Colorado led the way in juvenile justice reform. In 1993, Colorado developed a system that departed dramatically from the traditional division between juveniles and adults and provided for a "third system" to handle repeat and violent juvenile offenders who were to be punished as if they were adults but at the same time required that the offenders receive treatment and counseling. In 1994 and 1995, nine states passed meaningful legislation addressing juvenile gangs and violent youthful offenders. The trend for sweeping reform of juvenile justice systems continued in 1996 as two additional states addressed this critical problem (Kime, 1996: 8). In another instance, the IACP was involved during 1996 with the Public Safety Wireless

Advisory Committee in developing a report demonstrating the importance of wireless communications systems. The report pointed out the need for additional radio frequencies for public safety (Kime, 1996: 10-11).

In its monthly publication, the legislative counsel of IACP reviews national legislation as a means of alerting its members to bills that could affect their agency. The executive director of IACP, its legislative counsel, members of the organization, and its officers contact the House of Representatives and the Senate in support of or opposition to pending legislation. Typical of its efforts was the opposition to the repeal of the "assault weapons ban" during 1996. A bitterly divided House of Representatives voted to repeal the two-year-old law with a vote of 239 to 173, but there was not enough support for the bill to overcome a possible presidential veto. Roy Kime, legislative counsel for IACP, felt that the vote was a symbolic gesture by newly elected republican (70 out of 92 new members of the 104th Congress) representatives to appease the National Rifle Association (NRA). Political observers felt that the NRA was instrumental in electing them to office (Kime, 1996: 15).

Summary

Crime is of extreme concern to many Americans. Lifestyles are changed and many people are arming themselves. Newspapers, television, and the radio give a great deal of attention to crime presentations and in some instances take up twice as much time as reports on education or politics. More than one-half of the citizens feel that there is more crime today than previously, and feel it is a serious problem where they live. One observer pointed out that the sheer volume of crime overwhelms the criminal justice system that is collapsing.

Crime is declining, but no one really knows why. Many take credit, but there is no validity to their claims. Even with a decline in violent crime, it is excessive and its solution is beyond our present knowledge. The percentage difference between the FBI crime index and victimization studies is significant, but we still use the index as our primary measure of crime. In 1995, there was a 35 percent difference between the two rates. If the police are to deal realistically with crime statistics, victimization studies should be used as the key indicator of the level of crime.

Citizens' survey responses indicate that breaking into houses and the sale or use of drugs are real neighborhood problems. Slightly more than one-third had their homes invaded, which leaves one feeling helpless. The primary reason citizens report crime is just because one has been committed. This is followed by the desire to stop or prevent the crime. Violent crime is not a new phenomenon and is not endemic to America, but at the same time it must be dealt with.

The United States has the highest rate of gun ownership in the world (Wright, 1991: 1-42). One survey found that 50 percent of those questioned reported having a gun in their home or garage. Additionally, another survey found that 5.5 percent of all adults stated that they carried a gun with them or in their car at least once during 1994. The individual who is most likely to be armed, other than the criminal, is the white male who is beyond middle age and lives in a rural area. In recent years, the number of states that allow citizens to carry concealed weapons has increased dramatically.

Currently, 31 states have concealed weapons legislation and the last three states to enact such legislation were Virginia, Utah, and Arkansas. In some of the states that do not have a concealed weapons law, the restrictions are such that very few people can obtain a permit. One study in 1996 took the position that legally concealed weapons prevented 1,570 murders and 4,177 rapes, although some researchers have attacked this study, saying that there is no credible evidence to support such a conclusion.

Since the passing of the Brady Bill, 186,000 sales of weapons have not occurred because the potential purchaser had a criminal record. Nationally, nine major law enforcement groups supported the Brady Bill and its five-day waiting period. Under the bill, those who cannot obtain a permit include felons, illegal drug users, and fugitives from justice. As of July 1995, a total of seven persons have been prosecuted for making false statements on the Brady handgun purchase form.

In 1992, handgun crimes accounted for about 13 percent of all violent crimes. Approximately one percent of all victims of violent crimes used a firearm to defend themselves. Some 38 percent of the victims who defended themselves with a firearm attacked the offender, and the others threatened the offender with a weapon. Males were twice as likely as females to be victims of handgun crimes. Of all the groups studied, young African-American males continued to be the subgroup most vulnerable to handgun victimization, and five times more likely to be arrested for a weapons violation.

Crime has been the focal point of every political election at almost every level of government since the end of World War II. This was especially true in the presidential campaigns during 1988 and 1992. In the latter campaign, the Democrats changed from their traditional position, and ran on a crime control program. In the 1996 campaign, President Bill Clinton presented a broad crime control program, ranging from an emphasis on community policing to metal detectors in schools. After the election and in his State of the Union message, President Clinton called for a crackdown on drugs and gangs.

In local politics, many politicians have accused opponents of being soft on crime, and corruption has been an issue of primary concern in many elections. In most instances, the rhetoric of crime is seldom followed by policy implementation. Incumbents in some cities have manipulated crime statistics in order to reduce an artificially high crime rate. The crime rate is a salient issue to local politicians because it allows for posturing against crime that seems to always be of interest to the electorate.

Increasingly, police departments are becoming involved in the political process. Candidates are either supported or opposed, as is specific legislation. Some departments have a legislative liaison unit that monitors legislation that is of interest to law enforcement agencies. The International Association of Chiefs of Police (IACP) reviews pending federal legislation and takes a position either in support of or opposition to specific bills. Another unit that is of increasing importance is the Law Enforcement Steering Committee, which is composed of representatives from five major law enforcement associations, and represents more than 400,000 police officers before legislative entities.

References

Anderson, David C. (1995). *Crime and Politics of Hysteria.* New York: Random House.

Arizona Daily Star (1996). "Researcher Defends Gun-Law Study." January 3:A3.

Bas, Lisa (1995). *Criminal Victimization 1994.* Washington, DC: U.S. Department of Justice.

Burchell, Joe (1996). "City Cuts Theft of Gas From List of Crimes." *The Arizona Daily Star,* January 3:1, 8A.

Cannon, Carl M. (1995). "Media Violence Increases Violence in Society." In Carol Wekesser, *Violence in the Media.* San Diego, CA: Greenhaven Press.

Cook, Philip J. and Jens Ludwig (1997). *Guns in America: National Survey on Private Ownership and Use of Firearms.* Washington, DC: Office of Justice Programs.

Federal Bureau of Investigation (1976, 1977, 1986, 1987, 1988, 1993, 1994, 1995, 1996, 1997). *Crime in the United States, 1978, 1985, 1987, 1994, 1995, 1996.* Washington, DC: Department of Justice.

Greenfeld, Lawrence A. (1994). *Firearms and Crimes of Violence.* Washington, DC: Bureau of Justice Statistics.

Greenfeld, Lawrence A. and Marianne W. Zawitz (1995). *Weapons Offenses and Offenders.* Washington, DC: Bureau of Justice Statistics.

Heinz, Anne, Herbert Jacob, and Robert L. Lineberry (1983). *Crime in City Politics.* New York: Longman.

Jacob, Herbert (1984). *The Frustration of Policy.* New York: Little, Brown and Co.

Johnson, Jean (1997). "Americans' Views on Crime and Law Enforcement." *National Institute of Justice Journal.* Washington, DC: U.S. Department of Justice.

Karmen, Andrew (1996). "What's Driving New York's Crime Rate Down?" *Law Enforcement News,* Vol. XXI, No. 456:8-10.

Kellerman, Arthur L. (1996). *Understanding and Preventing Violence: A Public Health Perspective.* Washington, DC: Office of Justice Programs.

Kime, Roy Caldwell (1996). "Legislative Alert." *The Police Chief,* Vol. LXIII, No. 2:8.

Kime, Roy Caldwell (1996). "Assault Weapons Ban Repeal Effort." *The Police Chief,* Vol. LXIII, No. 5:15.

Kime, Roy Caldwell (1996). "Deferral of Technology Legislation Anticipated." *The Police Chief,* Vol. LXIII, No. 10:10-11.

Kirby, Bill (1996). "A Preview of the Supreme Court's 1996-1997 Term." *The Police Chief,* Vol. LXIII, No. 11:15.

Kleck, G. (1995). "Guns and Violence: An Interpretive Review of the Field." *Social Pathology,* Vol. 1, No. 1:12-47.

Kleck, G., and M. Gertz (1995). "Armed Resistance to Crime: The Prevalence and Nature of Self-defense With a Gun," *Journal of Criminal Law and Criminology* Vol. 86, No. 1:150-187.

Kopel, David B. (1995). "Guns, Germs, and Science: Public Health Approaches to Gun Control." *The Journal of the Medical Association of Georgia*, Vol. 84, No.2:269-273.

Kramer, Ronald and Raymond Michalowski (1995). "The Iron Fist and the Velvet Tongue: Crime Control in the Clinton Administration." *Social Justice*, Vol. 22, No. 2:87-100.

Kristof, Kathy (1996). "IRS is Happy to Take Care of Credit-Card Thief." *Arizona Daily Star*, October 21:2B.

Law Enforcement News (1996a). "Arresting Developments in LA." Vol. XXII, No. 442, March 31:1.

Law Enforcement News (1996b). "For One NYC Captain, Crime Reductions Are a Numbers Racket." Volume XXII, No. 457, December 15:9.

Law Enforcement News (1996c). "Fighting Gun Battles on Several Fronts." Vol. XXII, No. 458, December 31:23.

Law Enforcement News (1996d). "The Right to Bear Arms—Sort of." Vol. XXII, No. 438, January 31:1.

Lee, Robert W. (1995). "More Guns, Less Crime." *The New American*, Vol. 11, No. 14:15-16.

Maguire, Kathleen and Ann L. Pastore (eds.) (1993, 1994, 1995, 1996). *Sourcebook of Criminal Justice Statistics 1994, 1995, 1996, 1997*. Washington DC: USGPO.

Manson, Don and Gene Lauver (1997). *Pre-sale Firearm Checks*. Washington, DC: Office of Justice Programs.

Mena, Jennifer (1996). "Price Goes Up For Concealed Weapon License." *San Jose Mercury News*, May 2:5B.

Montgomery, Lon (1996). "Major Crimes Fell 2% in '95, Report Says." *The Arizona Daily Star*, May 6:1 and 8A.

Morgan, David R. (1989). *Managing Urban America*, Third Edition. Los Angeles, CA: Roxbury.

Nolan, William P. (1997). "Supreme Court Ruling Affects Brady Provisions." *The Police Chief*, Vol. LXIV, No. 8:20-24.

Poveda, Tony (1994). "Clinton, Crime and the Justice Department." *Social Justice*, Vol. 21, No. 3:73-84.

Rand, Michael R. (April 1994). "Guns and Crime." *Crime Data Brief*. Washington, DC: U.S. Department of Justice.

Rabkin, Norman J. (1996). *Gun Control: Implementing the Brady Handgun Violence Prevention Act*. Washington, DC: USGPO.

Reynolds, Morgan O. and W.W. Caruth III (1992). *Myths About Gun Control*. Dallas: National Center for Policy Analysis.

Rosen, Marie S. (1995/1996). "The Sweet Smell of Success, the Sour Taste of Bad Apples." *Law Enforcement News*, Vol. XXI, No. 436, 437, December 31/January 15:1.

Roth, Jeffery (1994). *Firearms and Violence*. Washington, DC: Office of Justice Programs.

Rothwax, Harold J. (1996). *Guilty: The Collapse of Criminal Justice*. New York: Random House.

Ruchelman, Leonard (1974). *Police Politics*. New York: Ballinger Publishing Co.

Spitzer, Robert J. (1995). *The Politics of Gun Control.* Chatham, NJ: Chatham House.

Taylor, Bruce M. (1997). *Changes in Criminal Victimization, 1994-1995.* Washington, DC: Bureau of Justice Statistics.

Travis, Jeremy (1995). *Arrestees and Guns: Monitoring the Illegal Firearms Market.* Washington, DC: National Institute of Justice.

U.S. Department of Justice (1992). *Criminal Victimization in the United States: 1973-90 Trends.* Washington DC: USGPO.

U.S. Department of Justice (1994). *Criminal Victimization 1992.* Washington, DC: Department of Justice.

U.S. Department of Justice (1997). *Criminal Victimization 1994.* Washington, DC: Department of Justice.

Valenti, Jack (1996). "The Danger of Demonizing Popular Culture." *American.* Washington, DC: American University.

Warner, John (1996). "Crime Control: America's Political Football." *Law Enforcement News*, Vol. XXII, No. 451:12.

Whitehead, Johnny C. (1993). "The Legislative Process—Law Enforcement's Role." *FBI Law Enforcement Bulletin,* Vol. 62, No. 7:5-10.

Whitman, David, Timothy M. Ito, and Amy Kost (1996). "Culture and Ideas." *U.S. News and World Report*, Vol. 120, No. 9:54-62.

Witkin, Gordon (1996). "A Very Different Gun Culture." *U.S. News and World Report*, Vol. 120, No. 10:32.

Wright, James D. (1991). "Guns and Crime." In Joseph F. Sheley, *Criminology: A Contemporary Handbook.* Belmont, CA: Wadsworth.

Wright, James D. (1995). "Ten Essential Observations on Guns in America." *Society*, March/April:63-68.

Zawitz, Marianne W. (1996). *Firearm Injury from Crime.* Washington, DC: Bureau of Justice Statistics.

THE EVOLVING POLICE FUNCTION: OBJECTIVES, ROLES, AND VALUES

2

The study of this chapter will enable you to:

1. Describe the major theme of Robert Peel's principles.

2. Compare the objectives of V.A. Leonard, J. Edgar Hoover, O.W. Wilson, and John P. Kenney.

3. List the two things that occur when a law enforcement agency defines its role.

4. Become aware of how the police protect the constitutional rights of citizens.

5. Identify the services that the police provide on an emergency basis.

6. Describe the importance of values to contemporary law enforcement.

7. List the five values of the Houston Police Department.

8. Write a short essay describing the core values of the Charlotte Police Department.

9. Compare the value statements of the Foster City Police Department and the Alexandria Police Department.

10. Describe how the Foster City Police Department ensures that integrity is basic to the accomplishment of its mission.

11. Write a short essay describing how the Alexandria Police Department strives for excellence.

12. List the police department goals created by the American Bar Association.

13. Describe the mission statement of the Charlotte Police Department.

The police field has wrestled for many years with the problem of defining the activities in which the police should engage. One of the earlier efforts was undertaken by Sir Robert Peel and his staff, in England, when they proclaimed nine principles of law enforcement. These principles are as applicable today as they were in 1822 and, most importantly, they reflect an outstanding example of understanding the relationship between the police and the public (Davis, 1977: 29-34; Patterson, 1995: 5-10; Harrison, 1996: 307).

- Prevention of crime is the basic mission of the police.
- Police must have the full respect of the citizenry.
- A citizen's respect for law develops respect for the police.
- Cooperation of the public decreases as the use of force increases.
- Police must render impartial enforcement of the law.
- Physical force is used only as a last resort.
- The police are the public and the public are the police.
- Police represent the law.
- The absence of crime and disorder is the test of police efficiency.

With the passage of *An Act for Improving the Police in and Near the Metropolis,* a mechanism came into existence that provided for the maintenance of law and order. This newly created police department had to deal with a constantly increasing crime rate. At the time of its implementation, the Peelian concept was ideal. It served as a bridge between either an antiquated police department or in some instances nonexisting police services. It turned out to be a renaissance of law, order, and justice (Radzinowicz, 1956: 572). One important contribution that Robert Peel made was to emphasize crime prevention rather than detection, but this concept never became a significant task of the earliest American police system. Each of these early principles represented a cooperative effort between the police and the public and set the tone for the professionalization of law enforcement. Even today, most police departments emphasize controlling and suppressing crime rather than prevention. This is changing slowly as community policing becomes more prevalent. This is a major philosophical shift and if it proves to be successful it will create a style of policing that is new to this nation. Only time will allow us to determine whether community policing is the wave of the future or an ill-conceived venture.

In the early part of this century, Leonhard F. Fuld pointed out that there was a need to identify the true purpose of policing (Fuld, 1909: 123). Highly visible and functioning 24 hours a day, the police assumed numerous duties outside the realm of law enforcement as politicians sought for ways to deal with community problems. The police became the dumping ground of municipal services that ran the gamut from running soup kitchens to chauffeuring the mayor. This was followed by a study of the American police, in 1915, by Elmer D. Graper that reinforced Fuld's position. He confirmed that the police had assumed too many extraneous activities that had a limited relationship to the enforcement of the law. Graper found that police departments performed a wide scope of duties, including censorship and tax collection (Graper, 1921: 29-42).

Can you imagine the problems the police would have today if they performed the functions of the Internal Revenue Service? In the early part of the twentieth-century, police agencies paid little heed to the nine principles of policing elicited by our English counterparts. Slowly but surely the police adopted a posture that moved them further and further away from the public as they enforced the law from a legalistic posture rather than a service orientation. It makes one wonder if our nation had followed the earlier precepts would we have had an entirely different type of police system and possibly a significant reduction in crime.

Police Objectives

A review of writings of former leading police administrators shows a consensus between the authors when listing the duties performed by law enforcement agencies. Typical of these are the objectives identified by the late V.A. Leonard, who suggested that the time-honored police role included (Leonard and More, 1974: 14):

- The protection of life and property.

- Maintenance of the peace and public order.

- Control and prevention of crime and vice.

- The regulation of traffic.

- Enforcement of regulatory responsibilities.

The role, as perceived by V.A. Leonard, is quite traditional in nature and the objectives are listed hierarchically with the protection of life and property as foremost. At the same time, Leonard saw the need for the police to deal with maintaining the peace and preventing crime. He also acknowledged the need for regulatory enforcement. Taken in the context of that period, this thought process was definitely ahead of its time and a significant shift in the way police viewed objectives in the early 1950s. It was a clear-cut acknowledgment that the police should function within the parameters of carefully defined objectives.

Another leading police administrator, the late O.W. Wilson, pointed out that police duties should be classified according to their more immediate objectives (Wilson and McLaren, 1972: 22):

- The prevention of the development of criminal and antisocial tendencies in individuals.

- The repression of criminal activities.

- The arrest of criminals, the recovery of stolen property, and the preparation of cases for court.

- The regulation of people in their non-criminal activities and the preparation of non-regulatory services.

Wilson recommended the expansion of the role into the area of prevention when he acknowledged that the police should prevent the development of anti-social tendencies. At the same time he expressed the need for repressing criminal activities, which is a traditional approach to law enforcement. The other objectives emphasized the more conventional approach to law enforcement and were representative of police duties performed in large cities during that era.

Another authority, John P. Kenney, stressed "It is well accepted that under our form of government, the general purpose of the police is to protect life and property and to preserve peace. In light of present trends, an additional end may be cited—rendering special services to the public." He identified the basic police functions as (Kenney, 1956: 70):

- The control of crime.

- The prevention of crime.

- Control of conduct.

- Provision of services.

The listing of provision of services as a police function suggested the need for the police to become involved in such activities as caring for the injured and assisting the impaired. It also calls for referring individuals to social service agencies and generally being concerned about the general welfare of citizens. This function is reminiscent of the earlier English principles. Kenney perceived crime prevention as a process primarily involving police involvement in the prevention and treatment of delinquents. He saw this function as one in which the police could make a significant impact not only on juveniles but contribute to the general welfare of the community. This marked a major departure from a general style of policing that emphasized repression and control of crime.

The late J. Edgar Hoover identified the basic responsibilities of the police as being (Hoover, 1961: 7):

- Protection of life and property.

- Preservation of the peace.

- Prevention of crime.

- Detection and arrest of violators of law.

- Enforcement of laws and ordinances.

- Safeguarding of individual rights.

Hoover was the only one who stressed the need for the police to be concerned with safeguarding the rights of individuals. This is not to say that other experts did not have a concern for this particular police objective, but they did not specifically express it. The identification of it as a specific goal leads to an acknowledgment of its importance and allows its use as a managerial guidepost. There is more commonality between the lists of objectives than disparity. Additionally, none of these experts consider the more ethical and philosophical principles listed by Sir Robert Peel. These include the following: "the police represent the law," "the police are the public and the public the police," and "the police must have the full respect of the citizenry." These factors represent some of the key components of value-oriented policing discussed later.

The authorities cited above reflect a general consensus about the fundamental tasks the police should perform. This general agreement shows the normal expectations of the public at large. Very simply, and in the broadest terms, the public expects the police to preserve the peace and protect society from crime through the enforcement of laws. The public views the police as a solid blue line protecting them from rampant crime. It is the governmental agency that separates the criminal from the law-abiding.

In recent years, the tasks performed by criminal justice agencies have become increasingly complex, especially those performed by local law enforcement agencies. Reviewing and assessing these tasks has never been more important or necessary than it is today. Time has caused many changes in our society. In the decades ahead, changes in our society will require law enforcement administrators to scientifically evaluate their programs and prepare their agencies to meet new challenges. Police administrators are increasingly accountable for what Robert Peal stressed—the absence of crime and disorder as the real test of police efficiency.

Historically, police executive officers have not been held responsible for the achievement of departmental objectives. It has been more of an approach that supports a managerial style that historically emphasized "don't rock the boat" and everything will be all right. With the trend toward contracts for police executives that spell out areas of accountability, it is anticipated that the achievement of clearly articulated objectives and their measurement will become more prevalent in the future (Greenberg, 1992: 70). For example, in Los Angeles the contract for the chief of police was not renewed for a second term because his management style and honesty came under fire. Willie Williams had been hired to restore confidence in the Los Angeles Police Department after the Rodney King riots. As part of the termination process, the Los Angeles City Council paid Chief Williams $375,000 in severance pay.

The Police Role

Law enforcement officials must make a serious and realistic attempt to outline a police role acceptable to all segments of society. It is also necessary for the public to understand the role (Dantzker, 1995: 12-25). Some authorities feel that the police must not reflect an attitude of moral self-righteousness—an attitude giving the public the impression that the sole purpose of law enforcement is to *enforce the laws*. The concept that the police are the only entity responsible for controlling crime is coming under increasing scrutiny. Through the years, the police have fostered the idea that they are solely responsible for controlling crime. Such a position is no longer tenable. The reality is that a simple solution and rhetoric are no longer viable responses to the crime problem. While some might view it as desirable, it is impossible for this nation to have a police officer on every corner, nor is it something that should occur in our republican form of government.

An analysis of actual police performance shows controlling crime by enforcing the laws is only one facet of police work. In one city, less than 20 percent of the calls received by a police department involved crimes. The remainder of the time dealt with a range of tasks such as responding to animal control calls, engaging in search and rescue activities, and directing and controlling traffic. It also included conducting traffic accident investigations and providing emergency medical services. The enforcement of the law cannot be underestimated, but the other functions cannot be ignored. If 80 percent of the time spent by police officers is in activities other than those involving crime, then serious consideration should articulate a police role that takes those activities into account. Adequately defining the role of the police is not easy. As our society changes, police administrators should constantly test departmental goals, and move toward a broadening of their objectives to meet the needs of the community.

Feature

Law Enforcement Agency Role

When a police agency defines its role, two things occur. First, officers know what is expected of them and can act without hesitation in complete harmony with departmental policy. Second, members of the public will have a general standard by which they are in a position to measure the tasks performed by their law enforcement agency. It is essential for an agency to set forth a written policy identifying the mission, goals, and basic programs and priorities. The departmental role should be responsive to the constitutional rights of the community.

Source: Commission on Accreditation for Law Enforcement Agencies (1996). *Standards for Law Enforcement Agencies*. Fairfax, VA: Commission on Accreditation for Law Enforcement Agencies, 1-1. Reprinted with permission.

Police Goals

The American Bar Association (ABA) developed a comprehensive set of police objectives that received wide acceptance. This professional entity acknowledged that many of the responsibilities assumed by the police were by default. This list of responsibilities definitely extends the police task beyond the basics as presented in the preceding lists. According to the ABA study, the police perform 11 distinct functions. They are especially important because they are transitional in nature and proved to be the forerunner of a police role that involved the public in the crime control process.

To identify criminal offenders and criminal activity and, where appropriate, to apprehend offenders and participate in later court proceedings. This is one of the traditional goals of the police, constituting what many would argue is the most significant contribution to community order: The specific control of conduct that is prohibited by the appropriate legislative body. It involves the identification of individuals believed to be guilty of committing a criminal offense and processing them through the legal system. This time-honored technique of investigation involves interviewing or interrogating victims, witnesses, and suspects. It also includes the collection and analysis of physical evidence, and taking into custody those responsible for the commission of an offense.

Figure 2-1
Standard 1-2.2: Major Current Responsibilities of Police

> In assessing appropriate objectives and priorities for police service, local communities should initially recognize that most police agencies are currently given responsibility, by design or default, to:
>
> (a) identify criminal offenders and criminal activity and, where appropriate, to apprehend offenders and participate in subsequent court proceedings;
>
> (b) reduce the opportunities for the commission of some crimes through preventive patrol and other measures;
>
> (c) aid individuals who are in danger of physical harm;
>
> (d) protect constitutional guarantees;
>
> (e) facilitate the movement of people and vehicles;
>
> (f) assist those who cannot care for themselves;
>
> (g) resolve conflict;
>
> (h) identify problems that are potentially serious law enforcement or governmental problems;
>
> (i) create and maintain a feeling of security in the community;
>
> (j) promote and preserve civil order; and
>
> (k) provide other services on an emergency basis.

Source: American Bar Association (1980). ABA Standards for Criminal Justice, Second Edition. "Standard 1-2.2: Major Current Responsibilities of Police," Volume I, Chapter 1: *Urban Police Function*. Copyright © 1980 American Bar Association. Reprinted by permission. All rights reserved.

Finally, it involves the preparation of the case for presentation in court, and follow-through as needed, to ensure a successful conclusion of the case. It is the role most often depicted on television, and from the viewpoint of many police officers it is *real* police work. A few traditionalists view all other police duties as meaningless and of little value.

A considerable amount of police work involves responding to information provided by citizens advising that a crime has occurred. It is a *reactive* process. Another aspect of police work involves the identification of individuals during the actual commission of an offense. While preventive patrol operates to reduce the desire of individuals to commit a crime, it also, on occasion, discovers offenders in the act of committing an offense. For example, officers have (on many occasions) arrested suspects who were in the act of stealing an automobile or committing a burglary. In other instances, officers on patrol, when enforcing traffic laws, have discovered weapons, drugs, or other evidence used in the commission of a criminal offense. The police also become involved in the investigation of a whole range of criminal activities committed over a period of time without an official agency becoming aware of it. This is true, for example, of offenses such as fraud, loan-sharking, environmental crimes, and fraudulent business practices. This secretive range of criminal activity, not easily discovered, occurs in some instances when the crime is of the type providing no victim or the victim is unaware that the offense has occurred. Since the investigative and prosecution functions under our system of justice can be of a highly selective nature, not every alleged offense is investigated. Indeed, many violations are ignored.

In some instances, criminal actions are only investigated after a complaint is filed. On the other hand, because of political or social pressures, the police have created investigative units to investigate certain crime. This has occurred in areas such as repeat offenders, domestic violence, missing children, bias-related, and environmental crimes (Reaves and Smith, 1995: 264-288).

Additionally, the decision by the police to investigate specific criminal activity is an internal administrative decision, having had limited review and scrutiny until recent years. The intent was to reduce political interference and allow for decisionmaking based on professional knowledge. As departments have entered into a community policing mode, shared decisionmaking has begun. This is a relatively recent occurrence, in which police operations are scrutinized by many citizens and organizations (Eck, 1992: 1-8).

To reduce the opportunities for the commission of some crimes through preventive patrol and other measures. This goal has receiving considerable attention in recent years, and will be increasingly emphasized as more and more departments move into a community policing mode. Many years ago, the late August Vollmer, Chief of Police of Berkeley, California, known as the father of modern police administration, stated, "I have spent my life enforcing the law. It is a stupid procedure and will never succeed until supplemented by preventive measures" (Vollmer, 1939: 407). With a large portion of police resources devoted to the enforcement function, the American people are slowly becoming aware of its futility as an approach to a significant social problem. Enforcement has definitely been given a fair trial. Police agencies are becoming increasingly involved in the area of prevention as noted by the fact that in one recent survey of police departments employing 100 or more officers, 97 percent were found to have specialized units dealing with community crime prevention (Reaves and Smith, 1995: 277-287).

Prevention programs vary considerably agency to agency, but generally considerable effort is given to informational activities and prevention seminars. During one fiscal year, the Tucson Police Department listed the following goals for its crime prevention program:

- Arrange departmental participation in 12 half-hour television programs promoting crime prevention.

- Produce at least two public service announcements promoting community participation in crime prevention.

- Make at least 12 presentations on Crime Prevention Through Environmental Design (CPTED), using trained officers, members of the development community, governing agencies, and the public.

- Review and make recommendations on all development, rezoning, and construction plans routed to the police department by other departments.

For years, most agencies have operated a variety of programs, including Neighborhood Watch, Operation Identification, security surveys, child abuse prevention, rape prevention, police athletic leagues, and child fingerprinting. One of the most popular programs is operation D.A.R.E. (Drug Abuse Resistance Education). This is true in spite of the fact that evaluation of the program indicates that it is effective for a short period of time, but does not have a lasting impact.

To aid individuals who are in danger of physical harm. The role of the police in this area is separate, unique, and in no way overlaps other goals. The police carry out a statutory and charter mandate to protect members of the community. This involves a wide range of activities, from rescuing individuals from burning buildings to securing hazardous substance areas. It also includes rescuing a drowning person, controlling traffic at the scene of an accident, and preventing someone from committing suicide. Additionally, the police play a major role during natural disasters. Fires, floods, tornadoes, and earthquakes ravage various sections of our nation frequently. The police respond to such catastrophes by protecting life and property, maintaining order, directing traffic, evacuating people, and caring for those who are in need. During such incidents, traffic control can prove to be a difficult task. This occurs as some seek to escape the devastation and others seek to enter an area to find and assist loved ones. Additionally, the police must deal with those who are just curious, as well as looters.

There is every reason to interpret the police role of protection beyond protecting individuals from crime. One aspect of this goal is the use of deadly force by the police. Throughout the nation, the police have altered departmental policies on the use of deadly force and restraint methods, to lessen the likelihood of injuring someone or taking someone's life. There is every reason to believe the review of all police policies dealing with the lessening of harm to individuals will be an ongoing process and will undergo dramatic change in the years ahead. This role is one of the most controversial, as injuries occur or someone is killed as the police attempt to exert control. Another chapter in this text addresses this acute problem.

To protect constitutional guarantees. As public officials, police officers, at the time of their appointment, take an oath to uphold the Constitution of the United States and the constitution and laws in their state of employment. In the past, many police officers have objected to court decisions curbing or restricting their powers to deal with crime and offenders. This has left them feeling that the Constitution and the Bill of Rights served to protect the offender at the expense of society.

With the beginning of civil disobedience and major disturbances caused by the Vietnam conflict, the police have revised the way they deal with such events. Today, the police protect the constitutional rights of citizens of every spectrum of our society. Currently, in various cities throughout the nation, the police protect the rights of the homeless to sit-in and demonstrate. They also protect the rights of homosexuals to advocate their rights, and even such a disparate group as the Ku Klux Klan (KKK), to the objections of numerous special interest groups. They also protect those who support and oppose abortion, and law enforcement agencies are making increasing use of court orders and injunctions to maintain order and protect the rights of demonstrators. The following Feature describes the action taken in the *Madesen* case by a state court. The decision prohibited anti-abortion protesters from demonstrating in certain places and in certain ways outside of an abortion clinic (McCormick, 1994: 29-30).

Feature

Injunction Prohibiting Anti-abortion Protesters

Protesters are prohibited from the following:

1. Demonstrating, at all times, within 36 feet of the clinic's property line.

2. Singing, chanting, whistling, shouting, yelling, using sound amplification equipment or other sounds or images observable to or within earshot of the patients inside the clinic during certain times and during surgical procedures.

3. Approaching at all times, any person seeking services of the clinic, unless the person indicates a desire to communicate by approaching the protesters.

4. Approaching, demonstrating, or using sound equipment, at all times, within 300 feet of the residences of clinic staff.

Source: William U. McCormick (1994). "Supreme Court Cases 1993-1994 Term." *FBI Law Enforcement Bulletin*, Vol. 63, No. 10:27-32.

The Supreme Court of the United States in *Madesen v. Women's Health Center, Inc.*, 114 S. Ct. 2516 (1994) held that the state had significant government interests in imposing the injunction. It also felt that there was a need to protect a woman's freedom to seek lawful medical services, ensuring public safety and order, providing for the free flow of traffic, and promoting residential safety. Overall, the Court accepted the primary content of the injunction while rejecting some specifics.

The causes change over the years, and the police are becoming increasingly aware of the need to take a positive role in ensuring that every citizen's constitutional rights are fully protected. Advocacy has led to legislation that allows officers to perform tasks more effectively when conflict occurs regarding volatile issues.

To facilitate the movement of people and vehicles. In urban America, the ability to move freely and easily from one location to another is an objective that few people accomplish. For many years, the police and traffic engineers have played an important part in creating a system that allows everyone to move freely and as rapidly as possible from one part of a community to another. Traffic units created in many cities have performed such activities as directing traffic, investigating accidents, enforcing the traffic code, promoting safety, regulating parking, and controlling pedestrians.

In some cities, police administrators, concerned with facilitating the movement of people and vehicles, have assigned a substantial portion of police resources to traffic units. Unfortunately, this has reduced the ability of the agency to accomplish other goals. The police have a dominant role in regulating traffic by utilizing motor vehicle codes that specify the rules of the road in minute detail. Vehicle codes give police officers the authority to exercise their traffic control and regulation responsibilities. A majority of larger law enforcement agencies maintain computerized files on traffic citations, accidents, stolen vehicles, and vehicle registration. Sixty-six percent of agencies with 100 or more officers have created special units to deal with drunk drivers (Reaves and Smith, 1995: 229-239).

For some time, the police have been very active in traffic safety programs extending well beyond that which is legally required. Most departments engage in a wide range of activities, including the supervision of school patrols. It also includes lecturing in schools at the elementary and high school levels, and participating in driver training programs. Experts have pointed out that public education will produce greater results in the reduction of traffic accidents than will either enforcement or engineering.

To help those who cannot care for themselves. Police officers constantly come into contact with those who need some type of aid. The aged, the impaired, the physically disabled, the youthful, the mentally ill, alcoholics, and those addicted to drugs are examples of those who constantly come to the attention of the police. Frequently, the initial involvement is the consequence of that person's criminal offense, such as public intoxication or trespassing. It also includes attempted suicide and traffic violations. Because the police are readily available 24 hours a day, they assume (in many instances) certain tasks simply because they are the only governmental agent available.

In some cities, when the temperature reaches a level close to freezing, a special program becomes operational and the police transport the homeless to shelters. They also remove the inebriated from the streets so they will not freeze to death. In addition, the police remove individuals from the street who engage in behavior that can prove harmful to themselves or others. They are then transported to appropriate facilities where they can receive help. This is especially true of individuals who exhibit signs of serious mental disorder. Many mental disorders include a number of symptoms that, particularly for the psychologically naïve, can be rather disconcerting. Although the more annoying symptoms of mental disorder, such as verbal abuse, belligerence, or disrespect, are not by themselves violations of any laws, such behavior may provoke a harsher response by the police officer, such as arrest. The police are becoming a major mental health resource, perhaps even more so in recent years as a result of deinstitutionalization. Generally, police officers do not rely excessively on conventional mental health resources and arrests are relatively rare. Informal dispositions are often the disposition of choice. Most police officers, based on prior experience, know precisely how to respond in order to soothe the mentally-disoriented person without medication or hospitalization. Police officers have and will continue to play a pivotal role in the mental health process (Teplin, 1986: 1-37).

To resolve conflict. Many police officers spend more time resolving conflict and disputes than they spend enforcing the criminal law. While the frequency will vary from community to community, the types of conflict include family disputes, conflict between neighbors, barking dogs, landlord and tenant disputes, and disagreements between merchants and customers.

Formerly termed *nuisance calls*, the police are becoming increasingly aware that handling these calls in a professional manner is essential to the maintenance of order in the community. Of genuine concern is that many of these incidents can escalate into violent confrontations. For many years, some police departments ignored family conflict. Now however, many police officers receive special training in crisis intervention counseling. Of agencies with 100 or more officers, 63 percent have created specialized domestic violence units. The police are increasingly becoming a significant part of a domestic violence response team by working with other agencies. This team can include a social worker, a member of the clergy, shelter personnel, and mental health experts (Brown, Unsinger, and More, 1990: 10). These teams have functioned successfully when a program protects the victim and helps them to cope with the situation. When prosecution proves necessary, members of the team help the victim to deal with the justice system. Family quarrels can prove to be quite dangerous for police officers. During the period from 1984 to 1993, 62 police officers were killed while responding to domestic disturbances (Federal Bureau of Investigation, 1994: 32). In recent years, the police have acknowledged the problem of domestic violence within its own ranks, and have moved to aggressively investigate incidents of domestic violence by police officers (Mader, 1997: 45).

To identify potentially serious law enforcement or government problems. The police are in an excellent position to identify problems as they occur and bring them to the attention of the appropriate government entity. It is quite common for legislative units to require police departments to report broken street lights, holes in streets, defective sidewalks, leaking water mains, shrubs obscuring traffic signs, inoperative or malfunctioning traffic lights, and toxic emissions. In recent years, the police have participated in the investigation of environmental cases. This has involved offenses such as: improper dumping or disposal of solid hazardous, medical/infectious or other wastes, and improper hauling/transportation of wastes (Travis, 1994: 1-11).

Feature

Drunk

A male who had been drinking considerably complains: "Two guys just strong-armed me and took my money and then ran away." An officer should determine the victim's state of intoxication. If he can tell a coherent story and give a description, the officer should handle the incident in the usual manner and take a robbery report. If the victim is unable to tell a coherent story, the officer should arrest him for public drunkenness. The report should include the victim's claims that he had been robbed before the arrest, but is unable to tell a coherent story.

Intoxicated

An officer answers a call at 3:00 A.M. to find a man drunk and laying on the floor, unable to care for himself. The man is in a hallway by his upstairs apartment. Inside the apartment, very young children are crying. He refuses to tell where his keys are, and no one answers the doorbell. The manager of the building is not available. The intoxicated person should be arrested and booked for violation of the appropriate law or ordinance. In addition, proper care of the children should be arranged. The room should be entered by using lock picks or by securing the services of a locksmith.

If the mother (or a reliable relative) is unavailable, a juvenile hall or a social agency should care for the children, pending the release of the suspect. Departmental policy will dictate whether to file an additional charge of child neglect.

Family Problems

A husband and wife agree to disagree and live separately. When he returns to get his clothes the wife will not let him in the house to get anything. In many states, the husband has as much right to enter the premises as the wife has, unless there is a court order to the contrary. In this situation, the officer should warn both parties that the officer is there merely to preserve the peace and not to settle a civil dispute. If there is a fight, or a disturbance takes place in the presence of the officer, those who participate in this illegal activity should be arrested for disturbing the peace.

A Family Dispute

An officer answers a disturbing the peace call. A man has thrown his wife's clothing on the front lawn and refuses to let her into the house. Generally, this is a civil matter, and the wife should be told to see her attorney. There is no crime unless a disturbance occurs. The officer should advise the wife to stay with some relatives or a friend. If she has none, there are several agencies that will give her overnight lodging, such as a Salvation Army facility or the YMCA. A complete report should be made on the incident.

Source: From John P. Kenney and Harry W. More (1986). *Patrol Field Problems and Solutions—476 Field Situations.* Courtesy of Charles C Thomas, Publisher, Springfield, Illinois.

The police also report any situation that negatively affects the welfare and safety of the community. The police have found they are in an excellent position to identify problems plaguing the community. They can then work for the resolution of the problem by referring complaints to the appropriate agency and, when appropriate, aid in problem resolution. One department takes the position that its members must become social activists and act as social change agents in order to foster positive change resulting in a better living environment (Santoro, 1993: 63). It is increasingly common for officers to work with representatives from a variety of city agencies and offices. It can include officials from planning, fire, streets, or the city attorney's office to improve neighborhood conditions and eradicate specific problems (Glensor and Peak, 1996: 14-21). One major federal commission suggested that police administrators should take an active role in supporting legislation addressing some of the major underlying problems of concern to the police. These include poverty, unemployment, homelessness, and discrimination.

To create and maintain a feeling of security in the community. The police in this nation are the primary governmental unit for ensuring a degree of tranquility in a community, and the police have not taken this commitment lightly. For many years the police have taken the position that they had the sole responsibility to control and suppress crime, and they have looked with disdain at others who have wanted to assume some responsibility in this area. Citizens who take reasonable precautions for their own protection have, historically, expected to engage in their ordinary daily activities without being endangered or becoming the subject of criminal attack.

The fear of crime is as much a problem as crime itself. In a nationwide survey, 20 percent of the respondents had a great deal of confidence in the ability of the police to protect them from violent crime. Thirty percent had quite a lot of confidence and 39 percent had not very much confidence. The remainder of the respondents (9%) had none at all (Maguire and Pastore, 1997: 127). Through the years, the police have dealt with this problem by preventive patrol in an effort to create an "omnipresence" and provide the community with a feeling of security. The American Bar Association has pointed out that "there is an illusory quality in this form of security, in that the actual potential of the police to guarantee the safety of residents (their persons and their property) is far less than suggested by the presence of police personnel. Few doubt the value in generating the illusion" (American Bar Association, 1972: 53-71). In recent years, consideration has been given to the concept of *broken windows*, which postulates that when consideration is given to the environment and its improvement, it has a significant impact on members of the community and their feeling of security and safety. One factor was to deal with neighborhood disorder, such as untended property, disorderly people, drunks, and obstreperous youths—all of which create fear in citizens and attract predators. Community policing has begun to address this goal and if it proves to be successful, it will go a long way toward maintaining a feeling of security within neighborhoods.

To promote and preserve civil order. Civil disturbances within our nation are the exception, but unfortunately we have had periods when the police (as well as national guard units) have had to engage in activities to preserve civil order. This has included occurrences such as the draft riots during the early part of the twentieth century and, most notably, the civil disturbances over the Vietnam War. The need to preserve public order is not new. Actually, a modern police agency came into existence in England because rioting and civil disorders occurred frequently. At that time, the parochial police forces were unable to control the acts of civil disobedience (Leonard and More, 1987: 3). With the occurrence of acts of civil disobedience, many police departments responded by creating tactical units. These units cope with critical temporary situations. They permit an overwhelming concentration of police power at a particular time and place to meet a specific problem, such as disorderly crowds or riotous situations.

The emphasis on this goal remains of interest to many in our communities, but it has lessened somewhat because of the reduction in the number of major disorders. There is a clear-cut need for agencies to have response plans that reduce the likelihood of minor disturbances evolving into widespread civil disorder (DeJong: 1994: 7). Although during the last few years in Miami there were five significant conflicts (with a loss of property and life) in reaction to the police use of deadly force. In one of the most recent disturbances, a Hispanic police officer was convicted of manslaughter in connection with the shooting of two African-American men. The officer claimed that the two men had tried to hit him with the motorcycle they were riding. Another major incident occurred in Los Angeles during the spring of 1992. Rioting started when four white police officers were acquitted in the videotaped beating of Rodney King. This riot was the deadliest in the twentieth century (Gates, 1992: 428-430; McCartney, 1992: 1). In 1996 in St. Petersburg, Florida, a riot broke out when officers stopped a speeding vehicle with two African-American men inside. The incident resulted in the eventual death of the 18-year-old driver of the vehicle. The riot, which involved 200 people, raged through the night as police strived to contain the violence.

To provide other services on an emergency basis. Through the years, the police have stepped in to fill voids in governmental response to the needs of members of the community. In most instances, there has been no one else to whom to turn. Readily available for a wide range of calls for help, the police have controlled minor fires and administered first aid. In addition, they have delivered babies, impounded stray animals, and created rescue units that are utilized to find lost children and hikers. When the volume of such services become excessive, alternative arrangements have been made in some communities. Other agencies (either public or private) have taken over such functions as animal control and emergency service. In the future, it is anticipated that other governmental and nongovernmental entities will be created to handle some of these tangential activities.

Through the years, the police have searched for a way to articulate their mission and it can be seen from the above discussion that it has been accomplished with some difficulty and variance. Goals and objectives in England started out with a serious consideration of the relationship of the police to the community and then shifted to an internalization of goals with an overriding professional model of policing. Then the 11 distinctive functions articulated by the American Bar Association study gave greater consideration to specific objectives, a number of which reflected a greater concern of individual and community needs.

Values in Policing

All organizations have values; police departments are no exception. Every action a department takes turns out to be an expression of the values of the department. When value statements are explicit, they actually set forth the real beliefs of that organization. These become standards for every member of the organization, and they provide the basis for the identification of the real mission the department expects to achieve through the tasks performed. In the field, there are many instances in which officers are thoroughly aware of the value dimensions involved when considering and selecting alternatives. In other instances, officers make decisions involving a complete lack of consideration of any value dimension. In reality, many of the tasks performed repetitively have become so routine that little consideration is given to the value base related to the performance of the task.

Even when values are positive, one value can conflict with another. Examples include when a fellow officer engages in an act of corruption and it is not reported, or an officer drinks on duty and it is ignored. Both these actions clearly conflict with professional conduct. The value of loyalty to a peer overrides other values the department has, such as performing tasks in a professional manner and abiding by a code of ethics. In some police departments, other values guide the actions of officers, such as: *never squeal, do not rock the boat, stay out of trouble*. These and other values can permeate the actual working values and alter the value structure of the agency. The informal structure of the organization too often decides what to take seriously and what to reject as immaterial or unsuitable. Humor, informal understandings, and attitudes of the members of the agency are examples of implicit values that can create a negative working environment. When this occurs it can create an atmosphere that is reflective of suspicion, cynicism, and bafflement rather than clarity and commitment to organizational values. Over time, the implicit value structure can become so dominate that the explicit value system takes a secondary position.

A contemporary management style demands that administrators develop values based on law and the Constitution. It truly represents the highest ideals and norms of the police profession—these values should be compatible with values expressed by the community. An explicit value structure within a police organization must exemplify the highest value structure possible. It must reflect absolute integrity and demand complete honesty on the part of every member of the organization. It should so imbue the total organization that everyone knows what to do and acts appropriately. There is no substitute for personal and organizational integrity that demands the highest moral response. Once values are established, they should be written in such a way that they are not ambiguous. A review should be conducted periodically to ensure that they are appropriately confronting the challenges facing today's police departments.

Value-oriented management requires that everyone be made aware of their existence starting with the initial interview and then at every annual performance evaluation. On appointment, each officer is given a copy of the organizational value statement and should be required to uphold the value statement at the official swearing-in ceremony. Newly hired officers should receive extensive training in the importance of values to the organization and they should be required to abide by the standards set forth in the value statement.

The departmental promotional system reinforces departmental values. The process should analyze behavior in terms of how values are applied. Job performance that is value-oriented translates to promotions. The department also reinforces the value system by acknowledging those who consistently perform within the framework of organizational values with preferential assignments or by sending them to special training programs. When value statements are part of the reward system, officers realize the importance of performing in ways that are compatible with departmental expectations. Additionally, management can reinforce the system by openly acknowledging work that successfully contributes to program achievement (Norman, 1992: 3).

Through the years, many police departments have expressed definitive statements reflecting the desired organizational response to crime and its related problems. Police officers and citizens (through policy statements and regulations) become aware of departmental values. This is especially true when departments issue policy statements on the use of deadly force. It becomes immediately apparent how the department views the value placed on human life. For example, should an officer be authorized to shoot at a vehicle driven by a fleeing felon who is considered dangerous? Should an officer shoot at an individual who is fleeing the scene of an armed robbery committed during the hours of darkness when that individual has a weapon?

These are difficult questions, but they address the problems involved in the decision-making process when developing value policies. The desirable factor is that value statements become viable and guide the officer during the decision-making process rather than being something serving only to prohibit actions. It is a radical switch in emphasis from one of command and control to one of allowing officers to consider a range of options rather than responding by the book. It calls for an officer to respond to a value orientation rather than providing a rote reaction to a situation. When properly implemented, it becomes a question of control by professional self-regulation and not the application of carefully defined rules trying to circumscribe every possible situation (Wasserman and Moore, 1988: 1-7).

A properly implemented values management system influences each and every administrative decision. As a consequence, management comportment becomes highly predictable. When operational personnel are presented with a stable working environment they are apt to use discretion more judiciously. This occurs because officers know exactly what contribution they are making to the organization. Consequently, there is less need for strong managerial control (Wasserman and Moore, 1988: 1). Values used by police departments have been highly specific in some situations, and in other instances they have been quite abstract. Either way, they should serve as a springboard that causes employees to become committed to the value process.

Values serve to clarify the abstract and provide meaning to the organization. A functioning value system causes police managers to make decisions within the context of that system providing guidance and support of operational personnel. A good value statement is one that expresses the specific individuality of the organization. It makes that organization unique and creates a working environment that fosters commitment to the organization. Consequently, the officers feel like they are a part of the agency and are making a significant contribution to the department. When employees are constantly reminded by supervisors and managers that value statements guide organizational actions, they react positively to this process. When officers know that value statements permeate every aspect of operational procedures, the process becomes real. The realities of value statements are such that in time they become a distinguishing characteristic of the agency. Over time, values can influence an organization to such an extent that they become the reason for existence (Leonard and More, 1993: 93-96).

A police agency can become an important part of government for maintaining democratic values and improving the quality of life in a city. The values expressed by an agency reflect two major viewpoints. First, a positive policing program takes the position that all members of the organization can contribute (by virtue of their experience and wisdom) to the effective operation of the department. Second, responsibility for making decisions is shared by the police and the community. It involves a legitimate partnership between the two groups. Citizens become a resource and the information they have is used to identify and prevent neighborhood crime (Brown, 1989: 1-10).

The Houston Police Department is an excellent example of the breadth of value statements (Wasserman and Moore, 1988: 1-7):

- The community is involved in all policing activities that directly affect the quality of community life.

- Strategies carried out by the department must reflect, preserve, and advance democratic values.

- The delivery of police services must be structured in such a way as to strengthen the city's neighborhoods.

- The public should have input into the development of policies directly affecting the quality of neighborhood life.

- The department will seek input from employees into matters involving job satisfaction and effectiveness.

Key elements of the Houston Police Department statement include a consideration of the quality of life, citizen and employee participation, the importance of the neighborhood, and the importance of democratic values. Another example of how values reflect this differing approach is illustrated by the mission statement of the Boston Police Department: "the department is committed to the positive evolution, growth, and livability of our city." Another statement created by a panel of experts developed a set of values representing the key elements of community policing as "a commitment to a problem-solving partnership: dealing with crime, disorder, and the quality of life" (Wasserman and Moore, 1988: 1-7).

Value-oriented policing marks a sharp departure from the professional crime-fighting model of policing that dominated the thinking of police administrators for many years. It encompasses a broader approach to policing through a set of values rather than a legalistic or technical orientation to the police function. Additionally, it reflects the genuine importance of every employee, when in the past the mission of a police department did not recognize the importance of employees.

Charlotte Police Department

This department has a unique approach to its concept of value-oriented policing. It utilizes a two-tiered approach. It starts with a mission statement: "the department is committed to fairness, compassion, and excellence while providing police services in accordance with the law and sensitive to the priorities and needs of the community" (*Law Enforcement News*, 1990: 9-14). This is followed by a set of core values:

- The protection of life and property is our highest priority.

- The department will respect and protect the rights and dignity of all persons and conduct all citizen contacts with courtesy and compassion.

- The department will strive for excellence in its delivery of police services and will utilize training, technology, and innovation to achieve that goal.

- The department recognizes its interdependent relationship with the community it serves and will remain sensitive to the community's priorities and needs.

- The law will be enforced impartially throughout the community.

- The department recognizes the individual worth of each of its members.

The Charlotte Police Department reiterates the time-honored objective of policing that is the protection of life and property. Listing this as its highest priority places the five other core values as secondary. It is interesting to note that one core value stresses that the law will be enforced impartially. In earlier listings of police objectives or goals this particular value was never given consideration. When all of the core values are considered, it clearly illustrates that previous styles of policing are rejected inasmuch as it involves providing police services based on core values rather than a legalistic orientation.

Foster City Police Department

Obviously, value statements vary from agency to agency because they reflect the differing views on communities and the managerial style of the police department. Figures 2-2 and 2-3 illustrate this difference wherein Foster City, California, lists five basic values and Alexandria, Virginia lists eight major value areas. The Houston Police Department listed five areas of concern while the Boston Police set forth a mission statement with limited specificity. Foster City, while listing five basic values, saw the need to have extensive amplification for each value. Similar to Charlotte, it indicated that it has a primary mission of dealing with dangerous and difficult situations. This basic value is similar to earlier police objectives in that it spells out the duty to prevent and investigate crimes, together with apprehension and vigorous prosecution. Of special importance is one of the basic values that stresses the need for innovation and the desire to encourage prudent risk-taking. Another value stresses the importance of personal and organizational integrity. Taken as a whole, the basic values provide a valuable frame of reference for the operation of the department.

Figure 2-2
Foster City Police Department Basic Values

---

1. **Integrity is basic to the accomplishment of the law enforcement mission. Both personal and organizational integrity are essential to the maintenance of the F.C.P.D. This means that we:**

   - Insure that accurate reporting occurs at all levels;
   - Promote and recognize ethical behavior and actions;
   - Value the reputation of our profession and agency, yet promote honesty over loyalty to the Department;
   - Openly discuss both ethical and operational issues that require change;
   - Collectively act to prevent abuses of the law and violations of civil rights.

2. **Due to the dynamic nature of our profession, the F.C.P.D. values innovation from all levels of the Agency. This means we:**

   - Reward and recognize those who contribute to the development of more effective ways of providing policing service;
   - Strive to minimize conflict which negatively impacts our work product, yet we support the constructive airing and resolution of differences in the name of delivering quality police services;
   - Listen to and promote suggestions emanating from all levels of the Department; and
   - Wish to promote an atmosphere that encourages prudent risk taking, and that recognizes that growth and learning may be spawned by honest mistakes.

3. **The law enforcement profession is recognized as somewhat close and fraternal in nature. The F.C.P.D. reflects this tradition, yet supports community involvement and ongoing critical self-appraisal by all its members. This means we:**

   - Encourage employees to socialize with employees and community members alike to promote the reputation of the Agency;
   - Promote programs that improve the relationship between our members and the community at large;

Figure 2-2—*continued*

- Report and confront employees who violate laws and the basic values of the organization; and
- Promote and discuss the positive aspects of the Agency and its product throughout the community.

4. **The provision of law enforcement services is a substantial expense to the taxpayer. The F.C.P.D. is obligated to provide the highest quality of police service for the resources expended. This means we:**

    - Regularly assess the cost vs. benefits of the various programs of the Agency;
    - Require a standard of professional performance for all members of the Department;
    - Administer the Departmental funds in a prudent, cost-effective manner;
    - Publicly acknowledge and praise employees that excel at their jobs; and
    - Support and encourage employees in their pursuit of higher education.

5. **Law enforcement, in the course of performing its primary mission, is required to deal with both dangerous and difficult situations. The F.C.P.D. accepts this responsibility and supports its members in the accomplishment of these tasks. This means we:**

    - Review and react to an individual's performance during such an event based upon the totality of the circumstances surrounding their decisions and actions;
    - Encourage all employees, as the situation permits, to think before they act;
    - Take all available steps and precautions to protect both the City's and employees' interests in incidents that provide either danger or civil exposure.
    - Keep our supervisor informed of any incident or pending action that jeopardizes either the reputation of the Agency or an individual employee;
    - Attempt, conditions permitting, to reason with individuals in the enforcement setting prior to resorting to the use of force; and,
    - Recognize that it is our duty to prevent, report, and investigate crimes, together with the apprehension and the pursuit of vigorous prosecution of lawbreakers. We also recognize that it is the domain of the court to punish individuals convicted of crimes.

Source: Correspondence from Robert G. Norman, Chief of Police, Foster City, CA (March 1, 1998).

Alexandria Police Department

Similar to other departments, the Alexandria Police Department acknowledges the need to serve the community by protecting life and property, preventing crime, maintaining order, and enforcing the law, which are all part of its mission statement. This department illustrates the variability in value statements and has a unique approach when one considers the values to which it gives consideration. It is the first department discussed here in which special consideration is given to identifying and solving community problems. Additionally, it acknowledges the need to actively seek the input of members of the community as well as the input of other agencies and organizations. Of special note is the indication that the members of the organization will lead by example and will strive to be role models for the community.

Figure 2-3
Alexandria Police—These are Our Values

The Alexandria Police Department exists to serve the community by protecting life and property; by preventing crime; by enforcing the laws; and by maintaining order for all citizens. Central to our mission are the values that guide our work and decisions, and help us contribute to the quality of life in Alexandria.

Our values are characteristics or qualities of worth. They are non-negotiable. Although we may need to balance them, we will never ignore them for the sake of expediency or personal preference. We hold our values constantly before us to teach and remind us, and the community we serve, of our ideals. They are the foundation upon which our policies, goals, and operations are built. In fulfilling our mission, we need the support of citizens, elected representatives, and City officials in order to provide the quality of service our values commit us to providing. We, the men and women of the Alexandria Police Department value:

HUMAN LIFE
INTEGRITY
LAWS AND CONSTITUTION
EXCELLENCE
ACCOUNTABILITY
COOPERATION
PROBLEM-SOLVING
OURSELVES

HUMAN LIFE

We value human life and dignity above all else.
Therefore:
>   We give first priority to situations which threaten life.
>   We use force only when necessary.
>   We treat all persons with courtesy and respect.
>   We are compassionate and caring.

INTEGRITY

We believe integrity is the basis for community trust.
Therefore:
>   We are honest and truthful.
>   We are consistent in our beliefs and actions.
>   We hold ourselves to high standards of moral and ethical conduct.
>   We are role models for the community.

LAWS AND CONSTITUTION

We believe in the principles embodied in our Constitution. We recognize the authority of federal, state, and local laws.
Therefore:
>   We respect and protect the rights of all citizens.
>   We treat all persons fairly and without favoritism.
>   We are knowledgeable of the law.
>   We enforce the law.
>   We obey the law.

EXCELLENCE

We strive for personal and professional excellence.
Therefore:
>   We do our best.
>   We have a vision for the future.
>   We seek adequate resources: staffing, facilities, equipment, training, salaries, and benefits.
>   We recruit and hire the best people.
>   We train and develop our employees to their highest potential.

Figure 2-3—*continued*

We are committed to fair and equitable personnel practices.
We provide organizational mobility.
We recognize and reward good performance.
We support reasonable risk-taking and are tolerant of honest mistakes.
We are receptive to new ideas and to change.
We work toward realistic, mutually-agreed-upon goals.
We meet nationally-recognized law enforcement standards.
We lead by example.

ACCOUNTABILITY

We are accountable to each other and to the citizens we serve, who are the source of our authority.
Therefore:

We communicate openly and honestly among ourselves and with the community.
We understand the importance of community values and expectations.
We are responsive to community concerns.
We acknowledge our mistakes and are open to constructive criticism.
We manage our resources effectively.
We thoroughly investigate complaints against our employees.

COOPERATION

We believe that cooperation and teamwork will enable us to combine our diverse backgrounds, skills, and styles to achieve common goals.
Therefore:

We work as a team.
We understand our role in achieving Department and City goals and objectives.
We share our responsibility to serve the citizens of Alexandria with many other agencies and organizations.
We strive to understand those who disagree with us.
We seek the help and cooperation of others.
We rely on community support and involvement.

PROBLEM-SOLVING

We are most efficient when we help identify and solve community problems.
Therefore:

We work to anticipate and prevent problems.
We give a high priority to preventing crime and helping citizens feel safe.
We actively seek opinions and ideas from others.
We plan, analyze, and evaluate.
We recognize that crime is a community problem.
We listen to problems and complaints with empathy and sensitivity.
We seek innovative solutions.

OURSELVES

We are capable, caring people who are doing important and satisfying work for the citizens of Alexandria.
Therefore:

We respect, care about, trust, and support each other.
We enjoy our work and take pride in our accomplishments.
We are disciplined and reliable.
We keep our perspective and sense of humor.
We balance our professional and personal lives.
We consult the people who will be affected by our decisions.
We have a positive, "can-do" attitude.
We cultivate our best characteristics: initiative, enthusiasm, creativity, patience, competence, and judgment.

Source: Correspondence from Charles E. Samarra, Chief of Police, Alexandria, VA (March 1, 1998).

Each agency places a differing emphasis on *community involvement*. The Charlotte Police Department has a broad mission statement followed by a list of core values that are much more specific, but does not reach the specificity apparent in statements set forth by other departments. The Alexandria Police Department has an extensive value statement and does an excellent job of considering the importance of the community and departmental employees. Especially outstanding is their coverage of *accountability*. Each of the value statements of the several departments provides a basis for personal commitment and provides a frame of reference for professional growth and development. The varying value statements range from specific to abstract, but are written in such a way that it is obvious they influence the decision-making process of each agency. The value statements definitely give organizational identity to each department and, when properly and consistently applied, create a positive working environment. The importance of values cannot be underestimated. They can and should be the lifeblood of the organization. When they become an integral part of each officer's behavior, and the basis for administrative decisionmaking, they serve as a basis for real professionalism.

Summary

Police administrators are fully aware of police work that is not devoted to crime, but many other human problems. In fact, the police have wrestled with the problem of defining the police role in a free world for more than 150 years. As early as 1823, police leaders in England enunciated nine principles of law enforcement. The primary focus was on the prevention of crime; this emphasis has been recaptured more recently by the American police. Since 1950, the leading police administration texts have identified an increasing number of police objectives that bear a striking similarity to each other. The tasks that the police perform reflect the general expectations of the public; to preserve the peace and protect society.

One of the most comprehensive lists of police tasks was put forth by the American Bar Association. The list includes such varied tasks as providing emergency services, creating and maintaining a feeling of security in the community, and protecting constitutional guarantees. Defining the role of law enforcement serves a dual purpose. First, the public is provided with a standard to measure police effectiveness. Second, police officers are made aware of the actions expected of them. Through the years, many police departments have expressed definitive statements that reflect the desired organizational response to crime and its related problems.

All organizations have value statements, and police departments are no exception. Whatever a police department does, it is an expression of its values. When values are expressed, they become a standard for every member of the organization. They provide the basis for identification of the real mission that the organization expects to achieve through the tasks performed. Value-oriented management that emphasizes values through a departmental value promotional system has proven to be a positive managerial approach in a contemporary environment.

The values of the four police departments discussed in this chapter have ranged from very specific to abstract. In every instance they have served as a springboard that has caused employees to become committed to the value process. Expressed values give life to the organizations and provide meaning to every action taken by the various departments. The value statements provide a basis for personal commitment and a frame of reference for professional growth and development.

References

American Bar Association (1980). *ABA Standards for Criminal Justice*, Second Edition. "Standard 1-2.2: Major Current Responsibilities of Police," Volume I, Chapter I: Urban Police Function. Chicago: American Bar Association.

Brown, John A., Peter C. Unsinger and Harry W. More (1990). *Law Enforcement and Social Welfare—The Emergency Response*. Springfield, IL: Charles C Thomas.

Brown, Lee P. (1989). *Community Policing: A Practical Guide for Police Officials*. Washington, DC: Office of Justice Programs.

Commission on Accreditation for Law Enforcement Agencies (1996). *Standards for Law Enforcement Agencies*. Fairfax, VA: Commission on Accreditation for Law Enforcement Agencies.

Dantzker, Mark L. (1995). *Understanding Today's Police*. Englewood Cliffs, NJ: Prentice Hall, Inc.

Davis, Edward M. (1977). "Professional Police Principles." *Federal Probation*, Vol. XXV, No. 1, March:29-34.

DeJong, Dean (1994). "Civil Disorder—Preparing for the Worst." *FBI Law Enforcement Bulletin*, Vol. 66, No. 3:1-7.

Eck, John E. (1992). *Helpful Hints for the Tradition-Bound Chief: Fresh Perspectives*. Washington, DC: Police Executive Research Forum.

Federal Bureau of Investigation (1994). *Law Enforcement Officers Killed and Assaulted 1993*. Uniform Crime Reports. Washington, DC: U.S. Department of Justice.

Fuld, Leonhard F. (1909). *Police Administration*. New York: Putnam.

Gates, Daryl F. (1992). *Chief*. New York: Bantam Books.

Glensor, Ronald W. and Ken Peak (1996). "Implementing Change: Community-Oriented Policing and Problem Solving." *FBI Law Enforcement Bulletin*, Vol. 74, No. 7:14-21.

Graper, Elmer D. (1921). *American Police Administration*. New York: Macmillan.

Greenberg, Sheldon F. (1992). *On the Dotted Line: Police Executive Contracts*. Washington DC: Police Executive Research Forum.

Harrison, Bob (1996). "More Harm Than Good?" *Law and Order*, Vol. 44, No. 1:307-310.

Hoover, J. Edgar (1961). *Should You Go into Law Enforcement?* New York: New York Life Insurance Co.

Kenney, John (1956). *Police Management Planning*. Los Angeles: author.

Kenney, John and Harry W. More (1986). *Patrol Field Problems and Solutions—476 Field Situations*. Springfield, IL: Charles C Thomas.

Law Enforcement News (1990). "Interview of Sam H. Killman, Police Chief of Charlotte, NC." Vol. XVI, No. 306, January 15:9-15.

Leonard, V.A. and Harry W. More (1974). *Police Organization and Management*, Third Edition. Mineola, NY: The Foundation Press.

Leonard, V.A. and Harry W. More (1987). *Police Organization and Management*, Seventh Edition. Mineola, NY: The Foundation Press.

Leonard, V.A. and Harry W. More (1993). *Police Organization and Management*, Eighth Edition. Westbury, NY: Foundation Press, Inc.

McCartney, Scott (1992). "Reeling LA Struggles to Recover From Deadly Riots." *The Arizona Daily Star*, Vol. 151, No. 126:1.

McCormick, William V. (1994). "Supreme Court Cases 1993-1994 Term." *FBI Law Enforcement Bulletin*, Vol. 63, No. 10:27-32.

Mader, Katherine (1997). *The Report of the Domestic Violence Task Force*. Los Angeles, CA: Los Angeles Police Department.

Madesen v. Women's Health Center, Inc., 114 S. Ct. 2516 (1994).

Maguire, Kathleen and Ann L. Pastore (1997). *Sourcebook of Criminal Justice Statistics—1996*. Washington, DC: Bureau of Justice Statistics.

Norman, Robert G. (1992). *Organizational Values: A Vision Becomes a Reality (One Man's Perspective) (Unpublished)*. Foster City, CA.

Patterson, Jeffrey (1995). "Community Policing—Learning the Lessons of History." *FBI Law Enforcement Bulletin*, Vol. 64, No. 11:5-10.

Radzinowicz, Leon (1956). *A History of English Criminal Law and its Administration from 1750*, Volume 4. London: Stevens and Sons, Ltd.

Reaves, Brian A. and Pheny Z. Smith (1995). *Law Enforcement Management and Administrative Statistics, 1993: Data for Individual State and Local Agencies with 100 or More Officers*. Washington DC: Office of Justice Programs, U.S. Department of Justice.

Santoro, Joseph, A. (1993). "A Department's Role as a Social Activist." *Law and Order*, Vol. 41, No. 5:63-66.

Teplin, Linda A. (1986). *Keeping the Peace: The Parameters of Police Discretion in Relation to the Mentally Disordered*. Washington, DC: National Institute of Justice.

Travis, Jeremy (1994). *Environmental Crime Protection: Results of a National Survey*. Washington, DC: U.S. Department of Justice.

Vollmer, August (1939). *Community Coordination*. Berkeley, CA: Coordinating Councils, Inc.

Wasserman, Robert and Mark H. Moore (1988). *Values in Policing*. Washington, DC: U.S. Department of Justice.

Wilson, O.W. and R.C. McLaren (1972). *Police Administration*, Third Edition. New York: McGraw-Hill.

POLICING THE COMMUNITY: A JOINT RESPONSE TO THE CRIME PROBLEM

3

The study of this chapter will enable you to:

1. Describe the characteristics of the professional policing model.

2. Contrast team policing and the community relations movement.

3. Identify five recommendations of the Independent Commission for changing the policing style of the Los Angeles Police Department.

4. List six different titles used for describing community policing.

5. Write a short essay describing the leadership style used in an organization utilizing COPPS.

6. List the five components that describe an effective neighborhood organization.

7. Describe the identifying characteristics of the police subculture.

8. List the four parts of the problem-solving process.

9. Identify the key features of the checklist for the analysis of a problem.

10. Describe in a short essay the benefits the community can derive from community policing.

11. List the benefits that the police can obtain from community policing.

12. Identify the goals of the Community Policing Consortium.

For more than one-half of the twentieth century, the move toward professionalism dominated the changes occurring in the American police system and, as a consequence, the police have become more and more isolated from the community they serve. While this was not the intent of professionalization, it was the result. The professional model swept across the nation like wildfire, including the trappings of the ideal bureaucracy set forth by Max Weber, and encompassing aspects of the scientific management movement of Frederick Taylor (Gerth and Mills, 1958: 196; Taylor, 1947: 129-130). Some police departments reacted to the development of contingency management theory (a blend of differing managerial approaches) in an effort to be effective when responding to a given situation (Hellriegel and Slocum, 1976: 5).

Professional Model of Policing

Over the years, these managerial philosophies affected law enforcement agencies as police executives wrestled with the demands of a changing society. Many departments responded with the creation of a legalistic style of policing, stressing impartiality and resistance to political influence. At the same time, a few agencies responded with a service model but it did not receive wide acceptance. Progressive managers adhered to strict civil service rules for hiring and promotion. Objectivity and efficiency dominated the police management style. The dominant approach was to centralize operations and, as a means of controlling operational personnel, agencies created standard operating procedures. Rules or regulations covered every conceivable contingency. Nothing was left to chance (Patterson, 1995: 5-10). For example, in one department, the manual states that officers will: "not loiter in cafes, drive-ins, service stations or other public places except for the purpose of conducting police business or taking regular meals or refreshments" (More and Shipley, 1987: 100). Over time, the police became increasingly bureaucratized and the semi-military managerial process prevailed.

The centralization process eliminated district stations and further removed officers from contact with the public. Standard Operating Procedures served to restrict officer discretion and force their continued and absolute acquiescence to the chain of command and superior authority. Centralization provided managers with a mechanism for controlling corruption and impeding political influence as officer discretion was restricted. Of all managerial contingencies present during the professionalization of law enforcement, the most important was the motorization of law enforcement. In the name of efficiency, the patrol officer no longer walked a beat or responded from the station house, because he or she took a seat in a patrol vehicle. Technology led the way and placed in the hands of each officer an array of resources to aid in the apprehension of offenders. Unfortunately this *incident-oriented* policing model failed to reduce actual crime numbers (Bobinsky, 1994: 17). This type of policing has aptly been described as *stranger policing* (Manus, 1995: 8).

Officers responded to calls for service and addressed the conditions present at each location. In this process, officers became acquainted with problem individuals and locations. The emphasis was on solving problems in a short time, and handling as many calls as possible. This essentially reactive process was controlled by the dispatcher who operated, in many instances, independently and essentially outside of the traditional chain of command. Under these circumstances, officers became so involved with handling calls that they had little time to become acquainted with or work with citizens (Farrell, 1988: 77). The features that best describe the professional model are set forth in Figure 3-1.

Figure 3-1
The Professional Policing Model

- A mechanistic organization
- Incident-oriented
- Legalistic approach to enforcement
- Limited input from the public
- A closed system
- Extensive polices, procedures, and rules
- An emphasis on control
- Limited contact with the public
- Effectiveness measured by the number of arrests and issuance of citations
- Hierarchical structure
- Chain of command
- Semi-military
- Non-risk-taking
- Reactive
- Rejection of failure
- Minimal response time
- Accountable to legal authority
- Rationality

Source: V.A. Leonard and Harry W. More (1993). *Police Organization and Management*, Eighth Edition. Westbury, NY: The Foundation Press.

In many instances, the police during the 1960s proved to be ineffective in handling urban unrest and were subjected to criticism by members of the community, of all political persuasions, as well as entrenched political leaders. These disturbing events were the subject of numerous national studies ranging from an analysis of riots, a study of violence, the President's Crime Commission, and the creation of standards and goals. Police authorities began to question time-honored techniques of deployment of personnel, types of patrol, and an extreme emphasis on response time. It soon became apparent that technological advances and the most advanced police procedures did little to reduce the fear of crime or crime itself.

Modifying the Professional Model

The professional model of policing proved not to be as successful as hoped, although it was viewed as a universal remedy for many years. The professional policing model has had an honored place in police history, as it dominated policing for an extended period. It was reasonably successful in cleansing law departments of political influence, but not quite as successful in reducing corruption. This model, like any managerial philosophy, has its pitfalls. It is those pitfalls that must be dealt with if community policing is to have any chance of succeeding. In any transitional period, the professional model can become into conflict with the community policing model. The professional model encompassed all of the trappings of the bureaucratic organization in which authority remained at the top; there was excessive specialization of tasks, and officers were never encouraged or rewarded for creativity or innovation (Leonard and More, 1993: 87). Efforts to modify the professional model of policing revolved around two different approaches—team policing and community relations.

Feature

The Professional Approach to Policing

At 1:32 A.M. a man we will call Fred Snyder dialed 911 from a downtown corner phone booth. The dispatcher noted his location and called the nearest patrol unit. Officer Knox arrived four minutes later. Snyder says he was beaten and robbed 20 minutes before, but did not see the robber. Under persistent questioning, Snyder admitted he was with a prostitute he had picked up in a bar. Later, in a hotel room, he discovered the prostitute was actually a man, who then beat Snyder and took his wallet.

Snyder wants to let the whole matter drop. He refuses medical treatment for his injuries. Knox finishes his report and lets Snyder go home. Later that day, Knox's report reaches Detective Alexander's desk. She knows from experience that the case will go nowhere, but she calls Snyder at work. Snyder confirms the report but refuses to cooperate further. Knox and Alexander go on to other cases. Months later, reviewing crime statistics, the city council discusses the difficulty of attracting businesses or people downtown.

Source: William Spelman and John E. Eck (1987). "Problem-Oriented Policing." *Research in Brief.* Washington, DC: National Institute of Justice.

Team Policing

In response to national commissions and societal changes, many departments implemented team policing. The team was viewed as a means of improving service to the community and improving the morale of police officers. For example, in Cincinnati, Ohio, team leaders were lieutenants (mini-chiefs); this organizational style threatened the authority and power of higher level administrators. The teams handled all calls, except homicides, and officers attended crime prevention meetings. The burglary rate fell and the crime rate remained the same for other offenses. Citizens still felt unsafe. Officers had to spend time with citizens, but this activity was never subject to measurement. The department retained the time-honored methods of measurement such as counting arrests and suspicious stops.

Overall, the results were disappointing (Silverman, 1978: 339-340). Other cities approached the team policing concept somewhat differently. A team usually consisted of eight to 10 officers with a team leader, which operated within a specified area. The central concept was to reduce the need for criminal investigation. The intent was to devote time to prevention, interception patrol, and arresting of offenders. Cooperation of the public was essential to the success of team policing. The public became fully aware of the team concepts and objectives. It was necessary to actively solicit public assistance and participation. This was done by continually seeking the opinions, ideas, and assistance of citizens in resolving problems of mutual interest (Leonard and More, 1993: 302-303).

The Los Angeles Police Department implemented a basic car plan. It consisted of small teams of officers responsible for a specific area, led by a senior lead officer (SLO). This leader was responsible for coordinating team efforts, monitoring beat conditions, creating neighborhood watches, and setting up crime prevention meetings. After a severe budget cut, this program ceased to exist. Efforts to work with the community took second place to the demand for statistics and rapid response. SLOs were retained, but their job was changed to emphasizing arrests, rather than community policing activities.

Community Relations

During the 1950s, police departments responded to pressure from many sources by creating community relations programs as a way to obtain community involvement in dealing with the crime problem.(Thurman, Giacomazzi, and Bogen, 1993: 554-558). Perceived as a universal remedy, community relations swept the police field. It became the "thing to do." A national commission recommended the establishment of programs in order to inform the public of the police role. Many different techniques and programs were used to resolve the failure of the police to communicate with the public. School resource officers became very popular, law enforcement explorer programs came into vogue, police athletic league programs were expanded, anti-burglary projects were implemented, and departments encouraged the community to participate in crime prevention programs. In today's overused phrase—*politically correct*— community relations became just that, an effort to pacify politicians, pressure groups, activists, and detractors of law enforcement. Most programs failed and those that appeared to work were never adequately evaluated, hence their worth was open to question. Over the years, the focus of community relations has shifted from opening communications with the public to improving race relations, then it expanded to emphasizing community involvement in specific crime prevention programs.

Many community relations programs had difficulty in relating to minority populations, the primary target, and internally many police officers felt that it was incompatible with *real* police work. In 1962, the San Francisco Police Department created a specialized unit with the goal of reducing crime by reducing despair. Officers assigned to this unit were viewed as *plastic cops* engaged in political games. The unit was to act as a social service agency. Unsure of what proved to be an equivocal mission, the unit was unable to function as a police agency and at the same time win the support of the minority community. The unit became alienated from its own department as well as the community. Eventually it ceased to function in the politically charged environment (Patterson, 1995: 8).

In fact, there were some instances in which factions within police departments worked diligently to disrupt and make sure that community relations programs failed. Community relations programs, in many instances, were innovative, but when superimposed on a professional policing model there was almost a guarantee that the programs would prove to be nonproductive. The philosophical base of professional policing was not a sound foundation to foster and develop such a divergent type of policing that was community-oriented. At this point, police executives began to look for a more innovative policing philosophy.

Transitional Problems

Community policing, if carried out properly, is a medium that offers the expectation of developing effective preventive programs and a means of improving relations with the community. In 1992, 10 of the largest cities in the United States expressed the need to move toward a community policing style (Cox, 1990: 168). These cities described community policing as a style that stresses values, problem-solving, accountability, and service orientation. This style cannot be superimposed on a professional model. When adopted, it should be done over a period of time, remembering that conflict is inevitable. It is such a significant departure from the professional model that internal opposition should be anticipated. The culture of an organization cannot be changed easily, and programs will have limited success if the mission statement and value structure permeate the organization. Change is occurring within the American police system, and while it might be occurring slowly, it is happening more rapidly than even the most optimistic would have anticipated (Zhao, 1996: 2-12).

Detractors of community policing are generally being proven wrong inasmuch as they have underestimated the viability and responsiveness of administrators and officers to the alternative that is known as community policing. When the policing style reflects the value structure of the agency, as a consequence of strong leadership, the status quo can be overcome and teamwork will become the rallying cry (Brown, 1991: 20-23). The concept of community policing stresses empowerment at the lowest level of the organization. It is difficult for agencies to disavow the security provided by a rigid structure based on command and control, but it has occurred. Police managers can be threatened

Feature

Recommendations of the Independent Commission for Changing the Los Angeles Police Department from a Professional to a Community Model of Policing

The Los Angeles Police Department was described by the Independent Commission, after its analysis following the Rodney King beating, as a department that utilized the professional style of policing. The Commission described the department as one that stressed arrests and control. It stated that community policing emphasizes restraint and mutual respect. They believed that LAPD officers used the professional model and the methods they used were incompatible with the behavior expected of officers under a community policing model. As professional, trained officers, situations were responded to by confronting and controlling, with limited concern for communicating or explaining.

The commission expressed the opinion that in spite of training, when officers are required to produce high arrest and situation statistics as rapidly as possible, they are just not in the position to explain why they doing something. Even if they make a mistake, they do not have time to express regret, let alone help citizens identify and resolve problems. Under the professional model, they must react and move on to the next call or incident

The Los Angeles Police Department at one time worked with the community to resolve problems. They created the Drug Abuse Resistance Education program in 1983. Other departments copied it and it is currently being used throughout the nation even though recent evaluation of the program has pointed out that its impact is short-term. In 1985, in response to demands from the public for better police service, the department implemented a Community Mobilization Project (CMP) in one area. The project called for the assignment of senior lead officers (SLOs) to deal with community needs. Officers went to block meetings and monitored the implementation of programs. Complaints were handled and community members were organized to paint over graffiti. When the response time for the area dropped to last place, the program was dropped and SLOs returned to patrol responsibilities. Efforts to work with the community went by the wayside, and the department in both of the above instances returned to the professional model of policing. The Commission recommended a community policing model in which patrol officers would interact with the public. It recognized that the culture of the organization, developed over many years, could not be changed easily, but there was a real need to develop programs that reduced the use of force. This was to be done by utilizing a *use of force continuum*. The commission felt that confrontation and physical force had a limited part to play when dealing with the public. It was hoped that the department would cultivate a different sentiment toward the population and help the public develop better reliance on their police department. Coveted assignments and promotions should go to officers who create and implement innovative crime prevention programs. The Commission felt that there was a definite opportunity for the department to change the value structure and recognize the importance of community involvement. Additionally, the department should be accountable to the community.

Source: City of Los Angeles (1991). *Report of the Independent Commission on the Los Angeles Police Department*. Los Angeles, CA: City of Los Angeles.

by the loss of power and status that took them years to attain. To empower operational personnel, it is necessary to flatten the organization, and give up the accoutrements of traditional positional authority. Change must be well-planned, flexible, and implemented in such a way as to minimize resistance. Planning for change should allow for incremental implementation of a new program, encourage officers to participation in the process, and provide for continual communications. Finally, every member of the department has to be trained (Johnson, 1994: 5-7). With well-planned change, it is anticipated that moderate or high correlations of effectiveness will be observed among community-oriented policing programs (Zhao and Thurman, 1996: 13).

Community policing varies considerably from department to department. Even defining community policing becomes a difficult task. The term has become so commonplace that just about every department claims to be operating under the rubric of community policing. Departments use the following terms for this process:

- Community Policing

- Community-Oriented Policing (COP)

- Problem-Solving Policing

- Problem-Oriented Policing

- Community-Based Policing

- Community-Oriented Policing and Problem Solving (COPPS)

- Community-Oriented Police Enforcement (COPE)

- Community Patrol Officer Program (CPOP)

- Community Policing Partnership Program

- Neighborhood-Oriented Policing (NOP)

- Citizen Contact Patrol

- Directed Area Response Team (DART)

- Community Mobilization Project (CMP)

Each of these terms is either a different approach, or in some instances the same program under a different title. Each term does little to provide guidance as to the philosophical underpinnings or the extent or true nature of the program. One common theme is that all of the terms infer a potential relationship with the community. They infer the opening up of two-way communication and allowing the public to become involved in making their community safer. One must realize that there is a possibility that an agency might state that it is involved in community policing, but in reality it is a means of placating the public and doing things the way things have always been done.

Community-Oriented and Problem-Oriented Policing

[A most promising approach to crime is the adoption of dual strategies that encompass both community-oriented policing and problem-oriented policing. Part of the growth of the police system in recent years has been experimentation and innovation as it has searched for a means of creating a modern police service that meets the exceptional demands currently being placed on the police of America. To most observers, it is clear that an extraordinary amount of effort is being placed on new and innovative programs that involve the marriage of the police and the community. There is a feeling of excitement and enthusiasm energizing the police service and it has allowed for actual experimentation, something that previously was not allowed (Goldstein, 1993: 1). The creation and extension of community policing has many barriers, pitfalls, and rocks in the roadway. This impeding factor can be overcome if the weaknesses of the professional policing model are dealt with and consideration is given to dealing with the ambiguity created by the implementation of a new system of policing. Agencies that become confused will announce the institution of community policing, but will seldom move beyond superficial programs such as mini-stations, bicycle patrol, or midnight basketball (Patterson, 1995: 9).

Leadership and Management

If the practices of community policing are superimposed on traditional policing strategies, it is necessary to make changes within the organization. Response-time policing is hierarchical and responsive to finite control, while community policing is flexible and the essence of operational discretion (Friedmann, 1992: 76). Under the concept of community policing, the primary role of management and staff is to support line operations. The importance of this approach should be set forth in the mission statement and values expressed by the department (see Chapter 2).

Organizational leaders, in dealing with subordinates, should reject the coercive leadership style and promote *Total Quality Management (TQM)*, which stresses listening to others, coaching, and fostering the personal development of employees (Couper, 1994: 12). Leaders must become change agents and involve all members of the organization in the development of the values statement that is compatible with the principles of COPPS (Glensor and Peak, 1996: 15). Involvement on the part of the members of the organization creates commitment, especially when they realize it involves their daily work (Stipak, Immer, and Clavadetscher, 1994: 120). Police executives must continuously support and reiterate the position that it will take a number of years to change an organization, and it takes constant and careful planning to achieve positive change. During this developmental process, it is essential to preclude undermining of the new program by involving all members of the organization in the philosophy of the new policing system. This is especially true of police middle managers who, with a perceived loss of prestige and power, have disrupted the implementation process of other attempts to introduce new programs. Middle managers should create an atmosphere that generates a sense of purpose. This can be based on the application of the art of influencing, guiding, instructing, directing, and controlling the activities of first-line supervisors and operational personnel.

First-line supervisors are essential constituents of this new style of policing. They must become part of the change process. Because of their influence over the attitudes and behavior of line personnel, they must be informed continuously and adequately trained. They should be trained as facilitators rather than controllers. First-line supervisors can effectively scuttle the implementation of community policing through the grapevine while openly expressing support to higher management.

Decisions that in the past were made at the supervisory or command level must become part of the working style of line personnel (Knowles, 1997: 43). Supervisors should arrange the schedules of officers so they can positively engage in problem-solving. They should work to remove barriers that impede or limit officers working with members of the community and other organizations. The operational guideline is: *facilitate–facilitate–facilitate*.

As officers are empowered, they find themselves in a new world where they have to make decisions. In fact, it is a process that is essential to the successful implementation of community policing. When operational personnel become increasingly independent and make decisions in a supportive atmosphere, errors can occur. This process is a far cry from the professional model of policing in which decisionmaking was the primary function of command personnel (Bennett, 1993: 86).

Formerly, risk taking, when making decisions, simply did not occur. It was incompatible with the regimentation of the bureaucratic agency. If one wanted a successful career, it was best not to rock the boat. The only decision was a benign one—put the problem in writing and buck it upstairs. Functioning under this method, mistakes were infrequent and the status quo was the operational guideline. Under community policing, mistakes are an allowable part of the process. When errors in judgment occur, they are accepted as a component of the learning process, and considered an essential ingredient of a managerial method with the fundamental goal of excellence.

If failure occurs, it must not only be acceptable but managed. This is best done by depicting failure as questionable judgment as it relates to a particular event or program and not a reflection on the individual decisionmaker (Garfield, 1986: 22-79). When failure is analyzed, and the reasons are shared with others, it can become a learning process for everyone concerned. The basic values of the Foster City Police Department (see Chapter 2) discuss this fundamental point by indicating that they "wish to promote an atmosphere that encourages prudent risk taking, and that recognizes that growth and learning may be spawned by honest mistakes," (Norman, 1992: 3).

Partnership With External Components

Ignored or accepted with reluctance under the professional policing model, the community policing style demands a new acceptance of the public and others outside of the police organization. Insularity must be rejected and others accepted as partners in reducing crime and improving the quality of life. Cooperative working relationships should be established between civic officials and representatives, businesses, members of the community, and providers of social services (Stipak, Immer, and Clavadetscher, 1994: 115).

The police should work with those who are affected by problems as a means of problem resolution. By initiating work with community groups, problems are more readily identified and neighbors can work together to resolve problems. It is most advantageous to work with citizens who are organized because experience shows there is a greater chance of focusing on and resolving problems. Additionally, once citizens are organized, the neighborhood entity is more apt to continue to exist once the immediate problem is resolved. Sustained effort and maintenance of citizen groups is critical inasmuch as problems quickly return (Friedman, 1996: 1). Research shows that neighborhood groups that are highly viable differ substantially from those that become inactive or expire. Effective neighborhood organizations give special consideration to a number of variables, including resource utilization, techniques of mobilization, organizational structure, extensive member participation, and responding to member opinions (Citizens' Committee for New York City, 1997: 3).

Resources. A significant characteristic of a strong neighborhood association is its ability to effectively utilize resources. The organization is more apt to make contact with and receive assistance from city departments, support organizations, and agencies. It utilized internal resources effectively by having members use their personal contacts to ensure that they obtained sufficient resources. Additionally, a strong block organization can network with nearby organizations in an effort to obtain information about issues of mutual concern.

Mobilization. Every effort is made to mobilize as many residents in the area as possible to become members of the organization. As much as possible, contributing members should be placed in positions of authority such as chairs of committees. Every member should be fully integrated into the organization and made to feel that they are a real member of the organization. Their contributions should be acknowledged whenever warranted, and new leaders should be cultivated by giving them positions of increasing responsibility. It has also been found that it is best to recruit new members by personal contact rather than using general announcements or by word-of-mouth. Communicating with members is essential and this should be done by a variety of means, including: flyers, newsletters, community newspapers, and bulletin boards.

Structure. Stronger neighborhood organizations are those that have numerous officers and committees, and were found to have written bylaws that specify roles, responsibilities, and operating procedures. Another important characteristic was the extensive use of written agendas and minutes as a means of conducting meetings in an orderly, timely, and predictable manner.

Member Participation. Strong associations employ democratic methods in all of their relationships with members. Everyone is allowed to participate in decision-making activities as well as every aspect of the planning process. Formalized voting procedures are followed and consensus rules. As a consequence of decentralization, responsibilities are delegated to a greater proportion of members and the democratic process permeates all activities. The organizational mandate is maximum participation and involvement. Time is scheduled for both business and pleasure. When time is provided for social interaction, it proves to be a catalytic process and helps to bond members to the organization.

Feature

Retaliation?

An anti-drug activist in Oakland, California, worked diligently in her neighborhood to eliminate rampant drug activities. She was very diligent and worked tirelessly on the goal of cleaning up the neighborhood. Her home had been firebombed on three separate occasions. On the last occasion, she was hospitalized for first- and second-degree burns. Fifteen percent of her body was burned in the latest bombing. She expressed the opinion that she could not believe that people could be so cruel. The Governor of California, Pete Wilson, offered a $50,000 reward for the arrest and conviction of those responsible for the firebombing, and the U.S. Drug Czar supported those who wanted the perpetrators caught and prosecuted. Several days later it was determined that the victim's sister had actually killed the crusader, by firebombing the house, hiding the dismembered body in a freezer, and assuming her identity. Contributions to help the burn victim were taken by the suspect and she forged her dead sister's name. Since then she has been arrested for forgery and murder.

Source: Adapted from *San Jose Mercury News* (1997a). "$50,000 Offered for Arrest, Conviction in Firebombing." July 10:1B; *San Jose Mercury News* (1997b). "Sister in Freezer, 'Scam-Artist' Suspect Still Puzzle Police." July 17:1A.

Member Opinion. Effective community organizations seriously consider the opinions of members. This process empowers members and provides a means for influencing organizational policies and actions. Empowerment places decisionmaking where it belongs—at the lowest level of the organization. This provides for less bureaucracy, and reduces red tape and delays. Additionally, empowerment allows members an opportunity to develop personal skills as an active member of the organization. Membership becomes real when empowerment becomes the operational mode of the community organization. Empowerment offers a win-win proposition (Ortiz and Peterson, 1994: 76). When integrated into the organization, new members should be given diverse assignments as a means of maintaining their interest.

During any implementation process, consideration should be given to joint planning or referral to health, probation, fire, zoning, or social service agencies.

The expertise of various agencies can be directed toward helping those in need, supporting victims, and focusing resources to ameliorate problems. Political leaders must support community policing efforts by providing continuing support and resources needed to ensure success. Also, the media needs to educate the public regarding the complexity of social issues and the need for joint response (Trojanowicz, 1994: 258-263).

Organizational Culture

The collective personality of a group is often referred to as culture. Over the years, a distinctive social orientation has developed within police organizations. Values, attitudes, expectations, norms, and behavioral patterns transfer from one generation of officers to the next and have become a way of life. For the most part, the police subculture remains isolated from the American mainstream. Officers share a common understanding, feelings, way of thinking, and methods of response, especially when the authority of the officer is questioned (More and Wegener, 1992: 240-241). Officers traditionally have been taught to maintain control of every situation and it is a major characteristic of officer behavior. They share a common language and argot of the trade. They support each other and are loyal to each other. They are a group that emphasizes the need for secrecy based on a time-honored position that policing is unique and a mindset that says *it is us against the world*. For years they have taken the position that they are proud members of *the thin blue line*, and the real protectors of society. Solidarity, esprit de corps, and isolation serve as pillars that serve to socialize officers more deeply into the police subculture. Many organizations have taboos and that is certainly true of law enforcement. Officers are never allowed to express fear or show a lack of courage. They must always back up fellow officers who are in danger or need assistance. Noncompliance with the taboos will lead to ostracism.

Figure 3-2
Characteristics of the Police Subculture

Solidarity	Secrecy
Loyalty	Esprit de corps
Isolation	Special argot
Semi-military	Control
Uniqueness	Bureaucracy
Conformity	Common values
Shared attitudes	Organizational norms
Social orientation	Authority
Legal foundation	Cohesiveness
Protectors	Professionals
Weapons	Taboos
Calm under stress	Code of silence
Group mores	Military rank

The culture of law enforcement is deep-seated and powerful. The police academy has usually been the first step in socializing new officers. They are taught how to act, think, and feel in the police subculture. After graduation, on-the-job experience reinforces the values of the organization, and the officer becomes a more integral part of the culture (Mollen, 1994: 51-69).

Organizational rank does not come easily in police organization. Few rise above the level of first-line supervisor. Consequently, those who have attained rank zealously protect their turf. Rank has its privileges and every effort is made to retain those privileges and deny them to others. The clearest illustration of this is the potential loss of power by allowing those of lower ranks to make decisions.

If the COPPS program is to become a reality, it must become a part of the organizational culture. This means that changes must occur that affect recruitment, selection, training, methods of evaluation, promotions, rewards, and disciplinary procedures (Glensor and Peak, 1996: 17). The need for officers to control every individual and situation must be replaced with a sharing of power with members of the community.

Forces Impeding Community Policing

Alteration of the traditional policing style is essential if community policing or any variations that fall under that umbrella term are to be successfully implemented. It is not known how much resistance will occur, but conflict is inevitable and should be anticipated. When community policing is being considered, one typical response is "there is not enough time." Initially, community policing can be viewed by officers as a process of loading on extra work, and they can be uncomfortable with the idea of policing in a different fashion (West, 1997: 51-53). The following Feature illustrates the conflict that can occur between the police and a neighborhood group.

Feature

Community Patrol Cuts Into Crime

A 20-member neighborhood watch in Sacramento, California, patrols midtown on foot, bicycles, and with canines. During the past year, they arrested more than one dozen suspects. One of the suspects was charged with nearly 50 graffiti taggings. Arrests have ranged from petty theft to auto burglary. In some instances, members of the patrol have videotaped suspects for later prosecution. All of this was done without the cooperation of the police department. The cops praise the work they have done, but are concerned about the danger. Civilian patrol members have been attacked with chemical spray, steel rods, and baseball bats. The patrol is currently working to improve communications with the police.

Source: Adapted from *San Jose Mercury News* (1997c). "Neighborhood Patrols Cut Into Crime, Community Watch Makes Citizen Arrests." July 25:3B.

Supporting or accepting resistance will lead to the eventual failure of community policing, whatever its form. Conflict can and should provide a stimulus for attaining organizational values and goals. It is a process that allows for organizational effectiveness and positive decisionmaking. Managing conflict creates an organizational psychology that emphasizes employee well-being. If conflict is not managed, negativism and rejection of the new policing style will be constantly reinforced

Community policing will be unsuccessful if a number of things occur that are set forth in Figure 3-3. The first thing to do is preserve the status quo and maintain that the department has always been involved in community policing. Describe the dedication of the department to continue such programs as *ride along* and *bicycle patrol,* which the department has used for years, and point out that citizens have responded enthusiastically to these programs. The detractor of community policing can add to this by extolling the *annual open house* as a significant part of the department's community policing program. This total posturing ensures that there is no need to change or get on the bandwagon of the currently mandated style of policing. The new system can be defeated by demanding acquiescence to the organizational chain of command, deference to rank, and the need to continue functioning as a quasi-military organization. At all costs, the department should retain the values of a professional police agency, ignore the advances in community policing, and just keep doing what they have been doing for many years.

Figure 3-3
Things to Do to Ensure That Community Policing Will Fail

• Retain rigid rules and regulations.
• Ignore or limit community input.
• Restrict or limit those involved in the problem identification or planning process.
• Ignore input from line personnel.
• Limit the authority of middle managers.
• Confine rewards to number of arrests and citations.
• Maintain the organizational hierarchy.
• Measure effectiveness by response time.
• Demand that all programs conform to the chain of command.
• Ignore efforts to sabotage community policing.
• Filter all communications from the bottom to the top of the organization.

Source: V.A. Leonard and Harry W. More (1993). *Police Organization and Management*, Eighth Edition. Westbury, NY: The Foundation Press.

Values-Driven Training

The training of recruits for law enforcement agencies is very different today. An example is the training of new police officers in the Massachusetts basic course for police, which emphasizes four guiding principles (Lebowitz, 1997: 2):

- Ethics (character)

- The law (constitutional basis)

- Fitness (both mental and physical)

- Community policing

The four principles listed above filter through every aspect of the content of the curriculum. The orientation, which lasts one week, requires students to think creatively and look for solutions to problems. It provides the foundation for the remainder of the curriculum, which stresses the following five fundamental objectives:

- Incorporate community policing throughout;

- Adopt a values-driven model of training;

- Integrate training and education;

- Train as a collaboration of police organizations with a shared history, a common body of knowledge, and an equal stake in self-evaluation; and

- Enhance character by examining the complexities of society and the choices of police officers.

Figure 3-4
Policing: The Basic Curriculum
A Values-Driven Educational Model of Police Education
Enforcement—Fear Reduction—Crime Prevention

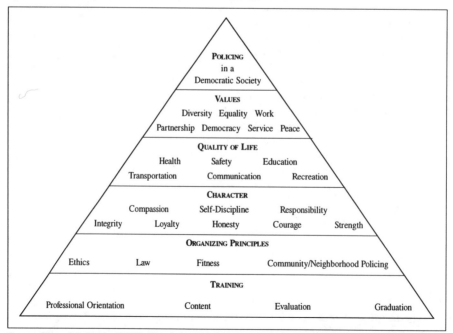

Source: Howard Lebowitz (1997). "Academy Training Curriculum Minimizes the Physical Factor, Emphasizes Moral Decision Making." Reprinted from Phase IV, No. 13 of *Community Policing Exchange*. For more information about this publication, call: 800-833-3085.

Each objective influences the curriculum and the methods of instruction. For example, the community policing philosophy talks about partnership, prevention, and problem solving. Officers are taught to identify and collaborate with partners, develop prevention strategies, and see police tasks as problems to be solved, not just calls to be cleared. Moral decisionmaking is discussed in every element of the curriculum. Difficult decisions are discussed with an emphasis on the outcomes of various actions.

When values are discussed, it is a great deal more than respect and politeness. The instruction takes the position that police and citizens share a set of values. Some of these values are safe schools, homes, and roadways; equality in the law and access to public services; a healthy environment and access to health service; freedom from fear; and protection from those who are a danger to others. The new curriculum emphasizes that, in the end, all police activities must be measured and communicated in terms of quality of life or community values. Finally, stress is placed on the fact that one cannot begin to talk about police-community partnerships without trust, communication, and integrity (Lebowitz, 1997: 2).

The Problem-Solving Process

A key characteristic of the modern approach to policing is a positive orientation to problem solving. It involves more than responding to 911 calls. It is a matter of viewing incidents from a community perspective to resolve the problem not just simply handling an incident. The following Feature graphically depicts the community policing methods of dealing with crime.

Problem-oriented policing shifts police efforts from a reactive to a proactive response to crime in which officers work with residents to prevent crime (Police Executive Research Forum, 1996: 5). Citizens, police departments, and other agencies work together to identify problems and apply appropriate problem-solving strategies (Rabkin, 1995: 1-21). This approach emerged in the late 1970s and was initially described by Herman Goldstein. It was his position that the police should be concerned with the problems that were of concern to residents of a community (Goldstein, 1990: 1-32). The central thesis of problem-oriented policing is that underlying incidents to which police respond are more general problems which, in order to be resolved, require a different type of response than do the incidents that are indicative of the problems. Problem solving requires analysis of the incidents by persons knowledgeable of the context in which they occur, followed by creative brainstorming about and experimentation with possible responses (Wycoff and Skogan, 1993: 9-10). While problem-oriented policing theoretically can be conducted in the absence of community-oriented policing, it is an excellent method of achieving the goals of community-oriented policing. This is why the model that is proposed in this chapter combines both under the term—community-oriented policing and problem solving (COPPS).

Feature

Community Collaboration in Problem Solving

Community policing partnership requires residents who are active at the community level to select problems and develop and implement strategies. But partnerships also require that the community have a say at the jurisdictional level, where the conditions of the partnership are set. Without give-and-take in establishing the guidelines of collaboration, partnerships will reflect the needs and concerns of police departments and not those of the neighborhood partners.

The police should be working very consciously in partnership with those who are affected by the problems and who are working or will work with their neighbors to solve them. There are two reasons for focusing on those who are organized. First, a collective community is more likely to be sustained and successful in solving as problem than an individual. Second, an organized effort is more likely to continue to exist after the problem is solved. The emphasis on working with residents who are organized does not mean that law enforcement agencies should stop responding to individual calls or refuse to work with individuals. It does mean that for community policing to be an effective crime-fighting strategy, there must be an emphasis on partners who can help produce long-term crime reduction. It does mean that where these partnerships do not exist or are weak, there must be an investment in creating or strengthening them.

Source: Warren Friedman (1996). *Community Collaboration: Essential for Long-Term Crime Reduction.* Washington, DC: Community Policing Consortium, September/October:1-8.

This process is a proactive philosophy that promotes the concept that incidents consuming patrol and investigative time can best be dealt with more effectively when consideration is given to underlying problems. It also assumes that the expertise and creativity of line officers are reliable sources when developing solutions to problems. Finally, if problem solving in the community is to be successful, then the police must work with the public to ensure that they are addressing the real needs of citizens.

Detectives and line officers are the personnel who can use the problem-solving approach. It allows them to continuously identify, analyze, and respond to the underlying causes that prompt citizens to request police services. It is not a one-shot project or program, but a comprehensive process for identifying, addressing, and resolving problems. It is a strategy consisting of four stages, called **SARA** (Spelman and Eck, 1987: 2):

Scanning—Identifying the problem;
Analysis—Learning the problem's causes, scope, and effects;
Response—Acting to alleviate the problem; and,
Assessment—Determining whether the response worked.

Once a problem is identified, information about the problem is collected. This information is then analyzed in detail. Action is then taken to correct the problem, and the final stage assesses whether the action had the desired effect on the problem.

Scanning

Instead of relying upon legal terms such as *robbery, burglary,* or *petty theft* to guide a response, officers analyze specific offenses in a broader context and address them as problems. Then these problems are dealt with according to their impact on the neighborhood or the community. For example, a police incident such as *auto theft* might be a part of a *chop* operation (cutting up an automobile into saleable or usable parts). A series of *house burglaries* might in reality be a school *truancy* problem.

Scanning initiates the problem-solving process. In a truly problem-oriented police department, every member scans for problems and brings the problem to the attention of a supervisor. With everyone involved, no one can assume that it is someone else's responsibility. In other words, passing the buck becomes somewhat limited. Some officers are better than others at identifying problems. Some accept the new process as a challenge, and others find it is extra work that is to be avoided at all costs. Other officers are reluctant to identify problems because they might be stuck with working on the problem (Eck and Spelman, 1987: 45). Over time, objections such as those mentioned above can be overcome as officers become more accustomed to the problem-solving process. The objectives of the scanning process include:

- Looking for problems

- Initial identification of possible problems

- Initial analysis to determine whether the problem exists and whether a detailed analysis is needed

- Prioritizing problems and assigning personnel

Agency personnel have numerous sources that can be used to identify problems, but in many instances officers will initially rely upon their own experience to identify problems. Most officers are cautious about announcing the identification of a problem until they truly feel that a problem actually exists. This usually means that problems have been rejected before bringing the problem to the attention of others. Sources available to officers are numerous and are identified in Figure 3-5. The list is not meant to be comprehensive, but it clearly reflects a wide range of information sources.

Figure 3-5
Possible Information Sources for Identifying Problems

Officer's Agency	Other Police Departments
Local Government Agencies	Elected Officials
Community Residents	Community Centers
Neighborhood Associations	Community-Based Organizations
Prosecutor's Office	Public Defender's Office
Mediation Centers	Social Service Agencies
Counseling Services	Agencies Serving the Elderly
Boards of Education	Teachers
School Principals	Housing Authorities
Businesses	Civic Clubs
Victim Service Agencies	Elected Officials
Neighborhood Watch	Chamber of Commerce
Youth Services	Health Services
Transit Agencies	Planning Agencies
Community Surveys	

Analysis

After identification of the problem, the officers assigned should collect information from every conceivable source even remotely related to the problem. This includes private as well as public sources. For example, it can include information from neighborhood associations and neighborhood watch groups. Other sources include elected officials or the news media as well as information from other law enforcement or governmental agencies. Officers can use a checklist to ensure all the needed information is collected. The three areas of concern include:

- Actors involved in the problem, including victims and offenders;

- Specific incidents, including the sequence of events and the physical contact involved in the incidents; and

- The responses by the community and institutional entities.

All the information gathered serves as a foundation for developing a thorough understanding of the real problem. This serves as a basis for identifying causes and developing options for its resolution. The checklist reminds officers of areas and topics open to consideration. Implicit in the list are potential sources of information that might not have been covered under the *scanning* part of the assessment process. During *analysis,* emphasis is given to external information sources such as: citizens, business leaders, community associations, and other community groups. The checklist also refers to the multitude of local, state, and federal agencies. One of the best sources, developed in recent years is the Community Policing Consortium (discussed later in this chapter) that can be accessed on the World Wide Web (www.communitypolicing.org). One can determine what is being done in other agencies by going to the consortium's home page and clicking on "Community Policing Resources." Additionally, a review of problem-solving strategies and success stories can be found by clicking on "Consortium Publications."

When utilizing the checklist, officers will not normally collect information from all of the sources listed, but only from those directly related to the problem under consideration. Another qualifier is the time the officer has available to search for an appropriate response to the problem under consideration (Eck and Spelman, 1987: 47). There is a tendency for officers to identify the response to the problem before completing the analysis and, if and when this occurs, options might be eliminated from consideration.

Figure 3-6
Checklist for the Analysis of a Problem

Actors	
Victims	Lifestyle
	Security measures taken
	Victimization history
	This victimization
Offenders	Identity and physical description
	Lifestyle, education, employment history, medical history
	Criminal history
Third parties	Personal data
	Connection to victimization
	Nature of involvement
	Expectations for police action
Incidents	
Sequence of events	Target of act
	Types of tools used by offenders
	Events preceding act
	Event itself
	Events following criminal act
Physical contact	Chronology
	Location
	Access control
	Surveillance
Social context	Likelihood and probable actions of witnesses
	Attitude of residents toward neighborhood
Responses	
Community	Neighborhood affected by problem
	City as a whole
	People outside the city
	Groups
Institutional	Criminal justice agencies
	Other public agencies
	Mass media
	Business sector

Source: William Spelman and John E. Eck (1987). "Problem Oriented Policing." *Research in Brief.* Washington, DC: National Institute of Justice.

Response

This stage requires initiative by the officer, as different solutions are identified and the best solution is selected and implemented. The potential solutions to a problem are increased by involving outside agencies that have resources and expertise seldom available within the police agency. This stage involves working with individuals, businesses, and private agencies. It also requires the officer to work with public agencies such as the probation department, health department, public works, and the social service department. All of these sources are important because other agencies and entities can come up with responses that fall outside of the normal expertise possessed by law enforcement agencies. Combined resources can prove to be the most effective response to the problem being studied. Officers striving to find a solution to a problem should have free rein for discovering the answer. In one city, the only restriction was that the solution had to be legally, financially, administratively, and politically possible (Spelman and Eck, 1987: 2).

Solutions to problems can be organized into five responses (Eck and Spelman, 1987: 49):

- Total problem elimination;

- Material reduction of the problem;

- Reduction of the harm caused by the problem;

- Dealing with the problem with the best possible solution; and

- Removal of the problem from police consideration.

When a solution becomes apparent, implementation should occur immediately or incrementally, depending upon the circumstances. Some problems are subject to immediate solution, because they are minor in nature or involve only a few people. Other solutions might involve broad social issues that require a complex response.

Assessment

Assessment is the final stage and it involves measuring how well the program performed. Was it effective? The agency and the community work together to answer these questions. Possibly the initial analysis was flawed, or the wrong response was selected. The process of assessment can provide an officer with the information needed to determine success. For some situations *assessment* is quite simple and the results are obvious. In other situations, it is complex and may involve the collection of complex data. Surveys are becoming increasingly common and can be used to achieve four goals (Bureau of Justice Assistance, 1993: 7):

- Gathering information on the public's attitudes toward police and neighborhood priorities (Gnagey and Henson, 1995: 25-27; Griffith, 1993: 37-40).

- Detect and analyze problems in neighborhoods or among special populations.

- Evaluate problem-solving efforts and other programs.

- Control crime and reduce fear of crime.

Feature

Community Policing and Problem Solving

Gang activity, drug dealing, shootings, prostitution—you name it, they all occur in Gill Park. The problem of the park was raised in beat community meetings. Selected as a neighborhood problem, beat officers discussed the problem with residents trained in cooperative problem solving. Analysis of the problem reflected the fact that the problem had three sides: offenders, victims, and location. The offenders were identified as gang members, drug dealers, and drug buyers. The victims were the adults and children who no longer could enjoy the park, and property owners whose buildings were devalued by the criminal presence in the park. The park was dark and unkempt. Officers did not have a good view of the park because of poor lighting, and overgrown trees and bushes. The physical layout of the park was conducive to crime.

Two sides of the crime triangle were addressed—the offenders and the location. Foot patrols were implemented in the park, and officers aggressively enforced curfew and loitering laws. Nearby residents of a high-rise agreed to use their bird's eye view to keep closer watch on the park and report suspicious activity. City crews trimmed the trees and installed more lighting. Residents secured permission from the Chicago Park District to renovate the park and eliminate the troublesome back area. A neighborhood architect donated plans for the park's renovation and showcased a baseball diamond as its central feature. The Chicago Cubs donated $20,000 for the new sports field and funds were received from other businesses and organizations. After a little more than one year, the renovations were completed. Results were evaluated and consideration was given to what worked and what did not work. Overall, everyone agreed that Gill Park was a glorious success.

Source: Barbara B. McDonald and Richard Glasser (1996). *Building a Field of Dreams: Anatomy of a Problem-Solving Strategy.* Washington, DC: Community Policing Consortium (November/December).

When evaluating a problem-solving program, multiple surveys can prove to be most effective. For example, before-and-after surveys can be used to determine changes in citizens' fear of crime as a result of a police intervention. Problem-solving units of the Baltimore County Police Department routinely use this technique to gauge their effectiveness. Another area in which surveys are most useful is the environment. By recording and analyzing the environmental characteristics of a problem area, environmental surveys can be used at each stage of the problem-solving process, from scanning through assessment. They help an officer analyze the nature of a problem by identifying what factors contribute to the crime and point to incivilities in the problem area. Used before and after implementing a problem-solving effort, environmental surveys enable the officer to measure the effectiveness of the effort (Bureau of Justice Assistance, 1993: 54).

The values of community policing are different from those practiced under the traditional response to crime. Expressed values, as set forth in the previous chapter, can serve as the basis for citizens understanding the police function in a democracy. The problem-solving process can be used to reinforce the values of the police department and the community, and have proven to be a vital tool for law enforcement.

Benefit to the Community

The community can benefit greatly from this new style of policing. One of the earlier experiments with community policing took place in the Houston, Texas Police Department. Under the leadership of Lee Brown, the Houston Police Department began to operate under a set of values during the 1980s. As the program evolved, it had its problems, but as a pioneering organization, it accomplished a great deal. This program emphasized problem solving and collaboration with the community. As part of this program, redesigning beats occurred, which reflected natural neighborhood boundaries. A variety of programs were started, emphasizing greater community involvement. The benefits to the community included the following (Brown, 1989: 1-7; Skolnick and Bayley, 1988: 67-70):

- **Commitment to Crime Prevention**. The basic mission of the department is the prevention of crime and disorder. This is in sharp contrast to the traditional policing concept, which focuses on responding to an incident. It is interesting to note that it reiterates the cornerstone of the Peelian reform discussed in Chapter Two.

- **Public Scrutiny of Police Operations**. The nature of community policing is such that there is an interactive process between the community and the police. They work together to identify and resolve community problems. This exposes the police to a critical evaluation of how they actually operate. It is a significant step and can revolutionize American law enforcement as it moves away from the professional model of policing.

- **Accountability to the Public**. As a typical bureaucracy, the police have traditionally operated under many regulations and police directives. In the traditional mode of policing, line officers were primarily accountable to police managers. Under community policing, officers are accountable not only to managers but to the public. This means that there is mutual accountability. As each group participates in policy development and plans for handling problems, they will need to become aware of (and more concerned about) the results of their actions.

- **Customized Police Service**. With the localization of police services, line officers increase their responsiveness to community problems identified by citizens. The creation of a police-citizen partnership allows the group to analyze and respond to problems. This is especially true of problems having a direct impact on the quality of life in the neighborhood. Commitment to a specific geographical area results in officers becoming genuinely concerned with neighborhood problems. In contrast to traditional approaches, officers functioning under community policing want to know what incidents occurred on the beat when they were off duty. A sense of obligation to the neighborhood develops as problems are looked at from a different perspective and the police deal with victims on a continuing and personal basis (Brown, 1989: 1-11).

- **Community Organization**. The greater the degree of public involvement in addressing community problems, the greater the potential for effective problem solving. Through the years, it has become increasingly clear that the cooperative approach of the police and the public results in the development of workable crime prevention programs. Constructive action with the police and the community working together is always better than the police operating alone. Community response allows citizens to accept personal responsibility for incidents and events that occur in their neighborhood rather than relying on the police as the agency that is solely responsible for controlling and reducing crime.

Before undertaking a program in the neighborhood, the appropriate community organizations are contacted and changes are discussed. The police must be willing to openly discuss the selection of problems, the establishment of priorities, and the methods used to deal with a problem. Such a commitment to public input reflects the high value the police place on the working partnership. It also recognizes the community as an important resource (Wasserman and Moore, 1988: 1-7).

Benefits of Community Policing to the Police

Community policing embodies both an operational and managerial philosophy that definitely benefits the organization and all its members (Skolnick and Bayley, 1988: 70-73):

- **Greater Citizen Support**. As members of the public work with the police, they become more knowledgeable about police operations. As knowledge increases, respect for the police increases. This in turn results in greater support for the police. Over a period of time, citizens become increasingly aware that the police have a real concern for those who live in a neighborhood. It becomes readily apparent that the police want to deal with the real concerns of citizens.

- **Shared Responsibility**. The value statement of the Houston Police Department clearly expresses the belief that the police should have input into policy development. This is especially true of problems affecting community life. Traditionally, the police assumed primary responsibility for resolving community crime. Under community policing, shared responsibility guides each officer's action. Both groups accept the viewpoint that the police alone cannot successfully suppress and reduce crime.

- **Greater Job Satisfaction**. Rather than taking report after report, officers work for the resolution of problems. Problem solving is accomplished within a reasonable period, resulting in greater job satisfaction. This is in sharp contrast to beats where officers have many 911 calls that are prioritized. Most officers working busy shifts do little but push papers and respond to calls. Problem resolution is different—it gives the job meaning and enhances job satisfaction.

- **Job Enlargement.** Under community policing, the individual officer is allowed to develop creative skills as he or she identifies and works to resolve problems of concern to members of the community. Additionally, they are given the opportunity to apply skills acquired from courses taken in institutions of higher learning. This is particularly true when an officer applies expertise to the identification, resolution, and assessment of community problems. Officers can grow in their job as they are allowed to make mistakes and learn from the process rather than being condemned. The high degree of freedom given to line officers under community policing enhances growth and the development of a true professional.

- **Better Internal Relationships**. Communications has long been a critical problem in many law enforcement agencies. Many observers of the police scene are familiar with departments in which one major unit dominates, and the barriers to communications are many. In one agency, two of the major units—field operations and investigations—are managed as if they were independent agencies. Under community policing, communications barriers can be breached and internal problems resolved because the emphasis is on accountability and problem-solving. Cooperation will improve as problems are approached mutually and various units within the department respond to neighborhood problems.

- **Support for Organizational Change.** Many changes are needed if community policing is to be successful. It starts with a change in management style. Authoritarian leadership has limited value and each employee must be viewed as a potential contributor to the organization. Additional changes must be made in performance evaluation criteria. The reward system must emphasize the attainment of the value structure of the department. In addition, the training system and its method of delivery should meet the expectations of a community-oriented police department.

As the organization shifts from a traditional role to a more contemporary role, it will be necessary to restructure the organization. Such units as patrol, investigation, planning, and records should be reorganized to meet the demands of the new delivery system. Change is not readily accepted in most instances. Strong resistance can be anticipated from those within the organization who will lose power. Others will resist because they will have to learn how to work under a system drastically different from the way the job has always been performed. Do not underestimate the fact that such a drastic change, unless carefully planned, can be unsettling to many and actually threatening to others. The reasons for opposing change are too numerous to include: "It cannot work," "this is not the way we do it," "we have been doing it this way ever since I joined the force," "no one asked me if this would work," "it is not police work," "it will cost too much money," and " if it's not broken, leave it alone" (Leonard, 1997: 64).

• **Enhanced Supervision**. First-line supervisors are critical to the strategy of problem solving. Supervisors are effective when they encourage officers to recognize problems, conduct attentive analysis, and search for a variety of responses. Supervisors must create an operational philosophy that emphasizes a supportive role. The key is to give officers as much discretion as they need as a means of performing effectively. Supervisors must give officers adequate time and support to deal with complex problems. Additionally, they must set work schedules that allow officers to adequately deal with problem-solving activities. In their supervisory role, they must follow up the problem-solving process and ensure that adequate resources are available and appropriately applied. This is particularly true of staffing. Supervisors must maintain staffing levels that will ensure that problems are confronted adequately. When problems are solved, supervisors must give credit to the officers who were responsible for the work (Eck and Spelman, 1987: 104-06).

Community Policing Consortium

The consortium is a Washington, D.C.-based organization that provides police departments and community groups with information on community-oriented policing. Additionally, it provides training sessions and seminars on community policing. The consortium consists of the following organizations: The International Association of Chiefs of Police, the National Sheriff's Association, the Police Executive Research Forum, the National Organization of Black Law Enforcement Executives, and the Police Foundation (Oliver, 1997: 45-49).

The consortium, through its publications, shares information with community policing practitioners. The *Community Policing Exchange* is published six times a year and has an extensive audience of law enforcement officials and city managers. The *Sheriff Times* provides community policing information to sheriffs and county administrators. A third publication is *Community Links*. Its audience includes civic activists and elected officials. It is published twice a year. It is anticipated that this publication will be converted to a computer bulletin board. Finally, the *Information Access Guide* provides monthly updates of community policing information and resources (Hoffman, 1997: 126-128).

Figure 3-7
Community Policing Consortium Resources on the World Wide Web

Publications:
Community policing practitioners share problem-solving strategies and success stories.
At our homepage, click on Consortium Publications.
• *Community Policing Exchange*
• *Sheriff Times*
• *Community Links*
• *Articles by Topic*

Resources:
At our homepage, click on Community Policing Resources.
Information Access Guide
The Guide is divided into six major categories and lists more than 450 community policing practitioners, community organizers and volunteers willing to share their practical experiences.

Communications:
Books
Clearinghouses
Newsletters
Videos

Community Initiatives:
Local Organizations
National Organizations
Regional Organizations
State and Federal Organizations

Government Contacts:
Bureau of Justice Assistance
National Institute of Justice
Office of Community Oriented
  Policing Services (COPS)
U.S. Department of Education

Law Enforcement:
Adopt-a-Cop
Asset Forfeiture
Bike Patrol
Community Mobilization
Crime Prevention
Cultural Diversity
Domestic Violence
Drug Abatement
Evaluation/Assessment
Implementing Community
  Policing
Investigators
Jail Management
Leadership
Maximizing Resources
Organizational Change
Partnerships/Corrections
Police Misconduct
Problem Solving
Recruitment/Selection
  Procedures
Residential Officer Programs
Strategic Planning
Strategies
Substations
Technology
Training
Volunteer Programs
Weed and Seed Sites

Upcoming Events:
Events, conferences, training sessions and seminars

Youth Initiatives:
Athletic Programs
At-Risk Youth Programs
Child Safety Programs
Community Involvement
Community Opportunities
Crime Prevention
Curfews
Gang Bibliography
Gang Prevention
Juvenile Justice
  Alternatives
Juvenile Probation
Leadership Programs
Police-Probation Partnerships
Police-School Partnerships
Underage Drinking
  Prevention
Violence
Weapons Initiatives
Youth Organizations

www.communitypolicing.org

COMMUNITY POLICING CONSORTIUM
1726 M. St. N.W., Suite 801, Washington, DC 20036
Phone (202) 833-3305 • Fax (202) 833-9295
E-mail: nsapubs@communitypolicing.org

Source: Reprinted from Phase IV, No. 13 of *Community Policing Exchange*. For more information about this publication call: 1-800-833-3085.

Summary

The professional model of policing dominated in America for a major part of the twentieth century. Many departments adopted a legalistic style of policing, while a few used a service model. As agencies evolved, the bureaucratic model dominated and the semi-military organizational style prevailed. Centralization was viewed as a means of eliminating political influence and reducing corruption. Advances in technology altered the mode of policing, but the crime rates increased and the police strategies proved to be ineffective in controlling major disturbances. Efforts to modify the professional model of policing revolved around two different approaches—team policing and community relations. Each of these efforts was not as successful as had been hoped because of internal conflict in some agencies. Community relations proved to be a forerunner of the current model of policing.

Community policing varies from agency to agency, and it appears that the adoption of a dual strategy can prove to be most viable. This a combination of community-oriented policing and problem-oriented policing. It utilizes a total quality management approach to policing, giving special consideration to leadership, external relationships, and organizational culture.

The traditional policing style must be altered if community policing is to succeed. Detractors are numerous and range from rigid rules to a retention of all of the aspects of a bureaucracy. To thwart the installation of community policing, departments can take the position that they have always been involved in community policing and can describe the programs that they have defined as representative of the new policing style.

Contemporary training for community policing involves the adoption of a values-driven training module. The philosophy of the new policing model is taught with an emphasis on partnership, prevention, and problem solving. Officers are taught to identify and collaborate with partners, develop prevention strategies, and see police tasks as problems to be solved. Throughout the training cycle, strong emphasis is given to moral decisionmaking.

A major element of COPPS is the stress that is placed on problem solving as a comprehensive process for identifying, addressing, and resolving problems. It is a strategy consisting of four parts: scanning, analysis, response, and assessment. It is a unique approach to dealing with community problems because it draws upon the experience of actual working personnel, other agencies, and members of the public (as individuals or collectively).

Benefits to the community that becomes involved in community policing vary from a commitment to crime prevention to customized police services. Of major significance is the fact that the police become accountable to the public. The police benefit from the partnership because they receive greater public support. Additionally, police officers find that they have greater job satisfaction and better internal relations.

The latest resource for community policing is the consortium. It consists of five national law enforcement agencies that have combined their expertise and serve as a clearinghouse on community policing. It provides police departments, civic activists, elected officials, sheriffs, city managers, and county administrators with information on community policing. It also provides seminars and training sessions and serves as a vehicle for the exchange of information between agencies.

References

Bennett, Charles W., Jr. (1993). "The Last Taboo of Community Policing." *The Police Chief*, Vol. LX, No. 8:86.

Bobinsky, Robert (1994). "Reflections on Community-Oriented Policing." *FBI Law Enforcement Bulletin*, Vol. 63, No. 3:15-20.

Brown, Lee P. (1989). *Community Policing: A Practical Guide for Police Officials*. Washington, DC: U.S. Department of Justice.

Brown, Lee P. (1991). "Policing in the '90s, Trends, Issues and Concerns." *The Police Chief*, Vol. LVIII, No. 3:20-23.

Bureau of Justice Assistance (1993). *A Police Guide To Surveying Citizens and Their Environment*. Washington, DC: Office of Justice Programs.

Citizens' Committee for New York City (1997). "What Makes a Community Organization Effective?" *Community Links*, Vol. 1, No. 1, Washington, DC: Community Policing Consortium.

City of Los Angeles (1991). *Report of the Independent Commission on the Los Angeles Police Department*. Los Angeles, CA: City of Los Angeles.

Couper, David C. (1994). "Seven Seeds for Policing." *FBI Law Enforcement Bulletin*, Vol. 63, No. 3:12-14.

Cox, Steven M. (1990). "Policing into the 21st Century." *Journal of Police Studies*, Vol. 13, No. 4:168-177.

Eck, John C., and William Spelman (1987). *Problem-Solving: Problem Oriented Policing in Newport News*. Washington, DC: U.S. Department of Justice and Police Executive Research Forum.

Farrell, Michael J. (1988). "The Development of the Community Patrol Officer Program: Community-Oriented Policing in the New York City Police Department." In Jack R. Greene and Stephen D. Mastrofski (eds.), *Community Policing: Rhetoric or Reality*? New York: Praeger.

Friedman, Warren (1996). *Community Collaboration: Essential for Long-Term Crime Reduction*. Washington, DC: Community Policing Consortium.

Friedmann, Robert R. (1992). *Community Policing: Comparative Perspectives and Prospects*. New York: Harvester and Wheatsheaf.

Garfield, Charles (1986). *Peak Performers: The New Heroes of American Business*. New York: William Morrow and Company.

Gerth, H.H. and C. Wright Mills (1958). *Max Weber: Essays in Sociology*. New York: Oxford University Press.

Glensor, Ronald W. and Ken Peak (1996). "Implementing Change—Community-Oriented Policing and Problem Solving." *FBI Law Enforcement Bulletin*. Vol. 65, No. 7:14-21.

Gnagey, John and Ronald Henson (1995). "Community Surveys Help Determine Policing Strategies." *The Police Chief*, Vol. LXII, No. 3:25-27.

Goldstein, Herman (1990). *Problem Oriented Policing*. New York: McGraw-Hill.

Goldstein, Herman (1993). *The New Policing: Confronting Complexity*. Washington, DC: U.S. Department of Justice, Office of Justice Programs.

Griffith, Douglas L. (1993). "Citizen Feedback Line." *Law and Order*, Vol. 412, No. 12:37-40.

Hellriegel, Don and John W. Slocum, Jr. (1976). *Organizational Behavior: Contingency Views.* St. Paul, MN: West Publishing.

Hoffman, John (1997). "Community Policing Consortium." *Law and Order*, Vol. 45, No. 5:126-128.

Johnson, Robert A. (1994). "Police Organizational Design and Structure." *FBI Law Enforcement Bulletin*, Vol. 63, No. 6:5-7.

Knowles, Terry L. (1997). "Meeting the Challenges of the 21st Century." *The Police Chief*, Vol. LXIV, No. 6:39-43.

Lebowitz, Howard (1997). "Academy Training Curriculum Minimizes the Physical Factor, Emphasizes Moral Decision Making." *Community Policing Exchange*. Washington, DC: The Community Policing Consortium.

Leonard, Karl S. (1997). "Making Change a Positive Experience." *Law and Order*, Vol 45, No. 5:63-65.

Leonard, V.A. and Harry W. More (1987). *Police Organization and Management*, Seventh Edition. Mineola, NY: The Foundation Press, Inc.

Leonard, V.A. and Harry W. More (1993). *Police Organization and Management*, Eighth Edition. Westbury, NY: The Foundation Press.

McDonald, Barbara B. and Richard Glasser (1996). *Building a Field of Dreams: Anatomy of a Problem-Solving Strategy.* Washington, DC: Community Policing Consortium (November/December).

Manus, Raymond P. (1995). "Misconceptions and 'Urban Village Policing.'" *Law Enforcement News*, Vol. XX, No. 448:8, 11.

Mollen, Milton (1994). *Commission Report: Commission to Investigate Allegations of Police Corruption and the Anti-Corruption Procedures of the Police Department.* New York, NY: The City of New York.

More, Harry W. and O.R. Shipley (1987). *Police Policy Manual—Personnel.* Springfield, IL: Charles C Thomas.

More, Harry W. and Fred W. Wegener (1992). *Behavioral Police Management.* New York: Macmillan.

Norman, Robert G. (1992). *Organizational Values: A Vision Becomes a Reality (One Man's Perspective)* (Unpublished). Foster City, CA: author.

Oliver, Willard M. (1997). *The COPS Office: The Office of Community Oriented Policing.* Washington, DC: Community Policing Consortium, 45-49.

Ortiz, Robert L. and Marilyn B. Peterson (1994). "Police Culture: A Roadblock to Change in Law Enforcement?" *The Police Chief,* Vol. LXI, No. 8:68-76.

Patterson, Jeffrey (1995). "Community Policing—Learning the Lessons of History." *FBI Law Enforcement Bulletin,* Vol. 64, No. 11:5-10.

Police Executive Research Forum (1996). *Themes and Variations in Community Policing: Case Studies in Community Policing.* Washington, DC: Police Executive Research Forum.

Rabkin, Norman J. (1995). *Community Policing: Information on the "COPS on the Beat" Grant Programs.* Washington, DC: U.S. General Accounting Office.

San Jose Mercury News (1997a). "$50,000 Offered for Arrest, Conviction in Firebombing." July 10:1B; *San Jose Mercury News* (1997b). "Sister in Freezer, 'Scam-Artist' Suspect Still Puzzle Police." July 17:1A.

San Jose Mercury News (1997c). "Neighborhood Patrols Cut Into Crime." July 25:3B.

Silverman, Charles E. (1978). *Criminal Violence*. New York: Vintage.

Skolnick, Jerome H. and David H. Bayley (1988). *Community Policing: Issues and Practices Around the World*. Washington, DC: U.S. Department of Justice.

Sparrow, Malcolm (1988). *Implementing Community Policing*. Washington, DC: U.S. Department of Justice.

Spelman, William and John E. Eck (1987). "Problem Oriented Policing." *Research in Brief*. Washington, DC: National Institute of Justice, U.S. Department of Justice.

Stipak, Brian, Susan Immer and Maria Clavadetscher (1994). "Are You Really Doing Community Policing?" *The Police Chief*, Vol. LXI, No. 10:115-123.

Taylor, Frederick W. (1947). *Scientific Management*. New York, NY: Harper and Brothers.

Thurman, Quint, Andrew Giacomazzi, and Phil Bogen (1993). "Research Note: Cops, Kids, and Community Policing—An Assessment of a Community Policing Demonstration Project." *Crime & Delinquency*, Vol. 39, No. 4:554-564.

Trojanowicz, Robert C. (1994). "The Future of Community Policing." In Dennis R. Rosenbaum (ed.), *The Challenge of Community Policing*. Thousand Oaks, CA: Sage Publications.

Wasserman, Robert and Mark H. Moore (1988). *Values in Policing*. Washington, DC: U.S. Department of Justice.

West, Marty L. (1997). "Gaining Employee Support for Community Policing." *Law and Order*, Vol. 45, No. 4:51-53.

Wycoff, Mary Ann and Wesley K. Skogan (1993). *Community Policing in Madison: Quality From the Inside Out*. Washington, DC: U.S. Department of Justice, Office of Justice Programs.

Zhao, Jihong (1996). *The Nature of Community Policing Innovations: Do the Ends Justify the Means?* Washington, DC: Police Executive Research Forum.

Zhao, Jihong and Quint Thurman (1996). *Why Police Organizations Change: A Study of Community-Oriented Policing*. Washington, DC: Police Executive Research Forum.

POLICE USE OF DEADLY FORCE: ENFORCING THE LAW IN A VIOLENT SOCIETY

4

The study of this chapter will enable you to:

1. Describe the trend in civilian deaths by legal intervention.

2. Define and explain the term *incident hit rate*.

3. Identify the most important findings of the Chicago study of police shootings.

4. List the reasons given by the Chicago police for shooting civilians.

5. Identify the three elements of the *Garner* decision.

6. Compare the constitutional standards of the *Garner* decision with the use of deadly force under common law.

7. Describe what occurred in four cities after the Rodney King verdict.

8. Write a short essay describing how the police and suspects use weapons during the commission of an offense.

9. Identify the key elements of the court's decision in the *Graham v. Connor* case.

10. Describe the findings in the *Plakas v. Drinski* case.

11. List ten less than lethal weapons used or currently under study.

12. Write a short essay on positional asphyxia.

13. Describe the use of force continuum.

One must constantly live with change, but sometimes it seems that change does not occur as rapidly as one would think, and sometimes not at all. In a 10-month period, four New York City police officers were killed in the line of duty.

Soon after these events, a police officer used his own weapon to shoot and kill a fleeing suspect in an unrelated case. A *New York Times* editorial pointedly criticized the incident, stating that "if an officer needed to defend his life, the use of force is permissible, but if he is chasing a suspect, he has no right to shoot the man." In this instance the grand jury declined to indict the officer. It is difficult to believe, but these events occurred in 1857 and 1858, rather than recently (Geller and Karales, 1981: 1).

After these events, other New York City police officers armed themselves as did officers in Boston. This practice spread to other departments and by the early 1900s, all cities began to issue revolvers to their officers (Matulia, 1982: 1). As of today, all police officers in the U.S. are armed with weapons ranging from semi-automatics to revolvers. The use of deadly force is as much an issue today as it was in the 1850s. The following incidents illustrate the continuing problem of the use of deadly force by the police in communities throughout the nation:

- In Arizona, a knife-wielding woman was shot by an officer. She was found hiding in a residential closet. The woman advanced on officers and refused to drop two knives. The officers sprayed her with a chemical but it did not deter her as she expressed the intent to kill the officers.

- In Connecticut, a man who appeared to be in his 40s stole a car from an automobile dealer and shot a salesman. Then the suspect commandeered a school van carrying two students—one was critically wounded. The suspect was killed in an exchange of gunfire with police after he crashed the van into a highway guardrail.

- Police in Nevada responded to a call that a man had a gun. While an officer was taking a report about that incident, another call was received, reporting that a man was chasing a woman with a knife. Then a report was received that officers needed assistance. The suspect was found at a residence and four officers surrounded him. The suspect implored the officers to shoot him before he lunged at them with a knife from a distance, estimated to be between four and eight feet away, and the suspect was shot. A police training expert testified at the inquest that the use of tear gas in this instance was not appropriate because officers have to be six to ten feet from a subject. The expert also stated that officers are trained to respond to deadly force with the highest force available.

- In California, a drifter wearing fatigues and a bullet-proof vest hijacked three cars, and with five weapons sprayed a neighborhood with more than 100 rounds. After a ferocious 25-minute gun battle, the suspect was shot to death by the police. During the gun battle, a police officer was killed and a paramedic and a bystander were wounded.

- In Missouri, the police responded to a report that someone had kicked in an apartment door. Residents of the apartment had observed a man running toward one of the nearby buildings. Entering the building, officers noticed that the door to one apartment was not tightly shut. They entered the apartment and one officer opened a bedroom door and encountered the occupant, unarmed, dressed in a T-shirt and boxer shorts standing near a bed five to eight feet from the door. The occupant ran at the officer and the officer shot the 24-year-old, who was a stockbroker.

- In front of the White House, a knife-wielding homeless man was shot when he refused to drop a knife that was taped to his hand. The suspect ignored repeated orders to drop his knife as he was chased some 60 yards across Pennsylvania Avenue. A videotape of the shooting showed the suspect standing motionless and surrounded by five police officers. When the suspect looked to his left he was shot twice by one of the officers.

As pointed out by one expert, the police are the "only representatives of governmental authority who (in the ordinary course of events) are legally permitted to use physical force against a citizen." (Kobler, 1975: 1). Other agencies have some degree of police power, but they rely upon request, persuasion, public opinion, custody, and legal processes to obtain compliance with regulations and laws. Of all the agencies that control conduct, only the police use firearms to obtain public compliance.

The police have a unique position in our society—they are sworn to enforce the law at all times. This is true even when they are off duty. In most jurisdictions, officers carry a weapon when they are not working. The chance of using excessive force in the course of police duties (and thus the power of life and death over the citizen) is truly a reality. The legal power and the responsibilities the police have in our society facilitate the application of deadly force when the law is enforced (Kobler, 1975: 163-165).

The debate on the use of deadly force goes on—it is as strong and divisive today as it was many years ago. Communities have been plunged into turmoil as a result of questionable police actions. It should be remembered that police action has never been identified as the sole precipitating factor leading to a major disturbance. Discrimination, unemployment, poor housing, inadequate social services, and other factors have all contributed significantly to major disturbances. Unfortunately, newspaper headlines suggest that, in many instances, rioting has been caused solely by the questionable use of deadly force, while other factors are ignored.

Whatever the underlying cause, riots do occur in our nation and, unfortunately, police action during the encounter has been a focal point of negative community reaction. For example, the Liberty City (Miami, FL) riot resulted in several deaths and millions of dollars in damage. The riot broke out when an all-white jury acquitted several white police officers accused of bludgeoning an African-American man to death. The deceased had allegedly resisted when arrested for a traffic violation.

The riot described above was one of five that occurred in the Miami area during the 1980s. The last riot in the same area occurred in the latter part of the decade, when a Hispanic police officer shot two African-American men to death.

In 1992, Jose Garcia was fatally shot during a confrontation with New York City police. Rioting broke out over a three-day period, during which two people died and 28 individuals were arrested. Streets in one area of the city were littered with glass, vandalized stores, overturned cars, and smoldering trash, and more than 1,000 police officers patrolled the area (*San Jose Mercury News*, 1992: 6A).

The Rodney King riot is described as the worst rioting in the United States during the twentieth century. The 81-second videotaping of the beating of King, an African-American man, by four police officers, while seven other officers watched, subsequently led to a massive riot involving more than 5,500 fires, the injury of 2,383 people, the deaths of 55 people, and the jailing of 13,379. It was estimated that 10,000 businesses were destroyed, resulting in 20,000 people becoming unemployed. The death toll surpassed the 1965 Watts riots during which 34 people died. President George Bush ordered federal troops to assist local law enforcement, which included 1,500 Marines, 3,000 members of the Army, 3,000 National Guard members, and 1,000 federal law officers who were specially trained for riot control. At one point, more than 13,000 police and troops patrolled the streets of Los Angeles. This was the first time that the military was ordered to engage in riot control since the anti-war demonstrations of 1972. Property damage in Los Angeles totaled at least $717 million (Drummond, 1992: 1-4A). Other cities' responses to the acquittal of the four white police officers erupted to varying degrees as illustrated by the Feature on page 91.

The actions of the Los Angeles police department were soundly criticized because command personnel ordered officers to leave the area where the rioting broke out and told them to not confront rioters in other parts of the city. A five-month study of the riot under the guidance of William H. Webster, former director of the Federal Bureau of Investigation, blamed the rioting on underlying social problems, inadequate crisis planning, and a failure to respond aggressively.

The nationwide response to the Rodney King beating, the initial acquittal of the officers in state court, and the subsequent conviction of the officers in federal court has done more to intensify the argument about the use of deadly force than any other event in recent history. The consequences resulting from the use of deadly force clearly call for continuing analysis of the need to use such extreme force. The problem is a real one and not easily solved.

The following event illustrates the fact that the use of deadly force is still a recurring event. During 1996, a police officer shot and killed an unarmed African-American motorist during a routine traffic stop. When stopped for speeding, the subject refused to get out of his automobile. When one of the two police officers broke one of the car windows, the automobile lurched forward, bumping one of the officers. The struck officer threatened to shoot and the car lurched again, striking the officer forcefully. The officer fired three shots, striking the subject in the arm and the chest. Later the police learned that the car was stolen and that the suspect was wanted on three arrest warrants. The death of the motorist sparked a riot that covered 20 square blocks, destroyed 29 buildings, and injured 11 people. Three weeks later a grand jury refused to indict the officer and civil unrest broke out again (Muwakkil, 1997: E3). An estimated 500,000 persons who had contact with the police (0.2 percent of the population over age 11) were hit, pushed, choked, threatened with a flashlight, restrained by a police dog, threatened or actually sprayed with chemical or pepper spray, threatened with a gun, or experienced some other form of force (Bureau of Justice Statistics, 1997: 1-10).

Feature

U.S. Cities Respond to the King Verdict
with Protest and Civil Disobedience

Las Vegas, Nevada

Rioting in this city resulted in the deaths of two people, and the injury of several dozen people. Additionally, numerous buildings were burned in a low-income section of the city. Approximately 400 National Guardsmen were activated to deal with the disobedience.

Atlanta, Georgia

In this community, 300 people were arrested and approximately 50 downtown stores were vandalized. A curfew was enforced for two nights, from 11:00 P.M. to 5:00 A.M. On the second day, 50 people were arrested when a disturbance broke out during the early evening at the Atlanta University Center when black students were forbidden to march from the campus to the downtown area. The Atlanta police, along with The Georgia State Patrol, ringed the campus and rock and bottle-throwers drove them back. A liquor store near the campus was looted and a car was overturned during the melee. During the disturbance, 17 Atlanta police officers were injured.

Seattle, Washington

A day after the Los Angeles riot, during the early morning, demonstrators in Seattle vandalized, looted stores, and set fires. Two pedestrians were assaulted and a police car was smashed with baseball bats and tire irons by approximately 100 youths. Police arrested 40 people who were characterized as "hooligans" and gang members. The mayor stressed that, regardless of the reason for the looting, violence and vandalism would not be tolerated.

San Francisco, California

A state of emergency was declared in San Francisco as a peaceful demonstration degenerated into a riotous situation. More than 100 businesses were either burned or looted. Fifty trash bins were set afire during the disturbance and city workers removed them from the streets the next day so as to prevent their being set afire again if an additional disturbance occurred. The initial confrontations led to the arrest of more than 1,100 people. One looter attacked a police officer with a bat and was shot in the leg.

Source: Adapted from B. Drummond Ayers, Jr. (1992). "U.S. Cities Handling Protests, Violence." *New York Times,* May 7:1A, 4A.

Accumulated evidence suggests that the debate about the police use of deadly force will intensify over the years ahead. The crime problem continues to plague our nation. This is especially true of violent crime. In 1996, there were 19,645 reported murders and non-negligent manslaughters. The type of weapon used to commit these offenses varied considerably, but firearms continued to be the weapon of choice with the preponderance being handguns. Seventy percent of these crimes involved the use of firearms. The victim/offender relationship has changed over the years. Approximately 13 percent of the offenders were strangers while 13 percent were related. Interestingly, the largest percentage of offenders was someone the victim knew (35.0 percent). During 1995, there were 1,119,950 aggravated assaults. Approximately one-fourth of the time, the assailant(s)used a firearm (Federal Bureau of Investigation, 1997: 15-34). In the United States, the public has ready access to firearms. There is, therefore, little evidence that gun control enthusiasts will succeed in curbing the possession or the sale of weapons, although it is anticipated that repeated efforts will be made to expand the Brady Bill and further limit public access to all types of weapons, especially automatic weapons.

Police Use of Deadly Force

Several issues need to be addressed about the shootings by police officers. Despite the increase in studies conducted over the last 15 years, there are still many unknowns. Some of the questions that need to be addressed include: Who gets shot and why? Is the current level of shooting too high? How can shootings be controlled? What rules govern officer discretion to shoot?

Knowledge of police shootings is uneven and intermittent. The Uniform Crime Reports annually set forth in minute detail the circumstances involving the killings of and assaults against police officers. The FBI Uniform Crime Reports Unit receives reports from some police agencies on police homicides, but these statistics are not published. These data are suspect because they are information given voluntarily, hence their reliability is open to question. Another problem is that deaths are identified by where they occur rather than by the officer's place of employment (Matulia, 1982: 10). Unfortunately, no agency regularly publishes extensive data on the police use of deadly force. General knowledge in this area would be greatly improved if the exact location of each death was known. It would also be helpful to have information on non-fatal shootings, and the number of individuals wounded, as well as incidents in which the police shoot and miss.

The only entity collecting data on justifiable homicides by the police is the Public Health Service. Published annually, these data are a part of the Vital Statistics of the United States. Data are taken from Standard Death Certificates that coroners and medical examiners submit from throughout the nation. These data are set forth in Table 4-1. Researchers in this area feel that the data are deficient for a number of reasons, varying from inferior quality of the medical diagnoses to errors in recording data. For these and other reasons, the researchers have concluded that the number of civilian deaths by legal intervention are underreported by about 50 percent. This figure is arrived at by reasoned judgment and as a consequence it can be either lower or higher. An additional problem with using data from this source is that the deaths are recorded by the county in which they occur rather than the community where the justifiable homicide occurred. Generally speaking, data from a community can prove to be more useful than data from a county. It pinpoints the occurrence of the event and makes for more meaningful data. Notwithstanding these limitations, the statistics from this source allow the consideration of the number of civilian deaths by legal intervention from several different positions (Brenner and Kravitz, 1979: 69-70).

Table 4-1
Civilian Deaths by Legal Intervention

Year	Total Civilian Deaths	White Deaths	Nonwhite Deaths
1968	343	159	184
1969	347	158	189
1970	331	155	176
1971	412	214	198
1972	296	132	164
1973	372	185	187
1974	370	183	187
1975	330	177	153
1976	286	146	140
1977	271	135	136
1978	265	147	118
1979	341	182	159
1980	303	190	113
1981	272	155	117
1982	276	162	114
1983	257	153	104
1984	253	154	99
1985	242	149	93
1986	247	148	99
1987	265	165	91
1988	237	158	71
1989	315	208	96
1990	297	186	102
1991	312	207	92
1992	314	216	87
Totals	**7,554**	**4,224**	**3,269**

Source: U.S. Department of Health and Human Services, Public Health Service (1995). *Vital Statistics of the United States, 1992, Volume II—General Mortality, Part A, Section 1.* Hyattsville, MD: Public Health Service. Statistics for the years from 1977 to 1992 were obtained from annual publications. Statistics for the years from 1968 to 1976 were cited in: Robert N. Brenner and Marjorie Kravitz, Compilers (1979). *Community Concerns: Police Use of Deadly Force.* Washington, DC: USGPO.

Of the civilian deaths recorded, the highest number (412) occurred in 1971 and the lowest (237) during 1988. This is a reduction of 41 percent and is considered somewhat significant. In addition, the number of nonwhite deaths for the same two years (1971 and 1985) decreased by 53 percent. The preponderance of the nonwhites killed were African-American. During the seven-year period from 1980 through 1986, only five percent of the minorities killed were not African-American. Studies also show that few women die at the hands of the police.

From 1952 to 1969, a total of 41 women died as a result of legal intervention (Brenner and Kravitz, 1979: 70). Hence, fewer than five women died annually at the hands of the police. Sixty-six women were killed by the police during the period from 1980 to 1990 (See Table 4-2). In the last two years (1991 and 1992) for which data are available, 17 women died as a result of legal intervention. It is anticipated that more women will die annually as the result of police shootings as women become more involved in violent crimes.

Table 4-2
Sex and Race of Civilians Killed: 1980-1992

Year	White		African-American	
	M	F	M	F
1980	189	1	111	0
1981	155	0	111	1
1982	158	4	111	1
1983	150	3	97	5
1984	152	2	91	2
1985	148	1	79	3
1986	144	4	90	2
1987	162	3	87	4
1988	151	7	70	1
1989	202	6	91	5
1990	179	7	98	4
1991	171	6	93	2
1992	180	6	95	3
Total	2,141	50	1,224	33

Source: U.S. Department of Health and Human Services, Public Health Service (1995). *Vital Statistics of the United States*, 1992, 238; 1991, 238; 1990, 370;,1989, 370;1988, 320; 1987, 304; 1986, 220; 1985, 220; 1984, 220; 1983, 220; 1982, 220; 1981,220; 1980, 218, *Volume II-General Mortality, Vol. II, Section 1.* Hyattsville, MD: Public Health Service.

Acknowledging the difficulty of actually determining the number of civilian deaths by legal intervention, most researchers estimate that publicly employed American law enforcement personnel kill about 600 criminal suspects each year. They shoot and wound another 1,200, and fire their weapons at 1,800 individuals. The hit rates and fatality rates making up national estimates vary from city to city. So, the number of people killed by different police departments is a poor basis for estimating and comparing the number of suspects they wound or try to shoot but miss entirely (Geller and Karales, 1981: 2). For example, over a five-year period, officers in Chicago and Los Angeles fatally shot similar numbers of people: 132 and 139 respectively. There the similarity ended, however, because the Chicago police shot 386 people non-fatally, compared to 238 for the Los Angeles police. The total number fired upon, including those missed, was 2,876 in Chicago and 611 in Los Angeles.

Chicago and Los Angeles are comparable-sized cities, but their populations (especially in high-crime areas, where most shootings occur) have markedly different chances of being exposed to police use of deadly force. Data regarding when officers shoot at criminal suspects, regardless of whether the intended victims were struck by bullets, are difficult to obtain. Fortunately, the Geller and Karales study group sheds some light on this topic. When analyzing data over a three-year period, the number of incidents in which civilians were shot by police resulted in what is termed an "incident hit rate." This rate is the percentage of incidents reported involving shootings in which one or more civilians were struck by police bullets.

Table 4-3 shows that slightly more than one-fourth of the 1,145 incidents resulted in a civilian being hit. In addition, Table 4-4 shows that an average of 2.9 bullets were fired at each shooting incident. Over the three-year period studied (involving the firing of 3,358 bullets), only 743 struck an individual (14.2 percent). These data suggest that an officer's inability to strike a target is, in all probability, due to something other than aiming incorrectly. Undoubtedly other factors are involved—such as the number of shots fired, the nature and type of incident, the distance between the officer and a suspect (Geller and Karales, 1981: 163), information received from the dispatcher, the number of officers involved in the incident, the number of suspects implicated, types of weapons used by the officers and suspects, the emotional state of the officer during the incident, and the type of cover and concealment. The firing of a weapon occurs during an exceedingly convoluted process and the fact that only 14.2 percent of the shots fired hit an individual clearly illustrates such complexity. This position is supported by one other study (Table 4-5). Out of 67 situations, the police did not fire in 16 incidents even though the suspect had fired. In 16 other incidents, the suspect and officer pointed weapons at each other and neither fired.

Table 4-3
Incidents of Shots Fired and Civilians Struck Over a Three-Year Period

Year	Incidents	Civilians Shot	Percentage of Hits
1975	482	138	28.6
1976	339	75	22.1
1977	324	95	29.3
Total	1,145	308	26.6

Source: William A. Geller and Kevin J. Karales (1981). *Split-Split-Second Decisions: Shootings of and by the Chicago Police*. Chicago: Chicago Law Enforcement Study Group. For further discussion of the use of deadly force by and against police officers see William A. Geller and Michael Scott (1992). *Deadly Force: What We Know*. Washington, DC: Police Executive Research Forum. Reprinted with permission. William A. Geller and Hans Toch (eds.) (1997). *And Justice For All: Understanding and Controlling Police Abuse*. Washington, DC: Police Executive Research Forum.

Critics of incidents of police shootings question why an officer did not shoot to hit the suspect in the leg or arm. How could this possibly be an expectation when the odds are that a suspect will not even be hit? An International Association of Chiefs of Police (IACP) survey of "justifiable homicides by police" in the nation's 57 largest cities demonstrated a wide difference in municipal rates for fatal incidents (Matulia, 1982: 9-15). Notably, police officers in New Orleans were 10 times more likely than officers in Newark to kill criminal suspects. This disparity holds true even when the rates are based on the number of violent crimes rather than the size of the police department.

Table 4-4
Hit Rate of Bullets Fired by the Chicago Police Department Over a Three-Year Period

Year	Bullets Fired	Number That Struck	Percentage of Hits	Average No. Fired
1975	1,481	480	14.7	3.1
1976	918	104	11.3	2.7
1977	959	159	16.6	3.0
Total	3,358	743	14.2	2.9

Source: William A. Geller and Kevin J. Karales (1981), *Split-Second Decisions: Shooting of and by Chicago Police*. Chicago: Chicago Law Enforcement Study Group, 163. Reprinted with permission of William A. Geller.

This tenfold difference is not typical, but many of the 57 cities differed by a factor of five. Noteworthy also is the incidence of extreme police-civilian violence being vastly different from neighborhood to neighborhood within a given city. In an average year in Chicago, the Near West Side was 27 times more likely than the Near North Side or the Near South Side to be the scene of a police shooting (Geller and Karales, 1981: 2).

Table 4-5
Police and Suspects' Use of Weapons During the Commission of an Offense

Situation	
1. The officer and the suspect pointed but neither fired	16
2. Both fired	17
3. Suspect pointed-officer fired	18
4. Suspect fired-officer did not	16
Total	67

Source: Committee on the Judiciary (1997). *Police Use of Deadly Force*. Subcommittee on Criminal Justice, House of Representatives, One Hundredth Congress, First Session, May 8, Serial No. 140: 58-125.

In Los Angeles, a review of nearly 700 shootings resulted in one-half of the officers being retrained, and one-fourth punished by reprimand, suspension, or dismissal. The remainder (one-fourth) of shooting incidents merited no action. In one situation, an officer shot another officer in the back as they converged upon a suspect in darkness. In other instances, three different officers shot out their own windshields while trying to stop suspects. In 230 of the shootings, the most frequently cited deficiency was poor communication. Some officers neglected to tell their partners that the suspect was armed, did not give suspects clear orders, or did not tell the command post what they were doing (*Los Angeles Times,* 1994: 3B). When three-fourths of shooting incidents require remedial action, it is essential that police management conduct an ongoing analysis of all such incidents in order to minimize the number of errors that occur during a shooting.

Placing Police Shootings in Perspective

Acknowledging local variations, one might wonder why police officers shoot at about 3,600 individuals annually. One approach is to ask: 3,600 compared to what? Undoubtedly, one's personal values will influence the comparison used. For example, one could compare the 3,600 incidents to the millions of offenders encountered annually by America's 518,510 publicly employed police officers. In one study, during one year, it was found that in the largest 33 cities the number of persons shot by the police ranged from 65 in Los Angeles to 18 in Dallas. Another way to view police shootings was to determine the officer-involved shootings per 100,000 population, where Kansas City had 1.80 as compared to St. Louis, which had 4.65. When two other communities were compared, based on the number of index crimes reported it was found that Denver had 5,268.43 as compared to Philadelphia with 3,803.05. None of the above statistics has any superiority over another nor does it tell us what is an acceptable level of police shootings, but it clearly illustrates the complexity of the problem and the variance in different communities (Committee on the Judiciary, 1997: 58-125).

Another way of viewing police shootings is against the backdrop of the *subculture of violence,* which characterized America from its revolutionary birth. Using the number of reported homicides in each city, it was found that El Paso had 8.3 percent of the police-related homicides, as compared to Pittsburgh with 2.9 percent of all homicides. As recently as 1995, there were 1,798,785 violent crimes in the United States and, of that number, 20,043 were murders and nonnegligent manslaughters (Maguire and Pastore, 1997: 332). Preliminary data for 1996 showed a 9.5 percent decline in violent crimes (Chaiken 1996: 4).

While the number of such crimes has declined, most citizens would agree that there is an excessive amount of violent crime in the majority of our cities and we have not made a great deal of progress either in understanding or reducing violent crime. Another variable in the violent crime patterns in our cities is the criminal. The following Feature describes the views of armed criminals in the United States.

Feature

The Armed Criminal

One reason criminals acquire and carry handguns is because many crimes are easier to commit if armed than if not. Beyond these obvious criminal motivations, however, the survey (1,800 incarcerated felons) also shows that criminals own and carry guns because they were raised around guns and have owned and used them all their lives. Most of them associated with other men who owned and carried guns as well.

Furthermore, the majority always kept their guns loaded and fired them regularly, often at other people. One-half of the men in the sample claimed to have fired a gun at someone at some time; one-half also claimed to have been fired upon (excluding military service in both cases). In fact, many respondents stated that a man who is armed with a gun is "prepared for anything that might happen." An opportunity to commit a crime can occur or there may be a need to defend oneself against the assaults or perditions of others. Therefore, while handgun carrying among felons is in part a rational response to the nature of their criminal activities, it is, in equal measure, an element of the lifestyle arising from early socialization and from fear. One-third of the sample (gun criminals) made it a practice to carry a gun all the time (more or less). Fifty percent describes the views of armed criminals in the United States, who carried a gun whenever the circumstances seemed potentially dangerous. This was when doing a drug deal, when going out at night, when they were with other men carrying guns or whenever their ability to defend themselves might be at issue. Only one in five of the gun criminals claimed that they carried a gun only when they intended to commit a specific crime.

Source: James D. Wright (1986). *Armed Criminals in America*, Research in Brief. Washington, DC: National Institute of Justice.

Against either of these backdrops, it is undoubtedly remarkable that the average American police officer completes a 20-year career without ever firing a weapon except in target practice. From another perspective, the 3,600 shootings are an example of lawful government decisions to implement justifiable homicides (Geller and Scott, 1992: 1-65). The government has an obligation to protect society from human predators who make it unsafe for many to lead a normal life in our society. Another approach is to compare the police homicides to the handful of individuals who, after lengthy court review, are given capital punishment. In 1994, there were 31 executions in the United States and of this number only 11 were African-American. In the years from 1930 through 1994, a total of 4,116 prisoners were executed (U.S. Bureau of the Census, 1996: 349). In 1995, there were 56 persons executed and a total of 3,054 prisoners under the sentence of death (Snell, 1996: 1-6). These numbers are significantly lower when one compares them with the estimated legal intervention incidents in which police officers have taken a life.

There is still another way to look at the deadly force process. The 3,600 shooting incidents could be assessed in light of the findings of several national commissions concerned about the questionable use of force that leads to unintended consequences. These events, coupled with other negative social conditions, can spark urban rebellion and tarnish the good image that a police department has painstakingly built through countless positive contacts with the citizenry.

Another way to think about the national and local levels of police shootings is to ask whether the numerous police goals could be accomplished as well or better without undue risk to police officers, if the number of shootings were less. Unfortunately, current data do not allow for a definitive assessment of this serious question.

Deadly Force—A Constitutional Standard

There has been a veritable revolution in state and local law enforcement in the United States. This has been brought about by successful challenges to law enforcement activities in federal courts, alleging violations of the Constitution (Hall, 1984: 26). In 1985 in *Tennessee v. Garner,* the U.S. Supreme Court ruled that the use of deadly force by police to apprehend a person is a "seizure." Consequently, it is subject to the reasonableness standard of the Fourth Amendment (Hall, 1988a: 27). Moreover, the Court held that it is constitutionally unreasonable to use such force unless it is necessary to prevent an escape. In addition, the officer must have probable cause to believe the suspect poses a significant threat of death or serious physical injury to the officer or others (*Tennessee v. Garner,* 471 U.S. 1, at 9, 1985).

As a prerequisite to understanding when the use of deadly force is constitutionally permissible, one must know what is meant by the expression "deadly force." Although the Court did not define the term anywhere in the *Garner* opinion, a workable definition—and one that seems consistent with the *Garner* case—is found in the Model Penal Code. There it is defined as "force that the actor uses with the purpose of causing or that he knows will create a substantial risk of causing death or serious bodily harm." (Model Penal Code 3.11: 2).

The Court provided some indications as to when the use of such force would be reasonable. It pointed out that "where the officer has probable cause to believe the suspect poses a threat of serious physical harm, either to the officer or to others, it is not constitutionally unreasonable to prevent escape by using deadly force."

Clearly, the *Garner* decision did not establish a blanket prohibition against the use of deadly force as a means of preventing escape. Rather, the decision requires that justification for the use of such force be based upon facts and circumstances that reasonably suggest to an officer that a person may be dangerous. This is in lieu of the simplicity of categorizing the suspect as a felon. The following Feature describes the *Garner* case in detail.

Feature

Challenging the "Fleeing Felon" Rule

Two Memphis, Tennessee police officers responded to a late night call of a burglary in progress at a private residence. Upon arriving at the scene, they learned from the woman who had made the call that she had heard glass breaking at the residence next to hers and someone was breaking in. As one officer radioed to report their location, the second officer walked to the back of the house, where he heard a door slam and saw someone running across the backyard.

The officer saw the fleeing suspect stop momentarily at a six-foot-high chainlink fence at the edge of the yard. With the aid of a flashlight, the officer was able to see the suspect's face and hands and concluded (although he was not certain), that the suspect was unarmed. The officer called out to the suspect, "Police, halt," and took a couple of steps in his direction. At that moment, the suspect began to climb the fence, and the officer fired one shot, which struck the suspect in the back of the head, inflicting a fatal wound.

The suspect was identified as Eugene Garner, a 15-year-old eighth grader, described as 5'4" tall and weighing 100-110 pounds. Ten dollars in a purse taken from the house were found on the body. In using deadly force to prevent Garner's escape, the officer was relying on the authority of a Tennessee statute which, like the common law rule, permitted the use of "all necessary means" to prevent the escape of a felony suspect if, "after notice of the intention to arrest . . . he either flees or forcibly resists . . ."

Source: *Tennessee v. Garner*, 471 U.S. 1, at 9 (1985).

This decision imposed a national minimum standard of force for the first time. The decision invalidated laws in almost one-half of the states that allowed the use of deadly force to prevent the escape of someone suspected of a felony. (Hayeslip and Preszler, 1993: 2).

The Supreme Court stated: ". . . if the suspect threatens the officer with a weapon or there is probable cause to believe he has committed a crime involving the infliction or threatened infliction of serious physical harm, deadly force may be used if necessary to prevent escape, and if, where feasible, some warning has been given." (Hall, 1988b: 23).

Three elements can be derived from this statement:

* The suspect threatens the officer with a weapon; or

* The officer has probable cause to believe that the suspect has committed a crime involving infliction or threatened infliction of serious physical harm; and

* The officer has given some warning, if feasible.

Either of the first two elements listed above satisfies the first part of the standard—i.e., reason to believe the suspect is dangerous. The third element applies to the other two.

As observed by the Supreme Court, at the time of the *Garner* decision, most law enforcement agencies had already developed departmental policies somewhat more restrictive than the common law fleeing felon rule. Whether such policies are within the constitutional boundaries now established by *Garner* is a matter that law enforcement administrators should carefully consider. Obviously, a policy more restrictive than the common law may nevertheless permit the unconstitutional use of deadly force. When such use of deadly force results from a policy or custom of a local governmental entity, that entity incurs a risk of liability under federal law (Hall, 1988b: 28).

Conversely, an overly restrictive policy can create increased risks to the lives of police officers and others in the community. Clearly that was not the intent, and it should not be the result, of the Supreme Court's decision in the *Garner* case. This decision sharply limited situations in which lethal force could be used by the police.

Since the *Garner* decision, the use of deadly force has been analyzed extensively and additional court cases have been decided on this critical issue. In the landmark decision of *Graham v. Connor,* the court interpreted the Fourth Amendment as the standard of "objective reasonableness" as being appropriate for assessing a police officer's use of force within the context of making an arrest. It is a standard that is not subject to a precise definition or mechanical application.

The Court emphasized that the issue is one of reasonableness at the moment. Another important feature of the decision is that the Court held that the inquiry must be limited to "the facts and circumstances confronting them (the officers) . . . judged from the perspective of a reasonable officer at the scene, rather than with 20/20 vision of hindsight . . ." (*Graham v. Connor,* 1989: 396-397). Thus, it is within this context and from this perspective that the reasonableness of an officer's judgment of the "necessity" to use deadly force must be viewed (Hall, 1995: 28).

In *Plakas v. Drinski,* a police officer shot and killed a handcuffed subject who attacked the officer with a fireplace poker. The primary argument of the plaintiff was that the officer could have and should have used alternatives short of deadly force. It was suggested that one of the officers on the scene had a canister of CS gas and there was a K-9 unit in the vicinity that could have been used to subdue the subject. The district court granted summary judgment for the police and the appellate court affirmed, explaining:

> There is no precedent in this Circuit (or any other) which says that the Constitution requires law enforcement officers to use all feasible alternatives to avoid a situation where deadly force can justifiably be used. There are, however, cases which support the assertion that where deadly force is otherwise justified, under the Constitution, there is no constitutional duty to use non-deadly alternatives first.

The court pointed out that there were three alternatives for the officers: (1) Maintain distance from the suspect and try to keep some barrier between him and them; (2) use some kind of disabling spray; or (3) use a dog to disarm the suspect. The court also considered that a decision made by an officer under these circumstances must be made after the briefest reflection.

> As the suspect moved toward the officer, was he supposed to think of an attack dog, of . . . CS gas, or of how fast he could run backwards? Our answer is, and has been, no, because there is little time for the officer to do so and too much opportunity to second guess the officer.

Needless to say, the decisions discussed above comply with the Supreme Court decision that has held that reasonableness under the Fourth Amendment does not require police officers to choose the least intrusive alternative, only a reasonable one (Hall, 1995: 28-32).

Alternatives to the Use of Deadly Force

Supreme Court and lower court decisions have been significant in creating the interest in developing less-than-lethal devices, particularly for use against fleeing felons (Hayeslip and Preszler, 1993: 5). Currently technology is not available to the police, allowing for the immediate apprehension, control of suspects, or stopping a fleeing felon with less than the use of deadly force. And unfortunately truly effective non-lethal weapons are not currently on the drawing board, although numerous studies are underway.

Taser

Some agencies use the Taser (stun gun) as a means of controlling suspects with less than lethal force. The U.S. Bureau of Alcohol, Tobacco and Firearms classifies the stun gun as non-lethal. The stun gun projects two electrically charged barbs at the end of 15-foot wires that carry 50,000 volts of electricity. The Taser has several limitations, including (McNaulty, 1994: 102-103):

1. The officer must be within 15 feet of a suspect.

2. There cannot be a physical barrier between the officer and the suspect. The darts will not penetrate such things as windows or heavy cardboard.

3. The darts cannot be used in an explosive atmosphere or near flammable liquids.

The Taser causes muscles to spasm uncontrollably and the suspect loses voluntary motor control. Normally suspects will fall within a few seconds and recover in a few minutes so it can readily be seen that under certain circumstances such a device can prove to be useful to a law enforcement officer when confronting a suspect.

Pepper Spray

Law enforcement agencies have used pepper spray since the mid-1970s. The active ingredient of the spray is oleoresin capsicum (OC), which is obtained from chili peppers. This organic ingredient is classified as an inflammatory and not an irritant, such as tear gas. In pepper sprays, OC is combined with other products that keep it suspended in a solution. A propellant is used to discharge the solution.

Figure 4-1
Less Than Lethal Weapons Used or Currently Under Study

Flash Bang Grenades	Robots
Kicks	Police Dogs
Upper Body Control Holds	Nets
Power Staff	Flashlights
Electrified Water Pistols	Claw
Mood-Altering Gases	Dart Guns
Tree-pole Trip Devices	Knockout
Air Bags	Sticky Stuff
Sleep Inducers	Aqueous Foam
Strob Light Grenade	Projectiles
Baton	Tear Gas
Electromagnetic Radiation Devices	Choke Holds
Stench Gases	Hog-tying

Source: L.C. Trostle (1990). "Force Continuum: From Lethal to Less-Than-Lethal Force." *Journal of Contemporary Criminal Justice*, February, Vol. 6, No. 2:23-36; Timothy M. Dees (1994). "The Quest for Less-Than-Lethal Weaponry." *Law and Order*, Vol. 42, No. 8: 49-52; David K. Dubay (1995). "Oleoresin Capsicum and Pepper Sprays." *Law and Order,* Vol. 43, No. 4: 65-67.

The spray is readily available in concentrations ranging from one to 10 percent. OC causes almost immediate swelling and burning of the eyes as well as coughing and shortness of breath from inflammation of the respiratory system. It can also cause an inflammation of exposed skin from very mild to acute burning (Reynolds and Burke, 1994: 87).

In a study conducted by the International Association of Chiefs of Police over a three-year period, a total of 30 incidents in which the death of a subject occurred following a spraying of OC. In every case, the decedents behaved in a combative and/or unusual manner and struggled with the arresting officers. In the majority of the cases, the pepper spray was either impotent or not completely effective. Prior to the use of the spray, restraint techniques were used, and in all but one instance, deaths occurred immediately or soon afterwards (Granfield, Onnen, and Petty, 1994: 1-2). Utilizing comprehensive autopsies and police reports it was determined, in 22 deaths, that OC was not the cause in any of these cases. The actual causes of death in 22 of the cases included positional asphyxia (discussed later in this chapter), with drugs, obesity, or disease as a contributing factor. In another study, conducted by the FBI over two years, 828 individuals were sprayed with OC (one and five percent varieties) and none of the subjects suffered from long-term ill effects (Reynolds and Burke, 1994: 87).

A detractor of OC is the American Civil Liberties Union, which released a study of 26 deaths in California. It concluded that while pepper spray was never found to be the cause of death, it might be because medical examiners do not know what to look for during autopsies. Roughly two-thirds of the law enforcement agencies in the state of California use pepper spray. The ACLU does not advocate banning OC, but would like to see tighter restrictions on its use until many questions can be answered about its effects (Fischer, 1994: 1B and 4B).

Unfortunately, the ability of the police to apprehend potentially dangerous criminal suspects without shedding blood, in some instances, is presently beyond officer capabilities. The current state of the art in the use of deadly force does not meet the standards the police and the community want, in order to preserve life. In recent years, we have become more knowledgeable about the nature and frequency of shootings in which police are involved, but there is a real need to learn more about the causes as well as techniques that can prevent a police shooting. The following Feature indicates the differing views regarding the use of deadly force.

Feature

Police Say Man Shot Was on Run, Lost Gun

The suspect was shot and killed as he ran away from an officer. The shooting occurred after a crime spree when the suspect allegedly robbed a bank, and fired randomly at motorists and into homes. The suspect was reported to be in a pawn shop with a pistol tucked in his waistband. Chased by the police, the suspect ran into a restaurant parking lot where he pointed a weapon at an employee. As the suspect ran he placed the weapon in his waistband and he was ordered to stop. The suspect raised his hands and walked briskly toward an officer. The officer fired two rounds at the suspect as he lowered his hands to his waistband. The suspect continued to run and only one out of three pursuing officers saw the gun fall from the suspect's waistband. Only one officer shot a weapon during the chase and the suspect received a grazing wound in the thigh and had entrance and exit wounds in his right arm. All of the other rounds struck the suspect in the back. The suspect was a strung-out cocaine addict with a history of forgery, burglary, fraud, and domestic violence. The autopsy report indicated that the suspect had a potentially lethal amount of cocaine in his body and a blood alcohol content of 0.16 percent. One witness felt that after the suspect was shot in the leg that it was unnecessary to shot the suspect in the back. The witness felt that the suspect received a death sentence without the benefit of a trial. The officer who fired the shots was cleared of criminal wrongdoing by the county attorney's office.

Source: Hipolito R. Corella (1992). "Officer's Killing of Fleeing Man Found Justified." *Arizona Daily Star*, October 30: 1B, 6B.

Positional Asphyxia

In recent years, a commonly used technique for controlling violent offenders has been to place them in a hog-tied and prone position by binding their hands and feet together behind their back and placing them on their stomach.

Positional asphyxia occurs when the position of the body interferes with a person's ability to breathe. Other readily observable factors that can increase a subject's susceptibility to sudden death include obesity and psychosis. A large, bulbous abdomen (such as a beer belly) can force the contents of the abdomen upward within the abdominal cavity when the body is in a prone position. The resulting pressure on the diaphragm can cause the person to stop breathing.

Feature

A Controversial Restraining Technique

In 1995, the hog-tie restraining technique was used on the 25-year-old son of a former police officer and the subject died while in custody. In 1997, the Los Angeles Police Commission agreed to settle the lawsuit filed by the family of the deceased for $750,000. Part of the settlement required the banning of the restraint technique and the city council is reviewing the recommended settlement. The current policy does not allow the suspect to be placed on their stomach. In addition, several years ago, the technique was modified to require sufficient slack in the strap so suspects could sit. Over the last five years, the police department has paid more than $2 million to settle the lawsuits involving the controversial restraining technique.

Source: *San Jose Mercury News* (1997). "LAPD to Settle Lawsuit With Ban on Hog-ties." July 6: 5B.

Figure 4-2
Caring for Subdued Subjects

To minimize the potential for in-custody injury or death, officers should:

- Prevent hog-tied subjects from laying on their stomachs.
- Determine whether subjects have used drugs or suffer from cardiac or respiratory diseases.
- Monitor subjects carefully for breathing difficulties or loss of consciousness.
- Be prepared to administer CPR.
- Obtain medical assistance immediately.
- Inform detention facility custodians of pre-existing medical conditions or respiratory difficulty.

Source: Donald T. Reay. (1996). "Suspect Restraint and Sudden Death." *FBI Law Enforcement Bulletin*, Vol. 65, No. 5, May: 22-26.

The second factor is psychosis, which is often induced by drugs or alcohol. Drugs such as LSD create a state of delirium frequently accompanied by violent muscular activity. Vigorous muscular activity, can cause individuals to stop breathing (Reay, 1996: 22-26). Figure 4-2 identifies measures that officers can take when caring for subdued subjects as a means of minimizing sudden death.

Use of Force Continuum

The use of force continuum has changed over the years as technology has provided new tools for controlling different situations (Prach, 1996: 89-93). The continuum is a guideline for officers that allows for the selection of a level of force needed to ensure that a situation is resolved (Jones, 1997: 84). It is a flexible sequence that is tailored to a specific situation. Normally, a use of force continuum consists of a number of levels with each successive level representing an escalation from the previous level (Niehaus, 1997: 103-105; Hunter, 1994: 25). The key is to use the lowest level possible in response to the level of force utilized by a suspect. With the use of neutralizing agents such as pepper spray, the continuum can include the following:

- Physical Presence
- Verbalization
- Neutralizing Agents
- Physical Contact
- Hand-held Impact Weapons
- Lethal Force

This expanded continuum provides officers with greater flexibility when dealing with a difficult individual. Whatever force is utilized, it must be appropriate for the situation. An officer must consider a wide range of factors, ranging from the perceived physical prowess of the subject to the types of non-lethal equipment that is readily available. While this model gives emphasis to neutralizing agents as key components of the continuum, it should be remembered that research shows that spraying an enraged intoxicated suspect or a suspect under the influence of drugs will in all likelihood not deter them from attacking an officer or completing an intended objective such as beating his wife or someone else. Pepper spray does not work on everyone—consequently, an officer should be alert to the necessity of using greater force (Reynolds and Burke, 1994: 90).

Departments employing a use of force continuum with adequate training and supervision have produced positive results. There have been fewer controversial shootings, fewer serious injuries of officers, no increase in the crime rate, and no fall-off in officers' aggressiveness in making arrests.

Summary

The police are the only agents of government who routinely have the authority to use physical force against a citizen. Consequently, it is a fact of life that the possibility of excessive use of force in the course of police duties can and will occur. Communities have been plunged into turmoil as the result of questionable police action. The worst rioting in the United States occurred in 1992 with the videotaped recording of the police beating of Rodney King. The 81-second videotape sent shock waves through police departments throughout the nation.

Our knowledge of the police use of deadly force is incomplete, but one cannot question the fact that it is an ongoing topic and of extreme concern to police administrators, pressure groups, and detractors of law enforcement. The Chicago study, although it is some what dated, found that over a three-year period, there were 1,145 incidents in which civilians were shot at, and slightly more than one-fourth of these civilians were actually hit. In these incidents, only 14.2 percent of the shots fired struck someone, which clearly reflects the complexity of police use of deadly force. In a study of another city, it was found that out of 67 situations the police did not fire in 16 incidents. In 16 other incidents, the officer and the suspect pointed weapons at each other and neither fired.

In *Tennessee v. Garner*, the U.S. Supreme Court ruled that the use of deadly force by police to apprehend a person is a *seizure* subject to the reasonableness standard of the Fourth Amendment. Moreover, the Court held that it is constitutionally unreasonable to use such force "unless it is necessary to prevent an escape and the officer has probable cause to believe the suspect poses significant threat of death or serious physical injury to the officer or others." The *Garner* decision established a national minimum standard for the use of deadly force by a police officer. While ambiguities remain, the ruling prohibits police from shooting at unarmed, nonviolent, fleeing felony suspects. In the years ahead, it is anticipated that a continuing effort will be placed on the development of shooting control techniques in order to reduce problematic violence.

In another case, *Graham v. Connor,* the Court interpreted the Fourth Amendment as the standard of "objective reasonableness" being appropriate for assessing a police officer's use of force within the context of making an arrest.

Supreme Court and lower court decisions have been significant in creating the interest in developing less-than-legal devices, particularly for use against fleeing felons. Two of the more prominent devises are the Taser and pepper spray. In recent years, positional asphyxia has become a topic of concern as a number of suspects have died while in custody. Guidelines have been developed to reduce injury to hog-tied subjects.

The use of force continuum serves as a guideline for officers that allows for the selection of a level of force needed to insure that a situation is resolved. The continuum has been expanded with the use of neutralizing agents.

References

Ayers, B. Drummond, Jr. (1992). "U.S. Cities Handling Protest, Violence." *New York Times,* May 7: 1A-4A.

Brenner, Robert N. and Marjorie Kravitz, Compilers (1979). *A Community Concern: Police Use of Deadly Force.* Washington, DC: USGPO.

Bureau of Justice Statistics (1997). *Police Use of Deadly Force: Collection of National Data.* Washington, DC: U.S. Department of Justice, 1-10.

Chaiken, Jan (1996). *Victims Report 9 Percent Fewer Crimes Last Year.* Press Release. Washington, DC: U.S. Department of Justice, 1-7.

Committee on the Judiciary (1997). Subcommittee on Criminal Justice, House of Representatives, One Hundredth Congress, First Session, Serial No. 140, *Police Use of Deadly Force.* Washington, DC: USGPO, 58-125.

Corella, Hipolito R. (1992). "Officer's Killing of Fleeing Man Found Justified." *Arizona Daily Star*, October 30:1B and 6B.

Dees, Timothy M. (1994). "The Quest for Less-Than-Lethal Weaponry." *Law and Order,* Vol. 42, No. 8:49-52.

Dubay, David K. (1995). "Oleoresin Capsicum and Pepper Sprays." *Law and Order*, Vol. 43, No. 4:65-68.

Federal Bureau of Investigation (1988). *Uniform Crime Reports, Law Enforcement Officers Killed and Assaulted 1987.* Washington, DC: USGPO.

Federal Bureau of Investigation (1996). *Crime in the United States 1997.* Washington, DC: USGPO, 15-34.

Fischer, Jack (1994). "Pepper Spray Remains Hot Issue." *San Jose Mercury News.* August 28:1B, 4B.

Geller, William A. and Kevin J. Karales (1981). *Split-Second Decisions: Shootings of and by Chicago Police.* Chicago: Chicago Law Enforcement Study Group.

Geller, William A and Michael Scott (1992). *Deadly Force: What We Know.* Washington, DC: Police Foundation.

Graham v. Connor, 490 U.S. 386, 396-397 (1989).

Granfield, John, Jami Onnen, and Charles S. Petty (1994). *Pepper Spray and In-Custody Deaths*, Executive Brief. Alexandria, VA: International Association of Chiefs of Police, March:1-5.

Hall, John C. (1984). "Deadly Force—the Common Law and the Constitution." *FBI Law Enforcement Bulletin*, Vol. 53, Number 4.

Hall, John C. (1988a). "Police Use of Deadly Force to Arrest—A Constitutional Standard." Part 1, *FBI Law Enforcement Bulletin*, Vol. 57, Number 5.

Hall, John C. (1988b). "Police Use of Deadly Force to Arrest—A Constitutional Standard." Conclusion. *FBI Law Enforcement Bulletin*, Volume, 57, Number 6.

Hall, John C. (1995). "Deadly Force: A Question of Necessity." *FBI Law Enforcement Bulletin.* Vol. 64, No. 2:27-32.

Hayeslip, David W. and Alan Preszler (1993). *NIJ Initiative on Less Than Legal Weapons.* Washington DC: Office of Justice Programs, National Institute of Justice, 1-5.

Hunter, John C. (1994). " Focus on Use of Force." *FBI Law Enforcement Bulletin*, Vol. 63, No. 5: 24-26.

Jones, Tony L. (1997). "Tactical Use of Force." *Law and Order*, Vol. 45, No. 2:84-86.

Kobler, Arthur L. (1975). "Police Homicide in a Democracy." *Journal of Social Issues*, Vol. 31, No. 1.

Law Enforcement News (1988). "NY Top Cop Proposes Training Cops in Avoiding Lethal-Force Situations." February 9:12.

Los Angeles Times (1994). "Police Reports Show Frequent Misuse of Guns by Officers." August 15:3B.

McNaulty, James F. (1994). "The Taser Alternative to Use of Force." *Law and Order*, Vol. 42, No. 10:102-104.

Maguire, Kathleen and Ann L. Pastore (eds.) (1997). *Sourcebook of Criminal Justice Statistics— 1966*. Washington, DC: USGPO, 307, 332.

Matulia, Kenneth J. (1982). *A Balance of Forces*. Gaithersburg, MD: International Association of Chiefs of Police.

Model Penal Code, § 3.11, 2, (1976).

Muwakkil, Salim (1997). "Police Who Kill Blacks Raise Little Concern." *The Arizona Daily Star*, January 5:E3.

Niehaus, Joe (1997). " Realistic Use-of-Force Training." *Law and Order,* Vol. 45, No. 6:103-105.

Plakas v. Drinski, 19 F.3d 1143 (7th Cir. 1988).

Prach, Mark (1996). "Less-Than-Lethal Force." *Law and Order*, Vol. 44, No. 10:89-93.

Reay, Donald T. (1996). "Suspect Restraint and Sudden Death." *FBI Law Enforcement Bulletin*, Vol. 65, No. 5, May:22-26.

Reynolds, Joseph and Tod W. Burke (1994). "Cheers or Tears? A Reevaluation of Pepper Spray." *Law and Order*, Vol. 42, No. 8:87-90.

San Jose Mercury News (1992). "NY Still Tense After Killing by Police." July 8:6A.

San Jose Mercury News (1997). "LAPD to Settle Lawsuit With Ban on Hog-Ties." July 6:5B.

Snell, Tracey L. (1996). *Capital Punishment in the United States*. Washington, DC: U.S. Department of Justice, Office of Justice Programs, 1-6.

Tennessee v. Garner, 471 U.S. 1, at 9 (1985).

Trostle, L.C. (1990). "Force Continuum: From Lethal to Less-Than-Lethal Force." *Journal of Contemporary Criminal Justice,* Vol. 6, No. 2:23-36.

U.S. Bureau of the Census (1996). *Statistical Abstracts of the United States*, 116th Edition. Washington, DC: USGPO, 349.

U.S. Department of Health and Human Services (1995). *Vital Statistics of the United States 1992, Volume II, General Mortality Part A, Section 1*. Hyattsville, MD: Public Health Service, 220.

Wright, James D. (1986). *The Armed Criminal in America*, Research in Brief. Washington, DC: National Institute of Justice, 1-5.

MURDER AND INJURY OF POLICE OFFICERS: NATURE, EXTENT, AND TRENDS

5

The study of this chapter will enable you to:

1. Compare the number of officers killed and assaulted in 1995 to the previous decade.

2. Discuss the three most dangerous situations in which officers were killed.

3. Describe the three most frequent assignments that officers were on when they were killed.

4. List the weapons used most often by offenders when they killed an officer.

5. Discuss the extent of body armor use by police officers.

6. Describe the places and times when officers were murdered.

7. Write a short essay describing the disposition of persons identified in the felonious killing of law enforcement officers.

8. Discuss the extent to which officers are assaulted and injured.

9. Describe the extent to which officers are accidentally shot.

10. Determine the type of research conducted in the special study of police killers.

11. List the factors that describe the offender in the special FBI study.

12. Discuss the offender's perspective when an officer is killed.

13. Describe some aspects of the family history of offenders.

14. List the elements that describe the antisocial personality.

15. Write a short essay describing the dependent personality.

16. Become aware of the demographic description of the officer-victim.

17. List five general areas of concern in procedural and training issues.

Death and injury are not continuously salient incidents in most people's lives (McConville and Shepherd, 1992: 114). In fact, the normal response is to be complacent and assume that if anything untoward occurs, it will happen to someone else. This myopic view is clearly not reality for some people and certainly not for some occupations. Police work, especially in urban areas, can be dangerous. Most agree that it is necessary to develop techniques and procedures to reduce the death or injury of police officers.

The first recorded police officer to be killed in the line of duty was U.S. Marshal Robert Forsyth in 1794. He was shot while attempting to serve an arrest warrant. The deadliest decade of the twentieth century was the 1970s, during which time an average of 215 officers died in the line of duty. The second deadliest decade was the 1980s, which averaged 185 fatalities each year. Prior to that time, the 1920s had an average fatality rate of 164 annually. So far, the first half of the 1990s has reflected an average death rate of 101. Hence, it would appear that officers are working in a less deadly period than previously. From the time that records have been kept of the killing of police officers, 13,294 have died while in the line of duty (*Parade*, 1992b: 20).

There are a number of occupations that over the years have proven to be more dangerous than police work. The risk of job-related death is reportedly lower in police work than in such industries as mining, agriculture, construction, and transportation. However, it is still a hazardous occupation. Other work that has been even more hazardous includes fire fighting, garbage collecting, and cab driving. Occupational deaths and injuries vary from community to community, and in one study of injuries to city workers in New York City, fire fighters were injured three times as often, and garbage collectors four times as often. Notwithstanding, too many officers are being killed, and from 1794 to 1991 New York City was the most dangerous city in the United States for police. During that period, 511 police officers were killed in the line of duty (*Parade*, 1992a: 8).

If this nation were fortunate enough to significantly reduce the death or injury of police officers by even one-half, there would be still be a need to reduce the number of such incidents. The nature of police work is such that there is always the potential for an officer to be injured or killed (Chapman, 1976: 1-74).

Ours is a violent society and many calls for service or contact with a citizen can result in either physical conflict or death (Boyd, 1986: 10-11). Many officers minimize the dangers of police work in certain situations, such as telling their spouse that there is nothing to worry about, and that there is an exaggeration of danger. They point out that injury or death occurs more frequently from automobile accidents. In other audiences, where war stories are appropriate, officers will discuss at length the danger and close calls.

Killed in the Line of Duty

The police function in a society that, in some instances, is becoming more and more violent. Hence our society has armed police and has given them the authority to use deadly force in given situations. Statistics on the killing of police officers are readily available. The Federal Bureau of Investigation (FBI) has collected and published these figures for many years. The annual publication, titled *Law Enforcement Officers Killed and Assaulted,* specified that during 1995, the number of law enforcement officers killed in the line of duty totaled 74. Officer deaths occurred in 27 states, the District of Columbia, Mariana Islands, and Puerto Rico. Of the victims, most were from city police departments, followed by officers from county police and sheriff's offices. Three officers from state agencies were killed. Puerto Rico reported two killings and the Mariana Islands reported one killing. Nine deaths were reported by federal agencies, which is unusually high for this level of law enforcement. Eight of these deaths occurred as a result of the crime of the century, the bombing of the Alfred P. Murrah Federal Building in Oklahoma City. This was a significant portion of the 20 federal officers killed over the last five years.

Feature

Robbery Suspect and a Burglary in Progress

While searching for a robbery suspect, a 44-year-old-officer with the Sparks, Nevada Police Department was shot and killed at approximately 10:00 P.M. on May 22. Shortly before the 11-year veteran's slaying, two robberies occurred, one at a grocery store and another at a bar. Witnesses directed officers to a residential area to which the suspect had fled. The first officer in the area was fired upon with a .357-caliber revolver. Taking cover behind his police vehicle, the officer returned fire beneath the vehicle and wounded the advancing suspect in the foot. Fleeing down the street, the suspect concealed himself in some bushes. The victim officer, wearing body armor, was assisting other officers in a foot search for the suspect. When the officers attempted to detain an individual exiting a residence, the victim moved to assist. The suspect, from a nearby hidden position, shot the officer in the leg and fatally in the upper chest. The bullet entered above the arm hole of his protective vest. Other officers returned fire, killing the 46-year-old assailant.

On January 15, at about 5:10 A.M., a San Antonio Police Department patrolman with more than two years' service was slain after intervening in a burglary in progress. The 29-year-old off-duty officer observed three males sitting in a car with the motor running. Upon approaching the vehicle, the officer, who was wearing body armor, was able to persuade the driver to turn off the ignition and hand over the keys. As the officer stood next to the right front door of the vehicle, the male seated closest to him fired three to four rounds from a .25-caliber semiautomatic handgun. One round struck the officer in his right eye, and he fell to the ground. Exiting the vehicle, the alleged assailant, age 19, then obtained the officer's service weapon and fired again, fatally shooting the victim officer in the head three times at very close range. The alleged assailant and the other two occupants, both age 17, fled the scene taking the officer's service weapon with them. After a high-speed chase, the suspects were arrested, and all were charged with capital murder. All stolen property from the burglary was recovered, as were the officer's service weapon and the suspect's pistol.

Source: Federal Bureau of Investigation (1996). Uniform Crime Reports, *Law Enforcement Officers Killed and Assaulted 1995.* Washington, DC: USGPO, 51-56.

Table 5-1
The Number of Police Officers Killed and Assaulted: 1960-1995

Year	Assaults		Deaths	
	Total Assaults	Percentage with Injury	Number of Officers Murdered	Number by Accidents
1960	9,621	NR*	28	20
1961	13,190	NR	37	34
1962	17,330	NR	48	30
1963	16,793	NR	55	33
1964	18,001	46.0	57	31
1965	20,532	33.0	53	30
1966	23,851	38.0	57	42
1967	26,755	40.0	76	47
1968	33,604	42.0	64	59
1969	35,202	34.0	86	39
1970	43,171	35.0	100	46
1971	49,768	35.0	126	52
1972	37,523	33.0	112	41
1973	32,535	40.0	127	40
1974	29,511	39.0	132	47
1975	44,867	42.0	129	56
1976	49,079	38.0	111	29
1977	49,156	36.0	93	32
1978	56,130	38.0	93	52
1979	59,031	37.0	106	58
1980	57,847	37.0	104	61
1981	57,116	35.0	91	66
1982	55,755	31.0	92	72
1983	62,324	33.0	80	72
1984	60,153	34.0	72	75
1985	61,724	34.0	78	70
1986	64,259	34.0	66	67
1987	63,842	33.0	73	74
1988	58,752	35.8	78	77
1989	62,172	35.2	66	79
1990	71,794	36.3	66	67
1991	62,852	37.6	71	52
1992	81,252	36.5	63	62
1993	66,975	35.9	70	59
1994	64,912	35.7	78	62
1995	56,686	28.5	74	55

Source: Federal Bureau of Investigation (1960-1996). Uniform Crime Reports, *Law Enforcement Officers Killed and Assaulted, 1961-1995*. Washington, DC: USGPO, 1-85. NR—Not reported until 1964; Kathleen Maguire and Ann L. Pastore (1996). *Sourcebook of Criminal Justice Statistics—1995*. Washington, DC: U.S. Department of Justice, Bureau of Justice Statistics, 380.

The 1995 total of officers killed was lower than the preceding year. Both of these years are in sharp contrast to 1974, when 132 officers died. This was the greatest number of officers killed in any single year since records have been kept on this type of incident. The fewest number of deaths was in 1960 when the number of officers murdered was 28. Comparisons for five- and ten-year periods show that the number of officers slain in 1995 was four percent higher than in 1991, and was 12 percent higher than the 1986 total. Table 5-1 sets forth the statistics about the number of officers assaulted or killed from 1960 through 1995. The good news is that, over all, the death rate of law enforcement officers has been declining for two decades.

Circumstances in Which Officers are Killed

In 1995, the largest number of officers were killed when making arrests. In that category, the most dangerous situations occurred when officers were responding to either a robbery in progress or when pursuing robbery suspects. The next largest number of officers were killed when responding to burglaries in progress or when officers were pursuing burglary suspects. Figure 5-1 identifies eight specific circumstances surrounding the deaths of or assaults on police officers.

Figure 5-1
Officers Assaulted and Killed, Circumstances at the Scene: 1986-1995

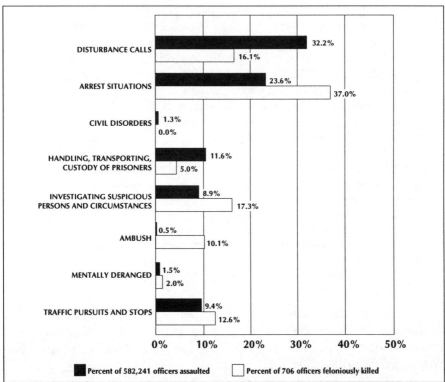

Source: Federal Bureau of Investigation (1996). Uniform Crime Reports, *Law Enforcement Officers Killed and Assaulted, 1995.* Washington, DC: USGPO, 28.

The next situation in which officers were apt to be killed was while investigating suspicious persons or circumstances. This was followed by ambush situations, in which six deaths occured, as a consequence of being trapped or the victim of a premeditated attack. The remainder of the ambushed officers died when they were attacked without provocation.

Feature

Ambush Situations

At approximately 9:40 P.M. on January 24, an off-duty detective with the Albertville, Alabama, Police Department was the victim of a fatal shooting at his residence. The 36-year-old detective answered a knock at his back door and was shot once in the front upper torso with a .38-caliber semiautomatic handgun. The alleged assailant was one of three male suspects, ages 32, 25, and 17. Allegedly, the trio had come to the victim's residence with the intention of preventing the detective from testifying against the 32-year-old in a theft by deception case. This suspect was a *habitual offender* and, if convicted, faced a possible life sentence. After managing to place an emergency call, the 14-year veteran detective was transported to the hospital, where he underwent surgery but died of his wound in the early morning hours of January 25. All three suspects were arrested and charged with capital murder.

At 5:30 A.M. on October 16, a Teller County Sheriff's Department patrol deputy with two years' experience, was ambushed while guarding an arson scene. The 27-year-old deputy responded to a reported structure fire, later found to have been deliberately set, in rural Teller County, Colorado. The victim was attacked while sitting alone in a patrol car at the fire scene awaiting arson investigators. The 28-year-old assailant apparently approached the deputy's vehicle from the left rear and fired one blast from a 12-gauge shotgun through either the open door or window of the car. The shot struck the deputy, who was wearing protective body armor, on the left front side of the face, mortally wounding him. The perpetrator, who was on parole and had a history of mental problems, then took the victim's 9-millimeter semiautomatic weapon and fled the scene. On the following day he took his own life, using the deputy's weapon. He left a confession and suicide note.

Source: Federal Bureau of Investigation (1996). Uniform Crime Reports, *Law Enforcement Officers Killed and Assaulted, 1995*. Washington, DC: USGPO, 41-57.

For some reason there have been a large number of ambushes in and around Washington, DC. Since 1990, there have been 31 unprovoked police murders—almost one-fourth of all the police killings that have occurred in the United States (Hoffman, 1997: 106-109).

Another dangerous situation was traffic stops or pursuits, and nine officers died in these situations As a result of nightly news stories and television programs, the public has been led to believe that drug arrests result in extreme violence. However, in 1995, there were only four officers killed in drug-related matters. Another surprise to some, because of publicity about the violence of family quarrels, is that the number of officers killed in these situations involved only six deaths. In terms of the circumstances resulting in the fewest or no deaths it proved to be, in the first instance, a situation in which one officer was slain while dealing with a mentally deranged individual. On the other hand, no officers were killed during civil disorders. Excluding the 1991 experience, the 21 officers killed while attempting to make arrests was the lowest in 10 years (Federal Bureau of Investigation, 1996: 1-85).

Types of Assignment

Of the 74 victims who died in 1995, 43 were patrol officers. The most dangerous duty for officers on patrol occurred when they were riding in one-officer vehicles—33 officers died in this situation. On the other hand, only 10 officers died when patrolling in two-officer vehicles. Eighteen victims were on investigative or special assignment, and the remainder were off duty but acting in an official capacity when slain. The fact that officers are more apt to die performing certain duties is not new. Statistics for the period from 1986 to 1995 reflect that the largest percentage of victim officers were on patrol when slain. Consistently, the most dangerous type of patrol duty for an officer has been the one-officer vehicle. Fifty-two percent of the vehicular patrol officers killed were alone and unassisted at the time of their death. Thirty-two percent of the victim officers on other types of assignments were alone and unassisted. A recent study suggests that state police or highway patrol officers assigned to one-officer patrol vehicles, in all probability, have a greater chance of dying in the line of duty. A factor that might contribute to this is the fact that state agencies have such an extensive area to patrol that backup does not occur rapidly enough (*Law Enforcement News*, 1997: 11-14).

Weapons

Firearms were used in a preponderance of incidents when officers were killed during the period from 1986 to 1995. Seventy-one percent of the murders involved the use of handguns. The remainder of weapons were primarily rifles and shotguns. Eighty-four officers were slain with their own weapons during the 10-year period. In the same time frame, the weapons of 126 officers were stolen. More than one-half of the officers killed by gunshots during this same period were within five feet of their assailants at the time of the attack. Fifty-eight percent of the firearm fatalities were caused by a wound to the head. This was followed by shots to the upper torso or below the waist.

During 1995, firearms were used in the vast majority of police slayings, and most unfortunate was the fact that six officers were shot with their own service weapons. The most common type of weapons used against officers were the .38 caliber, .380 caliber, and the nine millimeter. These three weapons jointly accounted for more than one-half of all handgun deaths. Twelve officers lost their lives to weapons other than firearms. Two were killed by knives, two were intentionally struck by vehicles, and eight federal officers were victims of the Oklahoma City bombing.

Body Armor

Protective body armor is being used by more and more law enforcement agencies. For example, in California, of 88 police departments with more than 100 sworn officers, almost three-fourths supply field officers with body armor, and two agencies provide some officers with vests. There is, of course, another variable involved inasmuch as a majority of these agencies have a policy that allows the officer to decide when to wear protective body armor. State law enforcement agencies present somewhat of a similar perspective. Forty states provide body armor, but only eight of these agencies require an officer to wear the vest when working (Reaves and Smith, 1995: 181-192).

During the past ten years, of 228 officers wearing body armor when slain, 142 suffered gunshot wounds to the head. Sixty-six suffered gunshot wounds to the upper torso and 20 suffered wounds below the waist. Thirty-three were shot between the panels of the vest or through the arm openings. Eleven officers died when bullets penetrated their protective vests. Although wearing body armor, one officer was beaten to death and another was killed when he was struck on the head with a bucket of spackling compound. In 1995, 32 officers were killed when wearing protective body armor, and 20 of those were shot in the head (Federal Bureau of Investigation, 1995: 15).

Places

The nation's most populous region, the South, recorded 32 of the 74 officer fatalities in 1995, and the western states reported 23 officers slain. Comparing the regional totals for two periods, 1986-1990 and 1991-1995, statistics indicate that the number of officers killed during the latter five-year span increased in all regions except the South. Forty-three percent of all officers killed were from the South (1986-1995). In that region, Texas, Florida, and Georgia were states where the death totals were the highest—64, 43, and 28 respectively. The South is clearly the most dangerous region and research is unable to explain this phenomenon. Figure 5-2 illustrates the number of officers killed according to the region in the following categories: as a percentage of the total United States population, as a percentage of all law enforcement officers employed, and as a percentage of all law enforcement officers killed.

Figure-5-2
Law Enforcement Officers Killed by Region: 1995

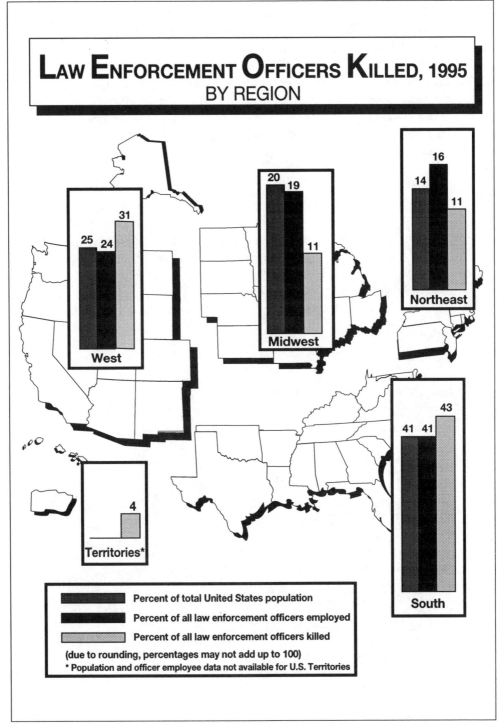

Source: Federal Bureau of Investigation (1996). Uniform Crime Reports, *Law Enforcement Officers Killed and Assaulted, 1995*. Washington, DC: USGPO, 22.

Times

In the past ten years, 63 percent of the incidents that resulted in officers' deaths occurred during the hours from 6:01 P.M. to 6:00 A.M. The four-hour period of 4:01 A.M. to 8:00 A.M. was the period when officers were at least risk, and the six-hour period from 8:01 P.M. to 2:00 A.M. was the most perilous. Additional statistics show that more officers died on Friday than on any other day of the week. The fewest fatalities occurred on Sundays. Monthly totals for the decade showed highs in January and April. During 1995, more officers were feloniously killed during April than any other month, followed by August. The smallest number of murders happened during the month of June.

Disposition of Offenders

Of those identified in connection with the murder of officers from 1984 to 1993, 115 were killed while committing an offense. Fifty-one others committed suicide, and five remain at large. Of those charged, almost three-fourths were found guilty of murder, and nine percent were found guilty of a lesser offense related to murder. Nine percent of the suspects were acquitted or had charges dismissed.

Table 5-2
Disposition of Offenders Identified in the Felonious Killing of Law Enforcement Officers: 1984-1993

Persons Identified	1984-1988	1989-1993	1984-1993
Known Persons	508	438	946
Fugitives	2	3	5
Justifiably Killed	66	49	115
Committed Suicide	23	28	51
Arrested and Charged	417	357	774
Arrested and Charged	417	357	774
Guilty of Murder	309	250	559
Guilty of Lesser Offense Related to Murder	31	35	66
Guilty of Crime Other than Murder	18	22	40
Acquitted or Otherwise Dismissed	49	19	68
Committed to Mental Institution	4	10	14
Case Pending or Disposition Unknown	0	12	12
Died in Custody	6	6	12
Probation	0	1	1
Indeterminate	0	2	2

Source: Federal Bureau of Investigation (1996). Uniform Crime Reports, *Law Enforcement Officers Killed and Assaulted, 1995*. Washington, DC: USGPO, 22.

Available data revealed that 113 of the 559 offenders found guilty of murder were sentenced to death, and 259 received life sentences. At the other extreme, one offender was placed on probation, and two were given indeterminate sentences (Federal Bureau of Investigation, 1996: 4).

Accidents Resulting in Deaths

Fifty-seven officers lost their lives due to accidents occurring while performing their official duties in 1995. Forty-three officers died in automobile, motorcycle, and aircraft accidents. Nine were accidentally struck by vehicles, and two were accidentally shot. The rest of the officers died in other types of accidents (e.g., drowning, asphyxiation, falls). Regionally, the southern states recorded 29 accidental deaths and the northeastern states had the fewest.

Since 1986, the number of officers killed accidentally totals 660. Of this number, the vast majority of officers died from injuries received in automobile accidents. Thirty-six officers died from accidental shootings that involved crossfires, mistaken identities, and firearm mishaps. Even training sessions can prove to be dangerous, inasmuch as during this 10-year period, seven officers died from being accidentally shot (Federal Bureau of Investigation, 1995: 63).

Assaulted and Injured in the Line of Duty

An average of 14 of every 100 officers were assaulted in 1995. The total number of assaults reported for the year was 56,686. Officers employed in the southern states were more apt to be assaulted than in other regions, inasmuch as that area registered the highest assault rate in the nation. Officers working in the midwestern states were assaulted the least—the states averaged nine assaults per 100 officers. In rural areas, officers performed in somewhat of a safer working environment where the assault rate was one-third that of cities with populations of 100,000-249,999. For 1995, the assault rate was one-fifth lower than that of the 1986 rate of 16.9 per 100 officers. In some instances, assaults on officers resulted in injuries. This rate has remained about the same in recent years and it has dropped over the years, with the highest percentage of injuries occurring in 1975 (Federal Bureau of Investigation, 1995: 72).

Twenty-nine percent of the assaults that caused injuries involved personal weapons such as hands, fists, and feet. When suspects assaulted officers using firearms, slightly more than one-sixth were injured. When officers were assaulted with knives or cutting instruments, slightly less than one-fourth received injuries.

Table 5-3
Law Enforcement Officers Assaulted by Population Group: 1995

Population Group of Victim Officer's Agency	Total	Rate per 100 Officers	Assaults with Injury	Rate per 100 Officers
Total	**56,686**	**13.5**	**16,181**	**3.8**
Group I (250,000 and over)	**17,316**	17.4	4,435	4.5
Group II (100,000 - 249,999)	**7,708**	21.3	2,357	6.5
Group III (50,000 - 99,999)	**6,621**	18.5	1,701	4.7
Group IV (25,000 - 49,999)	**4,121**	12.4	1,257	3.8
Group V (10,000 - 24,999)	**4,166**	10.9	1,295	3.4
Group VI (under 10,000)	**3,908**	7.8	1,251	2.5
Suburban Counties	**10,714**	11.1	3,252	3.4
Rural Counties	**2,132**	6.7	633	2.0

Source: Federal Bureau of Investigation (1996). Uniform Crime Report, *Law Enforcement Officers Killed and Assaulted, 1995*. Washington, DC: U.S. Department of Justice, USGPO, 67.

One-third of assaults against officers occurred when they responded to disturbance calls. This category included family quarrels, person with a gun, bar fights, and similar incidents. In all types of circumstances, one-fifth of the officers were making an effort to arrest a suspect when assaulted. The next category of assaults occurred when transporting, handling, or maintaining custody of prisoners. Twelve percent of the officers were assaulted in those situations. The next category involved assault situations in which officers were investigating suspicious persons or stops. This was followed by situations involving traffic pursuits or suspects.

During 1995, 80 percent of the law enforcement officers assaulted were on vehicular patrol. Almost two-thirds of the assault victims were patrolling alone, and 21 percent were assigned to two-officer vehicles. As in previous years, the most dangerous times for assaults was between 10:00 P.M. and 2:00 A.M. Combining five of the factors discussed above, it suggests that the possibility of being assaulted by personal weapons (hands, fists, feet, etc.) is greatest for officers patrolling alone during late evening and early morning duty shifts, while responding to disturbance calls.

Accidental and Self-Inflicted Shootings

It is also interesting to note that some shooting incidents are the result of officers not being shot by suspects. In the Chicago study (See Figure 5-3), 38 percent of the victim officers shot themselves or were victims of shots by other officers. Self-inflicted shootings by police accounted for 27 percent of all officer gunshot victims. These occurred in three situations: suicides, accidental discharges during the maintenance or other *non-combat* handling of the weapon, and accidental firings in the course of attempted arrests. Eleven percent of all officers shot during the study period were victims of shots by other officers. Shootings of this type resulted primarily from accidental gun discharges (Geller and Karales, 1981: 142-144). In a study conducted in New York City, a researcher stated that "police are at least as likely to be killed by themselves, their acquaintances, or their colleagues as by their professional clientele." (Fyfe, 1982: 18). Thus, one can see that the use of deadly force by the police can be injurious to the officers themselves.

Figure 5-3
Police Shot in Chicago

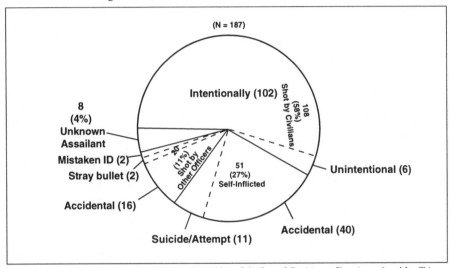

Source: William A. Geller and Kevin J. Karales (1981). *Split-Second Decisions: Shootings of and by Chicago Police.* Chicago: Chicago Law Enforcement Study Group, 142. Reprinted with the permission of William A. Geller.

In a study of the Metro-Dade Police Department over a five and one-half year period (1988-1994), of the shooting incidents studied (190), there were 44 incidents in which weapons were accidentally discharged. As a result of these shootings, four officers were shot, which suggests that even well-trained officers can, on occasion, discharge a weapon inappropriately. In one other shooting incident, an officer unwittingly shot an undercover police officer (Alpert and Dunham, 1995: 10-30).

Special Study of Selected Felonious Killings of Officers

Although the number of slayings of officers has declined in recent years, each tragic incident brings devastation and outrage to the community whose rights, lives, and property the victims are sworn to protect. Most directly affected, besides victims' families, are those fellow officers who are suddenly made starkly aware of the extremely hazardous nature of their profession and their vulnerability as they go about their everyday duties (Federal Bureau of Investigation, 1992: 1-60). A situation that results in the death of a law enforcement officer is exceedingly complex. It deals with two or more individuals, their life experiences and perceptions, as well as situational circumstances that brought them together and ultimately led to the death of an officer.

Circumstances Surrounding the Offense

A study by the FBI used 51 selected incidents and analyzed the psychology of the offender, the behavior of the law enforcement officer, and the circumstances in which the officer lost his or her life. These incidents resulted in the deaths of 54 law enforcement officers and involved 50 offenders. Included were two incidents involving the same offender and three incidents involving the slaying of two officers in each incident.

The Scene. Thirty-nine percent of the officers studied were involved in arrests or crime-in-progress situations, which is similar to data collected in nationwide studies. Next were traffic pursuits or stops, followed by situations involving disturbance calls. The remainder of the incidents involved handling prisoners, investigating suspicious situations, and other circumstances. Ambushes were not considered in the study because there was no possible preventive action the officers could have taken. Seventy-three of the killings occurred on a street, highway, or in a parking lot. The remainder occurred in private dwellings and public buildings. In terms of other aspects of the scene of the offense, the study found that 42 percent of the incidents occurred within five miles of the offender's residence (Federal Bureau of Investigation, 1992: 4).

In eight out of ten incidents, the initial encounter between the victim officer and the offender, whether questioning or confrontation, occurred in the same location as the assault that claimed the officer's life. Additionally, seventy-five percent of the offenders' means of transportation was a motor vehicle which is to be expected in our motorized society.

Environment. The time of day and the weather conditions at the time the incidents occurred were also factors contributing to the circumstances under which officers died. Sixty percent of the fatal incidents occurred during the nighttime hours, and visibility during these hours is likely to be a contributing factor to their outcome. Additionally, the majority of the incidents that occurred between 6:01 P.M. and 6:00 A.M. also involved snow, rain, or fog. While these conditions may not have a significant role in incidents, visibility issues may still play a role in the procedural safeguards that law enforcement officers may use and should be included in training sessions. These environmental conditions are for the most part uncontrollable, but their potential contributions to the fatal incidents are of importance to law enforcement survival training efforts (Federal Bureau of Investigation, 1992: 4-5).

Weapons Used in the Assault. The preponderance of the victim officers in the incidents selected for study died as a result of handgun wounds. Other weapons involved in the victimization of these officers included rifles at 13 percent, shotguns at nine percent, and the remainder were other weapons. The weapons of choice of the perpetrators were the .38 Smith & Wesson Special and the .357 Remington Magnum. Weapons used less frequently were the nine millimeter Luger Parabellum and the .32 Smith & Wesson. National studies show the use of similar weapons by assailants. This information about handgun type has implications for tactical training of officers. Interestingly, 85 percent of the victim officers in the study did not discharge their service weapons (Federal Bureau of Investigation, 1992: 5).

Geographical Variations. Regional variations are clearly evident in the deaths of police officers. It is also clear that there may be cultural and structural factors involved, but further study is needed to determine their contribution in this area. For years there have been a disproportionate number of law enforcement officers feloniously killed in the southern region of the United States, and the current study substantiates those findings. The South has other unusual characteristics, such as having the highest regional general homicide rate in the United States. This being true, it seems reasonable to assume that more police officer deaths will occur in the South. Other factors of interest are the number of law enforcement officers employed in the South and the concentration of population. The South has the largest population of any region in the United States, and employs the greatest number of officers, but neither of these factors explains the large disparity in officer deaths.

The Offender

There is no singular profile of an individual who kills a law enforcement officer. Rather, a variety of pictures are presented when the actual data are analyzed for physical, social, and psychological characteristics. Table 5-4 identifies some offender demographics.

The offenders in this study were predominately male, young, white, single, and high school educated. This profile corresponds to nationwide studies of offenders who have killed police officers.

Family History

From information obtained from offender interviews, it was determined that 82 percent of the killers reported that their natural mother was present most of the time during their pre-adult life, while only six percent reported that they had never lived with their natural mother. On the other hand, 44 percent of those interviewed stated that their natural father was present most of the time, and 14 percent reported that they had never lived with their natural father. More than one-half of the offenders reported that the most dominant parental figure in the home was the mother.

Table 5-4
Offenders: A Demographic Description

Gender:	96% male; 4% female
Average Age:	26 years
Race:	60% white; 40% nonwhite
Average Height:	5 feet 9 inches
Average Weight:	176 pounds
Marital Status:	12% married
	54% single
	2% separated
	32% divorced
Education:	34% no degree
	60% high school degree
	4% some college
	2% college degree

Source: Federal Bureau of Investigation (1992). *Killed in the Line of Duty: A Study of Selected Felonious Killings of Law Enforcement Officers.* Washington, DC: USGPO, 9.

Of particular note is that more than one-half of the offenders considered their pre-adult socioeconomic status to be at least average to comfortable. Within the home environment, 40 percent of the offenders pointed out that problem-solving in the home was accomplished rationally. On the other hand, more than one-half reported that verbal and physical abuse were common practices in resolving disputes. Forty-four percent of the offenders reported they had suffered some physical abuse by parental figures, and a little more than one-third claimed psychological abuse. This abuse involved neglect, verbal abuse, and cold, distant, uncaring, and indifferent treatment.

Criminal History

Slightly less than one-half of the offenders indicated during interviews that larceny was the first crime they committed, and this was done at an average age of 12. Drug offenses, larceny, burglary, weapons offenses, and robbery predominate the criminal history of the individuals who kill law enforcement officers. Of interest is the fact that commission of these offenses also predominates incarcerating offenses of individuals who have not killed law enforcement officers. Interestingly, just short of one-half of the offenders interviewed admitted that they had murdered or attempted to murder someone subsequent to the killing of the officer. These same offenders (18 percent) stated they had assaulted or had resisted arrest prior to killing an officer. Three offenders claimed to have had no criminal history prior to killing the officer (see Figure 5-4).

Figure 5-4
Self-Reported Criminal Involvement of Offenders

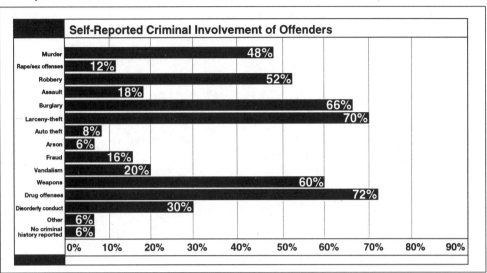

Source: Federal Bureau of Investigation (1992). *Killed in the Line of Duty: A Study of Selected Felonious Killings of Law Enforcement Officers.* Washington, DC: USGPO, 11.

When criminal arrest records were checked, it was found that 47 percent of the offenders had prior arrests for crimes of violence. There was also a clear presence of prior weapons and drug law violations in their history.

Weapons Usage

Of the 54 police officers killed, almost three-fourths were victims of handgun wounds. Therefore, use and familiarity with handguns appear to be contributing factors to these incidents. In fact, familiarity with handguns during childhood and teenage years was reported by as many as 64 percent of the offenders, and 60 percent had used a rifle in the past. Almost three-fourths of the offenders reported that they regularly carried a handgun, used these weapons during criminal behavior, and started carrying weapons when they were 18 years old. Twenty percent of the offenders carried their weapons in a pocket, and another 20 percent carried them in the small of their back. The other offenders carried weapons in various locations on their person. Slightly more than three-fourths of the perpetrators used the weapon they did because it was easily available and they were familiar with the weapon.

When in a vehicle, 34 percent of the offenders stated they kept their weapons on their person. While one-fifth kept the weapon beneath the seat, 12 percent kept them on the seat of the vehicle. Slightly more than one-half of the offenders practiced with their weapons at least once per month. The prevalence of handgun usage amongst offenders, in which they carry weapons on their person, and the placement of weapons in vehicles are important factors that can be considered in training police officers.

Alcohol/Drug Abuse

When drug or alcohol use or abuse is defined as any activity regarding the buying, selling, or use of these substances, 76 percent of the killers stated that they were engaged in drug or alcohol activity at the time of the killing of an officer. Slightly less than one-fourth of the offenders reported no drug or alcohol abuse. With the remainder of the study group, drug use was more prevalent than alcohol use (24 percent to 12 percent) at the time of the killings. Yet 41 percent of the offenders were using both when an officer was murdered.

Offender's Perspective

In the FBI study, the offenders were asked what, in their opinion, the victim officers could have done, if anything, to prevent their deaths. Forty-seven percent of the killers stated that there was nothing the victims might have done to prevent their deaths after the initial confrontation with the offender. Additionally, eight percent felt that if the officers had been more *professional,* they might not have lost their lives. However none of the offenders could articulate what they meant by *professional.* In three cases, the offenders stated that if the victim officers had identified themselves as law enforcement officers, they could have prevented their deaths. None of these officers were in uniform at the time of the killings. The offenders in these case claimed that the non-uniformed officers were mistaken for private citizens.

Each offender was questioned as to whether age, sex, or physical size of the victim had any influence on the decision to assault and kill the officer. Only four percent of the offenders stated that age was a contributing factor. Only a single offender advised that the size of the victim was a contributing factor. Yet seven offenders, all males who had killed male officers, stated that they would not have committed the act had the officer been a female.

Psychological Evaluation

The mental status and diagnosis of the personality of each of the offenders was accomplished by reviewing records. Additionally, a forensic psychologist interviewed 33 of the subjects. Using acceptable diagnostic criteria and terminology, three broad diagnostic categories were present. Two offenders were diagnosed as having organic personality disorder. They were victims of closed head injuries that occurred in circumstances distinct from the situation in which law enforcement officers were killed. Forty-three offenders received various diagnoses within the general category of personality disorders, and five offenders were not categorized within any diagnostic category. In this study, two personality types dominated, and these are discussed below and summarized in Figure 5-5.

Figure 5-5
Personality Typology of Offenders

Antisocial Personality	Dependent Personality
Sense of entitlement	Overcontrolled
Lack of remorse	Dependent and submissive
Disparity between behavior and	Inability to deal with anger,
socially accepted normative	frustration, and hostility
behavior	Passive compliance with the
Disregard for social obligations	wishes of others
Nonconformity to norms	Poor social interaction
Alienated from society	Inadequate
Lack of feelings for others	Weak and inefficient
Lack of conscience	Lacking energy
Blames others for their own	Passive
wrongdoing	
Projects negative consequences	
upon others	
Manipulative and cunning	
Irresponsible	
Affectively cold	

Source: Federal Bureau of Investigation (1992). *Killed in the Line of Duty: A Study of Selected Felonious Killings of Law Enforcement Officers.* Washington, DC: USGPO, 22.

Dependent Personality Type. These individuals have a pervasive pattern of dependent and submissive behavior, and a personality that is overcontrolled. These offenders have a personality best described as dependent, submissive, and full of anxiety. As they go through life, they are unable to deal with anger, frustration, and hostility. When this type of personality is involved in circumstances that cause stress and anxiety, the tension of what is described as an emotional spring can cause an explosive episode. There is no way to anticipate what will trigger an outburst or when it will be triggered. The next Feature is a case narrative of a dependent personality type.

Antisocial Personality Type. This personality type personifies the individual who is manipulative and cunning. They know right from wrong, but choose not to conform their behavior to what is socially acceptable. Typically, antisocial personality traits include a disregard for social obligations, and a gross disparity between their behaviors and the socially accepted normative behaviors. A lack of feelings for others is seen, especially in their social relationships. These individuals easily enter relationships that they feel they can work to their advantage.

Feature

Dependent Personality Type

Mary is a fictitious name for a woman who killed a law enforcement officer when she was 16 years old. She was born into a military family and was the oldest of three siblings. The father, although absent a great deal, was the dominant parental figure. Mary assessed the economic level of the family as comfortable. However, the overall stability and coherence of the family environment was unstable and disruptive. Mary characterized the quality of the relationship with parents as uncaring and indifferent. Family problem-solving involved frequent shouting, threats, and insults, as well as physical abuse.

Mary reported that the relationship with her father was emotionally and sometime physically abusive. She was unable to express her unhappiness and her anger at how she was being treated. Her relationship with her mother was antagonistic, and she felt she had no one to whom she could turn. At the age of eight her parents divorced. She lived with her father, then her mother for a while, and finally with her grandmother. By the age of 14 or 15 she lived regularly with her grandmother. She stated that she was average in school, but she dropped out before completing the twelfth grade. When she was 15, a small-time drug dealer came into her life. She recognized John as someone who would make decisions—which is something that Mary would avoid. She perceived the relationship with John as being a positive event in her life. She moved in with John and started experimenting with drugs. John taught her how to use a handgun and they shot at cans and other objects for fun.

After John and Mary had lived together for approximately six months, John robbed a drug dealer and obtained large amounts of drugs and money. Following the robbery, he ingested some of the drugs, then went into a convenience store to use the telephone. Because of his peculiar behavior, the proprietor called the police. Prior to the arrival of the police, Mary entered the store to determine why John had been gone so long. She found John sitting on the floor eating potato chips. When the police arrived they arrested John for disorderly conduct. Seeing this, Mary's world began to crumble. She perceived that her "knight in shining armor" was in trouble. She went to the car, retrieved a revolver, and returned to the store. She demanded that the arresting officer release John. When the officer refused, Mary shot and killed him.

Source: Federal Bureau of Investigation (1992). *Killed in the Line of Duty: A Study of Selected Felonious Killings of Law Enforcement Officers.* Washington, DC: USGPO, 18-19.

Their behavior is not readily modified by experience. They tend to project on others the bad or negative consequences of their own behavior. In other words, they tend to blame others for their own wrongdoing. People who know these individuals have commented on their high levels of aggression, irresponsibility, and low tolerance for frustration. The following Feature describes an individual with an antisocial personality.

Feature

The Antisocial Personality

Edward is a fictitious name for the individual who is responsible for the death of a law enforcement officer in the northeastern part of the country. At the time he killed the officer, Edward was 32 years of age. Edward is the oldest of eight siblings, and his father left the household when Edward was six months old. He lived with his mother and grandmother, who was the dominant person in the household. The grandmother's discipline was inconsistent. At times Edward was praised for doing something and then later punished for doing the same thing. The family's socioeconomic status was marginal, and Edward claimed that he was physically abused. In elementary school he had good grades but in junior high his grades dropped dramatically. He eventually dropped out of school and completed his GED in prison.

His social encounters were replete with conflict. Police reports described him as threatening and impulsive. His friends described him as dangerous. He had been found guilty of another homicide, which took place prior to the law enforcement officer shooting. Police and court reports described his ability to use and con others. After committing an armed robbery with two associates, they left the crime scene and drove the wrong way down a one-way street, attracting the attention of an officer who was on patrol in his marked vehicle. After the officer stopped the car, Edward opened the door of his car and walked back to the officer's vehicle. The officer ask Edward to return to his car and wait. While Edward was talking with the officer he noted that the officer was using the radio and not paying attention. When Edward returned to the car he told an individual in the back seat to get his shotgun ready because something is going to happen. Edward said that he was going to shoot the officer. When asked by the backseat passenger if he meant that he was going to kill the officer, Edward responded, "You're damn right I'm going to kill him." Edward reportedly walked back to the officer's car and stood to the side of the seated officer. Edward stated that when he arrived at the side of the car, the officer was "still looking at the radio when he was talking into the microphone. He didn't see me come to the car. He then looked up out of the corner of his eye for a fraction of a second and saw I had a gun. I shot him once in the chest and went back to the car."

Source: Federal Bureau of Investigation (1992). *Killed in the Line of Duty: A Study of Selected Felonious Killings of Law Enforcement Officers*. Washington, DC: USGPO, 21-22.

A major lesson learned from this study is that there is no single personality type that kills law enforcement officers. In the study, of those identified as having a personality disorder, the antisocial personality type was the most frequently diagnosed (56 percent) within the sample. There was also a relatively large number (23 percent) of individuals diagnosed as dependent personality types. People in this group appear to be too docile and easygoing to engage in violence. As such, officers need to be aware that a calm and agreeable surface may be hiding an emotional volcano.

The Victim

In the FBI study of 51 incidents involving the deaths of 54 officers, the victim's supervisors and co-workers were interviewed about the incidents. When provided, additional background records were reviewed. By studying the experiences and characteristics of previous victims, it was hoped that additional knowledge would be gained that might be used to save the lives of other officers.

Victim Demographics

The victim officers studied were predominately male, young (average age 34), white, married, and high school educated. They averaged 5 feet 10 inches in height and weighted 188 pounds. Seven percent of the sample were African-American and only two percent were female. Eleven percent were single, two percent were divorced, and six percent were separated. Nine percent of the officers possessed a college degree.

Table 5-5
Victims: A Demographic Description

Gender:	98% male; 2% female
Average Age:	34 years
Race:	93% white; 7% African-American
Average Height:	5 feet 10 inches
Average Weight:	188 pounds
Marital Status:	81% married; 11% single; 6% separated; 2% divorced
Education:	83% high school; 7% some college; 9% college degree

Source: Federal Bureau of Investigation (1992). *Killed in the Line of Duty: A Study of Selected Felonious Killings of Law Enforcement Officers.* Washington, DC: USGPO, 29.

This demographic description of the study group is similar to that of the offenders involved in these incidents. The victim officers were on average eight years older, more educated with higher percentages having completed both high school and college, and more likely to be married than were the offenders examined. There were, on average, no significant weight or height differences between the victim officers and the offenders studied.

Agency Affiliation

The victim officers were members of a variety of agencies at the time of their deaths. Clearly, municipal police, at 46 percent, and officers employed by sheriffs' offices at 26 percent, were the predominant victims in the incidents. The third highest number of victims were from state police agencies, followed by highway patrols. This distribution is similar to data gathered by the FBI in their annual survey of police killings.

Type of Assignment

Eight of ten officers in the study were assigned to vehicle patrol at the time of their deaths. Specifically, 70 percent were assigned to one-officer vehicles and nine percent to two-officer vehicles. Other victims studied served in varying capacities, with nine percent performing detective duties or special assignments. Six percent were serving in undercover, temporary, or administrative duties. Another six percent were off duty but acting in an official capacity when slain.

Years of Service

The victims averaged eight years of law enforcement service. None had less than one year of experience. Thirty-one percent had from one to five years of experience. At the other end of the spectrum, 30 percent were veterans with more than ten years of service. In nationwide surveys, the average length of service is nine years—similar to this study. It would seem that length of service has little bearing on officer deaths.

Work Performance

In spite of the difficulty in obtaining information on overall performance, a most surprising finding emerged. Ten victims had received successful or better than successful ratings over several rating periods, but just subsequent to their deaths received a lower assessment. The specific area in which the officers were found lacking could not be determined in all cases. Departments were reluctant to provide specific information from agency personnel records. In one case, an agency official stated that there were two areas of decline in the officer's last evaluation. The first was that the officer failed to maintain the department's weight guidelines—he was overweight. Second, the victim would not use the department-issued protective vest, stating it was uncomfortable to wear.

Behavioral Descriptors

The original purpose of the study did not include an intent to analyze the personalities of the victim officers. Consequently, no systematic approach to uncover behavioral patterns was made. It was only after several interviews that similar behavioral descriptors emerged. As the study continued, a list of common behavioral descriptors became apparent. Figure 5-6 lists the behavioral descriptors of victim officers.

Figure 5-6
Behavioral Descriptors of Victim Officers

Friendly to everyone
Well-liked by community and department
Tends to use less force than other officers felt they would in similar circumstances
Hard working
Tends to perceive self as more public relations than law enforcement
Uses force only as a last resort
 —peers claim they would use force at an earlier point in similar circumstances
Doesn't follow all the rules, especially regard to:
 —arrest
 —confrontation with prisoners
 —traffic stops
 —does not wait for backup (when available)
Feels she/he can *read* others and situations and will drop guard as a result
Tends to look for good in others
Laid back and easygoing

Source: Federal Bureau of Investigation (1992). *Killed in the Line of Duty: A Study of Selected Felonious Killings of Law Enforcement Officers.* Washington, DC: USGPO, 32.

Two points should be noted. First, it is obvious that not all descriptors are favorable. A statement that an officer uses force only as a last resort—even where most other officers would have used force earlier—suggests that the officer should have used more force. It also suggests that it should have been used earlier in order to protect both himself or herself, as well as other officers and/or civilians. Not following all of the procedures is another descriptor of importance. This too, could result in possible injury to oneself or others. If, for example, a prisoner is not handcuffed correctly, considering the offender's comfort more than officer's safety, the handguns might be used as a weapon against the officer and his or her partner. A second point to consider is that even some offenders, those who had timely contact with the officers prior to the killings, used these same behavioral descriptors when talking about officers. The most salient characteristics in relation to incidents of this nature appear to be those descriptors that characterize the officer as good-natured and conservative in his or her use of authority.

Procedural and Training Issues

One of the chief goals of the study was to analyze the incidents in the hope that the lives of law enforcement officers might be saved in the future. The study developed five general areas of concern in connection with law enforcement training and procedures:

- **Procedural Errors.** There were cases in which the officer did not follow accepted law enforcement procedures. Such examples include: failing to call for backup support when such backup was available and appropriate given the circumstances. Other situations involved acting alone prior to the

arrival of backup support, failure to search a suspect fully and completely, improper use of handcuffs, and positioning the police vehicle in front
of a target vehicle during a traffic stop.

- **Correct Procedure.** In some cases, the victim officers apparently followed all the acceptable procedures and yet were still killed. For example,
in one case the officer simply asked an individual to move a car that was
improperly parked. Without giving the officer any indication that he was
armed, the occupant of the car shot and killed the officer.

- **Absence of Procedures.** Certain situations arose for which the law
enforcement agency had no formalized or accepted procedures to handle
the circumstances. It is recognized that procedures cannot be formalized
to cover every situation that an officer may encounter; however, there are
some eventualities, given the nature of the profession, for which plans
should be made and then formalized in training. For example, how should
an officer respond to a situation in which he or she is faced with a drawn
weapon? Another example is illustrated by the lack of stated policies by
some departments, indicating whether the officer is to allow the occupants
of a vehicle in a traffic stop situation to exit the car or whether the officer
should instruct the occupants to remain in the car until the officer advises
them further. There is considerable variation in the philosophies for managing these circumstances.

- **Conflicting Procedures.** Procedures in which the officer was trained
were sometimes in conflict with his or her personal safety. In some jurisdictions, the written policy for traffic stops allows the officer to place the
driver of the target vehicle in the front seat of the officer's vehicle. This
procedure has the possible effect of placing the officer at a disadvantage.
When, for example, the radioed results of a National Crime Information
Center search reveals an existing arrest warrant, the situation turns into an
arrest event. Another example involving training procedures that may be
in conflict with an officer's safety may occur in jurisdictions where written departmental policies and procedures preclude an officer from drawing his or her service weapon unless drawn on first. Such a policy has the
potential of always placing the officer at a tactical disadvantage.

- **Training**. Agencies should continually strive to stay abreast of new methods, literature, studies, procedures, practices, concepts, court decisions,
and equipment, and develop procedures and training to keep their members informed and updated. Training issues include such things as:
approaching vehicles and suspects, conducting searches and seizures, controlling persons and situations, training at night, and first aid (Pinizzotto
and Davis, 1995: 1-6).

Survivors

The loss of a police officer is a traumatic event. The steps taken by the
agency can have a lasting impact on the well-being of the family, the community and the organization (Simms, 1996: 26-33). Following the tragic event, con-

sideration must be given to a wide range of events, such as: debriefings, benefits, and support groups (Gist and Taylor, 1996: 34-37). In a study by Concerns of Police Survivors, completed in 1997, only 39 percent of the police departments surveyed had a formal policy for officer deaths and survivor care (Concerns of Police Survivors, 1997: 1-4).

The federal government provides benefits available to survivors through the Public Safety Officers' Benefits Act. In order for survivors to receive benefits, an officer's death must have been the direct and proximate result of a traumatic injury sustained in the line of duty. Another section of the Act provides benefits to officers who have been permanently and totally disabled and cannot perform gainful work. The benefits are tied to the consumer price index, and in 1993 the payment totaled approximately $127,499, and 199 payments totaled awards of $24,123,153. Additionally, a total of $468,258 was awarded to four public safety officers who were permanently and totally disabled by a catastrophic line-of-duty injury (Bureau of Justice Assistance, 1997: 1). Since the program began in 1976, it has approved 3,557 death-benefit claims, resulting in total payments of approximately $240 million to eligible survivors (Gist, 1997: 1-4).

Another benefit source is the Social Security Administration. If the officer was paying FICA tax, the spouse and children would be eligible for a monthly survivors' benefit. Payments are based on the deceased officer's average annual income. Children of survivors are eligible to receive benefits until they reach age 18, and the surviving adult can receive benefits until the youngest child reaches age 16, providing that the beneficiary does not become employed. Another benefit from Social Security is a one-time death benefit of $255, payable to the surviving spouse. If a federal crime was involved in the death of an officer, benefits might be available from the U.S. Department of Labor (*Law and Order,* 1994: 153-154).

Concerns of Police Survivors (COPS) is an nationwide organization that was created to offer peer support to police survivors. This organization has developed guidelines for support services that should be provided to surviving families (Concerns of Police Survivors, 1994: 1-4). COPS has received funding for a number of years to conduct training sessions on "The Aftermath of Law Enforcement Officer Death." During 1976-1977, the organization trained 670 people in seminars held throughout the nation (Concerns of Police Survivors, 1997: 6).

Technology and Safety

A number of devices that can enhance the personal security of police officers are currently being tested and developed. The millimeter-wave camera is a detection device that seems to hold a great deal of promise. The human body emits a very strong electromagnetic signal with wavelengths in the millimeter range. Guns and knives emit almost no signal and block human emissions. This special camera projects a clear image on a monitor. It is anticipated that a police officer will be able to detect a weapon at a range of 30 to 60 feet. The camera could be handheld or mounted on a police vehicle and will detect both metallic and non-metallic weapons. It includes the potential for detecting plastic explosives. It is hoped that the device will be developed so it can be tested before the end of the decade. Overall the U.S. Justice Department is working on 12 promising weapons technologies.

Summary

While police work is not the most dangerous occupation, the death of a police officer is a traumatic event that affects the police department, the community, and the surviving family. During 1995, the number of officers killed in the line of duty totaled 74. Overall, the death rate has been declining for more than two decades, dropping from a high of 132 deaths in 1974. The largest number of officers were killed when making arrests. In that category, situations that proved to be most dangerous involved robberies in progress or the pursuit of robbery suspects.

Of the officers killed in 1995, a majority were on patrol and most of those were in one-officer vehicles. Eighteen victims were on detective or special assignment. Additionally, evidence suggests that state police or highway patrol officers have a greater chance of being killed while on duty in a one-person patrol vehicle. Firearms were involved in the vast majority of police slayings and the most common type of weapon used was the .38 caliber. Body armor is being used by more and more police officers, and during 1995, 32 officers were killed while wearing a vest. Two of these officers were killed when 7.62 x 39 millimeter bullets penetrated the vest.

The nation's most populous region, the South, recorded 32 of the 74 officer fatalities in 1995. The South is clearly the most dangerous region, but research is unable to explain this phenomenon. During 1995, more officers were feloniously killed during April than any other month, followed by August. Additionally, more officers died between 10:00 P.M. and midnight than any other time. Of those identified in connection with the murder of officers, 115 were killed at the scene of the officer's murder. One hundred thirteen of the offenders were found guilty of murder and sentenced to death and 259 received life imprisonment. The vast majority of officers who were accidentally killed were involved in automobile accidents. The tragic aspect of some at the accidents (36) during the last decade was that they involved shootings: crossfires, mistaken identities, and firearms mishaps.

An average of 14 out of 100 officers were assaulted in 1995. This rate was one-fifth lower than in 1986. Of those assaulted, a number are injured and this rate has remained relatively constant over recent years. In some instances, officers shoot themselves or other officers. These instances involve suicides, accidental discharges during maintenance of the weapon, and accidental firings in the course of attempted arrests. In the special study of the deaths of 54 officers, the FBI analyzed the psychology of offenders, the behavior of the involved officer, and the circumstance surrounding the death of the officer. With reference to the scene of the incident, 39 percent occurred when the officer was involved in an arrest or crime-in-progress situation. Just under three-fourths of the deaths occurred on a street, highway, or in a parking lot. Sixty percent of the fatalities happened between 6:01 P.M. and 6:00 A.M., and the majority of killings occurred when it was snowing, raining, or foggy. Additionally, 72 percent of the victims died as a result of handgun wounds. Similar to other studies, the South had the greatest number of felonious deaths of officers.

The offenders in the study were predominately male, young, white, single, and high school educated. From interview data it was determined that 82 percent of the offenders stated that their natural mother was present during most of their upbringing. More than one-half considered their pre-adult socioeconomic status to be at least average to comfortable. More than one-half of the offenders reported verbal and physical abuse. Abuse included neglect, verbal abuse, and cold, distant, uncaring, and indifferent treatment. Slightly less than one-half of the subjects indicated that their first crime was committed at age 12 and it was a crime of larceny. Their criminal history ran the gamut from drug offenses to weapons violations. They were familiar with handguns starting in childhood, and almost two-thirds had used a rifle in the past. Almost three-fourths of the offenders started carrying weapons when they were 18 years old. When in a vehicle, one-third were apt to keep a weapon on their person, while one-fifth kept the weapon under the seat of the vehicle.

A little more than three-fourths of the offenders were engaged in alcohol or drug use at the time they killed a law enforcement officer. During interviews, the offenders stated that they felt that there was nothing the victims might have done to prevent their deaths. The vast majority of the offenders were diagnosed as having personality disorders. The two dominant types of disorders were anti-social personality and dependent personality. The latter personality are described as individuals having a pervasive pattern of dependent and submissive behavior, and were overcontrolled. The antisocial personality exemplifies the individual who is manipulative and cunning. They know right from wrong but they choose not to conform.

The victim officers were predominately white, male, young, married, and high school educated. This description is similar to that of the offender study group, with the exception that the officers were eight years older, more educated, and more likely to be married. The officers were primarily from municipal agencies, assigned to patrol, averaged eight years of service, and just prior to their death received a lower performance rating than previously. These officers were found to be friendly to everyone, well-liked, tended to not follow the rules, and used force as a last resort. In terms of training needs, the researchers found the need to correct some procedures. Some of the officers failed to follow procedures, which pointed out the need for additional training. It was also determined that conflicting procedures had to be revised.

Survivors of officers should be debriefed, provided with information of benefits, and receive assistance from support groups. The federal government provides funds to survivors when an officer is killed in the line of duty. Another possible source of financial support is the Social Security Administration, which provides income for the surviving spouse and children. Peer support is essential and this can be obtained through such organizations as Concerns of Police Survivors (COPS).

Technology holds promise as federally supported research develops new devices such as the millimeter-wave camera, which can detect both metallic and non-metallic weapons. Currently the U.S. Department of Justice is working on 12 promising devices that can help improve the personal security of officers as well as members of the community.

References

Alpert, Geoffrey and Roger G. Dunham (1995). *Police Use of Deadly Force: A Statistical Analysis of the Metro-Dade Police Department.* Washington, DC: Police Executive Research Forum, 10-30.

Boyd, Gerald W. (1986). *The Will to Live—Five Steps to Officer Survival.* Springfield, IL: Charles C Thomas, 10-11.

Bureau of Justice Assistance (1997). Public Safety Officers' Benefit Program. Washington, DC: Office of Justice Programs, 1-4.

Chapman, Samuel G. (1976). *Police Murders and Effective Countermeasures.* Santa Cruz, CA: Davis Publishing, 1-75.

Concerns of Police Survivors (1977). "Study Reveals Most Departments Still Do Not Have Formal Policy for a Line-of-Duty Death—Is Your Agency Prepared?" *Rap Sheet!* Camdenton, MO: Concerns of Police Survivors, Inc. 1-4.

Concerns of Police Survivors (1994). *Supporting Services to Surviving Families of Line-of-Duty Death.* Camdenton, MO: Concerns of Police Survivors, Inc., 1-4.

Concerns of Police Survivors (1997). *COPS Newsletter.* Camdenton, MO: Concerns of Police Survivors, Inc., 1-19.

Federal Bureau of Investigation (1960-1996). Uniform Crime Reports, *Law Enforcement Officers Killed and Assaulted, 1961-1995.* Washington, DC: USGPO, 1-85.

Federal Bureau of Investigation (1988, 1989, 1990, 1991, 1992, 1993, 1993, 1994, 1995, 1996). Uniform Crime Reports, *Law Enforcement Officers Killed and Assaulted.* Washington, DC: USGPO, 1-85.

Federal Bureau of Investigation (1992). *Killed in the Line of Duty: A Study of Selected Felonious Killings of Law Enforcement Officers.* Washington, DC: USGPO, 1-60.

Federal Bureau of Investigation (1996). Uniform Crime Reports, *Law Enforcement Officers Killed and Assaulted, 1995.* Washington, DC: USGPO, 28.

Fyfe, James J. (1982). *Readings on Police Use of Deadly Force.* Washington, DC: Police Foundation, 18.

Geller, William A. (1987). *Deadly Force, Crime File, Study Guide.* Washington, DC: National Institute of Justice, 2-9.

Geller, William A. and Kevin J. Karales (1981). *Split-Second Decisions: Shootings of and by Chicago Police*. Chicago: Chicago Law Enforcement Study Group, 142-144.

Gist, Nancy E. (1997). *Public Safety Officers' Benefits Program*. Washington, DC: Bureau of Justice Assistance, 1-4.

Gist, Richard M. and Vickie Harris Taylor (1996). "Line-of-Duty Deaths and Their Effect on Co-Workers and Their Families." *The Police Chief*, Vol. LXIII, No. 5:34-37.

Hoffman, John (1997). "Unprovoked Police Murders." *Law and Order,* Vol. 45, No. 6:106-109.

Law Enforcement News (1997). "One-Officer State Police Cars Raise the Risk to Cops' Lives." Vol. XXIII, No. 461, February 14:11-14.

Law and Order (1994). "Special Supplement: Police Officer Deaths." Vol. 42, No. 9:130-169.

McConville, Mike and Dan Shepherd (1992). *Watching Police, Watching Communities*. London: Routland, 114.

Maguire, Kathleen and Ann L. Pastore (1996). *Sourcebook of of Criminal Justice Statistics—1995*. Washington, DC: Department of Justice, Bureau of Justice Statistics, 380.

Parade Magazine (1992a). "The Deadliest Decades for Cops." August 16:20.

Parade Magazine (1992b). "Deadliest for Cops." November 22:8

Pinizzotto, Anthony J. and Edward F. Davis (1995). "Killed in the Line of Duty: Procedural and Training Issues." *FBI Law Enforcement Bulletin,* Vol. 64, No.3:1-6.

Reaves, Brian A. and Pheny Z. Smith (1995). *Law Enforcement Management and Administrative Statistics, 1993: Data for Individual State and Local Agencies with 100 or More Officers*. Washington, DC: Department of Justice, Bureau of Justice Statistics, 181-192.

Simms, Thomas H. (1996). "Your Worst Nightmare Has Just Become True." *The Police Chief,* Vol. LXIII, No. 5:26-33.

DEVIATION FROM THE NORM: ABERRANT POLICE BEHAVIOR

6

The study of this chapter will enable you to:

1. List the five components of a viable complaint procedure.

2. Compare the review systems used in New York City and Kansas City.

3. Describe the 10 principles that can be followed in order to have an effective civilian review board.

4. Discuss the development of civilian review boards.

5. Compare COPWATCH and POLICE WATCH.

6. List the objectives of internal investigation.

7. Describe the three categories of complaints.

8. Write a short essay on how to classify complaints.

9. Identify the two due process clauses in the U.S. Constitution.

10. List the key elements of due process from *Morrissey v. Brewer*.

11. Describe how a trial board works.

12. List five of the elements usually included in a typical police bill of rights.

13. Write a short essay describing the handling of problem officers.

This nation entrusts every police officer with unique powers. It is a power not given to any other occupational group. The police function as society's governmental entity for maintaining ordered liberty. Unquestionably, this places the police at the cutting edge of society's ills. Law enforcement and all it entails impinge directly on the deeply prized values of life, freedom, and human dignity. Unlike many other government operations, the application of legal sanctions becomes a forcible and unwelcome intrusion into the affairs and fortunes of all who are drawn into the arms of justice (England, 1976: 241-277).

Enforcing the Law

The conduct of many individuals is under constant and continuing scrutiny on the part of the police, and this can lead to conflict. In some instances, police conduct becomes embroiled in the political process, and alleged police misconduct becomes a political issue. The romanticists become the champions of human rights and are in conflict with the pragmatists, whose concerns are to control and eradicate crime (Novick, 1991: 29-32; Sulc, 1995: 79-89).

The problem (review of police conduct) viewed in a total context must immediately acknowledge the complexity of society. The police are not responsible for the economic and political conditions that exist today, nor are they equipped to deal with the multitude of issues that are clearly beyond their control. Poverty, racism, inadequate housing, a lack of jobs, and many other negative aspects of our communities are the milieu in which the police operate.

Police officers, as governmental agents empowered to enforce the law, function at the fulcrum point of life. It is where the law, human tragedy, and society's expectations (for safety and security) come together (More and Wegener, 1994: 301). Referred to as the *thin blue line,* the police perform their duties by distinguishing between legal social control and the abuse of power that can lead to tyranny. Continual changes in the law, coupled with changes in our society, make the law enforcement job a highly complex and difficult task. The job can be ambiguous, stressful, and frustrating, as an officer is buffeted from all sides. Maintaining social control and dealing with crime can bombard an officer with a view of the seamy side of life, including all of its sordid aspects. An officer must deal with raw emotions, brutality, and the evil side of human behavior. Bizarre behavior, insanity, violence, and degradation are part of the daily routine on many beats in urban areas. While a part of society, police officers remain separate and, in some instances, isolated because of the awesome power they wield, the authority they represent, and the role they play in our communities. Many people never want to see an officer when they are commuting to work, but when trouble occurs they would like an officer on every corner. Police officers have a great deal of discretionary power that, at one extreme, can allow officers to enforce the law according to their own personal standards. On the other hand, some police administrators and the courts have worked to limit and circumscribe the powers exercised by officers. One cannot write regulations to address every situation with which an officer deals, but there have been many attempts to do just this. Many laws are ambiguous or vague because those who drafted them were unable to foresee the types of problems that would occur. Other laws came into existence because emotionally charged problems occurred, facilitating the passage of laws that should never have been approved in the first place. In addition, there are many laws that have been on the books for years, and are never enforced, such as social gambling laws.

It is within this highly complex environment that a police officer must work. Broad discretionary powers, the complexity of the law enforcement role, and the kind of people with whom officers continually interact place some officers in a highly vulnerable position. Some officers have succumbed to temptations and have become corrupt, while others have engaged in other types of malfeasance. Examples of these are an officer who lies to avoid criminal or civil liability, *fluffs up* evidence to make a more convincing case, or pushes and shoves a suspect unnecessarily (Barker and Carter, 1990: 61-73). Further examples are officers that illegally search for and actually plant evidence, or commit perjury in court (Dershowitz, 1992: 142-149). When considering the use of physical force by the police, it must be placed in proper perspective. Force is, in actuality, used infrequently, and is rarely used inappropriately. This is especially true when one considers the large number of contacts that police have with the public. However, the smaller the number of incidents of unnecessary force, the better (Worden, 1995: 59).

Watching the Police

Several organizations are involved in scrutinizing police conduct. In Los Angeles, Police Watch/Police Misconduct Lawyer Referral Service has been involved in assisting people whom they believe have used inappropriate and excessive use of force. It was founded in 1981 as a nonprofit civil rights organization by a group of community activists and civil rights attorneys who were concerned with the rising tide of police violence in Los Angeles. Police Watch provides consultation and assistance to anyone, regardless of income, in filing claims for damages against the police. It also provides referrals to a panel of private attorneys for representation in cases in which the conduct of the police has been improper and has caused injury or damages. Additionally, it conducts periodic workshops and seminars on the topic of police misconduct. It also organizes police abuse victims and provides surveillance of abusive police practices in targeted neighborhoods (Heppe, 1993: 1).

COPWATCH, in Berkeley, California, is a grassroots organization that is street oriented. It organizes and involves itself in protests and marches throughout the San Francisco Bay area. It trains people in their rights and assists victims of police misconduct in filing complaints. It also conducts demonstrations concerning police accountability. Considerable time is spent in giving speeches and lobbying public officials to change police practices. COPWATCH takes part in outreach and street patrols to directly help those targeted by police abuse. It has a quarterly publication that describes current issues of concern to the organization, such as the use of pepper spray and individual rights (COPWATCH, 1996: 1-12).

External Review

In the eyes of many police administrators, the effectiveness of law enforcement rests on the relative autonomy that society has given to the police. Therefore, any demands made for public review of police misconduct are typically regarded as intrusions upon that autonomy and as threats to effective law enforcement. Some administrators view such demands as an attempt to politicize the police. This is especially resented because during the last 35 years, police agencies have gained relative freedom from partisan political interference. Some police administrators believe that officers, when subjected to public review for their actions, will become (once again) instruments of pressure group politics. Finally, it is feared that public analysis of police conduct by review boards or other similarly constituted bodies will erode officers' morale by stripping away the self-contained authority of the department to discipline officers and to control misconduct. There are other objections to public review of police conduct.

One of the major contentions is that review boards threaten administrative authority. Management theory in all aspects of public administration repeatedly supports the position that the chief administrative officer is responsible for the conduct of the agency. In addition, the theory is that each assignment of responsibility carries commensurate authority to fulfill the obligation. There is also a general fear that diffusion of formal authority reduces the decisive and dramatic characteristics that are essential aspects of agency leadership (Leonard and More, 1993: 8).

The demand for a civilian review board usually emanates from police conduct that involves the perceived use of excessive force (Powers, 1995: 56). The board is perceived by proponents as a vehicle for restraining overzealous police officers. On the other hand, officers see boards as being anti-law enforcement. Some police departments have been successful in derailing efforts to create a citizen review board by establishing police advisory committees. Historically, the membership of such committees have been pro-police, and consequently not a threat to police managers (Petterson, 1991:270). Efforts to create civilian review boards, in most situations, have been fraught with conflict. Supporters and detractors gather their forces in an effort to influence the political decision-making process (American Civil Liberties Union, 1991: 135). For example, in the early part of this decade, the ill-fated Police Advisory Board of Philadelphia was created by the mayor. He was under enormous pressure from the local unit of the ACLU and established the board by executive order. The board was not funded for two years and because of lack of community and governmental support, ceased to exist after three years (Snow, 1992: 56). In 1995, the District of Columbia's highly criticized Citizen Complaint Review Board ceased to exist. The agency was eliminated from the city budget and the $1 million was used to hire additional police officers. A proposal to create a new board died due to lack of support (*Law Enforcement News*, 1995: 1). In New York City in 1994, the Mollen Commission recommended the creation of an external Police Commission after finding extensive corruption in the early part of the decade. This commission was to function as a corruption monitor outside of the traditional chain of command. It was empowered to conduct its own investigation, assess corruption controls, and identify corruption hazards (Mollen, 1994: 152-155).

Feature

Citizen's Police Review Board
of the City of Santa Cruz

915 Cedar St.
Santa Cruz, CA 95060
(408) 429-3262
429-9382 fax

WHAT WE DO

The **Citizens' Police Review Board** (CPRB) was established in 1994 by the Santa Cruz City Council to review the Police Department's Internal Affairs investigations of citizen complaints about the Police Department and to make recommendations to the City Council and City Manager regarding police policy and practices.

WHERE & WHEN

The CPRB holds regular meetings the second Monday of the month in the City Council Chambers, 809 Center St., at 5:30 p.m. Public input is encouraged. Meeting agendas and audio tapes of meetings are available at the Santa Cruz Central Library Reference Desk.

WHO

The CPRB is made up of seven volunteers from the community who have been appointed by City Councilmembers. The current Board members serve on the CPRB until their appointing City Councilmember's term expires.

MORE . . .

The CPRB office is located at 915 Cedar St., Santa Cruz, CA 95060. Office hours are Monday through Thursday, 9 a.m. to 1 p.m. The phone number is 429-3262. Staff invites you to stop in to find out more about the CPRB and the review process.

Complaint Form Locations

1. CPRB Office
   915 Cedar Street   (408) 429-3262
2. Santa Cruz Police Department Administration
   212 Locust Street   (408) 429-3714
   Santa Cruz Police Department Operations
   809 Center Street   (408) 429-3714
3. City Clerk's Office—Room 9 City Hall
   809 Center Street   (408) 429-3784
4. City Manager's Office—Room 10 City Hall
   809 Center Street   (408) 429-3540
5. Public Defender's Office
   2103 N. Pacific Ave.   (408) 426-2656
6. District Attorney's Office
   Governmental Center
   701 Ocean Street   (408) 454-2400
   Room 200
7. Santa Cruz County Jail—Booking
   259 Water Street   (408) 454-2420
8. Santa Cruz County Jail—Women's Facility
   141 Blaine Street   (408) 454-2177
9. Louden Nelson Community Center
   301 Center Street   (408) 429-3504
10. Resource Center for Nonviolence
    515 Broadway   (408) 423-1626

11. Public Library—Central Branch
    224 Church Street   (408) 429-3532
    Also, forms at each Branch Library in Reference Division
12. Downtown Information Center
    1126 Pacific Ave.   (408) 459-9486
13. Familia Center
    711 E. Cliff Drive   (408) 423-5747
14. River Street Shelter
    733 River Street   (408) 459-6644
15. Victim-Witness Assistance Program
    701 Ocean Street Room 200   (408) 454-2010
16. Beach Flats Community Center
    200 Raymond Street   (408) 429-3188
17. Drop-In Center
    412 Front Street   (408) 457-1163
18. Defensa de Mujeres
    555 Soquel Ave. #290   (408) 426-7273
19. Barrios Unidos
    313 Front Street   (408) 457-8208
20. Women's Crisis Support
    1658 Soquel Drive #A   (408) 477-4244
21. Valley Resource Center
    231 Main Street (PO Box 105)
    Ben Lomond, CA 95005   (408) 336-2553

Available in Spanish and English

Numerous cities have adopted citizen review boards during the last two decades. In 1991, in a survey of the 50 largest cities, it was determined that 60 percent had civilian review procedures (Walker and Bumphus, 1991: 2). Two years later, in a survey of local agencies with 100 or more officers, 92 agencies were identified as having civilian complaint review boards (Reaves and Smith, 1995: 253-263). After four years of public debate, the City of Santa Cruz, California, released a plan to create a civilian police review board. A member of the city council led the effort to establish a board, with the intent of improving public confidence in the handling of complaints against the police. Activists expressed the opinion that the board would not have enough power and it was structured to operate secretly. Police officers felt that the board was not needed. The chief expressed the position that there was not any problem with the current complaint procedure and the creation of a board was too strong of a remedy (Rogers, 1993: 1B). After hearings on the subject, the City Council approved the creation of a citizens' review board. The board's annual budget was estimated to be $80,000 when it was formally created in 1994. From a panel of 31 applicants, the city council appointed seven individuals to serve on the board, and it included none of the activists who supported its creation. The following Feature is a copy of an announcement describing the board.

The American Civil Liberties Union (ACLU) has developed a community action manual for fighting police abuse. It has proposed a number of principles that are needed if a civilian review board is to be effective and these are set forth in the following Feature.

If a department is confronted by a high-profile incident, and a review board is inevitable, it is best if the police executive takes the initiative and actually proposes a board. Ultimately, the police department exerts greater control over the process and the final product than reactive police managers (Tyre and Braunstein, 1994: 10-14; Watt, 1994: 1-8). It is anticipated that more and more cities will create civilian review boards, because there is reason to believe that many police officers will engage in excessive use of force (Powers, 1995: 56-60).

Internal Review

With more than 500,000 local police officers, misconduct will inevitably occur, as officers restrict the activities of others, enforce the law, and control behavior. Misconduct and/or malfeasance, it has been suggested, are in reality an occupational hazard (More and Wegener, 1994: 287). As complaints arise, the police department should respond in such a manner that the community and the officers view the total process as positive and responsive.

Several decades ago, the existence of internal affairs units in police departments was the exception rather than the rule. As situations and events occurred that called for an investigation, cases were assigned to varying units within the agency. Officers, supervisors, or command personnel were selected to conduct internal investigations because of their availability rather than their level of expertise in the area. Written policies and procedures were nonexistent, and there was no systematic method for filing the results of an investigation (Territo and Smith, 1976: 32).

As the courts increased their scrutiny of police activities and the various national commissions recommended internal change, police departments responded by developing policies and procedures for the investigation of complaints. If organized and operated properly, an internal affairs (IA) unit can be a vital organizational component (Schobel, 1996: 45-50). In some instances, this called for establishing IA units. In small police departments, the policy provided guidelines for investigating complaints in order to prove fairness and impartiality. In a number of large police departments, the officer in charge of the IA unit reports directly to the chief of police. This provides the chief with immediate access to information about ongoing investigations.

Feature

Ten Principles for an Effective Civilian Review Board

- **Independence.** The power to conduct hearings, subpoena witnesses, and report findings and recommendations to the public.

- **Investigation Power.** The authority to independently investigate incidents and issue findings on complaints.

- **Mandatory Police Cooperation**. Complete access to police witnesses and documents through legal mandate or subpoena power.

- **Adequate funding.** Should not be a lower budget priority than police internal affairs systems.

- **Hearings.** Essential for solving credibility questions and enhancing public confidence in the process.

- **Reflect Community Diversity.** Board and staff should be broadly representative of the community it serves.

- **Policy Recommendations.** Civilian oversight can spot problem policies and provide a forum for developing reform.

- **Statistical Analysis.** Public statistical reports can detail trends in allegations, and early warning systems can identify officers who are subjects of unusually numerous complaints.

- **Separate Offices.** Should be housed away from police headquarters to maintain independence and credibility with the public.

- **Disciplinary Role.** Board findings should be considered in determining disciplinary action.

Source: American Civil Liberties Union (1997). *Fighting Police Abuse, A Community Action Manual.* New York: American Civil Liberties Union, 14. Reprinted courtesy of the American Civil Liberties Union.

Organizationally, police departments respond to citizen complaints in entirely different fashions. In Philadelphia, the department responds to citizen complaints by having investigations conducted by the IA unit. Philadelphia has had its share of difficulties recently. In 1996, it was reported that the city had agreed to pay $2.4 million to settle 38 claims in which police officers planted false evidence, beat suspects, and lied in court. In Kansas City, the IA unit investigates allegations and forwards the results to the Office of Citizens' Complaints. In the County of San Diego, the Sheriff's Department has had a Citizens' Law Enforcement Review Board since 1992 (Walker, 1995: 2-53). The board receives, reviews, investigates, and reports on citizen complaints. In New York, internal affairs falls under the Office of Special Services. In Los Angeles, the internal affairs division (IAD) is in the Inspectional Services Bureau. Additionally, Los Angeles has established Community Police Advisory Boards in each area of the City and included civilians on the Department's Board of Rights (Los Angeles Police Department, 1997: 63). In each of the above departments, results of internal investigations are forwarded to the chief executive officer, who is responsible for rendering a decision. Two communities, Los Angeles and Kansas City, describe the function of the IA unit as reactive. Misconduct and corruption in those cities are not pursued proactively. On the other hand, both Philadelphia and New York identified the mission of the internal affairs unit to be both reactive and proactive.

Every department with an IA unit has detailed procedures for recording and processing citizen complaints of physical or verbal abuse by police officers. In Los Angeles and Philadelphia, the IA unit has primary responsibility for investigating serious complaints. Complaints of a less serious nature are handled by command personnel. In Kansas City and New York, there are separate organizations (independent of the IA unit) to review civilian complaints. The Civilian Complaint Review Board (CCRB) in New York reports to the police commissioner. When complaints are filed, they are immediately sent to the CCRB, which investigates the charges. Members of the board are appointed by the police commissioner, and there is a special conciliation unit within the board to informally resolve minor disputes. In 1990, the CCRB received 5,554 allegations of misconduct. Of this number, 43 percent involved force and the remainder were abuse of authority, discourtesy, and ethnic slurs (Walker, 1995: 1-69).

In Kansas City, complaints are handled by the Office of Civilian Complaints (OCC), which reports to the Board of Police Commissioners. This unit is staffed by civilians, and the director of the unit is appointed by the mayor. Complaints may be filed in person, by telephone, or by mail. After an initial inquiry, the head of the OCC may request an investigation by the internal affairs unit, may call for conciliation between the parties, or may determine that further action is not needed. If an investigation is conducted, the results are returned to the head of the OCC, who then forwards the report, together with a recommendation, to the chief of police. The chief makes the final decision, subject to approval of the Board of Commissioners. All parties are then notified of the outcome.

In Philadelphia, all citizen complaints are reviewed internally, and there is no provision for review by a formalized civilian board. In Los Angeles, the Police Commission acts as an *appellate court* where complainants can present their cases to the civilian members of the commission. Other cities have similar boards to investigate complaints against the police. The boards have power that varies considerably. In San Francisco, the Office of Citizens' Complaints was established in 1983. It receives and investigates all complaints about the conduct of officers. The Director of the Office is appointed by the Police Commission. In 1996, the office received 1,023 new cases. Of cases closed that year, 6.9 percent were sustained. Allegations (totaling 2,877) during 1996 involved 343 incidents of unnecessary force, 1,126 incidents of unwarranted action, and 673 incidents of neglect of duty (Dunlap, 1997: 22). The policy recommendations made by the office included the training of new captains in crowd control techniques; identification of transporting officer to youth guidance center; notifying psychological liaison personnel to come to the scene in cases in which a subject may be in need of psychiatric attention; citing motorists without insurance at the scene of a traffic violation; and using consistent racial identifiers on incident reports, citations, and other documents.

Critics of the Office of Citizen Complaints had previously pointed out that the unit lacked the staff and budget to adequately investigate citizen complaints. Additionally, they stressed that over a five-year period only 39 incidents that involved the use of excessive force were sustained out of 2,317 such incidents. They also objected to the fact that out of the 39 incidents, only 16 officers were suspended or received a written reprimand (Wallace, 1995: 1 and 4A). In 1996, the Charter of the City and County of San Francisco was amended by a ballot measure requiring the staff of the office of citizen complaints to consist of no fewer than one line investigator for every 150 sworn members. During that year, a total of eight new line investigators were hired and began to handle complaints (Dunlap, 1997: 5). In a study of the Los Angeles County Sheriff's Office, it was found that over a two and one-half year period, only six percent of alleged uses of excessive force were sustained. It was also found that when civilians attempted to lodge complaints at the charged officer's station, they were ignored, subjected to verbal abuse, and in some instances arrested. During the study period, there were 93 assault and battery cases that resulted in settlements and verdicts totaling $9,861,807 (Kolts, 1992: 99-100).

In smaller departments (fewer than 75 employees), the chief investigates citizen complaints, or they become a command responsibility. In one community, initial responsibility for investigating allegations of misconduct rests with the division commander. The commander forwards the personnel complaint form to the chief of police to determine whether the complaint should be investigated or referred to another division in the interest of integrity. The following Feature lists a variety of police misconduct that has occurred throughout the nation.

Feature

Incidents of Police Misconduct

- In 1997, a San Jose, California, police officer admitted to committing three burglaries while in uniform. He duped victims into believing that he was seeking the real thieves. The officer used the proceeds from the items that he took to support his gambling addiction. He took rings, bracelets, and a laptop computer. The San Jose Police Department had 20 investigators investigating the activities of Officer Johnny Venzon. The Department's position was that the officer had hurt the department, the citizens, and the integrity of the criminal justice system. He has been charged with a total of 14 crimes.

- A videotape rolled again, in 1994, in Compton, California, showing an African-American officer beating a Latino teenager. The tape shows the officer striking the victim and the victim kicking back. Then the officer strikes the victim several more times and kneels on his neck in order to handcuff him. Then the officer puts his baton through the handcuffs and leads the staggering victim away.

- In 1996, a New Jersey police officer was attending a law enforcement conference in Cincinnati, Ohio, where he allegedly robbed a bank. He was arrested after a lengthy car chase. In his hotel room, officers seized 346 packages containing heroin. He was believed to be the "Camouflage Bandit" who had robbed seven banks in New Jersey.

- In Detroit, Michigan, the suspended police chief stole approximately $2.6 million. The money was taken from a secret fund intended for use in paying informants and making drug buys. The chief used the funds to support his mistress. He was indicted on charges of conspiracy, tax evasion, and obstruction of justice.

- In 1995, it was reported that one in every six of the members of the Nogales, Arizona Police Department had been accused of misconduct. The officers were from all levels of the department and the charges included driving while under the influence, using excessive force, and false reporting.

- In New Orleans, Louisiana, a policewoman shot and killed her former patrol partner and two civilians. The incident occurred when she was holding up a restaurant with her nephew. She moonlighted at the restaurant and returned after working to stage the robbery. It was the first incident in the history of the department in which one police officer killed another while committing another crime.

- In Phoenix, Arizona, the police department arrested an officer for releasing a suspected prostitute in exchange for having sex with him. The officer was held on $10,000 bond and charged with misdemeanor assault and bribery, a felony. Following his arrest, the officer was fired.

- Nicknamed the "margarita crew," 11 police officers of the Mesa, Arizona Police Department spent $10,000 partying at the expense of taxpayers.

Feature—*continued*

The officers were sent to bars to find and develop sources of information about stolen property, but never developed a suspect or informant. Part of the funds were used to buy Groucho Marx masks for a staff photograph, a pornographic magazine, and other items. The officers were part of a multi-agency task force that investigated property crimes. Eight of the officers were suspended without pay for periods ranging from five to 18 days. The head of the unit was charged with tampering with public records, theft, and fraud.

- During August of 1997, four officers were arrested in New York City for being involved in the alleged sodomizing of a Haitian immigrant with a toilet plunger in the bathroom of a Brooklyn police station. The mayor relieved the commander, and the executive officer of the station where the incident occurred. He also ordered eight officers off duty and suspended a sergeant who was in the station when the incident occurred. Mayor Rudolph Giuliani assigned all 700 officers of the Internal Affairs unit to the investigation of the incident. Several weeks after the event, 7,000 people marched to protest the alleged act of police brutality.

Objectives of Internal Review

The objectives of internal investigation are fairly well standarized and should, at least, include the following (More and Shipley, 1987:214-215):

- **Protection of the Public.** The public has the right to expect efficient, fair, and impartial law enforcement. Therefore, any misconduct by department personnel must be detected, thoroughly investigated, and properly adjudicated, in order to assure the maintenance of these qualities.

- **Protection of the Department.** The department is often evaluated and judged by the conduct of individual members. It is imperative that the entire organization not be subjected to public censure because of misconduct by a few of its personnel. When an informed public knows that its police department honestly and fairly investigates and adjudicates all allegations of misconduct against its members, it will be less likely to feel any need to raise a cry of indignation over alleged incidents of misconduct.

- **Protection of the Employee.** Employees must be protected against false allegations of misconduct. This can only be accomplished through a consistently thorough investigative process.

- **Removal of Unfit Personnel.** Personnel who engage in serious acts of misconduct or who have demonstrated that they are unfit for law enforcement work must be removed for the protection of the public, the department, and department employees.

- **Correction of Procedural Problems.** The department constantly seeks to improve its efficiency and the efficiency of its personnel. Occasionally, personnel investigations disclose faulty procedures that would otherwise have gone undetected. These procedures can then be improved or corrected.

The fulfillment of these objectives would ensure that the department's reputation remains strong. It can be a process of positive control, creating a relationship of trust between the department and the community. Officers of the law have a special obligation to respect the rights of all persons. A sound complaint procedure, coupled with a positive and straightforward investigation, would subject officers to corrective action when they conduct themselves improperly, but also would protect them from unwarranted criticism when they discharge their duties properly (More and Shipley, 1987: 213-214).

Processing Complaints

The procedures to be followed in conducting complaint investigations vary, depending upon the origin, nature, and seriousness of an allegation. The types of complaints fall into one of the following categories (More and Wegener, 1994: 314):

- **Primary Complaint**. This type of complaint is filed by the alleged victim(s) of police malfeasance.

- **Secondary Complaint.** These are complaints filed by third parties about police malfeasance.

- **Anonymous.** This type of complaint is received from an unidentified source.

Each complaint should be handled in a professional manner and treated confidentially. In minor infractions, the problem usually is handled on the spot by a supervisor. The incident can be recorded and investigated at a later date to ensure that the problem has been rectified. When the complaint is serious, the investigation becomes more formalized and structured under departmental guidelines.

The steps followed in investigating serious charges of misconduct include:

- Determination of the extent and nature of the alleged malpractice.

- Determination of the extent to which the officer is culpable if the allegation is, in fact, sustained.

- Expeditious investigation of the complaint.

- Obtaining statements from witnesses, examining relevant physical evidence, and gathering all information pertinent to the allegation.

- Preparation of specific recommendations for disposition of the case.

- Affording the accused all of their rights as set forth under the Police Officer's Bill of Rights.

Figure 6-1
Internal Investigations Personnel Complaint Flow Chart

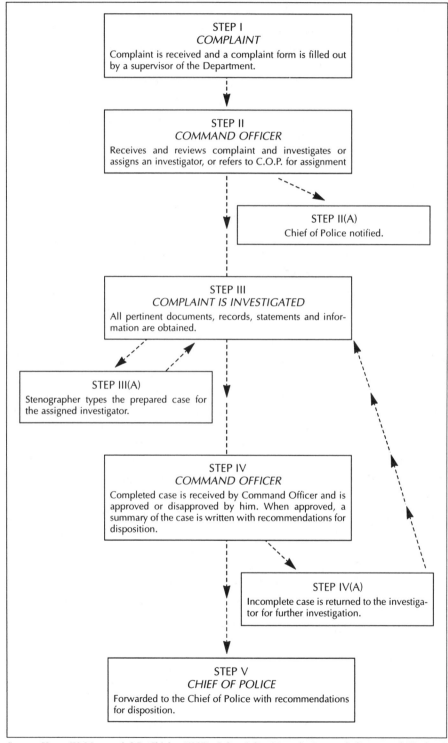

STEP I
COMPLAINT
Complaint is received and a complaint form is filled out by a supervisor of the Department.

STEP II
COMMAND OFFICER
Receives and reviews complaint and investigates or assigns an investigator, or refers to C.O.P. for assignment

STEP II(A)
Chief of Police notified.

STEP III
COMPLAINT IS INVESTIGATED
All pertinent documents, records, statements and information are obtained.

STEP III(A)
Stenographer types the prepared case for the assigned investigator.

STEP IV
COMMAND OFFICER
Completed case is received by Command Officer and is approved or disapproved by him. When approved, a summary of the case is written with recommendations for disposition.

STEP IV(A)
Incomplete case is returned to the investigator for further investigation.

STEP V
CHIEF OF POLICE
Forwarded to the Chief of Police with recommendations for disposition.

Source: Harry W. More and O.R. Shipley (1987). *Police Policy Manual—Personnel.* Courtesy of Charles C Thomas, Publisher, Springfield, Illinois.

Complaint Investigation

Figure 6-2 is a unique citizen complaint form that represents the diversity in the community. Note that the instructions are given in four languages. This form is completed by an investigating officer or the complaining citizen. The complainant should be given a copy of the report and advised of the procedures that are to be followed when the complaint is investigated. Complaints can be lodged in person, by mail, or by telephone. Investigators should be specifically trained for the task and given constant guidance and administrative support. Generally, the tools and techniques of this type of investigation do not vary substantially from the techniques employed in other types of investigation.

The initial step in a personnel investigation is to interview the complainant. If the accusation is anonymous, every effort should be made to gather evidence to support or refute the accusation. When filing a complaint, the investigator should obtain a wide range of information from the individual(s) making the complaint. This includes such things as personal identification of the complainant(s), identity of the officer(s), and a narrative description of the events giving rise to the complaint.

In non-criminal matters or upon consent in criminal matters, written statements should be taken from the accused, as well as from witnesses and complainants, when statements would be helpful in arriving at a sound conclusion. If the complaint is sustained, the statements must establish the basis for the disciplinary action to be taken.

The statements need not be in a formal question-and-answer style or even a narrative report. Instead, they may be in the form of a report from the investigator. Whatever the form of the report, all relevant information must be included (Mount Lebanon Police Department, 1987: 5-35). These statements, along with other evidence gathered by the investigator, should be submitted to the chief of police with a recommendation for disposition. During the investigation, if it is determined that the complaint is unfounded, the investigation should be terminated and copies of the report should be submitted to the chief executive officer. When the investigation is completed, the investigator classifies the complaint as follows:

- **Unfounded**—The allegation is false or not factual.

- **Exonerated**—Incident occurred, but was lawful and proper.

- **Not Sustained**—Insufficient evidence either to prove or disprove the allegation.

Figure 6-2
Office of Citizen Complaints

Police Commission for the City and County of San Francisco
OFFICE OF CITIZEN COMPLAINTS

~CITIZEN COMPLAINT FORM~

INSTRUCTIONS FOR COMPLETION OF THE CITIZEN COMPLAINT FORM:
Please answer questions in blocks 2, 3, 4, 5, 8, 11, 15, 17, 20, 21 & 22. Leave all other blocks blank unless you know the information requested. Please **print** all information in **English**. If you do not have a telephone number, enter a message number or the number of a neighbor, friend or relative in block 4. If witnesses are available, write their names, addresses and telephone numbers on a separate sheet of paper and attach it to your complaint. Do not write them on the complaint form. If you do not know the officers name or badge number, include a complete physical description in the narrative (22). **Print** your narrative. Explain what happened from beginning to end. Be specific as to the nature of your complaint against each officer. Include who, what, where, when and why. If you need additional space, use separate sheets of paper and attach them to the complaint. **YOUR STATEMENT MUST BE A TRUE AND ACCURATE ACCOUNT OF THE INCIDENT** to the best of your knowledge and belief, and <u>must be signed</u> by you in block 25. If you have questions or need help, please call the OCC at(415) 597-7711between 8:00 a.m. and 5:00 p.m., or leave a message with our answering service after 5:00 p.m. You may also contact your local neighborhood center for help. Interpreters can be provided at no charge.

填寫公民投訴書說明：
請回答第2，3，4，5，8，11，15，17，20，21及22項問題。除非您知道我們所要求的資料，否則請將其他各項留空。所有資料，務請以正楷填寫清楚。如果您沒有電話號碼，請在第4項填上有可能聯絡您的電話號碼，或鄰居、親戚、朋友的號碼。如果有證人，請用另一張紙寫上他們的姓名，地址及電話，和投訴書夾在一起；切勿寫在投訴書上。如果你不知道涉及事件的警務人員姓名或編號，請將該員的身體特徵，以正楷詳盡寫在第22項上。請清楚說明事件的過程，及投訴的類別，包括涉及何人、何事、何處、何時及何由。如您認為投訴書不夠您填寫，可以另紙填寫資料，夾在投訴書上。您應根據您所知道及所相信的事實填寫資料，必須真實及正確；填妥請在第26項簽名。如有疑問或需要幫助，請在上午八時至下午五時，致電 (415) 597-7711「公民投訴組」，或在下午五時後，在該組的電話錄音機上留言。您亦可以與有免費翻譯員服務的「華埠建民中心」求助，電話415-391-5099。

INSTRUCCIONES PARA LLENAR EL FORMULARIO DE QUEJAS DE LOS CIUDADANOS: Por favor
conteste las preguntas de las casillas 2, 3, 4, 5, 8, 11, 15, 17, 20, 21 & 22. Deje sin contestar las demas preguntas a menos que sepa la información solicitada. El formulario debe ser contestado en **Ingles**. Si usted no tiene telefono escriba en la casilla 4 el número de un servicio de mensajes, o el de un vecino, amigo o pariente. Escriba en una hoja separada los nombres, direcciones y telefonos de los testigos (si los hay), y adjunte ésta información al formulario. En caso de que no conozca el nombre o número de insignia de los oficiales, incluya una descripción fisica completa (22). Describa los hechos en forma completa, sea especifico. Incluya quien, que, donde, cuando y porque. Su declaración debe ser un recuento exacto y verdadero del incidente y debe estar firmada por usted (25). Para pedir información o solicitar ayuda visite nuestras oficinas locales o llamenos al numero(415) 597-7711 de 8:00 AM - 5:00 PM. El servicio de interpretacion es gratis. Formularios tambien pueden ser obtenidos en La Raza Information Center-- (415) 863-0764.

PARAAN NG PAGSAGOT   SA PORMANG ITO (CITIZEN COMPLAINT o REKLAMO NE MAMAMAYAN)
Mangyaring sagutin ang mga tanong sa blokeng 2, 3, 4, 5, 8, 11, 15, 17, 20, 21 , at 22. . Kung wala kayo ng impormasyon hinihingi dito, paki-iwanan blanko ang blokeng hindi masagot. **Paki-iimbag ang lahat na sagot ninyo.** Kung wala kayong telepono, paki-sulat lang ang inyong "message number", o ang numero ng inyong kapit-bahay, kaibigan, o kamaganak. Kung mayroon kayong mga saksi o testigo, isulat sa ibang papel ang kanilang mga pangalan, mga tirahan, at mga telepono at ikabit ito sa reklamo ninyo. Huwag gagamitin ang pormang ito. Kung hindi ninyo alam ang pangalan ng pulis o ang numero ng kanyang tsapa, isama sa inyong salaysay ang hitsura at pagmumukha ng pulis. Ilimbag ang inyong salaysay. Liwanagin lahat ang nangyari magmula sa umpisa hanggang sa katapusan. Tiyakin o siguraduhin ang inyong sinusumbong o renireklamo. Sabihin o ilarawan kung sino, ano, saan, kailan at bakit sa pangyayari. Kung kulang ang pagsusulatan dito gumamit ng ibang papel at ikabit ito sa sumbong ninyo. Sa inyong kaalaman at paniniwala, ang inilahad ninyong nangyari ay dapat lubos na katotohanan at walang kamali-mali at kailangan ninyong pirmahan ang sumbong ito sa blokeng bilang 25. Itanong sa amin kung alinman dito ang hindi maliwanag sa inyo. Kung kailangan ninyo ng tulong, paki-tawagan kami, OCC, telepono (415) 597-7711. Maaring tawagan din ninyo ang Philippines American Consul sa telepono(415) 626-0773 sa pagitan ng alas--otso ng umaga at alas--singko ng hapon o mag-iwan ng pahatid o "message" sa aming "answering service" paglampas dng alas--singko ng hapon.

SFPD/OCC FORM 293

Figure 6-2—*continued*

OFFICE OF CITIZEN COMPLAINTS - USE BLACK INK ONLY!

1 Day, Date & Time Complaint Received

Complaint Against: Personnel |_| Policy |_| Procedure |_|
How Received: Person |_| Phone |_| Letter |_| SFPD |_| Mail-In |_| Other |_| : (specify)_____

2 **Primary Complainant:**

Last Name First Name Middle Initial

HOME ADDRESS:_____
 Street Apartment

City State Zip

WORK ADDRESS:_____
 Street Apartment

City State Zip

3 **Personal Information**
Age:_____ Date of Birth:_____
Sex:_____
Ethnicity:_____
Occupation:_____

4 **Telephone Numbers:**
Home: (_____)_____
Work: (_____)_____

5 Location of Occurrence:

6 Type of Place **7** District

8 Day, Date, & Time Of Occurrence: A.M. / P.M.
(Circle one)

9 Incident Report or Citation No

10 SECONDARY COMPLAINANT? Yes|_| No|_| Witnesses? Yes |_| No |_| (If "Yes", attach separate sheet of paper.)
Taped Interview? Yes |_| No |_| Criminal Case Pending in Relation to this matter? Yes |_| No|_|

11 Injuries Claimed? Yes |_| No |_| Injuries Visible? Yes |_| No |_| Drug/Alcohol Related? Yes |_| No |_|
Photos Taken? Yes |_| No |_| By: Photo Lab |_| O.C.C. |_| Other:_____
Type of Injury: Medical Release Signed? Yes |_| No |_|

12 Activity	**13** Type	**14** DISP.	**15** Uniform Yes No	**16** Rank	**17** Member's Name & Star Number	**18** Unit	**19** Svc	**20** Sex	**21** Eth

Figure 6-2—*continued*

(22)   NARRATIVE OF INCIDENT:_____

_____

_____

_____

_____

_____

_____

_____

_____

_____

_____

_____

_____

_____

_____

_____

_____

_____

_____

_____

_____

_____

_____

_____

(State law passed in 1995 mandates that the following statement be provided to, read and signed by persons filing complaints. *The OCC encourages the filing of a complaint by anyone who believes he or she is a victim or a witness of improper police conduct or policies.)*

ACKNOWLEDGEMENT OF COMPLAINANT (148.6 P.C.)

YOU HAVE THE RIGHT TO MAKE A COMPLAINT AGAINST A POLICE OFFICER FOR ANY IMPROPER POLICE CONDUCT. CALIFORNIA LAW REQUIRES THIS AGENCY TO HAVE A PROCEDURE TO INVESTIGATE CITIZENS' COMPLAINTS. YOU HAVE A RIGHT TO A WRITTEN DESCRIPTION OF THIS PROCEDURE. THIS AGENCY MAY FIND AFTER INVESTIGATION THAT THERE IS NOT ENOUGH EVIDENCE TO WARRANT ACTION ON YOUR COMPLAINT; EVEN IF THAT IS THE CASE, YOU HAVE THE RIGHT TO MAKE THE COMPLAINT AND HAVE IT INVESTIGATED IF YOU BELIEVE AN OFFICER BEHAVED IMPROPERLY. CITIZEN COMPLAINTS AND ANY REPORTS OR FINDINGS RELATING TO COMPLAINTS MUST BE RETAINED FOR AT LEAST FIVE YEARS. IT IS AGAINST THE LAW TO MAKE A COMPLAINT THAT YOU KNOW TO BE FALSE. IF YOU MAKE A COMPLAINT AGAINST AN OFFICER KNOWING THAT IT IS FALSE, YOU CAN BE PROSECUTED ON A MISDEMEANOR CHARGE.

I HAVE READ AND UNDERSTOOD THE ABOVE STATEMENT.

Complainant Signature/Date:	Taken By (Name/#/Unit)/Date:
Assigned Investigator/Date:	Closure Approval/Date:

Source: Office of Citizen Complaints, Mary C. Dunlap, Director, City and County of San Francisco, 480 2nd Street #100, San Francisco 94107.

- **Sustained**—The allegation is supported by sufficient evidence. When the investigation is classified as sustained, the investigator (after consultation with the commanding officer of the accused) may recommend:

  - Oral Reprimand
  - Written Reprimand
  - Suspension
  - Demotion
  - Dismissal

Other possible remedies include reassignment, retraining, or counseling. Any of these recommendations can be imposed in combination: for example, 10-day suspension along with psychological counseling. Figure 6-3 lists some of the allegations that can be made against an officer, along with specific definitions of each category.

Due Process

Corrective measures should be taken to remedy the situation in such a way that job performance of the officer improves. Whatever steps are taken during the investigative process should comply with every aspect of due process. The U.S. Constitution contains two due process clauses. One is in the Fifth Amendment and the other is in the Fourteenth Amendment. These specifically state that neither the federal government nor the states may "deprive any person of life, liberty, or property, without due process of law . . ." If a department is to avoid conflict with these provisions and possible reversal by the courts, it must have a mechanism that provides appropriate procedural protections. Two areas of concern arise regarding this matter. The first has to do with whether the police officer's property or liberty interests have been impaired by the procedures used by the department. The second has to do with whether particular safeguards are required in a specific instance (Brancato and Polebaum, 1981:125).

In some instances, an officer is entitled to present a case before adverse action is taken. In other cases, the officer may receive a written statement detailing the action being taken after the decision has been made. Whatever the safeguards to which the employee is entitled, it is necessary for the department to differentiate between the following:

- The specific procedures to be followed in an adverse personnel action.

- The protection provided after an action is taken.

- The procedures followed if the department publicly states its position in the personnel decision.

Two of these provisions are concerned with an officer's desire to retain employment (property right), and the third deals with the officer's interest in his reputation (liberty). Experts have suggested that police departments should adhere to the following elements of procedural due process, as set forth in a case heard by the U.S. Supreme Court (*Morrissey v. Brewer*, 1972):

- Written notice of the claimed violations.

- Disclosure of evidence.

- Opportunity to be heard in person and to present witnesses and documentary evidence.

- Right to confront and cross-examine witnesses.

- Neutral and detached hearing body.

- Written statement by the fact finders as to the evidence relied on and reasons for the action taken.

Figure 6-3
Nature and Definition of Complaints

Nature	Definition
UF—Unnecessary Force:	Any use of force that exceeds the level of force reasonably needed to perform a necessary police action.
UA—Unwarranted Action:	An act or action not necessitated by circumstances or that does not affect a legitimate police function.
CRD—Conduct Reflecting Discredit on the Department:	An act or action which, by its nature, reflects badly on the Department and undermines public confidence.
ND—Neglect of Duty:	Failure to take action when some action is required under the applicable laws and regulations.
RS—Racial Slurs:	Behavior or use of language meant to belittle or defame because of race or ethnicity
SS—Sexual Slurs:	Behavior or use of language meant to belittle or defame because of sex or sexual preference.
D—Discourtesy:	Behavior or language commonly known to cause offense, including use of profanity.

Source: Office of Citizen Complaints, Mary C. Dunlap, Director, City and County of San Francisco, 480 2nd Street #100, San Francisco 94107.

These should be viewed as minimum guidelines and should be incorporated into departmental policy manuals. Procedural due process provides for absolute fairness in labor/management relations in police departments. Every part of procedural due process is expensive and time-consuming, but procedural due process is the professional means that a department should follow in order to ensure a positive and equitable disciplinary system.

The Trial Board

A number of police departments have established trial boards for the purpose of hearing serious disciplinary problems. The size and composition of these boards vary. In some instances, the board has five members, and in other cases, it is comprised of three members. In a department that has a three-member board, it is customary for the chief of police to designate a ranking officer to preside over the board and to choose one other member. The accused chooses the third member of the board.

A trial board may be convened by the investigator conducting the internal investigation, by the accused, by the chief of police, or by the city manager. A hearing is not a judicial trial, but the board functions as a quasi-judicial entity. The board considers the investigative reports, statements, other documents, and testimony of witnesses. It also considers previous disciplinary action taken against the accused, previous complimentary history, and such other evidence as it deems appropriate. The board may hear the plea of the accused and order other members of the department to appear (Mount Lebanon Police Department, 1987: 5-33).

The total process is administrative in nature. Hence, the prevailing guideline should be for members of the board to review evidence in terms of a "preponderance of the evidence" rather than "proof beyond a reasonable doubt" (More and Wegener, 1994: 287). The board recommends to the chief of police one of the following actions:

- Further investigation with specific recommendations
- Dismissal of the charge
- Charge sustained
- Charge not sustained

The chief of police reviews the recommendations of the board and prescribes disciplinary action if appropriate. Normally, the chief of police has five calendar days to notify the accused of the decision. When the decision is suspension, demotion, or dismissal, it is normal for the accused to have a specified period of time in which to appeal the decision. In many cities, the Civil Service Commission is empowered to hear appeals, and its action constitutes the final decision (Mount Lebanon Police Department, 1987: 5-34).

Public Safety Officers' Bill of Rights

During internal investigations, officers in most agencies are protected by a procedural bill of rights. These rights are either in the policy manual of the agency or determined by collective bargaining and included in the union contract or memorandum of understanding. While these bills of rights vary throughout the nation, they generally include the following (State of California, *Government Code*, Section 3303, 1981):

- The interrogation shall be conducted at a reasonable hour, preferably at a time when the public safety officer is on duty or during the normal waking hours for the public safety officer, unless the seriousness of the investigation requires otherwise. If such interrogation does occur during off-duty time of the public safety officer being interrogated, the public safety officer shall be paid for such off-duty time in accordance with departmental procedures.

- Before interrogation, the officer under investigation shall be informed of the rank, name, and command of the officer in charge of the interrogation. All questions directed to the officer under interrogation shall be asked by and through no more than two interrogators at one time.

- Before interrogation, the officer under investigation shall be informed of the nature of the investigation.

- The interrogation session shall be for a reasonable period of time, and what is "reasonable" shall be determined by taking into consideration the gravity and complexity of the issue being investigated. The person under interrogation shall be allowed to attend to his/her personal and physical needs.

- The officer under interrogation shall not be subjected to offensive language or threatened with punitive action, except that an officer refusing to respond to questions or submit to interrogations shall be informed that failure to answer questions directly related to the investigation or interrogation may result in punitive action. No promise of reward shall be made as an inducement to answer any question. The employer shall not cause the officer under interrogation to be subjected to visits by the news media without express consent of the officer. In addition, the home address or a photograph of the officer shall not be given to the news media without the officer's express consent.

- The complete interrogation of the officer may be recorded. If a tape recording is made of the interrogation, the officer shall have access to the tape. The officer shall be entitled to a transcribed copy of any notes made by a stenographer.

- If, prior to or during the interrogation of an officer, it is deemed that a criminal charge will be filed, the officer shall immediately be informed of his/her constitutional rights.

- Upon the filing of a formal, written statement of charges, or whenever an interrogation focuses on matters that are likely to result in punitive action, the officer shall have the right to be represented.

Internal discipline in police agencies often is crisis-oriented. Most agencies simply react to employee misconduct. They do a good job of investigation after incidents have occurred, but they do little to prevent them. The key question (concerning employee misconduct) that police chief executives should try to answer is: "Why?" Police supervisors should ask themselves: "What could have prevented the employee from engaging in this particular act of misconduct?" The answer should be made an integral part of the written recommendation for each complaint adjudication. The chief, even though ultimately responsible for internal discipline, should not bear the diagnostic responsibility alone. It is the responsibility of all employees to seek ways to maintain a disciplined police agency. Although preventive measures may not automatically produce disciplined performance, they may provide the impetus for the development of self-discipline. A self-disciplined employee saves a police agency time and money by reducing the need for much of the administration of internal discipline.

Control of Police Misconduct

In recent years, some police departments have developed procedures to determine patterns of officer misconduct. The problem was brought into sharp focus with the videotaped beating of Rodney King, and reinforced by the allegations made by Mark Fuhrman of systematic misconduct in the Los Angeles Police Department (Los Angeles Police Department, 1997: 1). Los Angeles was not alone in finally realizing that it had a problem in this area. Other cities, including New Orleans, Philadelphia, and Boston, have suffered similar problems. Historically, police departments handled complaints against officers on an individual basis, without paying any attention to patterns of misconduct or determining the types of repetitive occurrences (Ogletree, Prosser, Smith, and Talley, 1994: 45-99).

The Christopher Commission found that no area of police operations received more adverse comment than the department's handling of complaints against Los Angeles police officers. This was particularly true of allegations involving the use of excessive force. Over a four-year period the commission found that out of 2,152 citizen allegations of excessive force, only 42 were sustained (Christopher, 1991: 13). The Commission found that the complaint system was skewed against complainants. People who wanted to file complaints faced significant hurdles. Some intake officers actively discouraged filing by being uncooperative or requiring long waits before completing a complaint form. In many heavily Latino divisions, there was often no Spanish-speaking officer available to take complaints.

In Los Angeles, it was found that a significant group of problem officers were involved in incidents of excessive force or improper tactics. Of approximately 1,800 against whom an allegation had been made, 44 had six or more complaints against them. Figure 6-4 graphically illustrates the problem.

Figure 6-4
Comparison of Top 44 Officers Receiving Force Complaints With All Officers
Listed in Use of Force Reports in the Los Angeles Police Department
Average per Officer of Force-Related Complaint Allegations, Other Complaint
Allegations, and Use of Force Reports

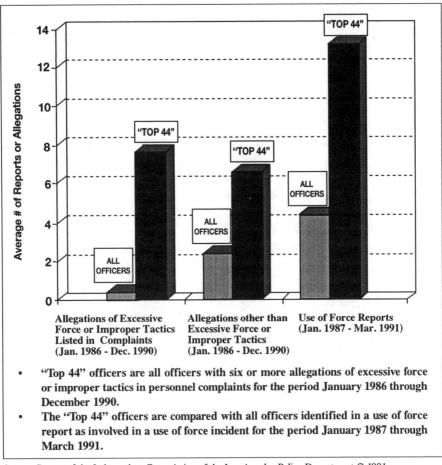

- "Top 44" officers are all officers with six or more allegations of excessive force or improper tactics in personnel complaints for the period January 1986 through December 1990.
- The "Top 44" officers are compared with all officers identified in a use of force report as involved in a use of force incident for the period January 1987 through March 1991.

Source: Report of the Independent Commission of the Los Angeles Police Department © 1991.

Beyond this, it was determined that one officer had 13 allegations of excessive force and improper tactics, five other complaint allegations, 28 use of force reports, and one shooting. When reviewing the personnel files of the 44 officers, it was found that the performance evaluation reports for the problem officers was very positive and expressed optimism about the officers' progress. The performance evaluations generally did not give an accurate picture of the of the officers' disciplinary history, and failed to record *sustained* complaints or discuss their significance (Christopher, 1991: 4). Since the issuance of the report, the Los Angeles Police Department has responded to the problem by utilizing the Human Resources Bureau and the Internal Affairs Group to monitor the list of the 44 officers to ensure that no unacceptable patterns emerge. Additionally, the

IAD now provides each command with a quarterly report on employees who receive three or more complaints per quarter. The department is also working on a Training Evaluation and Management System (TEAMS) which, when fully operational, will provide an incident-driven computerized database that will allow for a review of employee histories to better identify trends and patterns of behavior. The department has also developed a new *Use of Force Handbook* that was developed and distributed in 1995. The handbook serves as a guide for officers and supervisors on issues related to the use of force (Mader, 1997: 64-65.)

Domestic Violence by Police Officers

Domestic violence by law enforcement personnel has been something that has been ignored by police administrators, but in recent years it has received increasing attention. Police awareness of this critical issue parallels general public awareness. Domestic violence is a crime that must be energetically investigated and prosecuted. Statistics clearly support the fact that law enforcement agencies have been lax when dealing with this problem. The Office of the Inspector General of the Los Angeles Police Department reviewed investigations of domestic violence for the period from 1990 to 1997. In 40 percent of the 227 cases, internal investigations sustained the allegations of police misconduct and administered discipline. However, the discipline imposed was exceedingly light, and the case-by-case review determined that many of the investigations lacked requisite objectivity. Additionally, the investigation found that 30 employees accounted for 31 percent of all of the cases. When domestic violence cases occurred within the city limits, command staff ordered arrests in only six percent of the cases. When the incident occurred outside of city boundaries, arrests were made in 16 percent of the cases. Table 6-1 describes the adjudication of complaints.

Table 6-1
Results of Administrative Investigations of Domestic Violence by Year in the Los Angeles Police Department

YR.	Total	S	% S	N/R	% N/R	U	% U	E	% E
1990	21	8	38.1%	7	33.3%	3	14.3%	3	14.3%
1991	42	18	42.9%	19	45.2%	4	9.5%	1	2.4%
1992	25	8	32.0%	12	48.0%	4	16.0%	1	4.0%
1993	44	20	45.5%	19	43.2%	3	6.8%	2	4.5%
1994	41	21	51.2%	11	26.8%	7	17.1%	2	4.9%
1995	42	11	26.2%	21	50.0%	7	16.7%	3	7.1%
1996	11	4	36.4%	4	36.4%	2	18.1%	1	9.1%
1997	1	1	100.0%	0	—	0	—	0	—
Total	227	91	40.1%	93	41.0%	30	13.2%	13	5.7%

Classification of Complaint: S—Sustained; N/R—Not Resolved; U—Unfounded; E—Exonerated

Source: Katherine Mader (1997). *Domestic Violence in the Los Angeles Police Department: How Well Does the Los Angeles Police Department Police Its Own?* Los Angeles, CA: Los Angeles Police Department.

Following are several of the recommendations of The Office of Inspector General:

- A specialized unit should be created within the Internal Affairs Division with the primary responsibility to conduct investigations of Departmental personnel involved in domestic violence incidents.

- A Department employee should be treated no differently than any other citizen. A crime report should be taken in every instance in which a crime is alleged or there is evidence that a crime occurred. An arrest should be made in every instance in which it is legally mandated.

- When there is prima facie evidence of criminal misconduct, the investigation should be referred to the appropriate agency.

- Termination of employees should be a mandated penalty in serious cases of domestic violence in which an officer has demonstrated by a convincing pattern that he or she cannot control their abusive conduct.

It is essential that a police department vigorously investigate every allegation of domestic violence. This should be done even if the victim wants to drop any administrative or criminal charges. Officers are not exempt from the law. In the Chicago Police Department, the Office of Domestic Violence Advocate was created in 1995 to encourage abused spouses and partners of police officers to come forward and report incidents of domestic violence. The head of this office assists victims as much as possible, including accompanying the victim to court, referring the victim to counseling agencies, and other assistance as needed. The actual investigations are made by the Office of Professional Standards, which has assigned six investigators to these types of cases. In 1994, there were 304 domestic violence incidents investigated involving civilian and sworn personnel of the department (Clark, 1995: 1, 6).

Summary

Police conduct is under constant and continuing scrutiny that is both internal and external. In recent years, citizen review boards have become more prevalent. The complexity of the law enforcement role and the kind of people that constantly interact with police officers place some officers in a highly vulnerable position. Some officers have succumbed to temptations and become corrupt, while others have engaged in other types of malfeasance.

Public review of police conduct has been rejected by most police administrators because they fear that public review would reduce administrative control and expose the police to influence from pressure politics. Public clamor for a citizen review board usually occurs after a charge of police brutality. If a chief believes that the institution of a review board is inevitable, it would probably be best if the police departments supported and guided the development of such an agency. The ACLU has proposed 10 principles that should be followed if a civilian review board is to be effective.

There are two agencies that engage in external review of the police in Los Angeles and Berkeley, California. The *Police Watch* functions primarily as a legal referral agency to assist individuals who have been abused by the police. COP-WATCH, in Berkeley, is more of a grassroots organization. It engages in demonstrations, and conducts forums and organizes events. It also engages in street patrols to help those targeted by the police.

Most experts agree that every police department should have formal machinery for the investigation of complaints against police activity. In many departments, there is a board to investigate the facts of alleged dereliction and to make a recommendation to the chief administrative officer. If the complainant is dissatisfied with the decision of internal review, there is opportunity to appeal the decision to other agencies, such as the local district attorney, political entities, or the U.S. Department of Justice. All of these agencies are very traditional in their approach to such a problem, and they usually proceed slowly and are geographically far removed from the location where the event occurred.

The filing of a complaint should be relatively easy and the procedures should be acceptable to the public. The review procedure should be designed so that the public is convinced that an agency is truly receptive to complaints. Complaints can be received personally, by mail, or over the telephone. Larger police departments have detailed procedures for recording and processing citizen complaints of physical or verbal abuse by police officers. In some cities, units (such as the Office of Civilian Complaints in Kansas City) are staffed by civilians, while in other cities, sworn police personnel comprise IA units. In each of these cities, complaints are reviewed differently and investigative units have different responsibilities. In smaller police departments, the chief investigates complaints or assigns another officer to conduct the investigation. No matter who investigates complaints, the chief of police has ultimate responsibility for discipline.

The objectives of internal review include: protection of the employee, dismissal of unfit personnel, correction of procedural problems, protection of the public, and protection of the department. The fulfillment of these objectives ensures that the reputation of a police department remains strong. A process of positive control creates a relationship of trust between the department and the community. The investigation of complaints should be conducted in such a manner as to provide complete compliance with every aspect of procedural due process. The decision of the U.S. Supreme Court in *Morrissey v. Brewer* sets forth six elements to be considered in ensuring adherence to due process. Procedural due process provides for absolute fairness in labor/management relations.

In some police departments, the trial board is used as a vehicle for hearing serious disciplinary problems. The board recommends specific action to be taken, and it is up to the chief administrative officer to take final action. In some communities, the decision of the chief can be appealed to the city manager or a civil service commission. In all internal investigations, it is essential for investigators and administrative personnel to follow the procedural bill of rights afforded to police officers, and to ensure complete compliance. While the rights may vary slightly from community to community, they include such things as the right to be informed of the nature of the investigation prior to being interrogated and the right to be represented.

References

American Civil Liberties Union (1991). "Both Federal and Local Reforms are Needed to Stop Police Brutality." In William Dudley (ed.), *Police Brutality.* San Diego, CA: Greenhaven Press.

American Civil Liberties Union (1997). *Fighting Police Abuse: A Community Action Manual.* New York: American Civil Liberties Union.

Barker, T. and D. Carter (1990). "Fluffing Up the Evidence and Covering Your Ass." *Deviant Behavior,* Vol. 11, No. 3:61-73.

Brancato, Gilda and Elliot E. Polebaum (1981). *The Rights of Police Officers.* New York: A Discus Book/Avon Books.

Christopher, Warren (1991). *Report of the Independent Commission on the Los Angeles Police Department.* Los Angeles, CA: City of Los Angeles.

Clark, Jacob R. (1995). "When Brutality Hits Close to Home: Chicago PD Tackles Spouse Abuse by Officers." *Law Enforcement News,* Vol. LXII, No. 416, April 15:1, 6.

COPWATCH (1996). *COPWATCH Report,* (Fall) Berkeley, CA: COPWATCH.

Dershowitz, Alan M. (1992). *Contrary to Public Opinion.* New York: Pharos Books, 143-149.

Dunlap, Mary C. (1997). *Annual Report—1996.* San Francisco: CA: Office of Citizen Complaints, City and County of San Francisco.

England, Ralph W. (1976). "Criminal Justice in the American Democracy." *Current History,* Vol 70, No. 2:241-271.

Heppe, Karol (1993). *Remedies for Police Misconduct, Abuse of Power and Brutality* (brochure). Los Angeles, CA: Police Watch.

Kolts, James G. (1992). *The Los Angeles County Sheriff's Department.* Los Angeles, CA: Los Angeles County.

Law Enforcement News (1995). "In DC Area, One Review Board Dies, Another One is Stillborn." Vol. XXI, No. 427, August 20:1, 6.

Leonard, V.A. and Harry W. More (1993). *Police Organization and Management,* Eighth Edition. Westbury, NY: The Foundation Press.

Los Angeles Police Department (1997). *Executive Summary—Mark Fuhrman Task Force.* Los Angeles, CA: Los Angeles Police Department.

Mader, Katherine (1997). *Domestic Violence in the Los Angeles Police Department: How Well Does the Los Angeles Police Department Police Its Own? The Report of the Domestic Violence Task Force.* Los Angeles, CA: Los Angeles Police Department.

Mollen, Milton (1994). *Commission Report, Commission to Investigate Allegations of Police Corruption and the Anti-Corruption Procedures of the Police Department.* New York: The City of New York.

More, Harry W. and O.R. Shipley (1987). *Police Policy Manual—Personnel.* Springfield, IL: Charles C Thomas.

More, Harry W. and W. Fred Wegener (1994). *Effective Police Supervision,* Second Edition. Cincinnati, OH: Anderson Publishing Co.

Mount Lebanon Police Department (1987). "Commendations and Discipline." *Department Manual.* City of Mount Lebanon, PA.

Novick, Michael (1991). "Police Brutality is a Serious Problem." In William Dudley (ed.), *Police Brutality.* San Diego, CA: Greenhaven Press, Inc.

Ogletree, Charles J. Jr., Mary Prosser, Abbe Smith, and William Talley, Jr. (1994). *Beyond the Rodney King Story: An Investigation of Police Conduct in Minority Communities.* Boston: Northeastern University Press.

Petterson, Werner E. (1991). "Police Accountability and Civilian Oversight of Policing: An American Perspective." In Andrew J. Goldstein (ed.), *Complaints Against the Police: The Trend to External Review.* Oxford: Clarendon Press.

Powers, Mary D. (1995). "Civilian Oversight is Necessary to Prevent Police Brutality." In Paul A. Winters (ed.), *At Issue: Policing the Police.* San Diego, CA: Greenhaven Press, Inc.

Reaves, Brian A. and Pheny Z. Smith (1995). *Law Enforcement Management and Administrative Statistics, 1993: Data for Individual State and Local Agencies with 100 or More Officers.* Washington, DC: U.S. Department of Justice, Office of Justice Programs.

Rogers, Paul (1993). "Santa Cruz Plan for Police Review Board Attacked." *San Jose Mercury News,* July 27:1B, 2B.

Schobel, Gary B. (1996). "What Drives the Internal Affairs Investigator?" *The Police Chief,* Vol. LXIII, No. 4:45-50.

Snow, Robert (1992). "Civilian Oversight: Plus or Minus?" *Law and Order,* Vol. 40, No. 12:51-92.

State of California (1981). *Government Code,* Section 3303. Sacramento, CA: State of California.

Sulc, Lawrence B. (1995). "Police Brutality is not a Widespread Problem." In Paul A. Winters (ed.), *At Issue: Policing the Police.* San Diego, CA: Greenhaven Press, Inc.

Territo, Leonard and Robert L. Smith (1976). "The Internal Affairs Unit: The Policeman's Friend or Foe." *The Police Chief,* Vol. XLIII, No. 7:32.

Tyre, Mitchell and Susan Braunstein (1994). "Building Better Civilian Review Boards." *FBI Law Enforcement Bulletin,* Vol. 63, No. 12:10-14.

Walker, Samuel (1995). *Civilian Review Resource Manual.* Washington, DC: Police Executive Research Forum.

Walker, Samuel and Vic W. Bumphus (1991). *Civilian Review of the Police: A National Survey of the 50 Largest Cities, 1991."* Omaha, NE: University of Nebraska at Omaha.

Wallace, Bill (1995). "S.F. Police Discipline Questioned." *San Francisco Chronicle,* June 12:1, A4.

Watt, Susan (1994). "The Future of Civilian Oversight of Policing." *Another Viewpoint.* Cleveland, OH: IACOLE.

Worden, Robert E. (1995). "The Causes of Police Brutality: Theory and Evidence on Police Use of Force." In William A. Geller and Hans Toch (eds.), *And Justice for All: Understanding and Controlling Police Abuse of Force.* Washington, DC: Police Executive Research Forum.

POLICE UNIONS: CHALLENGING MANAGEMENT   7

The study of this chapter will enable you to:

1. Trace the evolution of police unionization in the United States.

2. Describe the reasons for the Boston police strike and the political response.

3. Discuss the various positions held by the International Association of Chiefs of Police toward police unions during early days.

4. Identify the key parts of the Pennsylvania Public Employee Act.

5. Compare the Fraternal Order of Police and the International Union of Police Associations.

6. Identify the goals of the International Brotherhood of Police Officers.

7. List five reasons for police unionization.

8. Identify the steps involved in interest-based bargaining.

9. List the three categories of what can and cannot be negotiated.

10. Draft a clause for management rights.

11. Describe the typical rights of employees that can be included in a Memorandum of Understanding.

12. Write a short essay describing ground rules for meeting and conferring.

13. Compare mediation and fact finding.

14. Describe the place for arbitration in collective bargaining.

Since the 1970s, overall union membership in the United States has dropped to the point where only 15 percent of all workers are unionized. During the 1996 presidential election, major unions strongly supported the Democratic party with large sums of money in the belief that returning the incumbent party to power would be of benefit to their membership. The Teamsters gave the Democratic Party $208,606 and the Republican Party $500 in *soft* money. Unions have moved vigorously to attract new members, particularly women and members of minority groups. During the last quarter-century, public unions have fared much better and their membership has increased as the worker base has increased. Public unions continue to challenge management for better working conditions. Initial concerns of police unions centered on such items as wages, benefits, working hours, and retirement (Guyot, 1991: 210-241). More recent concerns have extended to collective bargaining, grievance procedures, and the memorandum of understanding (MOU).

During the early part of this century, police officers joined social groups, societies, and clubs. Initially, these groups centered their activities around social events and benevolent endeavors, and slowly moved into labor matters. In some instances, these groups have functioned viably and contributed not only to the welfare of their members, but to the morale of the department and improvement of working conditions. In other departments, these organizations have served as a vehicle for departmental dissidents to promote their own welfare and to create conflict. Unfortunately, such actions have had a negative impact on departmental morale and efficiency (Leonard and More, 1993: 47)

Early Police Strikes

Whatever the nature and type of the organization, police unionization is not new. References from as early as the Civil War period reveal the existence of police employee organizations. Police strikes are not new either. In 1889, five police officers went on strike when the mayor of Ithaca, New York, reduced officers' wages by three dollars per week. After one week, the mayor restored the wage to 12 dollars per week, and the strike was canceled (O'Block, 1978: 56).

Another police strike occurred in 1918, when the chief of police in Cincinnati, Ohio, fired four police officers who attended a meeting to discuss a pay increase. In reaction to the chief's arbitrary and capricious action, departmental members joined the local Labor Council and went on strike. Approximately 450 officers refused to work until the public safety director agreed to consider reinstatement of the terminated officers (O'Block, 1978: 56). The police strikes described above attracted very little attention. It was not until the Boston police strike in 1919 that police unions and strikes caused a great deal of concern. Union supporters view the Boston strike as an important event in American police history. It became the *cause celebre*, giving labor problems in municipal government a great deal of notoriety (More and Wegener, 1996:343). From 1899 to 1919, the American Federation of Labor (AFL) rejected all efforts of police departments to affiliate. In June 1919, the AFL opened membership to law enforcement agencies and, in August, a charter was issued to the Boston police. The President of the American Federation of Labor stated, "[W]hen police officers accept charters from the American Federation of Labor, it is with the distinct understanding that strike action will not be resorted to . . ." (Sheehan, 1959: 1). The central issue precipitating the strike was an order issued by the commissioner of the Boston Police Department prohibiting officers from joining any organization other than a war group (Lyons, 1947: 28-33).

The nation was shocked by the strike, which served as a focal point in solidifying political opposition to unions and collective bargaining. The commissioner, Edwin Curtis, viewed the union as a threat to management and felt that unions did not belong in the public sector. One expert described what occurred as simply "power politics," and claimed that in no way did rationality prevail during the incident. This expert asserted that the winner of the game was preordained, and that the rules were determined in an arbitrary fashion (Shafritz, 1978: 51).

The suspension of the officers resulted in three-fourths of the department's officers going on strike at 5:45 P.M. on September 9, 1919. Only 427 officers remained on the job (Walker, 1983: 221). Most reasonable observers agreed that the officers had reason to create their own union. In 1919, Boston police officers earned an annual salary of $1,400 and had not received a pay raise in almost 20 years. From a salary of about $26.92 per week, the officers had to buy their own uniforms. They worked an average of 87 hours per week under inadequate working conditions. Promotions were political: it was *who* you knew, not *what* you knew. Morale was extremely low. The officers' request for a $200 increase in annual pay was rejected, and the officers voted to change the social club into a bonafide union. Subsequently, the union affiliated with the American Federation of Labor. Soon after the officers went on strike, the unprotected city was ravaged by mob action. Looting was rampant, people were killed, property damage was extensive, and lawlessness prevailed. About 15,000 people rioted in Scollay Square. The mayor declared a state of emergency and called upon the governor to restore law and order. Within three days, 7,000 fully armed members of the state militia, along with 825 civilian volunteers, assumed the law enforcement function in the city. Governor Calvin Coolidge, in defending the state's action said, "There is no right to strike against the public safety by anybody, anywhere, at any time" (More and Wegener, 1996: 344). This statement was reinforced by President Woodrow Wilson. At the height of the strike, Wilson stated:

> A strike of the policemen of a great city, leaving the city at the mercy of an army of thugs, is a crime against civilization. In my judgment, the obligation of a police officer is as sacred and direct as the obligation of a soldier. He is a public servant, not a private employee, and the whole honor and safety of the community is in his hands. He has no right to prefer any private advantage over the public's safety (Heustis, 1958: 44).

These statements served as a rallying point for an anti-unionism movement. Governor Coolidge took the position that the strikers were deserters and strongly opposed their reinstatement (Sheehan, 1959: 1-9). The striking officers were fired, even though they voted to return to work. The officers who did not strike received a $450 raise in annual pay. Despite extensive litigation, none of the striking officers was reinstated, and all of them lost their retirement benefits. As a result of the strong position that he took, Governor Calvin Coolidge emerged as a national hero. Eventually, he became vice president and then president of the United States (Russell, 1963: 79).

The Boston police strike has been one of the dominating elements in the slow development of police unions, but the incident remains a dark chapter in American history (Berkley, 1969: 52). In response to the strike, the American Federation of Labor immediately revoked all 37 local police charters in existence in 1919. In cities such as New York and Chicago, officers that had considered AFL affiliation abruptly backed off. Overall, the police strike had a chilling effect on police union organization efforts for several decades (Juris and Feuille, 1973: 2).

The Emergence of Police Unions

Even the Fraternal Order of Police (FOP), created to fulfill fraternal and social needs, was suspect because of the Boston police strike experiences. The efforts of the FOP to extend beyond Pittsburgh proved to be ineffective until well into the 1930s. Municipal managers openly opposed police efforts to organize and affiliate with any labor entity. In 1944, the International Association of Chiefs of Police concluded that "for the most part departmental rules, legal opinions or defined policies exist which permit the proper officials to ban a labor union . . ." The association also pointed out that not one of the unions in existence appealed to police managers. As late as 1958, the association cited the Boston police strike in a study that supported its opposition to police unions. This study suggested the meaninglessness of police membership in unions. It emphasized that police unions were inconsistent with employee-agency relations, that union membership requires dual allegiance, and that labor affiliation involves tacit acceptance of the right to strike (IACP, 1958: 6-9).

After the Great Depression of the 1930s, police officers began to question the significant gap between salary increases in the police field and those in business. Inadequate salaries, job dissatisfaction, and a lack of outlets for the redress of grievances led inevitably to frustration. Self-organization and militant action loomed as the primary alternative (Leonard and More, 1993: 42-48).

In the 1940s, the American Federation of Labor reactivated its program for the affiliation of police agencies. The program proved successful in a few cities but, overall, it had a limited impact on the police labor movement. As unions came into existence, they had no legal standing. A few of them experienced some success in negotiating with their employers, and the collective bargaining process began to emerge. Unfortunately, within a few years, the fledgling unions were crushed by restrictive legislation and unfavorable court decisions. In addition, there was firm opposition from police administrators, and local politicians refused to alter the balance of power. The governing bodies were in complete control and felt that compromise was to give up power that they wanted to retain.

Notwithstanding the anti-union sentiment, police employees continued to work for collective bargaining. Union-like professional associations were formed. These groups lobbied legislative bodies to change labor laws. Some associations, agitating for change, took illegal job actions. As the number of local and state employee organizations increased, the political power of these organizations increased accordingly.

The tide began to turn in 1958, when the mayor of New York approved the practice of collective bargaining. The following year, Wisconsin became the first state in the nation to grant public employees a limited right to bargain with employers. Bargaining was authorized in the areas of wages, hours, and working conditions. Wisconsin's public employees were specifically prohibited from striking, but the initial authorization opened the door for collective bargaining and the resolution of problems (More and Wegener, 1996: 345). Support also came from the President's office. In 1962, President John F. Kennedy signed Executive Order No. 10,988. This order extended recognition to employee groups, thereby authorizing collective negotiations (Juris and Hutchison, 1972: 4). During this period, teachers in different parts of the nation were becoming increasingly militant. Their efforts did not escape the attention of the police.

In a survey completed in 1968, police employee organizations were found in every part of the United States. In communities with populations greater than 10,000, there were 293 police agencies that had at least one employee organization (out of 347 responding departments). Most of these organizations limited membership to sworn police officers, and few of those actually affiliated with organized labor. Interestingly enough, about one-third of the employee groups in cities with populations of more than 50,000 engaged in collective bargaining (Juris and Hutchison, 1972: 16-21).

The late 1960s proved to be the period when chiefs of police began to change their attitude toward unions. In 1969, a special committee of the International Association of Chiefs of Police studied police employee organizations. The committee concluded that management should begin to work more closely with employee organizations (IACP, 1969: 23-24). During the 1960s, the right to bargain began to evolve. Thirteen states required the employer to bargain in good faith, nine permitted bargaining by local option, and four did not require bargaining. However, seven denied the right to bargain, and 17 were silent on the topic (Juris and Hutchison, 1972: 18-19). Figure 7-1 is an analysis of the Commonwealth of Pennsylvania's Public Employee Act. This act has served as a prototype for collective bargaining statutes throughout the United States.

The complexity of the problem of police unions and collective bargaining is well illustrated by the New York State Police, who negotiated for the first time under the Taylor Bill. The governor identified members of the state police as a separate negotiating unit, and the first hearings occurred in 1968. Upon completion of the hearings, the Public Employment Relations Board identified two negotiating units. One unit included middle management—lieutenants, captains, and majors. The second unit included troopers, sergeants, and criminal investigative personnel (Kirwin, 1969: 12-16).

Figure 7-1
Analysis of a Public Employee Act

[A] The Public Employee Act should be replaced by an entirely new law that would govern relationships between public employees and employers.

(1) The commission forged a single statute for all public instrumentalities and their employees in order to insure a uniform policy for all agencies of government.

[B] The new law should recognize the right of all public employees, including police and firemen, to bargain collectively, subject to enumerated safeguards.

(1) The bargaining unit should be determined in each instance by the Pennsylvania Labor Relations Board, following statutory guidelines.

(2) The bargaining agent should be determined only by elections supervised by the Labor Board.

(3) Bargaining should be permitted with respect to wages, hours, and conditions of employment, appropriately qualified by a recognition of existing laws dealing with aspects of the same subject matter and a carefully defined reservation of managerial rights.

(4) Employees should not be required to become members of an employee organization as a condition of employment. On the other hand, collecting dues from members of the organization (under appropriate safeguards) should be recognized as a bargainable issue.

[C] The law should require both parties to bargain in good faith through the following steps:

(1) Face-to-face collective bargaining between the parties, with the final agreement to be reduced to writing and signed by representatives of all parties.

(2) The utilization of the state mediation service, in the event that collective bargaining is not successful.

(3) Fact finding, recommendations, and publication thereof by a tribunal of three experienced arbitrators appointed by the Labor Board.

(4) In disputes involving policemen and firemen, if collective bargaining and mediation do not resolve the dispute, mandatory binding arbitration should be used.

[D] Except for policemen and firemen, a limited right to strike should be recognized, subject to these safeguards:

(1) No strike should be permitted for any reason whatsoever until all of the collective bargaining procedures outlined above have been followed.

(2) No strike should be permitted to begin or continue where health, safety, or welfare of the public is in danger.

(3) Unlawful strikes should be subject to injunctions and violations enforced by penalties that are effective against the bargaining agent or individual employee(s) or both.

Pennsylvania has two laws providing for collective bargaining for public employees. Act 111 provides for collective bargaining of police officers and firefighters of public jurisdictions. Binding arbitration is required for impasses, not for the right to strike. Despite the fact that the Pennsylvania Public Employee Act has been amended over the years, the basic thrust remains unchanged. Certainly, the act effectively encourages collective bargaining between local governments and certified employee groups that are authorized to represent police personnel.

Source: Commonwealth of Pennsylvania, *Employees Act of 1947*, As Amended, Commonwealth of Pennsylvania, 1968, 1-12.

When reviewing the many problems associated with the recognition of employee organizations and collective bargaining, the superintendent of the New York State Police advised, "[A]t the first sign of a desire to organize on the part of your employees, we suggest an attitude of 'join them' in the first instance rather than 'fight.'" He pointed out that it should never be management's intent to join the union. The intention should be to understand the union's goal and the objectives of the organization. Working with the union would allow for a better organization than otherwise would be possible. Management does not have to play a waiting game. The union may propose a resolution that is unacceptable to the management. By working together, he emphasized, mutual understanding can be achieved, and guidance can be given. The ultimate goal is to maintain harmonious relationships with employees (Kirwin, 1969: 12-28).

Dramatic changes have occurred. Today, more than 80 percent of the states have adopted legislation that permits public employees to participate in the collective bargaining process. In some states, public employees are allowed to strike, but this right has never been extended to the police. An example of this exception is Ohio's 1984 Public Bargaining Law. All employees except public safety personnel have the right to strike after a mandatory 10-day advance notice. By 1985, 24 states had labor laws that provided public employees with some type of arbitration instead of the right to strike (More and Wegener, 1996: 345).

Police Employee Organizations

Today, most public employees have some type of labor organization to represent them. One observer of the police scene has suggested that three-fourths of all American police officers are dues-paying members of police unions (Cole, 1986: 33). Obviously, the police union is no longer a myth; it is a reality. Some of the more prominent union organizations are described below.

AFSCME

The American Federation of State, County, and Municipal Employees (AFSCME) is one of the largest and most powerful unions in our nation (Stahl, 1983: 322). This union has 2,991 locals and more than one million members. There are 14,000 members from law enforcement agencies. AFSCME is affiliated with the American Federation of Labor and Congress of Industrial Organizations (AFL-CIO). The first local of police officers started in 1937 in Portsmouth, Virginia. At the end of World War II, there were 49 police locals, and this number grew to 66 by 1958. In its efforts to organize the police, AFSCME met resistance from police administrators and city managers. This happened in several large cities, including St. Louis, Chicago, and Los Angeles.

FOP

The Fraternal Order of Police (FOP) is the oldest national organization of affiliated police members. It came into existence in 1941, when police representatives met in Washington, D.C. to lobby against a bill that would have extended seemingly unnecessary Social Security coverage to police officers (Juris and Feuille, 1973: 17). Within two years, the FOP had 169 lodges. Faced with strong resistance from management, the FOP grew slowly until the 1960s. In 1997, there were 1,823 lodges in 42 states, representing about 215,000 members.

Since its inception, the FOP has served as a professional organization emphasizing fraternal and benevolent activities. In these areas, it certainly offers a great deal of power, influence, and service to its members. In recent years, the FOP has worked toward benefiting the economic and working conditions of its members. In this latter area, the FOP publishes updates on the Fair Labor Standards Act and a booklet on collective bargaining. It also conducts labor and grievance seminars as a means of informing its members of their rights.

FOP policy is reviewed annually, and conferences are attended by local and state lodge members as well as national officers. Although each local chapter is essentially autonomous, the National Office receives a small fee from each member. These funds, in addition to supporting the National Office, are used to support local police members during conflicts resulting from employment. Members are also kept up-to-date on matters involving labor relations and related matters via the *National Police Journal*. The most important functions of the National Office are political involvement and formal lobbying of Congress and other legislative bodies.

IUPA

In 1978, several local associations affiliated with the International Union of Police Associations (IUPA). This is a splinter group of the old International Conference of Police Associations (ICPA). One year after IUPA came into existence, the executive council of the AFL-CIO granted it a charter. IUPA has about 100 locals and seven State Councils. The organization has a membership of about 20,000 police officers. It works for just pay and reasonable working conditions. It functions as a coordinating body by providing training, information, and lobbying services to its members. The primary goal of IUPA is to bring police officers into the mainstream of the trade union membership. Dues provide for representation in Washington, and IUPA members have the right to call upon the assistance of AFL-CIO members/locals throughout the nation (Burpo, 1981: 11). IUPA encourages the formation of political action committees at the local level, and produces three publications: *Law Enforcement Quarterly, National Police Blue Book*, and *Police Union Quarterly*.

IBPO

Formed in 1964, the International Brotherhood of Police Officers (IBPO) is a national organization whose main office is in Boston, it also has a Washington, D.C. office that directs its lobbying activities in Congress. IBPO is affiliated with the Service Employees International Union. Latest available figures show that IBPO represents about 38,000 police officers who are members of about 175 chapters. The locals send all dues to IBPO. In turn, the main office or a regional staff representative provides labor relations services. The IBPO actively pursues a goal of becoming the bargaining agent for police officers. This goal distinguishes IBPO from other police labor organizations. This union is dedicated to the welfare and security of law enforcement personnel. It offers insurance programs and publishes a journal titled *The Police Chronicle*.

The above descriptions provide some insight into some of the major police unions and how they operate. No single organization dominates the labor scene and, from all available indications, the goal of combining the unions into one major police union is unattainable. Each organization appears to serve its constituency quite well, and the divergent philosophies are incompatible. This view is further supported by evidence that, over the last 20 years, several minority police associations have come into existence. These include the National Organization of Black Law Enforcement Executives (NOBLE), the Afro-American Patrolmen's League of the Chicago Police Department, and the Hispanic Caucus of the New York City Police Department (Garmire, 1982: 257). Generally speaking, it is still necessary to view police unionism as primarily a locally controlled phenomenon; the same is true for minority police organizations. Table 7-1 lists major police unions/associations and their memberships.

Table 7-1
Police Labor Organizations

Unit	Number of Members
Fraternal Order of Police (FOP)	215,000
International Union of Police Associations (IUPA)	20,000
Teamsters	10,000
National Troopers' Coalition	17,000
International Brotherhood of Police Officers (IBPO)	38,000
Peace Officers' Research Association (PORAC)	18,000
American Federation of State, County, and Municipal Employees (AFSCME)	14,000
Patrolmen's Benevolent Association (PBA) New York City	29,000

Management versus Labor

Contrary to the opinion held by police managers who continue to operate from an authoritarian posture, employee organizations are made, not born, it is a rare occurrence when a police union is able to develop within a well-managed police department. Whether intentional or not, the best boost for organizers of labor comes from managers who, through poor management, lack of concern for legitimate grievances, or just plain ignorance, antagonize officers. Officers then join a union or association that can engage in collective bargaining (Bingham, 1991: 248-249).

In some instances, management takes highly unusual and ridiculous steps to thwart labor members' attempts to organize. For example, in an incident that occurred several years ago, a chief of police transferred the president of the FOP 51 times in 49 days. This action was definitely something other than career development. It fact, it was simply a harassment technique designed to impede the birth of a police labor union (Salerno, 1981: 45). In a nationwide study of the impact of police unions, two experts stated:

> In sum, police unions have narrowed management discretion, fostered the development of management by policy, and they have protected employees against arbitrary or inconsistent treatment. In a few cases, contractual provisions negotiated between the union and the city have caused serious managerial problems, but the primary union impact has been to force police management to focus greater attention to the needs and wants of policemen and to improve personnel practices within the police department (Juris and Feuille, 1973: 2-10).

The reasons officers organize might not always be the same, but in most instances, they include one or more of the following (Sirene, 1981: 4-8; Crane, 1979: 231):

- Unsatisfactory working conditions
- Lack of an opportunity for advancement
- Lack of a grievance procedure
- Low salary
- No opportunity to be heard
- Need to be recognized
- Poor communications

Police managers are becoming increasingly aware that they need to become experts in labor relations. In agencies in which police managers have demonstrated a constant and continuing interest in the welfare of employees, unions have found limited support. Today, a police administrator must be knowledgeable in all aspects of labor relations, including collective bargaining, grievance procedures, negotiation tactics, and the memorandum of understanding.

Collective Negotiation

Once a union becomes a reality in a police organization, the issues with which it will deal vary, depending upon the needs and desires of its members. The extent to which police unions or associations have intruded into what traditionally was considered a managerial prerogative varies considerably from city to city. In any case, unions continue to challenge management as they engage in constructive conflict. The pervasive nature of police unionization requires administrators and elected officials to work with representatives of unions. One thing that police executives must do is recognize that police employees have a legal right, subject to certain reasonable limitations, to engage in activities protected by the First Amendment. They should also acknowledge the right of their employee to join (or not to join) employee organizations that represent employee interests, and they should give appropriate recognition to these organizations.

The First Amendment protects the rights of police officers to free association. Accordingly, police officers have a constitutionally protected right to form and join a labor union. The National Labor Relations Act (29 U.S.C.:151-168: 1976) specifies the rights of the typical employee.

It is important to note that this statute does not extend to public employees. It does not give police officers the right to bargain collectively or to strike. In fact, federal courts have suggested that police officers may be entitled to fewer constitutional protections in their labor-related associational rights than are other government employees, such as librarians (Brancato and Polebaum, 1981: 93-95).

In some instances, the negotiation process has been highly adversarial. Personal attacks, name calling, and bombastic tirades have proven to be symptomatic of the interplay between members of the union and management. Used initially by the Portland (Oregon) Police Association, interest-based bargaining has proven to be an effective means of resolving conflict between negotiating parties. It works out to be a process of consensus-building instead of a diatribe between loggerheaded negotiators. In order for this process to be effective, each side discusses its view and an effort is made to work together and solve the problem. Interest-based bargaining follows six steps (Johnson, 1995: 6):

1. Identify and document.

2. Ascertain the interests of each side for each problem.

3. Determine impartial criteria.

4. Brainstorm options.

5. Judge the worth of the options.

6. Select the best solution.

The total process has to focus on issues, not personalities, and the problem-solving process must dominate. In Portland, during one negotiation period, impasse occurred in only one instance. The following Feature illustrates the range of problems and conflict that occur between administrators and unions.

Feature

Management and Unions Confronting Issues

Job Security

In 1996, the Fraternal Order of Police (FOP), Lodge 7, which represents 17,000 members of the Chicago Police Department, negotiated a contract with the City. It was the first time since 1981 that a contract negotiation was concluded without going to arbitration. The contract provided for a 14 percent pay raise, job security provisions, and a cap on retirees' health care premiums. Uniform allowances were increased as well as an allowance for duty availability. The contract also provided for bilingual officers to be used as interpreters. Security was also given to detectives, gang investigators, and youth officers, who can only be removed from those positions for just cause.

Sick Call

Approximately 600 lieutenants, sergeants, detectives, and officers of the Los Angeles Police Department on the day shift called in sick. A six percent pay raise had been rejected. The Police Protective League wanted retroactive pay for the two years that the officers had worked without a contract. A court order prohibited the *Blue Flu,* but the union took the position that the walkout was initiated by officers, not the union. The department went on a modified tactical alert to ensure that it had the personnel it needed to police the city.

Getting Organized

Recently, the 1,200 member United States Capitol Police were allowed to organize under the Congressional Accountability Act. Numerous unions were courting the membership, including the Teamsters, the Fraternal Order of Police, and the International Brotherhood of Police Officers. The Teamsters took the position that they had the clout to deal with the political process. One Capitol police officer said the FOP was just a party organization while the Teamsters had influence. The head of the FOP stated they were in a better position to represent police officers than truck drivers. The FOP took the position that they would do whatever was needed to become the representing agency. It was anticipated that it would take months before the members of the department would vote for an organizing entity.

Kickback Scheme

In 1997, a scandal came to light in the Patrolmen's Benevolent Association of New York City while the union was in a contractual dispute with the City. The union had rejected a proposal for a pay raise and had been picketing and protesting for more than a month. Additionally, officers engaged in a ticket-writing slow down. Federal prosecutors had indicted the chief negotiator and two top lawyers of the union for corruption. Altogether, 11 people were named in a 13-count indictment. Charges included paying kickbacks to officials of the Transit Police union.

Source: *Law Enforcement News* (1997). "As Contract Disputes Simmers, Fed Prosecutors Charge: PBA lawyers, others in Kickback Scheme." Vol. XXIII, No. 461, February 28: 7; *Law Enforcement News* (1996). "Getting Organized." Vol. XXII, No. 442, March 3: 10; *Arizona Daily Star* (1994). "Hundreds of Los Angeles Cops Call in Sick over Pay Dispute." June 1: 1B; and *Law Enforcement News* (1996). "Job Security Boasted in New Chicago Pact." Vol. XXII, No. 454, October 31: 5.

What Can be Negotiated

Most public employee bargaining laws have come into existence since 1959, when Wisconsin passed a state collective bargaining law. Now more than two-thirds of the states have laws governing authorization of collective bargaining for police officers. For example, in California, the Meyers-Milias-Brown Act (Government Code 3500) along with the Public Safety Officer's Bill of Rights and city or county ordinances, defines the legal relationship between government entities and their employees.

Statutes limit collective bargaining. There are definite subjects that may or may not be negotiated (More and Wegener, 1996: 356-357):

- **Mandatory**. These are subjects falling under the category of working conditions. Examples are disability pay, shift assignment, and staffing requirements.

- **Voluntary**. These are topics that both sides of the bargaining table realize are outside the mandatory category. Examples are retirement benefits, health club memberships, and stress reduction programs. These topics are placed on the table for voluntary consideration and agreement. Neither party is required to bargain on these topics or to agree to include them in the contract.

- **Illegal**. These include activities that have been specifically prohibited by the public employee bargaining law. Examples are binding arbitration, union shop agreements, and the right to strike.

Collective negotiation between management and labor results in a union contract (Memorandum of Understanding). The contract usually runs from one to three years. Typically, the master agreement is a revision rather than a brand new document. In addition, the contract can be changed by what is normally called a sidebar agreement if the original document has a *re-opener* provision. Usually, sidebar agreements involve a single issue that was not addressed originally, or both parties agree that there is a need to clarify an issue. In many instances, the issue is the interpretation of a provision of the memorandum of understanding (Unsinger and More, 1989: 4-53). For example, in one west coast city, a sidebar agreement was drafted to clarify the process for withholding union dues.

Another type of negotiation is the day-to-day interpretation occurring between a union steward and management. This can involve a wide range of issues, such as resolving grievances, interpreting the contract, and handling disciplinary cases. Some of these issues are brought to the attention of management through the use of a *side letter*. In one instance, the issue in conflict involved salary adjustment of a police property clerk. The union in its side letter questioned the reduction process, expressing the opinion that the process was done arbitrarily and without the union's written agreement. The union requested that the discrepancy of the salary difference be set aside until the matter could be settled through further negotiations and or legal proceedings (Pang, 1992: 1).

Management Rights

Management in the public sector should be able to take action unilaterally when it is necessary to ensure the delivery of public services in an efficient and cost-effective manner. The authority and ability to make and implement decisions are *managerial rights* (Rynecki and Morse, 1981: 7). These rights are often derived from complex interaction between management and the union. Disputes regarding managerial rights are usually resolved by creating a *rights and responsibilities* clause, which becomes an integral part of the contract (memorandum of understanding).

The type of management rights clause that protects the employer most effectively is one that:

- Protects all residual managerial rights not mentioned in the collective bargaining agreement.

- Specifies rights important to effective departmental operations.

- Provides that the grievance arbitration procedure contained in the agreement does not limit management's exercise of enumerated rights (Rynecki and Morse, 1981: 7).

Typical of the rights a city can specify are the capacity to:

- Determine the mission of its constituent departments, commissions, and boards.

- Set standards of service, and determine the procedures and standards of selection for employment.

- Direct its employees.

- Take disciplinary action.

- Relieve its employees from duty because of lack of work or other legitimate reasons.

- Maintain the efficiency of governmental operations.

- Determine the methods, means, and personnel by which government operations are to be conducted.

- Determine the content of job classification.

- Determine when an emergency exists and take all necessary action to carry out the mission of the department in emergencies, including the requirement that employees work overtime.

- Exercise complete control and discretion over its organization and the technology of performing its work (Milpitas Police Department, 1996: 42).

The above list of city (management) rights reserves a great deal of power for management in the City of Milpitas. This fact is further reinforced by a section of the memorandum of understanding (contract) providing that neither the police association nor its agents or any employee, for any reason, will authorize, institute, aid, condone, or engage in a work stoppage, slowdown, strike, sick-out, or any other interference with the work and statutory functions or obligations of the city (Milpitas Police Department 1996:36). The enumeration of rights provides management with guidelines for exercising its legitimate authority. The following Feature describes how officers in one community circumvented a no-strike clause.

Feature

Police Force Leaves Town

California law prohibits strikes, but in one southern California community, most of the police officers went out on strike on one Friday evening when the entire swing shift did not show up for work. In total, 28 patrol officers and several ranking sergeants and lieutenants walked out. The officers had been working without a contract for four-and-one-half months, and negotiations over wages had been ongoing. The negotiations were at an impasse. When management obtained a contempt of court citation because of the illegal strike, the citation could not be served on the striking officers because they had left the state. Sequestered in the adjacent state, the officers could not be served with the contempt citation because its application was limited to the state of California. During the strike, the local sheriff's department and the adjacent community's police department handled calls for service.

Source: Adapted from *San Jose Mercury News* (1983). "Police Force Leaves Town." November 19:6B.

Employee Rights

It has become increasingly common for management to specify the rights of employees when negotiating a memorandum of understanding. These rights vary from community to community. Many of the rights included in the typical memorandum are embodied in the following example:

*   Any employee may join, organize, or maintain membership in a labor organization if she/he so desires. The right to join a labor union or association of municipal employees also includes the right not to join. Any employee desiring to join, remain a member, or become independent of any such organization or association must be free to exercise his/her right without undue influence, coercion, intimidation, or pressure of any kind from any person.

- City employees participating in organizational or other labor union activities or similar activities of any employee association are required to conduct such activities on their own time and not during regularly assigned working hours, with the following exceptions:

    a. A steward representing or assisting a fellow employee in the presentation of a grievance (including representation in disciplinary proceedings) may utilize such time as is essential for the presentation of the grievance to management during working hours; however, solicitation of grievances shall be on the employee's own time.

    b. Officials of any organization representing City employees may meet on City time with the City manager or other City officials when such meeting times are approved by the City Manager.

    c. Business agents or representatives of the union or other association, or their affiliates, having business (other than recruiting of members) with the officers or individual members of the union or association or other recognized employee group may meet and confer during the course of the day for a reasonable period of time providing that permission is first obtained from the department head, if on duty, and the employee's immediate supervisor, and further provided that the conduct of such business will in no way conflict with the performance of City business.

    d. The use of the workplace or premises for organizational activities other than the presentation of a grievance or the conduct of business as provided above, is permitted only after working hours, with the advance notice of the department head or City Manager and shall in no way interfere with the performance of official duties of on-duty personnel.

    e. For City employees who may wish to belong to a public employees union or association, the City will cause dues to be deducted where specifically authorized by the employee in advance.

    f. The City shall provide space approved by the Chief of Police to accommodate an Association file cabinet, bookcase, and answering machine.

    g. The City will provide paid release time for Association officers and members to conduct essential Association business, excluding political activity, upon reasonable written notice to and prior approval by the Chief of Police (Milpitas Police Department, 1996: 4-5).

When reviewing management and employee rights, one can see that there are numerous areas in which extensive negotiation may take place.

Memorandum of Agreement/Understanding

In most police departments across the nation, some type of contract or memorandum of understanding (MOU) governs the working relationship between management and the union (Los Angeles Police Department, 1994: 1-

79). Such agreements have replaced what some police officers had viewed as arbitrary and capricious management. On the other hand, some police executives view an MOU as something that limits their ability to manage the police organization. Figure 7-2 lists some of the issues that are typically included in a memorandum of understanding.

Management-labor relations govern almost every personnel action that takes place in today's contemporary police department. Whenever a manager or an employee takes an action, such an action is increasingly likely to take into account prior agreements between management and a union/association. This can involve anything from a grievance to special staffing assignments.

An MOU is defined as a written agreement prepared by management and an employee organization, reached through meet-and-confer procedures, and concerned with issues such as wages, hours, and working conditions. It is quite common for an MOU to have a statement providing ground rules for meeting and conferring. An example of this is one MOU that provided, "if unforeseen difficulties should arise, regarding safety, suitability, or acquisition of police vehicles during the life of this agreement, the parties shall meet and confer in an attempt to resolve said difficulties." (Milpitas Police Department, 1996: 24). Figure 7-3 sets forth an example of ground rules contained in an MOU for meeting and conferring.

Figure 7-2
Typical Issues Included in a Memorandum of Understanding

Employee Rights	Holidays
City Rights	Training
Grievance Procedures	Standby Assignment
Annual Vacation Leave	Safety Equipment
Sick Leave	Uniform Allowance
Family Leave	K-9 Premium
Military Leave	Educational Incentive Pay
Leave of Absence	Police Vehicles
Jury Leave	Stress Reduction Program
Compassionate Leave	Motorcycle Program
Hourly Rate and Overtime	Light Duty
Attendance	Benefits
Disciplinary Action	No Labor Action
No Discrimination	Resignation
Other Employment	Work-out-of-Class
Advance Notice	Pay Plan
Layoff	

Figure 7-3
Ground Rules for Meeting and Conferring

- Negotiation teams shall not exceed five representatives; however, expert testimony may be presented by one additional member at designated meetings.
- Employees who are members of the MPOA negotiating team shall be provided release time pursuant to Government Code Section 3505.3.
- Chief spokespersons shall be designated and shall be responsible for notifying respective team members as to meeting times, dates, and places.
- All communications by the MPOA to the City shall be directed to the City's designated chief negotiator.
- The City shall direct all communications to the MPOA's chief negotiator.
- All proceedings shall be confidential, and during the meet-and-confer process, there will be:
- No tape recording.
- No press release or public communications without notification.
- No contact by MPOA with the City Council on matters within the scope of bargaining after negotiations begin and prior to impasse.
- No management contacts with the general membership of the Police Association on matters within the scope of bargaining.
- Both parties agree to make a good faith effort to reach an agreement during the negotiations. In that regard, both parties agree that the negotiation process and all agreements will take place at the table.
- The MPOA will present a written initial proposal to the City, the receipt of which shall initiate the negotiation process.
- The initial proposals submitted by each party shall include all subject matters for negotiations, and no new subjects will be raised for negotiations without the concurrence of both parties.
- To the extent practicable, proposals and counterproposals should be written. Basic cost data is to be supplied when applicable.
- All agreements on individual proposals are tentative, pending mutual acceptance of a total package. Tentative agreements shall be in writing and initialed by both chief negotiators.
- There shall be no press releases during the meet and confer sessions without 24 hours notice to either party.
- If agreement is reached between the negotiating teams, the resulting MOU will be recommended to the MPOA membership. Upon acceptance, the City representative will recommend it to the City Council for ratification.
- In the event that no agreement has been reached by the expiration of the MOU, the provisions of the current agreement shall remain in effect.
- If an impasse is declared, resolution measures will be attempted in accordance with the City's employer/employee relations policy as described in the City Personnel Regulations.
- Violation of any of the above agreed-to ground rules shall constitute bad faith on the part of the violating party.

Source: Milpitas Police Department. (1996). *Memorandum of Understanding. January 1, 1996 – December 31, 1998.* Milpitas, CA: City of Milpitas, 1-38. Reprinted courtesy of Milpitas Police Officers Association.

Although the terms of agreement vary from one MOU to the next, it is becoming increasingly evident that the typical MOU covers two to four years. The actual drafting of an MOU requires the parties to review the past and take into consideration such things as new laws, ordinances, and programs that began since the last agreement. An important characteristic of an MOU is that it is not prepared by one party. It is prepared jointly by the representatives of management and the union. Another unique feature is that those who draft the memorandum of understanding are not responsible for signing the document. The agreement is submitted to the principals for both sides. In most instances, this means that the city council or its representatives are on one side and the members of the union are on the other side (Coble, 1989: 33-43).

Impasse Procedures

From time to time, the collective negotiation process becomes deadlocked, and something must be done if the two parties are to resolve an impasse. There are a number of impasse procedures that can be utilized. These are usually set forth in state statutes or, in some instances, city rules and regulations. Many of the present procedures have been borrowed from private sector labor relations. The major impasse procedures are discussed below.

Mediation

Of all the impasse procedures, mediation is the one used most frequently and the one that has proven to be highly successful when parties are deadlocked. It is a nonbinding, impasse resolution technique that involves a neutral third party whose role is to facilitate communications and help disputants reach a mutually acceptable agreement. Mediators facilitate communications, clarify issues, and explore possible avenues for agreement. Mediators have no authority to mandate settlement. Their value lies in their function as a neutral party that identifies the real needs of both parties and searches for solutions (McAndrews, 1989: 30-31).

Mediators are also valuable in reviewing disputes from a fresh perspective, objectively analyzing data, and injecting new ideas into a negotiation. When it is appropriate, mediators can extricate parties from difficult or untenable positions. A knowledgeable mediator can cut through the smoke screens projected by the parties involved and fine-tune the negotiation process. Professional mediation services are available at state and federal agencies. While mediation does not work in every instance, there are enough successes in the police field to recommend that parties on both sides use mediation if the opportunity presents itself (More and Wegener, 1996: 363).

Fact Finding

Fact finding is used less frequently than mediation in the resolution of police negotiation impasses. It is a nonbinding resolution technique. It is a quasi-judicial process in which a third party or a neutral panel gathers facts and takes testimony from the parties regarding disputed issues. An investigative report is prepared, and specific recommendations are made for resolving an impasse. Mediation can occur during this process if there appears to be a potential for settlement.

In some states, statutes provide for a tripartite fact-finding panel. In this case, the third-party neutral is joined by an advocate for each of the parties. One party represents the police union and the other the city. This format provides an additional opportunity for settlement as the fact-finding process evolves. Fact finding provides additional opportunity for negotiation, as recommendations are placed on the table. If a resolution does not occur, statutes in many states prevent a press release for a specific period (in some instances, 10 days). This provides a cooling-off period, and the parties then strive to negotiate a settlement. The parties can then release the report, and resolution is left to negotiation in an open forum (McAndrews, 1989: 31). Recent studies have shown that fact finding results in a success rate of about 70 percent (More and Wegener, 1996: 341).

Arbitration

Arbitration is a binding impasse resolution technique. Each side submits a proposal, and the arbitrator must select the final position of one of the parties. This final-offer method was created to encourage settlement short of an arbitration award. In actual operation, some arbitrators encourage negotiations through mediation. Whether this is done depends upon the persuasive skills of the arbitrator. In another type of arbitration, a neutral third party functions like a fact finder by gathering and interpreting data and obtaining testimony from both parties. In some instances, the disputants select the impasse process, and in other instances it is compulsory (McAndrews, 1989: 32). The arbitrator has the power to decide the issues, and the decision becomes legally binding and enforceable in the courts. In recent years, MOUs and contracts usually contain a section providing for arbitration. The American Arbitration Association maintains a list of qualified and experienced arbitrators.

Summary

Since the 1950s, police unions have emerged as a force to be taken into consideration. In many instances, they have evolved to the extent that they are able to challenge police management. Unions in the police field are not new. They can be traced back to the Civil War period. The same can be said for police strikes.

The most famous of these was the Boston police strike in 1919. That strike shocked the nation and served as a focal point in solidifying political opposition to unions and collective bargaining in the public sector.

This opposition continued for years. During the 1930s, municipal managers openly opposed the establishment of police unions. During the 1940s and 1950s, the International Association of Chiefs of Police condemned police unions. It was their position that police unions were inconsistent with employee-agency relations. In 1958, the tide began to turn when the mayor of New York accepted collective bargaining. This was followed by the action of the state government of Wisconsin, which granted public employees a limited right to bargain. Since that time, conditions have changed dramatically. Now, more than 80 percent of the states have adopted legislation permitting public employees to participate in collective bargaining. Available information suggests that three-fourths of all American police officers are dues-paying members of police unions. The police union is no longer a myth; it is a reality.

Whether intentional or not, the best boost to organized labor unions occurs when managers, through poor management, lack of concern for legitimate grievances, or just plain ignorance, antagonize officers to the point where they join a union or an association. Because police unions are here to stay, today's police administrator must be conversant in collective bargaining, grievance procedures, and negotiation techniques. Legal specialists have pointed out that the First Amendment protects the rights of police officers to free association. In recent years, interest-based bargaining has come into vogue.

Most public employee bargaining laws have come into existence since 1959. Currently, about two-thirds of the states have such laws. The authority and the ability to make and implement decisions are called *managerial rights*. Police managers strive to keep all of the rights needed to ensure the effective operation of the organization. This power source is further reinforced by clauses that prohibit police officers from engaging in any type of activity that interferes with the work and obligations of the city. On the other hand, most memoranda of understanding specify the employee's right to join and participate in union activities. Memoranda of understanding are becoming increasingly common. It is a written document reached through meet-and-confer procedures and concerns such issues as wages and working conditions.

If a collective bargaining negotiation process becomes deadlocked, the following impasse procedures can be invoked: mediation, fact finding, and arbitration. Each of these has special uses and characteristics.

References

Arizona Daily Star (1994). "Hundreds of Los Angeles Cops Call in Sick Over Pay Dispute." June 1:1B.

Berkley, George E. (1969). *The Democratic Policeman*. Boston, MA: Beacon Press.

Bingham, Richard D., et al. (1991). *Managing Local Government: Public Administration in Practice.* Newbury Park, CA: Sage Publications.

Brancato, Gilda and Elliot E. Polebaum (1981). *The Rights Of Police Officers.* New York: Avon Books, 93-95.

Burpo, John H.(1981). "The Police Labor Movement: Prospects for the 1980s." *FBI Law Enforcement Bulletin*, Vol. 50, No. 1, January:11.

Coble, Paul (1989). "Memoranda of Agreement/Understanding." In Peter C. Unsinger and Harry W. More (eds.), *Police Management—Labor Relations.* Springfield, IL: Charles C Thomas, 4-33.

Cole, George F. (1986). *The American System of Criminal Justice.* Monterey, CA: Brooks/Cole, 33.

Commonwealth of Pennsylvania (1968). Employee Act of 1947, As Amended. Harrisburg, PA: Commonwealth of Pennsylvania, 1-29.

Crane, Donald P. (1979). *Personnel: The Management of Human Resources*, Second Edition. Belmont, CA: Wadsworth, 231.

Garmire, Bernard L. (ed.) (1982). *Local Government Police Management*, Second Edition. Washington, DC: International City Management Association, 256-257.

Guyot, Dorothy (1991). *Policing as Though People Matter.* Philadelphia, PA: Temple University Press, 211-241.

Heustis, Carl E. (1958). "Police Union." *The Police Yearbook.* Washington, DC: International Association of Chiefs of Police, 44.

International Association of Chiefs of Police (1958). *Police Unions,* Revised Edition. Washington, DC: International Association of Chiefs of Police, 6-9.

International Association of Chiefs of Police (1969). *Report of the Special Committee on Police Employee Organizations.* Washington, DC: International Association of Chiefs of Police, 23-24.

Johnson, Mark (1995). "Interest-based Bargaining Shows Merit." *Law Enforcement News,* Vol. XXI, No. 423:6.

Juris, Hervey A. and Peter Feuille (1973). *Police Unionism, Power and Impact in Public-Sector Bargaining.* Lexington, MA: D.C. Heath, 2-10.

Juris, Hervey and Kay B. Hutchinson (1972). "The Legal Status of Municipal Police Employee Organizations." Working Paper Number 3. Madison, WI: University of Wisconsin, Center for Law and Behavioral Science, 2-21.

Kirwin, William E. (May 7, 1969). "The New York State Police: History and Development of Collective Bargaining (paper)." Albany, NY: 12-28.

Law Enforcement News (1996a). "Getting Organized." Vol. XXII, No. 442, March 31:7, 10.

Law Enforcement News (1996b). "Job Security Boosted in New Chicago Pact." Vol. XXII, No. 454, October 31:5.

Law Enforcement News (1997). "As Contract Dispute Simmers, Fed Prosecutors Charge: PBA Lawyers, Others in Kickback Scheme." Vol. XXIII, No. 461, February 20:7.

Leonard, V.A. and Harry W. More (1993). *Police Organization and Management*, Seventh Edition. Mineola, NY: Foundation Press, 47-345.

Los Angeles Police Department (1994). *Memorandum of Understanding.* Los Angeles, CA: City of Los Angeles, 1-79.

Lyons, Richard L. (June 1947). "The Boston Police Strike of 1919." *The New England Quarterly*, Vol. 20, No. 2:28-33.

McAndrews, Ian (1989). "The Negotiation Process." In Peter C. Unsinger and Harry W. More (eds.), *Police Management—Labor Relations*. Springfield, IL: Charles C Thomas, 30-32.

Milpitas Police Department (1996). *Memorandum of Understanding, January 1 1996-December 31, 1998*. City of Milpitas, Milpitas, CA: 1-42.

More, Harry W. and W. Fred Wegener (1996). *Effective Police Supervision*, Second Edition. Cincinnati, OH: Anderson Publishing Co., 47-344.

National Advisory Commission on Criminal Justice Standards and Goals (1973). *The Police*. Washington, DC: U.S. Government Printing Office.

O'Block, Robert (1978). "The Movement for Police Unionization." *The Police Chief*, Vol. XLV, No. 6:56.

Pang, Darryl (1992). *Side Letter Regarding Police Property Clerk Salary Adjustment*. Milpitas, CA: Correspondence, April 10:1.

Russell, Francis (1963). "The Strike that Made a President." *American Heritage*, October:14-79.

Rynecki, Steven B. and Michael J. Morse (1981). *Police Collective Bargaining Agreements—A National Survey*, Revised and Expanded Edition. Washington, DC: Police Executive Research Forum and National League of Cities, 7.

Salerno, Charles A. (1981). *Police at the Bargaining Table*. Springfield, IL: Charles C Thomas, 45.

San Jose Mercury News (1983). "Police Force Leaves Town." November 19:6B.

Shafritz, Jay M., et al. (1978). *Personnel Management in Government*. New York: Marcel Dekker, 51.

Sheehan, Robert (1959). "Lest We Forget." *Police*, September-October:1-9.

Sirene, Walt H. (1981). "Management—Labor's Most Effective Organizer." *FBI Law Enforcement Bulletin*, Volume 50, Number 1, January:4-8.

Stahl, O. Glen (1983). *Public Personnel Administration*. New York: Harper and Row, 322.

Unsinger, Peter C. and Harry W. More (eds.) (1989). *Police Management—Labor Relations*. Springfield, IL: Charles C Thomas, 4-53.

Walker, Samuel (1983). *The Police in America*. New York: McGraw-Hill Publishing, 221.

THE MALE-DOMINATED
POLICE CULTURE: *8*
REDUCING THE GENDER GAP

The study of this chapter will enable you to:

1. Write a short essay describing the early entry of women into police work.

2. List the typical police duties performed by women during the last century.

3. Describe how police departments in New York City, Miami, and Washington, D.C. assigned women to patrol.

4. List six reasons why Catherine Milton felt women should serve in all law enforcement capacities.

5. Compare the number of women employed as sworn officers in rural counties, suburban counties, and cities in the largest population group.

6. Describe the difficulties that women have when adjusting to the male-dominated police culture.

7. List eight responses that women give when asked what they think is the worst part of police work.

8. Define sexual harassment.

9. Refute four of the myths about sexual harassment.

10. Describe conduct that constitutes sexual harassment.

In the last 25 years, women have taken an increasingly important role in law enforcement agencies, but they still struggle for acceptance inside and outside of the department. Women have faced an ongoing battle not only to become police officers, but to gain acceptance once employed. Many people have not been stopped or questioned by a female police officer, but that is changing and more and more citizens will encounter female officers as their numbers increase.

The reasons for the late entry of women into sworn positions in law enforcement varies from agency to agency. In part, it stems from a long-standing belief that law enforcement agencies function to exercise authority and use force. Historically, these functions have been assigned to men; for years, women were never allowed to exercise authority and control over others. Another reason was that women, viewed as the weaker sex, were not permitted to serve as representatives of the state. In addition, it was believed that women did not have the physical capacity to perform effectively as police officers. The same was also true of shorter males, as height requirements were prevalent for many years.

Preference was given to taller males, who had the brawn to deal with situations requiring greater physical strength. It fact, it seemed that height was given greater weight than other selection factors. It was not until 1981 that the Los Angeles Police Department lowered its minimum height requirement from 5'8" to 5'0" (Segrave, 1995: 107-135).

This pattern of division of labor between males and females continued for many years, and dominated governmental hiring criteria. Social conditions, the narrow interpretation of the police role, and society's view of women have changed over the years, but one fact that was that clear for many years was that policing in reality was a male-dominated occupation.

There was a great deal of Victorian legislation designed to protect women against the evils of factories and mines. All of this contributed to the Victorian idea that women should be protected by men and the state. Limitations on work that could be performed by women were determined by what society thought women should and could do. Consideration was also given to limiting women to safe occupations that did not require physical strength. It was not until World War I that many of the conventions weakened, as women performed voluntary services that they never would have been permitted to do had they not volunteered to do the work (Carrier, 1988: xv).

For a good part of the twentieth century, police officers in the United States could only be described as conservative white males. Most of them came from working-class families and had been in the military (especially after World War II, when many veterans entered the police service). The majority of officers were high school graduates and had been previously employed in blue-collar or lower white-collar jobs.

Additionally, there were a number of departments in the United States in which certain fraternal, religious, or ethnic backgrounds proved important for entry and advancement in the police service. This was true for the Irish, Italians, Jews, Mormons, and Masons. More recently (with the advent of affirmative action), African-Americans, Latinos, and Asians have entered the police service in increasing numbers and have assumed leadership positions in many departments.

Police ranks (through the 1960s) were dominated by male recruits. Rookies learned from veteran officers that the way to get along in a police organization was to never rock the boat. Each new officer was expected to internalize norms and the value system of the department, and to accept the operating principle of maintaining the status quo. As new police officers, they were taught that criminals, civil rights activists, and feminists were the enemies. It was a question of us (the police) versus them (the criminal element). Shocked by the changes occurring at such a rapid pace, the police (during the 1960s) rejected charges of racism and sexism and viewed themselves as a minority and the last vestige of society's protectors. The real *thin blue line* was striving to contain the rabble that was trying to destroy the American way of life. All of this resulted in a continuing pattern of sexism, whereby women were discriminated against on the basis that change was not needed and that police work could only be performed by men. Unfortunately, vestiges of this attitude remain.

Early Entry of Women Into Police Work

Throughout history, but not with any great frequency, women have been used as spies, undercover agents, and detectives. Women performed exceptionally for such agencies as the Pinkerton Detective Agency and Wells Fargo, and for governmental entities during the Civil War. Toward the end of the nineteenth century, the most vociferous campaign for the introduction of women into the police service came from groups of women that were affiliated with the suffrage movement in Great Britain. This situation has been viewed as a classic example of a pressure group working to change the establishment (Carrier, 1988: 1). It was not until the latter part of the nineteenth century that women began to enter the police service with standard police powers (Horne, 1980: 17).

During the first one-half of the nineteenth century, efforts to change a number of police practices, along with the women's rights movement, served as the basis for the entry of women into American police agencies. The actual groundwork began prior to the Civil War, with what has been termed the *police women's movement*. Numerous reformers worked diligently to see that women and young girls being held in custody were supervised by women. In 1845, New York City succumbed to the pressures of an organization known as the American Female Society and hired its first jail matron. Over the next 25 years, women were appointed in increasing numbers to perform supervisory duties for women and girls in custody.

In 1888, Massachusetts and New York passed legislation making it mandatory for all communities with a population of more than 20,000 to employ police matrons to care for female prisoners (Horne, 1980: 17). In 1893, the mayor of Chicago appointed Marie Owens, the widow of an officer, to the position of patrol officer. She served in that position for 30 years before retiring. Her duties included assisting investigators in cases involving women and girls. She was called a police officer even though she did not have arrest powers (House, 1993: 1-3).

In 1905, Lola Baldwin became the first female police officer to have the powers of arrest. She served in Portland, Oregon, and was charged with helping women and children at the Lewis and Clark Exposition. Another landmark was established in the same department at the same time when it created a division for women in the police department. As women became employed in increasing numbers, national women's groups and the public expressed real concern for the social and moral conditions surrounding women and girls. Pressure groups called for special protection and guidance. All this led to the greater use of women by law enforcement agencies. Women were believed to be prepared to deal with the aspects of police work that males should not perform, including the handling of wayward young women and dealing with family conflict. In fact, for many years women were generally assigned to clerical duties or performed as matrons.

In 1910, social worker Alice S. Wells was appointed by the Los Angeles Police Department to the position of policewoman. She was a graduate theological student and social worker. She obtained her position by virtue of petitioning the city government for the job. Her petition was signed by many influential citizens that concurred with her point of view that with police powers (including the powers of arrest), a social worker could work more effectively in preventive and protective work for women and girls.

Officer Wells' duties included the supervision of women and girls in places of public recreation, such as dance halls, skating rinks, and theaters (Horne, 1980: 18). With the unique position she held, Wells immediately became a prime mover in the policewomen's movement. She had the support of the American Female Reform Society, the Women's Christian Temperance Union, and the League of Women Voters. Largely because of her efforts, within five years, 25 cities had appointed policewomen and, by the end of World War I, 200 cities had appointed policewomen (House, 1993: 139).

She immediately became the center of media attention and lectured throughout the United States and in other nations, and was called upon by numerous police departments to assist in the appointment of women. In 1915, Wells assisted in the creation of the International Association of Policewomen. The association functioned as a clearinghouse, providing information about the duties policewomen could perform, emphasizing preventive and protective services (Martin, 1979: 21). During the Great Depression, the organization lost its financial support and was not viable for an extended period. Many years later, the title of the organization was changed to International Association of Women Police in order to bring it into conformity with trends and changes occurring in our society. Currently, most women are appointed under the title of *police officer* not *policeman*.

In the early 1920s, August Vollmer, Chief of Police in Berkeley, California, created the first crime prevention unit in a police department. He appointed Elizabeth G. Lossing to head the new division. She held a B.S. from Mills College, and received additional education at the University of California, and the New York School of Social Work. She received additional training in psychiatric social work at the University of Michigan and the New School for Social Research. In Berkeley, her work consisted largely in dealing with pre-delinquency problems by bringing together all the agencies that could deal with the health, education, and morals of children.

World War I proved to be an event that changed women's lives in England and America, as it fostered the entry of additional women into the police service. Women performed a number of duties around military camps, including keeping prostitutes away from camps and supervising commercial and recreational locations near camps (Horne, 1980: 19).

The success of these women provided additional impetus in efforts to involve women in preventive and protective functions in police departments. In 1922, the International Association of Chiefs of Police, at its annual convention, passed a resolution supporting the use of policewomen. With this assistance and the increased knowledge that women had functioned successfully as police officers, the policewomen's movement became increasingly effective (Horne, 1980: 21).

In 1883, the Metropolitan Police in London appointed two women to supervise females that were detained in police stations. Subsequently, other women were employed part-time to assist male officers in the supervision of women in custody. In 1907, Eilide McDougall was hired by the Metropolitan Police Force to handle cases involving women and children. She was described as an experienced social worker who never viewed herself as a police officer (Carrier, 1988: 1). In 1914, the first uniformed policewoman was placed on actual police duty. This occurred because the Women's Central Committee of Grantham created a subcommittee and established a fund to maintain two policewomen. The civil and military authorities were required to make full use of the two women. In the city of Hull, policewomen arrested drunken and disorderly women for their own protection. They completed and signed the charge sheet and testified in court.

Mary S. Allen pointed out that "it was not unusual for a drunken woman to be so noisy and violent that she had to be half carried between two policewomen, whose progress through the streets was not made easier by the breathless interest of excited crowds, who would promptly attach themselves to the procession" (Allen, 1973: 46).

Before the end of World War I, policewomen in the United States served in numerous cities; their status in each community was varied. In some cities, they were sworn in and performed many police duties. In other cities, the functions that policewomen performed were limited because they did not have full police powers (Allen, 1973: 47). By 1924, the proportion of women police officers was 100 to 20,381 (0.5%), and by 1980, 8.5 percent of the officers were women (Carrier, 1988: xviii). On the other hand, when J. Edgar Hoover became the director of the FBI in 1924, he asked the only female agent, Alaska Davidson, to resign.

Susan Martin contended that the literature concerning policewomen has stressed the importance of their mission, that is, to perform as part of a larger social movement. It was a reform zeal second to none and was supported by an exceptional idealism.

Women wanted a different place in society, and it was felt that this could only be accomplished by altering society's major social institutions. Efforts to obtain employment in law enforcement agencies was part of the larger struggle to "save wayward youth and helpless women from the evils of industrialism, alcohol, and other abuses . . ." (Martin, 1980: 22). Entry into the police field was not easy for women. Barriers were numerous, including separate entrance requirements, limitations as to the number that could be employed and, of course, lower pay. Policewomen's duties were limited, but included performing delinquency prevention activities, dealing with lost children, handling various aspects of female criminality, and working with victims of sex offenses (Horne, 1980: 20). Eventually, preventive work proved to be acceptable for female officers because it was not viewed as "real" police work.

Anything that resembled social work was seen as "women's work." At the same time, male police officers questioned the physical ability of women, their emotional stability, and their capacity to work in a police environment. As more women entered the police service, integrating them into the department proved to be difficult. A number of larger agencies created separate women's bureaus. Consequently, many of the bureaus functioned as autonomous units and, in most instances, were totally isolated from the rest of the department. When not assigned to a bureau, the women functioned with limited organization and were powerless (Martin, 1980: 22).

In the early part of the twentieth century, the public administration reform movement swept the nation, including police agencies. People were dissatisfied with the results obtained from the traditional control methods used by the police, and prevention was given increasing importance. In 1915, one expert noted that one of the strategies the police should employ is crime prevention. He viewed this service as consisting of miscellaneous squads or units that would engage in identifying conditions creating crime and in suppressing offenses against the public morals (Fosdick, 1969: 268-270). The women's police movement grew in tandem with the larger public administration movement. Typical of the support for the women's police movement was that provided by Elmer D. Graper, who in 1921 published a handbook on American police administration. He stated that the use of policewomen was of recent origin and that it held great promise for the future. He noted that women's police work was frequently labeled *welfare work* and he saw it as means of widening the scope of police activities, including measures to prevent or minimize the factors contributing to vice, gambling, and lawlessness (Graper, 1921: 226-233).

Trained in social work, many of the early women officers possessed knowledge and skills that their male counterparts did not. The women used these assets to their advantage and carved out an important niche in the reform movement. As Susan Martin pointed out, they performed tasks that males did not want to do (such as clerical duties), and because of their specialization in protective activities, female officers were viewed as noncompetitive to the police tasks that were traditionally performed by male officers (Martin, 1980: 23-24). The 1930 census in the United States listed 1,534 policewomen and female detectives as being employed in public and private agencies. This number increased to 1,775 by 1940.

The Growth Period

The Great Depression and its severe impact on the well-being of the nation thwarted the hiring of policewomen. Women's bureaus were looked upon as organizational groups that could be eliminated so that all other governmental entities could survive. It was not until World War II that women saw an upsurge in their employment in law enforcement, but at the end of the war, many policewomen were laid off. By 1960, the census report indicated that the number of women employed in law enforcement had increased to 5,617, which was 2.3 percent of the total number of officers (Martin, 1980: 24). From 1940 on, some policewomen performed a few police duties other than in the area of prevention, but the evolution was extremely slow. Some departments had quotas and only hired a certain number of women, or they limited the hiring to replacements. Other departments resisted employing women. These departments took the position that women were not qualified to do police work. Starting in the late 1950s and the early 1960s, the trend reversed, and increased attention was given to the employment of women. Some state and federal agencies began employing women in sworn positions in the 1970s, but the majority of the women were employed by municipal and county agencies.

The traditional areas of employment for policewomen had been as clerks, secretaries, and switchboard operators. As their role expanded, policewomen were assigned to handle juvenile offenders or to deal with community relations. Furthermore, women began to participate in the special investigation of cases involving rape, obscene telephone calls, and voyeurism. Another area where the assistance of women was needed was in jails, where they became matrons. Slowly but surely, women were given assignments such as dispatching, criminalistics, and broader investigative duties.

The area of greatest controversy has always been the assignment of women to patrol. One of the first departments to make this assignment was Indianapolis, Indiana. In 1968, two female officers, Betty Blankenship and Elizabeth Coffal, began to patrol an assigned area and answer general purpose calls (Schulz, 1995: 1-7). As the two officers proved their effectiveness, additional women assumed patrol duties. New York City eliminated its women's bureau in 1968, and the members of the bureau were assigned to various duties inside the department. Within four years, women were assigned to patrol, and a study of their performance showed that they handled themselves very well (Horne, 1980: 25). By 1980, the New York City Police Department had 4,701 women working as civilians and 750 female police officers. Of those working as officers, 92 were inspectors or detectives and 13 were sergeants. There were also four female lieutenants, and two women held positions at a level above major (Police Executive Research Forum, 1981: 558).

In 1965, the Miami Police Department (after changing its entrance requirements) employed 29 women as sworn officers, and the majority of these women were assigned to field operations units. Fifteen years later, Miami had 212 women employed in civilian positions, and there were 47 women police officers.

Of those working as officers, seven functioned as first-line supervisors (Police Executive Research Forum, 1981: 558).

In 1967, the Metropolitan Police Department in Washington, D.C. dissolved its women's bureau, in which all the assigned policewomen had handled children and women offenders. A program was initiated to utilize women in nontraditional assignments, such as patrol duties. In an experiment conducted by the Police Foundation and the Urban Institute, the performances of male and female officers were compared. Women were found to have performed adequately. As of 1980, the Metropolitan Police Department had 277 female police officers. Twenty were either inspectors or detectives, and 16 were first-line supervisors. In addition, two women had attained the rank of lieutenant, and one was a captain (Police Executive Research Forum, 1981: 560). The adaptation of women to the Metropolitan Police Department was not easy, as pointed out by Susan Martin, who stated that female police officers had a great deal of difficulty in adapting to patrol and working with male officers. About one-half of the male officers were strongly opposed to working with female officers, (Martin, 1980: 49).

In 1973, the Los Angeles City Council approved a program for a *unisex* police department, scheduled to have women on patrol by the end of the year. A resolution was adopted to consolidate the classifications of "policeman" and "policewoman" into "police officers." Male and female officers would have equal opportunities for deployment and advancement (*Police Chief*, 1973: 3-4).

Catherine Milton, in her excellent study, *Women in Policing,* presented a very strong case supporting the position that women should serve in all law enforcement capacities and not limit their service to clerical and secretarial positions. She pointed out that (Milton, 1973: 3-4):

- Administrators are overlooking a significant resource of competent employees by de-emphasizing the potential role of women.

- Women are used extensively as line officers in Europe and Israel.

- A national commission recommended the recruitment of women into the police service.

- The number of women in police uniform is increasing steadily.

- Recruitment and promotional standards should be the same for men and women.

- The "weaker sex" is a misnomer and no longer a reason for overlooking the potential contributions of women to modern police service. (Milton cited the conclusion of the International Association of Chiefs of Police study which found that the highest single cause of police deaths was ambush, in which physical strength is not involved. The common denominator in all police murders has been the element of surprise.)

- Women want the job. There is increasing evidence that qualified women want to be police officers.

- By their visible presence and through their expanded contact with citizens, female officers have helped to improve the police image.

- Departments should train women officers to perform all police functions.

Table 8-1
Sex of Full-Time Sworn Personnel in Local Police Departments

Population Served	All sworn personnel		
	Total	Male	Female
All sizes	100%	91.2%	8.8%
1,000,000 or more	100	85.4	14.6
500,000 to 999,999	100	87.6	12.4
250,000 to 499,999	100	88.1	11.9
100,000 to 249,999	100	91.0	9.0
50,000 to 99,999	100	93.0	7.0
25,000 to 49,999	100	94.8	5.2
10,000 to 24,999	100	95.0	5.0
2,500 to 9,999	100	95.6	4.4
Less than 2,500	100	97.2	2.8

Source: U.S. Department of Justice (1996). *Local Police Departments, 1993.* Washington, DC: Bureau of Justice Statistics, USGPO, 3.

Transition

It is estimated that out of the total population in the United States, a little more than one-half are female. To ignore this large base of potential candidates is to ignore a majority of the population living in our nation. In 1994, out of a total employment of 130 million, 46 percent were female. Table 8-1 lists the number of employees in local law enforcement agencies by sex, according to population groups. The table shows that the larger the population served, the higher the percentage of female police officers. For example, in 63 cities with populations greater than 1,000,000, the percentage of female police officers was found to be 14.6, and in cities with populations between 500,000 and 999,999, the percentage was 12.4.

In smaller-sized departments, there are fewer women. In communities with populations from 10,000 to 24,999, only five percent were female officers. Overall, of 13,032 reporting agencies in 1992, the total percentage of female employees was 24, and there were 49,532 (7.9%) sworn female officers. When civilian employees of police agencies are included, the percentage of female employees increases dramatically to 63.5 percent (U.S. Department of Justice, 1996: 3).

A survey by the Department of Commerce in 1994 found that 13 percent of officer and detective positions were filled by females. Interestingly enough, 12 percent of police and detective supervisors were female. Additionally, 16 percent of the officers serving in the capacities of sheriffs, bailiffs, and other law enforcement positions were female (see Table 8-2).

Table 8-2
Percentage of Females in Selected Law Enforcement Occupations

Occupation	Percentage
Police and detectives	13
Sheriffs, bailiffs & other law enforcement	16
Supervisors of police and detectives	12

Source: Bureau of Labor Statistics (1995). *The Current Population Survey.* Washington, DC: Department of Commerce, USGPO, 1-38.

As women enter police service in ever-increasing numbers, they likewise will eventually assume positions of command in greater numbers. Obviously, evidence of this trend varies considerably from department to department. Currently in Palo Alto, California, out of 91 sworn positions, more than one-fourth are filled by female officers. In another California city, Chula Vista, out of 179 sworn positions, there are 20 women serving as peace officers. In the Sheriff's Department in Campbell County, Wyoming, the first woman joined the department in 1982 and currently females comprise 17 percent of the force (includes civilian positions). In Tallahassee, Florida, Syracuse, New York, and the Ohio State Highway Patrol, the hiring of women was the direct result of class action lawsuits and court decisions. In one survey, 11 percent of the respondents stated that they hired women because of government pressure, and seven percent stated they responded to outside pressure. It was also determined that 21 percent of the respondents stated that women have "a ways to go" to be totally integrated into the department (Sharp, 1993: 89-92).

Women have started to enter management ranks, and although the numbers are not large, it is anticipated that more women will become lieutenants or hold positions of higher rank. In Tallahassee, Florida, approximately 10 percent of the administrative positions are filled by women. In the Miami, Florida Police Department, about 16 percent of sworn officers are female and of those, five are serving in administrative positions (Sharp, 1995: 70). In Louisville, Kentucky, one-fifth of the administrative positions were found to be filled by women. It is anticipated that as more departments hire women in increasing numbers, they will move up through the ranks. In a survey of one metropolitan police department, the female officers expressed the opinion that they were confident that they would succeed in the department and gain a promotion. They felt that they would still have to struggle to gain the acceptance of their male counterparts, and also felt that they did not receive adequate credit for job performance even though they felt they were as competent as the male officers (Daum and Johns, 1994: 47-49).

In several instances, women have served as chief executive officers. One of the earlier female chiefs was Dolly Spencer, who served as chief of police in 1914. She received her appointment because of a gambling scandal. After two years, a newly elected mayor replaced her (Horne, 1980: 19). The woman who has held the position of chief in the largest city in the United States is Elizabeth Watson. She became the sixty-third police chief of the Houston Police Department (consisting of 3,900 total officers) in February 1990. She had been the first female captain on the department prior to assuming the position of deputy chief in 1987. After serving in Houston, she became the Chief in Austin, Texas, and currently is employed by the federal government. Another woman who served as the chief executive officer in Portland, Oregon was Penny Harrington. She served for 17 months, beginning in 1985, then resigned under fire (Schulz, 1995: 1-7). Harrington is currently the Director of the National Center for Women and Policing in Los Angeles. The center is the first nationwide resource for women police, law enforcement agencies, community leaders, and public officials seeking to increase the numbers of women police in their communities, raise awareness about the benefits of more women in policing, and improve police response to family violence (National Center for Women and Policing, 1995: 1). The following Feature sets forth the purpose and programs of the center.

Feature

National Center for Women and Policing

The purpose of the center is to significantly increase the numbers of women at all ranks in law enforcement as a strategy for reducing police brutality, improving police response to crimes of violence against women, and improving community-police relations. The center will achieve its purpose by working with women police, police agencies, and community and public leaders across the country to:

- Conduct educational campaigns to raise awareness among decisionmakers and the general public about the benefits of increasing the numbers of women in policing.

- Promote innovative action strategies to increase the numbers of women in policing and women's representation in policy-making positions.

- Conduct training programs for community and women leaders seeking reform.

- Promote specialized Family Violence Units within law enforcement agencies as a strategy for more effective police response to family violence crimes.

- Develop a *pro bono* attorney network for women in law enforcement agencies experiencing sexual harassment and discrimination.

- Publish and disseminate research and educational materials on women in policing.

Currently, the only head of a large police agency is Beverly J. Harvard, chief of police in Atlanta, Georgia. She is the first African-American woman to assume a leadership position in a large city. She had two years on a beat before moving to a desk job. Her assignments ranged from affirmative action to deputy chief of criminal investigation. She has two degrees, sociology and public administration, and has expressed the belief that because she is a woman she has been second-guessed throughout her career, but she has endured and proven to be a strong leader of the Atlanta Police Department. Currently, there are 58 women holding executive-level law enforcement positions across the country. In 1996, the National Sheriff's Association reported that, in the United States, 22 of the 3,094 sheriffs were female. One of these chief executive officers, Jacqueline Barrett, received nationwide publicity in 1992 as the first African-American female sheriff in the nation (Schmitt, 1996: 62-69).

Adjusting to a Male-Dominated Police Culture

The majority of women that entered law enforcement during its transition stage from a male-dominated occupational area have felt the impact of police culture. As minorities, women have been subjected to unyielding pressure from male officers and have been the objects of discrimination. For decades, law enforcement has portrayed the occupation as needing employees that are the equivalent of Dirty Harry: tall, tough, and ready to brawl. This macho ideal has made it difficult for women who have entered police service. As long as women stayed in their "place" and worked only with female offenders and children, they were accepted with reluctance and with minimal resistance. But when women entered patrol and investigative services, they crossed the threshold of a male-dominated world. Entry into patrol has been especially difficult for women. Many women find that they do not receive positive feedback from supervisors and fellow officers. Traditional values inculcated through the women's growing years compete and conflict with the newly defined role that she is attempting to assume in the police environment. Women raised to be compassionate, thoughtful, considerate, and motherly enter a working environment filled with pranks, profanity, and violence.

While law enforcement work can be infinitely boring at times, it can also be intense. Traumatized victims and witnesses must be interviewed. Some investigations involve minute details of sexual acts or other sensitive information. Furthermore, suspects must be restrained, as many of them are mentally unbalanced or under the influence of alcohol or drugs. Dealing with the derelicts and those deviating from society's norms can prove to be devastating (if not debilitating), as a new officer attempts to adjust to the job.

In the hiring process, there are usually a number of men that do not make it through the academy or the probationary period and are dismissed. Those that fail are described as "not having what it takes." The same situation applies to female police officers. A certain percentage fail at the academy; others are unable to successfully complete probation. A large majority of female candidates, however, like their male counterparts, become outstanding officers. When a woman fails, the response of male officers is often that "a woman should not have been hired in the first place" (Drummond, 1988: 93).

On entering the police service, women go through three stages. These stages can vary in length and/or intensity from individual to individual, and they can overlap. The initial stage is described as the *honeymoon stage*. It is a period of adjustment to the environment of the academy and the supervising tactical officer. After the initial introduction to the system, the officer (on probation) spends considerable time under the tutelage of one or more Field Training Officers (FTOs). Assuming that the candidate becomes reasonably adjusted to the initiation process, she then begins to receive positive feedback as she adapts to the challenges presented by the new occupation. In time, fears are overcome as successes occur and trepidation dissipates. Positive reinforcement provides a foundation, allowing the new officer to become self-confident. She slowly begins to realize that she can handle the demands of the job, a home life, and outside interests.

Over a period of time, the new officer may begin to doubt her ability to accept the new role; she now enters what is called the *ambivalent stage*. Traditional values, inculcated over a lifetime, can cause the officer to suffer from internal conflict as she attempts to assume the role demanded by the new occupation. Unusual demands can be placed on her, and these demands originate not only from the job but from her family. If not careful, she may become the victim of the *superwoman syndrome*. This condition, evidenced by a need to be all things to all people, can lead to a number of ailments, such as exhaustion or a sense of frustration (see Chapter 10 for a further discussion of stress).

The last stage that the female officer enters is the *transition stage*. This is a period when internal conflicts are resolved. As she begins to perform effectively, the officer acquires a feeling of status and self-fulfillment. Psychological rewards come from a job well done. The officer is motivated as she becomes committed to the job, and she really finds meaning in the work that she is doing. Making a good "bust," saving a life, assisting someone who needs help, and defusing a potentially violent family dispute are all experiences that make the job worthwhile and develop a sense of worth and self-esteem. Slowly but surely, the home and family life become only one of the numerous sources of role satisfaction for the officer (More and Wegener, 1992: 228-238).

A modification of the above stages is what is described as the *police personality*, which is characterized by an inherent need to control the situation. The officer with this "personality" has an authoritarian attitude and a need to be assertive and physically aggressive at certain times. These characteristics reflect society's view of the male role rather than the female role (Berg and Budnick, 1986: 182).

The female officer may experience true internal conflict as she tries to adapt to the stereotype of the male police personality. The female officer faces the difficult choice of retaining her basic femininity or emulating one or more aspects of the male police personality. The latter choice is termed *defeminization*. When a woman adjusts in this manner to the police occupation, she does so under the belief that male officers will accept her more readily. Her adjustment also makes it easier to establish a more trusting relationship (Martin, 1979: 88). One study supported this position, pointing out that female academy students who exhibited masculine behavior tended to get along better with their male counterparts (Gross, 1981: 4).

This presents a dilemma to female officers. If they retain their femininity, in all probability, their careers will be limited as long as the department is dominated by a system that rewards the "male" police personality. Female officers may be shunted to specialized jobs, such as juvenile work, where promotions are limited. Performance in a line function (in most instances) leads more readily to consideration for supervisory or managerial positions (Berg and Budnick, 1986: 174-182).

Other dilemmas await female officers in some agencies and communities. Some face discrimination not only by the department, but by members of the community. Women that serve in line positions are so new to the police field that they have numerous obstacles to overcome. The dominant obstacle is probably the attitude of male officers. The male attitude can be summed up as "police work is man's work" (Horne, 1980: 32).

A somewhat more rational argument against hiring females is that women are not physically qualified to serve as police officers. Current information supports the position that, in general, women have limited upper body and overall strength compared to men. However, experts have found that women can attain (through training) a level of fitness that is well within the requirements of contemporary police work.

Contrary to popular belief, policing is not always a physically demanding occupation. There are, of course, times when it becomes necessary for an officer to perform a physically demanding task, such as subduing a large or strong suspect or saving someone in a burning building, but such events do not occur frequently.

Because the preponderance of sworn officers are male, the attitude of male officers toward female officers remains important. Many male officers feel that women are not physically or psychologically able to handle "real" police work. They believe that if departments are forced to accept women, the women should serve in limited capacities and should never be allowed to serve in patrol or specialized units like SWAT teams. Not every male officer resists the entry of women into his department, but when resistance occurs, it can range from rational responses to illogical reactions.

In 1995, news reports surfaced that described tape-recorded interviews between Mark Fuhrman and Laura McKinny, an aspiring screenwriter. Fuhrman's comments referred to systematic misconduct within the Los Angeles Police Department. During the investigation of statements by Fuhrman, the Internal Affairs Division (IAD) found that four officers of the West Los Angeles Division created an association. This group became known as Men Against Women (MAW) and set out to create a hostile working environment for female officers. Officers that were interviewed said the working environment was unfriendly and aloof toward female officers. It was found that the conduct of MAW inhibited some women from safely and effectively performing their duties and created fear in many women that these male officers would not provide backup if they requested it in the field. Further, investigators determined that the MAW officers would ostracize male officers who did not support their boycott against female officers.

For the eight years following the initial investigation into MAW, the Los Angeles Police Department as a whole recognized the need to take more initiative in handling issues related to sexual harassment. In the Los Angeles Police Department, the type of sexual harassment used in West Los Angeles was about power—pure and simple. It was about the ability of the abuser to exert power over the abused. Supervisors have been known to show partiality to men in assigning officers to shifts, in assigning preferred beats, and in selecting officers for special assignments. The nature and type of discrimination varies considerably, depending upon the male involved. Certainly that recognition was bolstered by several court decisions in which employing agencies and supervisors themselves were held liable for failing to act when notified or becoming aware of harassment in the workplace. As a result, policies and procedures were changed and training was provided (Los Angeles Police Department, 1997: 1-69).

The extent to which discrimination can be carried out is illustrated by a study of a west coast police department in which the lack of respect and bad manners directed toward female officers included the use of the following expressions and terms: *c---, runt, pencilneck, gash,* and *wimp woman.* Abusive actions recorded in the study include placing a work application for a fast food restaurant, and later, a dead rat, in a female officer's departmental mailbox. These examples of abuse represent only a small part of what women who enter police work have had to endure (Drummond, 1988: 99).

Every officer must have a reserve of strength in order to respond to an emergency. Experts believe that, with careful and continuous training, an officer can maintain physical fitness. As a minimum requirement, an officer should exercise aerobically at least three times per week, with each session lasting from 20 to 40 minutes, in order to maintain a good level of fitness. Women are no exception. In fact, they need to participate in a physical training program that ensures that they can successfully perform as a police officer.

In the Long Beach study, when female officers were interviewed about their adjustment to police work, they stated that the best parts of police work included (Drummond, 1988: 97-98):

- The people with whom you work: the camaraderie; working with an outstanding partner; sharing tough and frightening circumstances; and working around men.

- The variety of work.

On the other hand, the female officers described the worst parts of police work as including:

- Poor working hours and days off that require missing family and community events.

- Stress on marriage and the family.

- Fear of the unknown.

- Fear of offering opinions.

- Working with an unlikeable partner.

- Men who are so macho that they cannot shed a tear and they have nothing good to say about anyone.

- The limited number of people that can give help and support.

- Internal strife (even the non-sworn could feel this).

- Arriving at a call and finding a dead cop.

- A "grapevine" that spreads malicious stories.

Interestingly enough, the female officers in the Long Beach Police Department study were nearly unanimous in stating that the most important and feasible remedy to the problems facing them in their work was the promotion of communication between the sexes. It was felt that communication could best be accomplished through carefully designed training programs.

It should be noted that women have brought a different set of tools to police work. They introduced the working police to good manners including clean language, courtesy, compassion, thoughtfulness, dignity, consideration for others, and improved communication as a means to solve problems (Drummond, 1988: 93-100). In a recent study, it was found that there are barriers for women who become police officers. Two of the most prominent barriers were found to be the stereotyping of female police officers by male officers and the preconception they have about female officers. Additionally, it was found that a barrier for female officers was their lack of knowledge of organizational politics. They were clearly not part of the informal organizational network, and the only hope is that over time this barrier will be eliminated (Molinaro, 1997: 62-66).

Typical of the problems that can occur are the conditions found in the Los Angeles Sheriff's Department. In a comprehensive investigation of the department, it was found that women found it very difficult to bring complaints of gender discrimination or sexual harassment. To do so, it was necessary to file a complaint that was invariably made public. Filing a complaint was widely perceived as a way to ruin one's career and give one a "jacket" as a troublemaker. The department did not have a policy that provided for achieving gender balance among different units. Women deputies comprised 12.5 percent of sworn personnel, but in six stations less than seven percent of the officers were female. No women were assigned to the elite Special Enforcement Bureau, which consisted of 91 sworn officers. The study found that job transfer policies posed significant barriers to women. The movement of officers within the department was far too dependent upon personnel connections, making such movement difficult for women. The "old boy" system dominated the transfer process and prevented desired movement by deputies without personal connections, who tended to disproportionately to be women (Kolts, 1992: 310-322).

Sexual Harassment

As more women now perform law enforcement duties, sexual harassment occurs more frequently than it did in the past. It is increasingly common for police agencies to strive for the creation of a working environment that is free of sexual harassment (Heckeroth, 1997: 56-62). Studies suggest that 40 percent of working women, and five to 10 percent of men have experienced some type of sexual harassment in the workplace (Thomann, Strickland, and Gibbons, 1989: 34-43). The public sector is not exempt. There are increasing numbers of complaints at every level of government.

The overwhelming number of incidents involved women complaining about unwanted attention from men. It is interesting to note that these women felt most vulnerable in working environments dominated by men. This is especially true in law enforcement, which still projects a masculine culture and a quasi-military administrative structure. Loyalty, teamwork, and the code of silence prevail in many law enforcement agencies.

The realities of police work foster a climate in which male officers ignore acts of sexual harassment. Loyalty to the group is more important than loyalty to an individual, particularly a female officer. An officer must depend upon other officers for mutual safety—consequently, it is becomes almost essential to ignore every form of sexual harassment. Group loyalty can supersede an officer's commitment to the profession of law enforcement. In fact, group loyalty can become a barrier to the implementation of a sexual harassment policy.

During 1994, the U.S. Equal Employment Opportunity Commission received 514 complaints from local and state law enforcement personnel that were sex-based charges This was 30.3 percent of all charges received (Gonzales, 1996: 1-2). Unfortunately, statistics are not available to reflect the number of complaints filed with individual law enforcement agencies.

Agencies should develop clear policies and procedures after taking into consideration a number of factors. First, every effort must be made to identify conduct that constitutes sexual harassment. Consideration should also be given to the creation of a training program, so that all employees are fully cognizant of what constitutes sexual harassment. It is imperative that the policy prohibit the offensive conduct and provide for remedial and punitive measures. In addition, a grievance procedure should be established, along with guidelines for the thorough and timely investigation of sexual harassment complaints (Higginbotham, 1988: 28-29). The following Feature sets forth some myths and facts about sexual harassment.

Feature

Some Myths and Facts About Sexual Harassment

MYTH: So-called sexual harassment is natural, normal behavior. People should feel complimented that they are considered desirable and attractive.

FACT: Sexual harassment is a power play that uses sexually directed behavior as a weapon. It is an inappropriate way to control another person through degradation and humiliation. It is not part of developing healthy human relationships, which are based on mutual caring and respect.

MYTH: Women should be held responsible for being sexually harassed because of their provocative dress, speech, and behavior.

FACT: The most common motivations for sexual harassment are power and aggression, not sexual desire. Victims who believe this myth have tried unsuccessfully to stop the harassment by making their physical appearance as unattractive as possible and by behaving in ways that are intended to discourage the harassment. Sexual harassment victims are not always young, physically attractive people.

MYTH: If one employee asks another employee for a date, this may be grounds for sexual harassment charges.

FACT: There is no sexual harassment in asking a co-worker for a date, so long as there is no coercion. The potential for sexual harassment arises when the person asked says no. Rejection is not cause to retaliate through sexual harassment. When a person makes it clear that the advances of the other person are unwelcome, his or her wishes must be respected.

MYTH: Women that enter a field that is dominated by men should expect to tolerate rough language, dirty jokes, and hazing. The women are not being treated any differently than the men treat each other.

FACT: This is a myth because the new woman in a previously all-male environment often is not treated as "one of the boys." Her treatment is not business as usual, that is, the men escalate the foul language or sexual conduct to test her or to make it difficult for her to succeed. While church-picnic behavior is not necessary, intensified and continued sexually directed conduct has been held to be sexual harassment. Being a woman in a nontraditional job is difficult. Women that take these types of jobs need support from their co-workers.

Source: Adapted from American Federation of State, County and Municipal Employees, *Stopping Sexual Harassment—An AFSCME Guide*, Washington, DC: AFSCME. Reprinted with permission.

Definition

A precise definition of what constitutes sexual harassment is not easily composed. On the surface, the term is more easily recognized than defined. Sexual harassment is a form of sex discrimination in violation of Title VII of the Civil Rights Act of 1964 (as amended). Specific guidelines on the types of conduct that constitute sexual harassment are provided in a publication of the Equal Employment Opportunity Commission:

Unwelcome sexual advances, requests for sexual favors, and other verbal or physical conduct of a sexual nature constitute sexual harassment when submission or rejection of this conduct explicitly or implicitly affects an individual's employment, unreasonably interferes with an individual's work performance, or creates an intimidating, hostile, or offensive work environment (EEOC, no date: 1).

Sexual harassment can occur in a variety of circumstances. It includes, but is not limited to:

- The victim as well as the harasser may be a woman or a man. The victim does not have to be of the opposite sex.

- The harasser can be the victim's supervisor, an agent of the employer, a supervisor in another area, a co-worker, or a non-employee.

- The victim does not have to be the person harassed, but can be anyone affected by the offensive conduct.

- Unlawful sexual harassment can occur without economic injury to or discharge of the victim.

- The victim has a responsibility to establish that the harasser's conduct is unwelcome.

It is in the victim's best interest to inform the harasser that the conduct is unwelcome and must stop. The victim should use any complaint mechanism or grievance system available.

Typically, sexual harassment occurs in one of two ways:

Quid Pro Quo Harassment. Unwelcome sexual advances, requests for sexual favors and other verbal or physical conduct of a sexual nature constitute sexual harassment when: (1) submission to such conduct is made either explicitly or implicitly a term or condition of an individuals employment; (2) submission to or rejection of such conduct by an individual is used as the basis for employment decisions affecting such individuals . . .

This form of harassment forces the employee to choose between the job and refusing to comply with the demands. When access to equal opportunities are blocked for refusing to capitulate to such demands, Title VII has been violated. The sexual advances must be *unwelcome*, which means undesired, uninvited, and unappreciated. The advances should also be *offensive*, although offensive behavior is harder to define because of its subjective nature (Rubin, 1995: 2-5).

Hostile Work Environment. This type of conduct occurs when such conduct has the purpose or effect of unreasonably interfering with an individual's work performance or creating an intimidating, hostile, or offensive work environment.

This form of sexual harassment was recognized by the United States Supreme Court in the case of *Meritor Savings Bank v. Vinson*, 106 S. Ct. 2399 (1986), which held that sexual harassment does not have to result in economic damage to the victim. The Court also made it clear that the hallmark of sexual harassment in a hostile work environment is that the conduct is *unwelcome*. A hostile work environment exists when the victim's employment is changed. This type of environment often entails repeated incidents or a series of events (Rubin, 1995: 1-7).

Police departments deal with sexual harassment by creating procedures that delineate conduct that is prohibited. Typical of such policy in this area is that set forth in Figure 8-2.

Figure 8-2
Prohibited Conduct

1. Expressed bias in the workplace, including any behavior that is potentially offensive to any employee on the basis of their protected status. Examples of such expressions of bias include, but are not limited to:
    *   Using degrading words, offensive slang labels or names, or profanity describing a person's protected status.
    *   Sexually suggestive, obscene, or lewd "jokes" or comments, or "jokes" or comments about a person's protected status.
    *   Inappropriate posters or posted "jokes."

2. Examples of such sexual harassment in the workplace include, but are not limited to:
    *   Sexually suggestive, obscene, or lewd comments or invitation.
    *   Gender related labels, such as "honey," "sweetie," "cutie," "boy," and "girl."
    *   Asking for sexual favors and implying that there will be economic or employment benefits.
    *   Leering, ogling, or drawing attention to a person's body.
    *   Sexual advances.
    *   Introduction into the workplace of pornographic pictures or written material, except in the course of official police investigations.

3. Failure to cooperate in any investigation of an EEO violation.

4. Taking any retaliatory action of any kind against any employee who has sought redress, filed a report, or made an inquiry concerning EEO matters, cooperated in an investigation, or otherwise participated in any way with the procedures outlined in this section.

Source: Tucson Police Department (1997). *Tucson Police Department Procedures,* Vol. I, 92-F-01.

Because a criminal justice agency may be liable when one employee sexually harasses another, it is important to have a policy that defines and prohibits sexual harassment. Failure to have such a policy may be construed as deliberate indifference by the agency, thus exposing it to liability. Those claiming sexual harassment will not have to prove economic injury, nor will they have to show severe psychological injury, in order to prevail (*Harris v. Forklift, Inc.,* 114 S. Ct. 367 [1993]).

Even when such a policy exists, the agency may nevertheless be held liable. It may also make no difference whether the employer knew or did not know of the offending conduct or events that took place. In most cases, employers will be liable for the acts of their supervisory employees.

Thus, complaints of sexual harassment should be taken seriously and acted upon immediately. Every complaint should be followed up, no matter how trivial or unlikely it may seem. It is a good idea to interview witnesses in private, maintain confidentiality, and document every step of the investigation. It is not uncommon for victims of sexual harassment to minimize the incident or fail to report it, all because of the embarrassing and personal nature of the complaint. Moreover, many victims are afraid of retaliation, reprisals, or even termination if they report the problem. For these reasons, discretion, sensitivity, and tact must be used when investigating and trying to remedy such claims. Remedial action may include warnings, reprimands, suspension, and dismissal. While the harshest penalty is not always required, aggressive remedial action is recommended whenever harassment is found (*Intlekofer v. Turnage,* 973 F.2d 773, [9th Cir. 1992]).

Prevention is the best tool to avert sexual harassment in the workplace. Employers should take the steps necessary to prevent sexual harassment from occurring. Employees should be informed of their rights, a complaint or grievance process should be established, and immediate and appropriate action should be taken when an employee complains. In the event that sexual harassment charges are not handled satisfactorily at the local level, the victim may file a charge of sexual harassment at any field office of the U.S. Equal Employment Opportunity Commission. A victim may also file suit under state laws that protect against assault, battery, intentional infliction of emotional distress, or intentional interference with an employment contract. If the person being harassed is subjected to sexual contact, there may be a violation of the criminal law against sexual assault. An interesting variable is that an employer may be held liable for acts of sexual harassment regardless of whether the employer knew or should have known of its occurrence (Vartanian 1992: 27). The following Features describe cases in which two different cities settled sexual harassment lawsuits brought by female police officers.

Feature

City to Pay Ex-Cop in Harassment Case

The City of San Jose agreed to pay a former police officer $350,000 to settle a lawsuit in which she claimed that management failed to protect her from harassment after she accused a sergeant of sexually assaulting her during an undercover assignment. The female officer stated that a sergeant kissed her, fondled her, and threw her onto a bed against her will while they were in a house conducting a burglary sting operation.

Harassment, she claimed, began with a broken chair at her desk and escalated into open statements of animosity and instances in which anonymous officers made kissing sounds over the police radio after she was called or while she spoke.

The former officer believes that she was being harassed for violating the officers' *code of silence,* an unwritten rule that cops should never report wrongdoing by their fellow officers. She reported the hostile treatment, but commanders did nothing about it. She was granted a disability retirement.

Source: Adapted from *San Jose Mercury News* (1990). "S.J. to Pay Ex-cop in Harassment Case." June 30:1B-4B. Reprinted with permission.

Feature

Former Detroit Policewoman Wins Half Million Dollars in Sexual Harassment Suit

A Michigan court awarded almost half a million dollars to former policewoman Cheryl Gomez-Preston. The award is one of the largest fines ever levied against a major urban police department for sexual harassment. The award marks the end of a six-year court battle to recognize the psychological and physical trauma that Gomez-Preston suffered in her 11-year tenure as a Detroit police officer. She was treated in a mental hospital and spent an extended time recuperating from a nervous breakdown induced by a command rank supervisor after Gomez-Preston refused his sexual advances. The commander, Mac Douglas, was also named in the civil suit.

Gomez-Preston was harassed by other squad members and she received racial hate mail and death threats. In one instance, she was deserted by her partner and other fellow officers in a dark alley while in pursuit of an armed robbery suspect. "At that time, I was hit with a large dose of reality," Gomez-Preston says. "These people meant business; they were really out to hurt me."

The ordeal cost Gomez-Preston her job, put tremendous strains on her marriage, and resulted in temporary separation from her children. At one point, she pulled out her service revolver and contemplated suicide. But Gomez-Preston decided to fight back in the courts and for her life. She started a self-help group for victims of sexual harassment in the workplace.

Gomez-Preston is now part of a research study on severe forms of sexual harassment. Preliminary results show that this kind of harassment can cause psychological and emotional devastation that is similar to the post-traumatic stress syndrome suffered by Vietnam veterans.

Source: Cheryl Gomez-Preston (no date). "Former Detroit Policewomen Wins Half Million Dollars in Sexual Harassment Suit." Press Release. Philadelphia, PA: Association for the Sexually Harassed, P.O. Box 27235, 19118, (215) 952-8037.

Cheryl Gomez-Preston currently conducts seminars on sexual harassment. Through her Association For The Sexually Harassed she works to help others. She believes that women in traditionally male-dominated jobs are more likely to be harassed (Lewis, 1993: 9A.)

Summary

Women have been used as spies, undercover agents, and detectives throughout history, but not until recent times did they enter the police service as sworn officers. At the turn of the twentieth century, the suffrage movements in Great Britain and the United States were instrumental in introducing women into police agencies. The International Association of Policewomen came into existence in 1915 and served as a clearinghouse that provided information about the tasks that policewomen could perform.

Initially, females performed preventive and protective duties, and for many years, they functioned as social workers in the police field. From 1940 on, the number of women in police service increased slowly, but it was not until the late 1950s and early 1960s that expanded attention was given to the employment of women.

The traditional areas of employment for women were as clerks, secretaries, and switchboard operators. Over many years, increasing numbers of women were assigned to handle juvenile offenders or to deal with community relations. Occasionally, women participated in special investigations of cases involving rape, obscene telephone calls, and voyeurism. It was not until 1968 in Indianapolis that women were assigned to patrol. At about the same time, a number of major departments dissolved separate women's bureaus and assigned women to patrol and other line units. Part of the impetus for these developments was the fact that several national commissions had recommended broadening the role of female officers.

In 1973, author Catherine Milton released a study that strongly supported the use of women in all capacities of law enforcement. Currently it is estimated that there are more than 50,000 sworn female officers serving in law enforcement agencies at local and state levels. Slowly but surely, women have also attained supervisory and command positions in law enforcement. For instance, in 1990, Elizabeth Watson was appointed to the position of chief of police in Houston, Texas, where she administered an agency of 3,900 officers.

The majority of women entering law enforcement have felt the impact of the male-dominated police culture. The dominant obstacle that women have had to overcome is the attitude of male officers. The male attitude can be summed up as: "police work is man's work." Many male officers feel that women are not physically or emotionally able to handle "real" police work. Women who have been successful in adjusting to police work feel that working relationships can be improved if there is open communication between male and female officers. These women contend that carefully designed training programs would serve as the vehicle for improving communication.

As more women enter the police service, sexual harassment occurs more frequently. In the last year for which statistics are available, the U.S. Equal Employment Opportunity Commission received 169 complaints from law enforcement personnel charging sexual harassment. Unfortunately, statistics are not available to reflect the number of complaints filed with individual law enforcement agencies. However, the problem is significant enough that agencies should develop clear-cut policies and procedures for handling complaints. Consideration should also be given to the creation of training programs, so that all employees are fully cognizant of what constitutes sexual harassment and of the techniques used in investigating such complaints.

References

Allen, Mary S. (1973). *The Pioneer Policewoman.* New York: AMS Press, 46.

American Federation of State, County, and Municipal Employees (no date). *Stopping Sexual Harassment—An AFSCME Guide.* Washington, DC: AFSCME, 1-31.

Berg, Bruce L. and Kimberly L. Budnick (1986). "Defeminization of Women in Law Enforcement: A New Twist in the Traditional Police Personality." *Journal of Police Science and Administration,* Vol. 14, No. 4:174-182.

Bureau of Labor Statistics (1995). *The Current Population Survey.* Washington, DC: Department of Commerce, USGPO, 1-38.

Carrier, John (1988). *The Campaign for the Employment of Women as Police Officers.* Brookfield, VT: Gower Publishing, xv, xvii, xviii, and 1.

Daum, James M. and Cindy M. Johns (1994). "Police Work From a Woman's Perspective." *The Police Chief,* Vol. LXI, No. 9:46-49.

Drummond, Douglas S. (1988). *Law Enforcement: The Cultural Impact of an Occupation.* Santa Ana, CA: Doctoral Project, August Vollmer University, 93-100.

Equal Employment Opportunity Commission (no date). *Facts About Sexual Harassment.* Washington, DC: Equal Employment Opportunity Commission.

Fosdick, Raymond B. (1969). *American Police Systems.* Montclair, NJ: Patterson Smith, 268-270.

Gonzales, Claire (1996). *Correspondence.* Washington, DC: U.S. Equal Employment Opportunity Commission, January 16:1-2.

Graper, Elmer D. (1921). *American Police Administration.* New York: Macmillan, 226-233.

Gross, S. (1981). *Socialization into Law Enforcement: The Female Police Recruit.* Miami, FL: Southeastern Institute of Criminal Justice, 4.

Harris v. Forklift, Inc., 114 S. Ct. 367 (1993).

Heckeroth, Sally and A. Michael Barker (1997). "Proactive Policies Deter Sexual Harassment." *Law and Order,* Vol. 45, No. 10:56-62.

Higginbotham, Jeffrey (1988). "Sexual Harassment in the Police Station." *FBI Law Enforcement Bulletin,* Vol. 58, No. 9:28-29.

Horne, Peter (1980). *Women in Law Enforcement.* Springfield, IL: Charles C Thomas, 17-32.

House, Cathryn H. (1993). "The Changing Role of Women in Law Enforcement." *The Police Chief,* Vol. LX, No. 10:1-3.

Intlekofer v. Turnage, 973 F.2d 773 (9th Cir. 1992).

Kolts, James G. (July 1992). *The Los Angeles Sheriff's Department.* Los Angeles, CA: Los Angeles County, 310-320.

Lewis, Claude (1993). "Preventing Sexual Harassment Means Understanding It." *Arizona Daily Star,* March 10:9A.

Los Angeles Police Department (1997). *Mark Fuhrman Task Force, Executive Summary.* Los Angeles, CA: Los Angeles Police Department, 1-69.

Martin, S. (1980). "Policewomen and Policewoman: Occupational Role, Dilemmas, and Choice of Female Officers." *Journal of Police Science and Administration,* Vol. 7, No. 3:21.

Meritor Savings Bank v. Vinson, 477 U.S. 57, 40 FEP Cases 1505, 106 S. Ct. 2399 (1986).

Milton, Catherine (1973). *Women in Policing.* Washington, DC: Police Foundation, 3-4.

Molinaro, L.A. (1997). "Advancement of Women in Law Enforcement." *Law and Order,* Vol. 45, No. 8:62-70.

More, Harry, W. and W. Fred Wegener (1992). *Behavioral Police Management*, Second Edition. New York: Macmillan Publishing, 228-238.

National Center for Women in Policing (February 1995). *Prospectus* (Brochure). Los Angeles, CA: A Project of the Feminist Majority Foundation, 1-4.

Police Chief (1973). "Los Angeles Councilmen Approve 'Unisex' Police Department." Vol. XXVI-II, No. 10:3-4.

Police Executive Research Forum (1981). *Survey of Police Operational and Administrative Practices—1981.* Washington, DC: Police Foundation, 558-560.

Rubin, Paula N. (1995). *Civil Rights and Criminal Justice: Employment Discrimination Overview.* Washington, DC: National Institute of Justice, 1-7.

San Jose Mercury News (1990). "S.J. to Pay Ex-cop in Harassment Case." June 30:1B and 4B.

Schmitt, Sheila (1996). "Sheriff Mom: Women Are Gaining in Numbers in a Traditionally Male Post." *Law and Order,* Vol. 44, No. 1:62-69.

Schulz, Dorothy Moses (1995). *From Social Worker to Crime-fighter: Women in United States Municipal Policing.* Westport, CT: Praeger, 1-7.

Segrave, Kerry (1995). *Policewomen: A History.* Jefferson, NC: McFarland & Company, 107-135.

Sharp, Arthur G. (1993) "Recruiting (& Retaining) Women Officers." *Law and Order,* Vol. 41, No. 5:89-92.

Sharp, Arthur G. (1995). "Rising Through the Ranks." *Law and Order,* Vol. 43, No. 5:70-74.

Thomann, Daniel A. and Tina M. Serritella (1994). "Preventing Sexual Harassment in Law Enforcement Agencies." *The Police Chief,* Vol. LXI, No. 9:31-35.

Thomann, Daniel A., D.E. Strickland, and J.L. Gibbons (1989). "An Organizational Development Approach to Preventing Sexual Harassment: Developing Shared Commitment Through Awareness Training." *College and University Personnel Association Journal,* Vol. 29, Vol. 3:34-43.

Tucson Police Department (1997). *Tucson Police Department Procedures*, Vol. I, 92-F-01. Tucson, AZ: Tucson Police Department.

U.S. Department of Justice (1996). *Local Police Departments, 1993.* Washington, DC: Bureau of Justice Statistics, USGPO, 3.

Vartanian, Elsie (1992). *A Working Woman's Guide to Her Job Rights,* Leaflet 55. Washington, DC: Department of Labor, USGPO, 27.

EQUALITY OF OPPORTUNITY: DISCRIMINATION AND ITS RESOLUTION

9

The study of this chapter will enable you to:

1. Describe the nature and extent of discrimination in law enforcement.

2. Distinguish between discrimination and prejudice.

3. Define *ethnocentrism*.

4. List five types of conduct prohibited by Title VII.

5. Identify key aspects of the Pregnancy and Maternity Act.

6. Define *bona fide occupational qualification*.

7. Describe how to prepare a *utilization analysis*.

8. Identify the primary consideration spelled out in the Age Discrimination Act.

9. Describe what constitutes religious discrimination.

10. Distinguish between a quota and a goal.

11. Write a short essay describing arguments against affirmative action.

12. Write a short speech supporting affirmative action.

13. Compare the trends in hiring women and minorities.

During this critical period, how the nation responds to its increasingly diverse population, the well-documented racial and ethnic tensions, and the frustration of unmet needs in our cities, will determine the future well-being and progress, not only of the urban communities, but of the nation as a whole (Fletcher, 1993: 1). In America's highly pluralistic society, discrimination based on race and sex has persisted over the years as a human relations problem. In spite of efforts to rectify the injustice created by discrimination, it continues to be a significant social problem. Discrimination is, in fact, part of our lifestyle, and it actually guides our interpersonal relationships with minorities (*de facto* discrimination). Additionally, discrimination has been institutionalized by our legal system (*de jure* discrimination). Sanctioned by the law, the government accepted and supported the social and political structure that discriminated against minorities. In our early history, slavery was supported by the government. Over the years, restrictive immigration laws have discriminated against certain racial and ethnic groups. Deep-seated prejudices based on race, sex, religion, and color fostered discrimination that permeated every facet of American life (More and Wegener, 1996: 389).

The *W*hite, *A*nglo-*S*axon, *P*rotestant (WASP) value system set the moral tone that guided our society. This process ensured that political power remained a tool of the majority. Subsequently, police departments followed this and supported the male-dominated political establishment. The objectives were to maintain the status quo and to never rock the boat. Comparatively, the enforcement of laws was applied differently in the white community than in minority communities. White citizens received the full benefits of the constitutional guarantees of due process and equal protection of the law. The reality of the situation proved to be that the Bill of Rights was meaningless in many minority neighborhoods. Rights that were guaranteed to the dominant group were denied to members of minority groups.

During this unsettled era, African-Americans had to sit at the back of buses, drink from specified water fountains, eat at designated locations, and use different bathroom facilities. Even the military followed suit. As recently as the Korean War (early 1950s), some military units were segregated and, in most instances, the officers were white. Employment and educational opportunities were limited for African-Americans.

The same conditions applied to law enforcement until the color barrier was breached. In 1944, five African-Americans were appointed to the Miami, Florida Police Department after receiving six weeks of secret training. Unlike white officers, the African-American officers were not allowed to drive departmental vehicles, so they patrolled their beats on foot or on bicycles.

The Nature of Discrimination

The full force of the law and the Constitution have little meaning to those harmed by discrimination. The values expressed by the law in terms of equal protection become abstract. When an individual or a group is discriminated against, that person or group is denied not only equal treatment, but equal opportunity, even though these benefits are retained by others. Discrimination can include a variety of actions, such as the refusal to employ, promote, or provide appropriate training to a specific group of people. The discriminatory denial of job-related privileges based upon such things as race, color, or religion has absolutely nothing to do with the skills needed to perform a job effectively (Reece and Brandt, 1987: 383).

Members of minority groups are distinguishable because they are usually fewer in number and easily identifiable. In other words, there is something about each minority that is obviously different from the majority. Some minorities can also be identified because of their political persuasion, race, religion, ethnic background, or age. Examples of minority ethnic groups include African-Americans, Native Americans, Filipinos, Mexican-Americans, Asian-Americans. Political minorities include communists, socialists, and other small political groups. Groups such as the Amish are easily identifiable because of their distinctive dress and appearance, which is based on their religious faith. Groups that are discriminated against because of their lifestyle include homosexuals (Radecic, 1993: 1-4; Uniform Crime Reports, 1997: 1-106). In 1997, the City of Los Angeles paid $325,000 to settle a claim regarding the beating of gay rights demonstrators outside of a GOP fundraiser. The settlement involved 28 individuals who alleged that they were falsely arrested and denied their civil rights (*San Jose Mercury News*, 1997: 3B).

The size of the minority group becomes less important when one considers women. They have suffered from numerous forms of discrimination, including sexual harassment, as well as other forms of discrimination that are traditionally practiced against minority groups (Reece and Brandt, 1987: 383). Chapter 8 discusses in detail the employment of women in law enforcement agencies.

Discrimination is not as blatant today as it was in the past. It is no longer discrimination in the workplace when job-hunting members of minority groups are told immediately upon arrival that they need not apply for employment. The situation has reached the point at which discrimination now takes the form of disparate treatment. The Justice Department and the Equal Employment Opportunity Commission found that Donald Rochon, an African-American FBI agent, was the victim of blatant racial harassment. The harassment occurred in the Omaha and Chicago offices of the FBI between 1983 and 1986. Of numerous incidents during that period, one incident involved a white agent who forged an application for death and dismemberment insurance for the Rochon family. The FBI paid Rochon $1 million to settle the case and then in 1994 he was paid an additional $50,000 for libelous statements in an authorized history of the FBI (*San Jose Mercury News,* 1994: 2D).

In another case, in Cleveland, Ohio, a federal jury awarded a white police officer $200,000 when it decided that the city refused to promote him because of his race. He was denied promotion to sergeant and the city took the position that he displayed questionable judgment because he had shot nine people over a span of 12 years. The officer scored third on the sergeant's examination and was the only one out of the top 50 officers not promoted (*Arizona Daily Star*, 1994: 3B). The Boston Police Department, under a consent decree mandating the hiring of one member of a minority group for every white officer hired, found a way to get around the decree. The order from the court did not apply to the department's cadet program and more than 90 percent of those appointed as cadets were white. Of those appointed to the cadet program, who you knew (political connection), proved to be most important if you wanted to become a cadet (*Law Enforcement News*, 1996: 1, 10).

It is obvious in the above situations that discrimination was the result of outright biases and prejudices against law enforcement officers by other law enforcement officers. These are examples of overt discrimination, but in many instances, the act of discrimination is quite subtle. In the Los Angeles County Sheriff's Department, the features of an "old boy" system prevented desired movement by deputies without personal connections, who tend disproportionately to be women and minorities (Kolts, 1992: 312). It can take place when managers take the position that certain minorities are not qualified to be hired or promoted. In some instances, the discrimination is an unconscious action on the part of the manager, but the action is based on the assumption that certain tasks cannot be performed by minorities. Discrimination can also result from poor communications, in which a manager perceives that top management has no real desire to promote minorities or to allow them to take specialized training, so the manager systematically excludes them. In another instance, the discriminatory act might be a manager taking the position that line personnel would never work well with members of a certain minority group, so the manager never hires a member of that group. Whether the act is intentional or not, the result is the same—discrimination.

Prejudice and Discrimination

Prejudice and discrimination are interrelated. Discrimination is behavior based upon an attitude of prejudice. Prejudice is defined as a judgment or opinion formed beforehand or without thoughtful examination of the pertinent facts, issues, or arguments. Good examples of prejudice are any unfavorable, irrational opinions (Funk and Wagnalls, 1987: 1063). A secondary definition states that prejudice is a hatred of, or dislike for, a particular group, race, or religion.

Prejudice comes into existence as a result of several factors; one is the process of contamination. Each of us is affected by this process from birth. We have a tendency to accept the attitudes and beliefs of those in positions of authority. The family, friends, and others with whom we come in contact teach us how to treat others concerning their racial, ethnic, and religious backgrounds. As we become adults, we retain these attitudes without testing them against experience and new knowledge. One of the difficulties with this process is that, if it is reinforced by a negative contact with a member of the minority community, the prejudice can extend to all members of that group (Reece and Brandt, 1987: 383). For instance, if one minority member is late to work or performs inadequately, care must be taken so as not to generalize this type of behavior by applying it to every member of the minority group. Additionally, bigoted speech and expression by officers is wrong by its very nature and destructive in its consequences. Law enforcement agencies have broad latitude in prohibiting employees from using ethnic slurs, racial epithets, or demeaning sexist insults (Delattre and Schofield, 1996: 27-32).

The second factor contributing to prejudice is ethnocentrism. It is the natural tendency of human beings to view their own culture and customs as right and superior, and to judge all others by those standards (Zastrow and Bowker, 1984: 231). It is hard to imagine any culture not being ethnocentric. As the United States becomes an increasingly pluralistic society, it will experience increased conflict between cultures. Many members of Asian and Pacific Island cultures strongly support law enforcement agencies, while members of some other cultures have had to deal with corrupt police agencies before leaving their homeland and the cultural conditioning is carried over after they enter the United States. Highly suspicious of law enforcement agencies, some cultures condition members not to cooperate with justice agencies. Very few members of such cultures become law enforcement officers.

Some cultures pride themselves on open and free communications, while other cultures condition members to be secretive and non-communicative. There are some cultures that value openness and emotionality, so feelings are expressed in a variety of situations, including verbal confrontation. Other cultures value the suppression of emotions, and members are careful to avoid verbal conflict. It is normal for people with the same beliefs and value system to enjoy being with others that view things the same way. It is the organization that is apt to bring together people that have been raised in different cultures, causing conflict in the work environment (Reece and Brandt, 1987: 381).

Acts of Discrimination

Humans have a strong need to be part of a small, select group. This is especially true in law enforcement. Sworn personnel feel that they differ from civilians employed by the department. Some members of specialized units such as SWAT teams and motorcycle patrol units view themselves as the elite and do whatever is necessary to separate themselves from other members of the department. In this way, these officers maintain their status and position within the department. Considerable effort is expended by members of such groups in order to maintain what they perceive as the purity of their unit. Only certain members are allowed to succeed within the unit. Subtle pressures are exerted against unwanted members that do not meet the informal standards established by the unit. These standards can be based on such factors as race or gender. In many instances, a specialized group promotes an *us versus them* attitude. In other departments, the process of discrimination can involve major departmental entities. Investigative units, in some instances, have functioned independently of patrol units, and the two have viewed each other with disdain. Organizations have become segregated in many instances, as favored individuals or groups have received appointments to certain units or to specific shifts. These acts of discrimination (buoyed by ingrained prejudice) can reduce the effectiveness of a law enforcement agency.

It has been more than 30 years since the passage of the Civil Rights Act. During this period, our nation has seen considerable progress, but there is still much that must be done.

Table 9-1
Discrimination Charges Filed Against State and Local Law Enforcement Agencies: 1995

Issue	Charges	Percentage
Race	662	39
Sex	514	30.3
Retaliation	398	23.4
National Origin	112	6.6
Religion	20	1.2

Source: Claire Gonzales (1996). *Correspondence.* Washington, DC: Equal Employment Opportunity Commission, January 16:1-2.

In the most recent data available, the federal Equal Employment Opportunity Commission kept track of the charges filed by law enforcement personnel against their employers and found that the issues that arose in the charges varied considerably. Table 9-1 lists the issues involved and the total number of charges and the percentage for each category.

Out of 1,305 charges of discrimination, 76.8 percent were filed under Title VII, and the remainder under other federal statutes during fiscal year 1994. The largest group of charges was race-based, followed by sex-based charges. The third largest group was based on retaliation charges, followed by charges of national origin and religion discrimination. An individual can file charges under more that one statute, for example, age discrimination (The American with Disabilities Act) combined with a race-based charge (Title VII).

Nationwide, individuals filed 382 charges under the Americans with Disabilities Act and 173 charges under the Age Discrimination in Employment Act. One other way to view the discrimination charges against state and local law enforcement agencies is the alleged issue promoting the charge. The most frequent were: terms of employment (384 charges), promotion (371 charges), discharge (321 charges), harassment (281 charges), and hiring (227 charges) (Gonzales, 1996: 2).

Discrimination occurs at several levels, including individual and organizational levels. It is an old concept that has endured since our society began. Discrimination refers to the negative and unfavorable treatment of people based on their membership in a minority group. It involves an act or an omission that hinders one person vis-à-vis another in order to satisfy some prejudice (More and Wegener, 1996: 366). In recent years, discrimination has become increasingly subtle. In fact, there are many times when those against whom discrimination is practiced cannot tell whether an act of discrimination has occurred. When a minority member is on a promotional list but is not promoted, it is difficult to ascertain whether discrimination has occurred. To complain without a factual basis may be perceived by the disappointed individual as something that should not be done because it could stereotype him or her as a troublemaker and could limit future promotions. It is a problem with which the individual must contend, even though retribution may occur. If the individual believes that he or she has been the victim of discrimination, he should pursue the matter. Most agencies strive to comply with civil rights laws and, except for cases in which there are extenuating circumstances, officers who feel that they have been discriminated against should initially file a complaint with the city, county, or state where they are employed.

The following Feature is a compilation of cases involving the disposition of discrimination complaints.

Feature

Incidents of Discrimination in Law Enforcement Agencies

- The U.S. Equal Opportunity Employment Commission, reacting to 32 minority officers, found that there was a pattern of discrimination against African-Americans, Hispanics, and females. These officers were subjected to repeated discrimination and were routinely denied promotion. The Commission also found that the Suffolk County, New York, police agency had failed to comply with a Justice Department consent decree, issued in 1986, to hire more women.

- In Washington, D.C., the chief of police considered firing a male lieutenant after a female sergeant filed a complaint against him for sexual harassment. The complaint was sustained by the police department's Office of Equal Employment Opportunity.

- Two Texas Rangers were reprimanded for making racial and sexual slurs against an African-American sergeant. The two officers were suspended with pay for more than four months during the investigation, and after the charges were sustained, the officers were placed on probation for six months.

- In Chicago, the police department came under fire because of a recently administered sergeant's examination. Charges of racial bias came to light after the results were published, indicating that those who passed included 1,453 whites, 300 African-Americans, 160 Hispanics, and 23 of other races. It was anticipated that only 62 minorities would be promoted out of 500 promotions to sergeant. The city spent $5 million to develop the test. Currently there are no plans to change the test.

- In Lawrence, Massachusetts, city officials agreed with community leaders to hire and promote more Hispanic police officers. It also agreed to create a special citizens' public safety commission, and a new stress-management program. Additionally, the city agreed to revamp the Spanish-language program.

- A U.S. district judge will preside over a class action suit filed by Hispanic agents of the U.S. Drug Enforcement Agency. The suit charged that the agents were locked out of promotions, given dangerous undercover assignments, and were required to perform mundane duties.

Overview of Relevant Statutes and Issues

Federal court rulings in education (beginning with the landmark case of *Brown v. Board of Education*), along with considerable racial unrest, laid the groundwork for the passage of the 1964 Civil Rights Act under President Lyndon Johnson. This has been the most important anti-discrimination law in American history. The act applies to private employers, labor unions, and employment agencies engaged in any industry affecting commerce and employing 25 or more employees. It was not until eight years after it was enacted that jurisdiction was extended to include public employers with 15 or more employees. The Equal Employment Opportunity Commission was created by Title VII to investigate allegations of discrimination. The commission is also responsible for enforcing other statutes, including: Age Discrimination Employment Act, Equal Pay Act, Pregnancy Discrimination Act, Americans with Disabilities Act, and Family Medical Leave Act. Combined, these laws give the commission a great deal of power over the discrimination process. Part of this power is delineated in Title VII, Section 703 of the Civil Rights Act, and is described in the following Feature.

Feature

Title VII, Section 703 of the Civil Rights Act

This section of the Act provides that it shall be unlawful employment practice for an employer: (1) to fail to or refuse to hire, or discharge any individual or otherwise to discriminate against any individual with respect to his compensation, terms, conditions, or privileges of employment, because of such individual's race, color, religion, sex, or national origin; (2) to limit, segregate, or classify his or her employees or applicants for employment in any way that would deprive or tend to deprive any individual of employment opportunity or otherwise adversely affect his or her status as an employee because of such individual's race, color, religion, sex, or national origin.

Source: Equal Employment Opportunity Commission (1988). *Title VII Enforces Job Rights.* Washington, DC: USGPO, October:1-12.

Under several laws, police agencies may not deny members of protected classes equal access to or the enjoyment of the privileges and benefits of employment. *Equal access* applies to recruitment, screening, interviewing, and hiring employees, as well as promoting employees and providing employee benefits. One factor that allows for excluding members of a protected class is discussed below.

Bona Fide Occupational Qualification

Law enforcement agencies may not deny members of protected classes equal access to or enjoyment of the privileges and benefits of employment. Equal access applies to recruiting, screening, interviewing, and hiring employees, as well as promoting employees and providing employee benefits. In the context of hiring, the laws allow exclusion of members of a protected class if there is a *bona fide occupational qualification* (BFOQ), that is, a valid job-related requirement reasonably necessary to the normal operation of that particular business. In other words, valid job requirements that tend to eliminate members of a protected class may still be permissible if the requirements are BFOQs.

Pregnancy and Maternity

This act outlaws discrimination on the basis of pregnancy, childbirth, or any medical condition that might be caused by pregnancy or childbirth. Without a BFOQ, employers may not refuse to hire an applicant solely because she is pregnant. This prohibition applies whether the woman is married or single. On the other hand, it is not unlawful to require employees to be able to perform the essential functions of the job or to complete a reasonable training period at the beginning of the employment relationship. Employers may be permitted to refuse to hire applicants who cannot complete the initial training period because of pregnancy.

Police departments may not fire, refuse to promote, or fail to provide equal access to benefits to a pregnant employee simply because she is pregnant. Nor can they force pregnant employees to take maternity leave if they are able and willing to work (Rubin, 1995: 3).

Family and Medical Leave

This act requires employers with 50 or more employees to provide 12 weeks unpaid leave to care for a newborn child, adopted child, or foster child. This requirement applies equally to men and women. Police agencies are allowed to require employees to use unpaid vacation and sick leave as part of the 12 weeks of leave. Agencies must offer employees taking leave under this law the same or equivalent job when they return from leave. Executive management employees are exempt from such reinstatement (Rubin, 1995: 3).

Age Discrimination

This act makes it illegal to discriminate against persons 40 years of age or older on the basis of age. Police departments should be aware of age issues in recruiting and hiring. For example, advertising that tends to discourage persons over the age of 40 might be deemed discriminatory. Without a BFOQ, terms such as *recent grad* or *young* should be avoided. A good rule of thumb is to look at the adjectives used in an advertisement to ensure that they describe the position's requirements. The law does not prevent police agencies from asking an applicant's age on an application. However, doing so invites extra scrutiny because such questions tend to discourage persons over the age of 40 from applying. One recommendation is to include a statement on the application that the agency complies with the ADEA as well as other relevant civil rights laws. Federal law does not prohibit agencies from imposing minimum age requirements (Rubin, 1995: 3).

Religious Discrimination

This act prohibits discrimination on the basis of religion, but the act does not define religion. However, religious practices can include traditional moral beliefs, ethical beliefs, and beliefs that individuals hold with the strength of traditional religious views. Moreover, atheists are protected from discrimination for not having religious beliefs.

The notion of what constitutes *religion* can include nontraditional practices as well. Even unusual cults may enjoy protection. Less traditional practices and beliefs might include, for example, *new age* training programs such as yoga, meditation, or biofeedback. Using these practices as part of motivational training may conflict with an employee's religious beliefs and therefore violate Title VII. Employees who notify their employer of a conflict between employment practices and their individual religious beliefs are entitled to *a reasonable accommodation,* which may include flexible scheduling, voluntary substitutions, reassignment, or lateral transfer. However, employers are not required to provide such an accommodation if it would create an undue hardship.

National Origin

Discrimination based on national origin can include elimination of applicants on the basis of physical appearance. To comply with the law, police agencies should avoid height and weight requirements that are not legitimately related to job performance. For the same reason, police departments should not refuse to hire or promote applicants and employees who speak with an accent. The guiding standard should be an ability to communicate effectively. Departments should not tolerate ethnic slurs, or verbal or physical abuse of employees based on their national origin or citizenship status. Any requirement, including *English-only* rules, should be job related.

Disability

Police administrators should ensure that individuals with disabilities are not treated differently than those without disabilities solely because of their disability. To be qualified, the job applicant or employee must be able to perform the essential functions of the job. Essential functions are those that are fundamental to the job. The Act does not require an agency to hire an unqualified candidate (Zappile and Jankowski, 1993: 51-53). It is important that written policies and procedures be in place and consistent with the law before a problem occurs. Job descriptions should be designed for each position. This process includes determining what physical and mental functions are needed to perform the essential functions of a position (Aaron, 1992: 35-37).

An Affirmative Action Program

As a means of fulfilling its mandate, the commission has forcefully supported affirmative action, which requires employers to take positive steps to overcome present and past discrimination in order to achieve absolute equity and employment opportunity. A realistic affirmative action plan is a mechanism through which an employer ensures equal opportunities for all personnel. It is a written commitment in which a community recognizes its responsibility to establish an ethnically integrated and highly productive workforce at every level of city employment.

An affirmative action program is a detailed, results-oriented set of procedures that, when carried out, results in full compliance with equal opportunity requirements through full use and equal treatment of all people. The creation of an affirmative action program is technical and somewhat complicated. There are several reasons for this. First, each city is subject to (and must address) a variety of state and federal laws and guidelines dealing with equal employment opportunity and affirmative action. In addition, relevant court decisions, which are often useful in interpreting guidelines, but sometimes conflict with them, must be taken into account when developing and implementing a program. Furthermore, in determining the current equal opportunity and affirmative action position (as well as anticipated achievements), it may first be necessary to perform a number of calculations when preparing a utilization analysis. The technical, legal, and mathematical aspects of an affirmative action program all have one common purpose, which is to allow the community to make three key determinations:

- Where does the community stand now?

- What must be done?

- How best to achieve what is desired?

The accomplishment of these determinations enables an employer to take the initiative in evaluating its employment practices. An effective plan identifies barriers to equal employment opportunity. A well-designed program aids the employer in taking action to eliminate discriminatory employment practices. An affirmative action program involves not only the elimination of barriers to equal employment opportunity, but also the development of an aggressive program to recruit, employ, train, and promote qualified minorities and women when analysis indicates an underutilization of these groups in the past (City of Campbell, CA, 1996: 1).

Utilization Analysis

In order to seek and achieve good faith results, a full and complete analysis of an employer's utilization of ethnic and gender groups should be undertaken. Federal agencies involved in ensuring compliance with equal employment laws and guidelines recognize the necessity for self-examination through a utilization analysis. As stated in the federal regulations: (EEOC, 1979:Section 1608.4)

> The objective of a self-analysis is to determine whether employment practices do, or tend to, exclude, disadvantage, restrict, or result in adverse impact or disparate treatment of previously excluded or restricted groups or leave uncorrected the effects of prior discrimination, and if so, to attempt to determine why.

Compliance agencies do not have a recommended or mandatory self-analysis method. Consequently, communities have selected their own methods for determining relevant labor markets. For example, in Palo Alto, California, each job group's labor market was determined. This was identified as the area from which the city normally recruited or obtained job applicants for the position of police officer. Availability was determined by identifying the percent of each gender and ethnic group in the applicant pool. The city took the position that applicant pool figures are better indicators of availability than the general labor figures or employment figures from census data. The data collected reflected the number and percentage of employees by sex and ethnic groups. It also indicates underutilization when the percentage of each group on the job was lower than the percentage available. From this information, the city was able to establish goals and timetables in order to correct the underutilization. In this instance, underutilization was indicated for African-Americans, Hispanics, and Native Americans. At the time of the survey, the city had 19 female officers and 15 officers from minority backgrounds. The minority officers included three African-Americans, nine Hispanics, and three Asians; these numbers constituted 26.9 percent of all employees. The department had higher percentages of whites, women, and Asian officers than those groups' respective percentages of availability, which suggests recruitment goals should be established for other groups of potential employees (City of Palo Alto, 1989: 1-10).

Goals and Timetables

When an employer's selection procedures intentionally or unintentionally result in a lower percentage of one gender or ethnic group in a particular job (e.g., police officer) than would be expected from availability data, positive steps should be taken to remedy the situation. An affirmative action program should set forth goals and timetables. These should take into account the availability of qualified persons in the relevant labor area. A goal, unlike a quota, does not require the hiring of persons when there are no vacancies, nor does it require the hiring of a person who is less likely to do well on the job (less qualified) over a person more likely to do well on the job (better qualified).

A major problem facing an employer lies in making proper distinctions between goals and timetables versus the concept of a quota. A goal and its associated timetable represent a guidepost against which an employer or a compliance agency can measure progress in remedying identified deficiencies in the department's workforce. When operating under a goal, an employer is not required to hire an unqualified person or a less qualified person over a better qualified person (City of Palo Alto, 1989: 18).

In addressing this issue, a federal agency stated:

> The terms *less qualified* and *better qualified* are not intended to distinguish among persons who are substantially equally qualified in terms of being able to perform the job successfully. Unlike quotas, therefore, which may call for a preference for the unqualified over the qualified, or for the less qualified over the better qualified to meet the numerical requirements, a goal recognizes that persons are to be judged on individual ability, and therefore is consistent with the principle of merit hiring (Equal Employment Opportunity Coordinating Council, 1973: 21).

In the 1971 case of *Griggs v. Duke Power Company*, the U.S. Supreme Court interpreted the Civil Rights Act of 1964, as amended. The Court asserted that, in short, the Act does not command that any person be hired simply because he or she was formerly the subject of discrimination or because he or she was a member of a minority group. Discriminatory preference for any group, minority or majority, is precisely (and only) what Congress has proscribed. What Congress intended was to remove artificial, arbitrary, and unnecessary barriers to employment (*Griggs v. Duke Power Company*, 1971: 521).

If a realistic goal is set on the basis of expected vacancies and anticipated availability of skills within a particular labor area, an affirmative action program will work. In order to attain success, an employer must conduct an effective recruitment program to ensure an adequate pool of minority and/or female qualified applicants from which to make selections. A public employer's goals and timetables must be consistent with *Griggs* and associated federal guidelines on employee selection procedures. Goals and timetables are designed to work for the elimination of discrimination by breaking down the barriers of habit, attitude, and training that prevent the recognition of individual capabilities.

Arguments Against Affirmative Action

Merit has been an honored tradition in civil service since the early part of the twentieth century, and opponents of affirmative action view it as a process that is destroying the merit system. Affirmative action can quickly become an emotionally charged issue that can tear an agency apart. It immediately divides employees into those that are helped by affirmative action and those who feel that they are victims of discrimination when an affirmative action program is implemented. There are numerous arguments that can be set forth against affirmative action; one of the major arguments is that the *quota* system is actually *reverse discrimination* (Skrentny, 1996: 19-66).

A major case in this area was decided by the U.S. Supreme Court in 1978. In *Regents of University of California v. Bakke*, the Court decided that an affirmative action program established by a university violated Title VI of the 1964 Civil Rights Act. The decision was highly complex and comprised 156 pages of text. The university had implemented an admissions program that excluded white applicants from 16 percent of the first-year medical school class. Fifty-five organizations filed *friends of the court* briefs, primarily arguing that the racial discrimination involved in the case was benign, not invidious, and was designed to further racial equality, not retard it (Heins, 1987: 53). In a split decision, Justice Powell wrote the opinion of the Court, arguing that the affirmative action program at the university was unconstitutional. On the other hand, in the same opinion, Justice Powell stated that a school may create an affirmative action program using race as a factor in admissions. At the time the decision was handed down, many white officers contended that it would turn the tide against affirmative action programs, but this position was never substantiated. Since the decision, a number of courts have referred to the *Bakke* case as the basis for decisions supporting affirmative action or, in other instances, for decisions finding affirmative action programs unlawful (Anderson and Levin-Epstein, 1982: 87).

The affirmative action guidelines actually prohibit reverse discrimination (EEOC, 1979: 1-36):

> Nothing contained in this title shall be interpreted to require any employer . . . subject to this title to grant preferential treatment to any individual or to any group because of the race, color, religion, sex, or national origin of such individuals or groups on account of an imbalance which may exist, with respect to the total number or percentage of persons of any race, color, religion, sex, or national origin employed by any employer . . . in comparison with the total number or percentage of persons of any race, color, religion, sex, or national origin in any community, state, section, or other area.

In discussing the quota system for racial promotions in the Detroit Police Department, the U.S. Civil Rights Commission took the position that the use of racially preferential employment techniques, such as quotas, should not be viewed as a situation pitting the interests of African-Americans against whites. Rather, each definitive preferential plan favors members of the preferred group (of whatever race or gender) at the expense of the non-preferred group, and each group inevitably includes persons of diverse ethnic, religious, or racial groups (U.S. Commission on Civil Rights, 1984: 197).

Further, the commission rejected the concept of an *operational justification* for racial quotas. In one major police department, African-American officers were promoted to all ranks under a quota system as a means of achieving more effective law enforcement and reducing discriminatory acts against African-American citizens. The commission rejected this system, pointing out that such an approach amounted to little more than a claim that only African-American officers could effectively provide law enforcement services to African-American citizens and that only an African-American supervisor should supervise African-American officers. The commission stated emphatically that such a claim has no place in a free, pluralistic society made up of many diverse ethnic and racial groups striving to achieve the goal of becoming one nation. If *operational justification* is accepted, it would lend credence to the claim that members of a racial or ethnic group can be properly served or treated only by fellow members of that group (U.S. Commission on Civil Rights, 1984: 196; U.S. Commission on Civil Rights, 1981: 84).

There may, of course, be many other arguments set forth when a case is being made against affirmative action. Figure 9-1 lists some of these arguments. It can readily be seen that the reasons for rejecting affirmative action vary from the philosophical to the pragmatic. It has been pointed out that when a less qualified person is hired, the service rendered suffers accordingly. Others argue that education and training could resolve this problem. Additionally, some suggest that the best way to support affirmative action would be to improve the economy. Several years ago, Secretary of the Interior James Watt stated that he had appointed a coal leasing board consisting of "a black, a woman, two Jews, and a cripple." Because of this and other remarks, Watt lost his job. However, it should be noted that some take the position that this illustrates the problem with affirmative action. When race, religion, gender, or an ethnic group is perceived as a factor in appointment, the issue of preferential treatment arises. This has led to resentment and in some cases has actually increased racial disharmony (Woods, 1989: 103).

In 1997, Proposition 209 was passed by voters in California. This measure prohibited race and sex preferences in affirmative action programs in state and local government, education, employment, and contracting. The U.S. Court of Appeals for the Ninth Circuit let the proposition stand and the U.S. Supreme Court concurred with the Circuit Court's decision. The full impact of this decision is unknown. The Supreme Court's decision was not a precedent and does not apply to other states.

Figure 9-1
Arguments Against Affirmative Action

- A less qualified individual is often hired or promoted.

- With less qualified people, poorer service is provided.

- Affirmative action presents the image that only race, sex, religion, and color enter into appointment or promotion.

- Artificial goals do not really promote civil rights.

- Minorities do not really benefit from affirmative action; only attorneys and bureaucrats benefit.

- Affirmative action programs generate a great deal of paper work and dilute limited resources.

- Reverse discrimination negatively affects white males.

- Affirmative action is the new racism.

- Better training and education would help minorities.

- The best way to help minorities is to improve the economy.

- Class preferences will be just as stigmatizing as racial preferences.

Sources: Geraldine Woods (1989). *Affirmative Action*. New York: Impact Books; Bureau of National Affairs (1986). *Affirmative Action Today: A Legal and Practical Analysis*. Rockville, MD: Bureau of National Affairs; and Richard Kahlenberg (1995). "Class Not Race." *The New Republic*, Vol. 215, No. 13, April 3:21-27.

Arguments for Affirmative Action

The debate about affirmative action began prior to the passage of the Civil Rights Act of 1964, and it continues today. Currently, in the U.S. Senate, the debate goes on in an effort to amend the Act in order to restore and strengthen civil rights laws banning discrimination in employment and other areas. The proposed amendment is in reaction to a series of recent decisions that addressed discrimination claims under federal law. The purpose of the legislation is to reverse the recent decisions made by the Supreme Court and to restore civil rights protection.

For 18 years following the unanimous opinion of the Supreme Court in the landmark case of *Griggs v. Duke Power Co.*, Title VII placed on employers the burden of proving that employment practices with a *disparate impact* (i.e., operating to exclude women and minorities disproportionately) were required by business necessity. In 1989, in *Wards Cove Packing Co. v. Atonio*, the Supreme Court effectively overruled the *Griggs* decision and held that, no matter how strong the proof of discriminatory effect, the employer need no longer prove that its practices are of business necessity. Instead, victims of discrimination must bear the burden of proving that the employer has no legal justification for its exclusionary practices. The Civil Rights Act of 1990 restores the *Griggs* rule by providing that, once a person proves that an employment practice has a disparate impact, the employer must justify the practice by showing that it is based upon business necessity (Senate of the United States, 1990: 11-16). The new Act was designed to overturn five 1989 Supreme Court decisions that made it increasingly difficult for minorities and women to win job discrimination suits.

Even if the Civil Rights Act of 1990 is not passed during the current session, there is every reason to believe that the Act, possibly with amendments, will eventually become law. Beyond the legal efforts calling for change, there are strong arguments that continue to support affirmative action. Figure 9-2 lists some of the contentions set forth by supporters of affirmative action. These arguments vary and include legal, philosophical, and pragmatic reasoning. The arguments center around the belief that to end discrimination, it is necessary to terminate the discrimination to which minorities and women have been subjected (Maguire, 1980: 186).

Supporters believe that hiring candidates with varying backgrounds actually benefits a police department because employees can contribute to the success of the organization in different ways. Thus, diversity brings strength to the workforce (Woods, 1989: 89). Another argument is that the minorities brought into the system have often proven to be highly successful (Skrentny, 1996: 67-222). Closely related to this is the fact that affirmative action has proven to be good business—that is, it works. Affirmative action is viewed as a process that expands the available pool of talented, productive, and creative people (Bureau of National Affairs, 1986: 11). Supporters of affirmative action believe that preferential treatment is not "reverse discrimination" if it remedies arbitrary or invidious discrimination. Affirmative action is, rather, an effort to reverse the white male quota system that existed for at least two centuries (Maguire, 1980: 186).

Figure 9-2
Arguments for Affirmative Action

- Diversity strengthens the workforce.

- Minorities and women have proven to be good employees.

- Affirmative action is good business—that is, it works.

- Preferential affirmative action reverses arbitrary and invidious discrimination.

- The labor force is shrinking.

- Merit never prevailed because of the "good old boy" system.

- The public supports affirmative action.

- Women and minorities were the victims of discrimination as a group. Only a remedy applying to the whole group is fair.

- Affirmative action is clearly defensible.

Sources: Daniel C. Maguire (1980). *The New American Justice: Ending the White Male Monopolies*. Garden City, New York: Doubleday; Geraldine Woods (1989). *Affirmative Action*. New York: Impact Books; Bureau of National Affairs (1986). *Affirmative Action Today: A Legal and Practical Analysis*. Rockville, MD; Bureau of National Affairs. Jeffrey Rosen (1995). "Affirmative Action: A Solution." *The New Republic*, May 8:20-25.

Quotas

There are a number of cities across the nation in which the courts have ordered the implementation of quota systems for police department hiring. These systems involve an effort to bring minorities and women into a police department because they are determined to be underrepresented when their numbers within the department are compared to those residing in the community. Such a statistical imbalance constitutes *prima facie* evidence of discrimination. Interestingly, Title VII of the Civil Rights Act of 1964 explicitly bans quota hiring (e.g., 23 percent of the members of a community are Hispanic, therefore, 23 percent of the police department must be Hispanic). However, the courts have ruled that this does not apply when quota hiring is used to remedy racial imbalance caused by unlawful discriminatory conduct (Bureau of National Affairs, 1986: 72). In recent years, diversity has been used as a means of having a law enforcement agency reflect the diversity of the community. This process is receiving increasing acceptance.

Trends in Hiring Minorities and Women

Since the passage of the Civil Rights Act of 1964 (as amended), an increasing number of minorities and women have entered the police service at all levels. The numbers of minorities vary greatly from agency to agency. In addition, the numbers vary considerably from level to level when statistics are reviewed for municipal, state, and federal law enforcement agencies.

In many of the larger cities throughout the nation, African-Americans are entering the police service in increasing numbers. During the last decade, the African-American population in many of these cities has increased considerably. African-Americans are also assuming positions of leadership in the police departments of major cities. Additionally, more and more members of minority groups serve on city councils and county boards of supervisors.

In the twenty-first century, it is anticipated that African-Americans will continue to assume positions at all managerial levels within police departments. As increasing numbers of African-Americans have entered the police service during the last quarter of a this century, the "trickle up" has become operational, and African-Americans are reaching the top.

The number of Hispanic officers employed by police departments with more than 100 sworn officers presents a somewhat different perspective (see Table 9-2). There are a number of reasons for this, including the fact that many cities do not have a large Hispanic population base. On the other hand, there are some cities located in the southwest that have large concentrations of Hispanics. Not surprising, in cities with populations of more than one million, the greatest number of Hispanics in a large city was in Los Angeles, which had 23.1 percent Hispanic officers, followed by New York with 14.1 percent Hispanic officers. In smaller cities, depending upon the geographical location, the percentage of Hispanic officers is exceedingly high. This is true in Laredo, Texas, with 99.5 percent; Brownsville, Texas with 82.4 percent; and Santa Fe, New Mexico, with 64.5 percent. There are several cities that have no Hispanic officers, including Decatur, Illinois; Boise, Idaho; Little Rock, Arkansas; and Pensacola, Florida,

Table 9-2
Full-Time Sworn Employees by Race and Place of Employment and Percentage in Each Group

Name Of Agency	Percentage By Race				
	White	Black	Hispanic	American Indian/ Alaskan Native	Asian/ Pacific Islander
New York	72.9	12.1	14.1	0.1	0.9
Chicago	66.6	24.7	7.9	0.2	0.6
Los Angeles	58.4	14.5	23.1	0.3	3.7
Philadelphia	69.8	26.2	3.3	0.4	0.4
Dallas	71.2	19.1	8.5	0.6	0.6
Phoenix	83.5	3.9	11.3	0.5	0.9
Baltimore	66.6	31.9	1.5	0.0	0.0

Source: Brian A. Reaves and Pheny Z. Smith (1995). *Law Enforcement Management and Administrative Statistics, 1993: Data for Individual State and Local Agencies with 100 or More Officers.* Washington, DC: U.S. Department of Justice, Bureau of Justice Statistics, 37-47.

Summary

As the United States has become an increasingly pluralistic society, discrimination based on race and sex has persisted as a human relations problem. In the past, deep-seated prejudices based on race, sex, religion, and color fostered discrimination that permeated every facet of life. When an individual is victimized by discrimination, he or she is denied not only equal treatment but equal opportunity.

Prejudice and discrimination are interrelated. Discrimination is based on an attitude of "prejudice." *Contamination* (passing down beliefs from generation to generation) is one factor that causes prejudice. The result of contamination is the assumption of the attitudes and beliefs of those in positions of authority, family members, friends, and others. Prejudice serves as a basis for how we treat others unless individuals change these attitudes. When belief systems are tested by experience and knowledge, prejudiced beliefs tend to weaken. Another influence is ethnocentrism, which is a person's tendency to view his own culture and customs as superior.

Since the passage of the Civil Rights Act of 1964, considerable progress has been made toward equality for all people, but there is still much that must be done. Studies by states and the federal government show that patterns of discrimination continue in a number of areas. For example, during 1994, police officers filed 1,305 discrimination charges with the Equal Employment Opportunity Commission against their employers.

Title VII of the Civil Rights Act of 1964 (as amended) is the most important antidiscrimination law in American history. In 1972, the Act became of special concern to law enforcement when the jurisdiction of the Equal Employment Opportunity Commission was extended to include public employers with 15 or more employees. Under the Act, a wide range of acts are illegal, such as specific types of recruitment, testing, promotion, and assignment.

The Equal Employment Opportunity Commission is responsible for investigating allegations of discrimination, including violations of the Age Discrimination in Employment Act, the Americans with Disabilities Act, the Pregnancy Discrimination Act, and the Family and Medical Leave Act. After a charge is filed, it is investigated by an EEOC investigator. If the investigation shows reasonable cause that discrimination has occurred, the agency makes an effort at conciliation, but if that does not resolve the issue, it can request that the Department of Justice sue a state or local government for violating Title VII.

References

Aaron, Titus (1992). "Federal Law Prohibits Disability Discrimination." *Law and Order,* Vol. 40, No. 5:35-37.

Anderson, Howard J. and Michael D. Levin-Epstein (1982). *Primer of Equal Employment Opportunity*, Second Edition. Washington, DC: Bureau of National Affairs, 87.

Arizona Daily Star (1994). "White Cop Wins Promotion-Bias Case." March 12:3B.

Bureau of National Affairs (1986). *Affirmative Action Today: A Legal and Practical Analysis.* Rockville, MD: Bureau of National Affairs, 1-72.

City of Campbell (1996). *Affirmative Action Program, As Amended by Resolution.* Campbell, CA: City of Campbell, March 15:1-8.

City of Palo Alto (1989). *Affirmative Action Plan,* revised annually, 1-18.

Delattre, Edwin J. and Daniel L. Schofield (1996). "Combating Bigotry in Law Enforcement." *FBI Law Enforcement Bulletin,* Vol. 65, No. 6:27-32.

Equal Employment Opportunity Coordinating Council (1973). *Federal Policy on Remedies Concerning Equal Employment Opportunity in State and Local Government Personnel Systems.* Washington, DC: USGPO, 1-21.

Equal Employment Opportunity Commission (1979). *Laws Enforced By the Equal Employment Opportunity Commission.* Washington, DC: Equal Employment Opportunity Commission.

Equal Employment Opportunity Commission (1988). *Title VII Enforces Job Rights.* Washington, DC: USGPO, October:1-12.

Fletcher, Arthur A. (1993). *Racial and Ethnic Tensions in American Communities: Poverty, Inequality, and Discrimination, Volume 1: The Mount Pleasant Report.* Washington, DC: U.S. Civil Rights Commission, 1-173.

Funk and Wagnalls (1987). *Standard College Dictionary.* New York: Funk and Wagnalls Publishing, 1063.

Griggs v. Duke Power Co., 401 U.S. at 431 (1971).

Gonzales, Claire (1996). *Correspondence.* Washington, DC: Equal Employment Opportunity Commission, January 16:1-2.

Heins, Marjorie (1987). *Cutting the Mustard.* Winchester, MA: Farber & Farber, 53.

Kahlenberg, Richard (1995). "Class, Not Race." *The New Republic,* Vol. 215, No. 13, April 3:21-27.

Kolts, James G. (1992). *The Los Angeles County Sheriff's Department.* Los Angeles, CA: Los Angeles County, 312.

Law Enforcement News (1996). "The Back Door to a Police Job." September 30:1, 10.

Maguire, Daniel C. (1980). *The New American Justice: Ending the White Male Monopolies.* Garden City, NY: Doubleday, 186.

More, Harry W. and W. Fred Wegener (1996). *Effective Police Supervision,* Second Edition. Cincinnati, OH: Anderson Publishing Co., 366.

Radecic, Peri J. (Winter 1993). "Letter From The Director." Washington, DC: National Gay & Lesbian Task Force, 1-4.

Reaves, Brian A. and Pheny Z. Smith (1995). *Law Enforcement Management and Administrative Statistics, 1993: Data for Individual State and Local Agencies with 100 or More Officers.* Washington, DC: U.S. Department of Justice, Bureau of Justice Statistics, 37-47.

Reece, Barry L. and Rhonda Brandt (1987). *Effective Human Relations in Organizations,* Third Edition. Boston, MA: Houghton Mifflin, 381.

Regents of University of California v. Bakke, 438 U.S. 265 (1978).

Rosen, Jeffery (1995). "Affirmative Action: A Solution." *The New Republic,* May 8:20-25.

Rubin, Paula N. (1995). *Civil Rights and Criminal Justice: Employment Discrimination Overview,* Research in Action. Washington, DC: National Institute of Justice, 1-8.

San Jose Mercury News (1994). "Harassed FBI Agent Will be Paid For Libel." July 13:2D.

San Jose Mercury News (1997). "Suit Alleging Violence Against Gays Settled." August 26:3B.

Senate of the United States (1990). *Civil Rights Act of 1990,* § 2104. 101st Congress, 2d Session, 11-16.

Skrentny, John D. (1996). *The Ironies of Affirmative Action.* Chicago, IL: University of Chicago Press, 19-222.

U.S. Commission on Civil Rights (1981). *Who is Guarding the Guardians?* Washington, DC: USGPO, 84.

U.S. Commission on Civil Rights (1984). *Statements on Civil Rights Concerning the Detroit Police Department's Racial Promotion Quota.* Washington, DC: USGPO, 196.

Uniform Crime Reports (1997). *Hate Crime Statistics 1995.* Washington, DC: Federal Bureau of Investigation, 1-106.

Wards Cove Packing Co. v. Atonio, 449 U.S. 191 (1989).

Woods, Geraldine (1989). *Affirmative Action.* New York: Impact Books, 89-103.

Zappile, Richard A. and Debbie Jankowski (1993). "The Philadelphia Police Department's Response to the Americans with Disabilities Act." *The Police Chief,* Vol. LX, No. 3:51-53.

Zastrow, Charles and Lee Bowker (1984). *Social Problems.* Chicago: Nelson Hall, 231.

STRESS: REACTING TO POLICE WORK

10

The study of this chapter will enable you to:

1. Differentiate between stress and eustress.

2. Define stress, job burnout, and organizational stress.

3. Identify four job-related stressors that are specifically associated with law enforcement.

4. Describe the characteristics of job burnout.

5. List five possible psychological responses to stress.

6. Identify the most prevalent stress warning signs.

7. Discuss the extent of alcoholism in law enforcement.

8. List the relaxation responses that can be used by police officers.

9. Identify the most prominent personal and organizational effects of occupational stress.

10. Describe the importance of a good exercise program.

11. List the items required in completing a viable needs assessment.

12. Identify the types of disorders included in a stress program.

13. Write a short speech describing LECLES.

The majority of people in our society pursue and actively engage in some type of work. Work is viewed as an integral part of each person's life cycle. It is a social as well as psychological response, and it is viewed by numerous experts as a natural aspect of life. Work is considered by psychologists to be an important developmental task. A successful effort at work is likely to yield such rewards as improved self-esteem and autonomy.

When a police officer's job requires thought, judgment, and analysis, the officer develops intellectually. Experts have taken the position that mental exercise seems to keep the mind in shape in much the same way that physical exercise keeps the body in shape (Bootzin, Bower, Zajonc, and Hall, 1986: 452).

A definition of work is: "an activity producing something of value for other people" (Task Force to the Secretary of Health, Education, and Welfare, 1973: 3). This definition is definitely one that falls into a social context, suggesting that work has a purpose. There is increasing evidence showing that an individual's sense of personal identity is, in most instances, obtained from his or her work. This is best illustrated by noting that many of us describe ourselves in terms of work groups or organizations. For example, most police officers will say that they work for the police department, not the city, state, or county. Officers identify strongly with policing and with the specific organization and unit for which they work.

Work provides more than the basic necessities of life. A job provides an individual with a sense of personal identity and accomplishment that is seldom provided by other activities. Satisfying work is usually that which challenges an individual's skills and requires ingenuity. When police work is intellectually demanding, it not only stimulates personal growth, it also affects the officer's personality (Bootzin, Bower, Zajonc, and Hall, 1986: 389).

Police work can become not only a place for mental and physical exertion, but the focal point of life. It is something that most officers live and breathe. At its extreme, the job can become an obsession. Police work itself can become more important than the economic reward that the job provides. The social interaction that occurs between officers, the support system, and the social bond that develops, provide officers with an experience that cannot be achieved in any other way (Leonard and More, 1993: 132).

The police *subculture* provides an arena for friendship and profound camaraderie (Albrecht, 1992: 13-14). Police managers are becoming increasingly aware of the need to create a working environment that allows an individual to grow, evolve, and obtain satisfaction from the job.

Job satisfaction is an emotional orientation toward one's work. It can be measured in terms of satisfaction from the job itself or toward specific facets of the job (Bootzin, Bower, Zajonc, and Hall, 1986: 450). Components of job satisfaction include:

- Attitude toward the agency.

- Attitude toward the work group.

- Attitude toward supervision.

- Working conditions.

- Monetary benefits (Rue and Byars, 1986: 342).

These are modified by other factors, such as the individual's attitude toward the type of work being performed and the general attitude that an individual has toward life in general. Other modifiers include one's health, age, level of aspiration, social status, and additional factors that are currently unidentified. It is immediately apparent that job satisfaction is highly complex and is of increasing concern not only to police managers, but to police officers themselves (especially when job dissatisfaction creates stress). In general, it is believed that a healthy, well-adjusted employee who finds a job rewarding and satisfying is preferable to a dissatisfied employee.

In our work-oriented society, there are many officers whose attitude toward work is such that they want not only a demanding, interesting, and challenging job, but one that allows them to focus totally on their work. These officers want to serve their community, make a contribution to society, and help those in need. A successful arrest not only leaves its mark by removing a criminal from the streets, but it has a positive impact on other members of the peer and managerial-level groups.

Ideally, the working life of a police officer consists of one rewarding experience after another. Realistically, this is not always the case. Policing is not exempt from the usual stresses that occur in many jobs. Police officers are not always held in the highest esteem by the public, and the pressures that exist as a result of this can take their toll on many police officers. The nature and actions of the citizens that the officer encounters when performing required duties can eventually leave him or her cynical. If this attitude is not controlled, it can distort the officer's attitudes toward everyone, not just toward those that violate the law (Goolkasian, Geddes, and DeJong, 1985: 4-10).

Other factors that make police work stressful include inadequate policies, excessive rules and regulations, the constant changing of shifts, poor supervision, non-supportive management, boredom, conflict with other criminal justice agencies, lack of public support, the potential for being injured or killed, and non-involvement in the decision-making process (Kroes, 1985: 29-33; Leonard and More, 1993: 132).

Over the years, numerous studies have concluded that police work is one of the most stressful jobs a person can hold. Meanwhile, other studies have listed police work as highly stressful, but not among the top ten most stressful occupations. Whether police work is ranked as one of the most stressful is not the real issue. What must be acknowledged is that police work can be stressful. Each police officer and manager must become knowledgeable about occupational stress and its consequences.

In recent years, police administrators have moved from a position of recognizing that stress is "just part of the job" to acknowledging that there are emotional hazards in police work. The police officer is no longer viewed as superhuman, but as human beings. The officer's image of being tough, hard, and unemotional is being replaced with the recognition that a cop is, in reality, someone in uniform trying to do a job. As such, they are subject to numerous on-the-job pressures that can prove to be perilous not only to the individual, but to the organization.

When stress is not alleviated, it can result in heart attacks, high blood pressure, ulcers, insomnia, chronic headaches, and a large number of other illnesses traceable to the pressures that officers encounter at work. Stress can lead to an increase in accidents, absenteeism, resignations, depression, suicides, alcohol and drug abuse, and aggression (Goolkasian, Geddes, and DeJong, 1985: 4-10). Occupational stressors affect officers' alertness, their physical stamina, and their ability to effectively perform their duties. Additionally, it causes psychological problems and physical health disorders (Brown and Campbell, 1994: 80). Organizational stress is readily apparent when an agency fails to define the goals of law enforcement, refuses to deal with personnel fairly, and refuses to allow personnel to have input into operational and policy matters (Law Enforcement News, 1995a: 12). Police administrators can no longer ignore on-the-job stress. The first-line supervisor (and anyone in a higher administrative position) cannot hide behind the statement: "if you don't like it, quit." Rather than waiting for something to happen, the progressive police administrator takes the position that it is possible to change the way that an officer reacts to stressors. Excessive absenteeism, disability, premature retirement, and high replacement costs are all factors that clearly behoove a police administrator to take positive action before, rather than after, the effects of stress become apparent.

Given the pressures experienced by police officers, it is essential that administrators address the problem of organizational stress by identifying recurring grievances among officers and working to change the policies that cause them. There is no question that when policies or procedures impair the ability to function properly, the sources of stress must be eliminated or reduced (Finn, 1997: 20-26).

Stress is a reality. It must be handled by the individual, the group, and the department. A working environment should be such that stress is accepted as a key part of organizational life and as an inevitable consequence of developing relationships. Stress has both positive and negative effects. It can contribute to personal growth and development and enhance mental health. Stress can cause an officer to perform successfully and feel satisfied with the working environment. On the other hand, excessive and prolonged stress can affect officers in negative ways. Performance can become inadequate, and there can be a negative impact on the officer's physical well-being (Blau, 1994: 184-193).

Defining Stress

Every individual reacts differently to stress. Some officers handle stress very well and perceive it as part of the job. Others react poorly to stress and respond negatively to specific job stressors. Stress is defined "as a situation in which some working conditions called stressors (or combination of conditions) interact with the worker and result in an acute disruption of psychological or behavioral homeostasis" (Murphy and Schoenborn, 1987: 48).

Implicit in this definition is that some aspect of the job causes an officer to react to the stressor. As a stressor is evaluated, there is an emotional and physical response. If there is any critical aspect of this evaluation, it is that the officer must consider the stressor to be a threat to his personal well-being. Otherwise, the physical and emotional response does not occur (Wilson, 1981: 218-221).

If a specific stressor (such as role ambiguity) is present, and it inhibits one's ability to do something, then stress will be rather high. This occurs because the officer has no idea how the situation will result. On the other hand, if the stressor is of no consequence and the result is inevitable, the stress-inducing factor is viewed as inconsequential. Another element to be taken into consideration is the significance of the situation resulting from the stressor. If the situation is perceived as insignificant, then there is no stress. In the case of Officer Ralph Cummings (discussed in the following Feature), there are a number of occupational stressors contributing to the way that he deals with his family, and all of these suggest that he has been unable to adjust to a number of aspects of his job.

Feature

Stressed Out

Officer Ralph Cummings was viewed by his peers as a "cop's cop." He was always in the thick of it. He was the first to respond to situations when another officer needed assistance or backup. He was a take-charge type who focused on the immediate accomplishment of a task, no matter what the consequences. He frequently felt frustrated by red tape and policies that limited or restricted officers' discretion.

Cummings liked to take risks, and had a need to be constantly stimulated by events. In fact, it seemed that in some instances, he created incidents that should never have occurred, such as the provocation of street people. He constantly harassed those that he viewed as "dirt bags" or "parasites." His enthusiasm for real police work seemed to have no bounds. Slowly, his overall attitude toward police work became one of "us against them."

Cummings' attitude toward the public was one of disdain and contempt. He performed his duty in such a manner as to feel justified in everything he did. He became convinced that the best way to handle the vast majority of incidents was to be tough and forceful. In other words, Cummings believed that an officer should never let anyone else get the upper hand, that an officer should play it just like he was told by the instructors in the police academy, and that an officer should take charge and always maintain control.

Married and the father of two children, Cummings began to have problems at home. His wife Cheryl found that he was becoming increasingly distant, authoritarian, demanding, and overbearing. She felt that she and the children were treated as the enemies and were the objects of continual derision and disdain. She discussed the problem with George Simmons, their minister, but Cummings refused to admit that there was a problem and adamantly refused counseling. Cummings came home from work at about 2 A.M. at one point and found a note from his wife stating that she had taken the children to his mother and that she was considering divorce.

What responsibility does the police department have in helping Officer Cummings resolve this family problem? If you were his immediate supervisor, what would you do? Is there a connection between the way that Cummings treats his family and the attitude that he holds toward police work? What occupational stressors played a part in the development of Officer Cummings' attitude toward his work?

Eustress

While stress is usually viewed as having negative connotations, many experts agree that stress can have either positive or negative effects (Goolkasian, Geddes, and DeJong, 1985: 3). This viewpoint leads to the concept of *good stress*. The term for this is *eustress* (Cherry, 1978: 42). It is not important to know whether the stressor is good or bad itself. Instead, one should know how an officer responds to the constraints and whether the consequences of the stressor are perceived as important. This means that how an individual responds to stress may depend on whether various events in life are viewed as positive occurrences.

A person's attitude determines whether a specific stressor, such as a restrictive policy on the use of force, is perceived as limiting that person's ability to protect himself. If an officer believes that the stressor increases the possibility of injury to himself, the stressor will be detrimental. On the other hand, if the new policy is viewed as something that should have been implemented many years ago, it may very well be accepted as an improvement and as a challenge. With a positive view of such a stressor, what might have been interpreted as a negative stressor becomes *good stress* (Leonard and More, 1993: 131-134).

When positive stressors are nurtured and developed by police administrators, the negative consequences of stressors can be eliminated and officers become more goal-oriented and perform more often at peak levels. Stress is always present, and officers react differently to stress stimuli. Consequently, it is important that management foster eustress and strive to eliminate or soften the impact of negative stress in the working environment.

The majority of police departments abound with regulations, as managers over the years have attempted to identify and clarify the principles and values that guide the performance of departmental activities. In one department, policy prohibits firing a weapon at a moving vehicle. An officer who violates this policy is suspended for five days without pay. In one situation, an officer who violated the policy was supported by many line officers and operational supervisors, all of whom had opposed the prohibitive policy when it was implemented. With this support, the officer responded positively to the potentially stressful situation. In fact, he viewed the suspension as a badge of honor conferred upon him by "real cops" (i.e., the operational personnel that work the streets and perform real police work) not the upper echelon of the hierarchy (i.e., *ivory tower* cops) (More and Wegener, 1991: 218).

It is important to realize that positive events can also be stressful. For example, there is clear-cut evidence showing that when an officer is promoted, successfully clears a case, or receives an award from a citizen's group, stress is experienced even though the event that has occurred is a positive event. It should be kept in mind that organizational stress can affect not only the individual, but the organization itself. Impact on the officer may result in alcohol or drug abuse, rigidity of behavior, or psychosomatic disorders. When an officer is under sustained periods of stress, the following types of behavior may be exhibited: anger, thoughtlessness, defensiveness, and irritability. A police manager may see productivity drop, morale decline, tasks not accomplished on time, an increase in the use of sick leave, or other signs of employee malfunctioning. Figure 10-1 sets forth a comprehensive list of occupational stressors.

Burnout

Most people who have been employed in law enforcement for at least a decade have come into contact (or worked closely) with a fellow officer who could be classified as suffering from burnout. A colleague who was once full of enthusiasm, action-oriented, and truly excited about police work slowly (in most instances) recedes into the background. The officer loses interest in the job and becomes someone who can only be described as a marginal employee. It is almost as if the officer has exhibited a split personality over the period; he has been a *Jekyll-and-Hyde*. What happened? How does a capable employee become, in some instances, a potential organizational liability? Is the problem something that should be identified and resolved in advance? When an employee becomes burned out, the organization and the community suffer. To the burned-out officer, work is unsatisfying, there is a general lack of involvement other than at a minimal level, and commitment to the tasks that need to be performed (as well as commitment to fellow officers) is usually lacking.

There are several types of burnout, including psychological, physiological, and behavioral. Burnout is most advantageously summarized as the final stage of mental or emotional exhaustion, in which the individual is unable to cope with the job. The term *burnout* is defined as "a debilitating psychological condition brought about by unrelieved work stress" (Veniga and Spradley, 1981: 6).

Figure 10-1
Occupational Stressors

Accidents	Inflated health-care costs
Thefts	Unpreparedness
Reduced productivity	Lack of creativity
High turnover	Increased sick leave
Increased errors	Premature retirement
Absenteeism	Organizational breakdown
Disability payments	Disloyalty
Damage and waste	Job dissatisfaction
Replacement costs	Antagonistic group action
Poor decisions	Resistance

Source: John W. Jones and David DuBois (1987). "A Review of Organizational Stress Assessment Instruments." In Lawrence R. Murphy and Theodore F. Schoenborn (eds.), *Stress Management in Work Settings*. Washington, DC: U.S. Department of Health and Human Services, 48.

Two experts in this field, Dennis T. Jaffe and Cynthia D. Scott, believe that burnout is a crisis of the spirit. It is their position that burnout is not caused by defective employees, but by difficult and demanding work environments. Most of us would agree that police work can be very stressful. Burnout has been found to have a high occurrence in the helping professions; police work falls into this category.

Experts who have listened to individuals suffering from burnout have pointed out a number of emerging themes. These include: feeling trapped, a need to get away, a feeling of being weighed down, feeling exhausted, a feeling of emptiness, and wanting to give up (Pelletier, 1984: 64). Unfortunately, these symptoms translate into poor performance in the workplace.

Fellow officers can be profoundly affected by the cynicism (Graves, 1996: 16-20; Guindon, 1995: 59-69) and overall negativism of burned-out officers. A team that once functioned superbly may become inept and perform poorly. Officers seldom burn out suddenly; burnout is usually something that develops gradually. Ordinary demands of the job can cause stress, but the impact of stress can vary from day to day. Once an officer is burned out, treatment is the only way to resolve the problem (Jaffe and Scott, 1988: 19).

The gradual onset of burnout proceeds through several stages. Stage one, the *honeymoon/enthusiasm* phase, is a positive one. New employees usually react enthusiastically to the working environment, and every new event becomes a challenge. This initial stage is a learning and growing period for the rookie. With their idealism, rookie officers are ready to confront criminals, save lives, and solve the most perplexing crimes. While stress can take its toll during this phase, many officers develop coping techniques that last throughout their careers. If the officer does not adapt to job stressors, the next stage occurs.

The second stage, *fuel shortage/stagnation*, is characterized by expending less energy, resulting in a reduction of enthusiasm. Conditions that were previously ignored, such as shift changes, long hours, or low pay, become important issues. The effects of personal deprivation of recognition, influence, or autonomy become significant (Edelwich & Brosky, 1980: 34). Work becomes routine and boring, as the officer has already mastered the skills needed to perform at an acceptable level. Unfortunately, new challenges are few and far between.

At some point in this stage, symptoms of job burnout appear. The specific symptoms vary from individual to individual, but they usually include: (1) job dissatisfaction, (2) inefficiency at work, (3) fatigue, (4) sleep disturbance, and (5) escape activities (e.g., daydreaming) (Veniga and Spradley, 1981: 7-10).

In the *chronic symptoms/frustration* stage, the officer has fewer reserves to cope with job frustrations. Anger and resentment evolve, and the officer begins to withdraw from the job. At the same time, physical as well as psychological problems become more pronounced. Three areas in which frustration manifests itself are: psychosomatic illness; unhealthy indulgence in food and drugs such as nicotine, caffeine, or alcohol; and damage to personal and family relationships (Edelwich & Brosky, 1980: 156).

The fourth stage, *crisis/apathy*, is one in which the symptoms reach the critical point by intensifying or increasing in number. For example, frequent headaches at this stage are diagnosed as migraine. The officer becomes obsessed with the frustrations created by the working environment. Pessimism sets in and self-doubt permeates the officer's thinking. Every burnout symptom becomes critical, and the officer develops an "escape mentality" (Veniga and Spradley, 1981: 68).

The last stage is *hitting the wall/intervention*, which is the point at which burnout becomes entwined with other problems such as alcoholism, drug abuse, heart disease, and mental illness. When intervention occurs, it breaks the cycle and can prevent suicide (Veniga and Spradley, 1981: 28).

Each of these stages overlaps with another, and it is very difficult to distinguish where one stage ends and another stage begins. It is possible for an officer to go through all of the stages in a relatively short period. Another officer will take a number of years. A key problem is that the cause-and-effect relationship between stress and health problems is not definitive. Consequently, many officers find it difficult to accept the fact that occupational stressors can cause physical and emotional problems (Blau, 1994: 193). It should also be kept in mind that the family of the officer can fall victim to the process of burnout and family members can exhibit symptoms of stress and become emotionally depleted over time. It is increasingly common for couples and families to be considered a treatment group (Ryan, 1997: 63-68).

Model of Job Stress and Health

Research psychologists at the National Institute for Occupational Safety and Health utilize a model to depict the relationship between working conditions and health consequences. Figure 10-2 identifies specific stressors and a combination of conditions that interact with the employee to result in an acute disruption of psychological or behavioral homeostasis. Such acute reactions or disruptions, if prolonged, lead to a variety of illnesses. These include such things as hypertension, coronary heart disease (Rachlin, 1996: 61-66), alcoholism, and mental illness (Murphy and Schoenborn, 1987: 18).

Various job conditions that produce psychological, physiological, and behavioral reactions in workers have been well documented. These fall into three broad categories: job/task demands, organizational factors, and physical conditions.

Job/Task Demands

Workload itself has been recognized as a source of stress, and is the subject of extensive research. For example, working excessive hours or holding more than one job has been associated with coronary heart disease (CHD) and mortality.

Figure 10-2
Model of Job Stress and Health

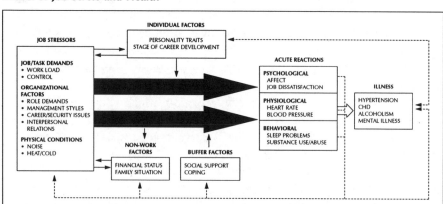

Source: Adapted from Lawrence R. Murphy and Theodore F. Schoenborn (1987) (eds.), *Stress Management in Work Situations*. Washington, DC: National Institute for Occupational Safety and Health.

This is especially critical in law enforcement because many officers seek part-time employment to supplement income. Many departments take the position that officers must obtain authorization prior to engaging in outside employment. This is an administrative technique used to ensure that the department receives full and faithful employment from its officers (More and Shipley, 1987: 147).

Recent studies have expanded this concept and show that the amount of work does not seem to be as critical to health as is the control that the worker has over the work rate and the related work processes. Employees that have large work-loads, many demands, and low control over those demands have an increased risk of coronary heart disease and high blood pressure. In law enforcement, administrators are becoming increasingly concerned about the excessive workload performed by officers when incoming calls are *stacked* and it becomes difficult for officers to handle them. This has forced some departments to prioritize calls, which may result in inefficient service. In some cities, crimes that were once investigated by an officer are closed after a telephone call to the victim or after the victim has completed an information form and mailed it to the department.

Shift work is another job demand that is thought to have health and safety consequences. There is substantial evidence that night and rotating-shift schedules, in particular, can lead to sleep disorders and gastrointestinal ailments. Other consequences include emotional disturbances and an increased risk of occupational injury (Murphy and Schoenborn, 1987: 48).

Organizational Factors

Organizational stress is defined as the general, unconscious, patterned mobilization of an individual's energy when confronted with any organizational or work demand (Quick and Quick, 1984: 75). In one study, it was found that officers who experienced role ambiguity had low self-confidence, higher job-related tension, and lower job satisfaction. Role ambiguity occurs when a person has a lack of clarity about the objectives associated with the work role, expectations concerning the work role, and confusion about the scope and responsibilities of the job. Likewise, workers who experienced role conflict (i.e., conflicting job demands) were found to experience more job-related tension and less job satisfaction. An analysis of 96 studies confirmed the connection between role conflict, ambiguity, and affective reactions. The analysis also suggested that these role stressors are related to absenteeism and poor job performance (Murphy and Schoenborn, 1987: 47-48; Kroes, 1985: 29-33).

Various management styles, such as allowing little or no participation in decisionmaking, providing ineffective consultation, and imposing restrictions on behavior, are organizational features also viewed as potentially stressful (Greene, 1997: 70-72). Early studies clearly demonstrated that greater participation in decisionmaking led to greater job satisfaction, lower turnover, better supervisor-subordinate relationships, and increased productivity (Leonard and More, 1993: 42).

Physical Conditions

Adverse environmental conditions appear to be associated with health disorders in a synergistic way. These conditions exacerbate the overall job demands placed on workers, thus lowering tolerance to other stressors and decreasing worker motivation. The conditions include factors such as excessive cold or heat, poor ventilation, and inadequate lighting. A reasonable temperature comfort zone ranges from 65 to 80 degrees. In one department, in an agricultural valley, the police cars were not air-conditioned, even though the summer temperatures often exceeded 100 degrees. The chief of the department conducted a study and found that, on an average summer day, in a vehicle without air-conditioning, the temperature was 135 degrees. The city manager had refused to purchase air-conditioned vehicles until it was shown that the increased cost of these vehicles was negligible when compared with the car's increased resale value (which, in fact, exceeded the cost of adding the air-conditioning by 50 percent).

Stressors Unique to Police Work

Many sources of police stress emerge from police work itself. Many officers feel that conflict is a constant feature of enforcing the law and serving the public. In part, the cumulative effects of stress can lead to:

* Impaired performance and reduced productivity.

* Reduced morale.

- Public relations problems.

- Labor-management friction.

- Civil suits stemming from stress-related shortcomings in personnel performance.

- Tardiness and absenteeism.

- Increased turnover due to leaves of absence and early retirements because of stress-related problems and disabilities.

- The added expense of training and hiring new recruits, as well as paying overtime, when the agency is left short-staffed as a result of turnover. (Finn and Tomz, 1997: 1-39)

Tasks performed by the police involve dealing with many negative stressors that present a very strong challenge not only to each officer, but to police administrators. Stress can be costly to a police department. A police officer's sudden heart attack can result in early disability retirement. Courts in the state of California have ruled for many years that coronary heart disease is occupationally related.

Stress experts support the position that stress is additive in nature (Robbins, 1986: 382-383). A single stressor may or may not have consequence, but if it is added to other stressors that are perceived as negative, the stressors become cumulative

James D. Sewell has developed a specific, critical life-events scale that has proven to be a significant tool for managers. This scale is called the Law Enforcement Critical Life-Events Scale (LECLES). It is an instrument that identifies critical life events specific to law enforcement. The scale identifies 144 events experienced by police officers, who rate each of the events on a scale of 1 to 100. The most stressful situation, violent death of a partner, was given a rating of 88 (the highest rating given), and the least stressful event, the completion of a routine report, was rated at the low point value of 13. Figure 10-3 is a partial rated listing of the 144 life events.

Of the police officers who participated in the development of this scale, slightly more than one-half (52.1%) stated that they had experienced at least one of eight stress-related illnesses. The most frequent illness was digestive disturbance (25.4%), while the second most frequent was the use of alcohol (19.9%).

The Law Enforcement Critical Life Event Scale (LECLES) can be used to administratively respond to a combination of stressful events. The items set forth in Figure 10-4 depict a series of events that negatively affect the health of an officer when these events occur within the space of a year. Depending upon the situation and the individual involved, a superior may counsel the officer, or professional counseling may be provided by mental health experts (Kirschman, 1997: 45-61). The goal is to help the officer to deal positively with the stressors involved, and to prevent negative psychological or physiological symptoms.

Comparisons of how stressful events are rated have been made between female and male police officers. Responses from the officers have indicated that the most significant stressors are in the following three areas: manpower, equipment, and supervision. In one study, male police officers expressed a greater concern about career issues than did female officers, and female officers rated personal safety issues as greater concerns (Pendergrass and Ostrove, 1984: 231-242).

Figure 10-3
Law Enforcement Critical Life Event Scale (LECLES)

Life Event	Value
1. Violent death of a partner in the line of duty	88
2. Dismissal	85
3. Taking a life in the line of duty	84
4. Shooting someone in the line of duty	81
5. Suicide of an officer who is a close friend	80
6. Violent death of another officer in the line of duty	79
7. Murder committed by a police officer	78
8. Duty-related violent injury (shooting)	76
9. Violent job-related injury of another officer	75
10. Suspension	72
11. Passed over for promotion	71
12. Pursuit of an armed suspect	71
13. Answering a call to scene involving violent non-accidental death of a child	70
14. Assignment away from home for a long period of time	70
15. Personal involvement in a shooting situation	70
16. Reduction in pay	70
17. Observing an act of police corruption	69
18. Accepting a bribe	69
***	
57. Physical assault on an officer	52
58. Disciplinary action against partner	52
59. Death notification	51
60. Press criticism of an officer's action	51
61. Polygraph examination	51
62. Sexual advancement toward you by another officer	51
63. Duty-related accidental injury	55
64. Changing work shift	50
***	

Source: This is a partial list of some of the critical life events out of a total of 144 developed by Dr. James D. Sewell. A copy of the instrument was obtained from the author. Reprinted with permission of James D. Sewell.

One other study of police officers in two states determined that female officers and male officers experienced the same level of work-related stress, with the exception of danger, which female officers rated higher (Davis, 1979: 89).

Figure 10-4
**Stressful Life Events Occurring in One Year That Require
a Positive Managerial Response**

Event	Value of Life Change Units
Marital separation	65
Oral promotion review	57
Written promotional review	55
Death notification	51
Changing work shifts	50
Reassignment/transfer	46
Unfair administrative policy	46
	370

Source: This is a partial list of some of the critical life events out of a total of 144 developed by Dr. James D. Sewell; Papalia, Diane E. and Sally W. Olds (1988). *Psychology* Second Edition. New York: McGraw-Hill Books, 312-314.

Stressors From the Criminal Justice System and the Community

During the last three decades, extensive consideration has been given to the relationship between the community and law enforcement agencies. Many studies acknowledge that the community is the source of considerable stress. The causes of stress, then, are a general lack of community support and, in many instances, segments of the community that hold the police in contempt and disdain. Even when officers are fortunate enough to work in a reasonably supportive community, there are always some individuals who are openly hostile to the police and are a constant source of negativism toward them (Ellison and Genz, 1983: 51).

Other stressors include distorted and unfavorable media accounts of incidents involving the police. This stressor is especially evident when an officer is familiar with the facts regarding a specific event, and the published account bears little relationship to reality.

Another community stressor comes from the political environment in which many officers operate. This stressor arises when political pressure is brought to bear, such that regulations are ignored or altered, so that a special privilege or favor is extended to someone who has political clout (Ellison and Genz, 1983: 50). Politicians have also been known to exert influence on the promotional process by interceding for an officer in an effort to obtain a special or preferred assignment for that officer.

During the years ahead, the police will have to meet the unprecedented challenges of societal change. Communities throughout the nation are changing rapidly as a consequence of urbanization, population explosion, immigration, changing morality, a transient lifestyle, and the aging of our population.

As the police are required to perform a variety of new tasks (many of which have not been identified at this point), the community will continue to be a source of stress. As the public continues to scrutinize police activities, there is speculation that the negative community attitude will endure. At the same time, it is believed that this type of stress can be reduced to a more acceptable level. Presently, police departments are expected to adopt a community problem-solving role in order to significantly reduce the tension between the police and the community.

The criminal justice system itself serves as a source of stress for many police officers. This is especially true of the courts and their influence on police operations. Numerous officers have expressed the opinion that courts are too lenient and that judges exhibit a greater concern for the welfare of defendants than for victims or the safety of the community at large. The frequent changes in penal codes and their interpretation are also stressful to officers who, in many instances, find that they are unaware of a change or nuance in the law until they are confronted with that change in court (Ellison and Genz, 1983: 49).

Another frequently cited source of stress is the lack of consideration by the courts in scheduling officers for court appearances. Delaying tactics by attorneys and changing court dates seem to constantly conflict with officers' work assignments, personal time, and sleeping schedules. This stress is further exacerbated by court decisions, especially when an officer's discretion is reduced or more closely circumscribed, and when the police role is limited or restricted. Furthermore, sentencing is often perceived as being too lenient. This occurs when offenders are released early or when they are placed on probation rather than sent to jail (Goolkasian, Geddes, and DeJong, 1985: 5).

Defense attorneys, in many instances, are another source of stress for officers. This is especially evident when the attorney searches diligently for a lenient judge or repeatedly obtains postponements of a trial until witnesses leave the area or memories fade. In one federal jurisdiction, a judge was nicknamed "Probation." During arraignments on Monday morning, he often proclaimed that he felt like it was "probation time" and that probation was available to anyone appearing before him. The only requirement was a guilty plea; the nature of the crime or previous convictions were never taken into consideration. Other stress inducers are the tactics used by defense attorneys when they attempt to discredit an officer. In effect, these tactics make it seem that the officer, not the defendant, is on trial (Ellison and Genz, 1983: 49).

Stress and Emotional Problems Among Police Officers

One recent study found that nearly 85 percent of the emotional problems suffered by officers involved alcoholism, depression, personality disorders, and exaggerated health problems. Overall, substance abuse (mostly alcohol) was found to be the most prevalent problem confronting male officers. Female officers suffered most frequently from depression, followed by substance abuse and distorted health problems (Rafilson and Heaton, 1995: 13). Another area of concern involves the psychological distress of officers involved in shooting incidents or critical incidents (Finn and Tomz, 1997: 125-137). There are, of course, other problems attributable to the stressful nature of police work. These include marital and family problems, sexual problems resulting from promiscuity, isolation from friends, suicide, and unnecessary risk-taking. The next Feature lists some of the stressors according to personal and organizational categories.

Suicide

While some studies support the belief that suicide is an occupational hazard for police officers, other studies refute this belief. When compared to other occupational groups, studies of data gathered from the 1930s through the 1960s by several different researchers supported the belief that police officers have a high suicide rate. These studies included officers from police departments in San Francisco, Chicago, and New York, as well as officers in Tennessee and Wyoming (Violanti, 1996a: 1-98). For example, in Wyoming during an eight-year period, researchers determined that the suicide rate for police officers was twice as high as the rate for physicians, which had the second-highest rate among occupational groups in the study.

Feature

Personal and Organizational Effects of Stressors

Personal

Alcohol abuse	Anxiety
Drug abuse	Psychosomatic diseases
Emotional instability	Eating disorders
Lack of self-control	Boredom
Fatigue	Mental illness
Marital problems	Suicide
Depression	Health breakdowns
Insomnia	Irresponsibility
Insecurity	Frustration

Organizational

Accidents	Inflated health-care costs
Reduced productivity	Lack of creativity
High turnover	Increased sick leave
Increased errors	Premature retirement
Absenteeism	Disloyalty
Disability payments	Job dissatisfaction
Organizational breakdown	Poor decisions
Damage and waste	Antagonistic group action

Source: Lawrence R. Murphy and Theodore F. Schoenborn (eds.) (1987). *Stress Management in Work Situations*. Washington, DC: National Institute for Occupational Safety and Health, 58.

A review of medical records in Tennessee by Wayne C. Richard and Ronald D. Fellin (in a 1975 report published by the federal government) found that police officers were third among occupational groups (behind laborers and pressmen) in terms of the suicide rate (Kroes and Hurrell, 1975: 234-246). In 1976, William H. Kroes concluded that police officers committed suicide less frequently than lumbermen and laborers and somewhat more frequently than physicians. In 1977, J. Dash and M. Reiser found that, in a six-year period during the 1970s, the suicide rate for police officers in Los Angeles was well below the average rate for the entire population of Los Angeles County (Goolkasian, Geddes, and DeJong, 1985: 8-9).

In 1995, the National Fraternal Order of Police, in a study of life insurance policies of 38,800 FOP members, concluded that suicide (37 percent) was the leading cause of accidental deaths among police officers (*Law Enforcement News*, 1995b: 1, 10). In 1996, a study of the deaths of Buffalo police officers determined that officers were eight times more likely to commit suicide than to be killed in a homicide, and three times more likely to commit suicide than to die in job-related accidents (*Law Enforcement News*, 1996: 1).

There is considerable difficulty in studying suicides of police officers. Many departments do not keep statistics on suicides and even if they do, they are reluctant to make the information available (Violanti, 1996b: 77-85). It is generally known that the figures on suicide for police officers are artificially low. Some suicides have been classified as either accidents or undetermined deaths. A cohesive sub-culture, the police shield victim officers, their families, and the department from the stigma of suicide (Violanti, 1995: 19-24).

In one instance, a police officer was found dead in his home. The barrel of a revolver was in the officer's mouth, and his finger was on the trigger. The cause of death was listed as accidental. The investigating officer knew that the survivors would receive a higher insurance benefit if the death were listed as accidental (Kroes, 1985: 27-34).

In another case, an officer radioed that he was stopping an individual for questioning. Later, the officer was found shot with his own weapon. A massive search, utilizing dogs and helicopters, was conducted for the suspect, but that person was never located. The medical examiner was unable to determine whether the officer took his own life or was shot by an unknown assailant. There were no powder burns, and the weapon was found next to the body. The autopsy did show that the officer was suffering from terminal cancer. There was also a reasonably large insurance policy on his life. The family of the officer was ruled eligible to receive funding from the Public Safety Officers' Benefits Act.

After 21 suicides in the New York Police Department over a two-year period, the Patrolmen's Benevolent Association trained 50 peer support officers for its Membership Assistance Program to help officers deal with stress and emotional problems. An additional goal was to train at least 200 more officers for the peer support program (Cohen, Hirsh, and Katz, 1996: 88). Additionally, in 1997 the Association received a federal grant to provide a stress-reduction education program for 1,500 officers and family members. Goals for the grant include

developing a handbook for peer support officers, expanding a network of referrals of mental health personnel, and forming permanent support groups (*Law
Enforcement News*, 1996: 5)

Alcoholism

In the United States, alcohol is number one in sales and consumption as the
drug of choice for reducing tension and stress. Interestingly, alcohol has been
purchased at a high rate even during periods of economic depression. Over a
recent 15-year period, the sale of hard liquor rose by 20 percent, and beer sales
increased by 25 percent. Needless to say, liquor consumption occurs for many
reasons other than stress reduction, but it remains a serious problem in the United States. The American Hospital Association has determined that there are
approximately 10 million alcoholics in the United States, including individuals
from every occupation and age level (Albrecht, 1979: 41).

Needless to say, police officers are as eager as other segments of the community to find something to reduce tension and stress. In fact, some researchers
have suggested that police work is especially conducive to the creation of problem drinkers. In many departments, the subculture supports drinking. *Choir
practice*, described by Joseph Waumbaugh (a former police officer) in his best-
selling books on police, refers to the practice of officers getting together at the
end of a shift to "hoist a few" and swap war stories. Drinking is considered
"macho" and is acceptable behavior. Officers who work undercover, especially
those who do vice work, are particularly vulnerable to excessive drinking
because (in many instances) the job requires it (Kroes, 1985: 27-34). In one
instance, an officer of a state alcoholic control agency became an alcoholic
because it was necessary when checking bars to drink as part of the assignment.

As in the situation with suicide, the research into the use of alcohol by police
officers has established a relationship between high job stress and excessive
drinking (Margolis, Kroes, and Quinn, 1974: 659-661). As early as 1955, the
Chicago Police Department began a police officer's fellowship for the purpose
of helping officers with drinking problems. In 1966, the New York Police
Department established a program to assist employees. One study of 2,300 officers, published in 1978, showed that 23 percent of the officers had serious
drinking problems. After another study of New York City officers, released in
1978, more than 1,000 officers were ordered to seek help for alcoholism (Ellison and Genz, 1983: 46; and Kroes, 1985: 47).

In Buffalo, New York, in 1995, it was found that 40 percent of the officers
found to be unfit had a substance abuse problem. Male officers were twice as
likely to have a drinking problem as compared to the second most frequent problem, which was depression. Twenty-one percent of the female officers in Buffalo suffered from substance abuse. Overall, this study found that problems developed and performance difficulties occurred after 10 years on the job (Rafilson
and Heaton, 1995: 13).

Informally, some police administrators have reported that 25 percent of the officers in their departments have alcohol abuse problems, while administrators in other departments have asserted that alcoholism in their departments is much less common (Goolkasian, Geddes, and DeJong, 1985: 9). There is some evidence that the police do not differ in rate of occurrence of alcohol abuse from the general population (Blau, 1994: 193). What is needed is a systematic study of a number of agencies to confirm or reject the widely held belief that the police suffer an unusually high rate of alcoholism.

Divorce

Police work has a definite influence on the family. What occurs at work can affect the family, and what occurs at home can influence job performance (Kannady, 1993: 92-95). Unfortunately, in many instances, the rigors of police work are factors that lead to divorce. The vast majority of police officers devote their entire lives to the job. As a result of this, the family suffers. Early research in the police field made findings that varied considerably as to the extent of divorce. In three communities, the number of divorced officers ranged from 17 to 33.3 percent. A nationwide study published in 1978 found a divorce rate of 30 percent. A study of the Los Angeles Police Department found a low divorce rate. In another study, only five percent of the officers interviewed were divorced (Ellison and Genz, 1983: 47).

In a review of research in this area, Marilyn Davidson and Arthur Veno pointed out that in the studies that purport to find a high divorce rate, there were a lack of control groups and a failure to consider a multitude of factors influencing divorce rates (such as age at marriage and the number of children) (Davidson and Veno, 1978: 190-191). Some departments have dealt with the problem of divorce by training spouses while the officer is in recruit training. Other departments conduct marriage seminars for couples, and offer the services of a police psychologist to assist families in coping with problems (Kannady, 1993: 92-95).

Critical Incidents

In a nationwide survey conducted on stress, respondents indicated that involvement in a shooting incident was the most dangerous and traumatic experience that an officer might have to face during his or her career. Even when an officer is not physically injured, the psychological stress caused by such an experience can be profound. Frequently cited reactions to this stress include guilt, anxiety, fear, nightmares, flashbacks, social withdrawal, and impaired memory and concentration. One expert has shown that the two most common problems of officers involved in an on-duty shooting were the inability to sleep and rumination about the event (Carson, 1987: 46). It seems obvious that an officer involved in a shooting is usually unprepared to cope with such an event, but the same is true of the officer's family, supervisors, and fellow officers. Chapter 4, Police Use of Deadly Force, is devoted to an extensive consideration of the use of deadly force by police officers.

Other critical incidents are of increasing concern to law enforcement (Fischer, 1997: 8-13). Extensive stress can be caused by an unusual occurrence. These events can include a line of duty death, an injury to a co-worker, a police suicide, a life-threatening assault on an officer, an accident involving multiple deaths, a traumatic death of a child, or a barricaded suspect (Brown and Campbell, 1994: 44-51). Critical incident stress manifests itself physically, cognitively, and emotionally. The officer may experience some or all of these reactions immediately, or perhaps not until after a delay. While in most instances the symptoms will subside in a matter of weeks, a few of those affected by such stress will suffer permanent emotional trauma (Kureczka, 1996: 10-16).

The Reduction of Stress

There are many things that can be done to deal with officer stress. Both the individual and the organization can use many resources to deal with the complexity of stress in the work setting. From the previous discussion, it is apparent that constructive stress can enhance work performance and negative stress cannot only impair job performance, but can be deleterious to an officer's health.

What is desirable is to manage stress in such a way that it is reduced or prevented from reaching excessive levels before performance is impaired or personal well-being is affected. Every officer in a police organization is important. If an agency is to function with any degree of effectiveness, the well-being of every officer must be taken into consideration. With an awareness of the importance of eustress and bad stress and their potential impact on both the individual and the organization, increased consideration is being given to developing wellness programs in law enforcement agencies.

Personal Strategies for Coping With Stress

The individual can respond to organizational stress by focusing on physical or behavioral strategies for handling stress and by becoming involved in a wide range of activities or functions, such as peer counseling or a running program. If at all possible, preventive programs should be emphasized; the individual and the organization should not wait until things are out of control. Unfortunately, many of us work from one day to the next and give little consideration to next week, next month, or next year. We fail to contemplate our life goals; we only manage to cope with the continuing difficulty of dealing with the demands of the job and the complexities generated by a rapidly changing society. There are also many other pressures felt by the officer who attempts to confront critical issues and prevent the occurrence of a stress-induced physical or psychological event (Reece and Brandt, 1987: 341).

Taking Charge of One's Life

There are many ways to minimize negative stress; one is to assess current and past job expectations, and compare the two in terms of the degree and extent of change from the past to the present. Examples of questions that should be asked include: Is there adequate time to perform the assigned tasks? Are deadlines realistic? Can tasks be handled differently? It is entirely possible that some behavior can be identified and changed. It might be that the individual should accept the fact that his working environment cannot be changed and that it is useless to keep fighting the organization. On the other hand, it is possible for an employee to be instrumental in changing working conditions.

Each individual officer should take charge of his own life; he should not wait for someone else or the organization to solve problems that he can solve himself. He does not know whether it can be done until he tries. In other words, an individual should plan ahead and should not wait until resolution of his or her problem becomes more difficult. It might be that court dates require an officer to return to duty after a limited amount of sleep. If this officer must perform at less than top efficiency, he or she should talk with his supervisor and the court liaison officer. It might be possible to change court dates. Perhaps the number of calls for service on an officer's beat are such that he or she is unable to answer all of them. The officer should ensure that his or her supervisor is fully aware of the problem because there is always a possibility that the beat can be restructured or that calls can be prioritized.

It is important to challenge every aspect of one job (within reason), so that the officer can control his or her working environment as much as possible. There are many ways to make police work more rewarding and more challenging. Officers in some agencies receive limited supervision; hence, they have considerable latitude regarding the way in which they perform their duties. Based upon an officer's experience, stressors can be anticipated and their impact can be lessened. Research suggests that many individuals expose themselves to unnecessary stress because they do not plan ahead (Baron, 1983: 281-295).

Relaxation

It has long been advocated that one way of dealing with stress is to take a vacation, enjoy a hobby, or participate in any type of activity found to be relaxing. In other words, the stressed-out individual should get away from the job and its pressures. This recommendation may be viewed as simplistic, but research has clearly pointed out the benefits to be obtained from participation in enjoyable activities. Interestingly enough, the individuals that benefit most from a change are those that suffer from the stress of negative life events (Baron, 1983: 281-299).

When an officer begins to feel tense or anxious, he should employ some type of stress reducer as soon as possible. This can be as simple as walking or running, or it can be accomplished by relaxation training. The majority of experts agree that relaxation techniques are useful in controlling and reducing stress.

Almost 30 years ago, Dr. Herbert Benson and his colleagues developed what has become known as the relaxation response. It involves an attempt to deal with stress through mastering techniques that induce deep muscle relaxation. The use of one of the numerous relaxation techniques decreases the heart rate, the metabolic rate, and the respiratory rate. It has also been found that, although blood pressure may remain the same at first, over a period of time, blood pressure will become lower (Quick and Quick, 1984: 75-83). Relaxation techniques include meditation, imagery, hypnosis, and biofeedback.

Exercise

If there is any proven way for an individual to become scientifically sound, it is to exercise. The benefits are numerous. Physical exercise can "ward off heart disease, colds, and influenza; maintain healthy and attractive weight goals; make sex more exciting; make food taste better and digest more efficiently; build up energy; and put one in a happier state of mind" (Papalia and Olds, 1988: 312-314).

Another outstanding benefit of physical exercise is stress reduction and the counteraction of some of the harmful physiological effects of stress. Each officer has the responsibility to maintain and enhance his own personal well-being; this is best accomplished through a disciplined approach to physical health. The officer must make a commitment to a lifestyle that includes positive involvement in physical exercise, and this should be done even if the agency does not have a physical fitness program.

Fortunately, more and more law enforcement agencies are promoting and sponsoring a wide range of exercise programs. These include such activities as 10K runs, marathons, the Police Olympics, and an annual football game known as the *Pig Bowl*. At the same time, police departments have opened weight rooms and provided other types of exercise equipment, including rowing machines, treadmills, and bicycles.

Although any kind of physical movement requires energy (calories), the type of exercise that uses the most energy is aerobic exercise. The term aerobic is derived from the Greek word meaning *with oxygen*. Jogging, brisk walking, swimming, biking, cross-country skiing, and aerobic dancing are some popular forms of aerobic exercise.

Aerobic exercises use the body's large muscle groups in continuous, rhythmic, sustained movement, which requires oxygen for the production of energy. When oxygen is combined with food (which can come from stored fat), energy is produced to power the body. The longer an individual moves aerobically, the more energy is needed and the greater the number of calories are used. Regular aerobic exercise improves cardiorespiratory endurance, which is the ability of the heart, lungs, blood vessels, and associated tissues to use oxygen to produce energy needed for activity. A person can build a healthier body while getting rid of excess body fat. Furthermore, experts recommend that aerobic exercises be supplemented by a program of muscle strengthening and stretching exercises. If a person's muscles are strong, he or she will be able to keep going longer during aerobic activity, and there is less chance of injury.

Experts recommend that aerobic exercise be performed at least three times a week for a minimum of 20 continuous minutes. Of course, if that is too much, one should start with a shorter time span and work up to the minimum. Then, one should gradually progress until he or she is able to work aerobically for 20 to 40 minutes. A person may engage in different types of aerobic activities. For example, walking one day, and riding a bicycle the next. The individual should be sure to choose an enjoyable activity that can be done regularly. The important thing to remember is that a person should not skip too many days between workouts, or fitness benefits will be lost. If a person must miss a few days, he or she should gradually work back into his routine as soon as possible.

Employee Assistance Programs

Employee counseling, especially for alcohol-related problems, has existed in the police field since before World War II. During the 1970s, Employee Assistance Programs (EAPs) were expanded, and consideration was given to other emotional and stress-related problems. An analysis of the brief history of existing stress programs reveals a number of different events or factors sparking program development. Precipitating elements included the inadequacy of previous department strategies for dealing with stress-related problems, the availability of funding, and legal requirements that departments be staffed by psychologically well-adjusted police officers who could perform their jobs properly (Goolkasian, Geddes, and DeJong, 1985: 25).

In Boston and San Francisco, dissatisfaction with the department's prior method of handling alcohol-related problems motivated line officers to develop programs of their own. In both of these departments, the stress programs were preceded by alcohol counselors who worked with troubled officers that had come to the attention of police supervisors or administrators (generally as part of official disciplinary proceedings). The dissatisfied officers wanted to develop a program that could address a broader range of problems, intervene before problems became severe, and offer assistance to officers' family members as well as to the officers themselves.

A number of stress programs were created in response to the concern for civil liability. Recent legal decisions have taken the position that law enforcement agencies are responsible for employee behavior and the psychological fitness of police officers. This responsibility falls under the term *negligent retention,* which emphasizes that police departments and supervisors can be held liable for the actions of their employees if they take no action even after they have indications that an officer is not performing adequately. It is important to create programs offering officers clinical services when they experience stress-related difficulties (Goolkasian, Geddes, and DeJong, 1985: 25).

The psychological services offered through the auspices of an EAP vary from agency to agency; some of the problems addressed by these services are listed in Figure 10-5. The majority of stress program managers assume that all personal problems and crises rendering an officer unable to perform his or her duties effectively, whatever the source, are legitimate concerns that warrant a response from the stress program (Goolkasian, Geddes, and DeJong, 1985: 29).

Figure 10-5
Types of Problems Addressed by Stress Programs

Alcoholism	Smoking
Substance abuse	Nutrition
Job stress	Exercise
Job burnout	Weight control
Anxiety	Divorce
Depression	Separation
Parent-child conflict	Police shooting
Single parenting	Gambling
Grief	Retirement
Suicide	

Source: John G. Stratton (1987). "Employee Assistance Programs—A Profitable Approach for Employees and Organizations." In Harry W. More and Peter C. Unsinger (eds.), *Police Managerial Use of Psychology and Psychologists*. Springfield, IL: Charles C Thomas, 63-84; Thomas E. Baker and Jane P. Baker (1996). "Preventing Police Suicide." *FBI Law Enforcement Bulletin*, Vol. 65, No. 10:24-27.

In recent years, peer support programs have been created throughout the nation. The program provides officers and members of their families the opportunity to confidentially discuss problems with a trained officer. The discussion can be about personal or professional problems. Officers are trained to recognize problems and make referrals when necessary. With proper support from a peer counselor, or professional help when needed, an event can be dealt with before it becomes a more serious problem (Greenstone, Dunn, and Leviton, 1995: 42-44; Janik, 1995: 38-40).

An effective EAP can benefit not only the individual, but the organization and the community. As police organizations become increasingly concerned about the quality of working life, it is anticipated that EAPs will play an important part in reducing organizational stress and helping officers to deal with all types of negative stress. Obviously, there is a critical need for law enforcement agencies to provide counseling, rehabilitation, and health promotion services for all personnel.

Summary

Stress is not only unique to the situation, but also to the individual. It is a fact of life and an integral part of the working environment. It has both positive and negative effects. It is present at both the operational level and at the managerial level. On one hand, stress can contribute to the personal growth and mental health of an officer, while in other situations, it can prove to be detrimental and have a negative impact on an officer's well-being.

The working life of a police officer is not simple; there can be pain and suffering as a result of performing police duties and fulfilling responsibilities to the community. The factors that make police work stressful include inadequate policies, excessive rules and regulations, the constant changing of shifts, poor supervision, non-supportive management, boredom, conflict with other criminal justice agencies, lack of public support, the potential for being injured or killed, and non-involvement in the decision-making process.

Job burnout has several components, including psychological, physiological, and behavioral, and it proceeds through several stages: honeymoon/enthusiasm, fuel shortage/stagnation, chronic symptoms/frustration, crisis/apathy, and hitting the wall/intervention. Each of these stages overlaps with another, but it is possible for one officer to go through all of the stages in a relatively short period, while another officer may take a number of years.

The National Institute for Occupational Safety and Health has created a model of job stress and health that depicts the relationship between specific working conditions and health consequences. These conditions fall into three broad categories: job/task demands, organizational factors, and physical conditions.

An assessment tool that has been used for a number of years by mental health practitioners is the Holmes-Rahe life stress inventory (Social Readjustment Rating Scale). It provides a rough measure of the degree of adjustment required of an individual over a specified period. Points are associated with each life event, e.g., "death of a spouse" is 100 points. There is also a Law Enforcement Critical Life Event Scale (LECLES), which consists of 144 life events experienced by police officers, e.g., "taking a life in the line of duty" is 84 points. Police managers and supervisors may use the events listed as a guide for deciding when consideration should be given to helping an officer deal with the combination of stressful events.

In some communities, there is a general lack of support for the police. Coupled with such factors as a negative press or political interference, this lack of support makes police work stressful. In one large community, a study determined that officers ranked poor community relations as fourth of all external stress inducers.

The criminal justice system itself serves as a source of stress. Some officers think that judges are soft on crime and have more concern for the defendant than for the protection of society. Stress can also result from dealing with court appearances. Court appearances are often rescheduled, creating havoc with officers' personal lives.

The preponderance of studies of stress and emotional problems among police officers have concentrated on the rates of suicide, divorce, and alcoholism, and on the psychological distress of officers involved in shooting incidents. The contention that in the first three areas (suicide, divorce, and alcoholism) the police have higher rates of incidence than other occupational groups has yet to be proven. Many of the early studies in this area proved to be faulty because of research design. However, it is not really important to know whether the police hold the top position in each of these categories. What is important is to be able to deal with the stressors that are unique to law enforcement.

There are many things that can be done to deal with the stress experienced by police officers. There are many ways that the individual and the organization can deal with the complexity of stress in the work setting. These include: taking charge of one's life, utilizing relaxation techniques, and developing an exercise program.

Employee Assistance Programs (EAPs) are becoming increasingly common in law enforcement. These programs are created for a number of reasons, including a concern for civil liability, the availability of funding, and the previous inadequacy of existing programs.

References

Albrecht, Karl (1979). *Stress and the Manager.* Englewood Cliffs, NJ: Prentice-Hall, Inc., 41.

Albrecht, Steve (1992). "Beating Burnout: Don't Let The Streets Get You Down." *Law And Order,* Vol. 40, No. 3:13-14.

Baker, Thomas and Jane P. Baker (1996). "Preventing Police Suicide." *FBI Law Enforcement Bulletin,* Vol. 65, No. 10:24-27.

Baron, Robert A. (1983). *Behavior in Organization: Understanding and Managing the Human Side of Work.* Newton, MA: Allyn and Bacon, 281-299.

Blau, Theodore, H. (1994). *Psychological Services for Law Enforcement.* New York: John Wiley, 184-193.

Bootzin, Richard R., Gordon H. Bower, Robert B. Zajonc, and Elizabeth Hall (1986). *Psychology Today,* Sixth Edition. New York: Random House, 389, 450-452.

Brown, Jennifer M. and Elizabeth A. Campbell (1994). *Stress and Policing: Sources and Strategies.* New York: John Wiley, 45-85.

Carson, Stephen L. (1987). "Post-Shooting Stress Reaction." *The Police Chief,* Vol. LVI, No. 9:46.

Cherry, L. (1978). "On the Real Benefits of Eustress." *Psychology Today,* Vol. 12, No. 3, March:42.

Cohen, Daniel, Ronnie M. Hirsh, and Rachelle Katz (1996). "Peer Support Programs: Officers Help Fellow Officers Deal With the Stressors of the Police Profession." *Law and Order,* Vol. 44, No. 9:88-90.

Davidson, Marilyn J. and Arthur Veno (1978). "Police Stress: A Multi-Cultural Interdisciplinary Review and Perspective, Part I." *Abstracts on Police Science,* July/August:190-191.

Davis, Richard H. (ed.) (1979). *Stress and the Organization.* Los Angeles: University of Southern California Press, 89.

Edelwich, Jerry and Archie Brodsky (1980). *Burnout: Stages of Disillusionment in the Helping Professions.* New York: Human Science Press, 34-156.

Ellison, Katherine and John L. Genz (1983). *Stress and the Police Officer.* Springfield, IL: Charles C Thomas, 45-51.

Finn, Peter (1997). "Reducing Stress—An Organization-Centered Approach." *FBI Law Enforcement Bulletin,* Vol. 66, No. 8:20-26.

Finn, Peter and Julie E. Tomz (1997). *Developing a Law Enforcement Stress Program for Officers and Their Families.* Washington, DC: Department of Justice, USGPO, 1-223.

Fischer, Russell (1997). "Emergency in the Everglades—The Recovery of ValuJet Flight 591." *FBI Law Enforcement Bulletin,* Vol. 66, No. 9:8-13.

Goolkasian, Gail A., Ronald W. Geddes, and William DeJong (1985). *Coping With Police Stress.* Washington, DC: National Institute of Justice, 3-10; 25-29.

Graves, Wallace (1996). "Police Cynicism: Causes and Cures." *FBI Law Enforcement Bulletin,* Vol. 65, No. 6:16-20.

Greene, Lorraine W. (1997). "Uplifting Resilient Police Families." *The Police Chief,* Vol. LXIV, No. 10:70-72.

Greenstone, James L., J. Michael Dunn, and Sharon C. Leviton (1995). "Fort Worth's Departmental Peer Counseling Program." *The Police Chief,* Vol. LXII, No. 1:42-44.

Guindon, Kurt (1995). "The Hidden Stressors of Law Enforcement." *Law and Order,* Vol. 43, No. 6:59-69.

Jaffe, Dennis T. and Cynthia D. Scott (1988). *Take This Job and Love It.* New York: Simon and Schuster, 19.

Janik, James (1995). "Who Needs Peer Support?" *The Police Chief,* Vol. LXII, No. 1:38-40.

Jones, John W. and David DuBois (1987). "A Review of Organizational Stress Assessment Instruments." In Lawrence R. Murphy and Theodore F. Schoenborn (eds.), *Stress Management in Work Situations.* Washington, DC: U.S. Department of Health and Human Services, 48.

Kannady, Grace (1993). "Developing Stress-Resistant Police Families." *The Police Chief,* Vol. LX, No. 8:92-99.

Kirschman, Ellen (1997). "Getting the Help You Need When You Need It." *The Police Chief,* Vol. LXIV, No. 10:45-62.

Kroes, William H. (1985). *Society's Victim—The Police, An Analysis of Job Stress in Policing.* Springfield, IL: Charles C Thomas, 29-47.

Kroes, William H. and Joseph J. Hurrell, Jr. (eds.) (1975). *Job Stress and the Police Officer.* Washington, DC: USGPO.

Kroes, W.H., Joseph Hurrell, and Bruce Margolis (1974). "Job Stress in Policemen." *Journal of Police Science and Administration,* Vol. 11, No. 3:234-236.

Kureczka, Arthur W. (1996). "Critical Incident Stress in Law Enforcement." *FBI Law Enforcement Bulletin,* Vol. 65, No. 2/3:10-16.

Law Enforcement News (1995a). "Tired? Stressed? Burned Out? Panel Seeks Answers for Phila. Police Officers." Vol. XXI, No. 419, April 15:15.

Law Enforcement News (1995b). "National FOP Looks at Police Suicide and How to Prevent It." Vol. XXI, No. 422, April 30:1, 10.

Law Enforcement News (1996). "What's Killing America's Cops? Mostly Themselves, According to a New Study." Vol. XXII, No. 455, November 15:1, 5.

Law Enforcement News (1997). "Stressed Out? Help May be on the Way." Vol. XXIII, No. 60, January 31:5.

Leonard, V.A. and Harry W. More (1993). *Police Organization and Management,* Eighth Edition. Westbury, NY: Foundation Press, 42, 131-134.

Margolis, B.L., W.H. Kroes, and R.P. Quinn (1974). "Job Stress: An Unlisted Occupational Hazard." *Journal of Occupational Medicine,* Vol. 16, No. 2:659-661.

More, Harry W. and O.R. Shipley (1987). *Police Policy Manual—Personnel.* Springfield, IL: Charles C Thomas, 147.

More, Harry W. and W. Fred Wegener (1991). *Behavioral Police Management.* New York: Macmillan Publishing, 218.

Murphy, Lawrence R. and Theodore F. Schoenborn (eds.) (1987). *Stress Management in Work Situations.* Washington, DC: National Institute for Occupational Safety and Health, USGPO, 18-48.

Papalia, Diane E. and Sally W. Olds (1988). *Psychology,* Second Edition. New York: McGraw-Hill Books, 312-314.

Pelletier, Kenneth R. (1984). *Healthy People in Unhealthy Places—Stress and Fitness at Work.* New York: Dell Publishing, 64.

Pendergrass, Virginia E. and Nancy M. Ostrove (1984). "Survey of Stress in Women in Policing." Paper presented at the American Psychological Association, 231-242.

Quick, James G. and Jonathan D. Quick (1984). *Organizational Stress and Preventative Management.* New York: McGraw-Hill Books, 75.

Rachlin, Harvey (1996). "Officers and Heart Disease." *Law and Order,* Vol. 44, No. 8:61-66.

Rafilson, Fred M. and Paul J. Heaton (1995). "Police Problems Identified: Officers Suffer Four Major Difficulties." *Law and Order,* Vol. 43, No. 5:13.

Reece, Barry L. and Rhoda Brandt (1987). *Effective Human Relations in Organizations,* Third Edition. Boston, MA: Houghton Mifflin, 341.

Robbins, James T. (1986). *Organizational Behavior—Concepts, Controversies, and Application.* Englewood Cliffs, NJ: 382-383.

Rue, Leslie and Lloyd L. Byars (1986). *Management Theory and Practice,* Fourth Edition. Homewood, IL: Richard D. Irwin, 342.

Ryan, Andrew H. (1997). "Afterburn: The Victimization of Police Families." *The Police Chief,* Vol. LXIV, No. 10:63-68.

Stratton, John G. (1987). "Employee Assistance Programs—A Profitable Approach for Employees and Organizations." In Harry W. More and Peter C. Unsinger (eds.), *Police Managerial Use of Psychology and Psychologists.* Springfield, IL: Charles C Thomas, 63-84.

Task Force to the Secretary of Health, Education and Welfare (1973). *Work in America.* Cambridge, MA: MIT Press.

Veniga, Robert L. and James Spradley (1981). *How to Cope With Job Burnout.* Englewood Cliffs, NJ: Prentice-Hall, 7-10, 28, 68.

Violanti, John M. (1995). "The Mystery Within: Understanding Police Suicide." *FBI Law Enforcement Bulletin,* Vol. 64, No. 2:19-24.

Violanti, John M. (1996a). *Police Suicide: Epidemic in Blue.* Springfield, IL: Charles C Thomas, 1-98.

Violanti, John M. (1996b). "Police Suicide: An Overview." *Police Studies,* Vol 19, No. 2:77-85.

Wilson, Marlene (1981). *Survival Skills for Managers.* Boulder, CO: Johnson Publishing, 218-221.

CORRUPTION: TARNISHING THE BADGE

11

The study of this chapter will enable you to:

1. List three things that occur when corruption is pervasive in a community.

2. Discuss why some police administrators have been reluctant to discuss police corruption openly.

3. Compare two of the different definitions of corruption.

4. Briefly describe the meaning of the term *material reward*.

5. Describe the contents of a regulation regarding rewards, gifts, and gratuities.

6. List eight types of people that are knowledgeable enough to consult regarding the nature of corruption in a city.

7. Identify the various groups that have members who have been convicted of crimes related to corruption.

8. Compare the type of corruption found by the Knapp Commission to that found by the Mollen Commission.

9. Describe the nature of police corruption identified by the Crime Commission in Pennsylvania with that found during the 1990s.

10. Distinguish between *grass eaters* and *meat eaters*.

11. Describe *crew corruption*.

12. Write a short essay describing the duties to be performed by a police commission.

13. Identify the features of command accountability.

Corruption in American law enforcement is a reality that is amply supported by evidence. It is invidious, and even a single incident of corruption can tarnish the badge of every honest officer. Indeed, since the inception of our nation, official corruption has existed and it is just as prevalent today as it was during the developmental stages of the United States. From an optimistic point of view, it would seem that police corruption could be eliminated with proactive investigative techniques by internal affairs units. From a pessimistic point of view, corruption will never be eliminated, let alone controlled (Getz, 1997: 35-42). In recent years, the problem of corruption has increased in some agencies because of the widespread availability of illicit drugs. Drugs have proved to be an opportunity for wrongdoing, stimulated by greedy conduct on the part of some officers. Millions of seized dollars have increased the temptations that officers confront. It is not just drug enforcement units that are confronted with temptation, it is patrol officers who encounter large supplies of drugs and cash. In fact, it can be most tempting to patrol officers, because they generally do not have the close supervision that is typical of officers assigned to narcotics units (Bureau of Justice Assistance, 1989: 5). Just to name a few communities, significant acts of corruption occurred within the past five years in Philadelphia, Chicago, Washington, D.C., New Orleans, Newark, and Atlanta (McCormick, 1996: 239-246). Smaller cities are not exempt. In Ford Heights, Illinois, an investigation determined that six current and former officers took bribes from approximately 20 drug dealers, and the police chief of the city helped in the distribution of drugs. Other nations have similar problems. In Australia, the New South Wales government overhauled the police service in reaction to allegations of corruption. In Hong Kong, the Independent Commission Against Corruption added 80 investigators to a special unit after a rise in reports of corruption.

If a chief ignores corruption within the department, it can prove to be fortuitous because it leaves his or her leadership record unblemished and the department may escape the embarrassment created by a scandal. If the chief reacts to corruption proactively and acknowledges that it occurred on his or her watch, the chief may find it necessary to look for employment elsewhere. It is common practice for governing entities to look for a scapegoat and the chief usually holds one of the most vulnerable positions in city government. Someone has to be blamed and take the fall. On the other hand, some police executive officers have survived such scandals, and this often seems to be best accomplished by blaming someone of lower rank (Rothlein and Lober, 1996: 32-34).

One of the essential qualities of a democracy is integrity in government, so everything possible should be done to ferret out wrongdoers in law enforcement agencies and other governmental entities. Individual or institutional corruption, by its very character, can devastate and demoralize not only a department, but it can cause citizens to question the integrity of every governing body. Every time there is an impairment of integrity or a violation of a moral principle, there is an erosion in the support that law enforcement needs in order to perform effectively (Sabato and Simpson, 1996: 1-10). Public confidence in the integrity and probity of law enforcement agencies is critical to effective law enforcement. Incorruptible law enforcement is a stubborn ideal that must be reached for if the citizens of this nation are to be the recipients of truly professional enforcement of the law (Miller, 1992: 359).

Numerous issues are of critical concern to police administrators, ranging from non-professional conduct to brutality, but none is more universal or persistent than police corruption. Corruption is not unique to law enforcement; it has occurred in all facets and at all levels of government. Police corruption in the United States is well-known and parallels the corrupt political regimes that prevailed in the nineteenth century and continued into the twentieth century. Through the years, many police departments have functioned as the military arm of incumbent political parties and have actively supported corrupt activities. Twenty-five years ago, a national commission reported that the public believed that corruption of public officials at all levels of government (federal, state, and local) was widespread. Such corruption results in a staggering cost to the American taxpayer and it is more than just a monetary cost—it is the erosion of confidence in government and a general decline in ethical standards and general morality. Additionally, the existence of corruption breeds further crime by providing the citizen with a model of official lawlessness that undermines the acceptable rule of law.

Confronting Corruption

Herman Goldstein, in his study of police corruption, pointed out that, until recently, it was almost impossible for police officers to generate an open discussion of corruption. One major reason for this unwillingness to discuss the problem is that it was difficult to do so without impugning the integrity of honest police personnel and contributing toward a stereotype that already labeled all police as corrupt (Goldstein, 1975: 1-45). Even today, many police officials feel that public discussion undermines public confidence in the police in a manner disproportionate to the prevalence and seriousness of the corrupt acts.

There is little doubt that disclosure of a single instance of corruption in a large police agency affects the reputation of the entire agency and makes all officers suspect in the eyes of a substantial segment of the community. This tends to be true even when an agency ferrets out its own corruption and when the disclosure reflects the agency's intense desire to rid itself of corrupt practices. Likewise, any effort by a newspaper, the mayor, citizen groups, or even the police administrator to stimulate a public discussion of police corruption tends to tarnish the reputation of all police personnel. The effect sometimes extends beyond the agency involved. The most isolated instance of corruption may affect the integrity of police personnel in agencies far removed from the area where the corruption is exposed (Hoffmann, 1997: 87-94). As a result, the low status accorded the police is reinforced, the respect upon which their effectiveness depends is further diminished, and their self-image suffers.

Given the far-reaching and rather indiscriminate effects that any exposure of corruption has on the reputation of police and their morale, the inclination of the police to suppress open discussion is understandable. Apart from these considerations, there is a strong feeling among police that they have been made scapegoats, and because they are responsible for policing the conduct of others, that some segments of the community delight in police corruption. Some personnel even argue that certain elements of the community, by seizing every opportunity to portray the police as corrupt, hope to convince themselves that their own corruption is less serious than that of the police.

A police officer can learn a great deal about the corruption of citizens, such as the exploitation of one individual by another, and of the existence of a multitude of corrupt schemes in a community. Overt corruption may be witnessed in the prosecutor's office, in the courts, and in relationships between lawyers and clients. It is frustrating to know that the institutions and professions that enjoy more prestige and status than do the police can be as corrupt, if not more corrupt, than the police, but that the police are most commonly singled out for attention. What we now know about corruption in government lends substantial support to this displeasure.

Yet, understandable as the reluctance to promote open discussion of corruption may be, it is impossible to deal innovatively with corruption and to develop community support for handling it, unless the problem is fully discussed (Cooksey, 1991: 5-9). Addressing the problem openly would have a less devastating effect than would the negative consequences of preventing open discussion.

At the same time, it should be apparent that the police administrator who addresses the problem must, in order to maintain credibility with personnel, constantly acknowledge the extent to which corruption constitutes a problem elsewhere in society. The administrator must argue convincingly that the existence of corruption elsewhere is no excuse for tolerating it among the police.

The police executive also must guard against becoming a fanatic, as the problem can arouse emotional involvement that can be dysfunctional. Important as it is to address corruption, concern with it must be related to the magnitude of the problem in the particular community and must be balanced by concern with other problems.

Definition

An accurate appraisal and assessment of police corruption can occur only after there is agreement as to what actually constitutes police corruption. In the past, studies of police corruption were primarily concerned with the *bad apple* theory. These studies proposed that the problem could best be remedied by dealing with the moral fiber of the police officer. The basic assumption was that the integrity of the department could be maintained by eliminating or prosecuting the officers who succumbed to the temptation of bribery or other illegal activities. The police profession took the position that this could be accomplished through internal investigation by police personnel.

Like many other areas in law enforcement, there is considerable disagreement over just what constitutes corruption. In some instances, the definition is exceedingly broad—that is, it includes such actions as the abuse of official authority by an officer. Other definitions include such acts as police brutality or the verbal attack of a citizen by an officer. An early study of the problem defined corruption by asserting that "a public official is corrupt if he accepts money or money's worth for doing something that he (she) is under a duty to do anyway, that he (she) is under a duty not to do, or to exercise a legitimate discretion for improper purposes" (McMullen, 1961: 183-184). The definition that arises from this statement is very broad, whereas other persons have developed a definition that applies directly to law enforcement.

In a study by the Police Foundation on the nature and control of police corruption, corruption was defined as "acts involving the misuse of authority by a police officer in a manner designed to produce personal gain for himself (herself) or for others" (Goldstein, 1975: 3). In the context of this book, the definition is narrowed somewhat, ensuring that a consideration of the topic excludes such acts as illegal seizure of evidence or police misconduct (discussed in Chapter 6, Deviation From the Norm). This study expressed the opinion that corruption has begun to breed when a police officer receives, or expects to receive, an unauthorized material reward or gain by virtue of occupying an official position.

These definitions express the position that corruption is not limited to its most egregious and sensational form, which is cash purchase of an official favor. Corruption includes all the circumstances in which the public officeholder or government employee sacrifices or sells all or part of his or her judgment on matters within his or her official purview in return for personal gain. Corruption thus defined includes a direct bargain: cash (or securities, or a share in a business venture, or the promise of a future job on the outside) in exchange for official action or inaction. Police officers should be mindful of instances in which the two may merge. For example, an officer might use force or threats to obtain payoffs (Goldstein, 1975: 3).

In order to assess the problem of corruption, it is necessary to have a definition in which acts and misdeeds fall into carefully specified categories. Operationally, corruption is defined as any act involving the misuse of authority, resulting in a law enforcement officer receiving a material reward or violating criminal laws.

A key term in this operational definition of corruption is *material reward*. While a few officers might disagree, this term must include the acceptance of such things as free coffee and meals. On the surface, such gratuities seem insignificant, but there is every reason to believe that they create an atmosphere conducive to corruption. If the police are to function effectively and responsibly as professionals, their integrity cannot be compromised. The police must serve all of the community and must not provide preferential services to those that offer gratuities.

The above definition clearly establishes the parameters of corruption and allows police executives an opportunity to formulate rules and regulations to govern officer conduct. Figure 11-1 sets forth a policy statement for a police department regarding rewards, gifts, and gratuities.

Figure 11-1
Rewards, Gifts, and Gratuities

> Rewards, gifts, and gratuities can compromise the integrity of a police department. . . . Officers and employees shall not, either in the course of regular duty or when off duty, through the representation of any position or connection held with the department, solicit (directly or indirectly) any person, firm, or organization for any reward, gratuity, contribution, or gift.
>
> Officers shall not accept any gratuity, fee, loan, reward, or gift whatsoever, directly or indirectly, from any person liable to arrest or to complaint, or in custody, or after discharge, or from any friend or friends, or person acting on behalf of any such person. Officers shall not conduct business with, or engage in any business transaction with, any person while he is confined in the city or county jail.

Source: From Harry W. More and O.R. Shipley (1987). *Police Policy Manual—Personnel*. Courtesy of Charles C Thomas, Publisher, Springfield, Illinois.

Assessment of Community Corruption

Several years ago, the federal government selected municipal corruption prevention (a training topic) as one of the most effective strategies for dealing with corruption. Figure 11-2 is a partial checklist of indicators that allow one to conduct an assessment of the integrity—maintenance and corruption-risk conditions of local government.

A simple and informal assessment of corruption in a community can be accomplished by talking to:

- Taxi drivers
- Newspaper reporters
- Chamber of Commerce members and staff
- Lawyers
- Clergy
- Bar owners and bartenders
- Law enforcement officers (local, state, and federal)
- Hotel employees
- Homeowners' association members
- Contractors (Dogin, 1978: 61-62)

Ask them:

- May I fix a traffic ticket?
- Where can I place a bet?
- Who is the best zoning attorney?

- How do I get a civil service position?

- Can I get a girl for my room?

- Who runs the gambling?

- Who really controls this city?

- Is this a good place to live?

- Where can I get some cocaine?

- How extensive is the drug problem?

- What are the politics of this city?

- How do I get a liquor license?

- Is it difficult to open a business?

- Whom do I see if I want to bid on a city contract?

- How good is the police department?

Crime and Corruption

It is impossible to measure precisely the extent of corruption in America today. However, the presence of one especially virulent species—the influence of organized crime syndicates on public officials—has been better documented than most. As long ago as 1930, the National Commission on Law Observance and Enforcement (also know as the Wickersham Commission) observed, "Nearly all the large cities suffer from an alliance between politicians and criminals" (National Commission on Law Observance and Enforcement, 1930: 1-85). The link has been condemned by successive attorneys general. The reform movement during the first part of the twentieth century confirmed what Lincoln Steffens observed: "efforts to control corruption have proven to be ineffective" (Steffens, 1902: 1-90). Even after corruption has been exposed and eliminated, it has been quite uncommon for it to return. In support of this idea is the concept that there is a 20-year cycle of corruption and reform that exists in the largest police departments in the United States (Sherman, 1974b: 5-15).

A national commission noted that the millions of dollars that organized crime spends on corrupting public officials gives it the power to:

- Maim or murder people with impunity.

- Extort money from businesses.

- Conduct businesses in such fields as liquor regulation.

- Avoid payment of income taxes.

- Secure public works contracts without competitive bidding.

Figure 11-2
Integrity Checklist for Policy Regarding Corruption

	Yes	No	Don't Know
In your jurisdiction, do statutes and ordinances clearly forbid (and clearly define) bribery, extortion, and other forms of official misconduct?	___	___	___
Does your jurisdiction have an official code of ethics specifying what conduct is officially desired and what is officially prohibited?	___	___	___
In addition to prohibiting cash payments, do rules prohibit the acceptance of meals, gratuities, discounts, and favors from any individual or firm doing business with the city or county or subject to regulation by the city or county?	___	___	___
Do rules forbid engaging in private business on city/county time or using city/county materials or equipment for private purposes?	___	___	___
Is outside employment that conflicts with official duties forbidden?	___	___	___
Are officials forbidden to represent private interests in dealing with city agencies or to take positions with firms that they have previously regulated?	___	___	___
Do campaign finance laws set limits on contributions from individuals or firms doing business with the city/county?	___	___	___
For those questions for which you answered "yes," additional factors to consider are:			
Are all personnel covered by the statutes, ordinances, and rules regularly informed of what is required of them in the conduct of their jobs?	___	___	___
Are there mechanisms for detecting and dealing with violations?	___	___	___
Does every detected violation result in an appropriate disciplinary action or in prosecution?	___	___	___

Source: Henry W. Dogin (1978). *Maintaining Municipal Integrity, Participant's Handbook.* Washington, DC: U.S. Department of Justice, 61-62.

In recent years, corruption has become less visible, more subtle, and more difficult to detect and assess than ever before. There is every indication that crime thrives when local officials are easily corrupted. Government officials at every level have become involved with crime as it has expanded its activities and as government has grown.

As government regulation expands into more and more areas of private and business activity, the power to corrupt likewise affords the corrupter more control over matters affecting the everyday life of each citizen. It is no wonder, then, that a poll conducted in 1971 revealed that the vast majority of the American people believed that organized crime had corrupted many politicians in the country (Harris Survey, 1971: 6).

Charges of corruption, some of which already have led to convictions, have been brought against many public officials throughout the United States in recent years. In one large eastern state, at least 57 elected or appointed officials were indicted or convicted on federal or state charges based on federal investigations. These officials include 10 mayors, two judges, three state legislators, various local officials, and several state officials, including two secretaries of state. Not all of these officials were charged while still in office. In another state, similar charges have been brought against at least 24 officials, including a former governor, two state senators, a state attorney general, and several other state and local officers or employees (*Arizona Daily Star,* 1991: 3A; *Arizona Daily Star,* 1995a: 1A). In Arizona, legislators were videotaped taking stacks of money in exchange for their votes (*Arizona Daily Star,* 1991: 1, 6A).

In recent years, the federal level of government, and even the judicial system, have not been exempt from corruption. In 1989, Judge Alcee Hastings, who was then serving on the federal bench in Florida, was impeached by the U.S. Senate for attempting to obtain a $150,000 bribe and for lying about the incident when he was tried. In November of 1989, the U.S. Senate impeached Judge Walter Nixon, Jr. after he was convicted of perjury. Nixon testified at his trial that he had lied to a grand jury about attempting to influence a prosecutor to delay indefinitely the investigation of the son of a friend for smuggling narcotics.

In August of 1990, Judge Robert P. Aguilar was convicted by a jury for lying to the Federal Bureau of Investigation and for telling Abe "The Trigger" Chapman, the last surviving member of Murder Inc., that Chapman was the subject of an FBI wiretap application. In 1994, the U.S. Court of Appeals for the Ninth Circuit threw out the conviction and in 1995 the U.S. Supreme Court reinstated the criminal charges. Aguilar has another appeal pending and eventually could be sent to prison for six months.

Likewise, elected officials continue to engage in corrupt practices. In Ohio, a judge pled guilty to distributing cocaine in 1995, after he invited an undercover Drug Enforcement Administration agent to snort a line of cocaine. The judge, Michael Gallagher, favored the legalization of drugs and said, "that only an idiot would use drugs" (*Arizona Daily Star,* 1995b: 11A). In 1994, Justice Rolf Larsen of the Pennsylvania Supreme Court was convicted of two counts of conspiracy by having a doctor issue prescriptions for him in his employee's name. Judge Larsen has appealed the conviction (*Arizona Daily Star,* 1994: 9A). In 1997, a massage parlor owner stood up at a city council meeting in Kentucky and accused police of taking payoffs, buying sex from her girls, and covering up two slayings (*Santa Cruz Sentinel,* 1997: 12B).

Lincoln Steffens' observation of more than a half-century ago that "the spirit of graft and of lawlessness is the American spirit" is far from outdated in these post-Watergate days. The American public's confidence in governmental purity was far from strong even before the disastrous disillusionment caused by Watergate and the resignation of President Nixon.

The direct costs of corruption are incalculable, but they are believed to be high enough to lend credence to the wry observation of one high-level U.S. Department of Justice official, who stated that "when we finally stop payoffs to public officials at all levels in this country, we will have found the cure to inflation." There is no dollar figure that adequately represents the debilitating effect on human life of such activities as narcotics operations, extortion rackets, prostitution rings, and gambling syndicates, which are permitted to flourish because of compliant and corrupt law enforcement (National Advisory Commission on Criminal Justice Standards and Goals, 1973: 205-207).

Figure 11-3
Specific Acts of Corruption in Communities Across The Nation

- Seven members of a tactical unit of the Chicago Police Department were charged with robbing and extorting more than $65,000 from undercover agents who were posing as drug dealers.

- The Director of the Newark, New Jersey, Police Department was placed on administrative leave because of allegations of corruption and malfeasance. The Director allegedly took protection money from drug dealers and sold transfers and promotions for as much as $500.

- In Mississippi, the Warren County Sheriff was ordered to resign from office, a position he had held since 1968. He was convicted on two federal perjury charges.

- In Fayetteville, Georgia, two uniformed officers were charged with murdering the owner of a bar. Several days later, a deputy sheriff was charged with murder. He was involved in planning the murder of the bar owner. This was followed by the arrest of two more officers for robbing a Home Depot store. One of these officers was on duty at the time of the robbery.

- In Los Angeles County, California, jurors deadlocked on 13 separate counts of corruption against six narcotics officers. They were charged with berating suspects and skimming money. One juror said the consensus was that the officers were guilty, but the evidence presented did not support such a verdict.

- In Buffalo, New York, four officers were caught on the film of a security camera eating snacks in a convenience store after they responded to an alarm. After the officers left, two burglars broke into the convenience store and were taped filling garbage bags with cigarettes, lottery tickets and other items. When the police returned to the second alarm, they were taped laughing, feasting, and drinking.

- In New York City, two officers were arrested and charged with soliciting payoffs from rabbis who had requested police escorts for religious processions.

- A $5.7 million suit was filed by 19 people, charging that three former Dallas police officers falsely arrested them for driving while drunk. It was alleged that the officers were stopping people so they could be paid for testifying in court.

- In Chicago, the former county chairman of the Republican Party, who formerly served as the undersheriff in Cook County, and an aide were charged with padding the sheriff's payroll with 22 individuals who had political connections. These "ghost employees" included two state senators and a state representative.

Corruption in New York City

Police corruption in New York City is classic in its nature, and parallels what has occurred in other cities. Although the names and dates change, corruption seems to recur periodically. The nature of the payoffs and their amounts may change, but corruption has become a perennial problem. It has led not only to the prosecution of numerous officers of varying ranks, but to the removal of police commissioners over the years. One key to eventually controlling corruption is to acknowledge its existence or the potential for its actuality. Charges of corruption must be investigated with all the resources available if the department is to maintain the highest integrity achievable. Faced with charges of corruption, the city of New York historically has responded by creating investigative bodies. In 1894, a New York State Senate Committee, known as the Lexow Committee, found systematic extortion and bribery among New York police. Almost 20 years later, the Curran Committee, appointed by the New York City Board of Aldermen, found systematic police extortion of gambling and prostitution houses. Twenty years later, in 1932, Samuel Seabury, counsel to a state legislative committee, conducted an investigation that found widespread police extortion of gamblers and bootleggers. On September 15, 1950, the Kings County District Attorney's Office arrested Harry Gross, the leader of a large-scale gambling racket, who cooperated with the district attorney and implicated 78 police officers for participating in an intricate and lucrative bribery scheme that included high-ranking members of the department. In 1972, the Knapp Commission issued its final report that declared police corruption to be a standardized and department-wide phenomenon (Mollen, 1994: 148-149).

The Knapp Commission

Corruption in New York City was found to be widespread and involved a wide range of illegal activities including payoffs, shakedowns, and bribery. The Knapp Commission found, in five of 17 plainclothes divisions, that corruption followed a strikingly similar pattern. Officers assigned to plainclothes duty to enforce vice and gambling laws routinely collected graft payments. Officers collected as much as $3,500 a month from each gambling location. This gave each officer from $300 to $1,500 a month as his or her share (or *nut*) of the so-called *pad* (payoff-list money). Functioning in bureaucratic fashion, those that were higher in the chain of command received greater rewards. Supervisors, sergeants, lieutenants, and high-ranking officers received a share and a half ($450-$2,250).

The practice of corruption in New York City created its own vocabulary. The terminology for the receipt of police graft by narcotics officers was defined as a *score*. This was a one-time payment to an individual officer. The payoff could be rather small, or it could be thousands of dollars. The largest narcotic score uncovered by investigators was found to be $80,000. Detectives assigned to general investigative duties also engaged in shakedowns of individual targets of opportunity. These scores were not as high as those in narcotics cases, but they frequently netted the recipients several thousand dollars for each score.

The corrupt practices carried on by uniformed officers assigned to normal patrol operations were reported to be the receipt of monies in much smaller amounts than those received by plainclothes officers. The uniformed officers shook down gambling locations and received payoffs from construction sites, bars, grocery stores, and other business establishments. Although the payments received by uniformed personnel were small (usually under $20), they were numerous and substantially enhanced an officer's income. Uniformed officers also received other payments, although less frequently, from after-hours bars, bottle clubs, motorists (for traffic violations), tow truck operators, cab drivers, parking lot operators, prostitutes, and defendants wanting to *fix* their court cases.

Another widespread practice was the payment of gratuities by one officer to another in order to expedite normal police procedures and paperwork or to gain favorable assignments. Sergeants and lieutenants could participate in the same kinds of corrupt practices as did their officers. Furthermore, some sergeants had their own *pads*, from which the officers who were working under the sergeants were excluded.

The Knapp Commission was unable to develop hard evidence that superior officers above the rank of lieutenant were receiving payoffs, although considerable circumstantial evidence and some testimony supported this possibility. It was reported that, if a superior officer was corrupt, a patrol officer would often serve as *bagman* for making collections and would keep some monies for himself or herself.

Two quite descriptive terms came out of the study of corruption in New York City. These terms are *meat eaters* and *grass eaters*. A meat eater is a police officer who aggressively misuses the police powers for personal gain, whereas the grass eater is one that simply accepts payoffs as part of performing normal police duties. In describing these categories of police officers, the report noted, "[A]lthough the *meat-eaters* get the huge payoffs getting the headlines, they represent a small percentage of all corrupt officers. The truth is, the vast majority on the take don't deal in huge amounts of graft" (Knapp, 1972: 23-89).

The Knapp Commission felt that the grass eaters were the heart of the problem because such a large number of officers were involved in this type of corrupt practice. In fact, its widespread nature of *grass eating* created an atmosphere of respectability. This, coupled with the code of silence existing among officers, served to brand anyone that exposed corrupt activities as a traitor.

The Mollen Commission

By 1994, the Mollen Commission had spent 22 months investigating the nature, extent, and causes of police corruption in the New York City Police Department. The following Feature describes some of the types of corruption found by the Mollen Commission.

Feature

The Nature of Corrupt Police Practices in New York City

Former police officer Michael Dowd, for example, did not just take bribes from drug traffickers to turn his head; he became a drug dealer himself and actually assisted and protected major drug operations. Former police officer Kevin Hembury did not only steal drugs, guns, and money in the course of a series of unlawful searches; he was part of a gang of cops that raided drug locations almost daily for the sole purpose of lining their pockets with cash. Former police officer Bernard Cawley—nicknamed "the Mechanic" by his sergeant because he so openly *tuned people up*, or beat them—not only used informants to identify drug locations for robberies, but beat people indiscriminately in crime-infested housing projects in his precinct. Additionally, it is alleged that former police officer Alfonso Compres, one of 14 officers arrested thus far in the 30th Precinct, did not just steal from drug dealers on the streets; he demanded regular payments to allow them to operate freely in his precinct and robbed those who did not pay. He even used his service revolver to shoot a dealer while stealing a package of cocaine while in uniform. To cover up their corruption, officers created even more: they falsified official reports and perjured themselves to conceal their misdeeds.

Source: Milton Mollen (1994). *Commission Report.* New York: City of New York, 1-158.

Investigative results found that, for at least a decade, the New York City Police Department had abandoned effective anti-corruption efforts and while it avoided public exposure of corruption, it actually fueled corruption. It sent a message throughout the department that integrity was not a high priority and that department bosses did not really want to know about corruption. In short, it gave everyone in the department an excuse for doing what was easiest: shutting their eyes to the corruption around them. This is precisely what happened. The principle of command accountability, which holds commanders responsible for fighting corruption, completely collapsed.

Corruption and Drugs. The Mollen Commission found that the drug trade caused the most serious police corruption. The eruption of the cocaine and crack trade in the mid-1980s fueled the opportunities for corruption by pouring drugs and cash into neighborhoods of the city. It created the opportunity for cops and the criminals to profit from each other. It also eliminated the unwritten rule of 20 years ago that narcotics graft was *dirty money*, not to be touched even by corrupt officers. With that change in attitude and opportunity came a wide spectrum of drug-related corruption, ranging from opportunistic thefts from street dealers, to carefully planned group assaults on drug locations, and long-term partnerships with narcotics offenders.

Today's narcotics corruption involves not only cops stealing from dealers, but cops using their authority to permit dealers and narcotic enterprises to flourish and operate freely. Even worse, this type of police corruption involves officers using their power to actively assist, facilitate, and strengthen the drug trade. Victims of this alliance are the thousands of law-abiding individuals who live in high-crime, drug-ridden precincts of the city.

Another feature of narcotics-related corruption is that it was found to be an activity carried out by uniformed patrol officers who are surrounded daily by drug traffickers operating in the streets, apartments, and storefronts. While some supervisors were involved, corruption did not reach high into the chain of command.

The New Character of Police Corruption. Twenty years ago, the most common form of corruption was relatively minor. Officers of all ranks took bribes to allow gamblers, prostitutes, and others to avoid the law and escape arrest. Minor corruption is no longer systemic among the ranks, but the meat-eaters are the rule rather than the exception. Currently, corruption is primarily characterized by serious criminal activity. Officers in numerous narcotics-infested precincts throughout the city routinely stormed drug locations and stole whatever drugs, money, or other property they could find; they stopped drug dealers and their vehicles and stole from them openly; and they sometimes used violence to carry out these activities. Many cops went so far as to assist criminals and used their police power to become criminals themselves.

Crew Corruption: A New Type of Corruption. Virtually all of the corruption uncovered by the Mollen Commission involved groups of officers—called *crews*—that protected and assisted other officers in criminal activities. This was accomplished in a variety of ways, including: identifying drug sites; planning raids; forcibly entering and looting drug trafficking locations; and sharing proceeds according to regular and agreed-upon principles. The crews varied in closeness, purpose, and size. In the 30th Precinct, a large group of cops worked in quasi-independent groups of three to five officers, each protecting and assisting the others' criminal activities. In the 73rd Precinct, a tightly knit group of eight to 10 officers who worked together on steady tours of duty, routinely conducted unlawful raids on drug locations while on duty from 1988 to 1992. Sometimes most of the squad, 10 to 12 officers, would attend clandestine meetings in desolate locations in the precinct—like one known as the *morgue*, an abandoned coffin factory—to drink, avoid patrol duties, and plan future raids. The 75th Precinct had a similar gathering location known as *The Pool*—an isolated inlet near Jamaica Bay—where as many as 15 officers from one crew would meet while on duty to drink, shoot their guns, meet their girlfriends, and plan future criminal activities. In the 9th Precinct, groups of officers would meet in a local store to drink, use cocaine, and avoid their duties.

Crews are more akin to street gangs: small, loyal, flexible, fast moving, and often hard-hitting. They establish areas to plan and discuss their operations. They often structure their legitimate police work to generate the leads they need to locate promising targets. They used the police radio network and code names to mount and coordinate operations. They often used police equipment to make forced entries. The manipulated fellow officers, their supervisors, and the courts to their advantage.

Motives Behind Corruption. The motive for corruption was more than greed. While money was still the primary cause of corruption, there was a complex array of other motives: to exercise power over their environment; to vent frustration and hostility over their inability to stem the tide of crime around them; to experience excitement and thrills; to prove their mettle to other officers and gain acceptance; and to administer their own brand of street justice, because they believed the criminal justice system administered none. Corrupt officers usually raided drug locations for profit, but sometimes also to show who was in control of the crime-ridden streets of their precincts; sometimes because they believed that vigilante justice was the only way to teach a lesson or punish those who might otherwise go unpunished.

Police falsifications and perjury also resulted from a variety of motives. Sometimes to cover up corruption or brutality; sometimes for personal gain; and sometimes for what was erroneously perceived as legitimate law enforcement needs. Additionally, through its investigation the Mollen Commission determined that in some instances force was used outside the bounds of necessity to: further corruption for profit; establish respect, exert power, and vent frustration; and administer what they believed was street justice (Mollen, 1994: 1-53).

The Police Culture. In New York City, the *code of silence* nurtured police corruption and impeded efforts at controlling corruption. This aspect of the police culture encouraged corruption by setting a standard that nothing is more important than the unswerving loyalty of officers to one another—not even stopping the most serious forms of corruption. This process emboldened corrupt cops and those susceptible to corruption. The code leads officers to protect or cover up for another officer's crimes—even crimes of which they disapproved. The pervasiveness of the code of silence was alarming. In fact, it was found to be the strongest where corruption was prevalent. The impact of the code was reinforced by the grave consequences for violating it. Officers who reported misconduct were ostracized and harassed; became targets of complaints and even physical threats; and were made to fear that they would be left alone on the streets in a time of crisis. This draconian enforcement of the code of silence fueled corruption because it made corrupt cops feel protected and invulnerable (Mollen, 1994: 53). The following Feature illustrates the impact of the code of silence.

Feature

The Reality of the Code Of Silence

Former police officer Bernard Cawley testified at a public hearing:

Question: Were you ever afraid that one of your fellow officers might turn you in?

Answer: Never.

Question: Why not?

Answer: Because it was the Blue Wall of Silence. Cops don't tell on cops. And if they did tell on them, just say if a cop decided to tell on me, his career's ruined. He's going to be labeled as a rat. So if he's got fifteen more years to go on the job, he's going to be miserable because it follows you wherever you go. And he could be in a precinct, he's going to have nobody to work with. And chances are if it comes down to it, they're going to let him get hurt.

Source: Milton Mollen (1994). *Commission Report,* Commission to Investigate Allegations of Police Corruption and the Anti-Corruption Procedures of the Police Department. New York: The City of New York, 53-54.

The code of the *blue fraternity* extends beyond the blue and into the communities they police. The loyalty ethic and insularity that breed the code of silence that protects officers from other officers also erects protective barriers between the police and the public. Far too many officers see the public as a source of trouble rather than as the people they are sworn to serve (*us versus them*). This attitude is powerfully reinforced on the job when recruits become full-fledged officers and interact with the public every day. It creates strong pressures on police officers to ally themselves with fellow officers, even corrupt ones, rather than reaching out to the public to create supportive and productive relationships with the communities they serve.

Corruption in Philadelphia

In a major study of the quality of law enforcement in Philadelphia, a special commission found that police corruption was ongoing, widespread, and systematic at all levels of the police department. Corrupt practices were uncovered in every police district during the investigation. The corrupt acts involved police officers at all levels, including inspector. Specific acts of corruption involved improper cash payments to the police by gamblers, racketeers, bar owners, business people, nightclub owners, after-hours club owners, and prostitutes. The investigation identified more than 400 officers (by name and badge or payroll number) as receiving improper payments in terms of cash, merchandise, sexual services, or meals.

Corruption and political influence are problems that have plagued the department in Philadelphia since its inception. In the twentieth century alone, there have been three special grand jury investigations, each of which found widespread corruption within the police force. Eighteen years ago, an investigation by the Pennsylvania Crime Commission found that corruption existed as a result of numerous interacting factors. These included the department's attitude toward the corruption problem, the vice enforcement policy, societal pressures on police officers, and the reaction to corruption by other parts of the criminal justice system and the public. The following Feature lists some of the types of corrupt police practices.

Feature

The Nature of Corrupt Police Practices in Philadelphia

- Falsifying official reports.
- Committing perjury in court.
- Falsely accusing individuals.
- Theft of drugs.
- Theft of money.
- Theft of weapons.
- Denying suspects their constitutional rights.
- Beating people.
- Performing illegal searches.
- Threatening to kill individuals.
- Conspiracy to commit robbery.
- Civil rights violations.
- Misconduct.

Source: *Law Enforcement News* (1995b). "Biggest Corruption Probe of the Decade Rocks Phila. P.D." March 31:10.

In Philadelphia, police officers saw the police commissioner held in contempt of court for *blatant disregard* of a court order. In addition, officers witnessed the department leadership failing to stop payoffs from businesses. At the same time, the courts treated officers as a special category of offenders. Few officers were actually put on trial, and even fewer served jail time. Furthermore, the public did not come forward to expose corruption, and overall, people were complacent about police corruption (Pennsylvania Crime Commission, 1974: 27-121). Figure 11-3 (page 278) lists more recent acts of police corruption in various cities throughout the nation. It can be seen that the large amounts of money generated by illegal narcotics and other drugs have created a financial temptation to which many officers have succumbed.

In February of 1995, a federal indictment was filed charging five current and former members of an anti-drug squad of the Philadelphia Police Department with criminal violations. The officers had stolen more than $100,000 in cash from numerous drug suspects, violated their rights, and committed acts of brutality. The officers conducted illegal searches of residences for the purpose of stealing money, drugs, and weapons. They also falsified police records as a means of covering up their crimes. Additionally, the officers maintained a stash of illegally seized drugs that they used to plant on individuals as a means of falsely accusing someone of a crime (*Law Enforcement News*, 1995b: 10).

The corrupt acts committed by these officers were reminiscent of vigilantes enforcing their own law at the expense of the rights of others, and for personal gain. A crime that corrupt officers committed that was of unusual significance and demonstrates their complete disregard of constitutional rights, was *flaking*— falsely accusing individuals for the sole purpose of earning additional pay when testifying in court. More than 1,500 cases over a period of eight years are believed to be tainted because of planted or fabricated evidence. Hundreds of convictions have been reversed and many victims have been released from prison or had their parole terminated. Nine former officers are serving long prison terms.

The ringleader, John Baird, received a 13-year federal prison sentence, and Steven Brown received a 10-year sentence for stealing $100,000 from drug dealers over a four-year period. By the end of 1996, 44 plaintiffs had sued the city and 42 of these cases settled for approximately $3.5 million in damages (*Law Enforcement News*, 1996: 1, 14).

Under the supervision of a federal judge, in response to an unfiled lawsuit by civil rights organizations, an agreement was reached with the city of Philadelphia in 1996 that proposals would be reviewed to identify new methods of fighting corruption. When the agreement was finalized, it included the creation of a 15-member task force to review all policies and procedures. The goal of the plaintiffs was to obtain changes that more effectively controlled corruption and misconduct, and eliminated racial abuse. The task force was to consist of a group of unpaid police experts who would study the department over an 18-month period.

Additionally, the agreement required the establishment of an integrity and accountability officer, and the development of procedures to identify officers who might be at risk for misconduct. The integrity officer was to monitor departmental ethics policies and review investigations conducted by the department's internal affairs division (*Law Enforcement News*, 1996: 1, 14).

Corruption in New Orleans

Over the years, the New Orleans Police Department has been criticized by different reviewing entities, which pointed out that the agency did not have a viable program to eliminate corruption, and the department proved inept in responding to charges of brutality and civil rights violations. Then, in 1993, the corruption problem reared its ugly head, and during the next few years more than 50 officers were arrested, indicted, or convicted for a wide range of charges ranging from rape to murder. Other offenses included drug trafficking, bribery, extortion, firearms violations, armed robbery, and aggravated battery. The most shocking act, which received nationwide attention, was the brutal murder of Kim Groves. A 32-year-old African-American and mother of three, she was a witness to the pistol-whipping of a teenager by a police officer and she filed a citizen's complaint against that officer, Len Davis. When arranging for the murder, he was being investigated by the FBI for corruption and was recorded giving a detailed description of Groves to a hit man and shouting into his cellular telephone, "Get that whore!" Soon after the murder, shouts of "Yeah" and "Rock, rock-a-by" were recorded over Officer Davis's cellular telephone. He was charged with contracting for the murder of Kim Groves (Smith, 1995: 5).

Officer Len Davis and eight other officers were also indicted for drug violations. Davis and his cohorts were paid by undercover officers to protect shipments of cocaine that was to be stored in an abandoned warehouse near the docks in New Orleans. These officers were the victims of a sting operation that led to charges against them for drug, civil rights, and arms violations. As the investigation widened, 22 more officers were arrested and charged with kidnapping, extortion, battery, and other violations (*Law Enforcement News*, 1995a: 1, 9). In another shocking incident, Officer Antoinette Frank was robbing a Vietnamese restaurant when she shot and killed a security guard. The guard was a moonlighting police officer and her former partner. Frank was charged with armed robbery and murder.

In response to the wanton acts of police violence, the superintendent replaced the Internal Affairs unit, strengthened entry standards, and limited moonlighting. Superintendent Richard Pennington also arranged for the development of an early warning system as a means of monitoring the conduct and behavior of officers. The intent of this system was to identify officers who needed to be counseled or retrained (*Law Enforcement News*, 1995a: 1, 9).

Controlling Corruption

Almost 20 years ago, police executives and criminal justice educators were of the opinion that corruption could primarily be controlled by the police department itself. Unfortunately, this has not proven to be a viable process, as the record reflects. One has only to look at the reoccurring patterns of corruption in cities throughout the nation, notably, New York City, Philadelphia, New Orleans, Chicago, and Miami. It should be emphasized that it is not just a big city problem. In recent years, many small cities have had officers succumb to the temptations offered by drugs and what seems to be a constant flow of illegal cash generated by the narcotics problem. For years, internal review was felt to be the way to deal with corruption—by instituting policies, procedures, and techniques that would easily detect corrupt activities, but reliance on this approach has left a great deal to be desired.

The second most important method that at one time was believed would control corruption was watchdog groups. Those that received a great deal of publicity included commissions operating in Chicago, New York, and Philadelphia. Commissions have proven to be more reactive than proactive and, as a consequence, particularly in hindsight, more competent at descriptive analysis rather than actively rooting out and preventing corruption.

Control by the mass media has proven to be just as ineffective. Investigative reporters have done an outstanding job of uncovering patterns of police corruption as well as reporting specific incidents, but their obligation is to report, not perform the function of controllers of corruption. The media has an important part to play in the total process of fettering out corruption, and without their efforts it is questionable whether the average citizen would be aware of police corruption. Investigative reporters can perform the function of watching over the watchers.

Many have held the position that the professionalization of law enforcement would emerge as the most important factor in the control of police corruption, but such is not the case. In fact, other than many individuals and a few departments, professionalization has evaded the American police system. The criteria utilized by other professions has never been fully applied to law enforcement and this is especially true of educational entry criteria.

Other factors that in earlier days were viewed as a prerequisite to controlling corruption are: improved supervision and training, ethical education, and the stringent prosecution of violators of the public trust. All of these elements have been known for decades, but across the board application has proven to be haphazard or nonexistent. There is no easy answer as to why this has not occurred, but maybe one has to take the position that corruption is inevitable. This is not to say that it has to be accepted, but it does call for continuing and constant vigilance. Too often, as reported by the Mollen Commission, whatever integrity controls are instituted will not last forever without the demand of the public and the commitment of the department to ensure that they remain effective. In the past, the New York Police Department placed absolute faith in the reforms it instituted to control corruption, but that faith was misplaced. If integrity rules are to be effective, they must be rooted in the pride of the organization. It was also determined that reform efforts could not be sustained without incentive and support from the outside.

The Mollen Commission took the position that it was impossible for the police department to bear the responsibility for corruption control without the help of independent, external oversight. It was felt that only the existence of an independent, external, effective corruption control monitor, outside the chain of command, could create a continuous pressure upon the agency to purge itself of corruption. At the same time, an independent monitor can serve to assure the public that corruption disclosures signal a vigilant department rather than a wholesale failure of its integrity. Only such a process can break the historical cycle of scandal, reform, and backsliding (Mollen, 1994: 1-158).

The experience of New York City suggests that a bifurcated approach to lasting corruption reform involves independent oversight and command account- ability. The anti-corruption control apparatus has to be strengthened to include improving the quality of recruits, enhancing police training, strengthening supervision, and upgrading methods of prevention. Additionally, there must be a strengthening of internal investigations, enforcement of command account- ability, and the causes and conditions that spawn corrupt acts need to be addressed.

A permanent external police commission should be created to:

- perform continuous assessments and audits of the department's systems for preventing, detecting, and investigating corruption;

- assist the department in implementing programs and policies to eliminate the values and attitudes that nurture corruption;

- ensure a successful system of command accountability; and

- conduct, when necessary, its own corruption investigations to examine the state of police corruption.

Such a police commission must have its own investigative capacity to carry out its mission of gauging the state of corruption, assessing corruption controls, and identifying corruption hazards. It must be empowered to conduct its own intelligence-gathering operations, self-initiated investigations, and integrity tests. The commission is not intended to replace the police department's corruption efforts. On the contrary, it is designed to ensure that the department continues to police itself by aggressively pursuing corruption. The police commission should be headed by five reputable and knowledgeable citizens appointed by the mayor, who will serve *pro bono*. The commissioners should have a limited, stag- gered term of office to guarantee turnover, avoid staleness, and prevent the development of a long-term bureaucratic relationship with the department that could compromise the police commission's independence. Such an entity should have unrestricted access to the department's records and personnel. It should have the power to subpoena witnesses and documents; the power to administer oaths; to take testimony in private and public hearings; and to grant immunity (Mollen, 1994: 153-154).

Summary

Police administrators are confronted with many critical goals, but few are more important than the eradication of corruption. Historically, the corruption of law enforcement in the United States parallels that of corrupt political regimes, especially those of the nineteenth century. Until recently, many police officials were reluctant to discuss corruption. A major reason for this was that discussing corruption meant impugning the integrity of honest police officers. Today, it is felt that the refusal to openly discuss corruption may have a more negative impact on officers.

There are numerous ways to define corruption, but defining corruption is an essential step in assessing the extent and nature of police corruption. The most acceptable definition of police corruption is "any act involving the misuse of authority that results in a law enforcement officer receiving a material reward for violating criminal laws." A key element of the definition is material reward, and this term must include such gratuities as free coffee and meals.

Anyone can conduct an assessment of the integrity-maintenance and corrupt-risk conditions of local government by using a checklist identifying the indicators of corruption. This checklist includes such items as whether a traffic ticket can be fixed or who is it that really runs a particular gambling operation. Questions such as the following can be asked: Are officers permitted to pursue outside employment that conflicts with their official duties? Is there an official code of ethics?

Since as long ago as 1930, alliances have existed between politicians and criminals. Numerous reform movements have come and gone, but corruption still exists. Criminal syndicates have spent millions of dollars in corrupting politicians and law enforcement agencies. Mayors, supervisors, state senators, state prosecuting attorneys, and numerous other officials have been convicted of violations of the law. The same can be said for judges at both state and federal levels. New York City and Philadelphia were investigated by crime commissions, and extensive corruption was found at all levels of law enforcement agencies in those cities.

Historically, the means for controlling police corruption included administrative control, control by the media, and control by watchdog groups. In the past, experts believed that administrative control was the most effective when it was coupled with internal investigation, but this has proven not to be an effective means of controlling corruption. The same can be said of efforts to control corruption by watchdog groups. They have proven most adept at describing corrupt conditions, but relatively ineffective at preventing corruption on an ongoing basis. The media has had its day over the years and has been effective at exposing corrupt conditions, but unsuccessful at preventing scandal. Other efforts of controlling have proven ineffective, and corruption continues to go through a 20-year cycle.

Departmental control of corruption must be accompanied by an independent police commission if the historical cycle of scandal is to be broken. The apparatus utilized by a police department must be strengthened if the problem of corruption is to be addressed. This should include improving the quality of recruits, enhancing training, strengthening supervision, and enforcing command accountability. A police commission should be independent and have full investigative powers. It should be responsible for performing the continuous assessment of the police department's efforts to control corruption.

References

Arizona Daily Star (1991a). "3 Lawmakers, Latest Indicted in S.C. Sting." February 21:3A.

Arizona Daily Star (1991b). "Videotapes Show Payoffs." February 8:1, 6A.

Arizona Daily Star (1994). "PA. Jurist in Drug Case is Guilty of Conspiracy." April 10:9A.

Arizona Daily Star (1995a). "13 Convicted Ex-Lawmakers are Still Drawing Pensions." March 28:1A.

Arizona Daily Star (1995b). "Judge Might Rethink Who is an 'Idiot.'" December 22:11A.

Bureau of Justice Assistance (1989). *Building Integrity and Reducing Drug Corruption in Police Departments.* Washington, DC: International Association of Chiefs of Police, 5.

Cooksey, Otis E. (1991). "Corruption—A Continuing Challenge for Law Enforcement." *FBI Law Enforcement Bulletin,* Vol. 60, No. 9:5-9.

Dogin, Henry S. (1978). *Maintaining Municipal Integrity, Participants Handbook.* Washington, DC: U.S. Department of Justice, USGPO, 61-62.

Getz, Ronald J. (1997). "Operation Broken Star—Revitalizing Chicago's Internal Affairs Division Results in Record Indictment of Officers." *Law and Order,* Vol. 45, No. 10:35-42.

Goldstein, Herman (1975). *Police Corruption: A Perspective on its Nature and Control.* Washington, DC: Police Foundation, 1-45.

Harris Survey (1971). "Public's Trust in Elected Officials has Diminished." New York, NY.

Hoffmann, John (1997). "Fighting Corruption—The U.S. Department of Justice Looks at Integrity and Ethics in Policing." *Law and Order,* Vol. 45, No. 3:87-94.

Knapp, Whitman (1972). *Commission Report—New York.* New York: Commission to Investigate Allegations of Police Corruption and the City's Anti-Corruption Procedures. September 15:20-99.

Law Enforcement News (1996). "Phila. Moves Against Misconduct." October 31:1, 14.

Law Enforcement News (1995a). "Murder, Corruption & Brutality Charges are Backdrop to New Orleans Reforms." January 31:1, 9.

Law Enforcement News (1995b). "Biggest Corruption Probe of the Decade Rocks Phila. PD." March 31:10.

McCormick, Robert J. (1996). "Police Perceptions and the Norming of Institutional Corruption." *Policing and Society,* Vol. 10, No. 3:239-246.

McMullen, M. (1961). "A Theory of Corruption." *Sociological Review.* Vol. 9, No. 2:183-184.

Miller, Nathan (1992). *Stealing from America: A History of Corruption from Jamestown to Reagan,* Revised Edition. New York: First Paragon House, 359.

Mollen, Milton (1994). *Commission Report,* Commission to Investigate Allegations of Police Corruption and the Anti-Corruption Procedures of the Police Department. New York: City of New York, 1-158.

More, Harry W. and O.R. Shipley (1987). *Police Policy Manual—Personnel.* Springfield, IL: Charles C Thomas, 120.

National Commission on Law Observance and Enforcement (1930). *Commission Report.* Washington, DC: USGPO.

Pennsylvania Crime Commission (1974). *Commission Report.* Harrisburg, PA: Pennsylvania Crime Commission, 27-121.

Rothlein, Steve and Richard Lober (1996). "The Ramification of Internal Affairs Investigation." *The Police Chief,* Vol. LXIII, No. 7:32-34.

Sabato, Larry and Glenn Simpson (1996). *Dirty Little Secrets—The Persistence of Corruption in American Politics.* New York: Times Books, 1-10.

Santa Cruz Sentinel (1997). "Allegations Rock Kentucky Town." July 22:12B.

Sherman, Lawrence W. (ed.) (1974a). *Police Corruption.* Garden City, NY: Doubleday Anchor Books, 25.

Sherman, Lawrence W. (1974b). *City Politics, Police Administrators, and Corruption Control.* New York: Criminal Justice Center, John Jay College of Criminal Justice, 5-15.

Smith, Gerald, (1995). "The Ones That Are Taking Money Are The Ones Giving the Beating." Berkeley, CA: *COPWATCH Report,* Winter:5.

Steffens, Lincoln (1902). *The Shame of the Cities.* New York: Hill and Wang, 1-95.

TERRORISM: DOMESTIC AND INTERNATIONAL VIOLENCE   *12*

The study of this chapter will enable you to:

1. Define *terrorism*.

2. List four new powers set forth in the latest U.S. Terrorism Act.

3. Trace the historical development of terrorism in the United States.

4. Distinguish between a terrorist incident and a *suspected* terrorist incident.

5. List four distinct species of political and social terrorism.

6   Describe how the Japanese Red Army functions.

7. Write a short essay describing radical Palestinian terrorism.

8. Compare the Skinheads and the Ku Klux Klan.

9. Describe the current threat in the United States from domestic terrorist groups.

10. Compare the Centennial Olympic Park bombing to the Oklahoma City bombing.

11. Identify the characteristics of a militia.

12. Describe the current threat in the United States from international terrorist groups.

13. Contrast the profiles of domestic and international terrorists.

Terrorism is a given. It will not go away. It has been with us for years, and it will continue into the future. Old terrorists are replaced by new ones, and terroristic groups come and go. We have always had political, social, and economical inequities and these conditions will continue to exist in the future. Unfortunately, there will always be individuals who will gravitate to violence as a means of remedying what they see as inequities (Long, 1990: 164).

The issue of terrorism is clouded by the aphorism "One man's terrorist is another man's freedom fighter." Therefore, even defining terrorism becomes a difficult task. The occurrence of a terrorist act generally evokes strong emotional responses from loved ones, victims, onlookers, and all the emergency personnel responding to such an incident. Anyone who viewed the wreckage caused by any of the following events on television could not regard the havoc with detachment or objectivity. This includes the bombing of Pan Am flight 103 over Lockerbie, Scotland, when 270 people died, and the bombing of the World Trade Center in 1993, in which six individuals died and approximately 1,000 were injured. Even more extreme was the truck bombing of the Alfred P. Murrah federal building in Oklahoma City, in which 168 died. It was the deadliest terrorist act ever committed on U.S. soil. It is relatively easy to feel that you might have been on the airplane or going into either of the bombed buildings. This creates a strong emotional identification with the victims, and clouds how one thinks about the subject. The term *terrorism* then becomes an instrument of condemnation rather than clarification (Sederberg, 1989: 23-24).

The Oklahoma City bombing shattered any complacency that Americans might have had toward domestic terrorism. In past years, the intensity of public response to terrorism has ebbed and flowed, based on the nature or frequency of outrageous acts. In the 1970s, hijackers represented the worst fear of air travelers worldwide (Sage, Wallace, and Wier, 1995: 8-11). This gave way during the 1980s to terrorist acts that involved fire bombings, pipe bombings, arson, and the malicious destruction of property. In the 1990s, the truck bomb became a part of the terrorist scene, and there has been an increasing interest in biological agents. In 1991, Iraq warned that if the United States attacked, there would be a wave of terrorism against Americans. Anti-terrorism security measures swept the nation. A chest-high fence was built on Pennsylvania Avenue in Washington, D.C. across from the White House. The Pentagon canceled all unscheduled building tours as it increased security. The New York City Police Department opened a terrorism 911 hotline, and a joint command center with other agencies was created. The Immigration and Naturalization Service began to photograph and fingerprint travelers carrying Iraqi passports and some diplomats of that country were expelled from the United States. At the Super Bowl in Tampa, Florida, fans had to run an anti-terrorism security gauntlet to enter the stadium, and fans cheered halftime reports on the activities of American troops in the Persian Gulf. At that time, the problem the United States had was how to put Americans on guard without panicking everyone. At the conclusion of Operation Desert Storm, things quieted down and the threat of terrorism ceased to be a concern of most citizens.

After the Oklahoma City bombing, 54 percent of U.S. adults expressed in an opinion poll the belief that the government must try to stop terrorists even if it means giving up some rights and privacy. In this opinion poll, respondents supported giving the following new powers to the government (*Arizona Daily Star*, 1995a: 1A, 3A):

- Power to quickly expel a citizen of another country who is suspected of planning a terrorist act.

- The power to infiltrate and spy on organizations that the government thinks might be planning a terrorist act.

- The power to search for and seize weapons from groups that might be planning terrorist acts.

- Power to ban information abut bomb-making from public computer networks.

The only power the respondents clearly opposed in the opinion survey was the banning of people from speaking on radio or television if they advocated anti-government violence. This survey was one of many circumstances that laid the foundation for the Clinton administration to introduce an anti-terrorism bill. Skeptics viewed it as oppressive. Specific provisions provided for deportation, and restricted fundraising for terrorist organizations. The bill passed after a considerable debate and delaying tactics. Part of the support for a terrorism bill was in reality political pandering, as everyone wanted to look tough on terrorism. The anti-terrorism legislation passed in the House of Representatives on the eve of the first anniversary of the Oklahoma City bombing. Elements of the domestic terrorism bill included:

- Augmented government authority to deport suspected terrorists without making the information public.

- Denial of visas for suspected terrorists or individuals associated with terrorist organizations.

- Augmented abilities to prosecute anyone raising money for terrorist organizations.

- Requiring terrorists to make restitution to their victims (*Arizona Daily Star*, 1996a:1A-3A).

Another key provision of the bill provided for an additional $1 billion to assist police agencies in coordinating efforts at suppressing domestic and international terrorism. Wiretapping and chemical identification markers in gunpowder were taken out of the bill after the National Rifle Association (NRA) and civil liberties groups opposed their inclusion.

Reacting to Terrorist Acts

Terrorism spreads fear that it is out of proportion to the specific damage perpetrated or the probability that one will be a victim of terrorism. Unfortunately, acts of terrorism exempt no one. A person may be in the wrong place at the wrong time. One does not even have to be a combatant to become a victim.

The fear generated by terrorism becomes increasingly acute when ordinary citizens become the targets of terrorist activities. Even commonplace, everyday activities that are normally perceived as safe can potentially be harmful.

Terrorist targets have included such places as train depots, bus terminals, airports, government buildings, and department stores. Almost no place can be looked upon as safe. Activities that formerly were routine must be viewed with suspicion, as terrorist acts weaken the ability to feel safe. One may ask: Should I go to that political event? Should I take that long-awaited vacation to Europe? Dare I go shopping at the neighborhood mall? (Sederberg, 1989: 41).

Terrorism is not predictable or calculable. It is not something for which a simple solution is readily apparent. History shows that it will never be completely eradicated. It is highly fluid and functions on a continuum spawned by political, economic, and social conditions (Long, 1990: 141-150). The tactics of the terrorist are numerous, and only limited by the creativity of the mind. Potential targets are so numerous that it defies one's imagination. Transportation, communications, hydro-electric, public buildings, and corporate buildings are all potential targets. It brings to mind such events as the lethal nerve gas (sarin) attack that occurred in the Tokyo subways, in which 12 people died, and 5,500 became ill (*Arizona Daily Star*, 1995b: 5A). Of special concern is the potential that someday some fanatic might resort to the use of chemical, biological, radiological, or nuclear weapons (DeGeneste, Silverstein, and Sullivan, 1996: 70-83; Rubin, 1996: 11, 51).

Terrorism continues to be a part of the American as well as the international scene. It is a way to influence those in power, and it is usually a violent act with either a political or social objective. It can be directed toward a government, the general population, or any segment of either. A significant goal of terrorism is destruction. The terrorist act usually occurs as a result of desperation. It is done with the belief that the violence is a legitimate form of protest that will cause government entities to act in a more acceptable fashion (Friedlander, 1983: 41).

Dissident political and social groups, which find themselves unable to achieve their goals, turn to coercive activities to change forms of government, replace governing bodies, and intimidate people. When a terrorist act occurs, it becomes an identifiable symbol of the group taking the action, and the act becomes a political statement. The goal of the terrorist is important. The desire to achieve a goal can approach fanaticism, wherein any type of atrocity becomes an acceptable tool. Commitment becomes all-important, and the terrorist act becomes central to the activities of the group. The goal of the group binds the members together, and every group activity focuses on attaining the revolutionary goal. To the terrorist, actions they take are acts of war and the end justifies the means (Friedlander, 1983: 43).

The Oklahoma bombing hardened many Americans against terrorist groups, and many politicians responded accordingly. In July of 1996, a bipartisan congressional task force tentatively agreed to expand wiretap authority and a taggants study. The wiretapping provision would allow the FBI to use roving wiretaps to listen to suspected terrorists who avoid detection by using cellular telephones and scramblers. The taggant study would determine whether to add chemical identification markers to black and smokeless gunpowder (*San Jose Mercury News*, 1996: 3A). The proposed bill has not become law.

In June of 1997, the U.S. Senate voted 94-0 to ban the publication of bomb-making information on the Internet. The ban also included alternative newspapers and books. Senator Dianne Feinstein of California sponsored the amendment. She had tried twice before to legislate a ban on such information. The ban would make such an offense a federal crime punishable by a $250,000 fine, up to 20 years in prison, or both. Senator Feinstein pointed out that there were 1,666 World Wide Web sites offering bomb-making information.

Brief Historical Perspective

The root of political terrorism is believed to reside with Hassan Ben Sabbah, 1070 A.D., who traveled the Middle East in an effort to convert Muslims to the Ishmaili philosophy. When people refused to follow his beliefs he resorted to terrorism. He became known as the First Grand Master of the Order of Assassins. He was responsible for the murder of innumerable political, military, and religious leaders (Mullins, 1988: 1-5)

Terrorism has played an important part in the history of the United States. Before the revolutionary war, loyalists were driven from their homes and their crops burned. In 1834, a Protestant mob burned a Catholic convent in Boston, and a few years later a writer, Alton P. Lovejoy, after his inflammatory oratory was killed by political mob action. In the middle of the nineteenth century, numerous eastern cities were the scenes of riots, and numerous Irish and Catholic citizens were beaten, stoned, and killed (Mullins, 1988: 19). In 1865, when John Wilkes Booth shot President Lincoln, he thought that he would be hailed as a hero by his fellow countrymen and by future generations. At that time, some Americans supported the assassination as necessary in order to resolve the conflict created by the Civil War. Some felt that the brutal killing of a leader was not only justified, but essential. Booth was not a revolutionary, but an overwrought Confederate sympathizer. After the war, the Ku Klux Klan, formed by former Confederates, worked its vengeance throughout the South. Lynching was common during this period, and violence became an integral part of the development of the West (Chalmers, 1965: 239).

From 1865 to 1875, business and labor fought each other in the streets of American cities. Typical of this conflict was that perpetrated by the Molly Maguires, a secret organization of Irish coal miners from Pennsylvania, who vigorously opposed the mine owners. Mining superintendents were assassinated, and numerous company police officers and members of the secret society were also killed (Parry, 1976: 93-95).

Many events occurred that subsequently contributed to unrest in the nation. One was the immigration of Johann Most to the United States in 1882. Most was a German anarchist who lectured with fire and brimstone throughout the nation.

He became the pride of the radicals when he published a manual giving detailed instructions on planting explosives in churches, palaces, ballrooms, and other gathering places. In the same publication, he listed poisons that could be effectively used against capitalists, politicians, spies, and other "traitors." In the opinion of Albert Parry, an expert on terrorism, Most's manual was a true predecessor to the later publications on guerrilla warfare and terrorism that were written by Mao Tse-tung and Che Guevara (Parry, 1976: 93-95).

In 1886, unemployment was high, and many of the jobless were exhorted to violence by socialists and anarchists. On May 3, strikers at the McCormick Harvester Plant in Chicago attacked replacement workers, and the police fired into the crowd of strikers. One striker was killed, and several were wounded. August Spies published an article in ALARM (an anarchist publication), calling all workers to arms. In response to this call, approximately 3,000 men, women, and children gathered in Chicago's Haymarket Square to listen to speeches by Albert Parsons and August Spies. Even with a steady rain falling, about 500 were still at the demonstration when 180 policemen arrived and ordered the dispersal of the crowd. Suddenly, a large bomb exploded. It had been thrown from a nearby alley, and landed between two companies of police. One officer died, and many were wounded. The police fired into the crowd amidst all the smoke and confusion. By the end of the short-lived battle, seven officers died, and 60 were wounded. The public demanded vengeance. Eventually, eight workers were found guilty. Two of those sentenced to death were Albert Parsons and August Spies. With their convictions, anarchist movement in the United States ceased to exist. However, what we know today as terrorism evolved from the anarchistic philosophy (Parry, 1976: 98-99).

Individual acts of violence tore at the basic fabric of the nation for decades. In 1933, the car in which President-elect Franklin D. Roosevelt was riding was riddled with bullets, and Anton J. Cermack, Mayor of Chicago, was killed. In 1935, Huey P. Long, a state senator from Louisiana, was murdered. In 1963, President John F. Kennedy was assassinated. This infamous act of violence was followed by the murder of civil rights leader Martin Luther King, Jr. in 1968, then by the shooting death of former U.S. Attorney General Robert F. Kennedy. None of these killings has been proven to have been committed by organized groups. One other near-tragedy, however, was a terrorist act that occurred in 1950, when a group of Puerto Rican extremists attempted to assassinate President Harry S. Truman.

Since these events, systematic violence has been increasingly common in the United States. Numerous radical groups have come on the scene, including the Black Panthers, the resurrected Ku Klux Klan, Students for a Democratic Society, the Weathermen, and the Symbionese Liberation Army (Sobel, 1975: 167-196). These groups are on both extremes of the political spectrum. Some terrorist groups have come into existence in order to right perceived (as well as real) racial wrongs. Other groups oppose the people who are thought to be a threat; these include both religious and racial groups. Some oppose warfare; these groups were especially active during the Vietnam War. Others include individuals that want to change the government or overthrow it (Sobel, 1975: 167). All of these types of groups have used varying means of violence to further a cause.

Terrorism Defined

Terrorism is not easily defined. It is best not to become caught up in the academic exercise engaged in by many as an effort to find a definition that meets all contingencies. Some distinguish violence and terrorism. Others argue for a separation, within the definition, of such terms as force and coercion. Some find it difficult to accept the fact that force can be a legitimate use of state power, as compared to force that is really just arbitrary violence (Wilkenson, 1977: 23).

The following definition of terrorism is becoming more and more accepted. It defines terrorism as: "the unlawful use of force or violence against persons or property to intimidate or coerce a government, the civilian population, or any segment thereof, in furtherance of political or social objectives." Additionally, this definition is refined by delineating the difference between domestic and international terrorism:

- Domestic terrorism involves groups or individuals who are based and operate entirely within the United States and Puerto Rico without foreign direction and whose acts are directed at elements of the U.S. Government or population.

- International terrorism is the unlawful use of force or violence committed by a group or individual, who has some connection to a foreign power or whose activities transcend national boundaries, against persons or property to intimidate or coerce a government, the civilian population, or any segment thereof, in furtherance of political or social objectives (Federal Bureau of Investigation, 1995: iii).

There are three types of terrorist-related activities:

- A *terrorist incident* is a violent act or an act dangerous to human life, in violation of the criminal laws of the United States or of any state, to intimidate or coerce a government, the civilian population, or any segment thereof, in furtherance of political or social objectives.

- A *suspected terrorist incident* is a potential act of terrorism in which responsibility for the act cannot be attributed at the time to a known or suspected terrorist group or individual.

- A *terrorism prevention* is a documented instance in which a violent act by a known or suspected terrorist group or individual with the means and a proven propensity for violence is successfully interdicted through investigative activity.

There is no federal crime that defines terrorism as a crime. Terrorists are arrested and convicted under existing criminal statues. Terrorists continue to improve their ability to support or conduct violent acts. Some extremists and their followers have demonstrated the ability to use advanced technology, travel undetected, and circumvent the letter and spirit of U.S. law.

Domestic terrorist groups usually represent extreme positions of either the left wing or the right wing. These groups seek to change the existing American social and political environment through violent means. Left-wing terrorist groups are generally of a Marxist-Leninist ideology and strive to bring about revolution in the United States. Right-wing terrorist groups are often influenced by a racist, anti-Semitic philosophy that advocates the supremacy of the white race. Included in the domestic category are Puerto Rican terrorist groups, Jewish terrorist elements, and other groups that resort to violent means to achieve their goals.

Terrorism in the United States

In past years, the American democracy seemed to be under frequent attack from terrorist activities although recently there has been a decline in terrorist incidents. Notwithstanding this fact, acts of terrorism are still a type of activity that cannot be tolerated. It is essential for law enforcement agencies to remain vigilant by preventing and responding to individuals and groups that use terrorism to achieve social or political ends.

Throughout the last three decades, leftist-oriented extremist groups posed the predominant domestic terrorist threat in the United States. During the last 20 years, many of the leaders of extremist groups have been arrested for conducting criminal activities. Another factor in the reduction of terrorism is the fact that the transformation of the former Soviet Union has deprived many leftists of a coherent ideology or spiritual patron. Hence, membership and support for these groups has waned (Federal Bureau of Investigation, 1995: 11). Two hundred fifty-nine terrorist incidents, 48 suspected terrorist incidents, and 84 terrorism preventions occurred in the United States and Puerto Rico during the period from 1980 to 1995 (see Figures 12-1, 12-2, 12-3).

However, during the five-year period ending in 1994, terrorist incidents totaled only 28, there were 16 terrorism preventions, and five suspected terrorist incidents (see Figure 12-4). During this period, bombing attacks were the most frequent, and commercial establishments were targeted most often. The North Central region was the scene of more attacks than any other region. What is significant about these events is the drop in terrorist activities in each category and especially the reduction of incidents that occurred in Puerto Rico. Between 1989 and 1993, there were 11 incidents of terrorism in Puerto Rico, but in the last three years there have been none. This apparent decrease, in part, is due to the plebiscite held in Puerto Rico in which a plurality voted to maintain their commonwealth status.

Figure 12-1
Terrorist Incidents: 1980-1995

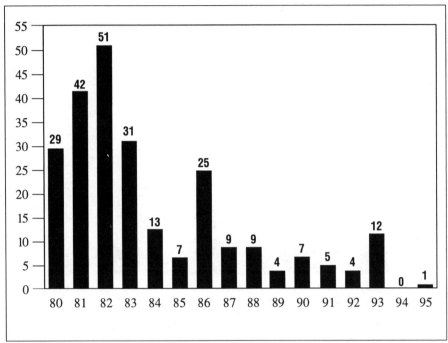

Source: Federal Bureau of Investigation (1996). *Terrorism in the United States 1995*. Washington DC: USGPO, 16.

Figure 12-2
Suspected Terrorist Incidents: 1982-1995

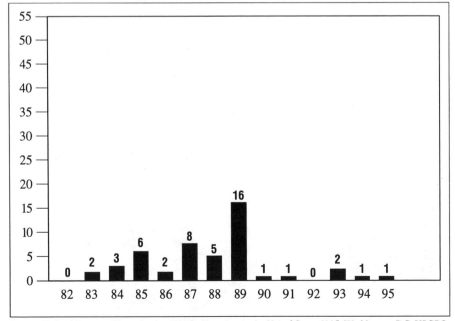

Source: Federal Bureau of Investigation (1996). *Terrorism in the United States 1995*. Washington, DC: USGPO, 16.

Figure 12-3
Terrorism Preventions: 1982-1995

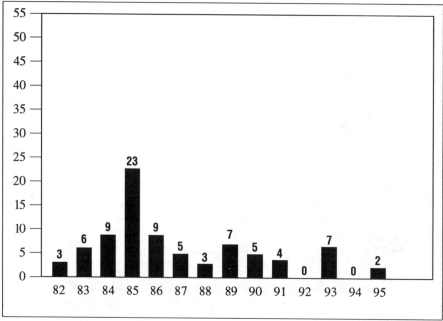

Source: Federal Bureau of Investigation (1996). *Terrorism in the United States 1995.* Washington, DC: USGPO, 16.

Figure 12-4
Terrorists Incidents By Type, Target, Group and Region: 1990-1994

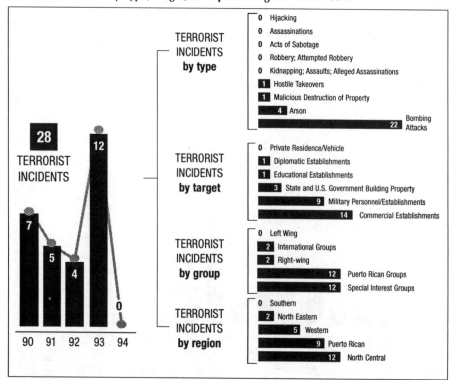

Source: Federal Bureau of Investigation (1995). *Terrorism in the United States 1994.* Washington, DC: USGPO, 8.

Bombings dominated the types of violence used by terrorists. These attacks included fire bombs, truck bombs, tear gas, pipe bombs, and rockets. It also included acts of shooting, arson, assassination, sabotage, hijackings, hostile takeovers, kidnapping, assaults, robbery, and malicious destruction of property. Of concern in the future is the potential use of chemical, biological, and nuclear weapons. Targets range from commercial establishments, military installations, government buildings, diplomatic establishments, and educational establishments. Terrorist groups include left-wing, right-wing, international, and special interest groups. Terrorist attacks by terrorist groups will continue to occur, as the perceived social and political conditions (often claimed as the basis for terrorist activities) have not changed to these groups' satisfaction.

In spite of the fact that there are fewer terroristic acts, it would be incorrect to conclude that there is no longer a threat for terrorism in the United States. Presently, there are representatives in the United States from foreign states that sponsor terrorism, including Iraq, Iran, Syria, Sudan, Cuba, North Korea, and Libya. In 1995, Egyptian Shaykh Omar Abdel Rahman, the spiritual leader of the militant Egyptian Islamic Group was tried on seditious conspiracy charges in New York. During the trial, a Sudanese national testified that Sudanese diplomats were aware of the conspiracy to bomb major landmarks. Allegedly one Sudanese diplomat offered to help the conspirators place a bomb at the United Nations by providing diplomatic license plates. In addition, members of subnational (anti-regime elements seeking political change) terrorist groups and other terrorist organizations maintain a presence in the United States.

Feature

International Acts of Terrorism

- On April 12, 1995, Michael "Mixie" Martin, a supporter of the Provisional Irish Republican Army (PIRA) pled guilty to conspiracy. Martin and two other supporters had conspired to purchase 2,900 detonators in Tucson in 1989 and a stinger missile in Florida in 1990. Martin was sentenced to 16 months incarceration and was deported in 1996.

- In January of 1995, Shaykh Omar Abdel Rahman and nine other defendants were placed on trial. They were charged with seditious conspiracy and other crimes in a June 1993 plot to bomb major landmarks in New York City and assassinate prominent politicians and foreign leaders. The landmarks were the United Nations Building, 26 Federal Plaza, which houses the FBI's New York Field Office, and the Lincoln and Holland Tunnels. The defendants were convicted on 48 of 50 charges. Rahman was convicted of seditious conspiracy, solicitation to murder President Hosni Mubarak, solicitation to attack a U.S. military installation, and conspiracy to conduct bombings. One of the defendants was convicted of the murder of militant Jewish leader Rabbi Meir Kahane.

Source: Federal Bureau of Investigation (1996). *Terrorism in the United States, 1995*. Washington, DC: Federal Bureau of Investigation, 1-17.

World Trade Center

On February 26, 1993, at 12:18 P.M. a massive explosion occurred on the B-2 level of the parking garage at the World Trade Center (WTC) in New York City. The explosion was caused by a bomb consisting of roughly 1,200 pounds of explosives. The blast created a crater 150 feet in diameter and five stories high. The attack caused enormous damage to the underground parking area and the connecting Vista Hotel. Six levels of the parking garage were perforated by the blast and hundreds of vehicles demolished. The Vista Hotel, located directly above the detonation site, took much of the force of the explosion and was badly damaged.

Property damage to the WTC amounted to more than one-half billion dollars, and caused serious disruption in international trade. The WTC had to be closed for one month to complete extensive structural repairs. At the time of the explosion, there were approximately 50,000 people on the WTC complex, six of whom died and 1,042 of whom were injured. Due to the loss of human life, serious bodily injuries, extensive property damage, and economic loss, the bombing of the WTC was considered to be the single largest international terrorist incident ever conducted in the United States.

In 1994, four of the six defendants indicted were convicted on all 38 counts against them. Each of these four defendants received sentences of 240 years in prison and fines of $250,000. The two remaining defendants were indicted in absentia. In 1995, one of these defendants, Ramzi Ahmed Yousef, was apprehended by Pakistani authorities and, after being returned to the United States, entered a plea of not guilty. He was convicted and sentenced to life imprisonment. One defendant, Abdul Rahman Yasin, remains at large.

The WTC bombing is an example of what has become known as international radical terrorism (IRT). Its adherents generally overcome traditional national differences by concentrating on a common goal of achieving social change, under the banner of personal beliefs, through violence. In this bombing, the defendants included: Egyptians, Iraqis, Jordanians, Palestinians, and U.S. citizens (Federal Bureau of Investigation, 1995: 14).

Oklahoma City Bombing

At approximately 9:02 A.M., on April 19, 1995, an improvised explosive device placed in a rental truck destroyed the Alfred P. Murrah Federal Building in Oklahoma City, Oklahoma. The blast killed 168 people and wounded hundreds of others. Property damage was in the hundreds of millions of dollars. On April 19, Timothy James McVeigh was arrested in Oklahoma for vehicle and weapons violations. Six days later McVeigh was charged with maliciously damaging and destroying a building by means of explosives. On May 11, 1995, Terry Lynn Nichols was charged with the same violation. McVeigh was allegedly an avid reader of *The Turner Diaries*. This novel describes the bombing of the FBI

Feature

Domestic Acts of Terrorism

- On October 9, 1995, a 12-car Amtrak train—the westbound Sunset Limited traveling from New Orleans to Los Angeles—derailed near Hyder, Arizona. The crash killed one person and seriously injured 12 others. Approximately 100 additional persons received minor injuries.

  FBI agents, Amtrak officials, and Southern Pacific Railroad personnel went to the site of the incident. Investigation revealed that a person or persons had deliberately tampered with the tracks, causing the train to derail. Investigators also found four typed letters. These letters mentioned the Bureau of Alcohol, Tobacco, and Firearms, the FBI, "Ruby Ridge," and "Waco." The signature on the letters was "Sons of the Gestapo." This suspected act of terrorism remains under FBI investigation.

- On March 9, 1995, Top Ten Fugitive Melvin Edward Mays, a member of the Chicago El Rukns street gang, was arrested by members of the FBI's Chicago Terrorism Task Force. He was charged with more than 40 federal counts related to a conspiracy to conduct terrorist activities on behalf of the Government of Libya. As part of the conspiracy, Mays purchased an inert light antitank weapon from an undercover agent. May eluded arrest and was placed on the FBI's Top Ten Most Wanted List on February 7, 1989. His conviction marked the first instance in U.S. history that an American citizen had planned terrorist acts on behalf of a foreign government for money.

- On December 18, 1995, an Internal Revenue Service employee discovered a 30-gallon plastic drum packed with 100 pounds of ammonium nitrate and fuel oil. The drum had been placed behind a vehicle in the parking lot of the IRS building in Reno, Nevada. On December 28, 1995, Joseph Martin Bailie and Ellis Edward Hurst were charged with planting the bomb. The two men tried to detonate the device the previous evening when the building was empty. A three-foot fuse had apparently been ignited, but went out prior to reaching the explosive.

- On February 25, 1995, the FBI concluded a terrorism prevention when a Minneapolis jury convicted Douglas Allen Baker and Leroy Charles Wheeler of violating the Biological Weapons Anti-Terrorism Act (BWAT). They had manufactured and intended to use ricin, a highly toxic biological substance made from castor beans. On October 25, 1995, Richard John Oelrich and Dennis Brett Henderson—both identified as co-conspirators in the plot—were convicted of identical BWAT charges.

  The Patriot's Council is a small, anti-government, tax protest group based in the Alexandria, Minnesota, area. Members advocate the violent overthrow of the U.S. government and the establishment of a new *truly constitutional* regime. In April 1991, Baker, Wheeler, Oelrich, and Henderson planned to kill a Deputy U.S. Marshal and a Sheriff who previously served papers on a Patriot's Council associate. They manufactured the ricin to use as a weapon. The amount of biological agent they eventually produced could have killed over 100 people if delivered effectively.

Source: Federal Bureau of Investigation (1996). *Terrorism in the United States, 1995*. Washington, DC: Federal Bureau of Investigation, 1-17.

national headquarters building. A truck was driven into the basement of the building without being stopped. The bomb was made by mixing heating oil with ammonium nitrate fertilizer and, when detonated, a sizable portion of the building was destroyed (McDonald, 1980: 38-40). The diary had a great deal of influence on McVeigh and in all probability was instrumental in his decision to plant a bomb.

Later in the year, an indictment charged both defendants with the bombing and the homicide of several law enforcement officers who were in the building. Following a petition by defense attorneys, U.S. District Judge Richard P. Matsch was appointed to hear the matter and the trial was held in Denver, Colorado. In the early part of June 1997, newspaper headlines read: "McVeigh Guilty: Conviction on All Counts." The verdict involved 11 counts; eight of which were murder. The jury deliberated for 23 hours before handing down the verdict. On June 13, 1997, the jury sentenced McVeigh to death. In the winter of 1997, Terry Lynn Nichols was found guilty of conspiracy and involuntary manslaughter for causing the deaths of eight federal agents.

Centennial Olympic Park Bombing

Three ten-inch-long pipe bombs detonated at 1:25 A.M. in a park near the Atlanta, Georgia, site of the 1996 Olympics. The explosives, which were in a knapsack, were next to a concert tower. The explosion killed one woman, and a cameraman died of a heart attack while rushing to capture the explosion on tape. One hundred eleven people were injured. Security officials reported that a person believed to be a white male telephoned 911, warning of the impending explosion.

After several days a security guard, Richard Jewell, who found the backpack bomb before it exploded, became the focus of the investigation. While investigating Jewell, the FBI obtained four search warrants, allowing them to search his home, a vehicle, and a storage unit. Several boxes of evidence, including firearms were removed from his home after a 12-hour search. The extensive coverage of Jewell as a hero and then a suspect brought into question media responsibility to individuals suspected of an offense but never charged. The *Atlanta Journal-Constitution*, the newspaper that initially identified Richard Jewell, refused to retract its identification of him as a suspect and Jewell has filed a civil suit against the newspaper. Additionally, he has pending suits against the *New York Post* and WABC radio in New York. Because of the way the accusations against Jewell were handled, he received more than $500,000 from NBC. Jewell also received settlements from CNN and an Atlanta radio station for undisclosed amounts (Cannon, 1997: 4A). After three months, federal prosecutors cleared Richard Jewell as a suspect. The bombing is still under investigation. In July of 1997, Attorney General Janet Reno apologized to Richard Jewell for disclosing that he was the prime suspect in the bombing.

Active Terrorist Groups

Contemporary terrorism is a threat to nations throughout the world. Terrorist groups have a wide spectrum of social and political beliefs. Some of these articulate grievances that have racial undertones. Others use violence to achieve a specific goal, such as liberation from what is perceived as a repressive regime (Homer, 1988: 200-203).

Ted Gurr, a terrorism expert, identified four distinct species of political and social terrorism that are based on the political status and situation of the perpetrators. These included *vigilante, insurgent, transnational*, and *state* terrorism. Historically, *vigilante terrorism* has been the most common in the United States. It involves terrorist activities by a private group directing its acts against another private group as a means of resisting or stopping change. The Ku Klux Klan is representative of vigilante terrorism.

Insurgent terrorism dominates the headlines. Acts in this category are directed by private groups against public agencies, with the expressed goal of achieving radical political change. Typical of this category would be the Patriot's Council.

The third category, *transnational terrorism*, originates in one country, while its acts are committed in another. Typical of this type of group are such organizations as Al Fatah—The Revolutionary Council, and the Liberation of Palestine—General Command.

The last category is *state terrorism*. It is used by authorities to intimidate either private citizens or groups. Typical of this are the acts committed by the government of England to control and suppress the Irish Republican Army (Gurr, 1988: 551-552).

In 1997, based on recently passed legislation, the U.S. Secretary of State, Madeleine Albright, released a list of terrorist groups for which fundraising would be prohibited in the United States. The list included 13 Islamic organizations and two Israeli groups. Others on the list included Asian and Latin American groups. Any money these organizations had in the United States was frozen, and it became a crime to provide money, weapons, or other types of tangible support to any of the listed organizations. Additionally, members and representatives of these organizations are ineligible for U.S. visas and are subject to exclusion.

The Japanese Red Army (JRA)

The Japanese Red Army (JRA) is typical of transnational terrorist groups. It is a Marxist-oriented group that was formed in the early 1970s. The group is believed to have a membership of about 18 to 20. It calls for a worldwide struggle against imperialism, and its ultimate goal is the *world revolution of communism.* The group emphasizes solidarity with the revolutionary forces in the world, especially those working for the Palestinian revolution (the struggle against Zionism and U.S. imperialism). The JRA regards international terrorism as an inseparable component of armed struggle against imperialism.

Figure 12-5

Foreign Terrorist Organizations Designated by the Secretary of State

Abu Nidal Organization (ANO)
Abu Sayyaf Group (ASG)
Armed Islamic Group (GIA)
Aum Shinrikyo (Aum)
Euzkadi Ta Askatasuna (ETA)
Democratic Front for the Liberation of Palestine-Hawatmeh Faction (DFLP)
HAMAS (Islamic Resistance Movement)
Harakat ul-Ansar (HUA)
Hizballah (Party of God)
Gama's al-Islamiyya (Islamic Group, IG)
Japanese Red Army (JRA)
al-Jihad
Kach
Kahane Chai
Khmer Rouge
Kurdistan Workers' Party (PKK)
Liberation Tigers of Tamil Eelam (LTTE)
Manuel Rodriguez Patriotic Front Dissidents (FPMR/D)
Mujahedin-e Khalq Organization (MEK, MKO)
National Liberation Army (ELN)
Palestine Islamic Jihad-Shaqaqi Faction (PIJ)
Palestine Liberation Front-Abu Abbas Faction (PLF)
Popular Front for the Liberation of Palestine (PFLP)
Popular Front for the Liberation of Palestine-General Command (PFLP-GC)
Revolutionary Armed Forces of Colombia (FARC)
Revolutionary Organization 17 November (17 November)
Revolutionary People's Liberation Party/Front (DHKP/C)
Revolutionary People's Struggle (ELA)
Shining Path (Sendero Luminoso, SL)
Tupac Amaru Revolutionary Movemement (MRTA)

The JRA was very active during the 1970s. After 1977, the group was fairly dormant until May 1986, when members were responsible for bombing attacks in Jakarta, Indonesia, at the American, Japanese, and Canadian embassies. Since then, the JRA has been responsible for numerous bombing attacks in Western Europe, targeting United States interests. On April 12, 1988, JRA member Yu Kikumura was arrested by the New Jersey State Police following the discovery of three bombs in his vehicle after he was stopped for a traffic violation. The bombs were modified fire extinguisher cylinders filled with a combination of bird-shot and gunpowder. At the time of his arrest, Kikumura possessed a stolen Japanese passport. Stamps in the passport indicated that he had entered the United States on March 8, 1988. Kikumura had in his possession various maps of the United States. Investigation determined that he had traveled throughout the northeastern United States, and it is believed that his intended target was a military recruiting station in New York City. The JRA is believed to possess wide-ranging capability for executing terrorist operations. This belief is based on the fact that the JRA appears to be a well-funded and entrenched terrorist group with the capability of conducting terrorist operations in any of the cities to which its members have traveled freely over the past several years (Federal Bureau of Investigation, 1988: 23-24). This group was relatively dormant for nine years between terroristic activities, hence it is still considered a threat. Syria still offers basing privileges or refuge to members of the JRA, and it is based in Syrian-controlled areas of Lebanon (Wilcox, 1997: 26).

Radical Palestinian Groups

When the state of Israel came into existence in 1948, many Palestinians fled due to the heavy fighting in the region, and they sought to live in Arab-controlled territories. By 1949, fewer than one-half of the original 1.3 million Palestinians remained in their original homes. Many terrorist groups have the common objectives of creating a Palestinian homeland and attaining self-government for Palestinians. During the 1950s, the Palestine National Liberation Movement (Al Fatah) was created by a group of Palestinian students led by Yassir Arafat. Al Fatah espoused a conservative, nationalist agenda that encouraged Palestinians to engage in armed struggle to pursue their goals of independence.

The *Palestine Liberation Organization (PLO)* was founded in 1964 as a Palestinian nationalist umbrella organization that included a number of radical terrorist components dedicated to the establishment of an independent Palestinian state. The PLO became an overtly political entity representing a *de facto* Palestinian government in exile. Al Fatah was the largest and most moderate of the Palestinian groups. Its leader, Yassir Arafat, was also the leader of the PLO. Al Fatah was responsible for operating guerrilla training bases throughout the Middle East and Near East, and was also responsible for a number of terrorist incidents committed against Israel. Al Fatah's activities in the United States have been largely limited to fund-raising activities.

On September 9, 1993, PLO Chairman Arafat committed the PLO to cease all violence and terrorism. The U.S. government continues to monitor PLO compliance with the commitment. One group under the PLO umbrella suspended its participation in the PLO in protest of the agreement and continues a sporadic campaign of violence.

The *Popular Front for the Liberation of Palestine (PFLP)* is a hard-line Palestinian group founded in 1967 and led by George Habbash. Historically, the PFLP is one of the more violent Palestinian groups. It is politically Marxist and advocates a communist Palestinian homeland. The PFLP was one of the first Palestinian terrorist groups to carry out an attack outside Israel. This occurred when it hijacked an El Al aircraft en route from Rome to Tel Aviv in 1968. The PFLP carries out numerous attacks against Israeli and moderate Arab targets. It has 800 members and receives most of its financial and military assistance from Syria and Libya. Ahmad Jabril split from the PFLP and formed the Popular Front for the Liberation of Palestine—General Command (PFLP—GC), whose headquarters are in Damascus with bases in Lebanon and cells in Europe. This group opposes any negotiated settlement with Israel.

The *Democratic Front for the Liberation of Palestine (DFLP)* was formed in 1969 when some members broke away from the PFLP. This group is a revolutionary Marxist-Leninist organization that advocates a communist Palestinian homeland. It seeks Palestinian liberation through a revolution of the masses. It opposes the Israel-PLO peace agreement and continues to be involved in border raids. It has 500 members and receives financial and military aid from Syria and Libya.

The *Palestine Liberation Front (PLF)* was founded in 1977. The PLF subsequently split into three factions. One was led by Abu Abbas. This faction was responsible for hijacking the Achille Lauro ocean-liner, during which an American was murdered. In 1993, Khalid Al Jawary, a Palestinian terrorist, was convicted for his part in an attempted bombing of three vehicles in New York City that had occurred 20 years earlier. He was sentenced to 10 years imprisonment. He was a member of the Black September Organization (BSO) that was the operational wing of PLF. The PLF currently has about 50 members and is based in Iraq. It receives logistic and military support from the PLO, Libya, and Iraq.

One of the most violent Palestinian groups is the *Abu Nidal Organization (ANO)*, officially known as Al Fatah—The Revolutionary Council (Streissguth, 1993: 75-94). At various times, this group has also been known as the Black June Organization, Arab Revolutionary Brigades, and the Revolutionary Organization of Socialist Moslems. ANO member Saif Nijmeh was arrested in 1993 in St. Louis County, Missouri, following his indictment for violations of the Racketeer Influenced and Corrupt Organizations Act (RICO).

Three other ANO members were arrested later, based on the primary charge of traveling in interstate and foreign areas in aid of racketeering enterprise (Federal Bureau of Investigation, 1994: 8). The ANO opposes all efforts toward political reconciliation in the Middle East and views armed struggle against Zionism as the first priority of the Palestinian resistance movement.

The ANO is thought to be responsible for more than 90 terrorist attacks throughout the world in the last 14 years. It has carried out terrorist attacks in 20 countries, killing or injuring almost 900 people. It is based in Libya and has a presence in Lebanon. It has received support from Iraq and Syria.

HAMAS (Islamic Resistance Movement) was formed as an outgrowth of the Palestinian branch of the Muslim Brotherhood. It has used both political and violent means, including terrorism, to pursue the goal of establishing an Islamic Palestinian state in place of Israel. Its strength is located in the Gaza Strip and a few areas of the West Bank. It has engaged in peaceful political activities in contrast to the many attacks it has made against Israeli civilian and military targets. It conducts some fundraising in North America.

The *Palestine Islamic Jihad (PIJ)* is a series of loosely affiliated factions rather than a cohesive group. It is committed to the creation of a Palestinian state and the destruction of Israel through holy war. The PIJ has identified the United States as an enemy and has threatened and attacked United States' interests in Jordan. It has carried out suicide bombing attacks against Israeli targets. It is believed that PIJ receives financial assistance from Iran and Syria. These groups generally have the sympathy of certain radical elements of Middle Eastern communities in the United States.

Skinheads

The number of youth gangs who call themselves *Skinheads* or *Skins* have increased during the last decade. Members of these gangs are recognizable by their shaved heads and their uniform, which consists of shirts buttoned to the neck, flight jackets, and black English workboots. Skinheads are generally young, ranging in age from 15 to 25. Although exact numbers are difficult to determine, it is estimated that there are approximately 500 to 1,000 Skinheads in the United States, belonging to about 10 major gangs, each of which have several subgroups. The gangs usually have 15 to 50 members each.

The Skinhead movement originated in England in the 1970s, as a protest to social unrest and high unemployment. Skinheads began as individuals who emphasized racial (white) pride, patriotism, support of the working class, and anti-immigration views (Stern, n.d.: 1-21). Neo-Nazi groups in England noticed this trend and successfully began to recruit members.

Skinheads first appeared in the United States around 1980, as certain British rock groups, some of which were racist-oriented, gained American followers. These British rock groups had song titles such as "White Power." White racist philosophy appeared in the lyrics of many of these groups' songs. Skinheads in the United States usually listened to the same music and dressed the same, but not all of them believed in a racist philosophy of neo-Nazism and hatred of African-Americans, Jews, and Hispanics. At the end of the 1980s it was reported that there were numerous activist skinheads in 31 states. They were mostly concentrated in the West and the South (Ridgeway, 1990: 165)

Skinheads in the United States are now split into two factions of opposing philosophies. One faction believes in racial harmony; these are known as *straight-edge* Skins. The other faction follows the extreme right-wing philosophies of racism. As in England, some of the older white supremacist groups in the United States have allegedly begun to recruit Skinheads. White supremacist groups such as the Ku Klux Klan (KKK) and the National Socialist White American Party (NSWAP) have used Skinheads as *foot soldiers*, security guards (at their meetings and demonstrations), and distributors of newsletters and pamphlets.

Law enforcement authorities are concerned about the growing number of Skinheads because they have been known to commit violent crimes. Skinheads are very defensive of their *turf* and their arsenals reportedly consist of knives, handguns, and even machine guns. Law enforcement officers are also concerned about the recruiting of Skinheads by white supremacist groups whose philosophies include racial violence.

In 1993, the American Front Skinheads, located on the West Coast, engaged in two acts of domestic terrorism. They targeted the National Association for the

Advancement of Colored People (NAACP) headquarters in Tacoma, Washington, and a bar frequented by homosexuals in the Seattle, Washington, area. In the summer of 1993, law enforcement officials arrested eight individuals who were about to launch an anti-black revolution. They were arming themselves in preparation for the riot they expected to occur following the Rodney King verdict. King gained national media attention when he was assaulted during his arrest by members of the Los Angeles Police Department. When the riot did not occur, the Skinheads—members of the Fourth Reich Skinheads—plotted to assassinate prominent members of the African-American and Jewish communities in Los Angeles. Fortunately, they were arrested before the revolution and all suspects either pled guilty or were convicted of the charges against them (Federal Bureau of Investigation, 1994: 22).

In Denver, Colorado, on November 19, 1997, a Skinhead murdered a police office and later killed himself. Eight days later, an officer was fired upon and this attack renewed a concern about Skinheads. In another incident, a Skinhead admitted to killing a West African immigrant and shooting a white nurse who rushed to help because he did not want to live with African-Americans.

Militias

The *Posse Comitatus* and *Christian Patriots* were spearheads of the current militia movement in the United States, but remain separate entities with their own agendas. The members of these two groups are not as mainstream as some militia entities. They are more anti-black and anti-Semitic, but definitely share the anti-government sentiments of white supremacists. They protest many of the things that militias protest, such as taxes and the use of Social Security numbers. They have moved toward greater solidarity and disclaim federal and state powers. They have formed their own court system and threaten government workers who oppose them (Ross and Mauney, 1996: 1-10).

The Southern Poverty Law Center has pointed out that militia groups are more dangerous than ever (Dees and Corcoran, 1996: 1-90). They have organized into small cells in order to thwart infiltration. As of 1996, it was estimated that there were 858 patriot groups, including 380 armed militias. This is a six percent increase over the number of groups identified in 1994. Patriot groups are active in all 50 states (Klanwatch and Militia Task Force, 1997: 1). Since militia groups attracted national attention after the Oklahoma City bombing, they have become increasingly popular and militia leaders have been keynote speakers at *Preparedness Expos*, where the average attendance has been 6,000 people (Thrap and Holstein, 1997: 24-37).

Many of the individuals joining militia groups feel displaced by rapid changes in the U.S. culture and economy, or are seeking some type of personal affirmation. Another factor that contributes to the increase in membership is the anti-government movement. The changing political environment, issues such as gun control legislation, United Nations involvement in international affairs, and clashes between dissidents and law enforcement, are cornerstones of militia ideology. A significant part of the movement are common law courts. These courts—which have no legitimate legal authority—consist of self-appointed judges and juries who sometime issue fraudulent indictments and warrants.

Some militia members believe that the U.S. Government is part of a conspiracy to create a *New World Order*. According to adherents, in this new order, existing international boundaries will be dissolved and the world will be ruled by the United Nations. Other militia supporters believe that the federal government is either too powerful or simply illegal (Federal Bureau of Investigation, 1995: 11).

Ku Klux Klan

After the Civil War, the Ku Klux Klan (KKK) spread throughout the South, rendering brutal revenge on its victims (Parry, 1976: 93). The Klan used unspeakable terror in its opposition to Reconstruction policies. Klan members aimed to gain control over former slaves and to render vengeance on former supporters of the northern cause. Hooded Klansmen led campaigns of violence against freed slaves and their supporters (Gurr, 1988: 550). Klansmen administered beatings and openly killed opponents. In a few years, the Klan became so powerful that white, southern Democrats were unable to wrest control of state governments from both the northern-imposed military rule and the elected, biracial state governments (Chalmers, 1965: 27-92).

By the 1920s, the Klan was a nationwide movement (Katz, 1986: 63-107). It operated openly as a respected middle-class movement until the extreme violence and scandalous conduct of some of its leaders led the Klan into disrepute (Chalmers, 1965: 103-131). Following World War II, the resurrected KKK reappeared in the South as splinter groups and competing factions. In 1945, crosses burned in three southern states and as far north as New Jersey. Three years later, the Birmingham, Alabama, area was the site of many instances of kidnapping, flogging, and cross burning.

In the 1960s, as the civil rights movement expanded, the KKK perpetrated a rash of bombings and assassinations in protest to the movement. In 1966, the House Un-American Activities Committee denounced the KKK as terrorists who engaged in "threats, cross burnings, the firing of churches and schools, bombings, beatings, maimings, and murders" (Schlagheck, 1988: 64-66; Sobel, 1975: 178).

After members of the Ku Klux Klan attacked civil rights marchers in Decatur, Alabama, in 1979, the Southern Poverty Law Center created *Klanwatch*, which filed suit on behalf of the civil rights marchers. Klanwatch investigators presented evidence to the U.S. Department of Justice that resulted in 10 indictments of KKK members in 1984. Five years later, the civil case was settled, and Klan members were required to pay damages, perform community service, and attend a race relations course taught by African-American civil rights

Figure 12-6
The Klanwatch in Court

- A court ordered Texas Klansmen to refrain from harassing immigrant Vietnamese fisherman in Galveston Bay. The Klansmen were led by Texas Grand Dragon Louis Beam, who was considered the most radical and inflammatory racist in the country. Klanwatch was also successful in shutting down Beam's paramilitary camp, where Klansmen and American fishermen were trained in guerrilla warfare.

- In 1990, the out-of-court settlement of a civil suit ended paramilitary activity of the Klan in Alabama. Klan members were required to pay damages, perform community service, and attend a course on race relations and prejudice. Prior to this, nine Klansmen were convicted of criminal charges stemming from an attack on civil rights marchers in Decatur, Alabama.

- A court ordered the Confederate Knights of the KKK (later known as the White Patriot Party) to halt paramilitary training and refrain from harassing blacks. The order resulted from a lawsuit brought by Klanwatch on behalf of Bobby Person, a black correctional officer. A federal jury found the White Patriot Party and its top leaders Glenn Miller and Stephen Miller guilty of contempt of court for violating the order. The lawsuit also exposed the training of U.S. military personnel by the Klan and led to new regulations restricting the military in Klan activities.

- A Mobile, Alabama, jury awarded $7 million in damages to the mother of 19-year-old Michael Donald, who was lynched by United Klans of America members in 1981. Once the largest Klan group, the UKA was forced to turn over its national headquarters to the youth's mother, and the organization was virtually destroyed. The evidence gathered by Klanwatch investigators for the 1987 civil trial led to the murder indictments of UKA members Benjamin Cox, who was sentenced to life in prison, and Bennie Jack Hays, who now awaits trial. Klansmen James "Tiger" Knowles, serving life in prison, and Henry Hays, presently on death row, were sentenced on federal civil rights charges.

- An Atlanta jury awarded nearly $1 million in damages to civil rights marchers who were attacked by a Klan-led mob in all-white Forsyth County, Georgia. Klanwatch filed the suit against the Invisible Empire of the Southern White Knights, its leader Dave Holland, and 10 other individuals. The case was concluded in 1994 and, interestingly, the office equipment was given to the NAACP.

- In 1988, Tom and John Metzger sent members of the White Aryan Resistance to Portland, Oregon to organize a chapter of Skinheads. Members killed an Ethiopian student and Tom Metzger praised them for doing their "civic duty." A civil suit was filed against the Metzgers and in 1990 a court awarded $12.5 million in damages to the family of the victim. In 1994, the U.S. Supreme Court refused to review the appeal.

Source: *SPLC Report* (1996). "25 Years of Seeking Justice." Montgomery, AL: Southern Poverty Law Center, 2-95; Morris Dees and Steve Fiffer (1993). *Hate on Trial.* New York: Villard Books, 3-50; Bill Stanton (1991). *Klanwatch: Bringing the Ku Klux Klan to Justice.* New York: Grove Weidenfeld, 4-80.

leaders (Klanwatch, 1990: 23). Klanwatch has been very effective and, as a result of their investigations, obtained convictions against 37 individuals and seven major white supremacist organizations. Klanwatch is the most comprehensive source of information on hate groups (Klanwatch, 1990: 12; Dees and Fiffer, 1991: 4-39).

In 1993, in Austin, Texas, approximately 50 Ku Klux Klan members gathered to protest the Martin Luther King, Jr. holiday and were confronted by 5,000 opponents who threw eggs, beat drums, and shouted them down. A similar rally was held in Montgomery, Alabama, and another in Miami, Florida, where the KKK won a court order allowing a rally in Davie, Florida. In the summer of 1993, in Corsicana, Texas, a KKK rally was held to show support for the police, who had been the subject of sporadic protests. The protest against the police occurred because of the death of an African-American man while he was in custody. The death was ruled accidental, although officials criticized the use of restraint methods (*San Jose Mercury News*, 1993: 11A). In April of 1997, approximately 50 members of the KKK held a rally in downtown Pittsburgh, Pennsylvania. The gathering was organized by the Grand Dragon of the Keystone Knights of the KKK (*Arizona Daily Star*, 1997: 16A). For the last 10 years, the Klan has marched in Pulaski, Tennessee, the birthplace of the Klan, without significant incidents (Newton and White, 1997: 124-129). Figure 12-6 lists the results of a number of cases in which Klanwatch has opposed the Klan in the courtroom.

The Klan is not as prominent as it once was, but it is still a hate group with which society and law enforcement must contend. In spite of declining membership, the KKK and other white supremacist groups remain a threat to our nation.

The Current Threat—Domestic Groups

During the 1990s, the *Popular Liberation Army (PLA)*, a Puerto Rican group, claimed credit for three terrorist attacks involving bombings and arson. One other incident of arson was perpetrated by an unknown Puerto Rican group. Of special significance was the surrender of two Top Ten Fugitives on December 6, 1994. Claude Daniel Marks and Donna Jean Willmott were supporters of the Prairie Fire Organizing Committee and the Armed Forces for National Liberation (AFNL). The AFNL was a clandestine Puerto Rican terrorist group based in the continental United States. Since 1974, the AFNL had been linked to more than 130 bombings which resulted in more than $3.5 million in damages, five deaths, and 84 injuries. Prairie Fire and the AFNL shared similar extreme leftist ideologies (Federal Bureau of Investigation, 1995: 5).

In the past, Puerto Rican terrorist groups committed bombings, shootings, and arson in their campaign against the U.S. government. Their targets were U.S. government buildings, military and National Guard personnel and facilities, and police officers, among others. Two of the groups, EPB-Macheteros and the Organization of Volunteers for the Puerto Rican Revolution, once considered the most violent of the Puerto Rican organizations, have not claimed any terrorist acts since late 1986. It is thought that this inactivity is the result of court proceedings in Connecticut, stemming from the September 1983 robbery of $7.2 million from a Wells Fargo terminal in West Hartford. In 1990, two members of the EPB-Macheteros, Filiberto Ojeda Rios and Luis Alfredo Colon Osorio, defaulted on their bonds while awaiting trial and went underground. Since 1993, there has not been one violent act perpetrated by Puerto Rican terrorist extremists. Notwithstanding, it is anticipated that a few extremists are willing to plan and conduct terrorist acts as a primary method of operation (Federal Bureau of Investigation, 1995: 11).

Left-wing terrorism has a definite Marxist-Lenin orientation. Groups such as the African National Ujammu, the Dar-Ul Movement, and the Ansaru Allah Community are defined as being leftist in orientation (Federal Bureau of Investigation, 1995: 11). Many of the Puerto Rican terrorist groups, such as the Armed Forces of National Liberation and the Macheteros also fall into this category. Left-wing terrorism has declined dramatically, with no incident occurring during the last five years. Unfortunately, the threat from this quarter has not been eliminated; it only lies dormant. The reason for this is the number of arrests and trials that have occurred during the past several years.

Subsequent convictions removed many, but not all, of the left-wing terrorists responsible for or capable of committing terrorist acts from the streets. These groups continue to pose a threat to American society, as long as they maintain a propensity for violence in their bid to achieve their objectives (Federal Bureau of Investigation, 1995: 11).

Previously, leftist revolutionaries undertook an armed campaign against the U.S. government to eliminate what (in their view) was imperialism, militarism, and corporate exploitation of Third World nations. Bombings were committed against government, military, and corporate facilities as part of this armed action. This campaign is usually financed through bank and/or armored truck robberies that are called *expropriations* by the perpetrators.

Despite various law enforcement successes, fugitive revolutionaries remain at large, including two individuals who are listed in the FBI's Top Ten Fugitives. These two are quite capable of conducting terrorist acts. Many of their associates who support the use of armed action to eliminate perceived ills in this country also remain at large. Many of the wrongs that these revolutionaries perceived actually exist. The problem is their belief that the only way to correct the wrongs is through revolution.

Reactionary right-wing terrorist acts were also rare in 1995, compared to past years, when bombings, armed robberies, and other acts committed to further the white supremacist cause were more commonplace. During the past five years, there were two acts of terrorism and one prevented act of terrorism attributed to right-wing extremists.

The members of the ultra-right usually espouse beliefs that are anti-tax, anti-government, anti-Semitic, and anti-Communist, and they often support the idea of white supremacy. In addition, these groups have engaged in acts of provocation and assault against federal and state law enforcement officials. These groups include the Aryan Nation, the Order, and Posse Comitatus. Many ultra-rightists realize that their views neither conform with, nor are acceptable to, the majority of Americans. They seek, therefore, to establish an all-white homeland in five states of the northwest United States. Several years ago, the group known as *The Order* began to commit a series of armed robberies to finance a campaign to create this homeland. Their enemies were the agents of Zionist Occupation Government (ZOG), police officers, and anyone else that stood in their way.

More than 50 members of The Order and other ultra-rightist groups were arrested, tried, and convicted of weapons violations, bombings, murders, counterfeiting, and other criminal acts. Because many right-wing radicals have been incarcerated, law enforcement actions can be seen as largely responsible for the decrease in activity by the ultra-right.

Ultra-right terrorist groups remain a viable threat, albeit less so than in the past. Many associates of those imprisoned hold the same white supremacist, anti-Semitic, and anti-government beliefs, and these supporters also are capable of committing violence. Many violent individuals are in custody, and this fact may cause those remaining to be less inclined to act. The leadership of the movement is also growing old, but a more youthful and more aggressive leadership may soon take control.

A significant element of the ultra-right movement in past years was the Nazi Skinheads. Some Skinheads have been associated with violence and crimes such as vandalism, weapons violations, assaults, and murders. Skinheads have been known to associate with white supremacists at rallies, demonstrations, and other such gatherings. Wherever these racist Skinheads appear, whether on national television or at counter-demonstrations, they are controversial and may cause violence to erupt. It may be because of this controversy that the ultra-right movement uses the Skinheads. The attention generated may continue to lead to an increase in membership just when the movement needs new members the most.

In addition to Puerto Rican, left-wing, and right-wing groups, which have traditionally committed terrorist acts in the United States, several new and entirely different groups have made themselves known in the last few years. The factor distinguishing these groups from the others is that the new groups employ violence and criminal acts to bring about social rather than political change. These groups are known as the Evan Mecham Eco-Terrorist International Conspiracy (EMETIC), Up the IRS, Earth Night Action Group, Earth First, and the Animal Liberation Front (ALF). These groups are loosely known as *special interest* terrorist groups, who seek specific issue resolution rather than widespread political changes (Eagan, 1996: 1-18).

EMETIC is a group of persons seeking to preserve the earth's ecological system by committing destructive acts of sabotage (or *ecotage*) against those considered to be spoilers of the ecology. ALF, in contrast, is a group of persons seeking to eliminate the use of animals in medical research and other industries through direct criminal action.

In the five years prior to 1995, there were 12 incidents of terrorism associated with special interest terrorist groups. These included such groups as the American Liberation Front, which claimed to have placed nine incendiary devices in four department stores. It also included the arson at a mink research facility at Michigan State University. Rodney Coronado, a member of ALF, pled guilty to the arson and was sentenced to 57 months in prison.

The Current Threat—International Groups

Although the United States has not yet experienced the level of terrorism that has occurred in some regions of the Middle East, Western Europe, and Latin America, there are active international terrorist groups whose transnational character makes international terrorist acts possible within our borders.

State-sponsored activity worldwide has been most prominent among Middle Eastern governments (e.g., Iran, Libya, and Syria). Subnational groups that are currently active include Palestinian, Armenian, Sikh, and Irish organizations. There are several international terrorist groups that have shown both the willingness and the capability to conduct violent acts on U.S. soil. In the past, members of international terrorist groups have conducted bombings, murders, assassinations, and acts of extortion in the United States. However, to date, none of these attacks has been against a U.S. target. Rather, the attacks have been committed by groups against their historic enemies, such as Armenians against Turks, or against groups that hold opposing political or religious views, such as pro-Khadaffy Libyans against Libyan dissidents. Other international terrorist groups are primarily active in collecting funds and distributing propaganda.

The major international terrorist threat in the United States emanates from state sponsors of terrorism such as Iran, Libya, and Syria. Other threats include Palestinian terrorist organizations and various subnational groups such as the Japanese Red Army (JRA). These entities have a presence in this country that would be able to support the commission of a terrorist act. In addition, many state sponsors of terrorism maintain a number of students enrolled in U.S. colleges and universities. Although the vast majority of these students do not support terrorism, a minority of them have demonstrated a fanatical dedication to their regimes.

Despite the success of the U.S. counterterrorism program, the violent and unpredictable nature of international terrorism continues to pose a threat to the security of the United States. The explosive situation in the Middle East, opposition to U.S. foreign policy in Central America, and the existence of potential terrorist networks in the United States increase the possibility that future international terrorist attacks may occur within our borders. The following Feature describes critical aspects of a terrorist entity and some characteristics of a "terrorist."

Feature

Profile of a Terrorist

In dealing with any terrorist group, the law enforcement officer must keep in mind three important factors separating terrorist groups from other groups involved in criminal acts. Terrorist groups are distinct in that:

- Their organization is usually structured, regardless of the size of the group.

- Secrecy is their best defense, and they utilize it to its fullest capacity.

- They are highly disciplined.

These three traits pose a real threat to law enforcement. When combined in an effort against an appropriate target, they often lead to overreaction by the police, which is one of the aims of the terrorist. When the police overreact in their response, the public often feels that government agencies are unable to cope with terrorism. This turns people away from the side of the police and aligns them with the terrorist.

There have been numerous attempts to build profiles of the "average American terrorist" to aid the law enforcement officer in identification. Such attempts have not been very successful. There are some common characteristics of terrorists, but not enough to build a usable profile. Some of the commonalities are:

- Age—early 20s and 30s.

- Sex—both male and female (some known groups are up to 70 percent female).

- Education—some have college or graduate degrees.

- Race—all represented, but predominantly white.

- Religion—all denominations represented.

- Criminal background—almost without exception, the terrorist had no criminal record for violence prior to becoming involved in terrorist movements.

Contrast these characteristics with a recent profile developed on 350 known terrorists from 18 Middle-Eastern, Latin American, West European, and Japanese groups:

- Age—22 to 24.

- Sex—mostly male.

- Education—some college education (usually humanities).

- Prior vocation—law, medicine, journalism, and teaching (in Turkey and Iran, most terrorists came from engineering and technical backgrounds).

- Upbringing—from middle-class to upper-class families.

- Recruitment—almost without exception, they were recruited into terrorist activities on a university campus.

Source: Adapted from Earl W. Robitaille (1981). "Terrorism and the Role of the Police." *Law and Order*, Vol. 29, No. 9, September:45-47. Reprinted with permission. Maxwell Taylor (1988). *The Terrorist*. London: Brassey's Defence Publishers, 122-197.

Since 1990, at the federal level, the counterterrorism response has successfully taken a consistent, aggressive, proactive approach to the problem of terrorism. Greater emphasis has been placed on acquiring intelligence information related to groups or individuals who would choose terrorism as a means to threaten or attack U.S. interests, or foreign nationals within the United States. A major step for law enforcement has been the development of joint counterterrorism efforts among U.S. law enforcement agencies. Joint task forces and greater cooperation between federal and state agencies has created a mechanism for an improved response to terrorism.

Summary

Terrorism is a very old technique. It seems to be ageless. Unfortunately, it has played an important part in the history of our nation. The bombings of the World Trade Center and the federal building in Oklahoma City brought into sharp focus the travesty of terrorism. After the last major bombing, a federal terrorist act gave additional powers to federal agencies to investigate and prevent terrorism. Terrorism continues to be a part of the American and international scene. Dissident political and social groups attempt to achieve their goals by engaging in coercive activities.

Terrorism existed as early as 1070 A.D. and played an important part in the development of this country. For years after the Civil War, the Ku Klux Klan spread its violence with near impunity. The Molly Maguires and the mine owners vigorously opposed each other, and assassinations and murders were commonplace. These situations were followed by riots in Chicago, in which seven police officers were killed and 60 were wounded. Following numerous assassinations of public figures during the 1960s, many terrorist groups came on the scene. These included the resurrected Ku Klux Klan and the Symbionese Liberation Army. Other organizations came into existence over the years with new groups such as militias, on the scene.

When considering terrorism, a distinction must be made between domestic and international terrorism and the extent to which each is a risk to the United States. Left-wing terrorists are generally of a Marxist-Leninist philophosy, and the right-wing groups are generally influenced by a racist, anti-Semitic philosophy.

In recent years, terrorist events have occurred less frequently, but the threat remains. There are several reasons for this. Many of the leaders of terrorist groups are in prison, and the demise of the Soviet Union has deprived many leftists of a philosophical base. Prior to 1993, the majority of these acts occurred in Puerto Rico, followed by the northeastern and western regions. The reduction of incidents in Puerto Rico has occurred because of the plebiscite in which a plurality voted to maintain Puerto Rico's commonwealth status.

Three major events have shocked the United States in recent years because of bombings: the World Trade Center, Oklahoma City, and the Centennial Olympic Park, all of which have occurred since 1992.

Terrorist groups have a wide spectrum of social and political beliefs, of which there are distinct types: vigilante, insurgent, transnational, and state. Vigilante terrorism is represented by the Ku Klux Klan (KKK). Insurgent groups include such organizations as the Patriot's Council. The Japanese Red Army (JRA) is typical of transnational terrorist groups, as are radical Palestinian groups. The last category is state terrorism and it is represented by the government of England in its effort to suppress the Provisional Irish Republican Army (PIRA).

Currently, there are a number of domestic terrorist groups capable of committing terrorist acts in the United States. The same is true for international groups. The Japanese Red Army (JRA), although currently dormant, is still considered to be a very dangerous terrorist group. Radical Palestinian groups engage in terrorist activities with the objective of creating a Palestinian homeland and attaining self-government. Terroristic acts by Skinheads are not as frequent as they have been in past years, but they are still of concern to law enforcement agencies. In 1993, Skinheads were involved in three terrorist incidents. In the last few years, militia groups have become of increasing concern. Many of them are anti-government and support white supremacy. Some of these groups have set up their own court systems, and threaten government workers who oppose them. Other groups that are of concern are loosely known as special interest groups. They include such groups as Earth First, the Animal Liberation Front (ALF), the Earth Night Action Group, and Up the IRS.

There is a strong need for local, state, and federal agencies to improve their cooperation and coordination in the prevention and response to terrorist groups.

References

Arizona Daily Star, (1995a). "Broad Powers Supported in Terrorist Fight." May 5:1, 3A.

Arizona Daily Star (1995b). "Cult Leader's Aide Admits to Making Sarin in Japan." October 25:5A.

Arizona Daily Star (1996). "Terrorism Bill Goes to Clinton." April 19:1, 3B.

Arizona Daily Star (1997). "Klan Rally in Pittsburgh Sparks Rage in Thousands." April 6:16A.

Bizzack, John (1989). *Police Management for the 1990s: A Practitioner's Road Map.* Springfield, IL: Charles C Thomas, 29.

Cannon, Angie (1997). "Jewell: Investigates the FBI." *San Jose Mercury News.* July 3:4A.

Chalmers, David, M. (1965). *Hooded Americanism: The History of the Ku Klux Klan.* Chicago: Quadrangle Books, 103-131, 239.

Clutterbuck, Richard (1978). *Kidnap and Ransom.* London, UK: Faber and Faber Limited, 27.

Dees, Morris and Jim Corcoran (1996). *Gathering Storm: America's Militia Network.* New York: Harper Collins, 1-223.

Dees, Morris and Steve Fiffer (1991). *A Season For Justice.* New York: Charles Scribners, 2-95.

Dees, Morris and Steve Fiffer (1993). *Hate on Trial.* New York: Villard Books, 3-50.

DeGeneste, Henry, I., Martin E. Silverstein, and John Sullivan (1996). "Chemical and Biological Terrorism: Upping the Ante?" *The Police Chief,* Vol. LXIII, No. 10:70-83.

Eagan, Sean P. (1996). "From Spikes to Bombs: The Rise of Eco-Terrorism." *Studies in Conflict & Terrorism,* Vol. 19, No. 1:1-18.

Elliot, John D. (1978). "Contemporary Terrorism and the Police Response." *The Police Chief,* Volume XLV, No. 2, February:32.

Federal Bureau of Investigation (1988, 1995, 1996, 1997). *Terrorism in the United States, 1989, 1994, 1995, 1996.* Washington DC: Federal Bureau of Investigation, 23-24; 1-22; 1-11; 1-17.

Friedlander, Robert A. (1983). *Terror-Violence: Aspects of Social Control.* New York: Oceana Publications, Inc., 41-43.

Gates, Daryl (1989). "The Role of Analysis in Combating Modern Terrorism." *FBI Law Enforcement Bulletin.* Vol. 59, June:No. 6.

Gurr, Ted R. (1988). "Political Terrorism in the United States: Historical Antecedents and Contemporary Trends." In Michael Stohl (ed.), *The Politics of Terrorism.* New York: Marcel Dekker, Inc. 550-552.

Homer, Frederic (1988). "Terror in the United States: Three Perspectives." In Michael Stohl (ed.), *The Politics of Terrorism.* New York: Marcel Dekker, Inc., 200-203.

Katz, William L. (1986). *The Invisible Empire: The Ku Klux Klan Impact on History.* Seattle, WA: Open Hand Publishing, Inc., 63-107.

Klanwatch (1990). *Intelligence Report, Number 49.* Montgomery, AL: The Southern Poverty Law Center, 12, 23.

Klanwatch and Militia Task Force (1997). *Two Years After: The Patriot Movement Since Oklahoma City.* Montgomery, AL: Southern Poverty Law Center, 1.

Law Enforcement News (1990). "Sheriff Purges Klansmen." Vol. XVI, No. 309, February 20:3.

Long, David E. (1990). *The Anatomy of Terrorism.* New York: The Free Press, 141-219.

McDonald, Andrew (1980). *The Turner Diaries.* Hillsboro, WV: National Vanguard Books, 38-42.

Mullins, Wayman C. (1988). *Terrorist Organizations in the United States: An Analysis of Issues, Organizations, Tactics, and Responses.* Springfield, IL: Charles C Thomas, 1-118.

Newton, Stanley E. and John L. White (1997). "Extremists: A Small Town Under Attack." *The Police Chief,* Vol. LKIV, No. 10:124-129.

Olin, W. Ronald (1986). "Current Trends in the Terrorist War." *The Police Chief,* Vol. LX, No. 4, April:25-32.

Parry, Albert (1976). *Terrorism from Robespierre to Arafat.* New York: The Vanguard Press, Inc. 93-95; 98-99.

Revell, Oliver (1985). "Responding to the Terrorist Threat: The Need for International Liaison and Cooperation." *The Police Chief.* Vol. XLIIV, No. 4, March:29-32.

Ridgeway, James (1990). *Blood in the Face.* New York: Thunder Mouth Press.

Robitaille, Earl W. (1981). "Terrorism and the Role of the Police." *Law and Order,* Vol. 29, No. 9, September:45-47.

Ross, Loretta J. and Mary Ann Mauney (1996). *The Changing Faces of White Supremacy.* Atlanta, GA: The Center for Democratic Renewal, 1-10.

Rubin, Trudy (1996). "It's Time For America to Wake Up." *San Jose Mercury News.* July 21:11, 51.

Sage, Byron A., Mack Wallace, and Carolyn Wier (1995). "The Central Texas Counterterrorism Working Group." *FBI Law Enforcement Bulletin.* Vol. 64, No. 3:8-11.

San Jose Mercury News (1990). "Terror Group Declares War on 4th Reich." August 1:4A.

San Jose Mercury News (1993). "Klan Rally Stirs Tensions in Texas Town." June 20:11A.

San Jose Mercury News (1996). "Task Force Agrees to Expanding Wiretaps." July 31:3A.

Schlagheck, Donna M. (1988). *International Terrorism.* New York: Lexington Books, 64-66.

Seddon, Alfred E. (1987). "The Domestic Threat: An FBI View." *Terrorism,* Vol. 57, No. 3:217-218.

Sederberg, Peter C. (1989). *Terrorist Myths: Illusions, Rhetoric, and Reality.* Englewood, Cliffs, NJ: Prentice Hall, 23-41.

Sobel, Lester A. (ed.) (1975). *Political Terrorism.* New York: Facts on File, Inc., 1-309.

SPLC (1996). *25 Years of Seeking Justice.* Montgomery, AL: Southern Poverty Law Center, 2-90.

Stanton, Bill (1991). *Klanwatch: Bringing the Ku Klux Klan to Justice.* New York: Grove Weidenfeld, 4-80.

Stern Kenneth S. (n.d.). *Skinheads: Who They Are & What To Do When They Come to Town.* New York: The American Jewish Committee, 1-21.

Streissguth, Thomas (1993). *International Terrorists.* Minneapolis, MN: The Oliver Press, 75-94.

Taylor, Maxwell (1988). *The Terrorist.* London: Brassey's Defence Publishers, 122-197.

Thrap, Mike and William J. Holstein (1997). "Mainstreaming the Militia." *U.S. News & World Report.* April 21:24-37.

Wardlaw, Grant (1982). *Political Terrorism: Theory, Tactics.* Cambridge, MA: University of Cambridge, 92-95.

Wilcox, Philip C., Jr. (1997). *Patterns of Global Terrorism 1996.* Washington, DC: U.S. Department of State, 26.

Wilkenson, Paul (1977). *Terrorism and the Liberal State.* New York: John Wiley and Sons, 23.

Williams, Hubert and James Ginger (1987). "The Threat of International Terrorism in the United States: The Police Response." *Terrorism,* Volume 10, Number 3:219-223.

INDEX

SECRETS OF A BILLIONAIRE'S MISTRESS

SECRETS OF A BILLIONAIRE'S MISTRESS

BY

SHARON KENDRICK

First published in Great Britain 2017
By Mills & Boon, an imprint of HarperCollins*Publishers*
1 London Bridge Street, London, SE1 9GF

Large Print edition 2017

© 2017 Sharon Kendrick

ISBN: 978-0-263-07109-2

Printed and bound in Great Britain
by CPI Antony Rowe, Chippenham, Wiltshire

For three fabulous writers who helped with the Australian detail in my 100th book, *A Royal Vow of Convenience.*

Helene Young and Margareta Young, for the inspiration and the insight— and Rachael Johns, for the Tim-Tams!

CHAPTER ONE

RENZO SABATINI WAS unbuttoning his shirt when the doorbell rang. He felt the beat of expectation. The familiar tug of heat to his groin. He was half-tempted to pull the shirt from his shoulders so Darcy could slide her fingers over his skin, closely followed by those inventive lips of hers. The soft lick of her tongue could help him forget what lay ahead. He thought about Tuscany and the closing of a chapter. About the way some memories could still be raw even when so many years had passed and maybe that was why he never really stopped to think about them.

But why concentrate on darkness when Darcy was all sunshine and light? And why rush at sex when they had the whole night ahead—a smorgasbord of sensuality which he could enjoy at his leisure with his latest and most unexpected lover? A woman who demanded nothing other than that he satisfy her—something which was easy since he had only to touch her pale skin to grow so hard that it hurt. His mouth dried. Four months in and he was as bewitched by her as he had been from the start.

In many ways he was astonished it had continued this long when their two worlds were so different. She was not his usual type of woman and he was very definitely not her type of man. He was into clean lines and minimalism, while Darcy was all voluptuous curves and lingerie which could barely contain her abundant flesh. His mouth curved into a hard smile. In reality it should never have lasted beyond one night but her tight body had been difficult to walk away from. It still was.

The doorbell rang again and the glance he shot at his wristwatch was touched with irritation. Was she daring to be *impatient* when she wasn't supposed to be here for another half hour? Surely she knew the rules by now…that she was expected to fit around his schedule, rather than the other way round?

Barefooted, he walked through the spacious rooms of his Belgravia apartment, pulling open the front door to see Darcy Denton standing there—small of stature and impossible to ignore—her magnificent curls misted with rain and tugged back into a ponytail so that only the bright red colour was on show. She wore a light raincoat, tightly belted to emphasise her tiny waist, but underneath she was still in her waitress's uniform because she lived on the other side of London, an area Renzo had never visited—and he was perfectly content for it to stay that way. They'd established very quickly that if she went home after her shift to change, it wasted several hours—even if he sent his car to collect her. And Renzo was a busy man with an architectural practice which spanned several continents. His time was too precious to waste, which was why she always came straight from work with her overnight bag—though that was a largely unnecessary detail since she was rarely anything other than naked when she was with him.

He stared down into her green eyes, which glittered like emeralds in porcelain-pale skin and, as always, his blood began to fizz with expectation and lust. 'You're early,' he observed softly. 'Did you time your visit especially because you knew I'd be undressing?'

Darcy answered him with a tight smile as he opened the door to let her in. She was cold and she was wet and it had been the most awful day. A customer had spilt tea over her uniform. Then a child had been sick. She'd looked out the window at the end of her shift to discover that the rain had started and someone must have taken her umbrella. And Renzo Sabatini was standing there in the warmth of his palatial apartment, looking glowing and delectable—making the assumption that she had nothing better to do than to time her visits just so she would find him half-naked. Could she ever have met a man more arrogant?

Yet she'd known what she was letting herself

in for when she'd started this crazy affair. When she'd fought a silent battle against everything she'd known to be wrong. Because powerful men who dallied with waitresses only wanted one thing, didn't they?

She'd lost that particular battle and ended up in Renzo's king-size bed—but nobody could say that her eyes hadn't been open at the time. Well, some of the time at least—the rest of the time they'd fluttered to a quivering close as he had thrust deeply inside her until she was sobbing with pleasure. After resisting him as hard as she could, she'd decided to resist no more. Or maybe the truth was that she hadn't been able to stop herself from falling into his arms. He'd kissed her and that had been it. She hadn't known that a kiss could make you feel that way. She hadn't realised that desire could make you feel as if you were floating. Or flying. She'd surrendered her virginity to him and, after his shocked reaction to discovering he was her first lover, he had introduced her to more pleasure than she'd thought possible, though in a life spectacularly short on the pleasure front that wouldn't have been difficult, would it?

For a while things had been fine. More than fine. She spent the night with him whenever he was in the country and had a space in his diary—and sometimes she spent the following day there, too. He cooked her eggs and played her music she'd never heard before—dreamy stuff featuring lots of violins—while he pored over the fabulously intricate drawings which would one day be transformed into the glittering and iconic skyscrapers for which he was famous.

But lately something had started to niggle away inside her. Was it her conscience? Her sense that her already precarious self-worth was being eroded by him hiding her away in his palatial apartment, like a guilty secret? She wasn't sure. All she knew was that she'd started to analyse what she'd become and hadn't liked the answer she'd come up with.

She was a wealthy man's plaything. A woman

who dropped her panties whenever he clicked those elegant olive fingers.

But she was here now and it was stupid to let her reservations spoil the evening ahead, so she changed her tight smile into a bright smile as she dumped her overnight bag on the floor and tugged the elastic band from her hair. Shaking her damp curls free, she couldn't deny the satisfaction it gave her to see the way Renzo's eyes had darkened in response—although her physical appeal to him had never been in any question. He couldn't seem to get enough of her and she suspected she knew why. Because she was different. Working class, for a start. She hadn't been to college—in fact, she'd missed out on more schooling than she should have done and nearly everything she knew had been self-taught. She was curvy and red-headed, when usually he went for slender brunettes—that was if all the photos in the newspapers were to be believed. They were certainly mismatched on just about every level, except when it came to bed.

Because the sex was amazing—it always had

been—but it couldn't continue like this, taking her on an aimless path which was leading nowhere. Darcy knew what she had to do. She knew you could only fool yourself for so long before reality started hurting and forced you to change. She'd noticed Renzo was starting to take her for granted and knew that, if it continued, all the magic they'd shared would just wither away. And she didn't want that, because memories were powerful things. The bad ones were like heavy burdens you had to carry around with you and she was determined to have some good ones to lighten the load. So when was she going to grab the courage to walk away from him, before Renzo did the walking and left her feeling broken and crushed?

'I'm early because I sent your driver away and took the Tube instead,' she explained, brushing excess raindrops from her forest of red curls.

'You sent the driver away?' He frowned as he slid the damp raincoat from her shoulders. 'Why on earth would you do that?'

Darcy sighed, wondering what it must be like

to be Renzo Sabatini and live in an enclosed and protected world, where chauffeur-driven cars and private jets shielded you from rain and snow and the worries of most normal folk. Where people did your shopping and picked up your clothes where you'd left them on the bedroom floor the night before. A world where you didn't have to speak to anyone unless you really wanted to, because there was always some minion who would do the speaking for you.

'Because the traffic is a nightmare at this time of day and often we're forced to sit in a queue, moving at a snail's pace.' She took the coat from him and gave it a little shake before hanging it in the cupboard. 'Public transport happens to have a lot going for it during the rush hour. Now, rather than debating my poor timekeeping can I please have a cup of tea? I'm f-f-freezing.'

But he didn't make any move towards the kitchen as most people might have done after such a wobbly request. He took her in his arms and kissed her instead. His lips were hard as they pressed against hers and his fingers caressed her bottom through her uniform dress as he brought her up close to his body. Close enough for her to feel the hardness of his erection and the warmth of his bare chest as he deepened the kiss. Darcy's eyelids fluttered to a close as one hard thigh pushed insistently against hers and she could feel her own parting in automatic response. And suddenly her coldness was forgotten and tea was the last thing on her mind. Her questions and insecurities dissolved as he deepened the kiss and all she was aware of was the building heat as her chilled fingers crept up to splay themselves over his bare and hair-roughened torso.

'Hell, Renzo,' she breathed.

'Is it really hell?' he murmured.

'No, it's...' she brushed her lips over his '...heaven, if you must know.'

'That's what I thought. Are you trying to warm your hands on my chest?'

'Trying. I don't think I'm having very much luck. You do many things very well, but acting as a human hot-water bottle isn't one of them.'

'No. You could be right. My skills definitely lie in other directions. Perhaps I could demonstrate some of them to you right now.' He moved his hand from her bottom and curled his fingers round hers as he guided her hand towards his groin. 'In which case I think you'd better join me in the shower, don't you?'

She couldn't have said no even if she'd wanted to. One touch from Renzo was like lighting the touchpaper. Two seconds in his arms and she went up in flames.

In the bathroom, he unzipped her drab beige uniform, soft words of Italian falling from his lips as her breasts were revealed to him. Disproportionately big breasts which had always been the bane of her life, because she'd spent her life with men's attention being constantly homed in on them. She'd often thought longingly of a breast reduction—except who could afford an operation like that on the money she earned waiting tables? So she'd made do with wearing restrictive bras, until Renzo had taught her to love her body and told her that her breasts were the most magnificent thing he'd ever seen. To enjoy being suckled or having his teeth tease the sensitive flesh until she was crying out with pleasure. He'd started to buy lingerie for her, too—the only thing she'd ever allowed him to buy for her and only because he'd insisted. He couldn't understand why she wouldn't let him spend money on her, but her reasons were raw and painful and she had no intention of letting him in on her secret.

But she let him buy her pretty underclothes, because he insisted that it enhanced their sex play—balcony bras and tiny matching panties, which he said made the most of her curvy hips. And didn't it make her feel rather decadent when she was at work, knowing she was wearing the finest silk and lace beneath the drab check of her waitress uniform? Hadn't he told her that he *wanted* her to think about him when he wasn't there? That when he was far away on business he liked to imagine her touching herself until she was wet between the legs and her body bucking helplessly as she thought about *him*. And although his fantasy about how she lived when he wasn't there was just that—fantasy—she couldn't deny that it also turned her on. But then, everything about Renzo Sabatini turned her on. His tall and powerful frame. His black hair and black eyes and those dark-rimmed spectacles he wore when he was working on one of his detailed plans. That way he had of watching her as she moved around the room. And stroking her until she was trembling with helpless need for him. Like now.

Her dress fell to the floor and the delicate underwear quickly followed. A master in the art of undressing, her Italian lover was soon as naked as she, and Darcy sucked in an instinctive gasp when she saw how aroused he was.

'Daunting, isn't it?' His sensual lips curved into a mocking smile. 'Want to touch me?'

'Not until I've got hot water gushing over me. My hands are so cold you might recoil.'

'I don't think so,' he said softly.

His eyes glittered as he picked her up and carried her into the wet room, where steaming water streamed down from a huge showerhead and the sensory impact of the experience threatened to overwhelm her. Hot water on icy skin and a naked Renzo in her arms. In the steamy environment, which made her think of a tropical forest, his lips were hungry, one hand stroking between her legs while the other played with one aching nipple. The warm water relaxed her, made her aware of the fierce pounding of her heart and the sudden rush of warmth at her groin. She ran her hands over the hard planes of his body, enjoying the sensation of honed muscle beneath his silken olive skin. Boldly she reached down to circle his erection, sliding her thumb and forefinger lightly up and down the rocky shaft the way she knew he liked it. He gave a groan. Hell. *She* liked it, too. She liked everything he did to her…and the longer it went on, the more difficult it was to imagine a life without him.

She closed her eyes as his fingers moved down over her belly until they were tangling in the wet hair at the juncture of her thighs. One finger took a purposeful route farther, until it was deep inside her and she gave a little yelp of pleasure as he strummed the finger against swollen flesh, the rhythmical movement taking her closer to the edge. And now it was her turn to writhe her hips against him, wanting release—and wanting oblivion, too.

'Now,' she breathed. 'Make love to me now.'

'You are impatient, little one.'

Of course she was impatient. It had been nearly a month since she'd seen him. A month when he'd been hard at work in Japan, before flying to South America to oversee the enormous new hotel complex he'd designed which was creating a lot of waves in the high-octane world of architecture. And yes, there had been the occasional email—an amusing description about a woman who had propositioned him after a boardroom meeting, which Darcy had managed to laugh off and act as if it didn't hurt. He'd even phoned her once, when his plane had been delayed at the airport in Rio de Janeiro and presumably he must have had time to kill. And even though she'd been battling through the wind on her way back from the discount supermarket at the time, she'd managed to find shelter in a shop doorway and make like it was a normal conversation. She'd tried to tell herself that she didn't mind his total lack of commitment. That they didn't have an ordinary relationship and that was what made it so interesting.

He'd told her right from the start what she could expect and what she must not expect, and number one on his list had been commitment, closely followed by love. She remembered turning round as he'd spoken, surprising an unexpectedly bleak look in his gaze—unexpected because those ebony eyes usually gave nothing away. But she hadn't probed further because she'd sensed he would clam up. Actually, she never probed—because if you asked someone too many questions about themselves, they might just turn around and ask them back and that was the last thing she wanted.

And she had agreed to his emotionally cold terms, hadn't she? She'd acted as if they were the most reasonable requests in the world. To be honest, she hadn't been able to think beyond the next kiss—and every kiss had the effect of binding her ever tighter to him. But several months had passed since he'd extracted that agreement from her and time changed everything. It always did. Time made your feelings start to deepen and made you prone to foolish daydreams. And what could be more foolish than imagining some kind of future with the billionaire designer with his jet-set lifestyle and homes all around the world? She, without a single qualification to her name, whose only skill was her ability to multitask in a restaurant?

She pressed her lips against his shoulder, thinking how best to respond to his question— to show him she still had some control left, even if it was slipping away by the second. 'Impatient?' she murmured into his wet, bare skin. 'If I'm going too fast for you, we could always put this on hold and do it later. Have that cup of tea after all. Is that what you'd like, Renzo?'

His answer was swift and unequivocal. Imprisoning her hands, he pushed her up against the granite wall of the wet room, parted her legs and thrust into her, as hot and hard as she'd ever felt him. She gasped as he filled her. She cried out as he began to move. From knowing nothing, he'd taught her everything and she had been his willing pupil. In his arms, she came to life.

'Renzo,' she gasped as he rocked against her.

'Did you miss me, *cara*?'

She closed her eyes. 'I missed…this.'

'But nothing else?'

She wanted to say that there *was* nothing else, but why spoil a beautiful moment? No man would want to hear something like that, would they—even if it was true? Especially not a man with an ego the size of Renzo's. 'Of course,' she said as he stilled inside her. 'I missed you.'

Did he sense that her answer was less than the 100 per cent he demanded of everything and everyone? Was that why he slowed the pace down, dragging her back from the brink of her orgasm to tantalise her with nearly there thrusts until she could bear it no more?

'Renzo—'

'What is it?'

How could he sound so calm? So totally in control. But control was what he was good at, wasn't it? He was the master of control. She squirmed. 'Don't play with me.'

'But I thought you liked me playing with you. Perhaps...' he bent his head to whisper in her water-soaked ear '...I shall make you beg.'

'Oh, no, you won't!' Fiercely, she cupped his buttocks and held him against her and he gave an exultant laugh as at last he gave her exactly what she wanted. He worked on her hard and fast, his deep rhythm taking her up and up, until her shuddered cries were blotted out by his kiss and he made that low groaning sound as he came. It was, she thought, about the only time she'd ever heard him sound helpless.

Afterwards he held her until the trembling had subsided and then soaped her body and washed her hair with hands which were almost gentle—as if he was attempting to make up for the almost-brutal way he'd brought her gasping to orgasm. He dried her carefully, then carried her into the bedroom and placed her down on the vast bed which overlooked the whispering treetops of Eaton Square. The crisp, clean linen felt like heaven against her scented skin as he got into bed beside her and slid his arms around her waist. She was sleepy and suspected he was, too, but surely they needed to have some sort of *conversation* instead of just mating like two animals and then tumbling into oblivion.

But wasn't that all they were, when it boiled down to it? This affair was all about sex. Nothing except sex.

'So how was your time away?' she forced herself to ask.

'You don't want to know.'

'Yes, I do.'

'All good.' He yawned. 'The hotel is almost complete and I've been commissioned to design a new art gallery just outside Tokyo.'

'But you're tired?' she observed.

His voice was mocking. '*Sì, cara.* I'm tired.'

She wriggled her back against him. 'Ever

thought of easing off for a while? Taking a back seat and just enjoying your success?'

'Not really.' He yawned again.

'Why not?' she said, some rogue inside her making her persist, even though she could sense his growing impatience with her questions.

His voice grew hard. 'Because men in my position don't *ease off*. There are a hundred hot new architects who would love to be where I am. Take your eye off the ball and you're toast.' He stroked her nipple. 'Why don't you tell me about your week instead?'

'Oh, mine was nothing to speak about. I just *serve* the toast,' she said lightly.

She closed her eyes because she thought that they might sleep but she was wrong because Renzo was cupping her breasts, rubbing his growing erection up against her bottom until she gave an urgent sound of assent and he entered her from behind, where she was slick and ready.

His lips were in her hair and his hands were playing with her nipples as he moved inside her again. Her shuddered capitulation was swift and two orgasms in less than an hour meant she could no longer fight off her fatigue. She fell into a deep sleep and sometime later she felt the bed dip as Renzo got up and when she dragged her eyelids open it was to see that the spring evening was still light. The leaves in the treetops outside the window were golden-green in the fading sunlight and she could hear a distant bird singing.

It felt surreal lying here. The prestigious square on which he lived sometimes seemed like a mirage. All the lush greenery gave the impression of being in the middle of the country—something made possible only by the fact that this was the most expensive real estate in London. But beyond the treetops near his exclusive home lay the London which was *her* city. Discount stores and tower blocks and garbage fluttering on the pavements. Snarled roads and angry drivers. And somewhere not a million miles from here, but which felt as if it might as well be in a different universe, was the tiny bedsit she called home. Sometimes it seemed like something out of some corny old novel—the billionaire boss and his waitress lover. Because things like this didn't usually happen to girls like her.

But Renzo hadn't taken advantage of her, had he? He'd never demanded anything she hadn't wanted to give. She'd accepted his ride home—even though some part of her had cried out that it was unwise. Yet for once in her life she'd quashed the voice of common sense which was as much a part of her as her bright red hair. For years she had simply kept her head down and toed the line in order to survive. But not this time. Instead of doing what she knew she *should* do, she'd succumbed to something she'd really wanted and that something was Renzo. Because she'd never wanted anyone the way she'd wanted him.

What she was certain he'd intended to be just one night had become another and then another as their unconventional relationship had developed. It was a relationship which existed only within the walls of his apartment because, as if by some unspoken agreement, they never went out on dates. Renzo's friends were wealthy and well connected, just like him. Fast-living powerbrokers with influential jobs and nothing in common with someone like her. And anyway, it would be bizarre if they started appearing together in public because they weren't really a *couple*, were they?

She knew their relationship could most accurately be described as 'friends with benefits,' though the benefits heavily outweighed the friendship side and the arrogant Italian had once told her that he didn't really have any female *friends*. Women were for the bedroom and kitchen—he'd actually said that, when he'd been feeling especially uninhibited after one of their marathon sex sessions, which had ended up in the bath. He'd claimed afterwards that he'd been joking but Darcy had recognised a grain of truth behind his words. Even worse was the way his masterful arrogance had thrilled her, even though she'd done her best to wear a disapproving expression.

Because when it boiled down to it, Darcy knew the score. She was sensible enough to know that Renzo Sabatini was like an ice cream cone you ate on a sunny day. It tasted amazing—possibly the most amazing thing you'd ever tasted—but you certainly didn't expect it to last.

She glanced up as he walked back into the bedroom carrying a tray, a task she performed many times a day—the only difference being that he was completely naked.

'You're spoiling me,' she said.

'I'm just returning the favour. I'd like to ask where you learned that delicious method of licking your tongue over my thighs but I realise that—'

'I learned it from you?'

'*Esattamente.*' His eyes glittered. 'Hungry?'

'Thirsty.'

'I expect you are,' he said, bending over to brush his lips over hers.

She took the tea he gave her and watched as he tugged on a pair of jeans and took his glass of red wine over to his desk, sitting down and putting on dark-framed spectacles before waking his computer from sleep mode and beginning to scroll down. After a couple of minutes he was completely engrossed in something on the screen and suddenly Darcy felt completely excluded. With his back on her, she felt like an insignificant cog in the giant wheel which was his life. They'd just had sex—twice—and now he was burying himself in work, presumably until his body had recovered enough to do it to her all over again. And she would just lie back and let him, or climb on top of him if the mood took her—because that was her role. Up until now it had always been enough but suddenly it didn't seem like nearly enough.

Did she signal her irritation? Was that why he rattled out a question spoken like someone who was expecting an apologetic denial as an answer?

'Is something wrong?'

This was her cue to say no, nothing was wrong. To pat the edge of the bed and slant him a compliant smile because that was what she would normally have done. But Darcy wasn't in a compliant mood today. She'd heard a song on the radio just before leaving work. A song which had taken her back to a place she hadn't wanted to go to and the mother she'd spent her life trying to forget.

Yet it was funny how a few random chords could pluck at your heartstrings and make you want to screw up your face and cry. Funny how you could still love someone even though they'd let you down, time after time. That had been the real reason she'd sent Renzo's driver away. She'd wanted to walk to the Tube so that her unexpected tears could mingle with the rain. She'd hoped that by coming here and having her Italian lover take her to bed, it might wipe away her unsettled feelings. But it seemed to have done the opposite. It had awoken a new restlessness in her. It had made her realise that great sex and champagne in the shadows of a powerful man's life weren't the recipe for a happy life—and the longer she allowed it to continue, the harder it would be for her to return to the real world. Her world.

She finished her tea and put the cup down, the subtle taste of peppermint and rose petals still lingering on her lips. It was time for the affair to fade out, like the credits at the end of the film. And even though she was going to miss him like crazy, she was the one who needed to start it rolling.

She made her voice sound cool and non-committal. 'I'm thinking I won't be able to see you for a while.'

That had his attention. He turned away from the screen and, putting his glasses down on the desk, he frowned. 'What are you talking about?'

'I have a week's holiday from work and I'm planning to use it to go to Norfolk.'

She could see he was slightly torn now because he wasn't usually interested in what she did when she wasn't with him, even if he sometimes trotted out a polite question because he obviously felt it was expected of him. But he was interested now.

'What are you doing in Norfolk?'

She shrugged her bare shoulders. 'Looking for a place to rent. I'm thinking of moving there.'

'You mean you're leaving *London*?'

'You sound surprised, Renzo. People leave London all the time.'

'I know. But it's…' He frowned, as if such an option was outside his realm of understanding. 'What's in Norfolk?'

She'd been prepared to let him think that she just wanted a change—which was true—and to leave her real reasons unspoken. But his complete lack of comprehension angered her and when she spoke her voice was low and trembling with an anger which was directed as much at herself as at him.

'Because there I've got the chance of renting somewhere that might have a view of something which isn't a brick wall. As well as a job that doesn't just feature commuters who are so rushed they can barely give me the time of day, let alone a *please* or a thank you. The chance of fresh air and a lower cost of living, plus a pace of life which doesn't wear me out just thinking about it.'

He frowned. 'You mean you don't like where you're living?'

'It's perfectly adequate for my *needs*,' she said carefully. 'Or at least, it has been until now.'

'That's a pretty lukewarm endorsement.' He paused and his frown deepened. 'Is that why you've never invited me round?'

'I guess.' She'd actually done it to save his embarrassment—and possibly hers. She'd tried to imagine him in her humble bedsit eating his dinner off a tray or having to squeeze his towering frame into her tiny bathroom or—even worse—lying on her narrow single bed. It was a laughable concept which would have made them both feel awkward and would have emphasised the vast social gulf between them even more. And that was why she never had. 'Would you really have wanted me to?'

Renzo considered her question. Of course he wouldn't, but he was surprised not to have got an invite. You wouldn't need to be a genius to work out that her life was very different from his and perhaps if he'd been confronted by it then his conscience would have forced him to write a cheque, and this time be more forceful in getting her to accept it. He might have told her to buy some new cushions, or a rug or even a new kitchen, if that was what she wanted. That was how these things usually worked. But Darcy was the proudest woman he'd ever encountered and, apart from the sexy lingerie he'd insisted she wear, had stubbornly refused all his offers of gifts. Why, even his heiress lovers hadn't been averse to accepting diamond necklaces or bracelets or those shoes with the bright red soles. He liked buying women expensive presents—it made him feel he wasn't in any way *beholden* to them. It reduced relationships down to what they really were...transactions. And yet his hard-up little waitress hadn't wanted to know.

'No, I wasn't holding out for an invite,' he said slowly. 'But I thought you might have discussed your holiday plans with me before you went ahead and booked them.'

'But you never discuss your plans with me, Renzo. You just do as you please.'

'You're saying you want me to run my schedule past you first?' he questioned incredulously.

'Of course I don't. You've made it clear that's not the way you operate and I've always accepted that. So you can hardly object if I do the same.'

But she was missing the point and Renzo suspected she knew it. *He* was the one who called the shots because that was also how these things worked. He was the powerbroker in this affair and she was smart enough to realise that. Yet he could see something implacable in her green gaze, some new sense of determination which had settled over her, and something else occurred to him. 'You might stay on in Norfolk,' he said slowly.

'I might.'

'In which case, this could be the last time we see one another.'

She shrugged. 'I guess it could.'

'Just like that?'

'What were you expecting? It had to end some-time.'

Renzo's eyes narrowed thoughtfully. Up until a couple of hours ago it wouldn't *really* have bothered him if he'd been told he would never see her again. Oh, he might have experienced a faint pang of regret and he certainly would have missed her in a physical sense, because he found her enthusiastic lovemaking irresistible. In fact, he would go so far as to say that she was the best lover he'd ever had, probably because he had taught her to be perfectly attuned to the needs of *his* body. But nothing was for ever. He knew that. In a month—maybe less—he would have replaced her with someone else. Someone cool and presentable, who would blend more easily into his life than Darcy Denton had ever done.

But she was the one who was doing the with-drawing and Renzo didn't like that. He was a natural predator—proud and fiercely competi-tive. Perhaps even prouder than Darcy. Women didn't leave *him*… He was the one who did the walking away—and at a time of *his* choosing.

And he still wanted her. He had not yet reached the crucial boredom state which would make him direct her calls straight to voicemail or leave a disproportionately long time before replying to texts. Lazily, he flicked through the options available to him.

'What about if you took a holiday with me, instead of going to Norfolk on your own?'

He could tell from the sudden dilatation of her eyes that the suggestion had surprised her. And the hardening of her nipples above the rumpled bedsheet suggested it had excited her. He felt the sudden beat of blood to his groin and realised it had excited him, too.

Her emerald eyes were wary. 'Are you serious?'

'Why not?'

He got up from the chair, perfectly aware of the powerful effect his proximity would have on her as he sat down on the edge of the bed. 'Is that such an abhorrent suggestion—to take my lover on holiday?'

She shrugged. 'It's not the type of thing we usually do. We usually stay in and don't go out.'

'But life would be very dull if only the expected happened. Are you telling me that the idea of a few days away with me doesn't appeal to you?' He splayed his palm possessively over the warm weight of her breast and watched as her swanlike neck constricted in a swallow.

She chewed on her lip. 'Renzo—'

'Mmm...?'

'It's...it's quite difficult to think straight when you're touching my nipple like that.'

'Thinking in the bedroom can be a very over-rated pastime,' he drawled, subtly increasing the pressure of his fingers. 'What's to think about? My proposition is perfectly simple. You could come out to Tuscany with me. I need to make a trip there this weekend. We could spend a few days together and you would still have time to go to Norfolk.'

She leaned back against the pillows and her eyes closed as he continued to massage her breast. 'You have a house there, don't you?' she breathed. 'In Tuscany.'

'Not for much longer. That's why I'm going. I'm selling it.' The pressure on her breast increased as his voice hardened. 'And you can keep me company. I have to take an earlier flight via Paris to do some business but you could always fly out separately.' He paused. 'Doesn't the idea tempt you, Darcy?'

His words filtered into her distracted mind as he continued to tease her exquisitely aroused nipple and her lashes fluttered open. His black eyes were as hard as shards of jet but that didn't affect the magic he was creating with the slow movement of his fingers as she tried to concentrate on his question.

Her tongue flicked out to moisten her lips. Of course a few days away with him tempted her—but it wasn't the thought of flying to Tuscany which was making her heart race like a champion stallion. *He* tempted her. Would it be so wrong to grab a last session of loving with him—but in a very different environment? Because although his apartment was unimaginably big, it had its limitations. Despite the pool in the basement, the heated roof terrace and huge screening room, she was starting to feel like part of the fixtures and fittings. Couldn't she go out to Italy and, in the anonymous setting of a foreign country, pretend to be his *real* girlfriend for a change? Someone he really cared about—rather than just someone whose panties he wanted to rip off every time he saw her.

'I guess it does tempt me,' she said. 'A little.'

'Not the most enthusiastic response I've ever had,' he commented. 'But I take it that's a yes?'

'It's a yes,' she agreed, relaxing back into the feathery bank of pillows as he turned his attention to her other aching breast.

'Good.' There was a pause and the circular movement of his fingers halted. 'But first you're going to have to let me buy you some new clothes.'

Her eyes snapped open and she froze—automatically pushing his hand away. 'When will you get it into your thick skull that I'm not interested in your money, Renzo?'

'I think I'm getting the general idea,' he said drily. 'And although your independence is admirable, I find it a little misguided. Why not just accept gracefully? I like giving presents and most women like receiving them.'

'It's a very kind thought and thank you all the same,' she said stiffly, 'but I don't want them.'

'This isn't a question of *want*, more a case of *need* and I'm afraid that this time I'm going to have to insist,' he said smoothly. 'I have a certain…*position* to maintain in Italy and, as the woman accompanying me, you'll naturally be the focus of attention. I'd hate you to feel you were being judged negatively because you don't have the right clothes.'

'Just as you're judging me right now, you mean?' she snapped.

He shook his head, his lips curving into a slow smile and his deep voice dipping. 'You must have realised by now that I prefer you wearing nothing at all, since nothing looks better than your pale and perfect skin. But although it's one of my biggest fantasies, I really don't think we can have you walking around the Tuscan hills stark naked, do you? I'm just looking out for you, Darcy. Buy yourself a few pretty things. Some dresses you can wear in the evenings. It isn't a big deal.'

She opened her mouth to say that it *was* a big deal to her but he had risen to his feet and his shadow was falling over her so that she was bathed in darkness as she lay there. She looked up into lash-shuttered eyes which gleamed like ebony and her heart gave a funny twist as she thought about how much she was going to miss him. How was she going to return to a life which was empty of her powerful Italian lover? 'What are you doing?' she croaked as he began to unzip his jeans.

'Oh, come on. Use your imagination,' he said softly. 'I'm going to persuade you to take my money.'

CHAPTER TWO

RENZO LOOKED AT his watch and gave a click of impatience. Where the hell *was* she? She *knew* he detested lateness, just as she knew he ran his diary like clockwork. In the exclusive lounge at Florence airport he crossed one long leg over the other, aware that the movement had caused the heads of several women instinctively to turn, but he paid them no attention for there was only one woman currently on his mind—and not in a good way.

The flight he had instructed Darcy to catch—in fact, to purchase a first-class ticket for—had discharged its passengers twenty minutes earlier and she had not been among their number. His eyes had narrowed as he'd stared at the hordes of people streaming through the arrivals section, fully expecting to see her eagerly pushing her way through to see him, her pale face alight with excitement and her curvy body resplendent in fine new clothes—but there had been no sight of her. A member of staff had dealt with his irritation and was currently checking the flight list while he was forced to consider the unbelievable...*that she might have changed her mind about joining him in Italy.*

He frowned. Had her reluctance to take the cash he had insisted she accept gone deeper than he'd imagined? He'd thought she was simply making a gesture—hiding the natural greed which ran through the veins of pretty much every woman—but perhaps he had misjudged her. Perhaps she really *was* deeply offended by his suggestion that she buy herself some decent clothes.

Or maybe she'd just taken the money and done a runner, not intending to come here and meet him at all.

Renzo's mouth hardened, because wasn't there a rogue thought flickering inside his head which almost wished that to be the case? Wouldn't he have welcomed a sound reason to despise her, instead of this simmering resentment that she was preparing to take her leave of him? That she had been the one to make a decision which was usually *his* province. He glanced again at his wristwatch. And how ironic that the woman to call time on a relationship should be a busty little red-headed waitress he'd picked up in a cocktail bar rather than one of the many more eligible women he'd dated.

He hadn't even been intending to go out the night he'd met her. He'd just planned to have a quick drink with a group of bankers he'd known from way back who had been visiting from Argentina and wanted to see some London nightlife. Renzo didn't particularly like nightclubs and remembered the stir the six men had made as they'd walked into the crowded Starlight Room at the Granchester Hotel, where they'd ordered champagne and decided which of the women sipping cocktails they should ask to dance. But Renzo hadn't been interested in the svelte women who had been smiling invitingly in his direction. His attention had been caught by the curviest little firecracker he'd ever seen. She'd looked as if she had been poured into the black satin dress which had skimmed her rounded hips, but it had been her breasts which had caused the breath to dry in his throat. *Madonna, che bella!* What breasts! Luscious and quivering, they had a deep cleavage he wanted to run his tongue over and that first sight of them was something he would remember for as long as he lived.

He had ended up dancing with no one, mainly because he'd been too busy watching her and his erection had been too painful for him to move without embarrassment. He'd ordered drinks only from her, and wondered afterwards if she noticed he left them all. Each time he'd summoned her over to his table he could sense the almost palpable electricity which sizzled in the air—he'd certainly never felt such a powerful attraction towards a total stranger before. He'd expected her to make some acknowledgement of the silent chemistry which pulsed between them, but she hadn't. In fact the way her eyelids had half shielded her huge green eyes and the cautious looks she'd been directing at him had made him think she must either be the world's greatest innocent, or its most consummate actress. If he had known it was the former, would he still have pursued her?

Of course he would. Deep down he recognised he wouldn't have been able to stop himself because hadn't he been gripped by a powerful hunger which insisted he would never know peace until he had possessed her?

He'd been waiting outside when eventually she had emerged from the club and had thanked the heavens for the heavy downpour of rain which had been showering down on her. She hadn't looked a bit surprised to see him as she'd opened up her umbrella and for a moment it had crossed his mind that she might take a different man home with her every night, though even that had not been enough to make him order his driver to move on. But when he'd offered her a lift she'd refused, in an emphatic manner which had startled him.

'No, thanks.'

'No?'

'I know what you want,' she'd said, in a low voice. 'And you won't get it from me.'

And with that she'd disappeared into the rain-wet night and Renzo had sat in the back seat of the limousine, watching her retreating form beneath her little black umbrella, his mouth open and his body aching with frustration and unwilling admiration.

He'd gone to the club the next night and the weekend when he'd returned from a work trip to New York. Some nights she'd been there and some she hadn't. He'd discovered she only worked there at weekends and it had only been later he'd found out she had a daytime job as a waitress somewhere else. Extracting information from her had been like trying to get blood from a stone. She was the most private woman he'd ever met as well as the most resistant and perhaps it was those things which made Renzo persist in a way he'd never had to persist before. And just when he'd been wondering if he was wasting his time, she had agreed to let him drive her home.

His voice had been wry as he'd looked at her. '*Madonna mia!* You mean you've decided you trust me enough to accept the lift?'

Her narrow shoulders had shrugged, causing her large breasts to jiggle beneath the shiny black satin of her dress and sending a shaft of lust arrowing straight to his groin. 'I guess so. All the other staff have seen you by now and you've been captured on CCTV for all eternity, so if you're a murderer then you'll be apprehended soon enough.'

'Do I look like a murderer?'

She had smiled then, and it had been like the sun coming out from behind a cloud.

'No. Although you look just a little bit dangerous.'

'Women always tell me that's a plus.'

'I'm sure they do, though I'm not sure I agree. Anyway, it's a filthy night, so I might as well get a lift with you. But I haven't changed my mind,' she'd added fiercely. 'And if you think I'm going to sleep with you, then you're wrong.'

As it happened, she was the one who'd been wrong. They'd driven through the dark wet streets of London and he'd asked her to come in for coffee, not thinking for a moment she'd accept. But maybe the chemistry had been just as powerful for her. Maybe her throat had also been tight with tension and longing and she'd been finding it as difficult to speak as he had, as she'd sat beside him in the leather-scented car. He'd driven her to his apartment and she'd told him primly that she didn't really like coffee. So he'd made her tea flavoured with peppermint and rose petals, and for the first time in his life he'd realised he might lose her if he rushed it. He'd wondered afterwards if it was his unfamiliar restraint which had made her relax and sink into one of his huge sofas—so that when at last he'd leaned over to kiss her she'd been all quivering acquiescence. He'd done it to her right there—pulling her panties down and plunging right into her—terrified she might change her mind during the long walk from the sitting room to the bedroom.

And that had been when he'd discovered she was a virgin—and in that moment something had changed. The world had tipped on its axis because he'd never had sex with a virgin before and had been unprepared for the rush of primitive satisfaction which had flooded through him. As they'd lain there afterwards, gasping for breath among all the cushions, he'd pushed a damp curl away from her dewy cheek, demanding to know why she hadn't told him.

'Why would I? Would you have stopped?'

'No, but I could have laid you at the centre of my big bed instead of the sofa if I'd known this was your first sexual adventure.'

'What, you mean like some sort of medieval sacrifice?' she'd murmured and that had confused him, too, because he would have expected high emotion at such a moment, not such a cool response.

Had it been her coolness which had made him

desire her even more? Possibly. He'd thought it would be one night, but he'd been mistaken. He'd never dated a waitress before and he acknowledged the cold streak of snobbery in his nature which told him it would be unwise to buck that trend. But Darcy had confounded him. She read just as many books as an academic he'd once dated—although admittedly, she preferred novels to molecular biology. And she didn't follow the predictable path of most women in a sexual relationship. She didn't bore him with stories of her past, nor weigh him down with questions about his own. Their infrequent yet highly satisfying meetings, which involved a series of mind-blowing orgasms, seemed to meet both their needs. She seemed instinctively to understand that he wasn't seeking a close or lasting connection with a woman. Not now and not ever.

But sometimes an uncomfortable question strayed into his mind to ask why such a beauty would have so willingly submitted her virginity to a total stranger. And didn't he keep coming up with the troublesome answer that maybe she had been holding out for the highest bidder—in this case, an Italian billionaire...?

'Renzo?'

The sound of her voice dragged him away back into the present and Renzo looked up to see a woman walking through the airport lounge towards him, pulling behind her a battered suitcase on wheels. His eyes narrowed. It was Darcy, yes—but not Darcy as he knew her, in her drab waitress uniform or pale and naked against his pristine white sheets. Renzo blinked. This was Darcy in a dress the colour of sunshine, dotted with tiny blue flowers. It was a simple cotton dress but the way she wore it was remarkable. It wasn't the cut or the label which was making every man in the place stare at her—it was her youthful body and natural beauty. Fresh and glowing, her bare arms and legs were honed by honest hard work rather than mindless sessions in the gym. She looked *radiant* and the natural bounce of her breasts meant that no man could look at her without thinking about procreation. Renzo's mouth dried. Procreation had never been on *his* agenda, but sex most definitely was. He wanted to pull her hungrily into his arms and to kiss her hard on the mouth and feel those soft breasts crushing against him. But Renzo Sabatini would never be seen in any airport—let alone one in his homeland—making such a public demonstration of affection.

And wasn't it time he reinforced the fact that nobody—nobody—ever kept him waiting?

'You're late,' he said repressively, throwing aside his newspaper and rising to his feet.

Darcy nodded. She could sense his irritation but that didn't affect her enjoyment of the way he was looking at her—if only to reassure her she hadn't made a terrible mistake in choosing a cheap cotton dress instead of the clothes he must have been expecting her to wear. Still, since this was going to be the holiday of a lifetime it was important she got it off to a good start and the truth of it was that she *was* late. In fact, she'd started to worry if she would get here at all because that horrible vomiting bug she'd had at the beginning of the week had really laid her low.

'Yes, I know. I'm sorry about that.'

He commandeered her wheeled case and winced slightly as he took her hand luggage. 'What have you got in here? Bricks?'

'I put in a few books,' she said as they set off towards the exit. 'Though I wasn't sure how much time I'd have for reading.'

Usually he would have made a provocative comment in response to such a remark but he didn't and the unyielding expression on his face told her he wasn't ready to forgive her for making him wait. But he didn't say anything as they emerged into the bright sunshine and Darcy was too overcome by the bluest sky she'd ever seen to care.

'Oh, Renzo—I can't believe I'm in Italy. It's so beautiful,' she enthused as she looked around, but still he didn't answer. In fact, he didn't speak until his shiny black car had pulled out of the airport and was heading towards a signpost marked Chiusi.

'I've been waiting at the damned airport for

over an hour,' he snapped. 'Why weren't you on the flight I told you to get?'

Darcy hesitated. She supposed she could come up with some vague story to placate him but hadn't she already shrouded so much of her life with evasion and secrets, terrified that someone would examine it in the harsh light of day and judge her? Why add yet another to the long list of things she needed to conceal? And this was different. This wasn't something she was ashamed of—so why not be upfront about the decision she'd made when he had stuffed that enormous wad of cash into her hand and made her feel deeply uncomfortable?

'Because it was too expensive.'

'Darcy, I *gave* you the money to get that flight.'

'I know you did and it was very generous of you.' She drew in a deep breath. 'But when I saw how much it cost to fly to Florence first class, I just couldn't do it.'

'What do you mean, you couldn't do it?'

'It seemed a ludicrous amount of money to

spend on a two-hour flight so I bought a seat on a budget airline instead.'

'You did *what*?'

'You should try it sometime. It's true they ran out of sandwiches and the tea was stone-cold, but I saved absolutely loads of money because the price difference was massive. Just like I did with the clothes.'

'The clothes,' he repeated uncomprehendingly.

'Yes. I went to that department store you recommended on Bond Street but the clothes were stupidly overpriced. I couldn't believe how much they were asking for a simple T-shirt so I went to the high street and found some cheaper versions, like this dress.' She smoothed the crisp yellow cotton down over her thighs and her voice wavered a little uncertainly. 'Which I think looks okay, doesn't it?'

He flashed a glance to where her hand was resting. 'Sure,' he said, his voice sounding thick. 'It looks okay.'

'So what's the problem?'

He slammed the palm of his hand against the

steering wheel. 'The problem is that I don't like being disobeyed.'

She laughed. 'Oh, Renzo. You sound like a headmaster. You're not my teacher, you know—and I'm not your pupil.'

'Oh, really?' He raised his eyebrows. 'I thought I'd been responsible for teaching you rather a lot.'

His words made her face grow hot as they zoomed past blue-green mountains, but suddenly Darcy was finding the sight of Renzo's profile far more appealing than the Tuscan countryside. He was so unbelievably gorgeous. Just the most gorgeous man she'd ever seen. Would she ever feel this way about anyone again, she wondered—with a chest which became so tight when she looked at him that sometimes it felt as if she could hardly *breathe*? Probably not. It had never happened before, so what were the chances of it happening again? How had Renzo himself described what had happened when they first met? *Colpo di fulmine*—that was it. A lightning strike—which everyone knew was extremely rare. It was about the only bit of Italian she knew.

She sneaked another glance at him. His black hair was ruffled and his shirt was open at the neck—olive skin glowing gold and stunningly illuminated by the rich Tuscan light. His thighs looked taut beneath his charcoal trousers and Darcy could feel the sudden increase of her pulse as her gaze travelled along their muscular length. She'd rarely been in a car with him since the night he had seduced her—or rather, when she had fallen greedily into his arms. She'd hardly been *anywhere* with him other than the bedroom and suddenly she was glad about something which might have bothered other women.

Because with the amazing landscape sliding past like a TV commercial, she thought how easy it would be to get used to this kind of treatment. Not just the obvious luxury of being driven through such beautiful countryside, but the chance to be a bona fide couple like this. And she mustn't get used to it, because it was a one-off. One last sweet taste of Renzo Sabatini before she began her new life in Norfolk and started to forget him—the man with the cold heart who had taught her the definition of pleasure. The precise and brilliant architect who turned into a tiger in the bedroom.

'So what exactly are we going to be doing when we get to this place of yours?' she said.

'You mean apart from making love?'

'Apart from that,' she agreed, almost wishing he hadn't said it despite the instant spring of her breasts in response. Did he need to keep drumming in her sole purpose in his life? She remembered the hiking shoes she'd packed and wondered if she'd completely misjudged the situation. Was he planning to show her anything of Tuscany, or would they simply be doing the bed thing, only in a more glamorous location? She wondered if he had sensed her sudden discomfiture and if that was the reason for his swift glance as they left the motorway for a quieter road.

'The man who is buying the estate is coming for dinner,' he said, by way of explanation.

'Oh? Is that usual?'

'Not really, but he's actually my lawyer and I want to persuade him to keep on the staff who have worked at Vallombrosa for so long. He's bringing his girlfriend with him, so it'll be good to have you there to balance the numbers.'

Darcy nodded. To balance the numbers. Of course. She was there to fill an empty chair and warm the tycoon's bed—there was nothing more to it than that. Stupidly, his remark hurt but she didn't show it—something in which she'd learned to excel. A childhood of deprivation and fear had taught her to hide her feelings behind a mask and present the best version of herself to the world. The version that prospective foster parents might like if they were looking for a child to fit into their lovely home. And if sometimes she wondered what she might reveal if that mask ever slipped, she didn't worry about it for too long because she was never going to let that happen.

'So when were you last abroad?' he questioned, as they passed a pretty little hilltop village.

'Oh, not for ages,' she answered vaguely.

'How come?'

It was a long time since she'd thought about it and Darcy stared straight ahead as she remembered the charity coach trip to Spain when she'd been fifteen. When the blazing summer sun had burned her fair skin and the mobile home on the campsite had felt like sleeping in a hot tin can. They were supposed to be grateful that the church near the children's home had raised enough money to send them on the supposed trip of a lifetime and she had really tried to be grateful. Until somebody had drilled a peephole into the wall of the female showers and there had been a huge fuss about it. And someone had definitely stolen two pairs of her knickers when she'd been out swimming in the overcrowded pool. Somehow she didn't think Renzo Sabatini's Tuscan villa was going to be anything like that. 'I went on a school trip when I was a teenager,' she said. 'That was the only time I've been abroad.'

He frowned. 'You're not much of a traveller, then?'

'You could say that.'

And suddenly Darcy scented danger. On the journey over she'd been worried she might do something stupid. Not something obvious, like using the wrong knife and fork at a fancy dinner, because her waitressing career had taught her everything there was to know about cutlery. But she realised she'd completely overlooked the fact that proximity might make her careless. Might make her tongue slip and give something away—something which would naturally repulse him. Renzo had told her that one of the things he liked about her was that she didn't besiege him with questions, or try to *dig deep* to try to understand him better. But that had been a two-way street and the fact he didn't ask about *her* past had suited her just fine. More than fine. She didn't want to tell any lies but she knew she could never tell him the truth. Because there was no point. There was no future in this liaison of theirs, so why tell him about the junkie mother who had given birth to her? Why endure the pain of seeing his lips curve with shock and contempt as had happened so often in the past? In a world where everyone was striving for perfection and judging you, it hadn't taken her long to realise that the best way to get on in life was to bury all the darkness just as deep as she could.

But thoughts of her mother stabbed at her conscience, prompting her to address something which had been bothering her on the flight over.

'You know the money I saved on my airfare and clothes?' she began.

'Yes, Darcy. I know. You were making a point.' He shot her a glance, his lips curving into a sardonic smile. 'Rich man with too much money shown by poor girl just how much he could save if he bothered to shop around. I get the picture.'

'There's no need to be sarcastic, Renzo,' she

said stiffly. 'I want you to have it back. I've put most of it in an envelope in my handbag.'

'But I don't want it back. When are you going to get the message? I have more than enough money. And if it makes you feel better, I admire your resourcefulness and refusal to be seduced by my wealth. It's rare.'

For a moment there was silence. 'I think we both know it wasn't your wealth which seduced me, Renzo.'

She hadn't meant to say it but her quiet words reverberated around the car in an honest explanation of what had first drawn her to him. Not his money, nor his power—but him. The most charismatic and compelling man she'd ever met. She heard him suck in an unsteady breath.

'Madonna mia,' he said softly. 'Are you trying to tempt me into taking the next turning and finding the nearest layby so that I can do what I have been longing to do to you since last I saw you?'

'Renzo—'

'I don't want the damned money you saved!

I want you to put your hand in my lap and feel how hard I am for you.'

'Not while you're driving,' said Darcy and although she was disappointed he had turned the emotional into the sexual, she didn't show it. Because that was the kind of man he was, she reminded herself. He was never emotional and always sexual. She didn't need to touch him to know he was aroused—a quick glance and she could see for herself the hard ridge outlined beneath the dark trousers. Suddenly her lips grew dry in response and she licked them, wishing they *could* have sex right then. Because sex stopped you longing for things you were never going to have. Things other women took for granted—like a man promising to love and protect you. Things which seemed as distant as those faraway mountains. With an effort she dragged her attention back to the present. 'Tell me about this place we're going to instead.'

'You think talking about property is a suitable substitute for discovering what you're wearing underneath that pretty little dress?'

'I think it's absolutely vital if you intend keeping your mind on the road, which is probably the most sensible option if you happen to be driving a car.'

'Oh, Darcy.' He gave a soft laugh. 'Did I ever tell you that one of the things I admire about you is your ability to always come up with a smart answer?'

'The *house*, Renzo. I want to talk about the house.'

'Okay. The house. It's old,' he said as he overtook a lorry laden with a towering pile of watermelons. 'And it stands against a backdrop that Leonardo should have painted, instead of that village south of Piacenza which is not nearly as beautiful. It has orchards and vineyards and olive groves—in fact, we produce superb wines from the Sangiovese grape and enough olive oil to sell to some of the more upmarket stores in London and Paris.'

The few facts he'd recited could have been lifted straight from the pages of an estate agent's website and Darcy felt oddly disappointed. 'It sounds gorgeous,' she said dutifully.

'It is.'

'So…why are you selling it?'

He shrugged. 'It's time.'

'Because?'

Too late, she realised she had asked one question too many. His face grew dark, as if the sun had just dipped behind a cloud and his shadowed jaw set itself into a hard and obdurate line.

'Isn't one of the reasons for our unique chemistry that you don't plague me with questions?'

She heard the sudden darkness underpinning his question. 'I was only—'

'Well, don't. Don't pry. Why change what up until now has been a winning formula?' His voice had harshened as he cut through her words, his hands tensing as a discreet sign appeared among the tangle of greenery which feathered the roadside. 'And anyway. We're here. This is Vallombrosa.'

But his face was still dark as the car began to ascend a tree-lined track towards an imposing pair of dark wrought-iron gates which looked like the gates of heaven.

Or the gates of hell, Darcy thought with a sudden flash of foreboding.

CHAPTER THREE

'HOW ON EARTH am I going to converse with everyone?' questioned Darcy as she stepped out onto the sunny courtyard. 'Since my Italian is limited to the few words I learnt from the phrasebook on the plane and that phrase about the lightning strike?'

'All my staff are bilingual,' Renzo said, his show of bad temper in the car now seemingly forgotten. 'And perfectly comfortable with speaking your mother tongue.'

The words mocked her and Darcy chewed on her lip as she looked away. Mother tongue? Her own mother had taught her to say very little—other than things which could probably have had her prosecuted if she'd repeated them to the authorities.

'Pass Mummy that needle, darling.'

'Pass Mummy those matches.'

'If the policewoman asks if you've met that man before, tell her no.'

But she smiled brightly as she entered the shaded villa and shook hands with Gisella, the elderly housekeeper, and her weather-beaten husband, Pasquale, who was one of the estate's gardeners. A lovely young woman with dark hair helped Gisella around the house and Darcy saw her blush when Renzo introduced her as Stefania. There was also a chef called Donato, who apparently flew in from Rome whenever Renzo was in residence. Donato was tanned, athletic, amazingly good-looking and almost certainly gay.

'Lunch will be in an hour,' he told them. 'But sooner if you're hungry?'

'Oh, I think we can wait,' said Renzo. He turned to Darcy. 'Why don't we take a quick look around while our bags are taken to our room?'

Darcy nodded, thinking how *weird* it felt to be deferred to like that—and to be introduced to his staff just like a real girlfriend. But then she reminded herself that this was only going to work if she didn't allow herself to get carried away. She followed him outside, blinking a little as she took in the vastness of his estate and, although she was seeing only a fraction of it, her senses were instantly overloaded by the beauty of Vallombrosa. Honeybees flitted over purple spears of lavender, vying for space with brightly coloured butterflies. Little lizards basked on baked grey stone. The high walls surrounding the ancient house were covered with scrambling pink roses and stone arches framed the blue-green layers of the distant mountains beyond. Darcy wondered what it must be like growing up somewhere like here, instead of the greyness of the institution in the north of England, which had been the only place she'd ever really called home.

'Like it?' he questioned.

'How could I not? It's beautiful.'

'You know, you're pretty beautiful yourself,' he said softly as he turned his head to look at her.

Remembering the way he'd snapped at her in the car, she wanted to resist him, but the light touch of his hand on her hip and brush of his fingers against her thighs made resistance impossible and Darcy was shaking with longing by the time they reached the shuttered dimness of his bedroom. It was a vast wood-beamed room but there was no time to take in her surroundings because he was pulling her into his arms, his lips brushing hungrily over hers and his fingers tangling themselves in her curls.

'Renzo,' she said unsteadily.

'What?'

She licked her lips. 'You know what.'

'I think I do.' His lips curved into a hard smile. 'You want this?'

Sliding down the zip of her cotton dress, he peeled it away from her and she felt the rush of air against her skin as it pooled to the ground around her ankles. 'Yes,' she breathed. 'That's what I want.'

'Do you know,' he questioned as he unclipped her lacy bra and it joined the discarded dress, 'how much I have been fantasising about you? About this?'

She nodded. 'Me, too,' she said softly, because the newness of the environment and the situation in which she found herself was making her feel almost *shy* in his presence.

But not for long. The beat of her heart and the heat of her blood soon overwhelmed her and had her fumbling for his belt, her fingers trembling with need. Very quickly she was naked and so was he—soft, shuttered light shading their bodies as he pushed her down onto the bed and levered his powerful form over hers. She gripped at the silken musculature of his broad shoulders as he slowly stroked his thumb over her clitoris. And she came right then—so quickly it was almost embarrassing. He laughed softly and eased himself into her wet heat and for a moment he was perfectly still.

'Do you know how good that feels?' he said as he began to move inside her.

She swallowed. 'I've…I've got a pretty good idea.'

'Oh, Darcy. It's you,' he groaned, his eyes closing. 'Only you.'

He said the words like a ragged prayer or maybe a curse—but Darcy didn't read anything into them because she knew exactly what he meant. She was the first and only woman with whom he hadn't needed to wear a condom, because her virginity had elevated her to a different status from his other lovers—he'd told her that himself. He told her she was truly pure. He'd been fascinated to find a woman of twenty-four who'd never had a lover before and by her fervent reply when he'd asked if she ever wanted children.

'Never!'

Her response must have been heartfelt enough to convince him because in a rare moment of confidence he told her he felt exactly the same. Soon afterwards he had casually suggested she might want to go on the pill and Darcy had eagerly agreed. She remembered the first time they'd left the condom off and how it had felt to have his naked skin against hers instead of '*that damned rubber*'—again, his words—between them. It had been...*delicious*. She had felt dangerously close to him and had needed to give herself a stern talking-to afterwards. She'd told herself that the powerful feelings she was experiencing were purely physical. Of course sex felt better without a condom—but it didn't *mean* anything.

But now, in the dimness of his Tuscan bedroom, he was deep inside her. He was filling her and thrusting into her body and kissing her mouth until it throbbed and it felt so amazing that she could have cried. Did her low, moaning sigh break his rhythm? Was that why, with a deft movement, he turned her over so that she was on top of him, his black eyes capturing hers?

'Ride me, *cara*,' he murmured. 'Ride me until you come again.'

She nodded as she tensed her thighs against his narrow hips because she liked this position. It gave her a rare feeling of power, to see Renzo lying underneath her—his eyes half-closed and his lips parted as she rocked back and forth.

She heard his groan and bent her head to kiss it quiet, though she was fairly sure that the walls of this ancient house were deep enough to absorb the age-old sounds of sex. He tangled his hands in her hair, digging his fingers into the wayward curls until pleasure—intense and unalterable—started spiralling up inside her. She came just before he did, gasping as he clasped her hips tightly and hearing him utter something urgent in Italian as his body bucked beneath her. She bent her head to his neck, hot breath panting against his skin until she'd recovered enough to peel herself away from him, before falling back against the mattress.

She looked at the dark beams above her head and the engraved glass lampshade, which looked as if it was as old as the house itself. Someone had put a small vase of scented roses by the window—the same roses which had been scrambling over the walls outside—and all the light in that shadowy room seemed to be centred on those pale pink petals.

'Well,' she said eventually. 'That was some welcome.'

Deliberately, Renzo kept his eyes closed and his breathing steady because he didn't want to talk. Not right now. He didn't need to be told how good it was—that was a given—not when his mind was busy with the inevitable clamour of his thoughts.

He'd felt a complex mixture of stuff as he'd driven towards the house, knowing soon it would be under different ownership. A house which had been in his mother's family for generations and which had had more than its fair share of heartbreak. Other people might have offloaded it years ago but pride had made him hold on to it, determined to replace bad memories with good ones, and to a large extent he'd succeeded. But you couldn't live in the past. It was time to let the place go—to say goodbye to the last clinging fragments of yesterday.

He looked across the bed, where Darcy was lying with her eyes closed, her bright red hair spread all over the white pillow. He thought about her going to Norfolk when they got back to London and tried to imagine what it might be like sleeping with someone else when she was no longer around, but the idea of some slender-hipped brunette lying amid his tumbled sheets was failing to excite him. Instinctively he flattened his palm over her bare thigh.

'And was it the perfect welcome?' he questioned at last.

'You know it was.' Her voice was sleepy. 'Though I should go and pick my dress up. It's the first time I've worn it.'

'Don't worry about it.' He smiled. 'I'll have Gisella launder it for you.'

'There's no need for that.' Her voice was suddenly sharp as her eyes snapped open. 'I can do my own washing. I can easily rinse it out in the sink and hang it out to dry in that glorious sunshine.'

'And if I told you I'd rather you didn't?'

'Too bad.'

'Why are you so damned stubborn, Darcy?'

'I thought you *liked* my stubbornness.'

'When appropriate, I do.'

'You mean, when it suits *you*?'

'Esattamente.'

She lay back and looked up at the ceiling. How could she explain that she'd felt his house-keeper looking at her and seeing exactly who she was—a servant, just as Gisella was. Like Gisella, she waited tables and cleared up around people who had far more money than she had. That was who she was. She didn't want to look as if she'd suddenly acquired airs and graces by asking to have her clothes laundered. She wasn't going to try to be someone she wasn't—someone who would find it impossible to settle back into her humble world when she got back to England and her billionaire lover was nothing but a distant memory.

But she shouldn't take it out on Renzo, because he was just being Renzo. She'd never objected to his high-handedness before. If the truth were known, she'd always found it a turn-on—and in a way, his arrogance had provided a natural barrier. It had stopped her falling completely under his spell, forcing her to be realistic rather than dreamy. She leaned over and brushed her mouth against his. 'So tell me what you've got planned for us.'

His fingers slid between the tops of her thighs. 'Plans? What plans? The sight of your body seems to have completely short-circuited my brain.'

Halting his hand before it got any further, Darcy enjoyed her brief feeling of power. 'Tell me something about Vallombrosa—and I'm not talking olive or wine production this time. Did you live here when you were a little boy?'

His shuttered features grew wary. 'Why the sudden interest?'

'Because you told me we'd be having dinner with the man who's buying the place. It's going to look a bit odd if I don't know anything about your connection with it. Did you grow up here?'

'No, I grew up in Rome. Vallombrosa was our holiday home.'

'And?' she prompted.

'And it had been in my mother's family for

generations. We used it to escape the summer heat of the city. She and I used to come here for the entire vacation and my father would travel down at weekends.'

Darcy nodded because she knew that, like her, he was an only child and that both his parents were dead. And that was pretty much all she knew.

She circled a finger over the hardness of his flat belly. 'So what did you do when you were here?'

He pushed her hand in the direction of his groin. 'My father taught me to hunt and to fish, while my mother socialised and entertained. Sometimes friends came to visit and my mother's school friend Mariella always seemed to be a constant fixture. We were happy, or so I thought.'

Darcy held her breath as something dark and steely entered his voice. 'But you weren't?'

'No. We weren't.' He turned his head to look at her, a hard expression suddenly distorting his features. 'Haven't you realised by now that so few people are?'

'I guess,' she said stiffly. But she'd thought…

What? That other people were strangers to the pain she'd suffered? That someone as successful and as powerful as Renzo had never known emotional deprivation? Was that why he was so distant sometimes—so shuttered and cold? 'Did something happen?'

'You could say that. They got divorced when I was seven.'

'And was it…acrimonious?'

He shot her an unfathomable look. 'Aren't all divorces acrimonious?'

She shrugged. 'I guess.'

'Especially when you discover that your mother's best "friend" has been having an affair with your father for years,' he added, his voice bitter. 'It makes you realise that when the chips are down, women can never be trusted.'

Darcy chewed on her lip. 'So what happened?'

'After the divorce, my father married his mistress but my mother never really recovered. It was a double betrayal and her only weapon was me.'

'Weapon?' she echoed.

He nodded. 'She did everything in her power to keep my father out of my life. She was depressed.' His jaw tightened. 'And believe me, there isn't much a child can do if his mother is depressed. He is—quite literally—helpless. I used to sit in the corner of the room, quietly making houses out of little plastic bricks while she sobbed her heart out and raged against the world. By the end of that first summer, I'd constructed an entire city.'

She nodded in sudden understanding. Had his need to control been born out of that helplessness? Had the tiny plastic city he'd made been the beginnings of his brilliant architectural career? 'Oh, Renzo—that's...*terrible*,' she said.

He curled his fingers over one breast. 'What an innocent you are, Darcy,' he observed softly.

Darcy felt guilt wash over her. He thought she was a goody-goody because she suspected he was one of those men who divided women into two types—Madonna or whore. Her virginity had guaranteed her Madonna status but it wasn't that simple and if he knew why she had kept herself pure he would be shocked. Married men having affairs was hardly ground-breaking stuff, even if they chose to do it with their wife's best friend—but she could tell him things about *her* life which would make his own story sound like something you could read to a child at bedtime.

And he wasn't asking about *her* past, was he? He wasn't interested—and maybe she ought to be grateful for that. There was no point in dragging out her dark secrets at this late stage in their relationship and ruining their last few days together. 'So what made you decide to sell the estate?'

There was a pause. 'My stepmother died last year,' he said flatly. 'She'd always wanted this house and I suppose I was making sure she never got her hands on it. But now she's gone—they've all gone—and somehow my desire to hang on to it died with her. The estate is too big for a single man to maintain. It needs a family.'

'And you don't want one?'

'I thought we'd already established that,' he said and now his voice had grown cool. 'I saw enough lying and deceit to put me off marriage for a lifetime. Surely you can understand that?'

Darcy nodded. Oh, yes, she understood all right. Just as she recognised that his words were a warning. A warning not to get too close. That just because she was here with him in the unfamiliar role of girlfriend, nothing had really changed. The smile she produced wasn't as bright as usual, but it was good enough to convince him she didn't care. 'Shouldn't we think about getting ready for lunch?' she questioned, her voice growing a little unsteady as his hand moved from her breast to the dip of her belly. 'Didn't...didn't Donato say it would be ready in an hour?'

The touch of her bare skin drove all thoughts from Renzo's mind until he was left with only one kind of hunger. The best kind. The kind which obliterated everything except pleasure. He'd told her more than he usually told anyone and he put that down to the fact that usually she didn't ask. But she needed to know that there would be no more confidences from now on. She needed to know that there was only one reason she was here—and the glint of expectation in her eyes told him that she was getting the message loud and clear. He felt his erection grow exquisitely hard as he looked at the little waitress who somehow knew how to handle him better than any other woman.

'I employ Donato to work to my time frame, not his,' he said arrogantly, bending his head and sucking at her nipple.

'Oh, Renzo.' Her eyes closed as she fell back against the pillow.

'Renzo, what?' he taunted.

'Don't make me beg.'

He slid his finger over her knee. 'But I like it when you beg.'

'I know you do.'

'So?'

She groaned as her hips lifted hungrily towards his straying finger. 'Please…'

'That's better.' He gave a low and triumphant laugh as he pulled her towards him. 'Lunch can wait,' he added roughly, parting her thighs and positioning himself between them once more. 'I'm afraid this can't.'

CHAPTER FOUR

'THIS?' DARCY HELD up a glimmering black sheath, then immediately waved a flouncy turquoise dress in front of it. 'Or this?'

'The black,' Renzo said, flicking her a swift glance before continuing to button up his shirt.

Her skin now tanned a delicate shade of gold, Darcy slithered into the black dress, aware that Renzo was watching her reflection in the glass in the way a hungry dog might look at a butcher, but she didn't care. She found herself wishing she had the ability to freeze time and that the weekend wasn't drawing to a close because it had been the best few days of her life.

They'd explored his vast estate, scrambling up hilly roads to be rewarded with spectacular views of blue-green mountains and the terracotta smudge of tiny villages. Her hiking boots had come in useful after all! He'd taken her to a beautiful village called Panicale, where they'd drunk coffee in the cobbled square with church bells chiming in stereophonic all around them. And even though Renzo had assured her that May temperatures were too cold for swimming, Darcy wasn't having any of it. She'd never been anywhere with a private pool before—let alone a pool as vast and inviting as the one at Vallombrosa.

Initially a little shy about appearing in her tiny bikini, she'd been quickly reassured by the darkening response in his eyes—though she'd been surprised when he'd changed his mind and decided to join her in the pool after all. And Renzo in sleek black swim shorts, olive skin gleaming as he shook water from his hair, was a vision which made her heart race. She could have spent all afternoon watching his powerful body ploughing through the silky water. But he'd brought her lazy swim to a swift conclusion with some explicit suggestions whispered in her ear and they had returned to his bedroom for sex which had felt even more incredible than usual.

Was it because her senses had been heightened by fresh air and sunshine that everything felt so amazing? Or because Renzo had seemed unusually accessible in this peaceful place which seemed a world away from the hustle and bustle of her normal life? Darcy kept reminding herself that the reasons why were irrelevant. Because this was only temporary. A last trip before she moved to Norfolk—which was probably the only reason he had invited her to join him. And tonight was their final dinner, when they were being joined by Renzo's lawyer, who was buying the Sabatini estate.

Their eyes met in the mirror.

'Will you zip me up?'

'Certo.'

'So tell me again,' she said, feeling his fingers brushing against her bare skin as he slid the zip of the close-fitting dress all the way up. 'The lawyer's name is Cristiano Branzi and his girlfriend is Nicoletta—'

'Ramelli.' There was a moment of hesitation and his eyes narrowed fractionally. 'And—just so you know—she and I used to have a thing a few years back.'

In the process of hooking in a dangly earring, Darcy's fingers stilled. 'A *thing*?'

'You really are going to have to stop looking so shocked, *cara*. I'm thirty-five years old and in Rome, as in all cities, social circles are smaller than you might imagine. She and I were lovers for a few months, that's all.'

That's all. Darcy's practised smile didn't waver. Just like her. Great sex for a few months and then goodbye—was that his usual pattern? Had Nicoletta been rewarded with a trip abroad just before the affair ended? But as she followed Renzo downstairs she was determined not to spoil their last evening and took the champagne Stefania offered, hoping she displayed more confidence than she felt as she rose to greet their guests.

Cristiano was a powerfully built man with piercing blue eyes and Darcy thought Nicoletta the most beautiful woman she'd ever seen. The Italian woman's sleek dark hair was swept up into a sophisticated chignon and she wore a dress which was obviously designer made. Real diamond studs glittered at her ears, echoing the smaller diamonds which sparkled in a watch which was slightly too loose for her narrow wrist. Darcy watched as she presented each smooth cheek in turn to be kissed by Renzo, wondering why she hadn't worn the turquoise dress after all. Why hadn't she realised that of *course* the Italian woman would also wear black, leaving the two of them wide open for comparison? How cheap her own glimmering gown must seem in comparison—and how wild her untameable red curls as they spilled down over her shoulders towards breasts which were much too large by fashionable standards.

'So...' Nicoletta smiled as they sat down to prosciutto and slivers of iced melon at a candlelit table decorated with roses. 'This is your first time in Italy, Darcy?'

'It is,' answered Darcy, with a smile.

'But not your last, I hope?'

Darcy looked across the table at Renzo, thinking it might bring the mood down if she suddenly announced that they were in the process of splitting up.

'Darcy isn't much of a traveller,' he said smoothly.

'Oh?'

Something made her say it. Was it bravado or stupidity? Yet surely she wasn't *ashamed* of the person she really was. Not unless she honestly thought she could compete with these glossy people, with their Tuscan estates and diamond wristwatches which probably cost as much as a small car.

'To be honest, I don't really have a lot of money to go travelling.' She slanted Nicoletta a rueful smile. 'I'm a waitress.'

'A *waitress*?' Nicoletta's silver fork was returned to her plate with a clatter, the dainty morsel she'd speared remaining untouched. 'That is a very unusual job.' There was a slightly perplexed pause. 'So how did you and Renzo actually meet?'

Darcy registered the faint astonishment on Nicoletta's face, but what had she expected? And now she had dropped Renzo in it. He was probably going to bluster out some story about how he'd bumped into her in a bookshop or been introduced at a party by a friend of a friend. Except he'd told her very specifically that he didn't like lies, hadn't he?

'I met Darcy when she was working in a nightclub in London,' Renzo said. 'I walked in with some visiting colleagues and saw her serving cocktails to the people on the next table. She turned round and looked at me and that was it. I was completely blown away.'

'I'm not surprised,' murmured Cristiano. 'I have never seen hair as bright as yours before, Darcy. I believe this is what they call the show-stopping look?'

The compliment was unexpected and Darcy met Renzo's eyes, expecting to find mockery or anger in them but there was none. On the contrary, he looked as if he was *enjoying* the praise being directed at her and suddenly she wanted to turn and run from the room. Or tell him not to look at her that way because it was making her fantasise about a life which could never be hers.

She cleared her throat, trying to remember back to when she'd worked in that very hip restaurant which had been frequented by the media crowd. To remember how those high-profile people used to talk to each other when she arrived to offer them a bread roll, which they inevitably refused. They used to play everything down, didn't they? To act as if nothing really mattered.

'Oh, that's quite enough about me,' she said lightly. 'I'd much rather talk about Tuscany.'

'You like it here?' questioned Nicoletta. 'At Vallombrosa?'

'Who could fail to like it?' questioned Darcy simply. 'There can't be anywhere in the world as beautiful as this. The gardens are so lovely and the view is to die for.' She smiled as she reached for a piece of bread. 'If I had the money I'd snap it up in a shot. You're a very lucky man, Cristiano.'

'I'm very aware of that.' Cristiano's blue eyes

crinkled. 'Nobody can quite believe that Renzo has put it on the market at last, after years of everyone offering him vast amounts of money to sell it. And he won't say what has suddenly changed his mind.'

But Darcy knew why. She'd seen the pain in his eyes when he'd talked about his parents' divorce and suspected his stepmother's death had made him want to let all that painful past go. He hadn't said that much but it surprised her that he'd confided in her at all. For a little while it had made her feel special—more than just his 'friend with benefits.' But that was fantasy, too. It was easy to share your secrets with someone you knew was planning to leave you.

Except for her, of course. She was one of those people whose secrets were just too dark to tell.

Course after course of delicious food was served—stuffed courgette flowers, ultra-fine pasta with softshell crab and a rich dessert of cherries and cream—all accompanied by fine wines from Renzo's cellar. Nicoletta skilfully fired a series of questions at her, some of which

Darcy carefully avoided answering but fortunately Nicoletta enjoyed talking about herself much more. She waxed lyrical about her privileged upbringing in Parioli in Rome, her school in Switzerland and her fluency in four languages. It transpired that she had several dress shops in Rome, none of which she worked in herself.

'You should come visit, Darcy. Get Renzo to buy you something pretty.'

Darcy wondered if that was Nicoletta's way of subtly pointing out that the cheapness of her clothes hadn't gone unnoticed, but if it was, she didn't care. All she could think about right then was being alone with Renzo again as she tried not to focus on time slipping away from them. She returned to their room while he waved their guests goodbye and was naked in bed waiting for him when at last he came in and shut the door behind him.

'You were very good during dinner,' he said, unbuckling the belt of his trousers.

'Good? In what way?'

'A bewitching combination. A little defiant

about your lowly job,' he observed as he stepped out of his boxer shorts. 'And there's no need to look at me that way, Darcy, because it's true. But your heartfelt praise about the property pleased Cristiano very much, though he's always been a sucker for a pretty girl. He's going to keep Gisella, Pasquale and Stefania on, by the way. He told me just before they left for Rome.'

'So all's well that ends well?' she questioned brightly.

'Who said anything about it ending?' he murmured, climbing into bed and pulling her into his arms so that she could feel the hard rod of his arousal pushing against her. 'I thought the night was only just beginning.'

They barely slept a wink. It was as if Renzo was determined to leave her with lasting memories of just what an amazing lover he was as he brought her to climax over and over again. As dawn coated the dark room with a pale daffodil light, Darcy found herself enjoying the erotic spectacle of Renzo's dark head between her thighs, gasping as his tongue cleaved over her exquisitely aroused flesh, until she quivered helplessly around him.

She was slow getting ready the next morning and when she walked into the dining room, Renzo glanced up from his newspaper.

'I need to leave for the airport soon,' she said.

'No, you don't. We'll fly back together on my jet,' he said, pouring her a cup of coffee.

Darcy sat down and reached for a sugar cube. *Start as you mean to go on. And remember that your future does not contain billionaire property tycoons with an endless supply of private transport.*

'Honestly, there's no need,' she said. 'I have a return ticket and I'm perfectly happy to go back on FlyCheap.'

The look he gave her was a mixture of wry, indulgent—but ultimately uncompromising. 'I'm not sending you back on a budget airline, Darcy. You're coming on my jet, with me.'

And if Darcy had thought that travelling in a chauffeur-driven car was the height of luxury, then flying in Renzo's private plane took luxury onto a whole new level. She saw the unmistakable looks of surprise being directed at her by two stewardesses as they were whisked through passport control at Florence airport. Were they thinking she didn't look like Renzo's usual *type*, with her cheap jewellery, her bouncing bosom and the fact that she was clearly out of her comfort zone?

But Darcy didn't care about that either. She was just going to revel in her last few hours with her lover and as soon as he'd dismissed the flight crew she unzipped his jeans. As she pulled down his silk boxers she realised this was the last time she would ever slide her lips over his rocky length and hear his helpless groan as he jerked inside her mouth. The last time he would ever give that low, growling moan as he clamped his hands possessively around her head to anchor her lips to the most sensitive part of his anatomy. Afterwards, he made love to her so slowly that she felt as if she would never come down to earth properly.

But all too soon the flight was over and they

touched down in England where his car was waiting. Darcy hesitated as the driver held open the door for her.

'Could you drop me off at the Tube on the way?'

Renzo frowned, exasperation flattening his lips. 'Darcy, what is this? I'm not dropping you anywhere except home.'

'No. You don't have to do that.'

'I know I don't.' He paused before giving a flicker of a smile. 'You can even invite me in for coffee if you like.'

'Coffee?'

'There you go. You're sounding shocked again.' He shook his head. 'Isn't that what normally happens when a man takes a woman home after the kind of weekend we've just had? I've never even seen where you live.'

'I know you haven't. But you're not interested in my life. You've always made that perfectly clear.'

'Maybe I'm interested now,' he said stubbornly.

And now was too late, she thought. Why

hadn't he done this at the beginning, when it might have meant something? He was behaving with all the predictability of a powerful man who had everything he wanted—his curiosity suddenly aroused by the one thing which was being denied him.

'It's small and cramped and all I can afford, which is why I'm moving to Norfolk,' she said defensively. 'It's about as far removed from where you live as it's possible to be and you'll hate it.'

'Why don't you let me be the judge of that? Unless you're ashamed of it, of course.'

Furiously, she glared at him. 'I'm not *ashamed* of it.'

'Well, then.' He shrugged. 'What's the problem?'

But Darcy's fingers were trembling as she unlocked her front door because she'd never invited *anyone* into this little sanctuary of hers. When you'd shared rooms and space for all of your life—when you'd struggled hard to find some privacy—then something which was completely your own became especially precious. 'Come in, then,' she said ungraciously.

Renzo stepped into the room and the first thing he noticed was that the living, dining and kitchen area were all crammed into the same space. And…his eyes narrowed…was that a narrow *bed* in the corner?

The second thing he noticed was how clean and unbelievably tidy it was—and the minimalist architect in him applauded her total lack of clutter. There were no family photos or knick-knacks. The only embellishment he could see was a cactus in a chrome pot on the window sill and an art deco mirror, which reflected some much-needed extra light into the room. And books. Lots of books. Whole lines of them, neatly arranged in alphabetical order.

He turned to look at her. She had been careful about sitting in the Tuscan sun but, even so, her fair skin had acquired a faint glow. She looked much healthier than she'd done when she'd arrived at Vallombrosa, that was for sure. In fact, she looked so pretty in the yellow dress with blue flowers which she had stubbornly insisted on laundering herself, that he felt his heart miss a beat. And suddenly Renzo knew he wasn't ready to let her go. Not yet. He thought about the way she'd been in his arms last night. The way they'd taken their coffee out onto the terrace at Vallombrosa to stare at the moon, and he'd known a moment of unexpected peace. Why end something before it fizzled out all of its own accord, especially when it still had the potential to give him so much pleasure?

He glanced over towards her neat little kitchenette. 'So… Aren't you going to offer me coffee?'

'I've only got instant, I'm afraid.'

He did his best to repress a shudder. 'Just some water, then.'

He watched as she poured him a glass of tap water—he couldn't remember the last time he'd drunk *that*—and added an ice cube. But when she put the drink down on the table, he didn't touch it. Instead, he fixed her with a steady gaze.

'I've had a good weekend,' he said slowly.

'Me, too. Actually, it was more than good.' She gave him a quick smile. 'Thank you.'

There was a pause. 'Look, this move to Norfolk seems a little…hasty. Why don't you stay in London a bit longer?'

'I told you why—and now you've seen for yourself my reasons. I want to start living differently.'

'I can understand that. But what if I told you I had an apartment you could use—somewhere much bigger and more comfortable than this? What then?'

'What, just like that? Let me guess.' Her emerald gaze bored into him. 'Even if you don't have one available, you'll magically "find" an apartment for me? Browse through your extensive property portfolio or have one of your staff discreetly rent somewhere? Thanks, but no, thanks. I'm not interested, Renzo. I have no desire to be a "kept woman" and fulfilling the stereotype of being a rich man's mistress, even if that's the way I'm currently heading.'

Her stubbornness infuriated him but it also produced another spark of admiration. How could a woman with so little be so proud and spirited and turn down an offer anyone else in her position would have leapt at? Renzo picked up the iced water and sipped it before walking over to the window and looking out at a red-brick wall. He wondered what it must be like to wake up to this view every morning, before putting on some drab uniform to spend the rest of the day carrying trays of food and drink.

He turned round. 'What if I asked you to delay going to Norfolk?'

She raised her eyebrows. 'And why would you do that?'

'Oh, come on, Darcy,' he said softly. 'You may have been an innocent when I bedded you, but you're not so innocent now. I have taught you a great deal—'

'Perhaps there's some kind of certificate I could nominate you for, if it's praise you're after?'

He gave a low laugh, turned on by an insolence he encountered from nobody else. He could see the wariness on her face as he took a step towards her, but he could also see the darkening of her eyes and the sudden stiffness of her body, as if she was using every bit of willpower not to give into what she really wanted. And Renzo knew enough about women to realise that this wasn't over. Not yet.

'It's not praise I want,' he said softly. 'It's you. I'm not ready to let you go.' He reached out to smooth down her riotous curls and felt the kick of lust as he pulled her into his arms. 'What if I told you that I liked the way you were with Cristiano and Nicoletta? That I find you charming in company as well as exquisite in bed and that maybe I'd like to take you out a little more. Why shouldn't we go to the theatre, or a party or two? Perhaps I've been a little selfish keeping you locked away and now I want to show you off to the world.'

'You make it sound as if I've passed some sort of hidden test!' she said indignantly.

'Maybe you have,' came his simple reply.

Darcy was torn, because his words were dangerous. She didn't want him *showing her off to the world*. What if someone remembered her? Someone who knew who she really was? And yet Renzo was only echoing the things she'd been thinking. Things she'd been trying and failing to deny—that she wasn't yet ready to walk away either.

'What if I gave you a key to my apartment?' His voice broke into her thoughts.

'A key?' she echoed.

'Why not? And—just so you know—I don't hand out keys every day of the week. Very few people are given access to my home because I value my privacy very highly.'

'So why me? To what do I owe this huge honour?'

'Because you've never asked me for anything,' he said quietly. 'And nobody's ever done that before.'

Darcy tried telling herself it was just another example of a powerful man being intrigued by the unfamiliar. But surely it was more than that. Wasn't the giving of a key—no matter how temporary—a sign that he *trusted* her? And wasn't trust the most precarious yet most precious thing in the world, especially considering Renzo's lack of it where women were concerned?

She licked her lips, tempted beyond reason, but really—when she stopped to think about it—what was holding her back? She'd escaped her northern life and left that dark world behind as she'd carved out a new identity for herself. She'd been completely underqualified and badly educated but night classes had helped make up for her patchy schooling—and her sunny disposition meant she'd been able to find waitressing work whenever she had put her mind to it. She wasn't quite sure where she wanted to be but she knew she was on her way. And who would possibly remember her after all this time? She'd left Manchester for London when she was sixteen and that was a long time ago. Didn't she deserve a little fun while she had the chance?

He was watching her closely and Darcy was

savvy enough to realise her hesitation was turning him on. Yet she wasn't playing games with him. Her indecision was genuine. She really *was* trying to give him up, only it wasn't as easy as she'd imagined. She was beginning to suspect that Renzo Sabatini was becoming an addiction and that should have set off every alarm bell in her body because it didn't matter if it was drink or drugs or food—or in this case a man—addictions were dangerous. She knew that. Her personal history had taught her that in the bleakest way possible.

But now he was pulling her against him and she could feel all that hard promise shimmering beneath the surface of his muscular body. Enveloped by his arms, she found herself wanting to sink further into his powerful embrace, wanting to hold on to this brief sense of comfort and safety.

'Say yes, Darcy,' he urged softly, his breath warm against her lips. 'Take my key and be my lover for a little while longer.'

His hand was on her breast and her knees were

starting to buckle and Darcy knew then that she wasn't going to resist him anytime soon.

'Okay,' she said, closing her eyes as he began to ruck up her dress. 'I'll stay for a bit longer.'

CHAPTER FIVE

THE LIMOUSINE SLID to a halt outside the Granchester Hotel as Renzo was caressing Darcy's thigh and he found himself thinking that she'd never looked more beautiful than she did tonight. Hungrily, he ran his gaze over the emerald shimmer of her gown, thinking that for once she looked like a billionaire's mistress.

He gave an almost imperceptive shake of his head. Didn't she realise that, despite her initial reluctance, she was entitled to a mistress's perks? He'd tried to persuade her that it would be easier all round if she enjoyed *all* the benefits of his wealth and made herself more available to him by giving up her lowly job, but she had stubbornly refused to comply. She'd told him he should be grateful she was no longer working in the nightclub and he had growled at the thought of her curvy body poured into that tight black satin while men drooled over her.

But tonight, a small victory had been won. For once she'd accepted his offer of a custom-made gown to wear to the prestigious ball he was holding in aid of his charity foundation, though it had taken some persuasion. His mouth flattened because where once her stubborn independence had always excited him, her independence was starting to rankle, as was her determination to carry on waiting tables even though it took up so much of her time.

'The princess is supposed to be smiling when she goes to the ball,' he observed wryly, feeling her sequin-covered thigh tense beneath his fingers. 'Not looking as if she's walking towards her own execution.'

'But I'm not a princess, Renzo. I'm a waitress who happens to be wearing a gown which cost as much as I earn in three months.' She touched her fingertips to one of the mother-of-pearl clips which gleamed like milky rainbows against the abundant red curls. 'If you must know, I feel like Cinderella.'

'Ah, but the difference is that your clothes will not turn into rags at midnight, *cara*. When the witching hour comes you will be doing something far more pleasurable than travelling home in a pumpkin. So wipe that concerned look from your face and give me that beautiful smile instead.'

Feeling like a puppet, Darcy did as he asked, flashing a bright grin as someone rushed forward to open the car door for her. Carefully, she picked up the fishtail skirt of her emerald gown and stepped onto the pavement in her terrifyingly high shoes, thinking how quickly you could get used to being driven around like this and having people leap to attention simply because you were in the company of one of the world's most powerful men. What was not so easy was getting rid of the growing feeling of anxiety which had been gnawing away inside her for weeks now—a sick, queasy feeling which just wouldn't shift.

Because she was starting to realise that she was stuck. Stuck in some awful limbo. Living in a strange, parallel world which wasn't real and locked into it by her inability to walk away from the only man who had ever been able to make her feel like a real woman.

The trouble was that things had changed and they were changing all the time. Why hadn't she realised that agreeing to accept the key to his apartment would strengthen the connection between them and make it even harder for her to sever her ties with him? It had made things... *complicated*. She didn't want her heart to thunder every time she looked at him or her body to melt with instant desire. Her worst fears had been realised and Renzo Sabatini had become her addiction. She ran her tongue over her lips. She knew he was bad for her yet she couldn't seem to give him up.

Sometimes she found herself longing for him to tire of her and kick *her* out since she didn't have the strength to end it herself. Wouldn't such a move force her to embrace the new life in Norfolk which she'd done absolutely nothing about—not since the day he'd given her his key and then made her come on the narrow bed in her humble bedsit, which these days she only ever visited when Renzo was away on business?

She could hear him telling his driver to take the rest of the night off and that they'd get a taxi home when the ball was over and she wished he wouldn't be so thoughtful with his staff. No wonder they all thought the world of him. But Darcy didn't need any more reasons to like him. Hadn't it been easier not to let her heart become involved when their affair had been more low-key, rather than this new-found openness with trips to the opera and theatre and VIP balls?

And now he was taking her arm and leading her towards the red-carpeted marble staircase where the paparazzi were clustered. She'd known they were going to be there, but had also known she couldn't possibly avoid them. And anyway, they weren't going to be looking at *her*. They would be far too busy focussing on the Hollywood actress who was wearing the most revealing dress Darcy had ever seen, or the married co-star she was rumoured to be having an affair with.

Flashbulbs exploded to light up the warm night and although Darcy quickly tried to turn her head away, the press weren't having any of it. And wasn't that a TV camera zooming in on her? She wondered why she had let the dress designer put these stupid clips in her hair which meant she couldn't hide behind the usual comforting curtain of her curls. This was the most high-profile event they'd attended as a couple but there had been no way of getting out of it—not when it was Renzo's foundation and he was the man who'd organised it.

She felt like a fox on the run as they entered the ballroom but the moment she was swallowed up by all that glittering splendour, she calmed down. The gilded room had been decked out with giant sprays of pink-and-white cherry blossoms, symbolising the hope which Renzo's foundation brought to suffering children in war-torn areas of the world. Tall, guttering candles gave the place a fairy-tale feel. On a raised dais, a string quartet was playing and the exquisitely dressed guests were mingling in small chattering groups. It was the fanciest event she'd ever attended and dinner had been prepared by a clutch of award-winning chefs. But the moment the first rich course was placed in front of her, Darcy's stomach did an intricate kind of twist, which meant she merely pushed the food around her plate and tried not to look at it. At least Renzo didn't notice or chide her for her lack of appetite as he might normally have done—he was too busy talking to fundraisers and donors and being photographed next to the diamond necklace which was the star lot for the night's auction.

But after disappearing into one of the restrooms, where a splash of her face with cold water made her queasiness shift, Darcy became determined to enjoy herself. *Stop living so fearfully*, she chided herself as she chatted attentively whenever she was introduced to someone new and rose eagerly to her feet when Renzo asked her to dance. And that bit felt like heaven. His cheek was warm against hers and her body fitted so snugly into his that she felt like one of those salt and pepper shakers you sometimes found in old-fashioned tea rooms—as if they were made to be together. But they weren't. Of course they weren't.

She knew this couldn't continue. She'd been seduced into staying but if she stayed much longer she was going to have to tell him the truth. Open up about her past. Confess to being the daughter of a junkie and all the other stuff which went with it. He would probably end their affair immediately and a swift, clean cut might just be the best thing. She would be heartbroken for a while of course, but she would get over it because you could get over just about anything if you worked at it. It would be better than forcing herself to walk away and having to live with the stupid spark of hope that maybe it *could* have worked.

'So… How is the most beautiful woman in the

room?' He bent his head to her ear. 'You seem to be enjoying yourself.'

She closed her eyes and inhaled his sultry masculine scent. 'I am.'

'Not as bad as you thought it was going to be?'

'Not nearly so bad.'

'Think you might like to come to something like this again in the future?'

'I *could* be persuaded.'

He smiled. 'Then let's go and sit down. The auction is about to begin.'

The auctioneer stepped onto the stage and began to auction off the different lots which had been donated as prizes. A holiday in Mauritius, a box at the opera and a tour of Manchester United football ground all went under the hammer for eye-watering amounts, and then the diamond necklace was brought out to appreciative murmurs.

Darcy listened as the bidding escalated, only vaguely aware of Renzo lifting a careless finger from time to time. But suddenly everyone was clapping and looking at *them* and she realised that Renzo had successfully bid for the neck-lace and the auctioneer's assistant had handed it to him and he was putting it on *her* neck. She was aware of every eye in the room on them as he fixed the heavy clasp in place and she was aware of the dazzle of the costly gems.

'In truth you should wear emeralds to match your eyes,' he murmured. 'But since diamonds were the only thing on offer they will have to do. What do you think, *cara*?'

Darcy couldn't get rid of the sudden lump in her throat. It felt like a noose. The stones were heavy and the metal was cold. But there was no time to protest because cameras were flashing again and this time they were all directed at her. Sweat beaded her forehead and she felt dizzy, only able to breathe normally when the rumour went round that the Hollywood star was exiting through the kitchens and the press pack left the ballroom to follow her.

Darcy turned to Renzo, her fingertips touch-ing the unfamiliar stones. 'You do realise I can't possibly accept this?' she questioned hoarsely.

'And you do realise that I am not going to let you give it back? Your tastes are far too modest for a woman in your position. You are the lover of a very wealthy man, Darcy, and I want you to wear it. I want you to have some pretty jewels for all the pleasure you've given me.'

His voice had dipped into a silken caress, which usually would have made her want to melt, but he made it sound like payment for services rendered. Was that how he saw it? Darcy's smile felt as if someone had stitched it onto her face with a rusty needle. Shouldn't she at least try to look as a woman *should* look when a man had just bought something this valuable? And wasn't she in danger of being a hypocrite? After all, she had a key to his Belgravia home—wasn't that just a short step to accepting his jewels? What about the designer dress she was wearing tonight, and the expensive shoes? He'd bought those for her, hadn't he?

Something like fear clutched at her heart and she knew she couldn't put it off any longer. She was going to have to come clean about her mum and the children's home and all the other sordid stuff.

So tell him. Explain your aversion to accepting gifts and bring this whole crazy relationship to a head, because at least that will end the uncertainty and you'll know where you stand.

But in the car he kissed her and when they reached the apartment he kissed her some more, unclipping the diamond choker and dropping it onto a table in the sitting room as casually as if it had been made of paste. His hands were trembling as he undressed her and so were hers. He made love to her on one of the sofas and then he carried her into the bedroom and did it all over again—and who would want to talk about the past at a moment like that?

They made love most of the night and because she'd asked for a day off after the ball, Darcy slept late next morning. When she eventually woke, it was getting on for noon and Renzo had left for the office long ago. *And still she hadn't told him.* She showered and dressed but her queasiness had returned and she could only manage some mint tea for breakfast. The morning papers had been delivered and, with a growing sense of nervousness, she flicked through the pages until she found the column which listed society events. And there she was in all her glory—in her mermaid dress of green sequins, the row of fiery white diamonds glittering at her throat, with Renzo standing just behind her, a hint of possessiveness in the sexy smile curving his lips.

She stood up abruptly, telling herself she was being paranoid. Who was going to see, or, more important, to *care* that she was in the wretched paper?

The morning slipped away. She went for a walk, bought a bag of oranges to put through the squeezer and was just nibbling on a piece of dry toast when the doorbell rang and Darcy frowned. It never rang when Renzo wasn't here—and not just because his wasn't a lifestyle where people made spontaneous visits. He'd meant what he said about guarding his privacy; his home really was his fortress. People just didn't come round.

She pressed the button on the intercom.

'Yes?'

'Is that Darcy Denton?' It was a male voice with a broad Manchester accent.

'Who is this?' she questioned sharply.

'An old friend of yours.' There was a pause. 'Drake Bradley.'

For a minute Darcy thought she might pass out. She thought about pretending to be someone else—the housekeeper perhaps. Or just cutting the connection while convincing herself that she didn't have to speak to anyone—let alone Drake Bradley. But the bully who had ruled the roost in the children's home had never been the kind of person to take no for an answer. If she refused to speak to him she could imagine him settling down to wait until Renzo got home and she just imagined what he might have to say to him. Shivering, she stared at her pale reflection in the hall mirror. What was it they said? Keep your friends close but your enemies closer.

'What do you want?'

'Just a few minutes of your time. Surely you can spare that, Darcy.'

Telling herself it was better to brazen it out, Darcy pressed the buzzer, her heart beating out a primitive tattoo as she opened the door to find Drake standing there—a sly expression on his pockmarked face. A decade had made his hair recede, but she would have recognised him immediately and her blood ran cold as the sight of him took her back to a life she'd thought she'd left for ever.

'What do you want?' she asked again.

'That's not much of a welcome, is it? What's the matter, Darcy? Aren't you going to invite me in? Surely you're not ashamed of me?'

But the awful thing was that she *was*. She'd moved on a lot since that turbulent period when their lives had merged and clashed, yet Drake looked as if he'd been frozen in time. Wearing clothes which swamped his puny frame, he had oil beneath his fingernails and on the fingers of his left hand were the letters *H, A, T, E. You have no right to judge him*, she told herself. He was simply another survivor from the shipwreck of their youth. Surely she owed him a little hospitality when she'd done so well for herself.

She could smell stale tobacco and the faint underlying odour of sweat as she opened the door wider and he brushed past her. He followed her into the enormous sitting room and she wondered if he was seeing the place as she had seen it the first time she'd been here, when she'd marvelled at the space and light and cleanliness. And, of course, the view.

'Wow.' He pursed his lips together and whistled as he stared out at the whispering treetops of Eaton Square. 'You've certainly landed on your feet, Darcy.'

'Are you going to tell me why you're here?'

His weasel eyes narrowed. 'Not even going to offer me a drink? It's a hot day outside. I could murder a drink.'

Darcy licked her lips. *Don't aggravate him. Tolerate him for a few minutes and then he'll go.* 'What would you like?'

'Got a beer?'

'Sure.'

Her underlying nausea seemed to intensify as Darcy went to the kitchen to fetch him a beer. When she returned he refused her offer of a glass and began to glug greedily from the bottle.

'How did you find me?' she asked, once he had paused long enough to take a breath.

He put the bottle down on a table. 'Saw you on the news last night, walking into that big hotel. Yeah. On TV. Couldn't believe my eyes at first. I thought to myself, that can't be Darcy Denton—daughter of one of Manchester's best known hookers. Not on the arm of some rich dude like Sabatini. So I headed along to the hotel to see for myself and hung around until your car arrived. I'm good at hanging around in the shadows, I am.' He smiled slyly. 'I overheard your man giving the address to the taxi driver so I thought I'd come and pay you a visit to catch up on old times. See for myself how you've come up in the world.'

Darcy tried to keep her voice light. To act as if her heart weren't pounding so hard it felt as if it might burst right out of her chest. 'You still haven't told me what you want.'

His smile grew calculating. 'You've landed on your feet, Darcy. Surely it's no big deal to help out an old friend?'

'Are you asking for money?' she said.

He sneered. 'What do you think?'

She thought plenty but nothing she'd want *him* to hear. She thought about how much cash she had squirrelled away in her bank account. She'd amassed funds since she'd been with Renzo because he wouldn't let her pay for anything. *But it was still a pitiful amount by most people's standards, and besides...if you gave in to blackmail once then you opened up the floodgates.*

And she didn't need to give into blackmail because hadn't she already decided to tell Renzo about her past? This might be the push she needed to see if he still wanted her when he discovered who she really was. Her mouth dried. Dared she take that risk?

She had no choice.

Drawing her shoulders back, she looked

straight into Drake's shifty eyes. 'You're not getting any money from me,' she said quietly. 'I'd like you to leave and not bother coming back.'

His lip curled and then he shrugged. 'Have it your own way, Darcy.'

Of course, if she'd thought it through properly, she might have wondered why he obeyed her quite so eagerly...

Renzo's eyes narrowed as the man with the pockmarked face shoved his way past, coming out of *his* private elevator as if he had every right to do so. His frown deepened. Had he been making some kind of delivery? Surely not, dressed like *that*? He stood for a moment watching his retreating back, instinct alerting him to a danger he didn't quite understand. But it was enough to cast a shadow over a deliciously high mood which had led to him leaving work early—something which had caused his secretary to blink at him in astonishment.

In truth, Renzo had been pretty astonished himself. Taking a half-day off wasn't the way he usually operated, but he had wanted to spend the rest of the afternoon with Darcy. Getting into bed with her. Running his fingers through her silky riot of curls. Losing himself deep in her tight, tight body with his mouth on her breast. Maybe even telling her how good she made him feel. Plus he'd received an urgent message reminding him that he needed to insure the necklace he'd spent a fortune on last night.

After watching the man leave the building, Renzo took the penthouse elevator where the faint smell of tobacco and beer still tainted the air. He unlocked the door to his apartment just as Darcy tore out of the sitting room. But the trouble was she didn't look like the Darcy of this morning's smouldering fantasies, when somehow he'd imagined arriving home to see her clad in that black satin basque and matching silk stockings he'd recently bought. Not only was she wearing jeans and a baggy shirt—her face was paler than usual and her eyes looked huge and haunted with something which looked like guilt. Now, why was that? he wondered.

'Renzo!' she exclaimed, raking a handful of bouncing red curls away from her forehead and giving him an uncertain smile. 'I wasn't expecting you.'

'So I see.' He put his briefcase on the hall table. 'Who was the man I saw leaving?'

'The man?' she questioned, but he could hear the sudden quaver in her voice.

Definitely guilt, he thought grimly.

'The man I met coming down in the elevator. Bad skin. Bad smell. Who was he, Darcy?'

Darcy met the cool accusation in Renzo's eyes and knew she had run out of reasons not to tell him.

'I need to talk to you,' she said.

He didn't respond straight away, just walked into the sitting room leaving her to follow him, her senses alerted to the sudden tension in his body and the forbidding set of his shoulders. Usually, he pulled her into his arms and kissed all the breath out of her when he arrived home but today he hadn't even touched her. And when he turned around, Darcy was shocked by the cold expression on his face.

'So talk,' he said.

She felt like someone who'd been put on stage in front of a vast audience and told to play a part she hadn't learnt. Because she'd never spoken about this before, not to anyone. She'd buried it so deep it was almost inaccessible. But she needed to access it now, before his irritation grew any deeper.

'He's someone I was in care with.'

'In care?'

She nodded. 'That's what they call it in England, although it's a bit of a misnomer because you don't actually get much in the way of care. I lived in a children's home in the north for most of my childhood.'

His black eyes narrowed. 'What happened to your parents?'

Darcy could feel a bead of sweat trickling its way down her back. Here it was. The question which separated most normal people from the unlucky few. The question which made you feel a freak no matter which way you answered it. Was it any wonder she'd spent her life trying to avoid having to do so?

And yet didn't it demonstrate the shallowness of her relationship with Renzo that in all the time she'd known him—this was the first time he'd actually asked? Dead parents had been more than enough information for him. He hadn't been the type of person to quiz her about her favourite memory or how she'd spent her long-ago Christmases.

'I'm illegitimate,' she said baldly. 'I don't know who my father was and neither did my mother. And she… Well, for a lot of my childhood, she wasn't considered fit to be able to take care of me.'

'Why not?'

'She had…' She hesitated. 'She had a drug problem. She was a junkie.'

He let out a long breath and Darcy found herself searching his face for some kind of understanding, some shred of compassion for a situation which had been out of her control. But his expression remained like ice. His black eyes were stony as they skimmed over her, looking at her as if it was the first time he'd seen her and not liking what they saw.

'Why didn't you tell me any of this before?'

'Because you didn't ask. And you didn't ask because you didn't want to know!' she exclaimed. 'You made that very clear. We haven't had the kind of relationship where we talked about stuff like this. You just wanted…sex.'

She waited for him to deny it. To tell her that there had been more to it than that—and Darcy realised she was already thinking of their relationship in the past tense. But he didn't deny it. His sudden closed look made his features appear shuttered as he walked over to the table near where he'd undressed her last night and her heart missed a beat as she saw him looking down at the polished surface, on which stood a lamp and nothing else.

Nothing else.

It took a moment for her to register the significance of this and that moment came when he lifted his black gaze to hers and slanted her an unfathomable look. 'Where's the necklace?' he questioned softly.

Darcy's mind raced. In the heat of everything that had happened, she'd forgotten about the diamond necklace he'd bought last night for her at the auction. She vaguely remembered the dazzle of the costly gems as he'd dropped them onto the table, but his hands had been all over her at the time and it had blotted out everything except the magic of his touch. Had she absent-mindedly tidied it away when she was picking up her clothes this morning? No. It had definitely been there when…

Fear and horror clamped themselves around her suddenly racing heart.

When…

Drake! Her throat dried as she remembered leaving him alone in the room while she went to fetch him a beer. Remembered the way he'd hurriedly left after his half-hearted attempt at blackmail. Had Drake stolen the necklace?

Of course he had.

'I don't—'

His voice was like steel. 'Did your friend take it?'

'He's not—'

'What's the matter, Darcy?' Contemptuously, he cut through her protest. 'Did I arrive home unexpectedly and spoil your little plan?'

'What *plan*?'

'Oh, come on. Isn't this what's known in the trade as a scam? To rob me. To cheat on me.'

Darcy stared at him in disbelief. 'You can't honestly believe that?'

'Can't I? Perhaps it's the first clear-headed thought I've had in a long time, now that I'm no longer completely mesmerised by your pale skin and witchy eyes.' He shook his head like a man who was emerging from a deep coma. 'Now I'm beginning to wonder whether something like this was in your sights all along.'

Darcy felt foreboding icing her skin. 'What are you talking about?' she whispered.

'I've often wondered,' he said harshly, 'what you might give a man who has everything. Another house, or a faster car?' He shook his head. 'No. Material wealth means nothing when you have plenty. But innocence—ah! Now that is a very different thing.'

'You're not making sense.'

'Think about it. What is a woman's most prized possession, *cara mia*?' The Italian words of endearment dripped like venom from his lips. '*Sì*. I can see from your growing look of comprehension that you are beginning to understand. Her virginity. Precious and priceless and the biggest bartering tool in the market. And hasn't it always been that way?'

'Renzo.' She could hear the desperation in her voice now but she couldn't seem to keep it at bay. 'You don't mean that.'

'Sometimes I would ask myself,' he continued, still in that same flat tone, 'why someone as beautiful and sensual as you—someone hard-up and working in a dead-end job—hadn't taken a rich lover to catapult herself out of her poverty before I came along.'

Desperation morphed into indignation. 'You mean…use a man as a meal ticket?'

'Why are you looking so shocked—or is that simply an expression you've managed to perfect over the years? Isn't that what every woman does ultimately—feed like a leech off a man?' His black gaze roved over her. 'But not you. At least, not initially. Did you decide to deny yourself pleasure—to look at the long game rather than the lure of instant gratification? To hold out for the richest man available, who just happened to be me—someone who was blown away by your extraordinary beauty coupled with an innocence I'd never experienced before?' He gave a cynical smile. 'But you were cunning, too. I see that now. For a cynic like me, a spirited show of independence was pretty much guaranteed to wear me down. So you refused my gifts. You bought cheap clothes and budget airline tickets while valiantly offering me the money you'd saved. What a touching gesture—the hard-up waitress offering the jaded architect a handful of cash.

And I fell for it—hook, line and sinker! I was sucked in by your stubbornness and your pride.'

'It wasn't like that!' she defended fiercely.

'You must have thought you'd hit the jackpot when I gave you the key to my flat and bought you a diamond necklace,' he bit out. 'Just as I did when you gave yourself so willingly to me and I discovered you were a virgin. I allowed my ego to be flattered and to blind myself to the truth. How could I have *been* so blind?'

Darcy felt her head spin and that horrible queasy feeling came washing over her again, in giant waves. This couldn't be happening. In a minute she would wake up and the nightmare would be over. But it wouldn't, would it? She was living her nightmare and the proof was right in front of her eyes. In the midst of her confusion and hurt she saw the look of something like satisfaction on Renzo's face. She remembered him mentioning his parents' divorce and how bitterly he'd said that women could never be trusted. Was he somehow pleased that his prejudices had been reinforced and he could continue thinking that way? Yes, he was, she realised. He *wanted* to believe badly of her.

She made one last attempt because wasn't there still some tiny spark of hope which existed—a part which didn't want to let him go? 'None of that—'

'Save your lying words because I don't want to hear them. You're only upset because I came home early and found you out. How were you going to explain the absence of the necklace, Darcy?' he bit out. 'A "burglary" while you were out shopping? Shifting the blame onto one of the people who service these apartments?'

'You think I'd be capable of that?'

'I don't know what you're capable of, do I?' he said coldly. 'I just want you to listen to what I'm going to say. I'm going out and by the time I get back I want you out of here. Every last trace of you. I don't ever want to see your face again. Understand? And for what it's worth— and I'm sure you realise it's a lot—you can keep the damned necklace.'

'You're not going to go to the police?'

'And advertise exactly what kind of woman my girlfriend really is and the kind of low-life company she keeps? That wouldn't exactly do wonders for my reputation, would it? Do whatever you'd planned to do with it all along.' He paused and his mouth tightened as his black gaze swept down over her body. 'Think of it as payment for services rendered. A clean-break payoff, if you like.'

It was the final straw. Nausea engulfed her. She could feel her knees buckling and a strange roaring in her head. Her hand reached out to grab at the nearest chair but she missed and Darcy felt herself sliding helplessly to the ground, until her cheek was resting on the smooth silk of the Persian rug and her eyes were level with his ankles and the handmade Italian shoes which swum in and out of focus.

His voice seemed to come from a long way off. 'And you can spare me the histrionics, Darcy. They won't make me change my mind.'

'Who's asking you to change your mind?' she managed, from beneath gritted teeth.

She saw his shadow move as he stepped over her and a minute later she heard the sound of the front door slamming shut.

And after that, thankfully, she passed out.

CHAPTER SIX

'YOU CAN'T GO ON like this, Darcy, you really can't.'

The midwife sounded both kind and stern and Darcy was finding it difficult keeping her lips from wobbling. Because stern she could handle. Stern was something she was used to. It was the kindness which got to her every time, which made her want to cover her face with her hands and howl like a wounded animal. And she couldn't afford to break down, because if she did—she might never put herself back together again.

Her hand slipped down to her belly. 'You're sure my baby's okay?' she questioned for the fourth time.

'Your baby's fine. Take a look at the scan and see. A little bit on the small side perhaps, but thriving. Unlike you. You're wearing yourself out,' continued the midwife, a frown creasing her plump face. 'You're working too hard and not eating properly, by the look of you.'

'Honestly, I'll try harder. I'll…I'll cut down on my hours at work and start eating more vegetables,' said Darcy as she rolled up her sleeve. And she would. She would do whatever it took because all she could think about was that her baby was safe. *Safe.* Relief washed over her in almost tangible waves as the terror she'd experienced during that noisy ambulance ride began to recede. 'Does that mean I can go home?'

'I wanted to talk to you about that. I'm not very happy about letting you go anywhere,' said the midwife. 'Unless you've got somebody who can be there for you.'

Darcy tried not to flinch. She supposed she could pretend she had a caring mother or protective sister or even—ha, ha, ha—a loving husband. But that would be irresponsible. Because it wasn't just her she was looking out for any more. There was a baby growing inside her. Her throat constricted. Renzo's baby.

She tried not to tense up as the midwife began to measure her blood pressure. Things hadn't been easy since Renzo had left her lying on the floor of his Belgravia apartment, accusing her of histrionics before slamming the door behind him. But Darcy's unexpected faint hadn't been caused by grief or anger, though it had taken a couple of weeks more to realise why a normally healthy young woman should have passed out for no apparent reason. It was when she'd found herself retching in the bathroom that she'd worked it out for herself. And then, of course, she wondered how she could have been so stupid to have not seen it before. It all added up. But her general queasiness and lack of appetite—even the lateness of her period—had been easy to overlook after Renzo had dumped her.

Of course she'd hoped. Hoped like mad she'd somehow got her dates muddled, but deep down she'd known she hadn't because the brand-new aching in her breasts had told her so. She'd gone out to buy a pregnancy kit and the result had come as a shock but no great surprise. Heart racing, she'd sat on the floor of her bathroom in Norfolk staring at the blue line, wondering who to tell. But even if she *had* made some friends in her new home town, she knew there was only one person she *could* tell. Tears of injustice had stung her eyes. The man who thought she was a thief and a con woman. Who had looked at her with utter contempt in his eyes. But that was irrelevant. Renzo's opinion of her didn't really matter—all that mattered was that she let him know he was going to be a father.

If only it had been that easy. Every call she'd made had gone straight through to voicemail and she'd been reluctant to leave him her news in a message. So she'd telephoned his office and been put through to one of his secretaries for another humiliating experience. She'd felt as if the woman was reading from a script as she'd politely told her that Signor Sabatini was unavailable for the foreseeable future. She remembered the beads of sweat which had broken out on her forehead as she'd asked his secretary to have him ring her back. And her lack of surprise when he hadn't.

'Why…?' Her voice faltered as she looked up into the midwife's lined face. 'Why do I have to have someone at home with me?'

'Because twenty-eight weeks is a critical time in a woman's pregnancy and you need to take extra care. Surely there must be someone you could ask. Who's the baby's father, Darcy?'

Briefly, Darcy closed her eyes. So this was it. The point where she really needed to be self-sacrificing and ignore pride and ego and instinct. For the first time in a long time images of Renzo's darkly rugged face swam into her mind, because she'd been trying her best not to think about him. To forget that chiselled jaw and lean body and the way he used to put on those sexy, dark-rimmed glasses while he was working on plans for one of his buildings. To a large extent she had succeeded in forgetting him, banishing memories of how it used to feel to wake up in his arms, as she concentrated on her new job at the local café.

But now she must appeal for help from the man who had made her feel so worthless—whose final gesture had taken her back to those days when people used to look down their noses at her and not believe a word she said. She told herself it didn't matter what Renzo thought when the hospital phoned him. That she didn't care if he considered her a no-good thief because she knew the truth and that was all that mattered. Her hand reached down to lie protectively over her belly, her fingers curving over its hard swell. She would do anything to protect the life of this unborn child.

Anything.

And right at the top of that list was the need to be strong. She'd been strong at the beginning of the affair and it had protected her against pain. She'd done her usual thing of keeping her emotions on ice and had felt good about herself. Even during that weekend when he'd taken her to Tuscany and hinted at his trust issues and the fickleness of women, she had still kept her feelings buried deep. She hadn't expected anything—which was why it had come as such a surprise to her when they'd got back to England and he'd offered her the key to his apartment.

Had that been when she'd first let her guard down and her feelings had started to change? Or had she just got carried away with her new position in life? Her plans to move to Norfolk had been quietly shelved because she'd enjoyed being his mistress, hadn't she? She'd enjoyed going to that fancy ball with him, when—after her initial flurry of nerves—she'd waltzed in that cherry blossom–filled ballroom in his arms. And if things hadn't gone so badly wrong and Drake hadn't turned up, it probably wouldn't have taken long for her to get used to wearing Renzo's jewels either.

She'd been a fool and it was time to stop acting like a fool.

Never again would she be whimpering Darcy Denton, pleading with her cruel Italian lover to believe her. He could think what the hell he liked as long as he helped take care of her baby.

She opened her eyes and met the questioning look in the midwife's eyes.

'His name is Renzo Sabatini,' she said.

Feeling more impotent than he'd felt in years, Renzo paced up and down the sterile hospital corridor, oblivious to the surreptitious looks from the passing nurses. For a man unused to waiting, he couldn't believe he was being forced to bide his time until the ward's official visiting hours and he got the distinct impression that any further pleas to be admitted early would by vetoed by the dragon-like midwife he'd spoken to earlier, who had made no secret of her disapproval. With a frown on her face she'd told him that his girlfriend was overworked and underfed and clearly on the breadline. Her gaze had swept over him, taking in his dark suit, silk tie and handmade Italian shoes and he could see from her eyes that she was sizing up his worth. He was being judged, he realised—and he didn't like to be judged. Nor put in the role of an absentee father-to-be who refused to accept his responsibilities.

But amid all this confusion was a shimmering of something he couldn't understand, an emotion which licked like fire over his cold heart and was confusing the life out of him. Furiously, he forced himself to concentrate on facts. To get his head around the reason he was here—why he'd been driven to some remote area of Norfolk on what had felt like the longest journey of his life. And then he needed to decide what he was going to do about it. His head spun as his mind went over and over the unbelievable fact.

Darcy was going to have a baby.

His baby.

His mouth thinned.

Or so she said.

Eventually he was shown into the side room of a ward where she lay on a narrow hospital bed—her bright hair the only thing of colour in an all-white environment. Her face was as bleached as the bed sheets and her eyes were both wary and hostile as she looked at him. He remembered the last time he'd seen her. When she'd slid to the floor and he had just let her lie there and now his heart clenched with guilt because she looked so damned fragile lying propped up against that great bank of pillows.

'Darcy,' he said carefully.

She looked as if she had been sucking on a lemon as she spoke. 'You came.'

'I had no choice.'

'Don't lie,' she snapped. 'Of course you did! You could have just ignored the call from the hospital, just like you've ignored all my other calls up until now.'

He wanted to deny it but how could he when it was true? 'Yes,' he said flatly. 'I could.'

'You let my calls go through to voicemail,' she accused.

Letting out a breath, Renzo slowly nodded. At the time it had seemed the only sane solution. He hadn't wanted to risk speaking to her, because hadn't he worried he would cave in and take her back, even if it was for only one night?

Because after she'd gone he hadn't been able to forget her as easily as he'd imagined, even though she had betrayed his trust in her. Even when he thought about the missing diamonds and the way she'd allowed that creep to enter his home—that still didn't erase her from his mind. He'd started to wonder whether he'd made a big mistake and whether he should give her another chance, but pride and a tendency to think the worst about women had stopped him acting on it. He'd known that 50 per cent of relationships didn't survive—so why go for one which had the odds stacked against it from the start? Yet she'd flitted in and out of his mind in a way which no amount of hard work or travelling had been able to fix.

'Guilty as charged,' he said evenly.

'And you told your secretary not to put me through to you.'

'She certainly would have put you through if she'd known the reason you were ringing. Why the hell didn't you tell her?'

'Are you out of your mind? Is that how you like

to see your women, Renzo?' she demanded. 'To have them plead and beg and humiliate themselves? *Yes, I know he doesn't want to speak to me, but could you please tell him I'm expecting his baby?* Or would you rather I had hung around outside the Sabatini building, waiting for the big boss to leave work so I could grab your elbow and break my news to you on a busy London street? Maybe I should have gone to the papers and sold them a story saying that my billionaire boyfriend was denying paternity!'

'Darcy,' he said, and now his voice had gentled. 'I'm sorry I accused you of stealing the necklace.'

Belligerently, she raised her chin. 'Just not sorry enough to seek me out to tell me that before?'

He thought how tough she was—with a sudden inner steeliness which seemed so at odds with her fragile exterior. 'I jumped to the wrong conclusions,' he said slowly, 'because I'm very territorial about my space.' But he had been territorial about her, too, hadn't he? And old-fashioned enough to want to haul that complete stranger up against the wall and demand to know what he'd been doing alone with her. 'Look, this isn't getting us anywhere. You shouldn't be getting distressed.'

'What, in my *condition*?'

'Yes. Exactly that. In your condition. You're pregnant.' The unfamiliar word sounded foreign on his lips and once again he felt the lick of something painful in his heart. She looked so damned vulnerable lying there that his instinct was to take her in his arms and cradle her—if the emerald blaze in her eyes weren't defying him to dare try. 'The midwife says you need somebody to take care of you.'

Darcy started biting her lip, terrified that the stupid tears pricking at the backs of her eyes would start pouring down her cheeks. She hated the way this new-found state of hers was making her emotions zigzag all over the place, so she hardly recognised herself any more. She was supposed to be staying strong only it wasn't easy when Renzo was sounding so...*protective*. His words were making her yearn for something she'd never had, nor expected to have. She found herself looking up into his darkly handsome face and a wave of longing swept over her. She wanted to reach out her arms and ask him to hold her. She wanted him to keep her safe.

And she had to stop thinking that way. It wasn't a big deal that he'd apologised for something he needed to apologise for. She needed to remind herself that Renzo Sabatini wouldn't even *be* here if it weren't for the baby.

'It's the unborn child which needs taking care of,' she said coldly. 'Not me.'

His gaze drifted down to the black-and-white image which was lying on top of the locker. 'May I?'

She shrugged, trying to ignore the tug at her heart as he picked it up to study it, as engrossed as she had ever seen him. 'Suit yourself.'

And when at last he raised his head and looked at her, there was a look on his face she'd never seen before. Was that wonder or joy which had transformed his dark and shuttered features?

'It's a boy,' he said slowly.

She'd forgotten about his precise eye and attention to detail, instantly able to determine the sex of the baby where most men might have seen nothing but a confusing composition of black and white.

'It is,' she agreed.

'A son,' he said, looking down at it again.

The possessive way his voice curled round the word scared her. It took her back to the days when she'd been hauled in front of social services who'd been trying to place her in a stable home. Futile attempts which had lasted only as long as it took her mother to discover her new address and turn up on the doorstep at midnight, high on drugs and demanding money in 'payment' for her daughter. What had those interviews taught her? That you should confront the great big elephant in the room, instead of letting it trample over you when you weren't looking.

'Aren't you going to ask whether it's yours?' she said. 'Isn't that what usually happens in this situation?'

He lifted his gaze and now his eyes were flinty. 'Is it?'

Angered by the fact he'd actually *asked* despite her having pushed him into it, Darcy hesitated—tempted by a possibility which lay before her. If she told him he wasn't the father would he disappear and let her get on with the rest of her life? No, of course not. Renzo might suffer from arrogance and an innate sense of entitlement but he wasn't stupid. She'd been a virgin when she met him and the most enthusiastic of lovers during their time together. He must realise he was the father.

'Of course it's yours,' she snapped. 'And this baby will be growing up with me as its mother, no matter how hard you try to take him away!'

As he put the photo back down with a shaking hand she saw a flash of anger in his eyes. 'Do you really think I would try to take a child away from its mother?'

'How should I know what you would or wouldn't do?' Her voice was really shaking now. 'You're a stranger to me now, Renzo—or maybe you always were. So eager to think badly of someone. So quick to apportion blame.'

'And what conclusion would you have come to,' he demanded, 'if you'd arrived home to find a seedy stranger leaving and a costly piece of jewellery missing?'

'I might have stopped to ask questions before I started accusing.'

'Okay. I'll ask them now. What was he doing there?'

'He turned up out of the blue.' She pushed away a sweat-damp curl which was sticking to her clammy cheek. 'He'd seen a photo of me at the ball. He was the last person I expected or wanted to see.'

'Yet you offered him a beer.'

Because she'd been afraid. Afraid of the damage Drake could inflict if he got to Renzo before she did because she hadn't wanted her golden present to come tumbling down around her ears. But it had come tumbling down anyway, hadn't it?

'I thought he would blackmail me by telling

you about my mother,' she said at last, in a low voice. 'Only now you know all my secrets.'

'Do I?' he questioned coolly.

She didn't flinch beneath that quizzical black gaze. She kept her face bland as her old habit for self-preservation kept her lips tightly sealed. He knew her mother had been a drug addict and that was bad enough, but what if she explained how she had funded her habit? Darcy could imagine only too well how that contemptuous look would deepen. Something told her there were things this proud man would find intolerable and her mother's profession was one of them. Who knew how he might try to use it against her?

Suddenly, she realised she would put nothing past him. He had accused her of all kinds of things—including using her virginity as some kind of bartering tool. Why shouldn't she keep secrets from him when he had such a brutal opinion of her?

'Of course you do. I'm the illegitimate daughter of a junkie—how much worse could it be?' She sucked in a deep breath and willed herself to keep her nerve. 'Look, Renzo, I know I'm expecting your baby and it must be the last thing you want but maybe we can work something out to our mutual satisfaction. I don't imagine you'll want anything more to do with me but I shan't make any attempt to stop you from having regular contact with your son. In fact, I'll do everything in my power to accommodate access to him.' She forced a smile. 'Every child should have a father.'

'That's good of you,' he said softly before elevating his dark eyebrows enquiringly. 'So what do you propose we do, Darcy? Perhaps you'd like me to start making regular payments until the baby is born? That way you could give up work and not have to worry.'

Hardly able to believe he was being so acquiescent, Darcy sat up in bed a little, nervously smoothing the thin sheet with her hand. 'That's a very generous offer,' she said cautiously.

'And in the meantime you could look for a nice house to live in for when our son arrives—budget no obstacle, obviously. In the country of your choice—that, too, goes without saying.'

She flashed him an uncertain smile. 'That's… that's unbelievably kind of you, Renzo.'

'And perhaps we could find you a street paved with gold while we're at it? That way you could bypass me completely and simply help yourself to whatever it was you wanted?'

It took a moment or two for her to realise he was being sarcastic but the darkly sardonic look on his face left her in no doubt. 'You were joking,' she said woodenly.

'Yes, I was *joking*,' he bit back. 'Unless you think I'm gullible enough to write you an open cheque so you can go away and bring up my son in whatever chaotic state you choose? Is that your dream scenario? Setting yourself up for life with a rich but absent babyfather?'

'As if,' she returned, her fingers digging into the thin hospital sheet. 'If I had gone looking for a wealthy sperm donor, I'd have chosen someone with a little more heart than you!'

Her words were forceful but as Renzo absorbed

her defiant response he noticed that her face had gone as white as the sheet she was clutching. 'I don't want to hurt you, Darcy,' he said, self-reproach suddenly rippling through him.

'Being able to hurt me would imply I cared.' Her mouth barely moved as she spoke. 'And I don't. At least, not about you—only about our baby.'

Her fingers fluttered over the swell of her belly and Renzo's heart gave a sudden leap as he allowed his gaze to rest on it. 'I am prepared to support you both.' His voice thickened and deepened. 'But on one condition.'

'Let me guess. Sole custody for you, I suppose? With the occasional access visit for me, probably accompanied by some ghastly nanny of your choice?'

'I'm hoping it won't come to that,' he said evenly. 'But I will not have a Sabatini heir growing up illegitimately.' He walked over to the window and stared out at the heavy winter clouds before turning back again. 'This child stands to inherit my empire, but only if he or she bears my name. So yes, I will support you, Darcy—but it will be on my terms. And the first, non-negotiable one is that you marry me.'

She stared at him. 'You have to be out of your mind,' she whispered.

'I was about to say that you have no choice but it seems to me you do. But be warned that if you refuse me and continue to live like this—patently unable to cope and putting our child at risk—I will be on my lawyers so fast you won't believe it. And I will instruct them to do everything in their power to prove you are an unfit mother.'

Darcy shivered as she heard the dark determination in his voice. Because wouldn't that bit be easy? If that situation arose he would start digging around in her past—and what a bonanza of further unsavoury facts he would discover. The drug addict bit was bad enough, but would the courts look favourably on the child of a prostitute without a single qualification to her name, one who was struggling to make ends meet and who had been admitted to hospital with severe exhaustion? Of course they wouldn't. Not when she was up against a world-famous architect with more money than he knew what to do with.

She licked her lips, naked appeal in her eyes. 'And if the marriage is unbearable, what then? If I *do* want a divorce sometime in the future, does that mean you won't give me one?'

He shook his head. 'I'm not going to keep you a prisoner, Darcy—you have my word on that. Perhaps we could surprise ourselves by negotiating a relationship that works. But that isn't something we need to think about today. My priority is to get you out of here and into a more favourable environment, if you agree to my terms.' His gaze swept over her, settling at last on her face so that she was captured by the dark intensity of that look. 'So…do I have your consent? Will you be my wife?'

A hundred reasons to refuse flooded into her mind but at that precise moment Darcy felt her son kicking. The unmistakable shape of a tiny heel skimmed beneath the surface of her belly and a powerful wave of emotion flooded over her. All she wanted was the best for her child, so how could she possibly subject him to a life like the one she had known? A life of uncertainty, with the gnawing sense of hunger. A life spent living on the margins of society with all the dangers that entailed. Secondhand clothes and having to make do. Free meals at school and charity trips to the seaside. Did she want all that for her little boy?

Of course she didn't.

She stared into Renzo's face—at all the unshakable confidence she saw written on his shuttered features. It would be easier if she felt nothing for him but she wasn't self-deluding enough to believe that. She thought how infuriating it was that, despite his arrogance and determination to get his own way, she should still want him. But she did. Her mind might not be willing but her flesh was very weak. Even though he'd wounded her with his words and was blackmailing her into marriage—she couldn't deny the quiver of heat low in her belly whenever he looked at her.

But sex was dangerous. Already she was vulnerable and if she fell into Renzo's arms and let him seduce her, wouldn't that make her weaker still? Once their relationship had been about passion but now it was all about possession and ownership. And power, of course—cold, economic power.

But a heady resolve flooded through her as she reminded herself that she'd coped with situations far worse than this. She'd cowered in cupboards and listened to sounds no child should ever have had to hear. She'd stood in courtrooms where people had talked about her future as if she weren't there, and she'd come through the other side. What was so different this time?

She nodded. 'Yes, Renzo,' she said, with a bland and meaningless smile. 'I will marry you.'

CHAPTER SEVEN

DARCY ALMOST LAUGHED at the pale-faced stranger in the mirror. What would the child she'd once been have thought about the woman whose reflection stared back at her? A woman dressed in clothes which still made her shudder when she thought about the price tag.

Her floaty, cream wedding gown had been purchased from one of Nicoletta's boutiques in Rome and the dress cleverly modified to conceal her baby bump but nonetheless, Darcy still felt like a ship in full sail. Her curls had been tied and tamed by the hairdresser who'd arrived at the Tuscan villa they were renting now that Vallombrosa had been sold, and from which they had been married that very morning. Darcy had wanted to wear normal clothes for her marriage to Renzo, as if to reinforce that it was merely a formality she was being forced to endure, but her prospective husband had put his foot down and insisted that she at least *looked* like a real bride...

'What difference does it make whether I wear a white dress or not?' she'd questioned sulkily.

'The difference is that it will feel more real if you wear white and carry flowers. You are a very beautiful woman, *cara*—and you will make a very beautiful bride.'

But Darcy had not felt at all real as she'd walked downstairs—though she couldn't deny that the dark blaze in Renzo's eyes *had* made her feel briefly beautiful. He had insisted they marry in Italy, presumably on the advice of his lawyers, who seemed to be running the whole show. But that part Darcy didn't mind. A wedding in Italy was bound to be more low-key than a wedding in England, where the press were much more curious and there was the possibility of someone from her past getting wind of it. With all the necessary paperwork in place, they had appeared before the civil registrar in the beautiful medieval town of Barga, with just Gisella and Pasquale as their witnesses. And just four days later they had been legally allowed to wed.

It had been the smallest and most formal of ceremonies in an ancient room with a high, beamed ceiling and although Gisella had voiced a slight wistfulness that they weren't having a religious service, Darcy, for one, was glad. It was bad enough having to go through something you knew was doomed, without having to do so before the eyes of the church.

But there had been a point when her heart had turned over and she'd started wishing it *were* real and that had been when Renzo had smiled at her once they'd been legally declared man and wife—his black eyes crinkling with a smile which had reminded her of the first time she'd met him. With his dark suit echoing the raven hue of his hair he'd made a sensational groom. And when he'd looked at her that way, he'd looked as if he actually *cared*—and she'd had to keep reminding herself that he didn't. It had all been an act for the benefit of those around them. She was here because she carried his child and for no other reason. But it had been difficult to remember that when he'd pulled her into his arms in full view of everyone.

She'd felt so torn right then. Her instinctive response had been to hug him back because that was how she always responded and they hadn't touched one another in any way since he'd turned up at the hospital with his ultimatum of a marriage proposal. But too much had happened for her to ever go back to that easy intimacy. How could she possibly lie in his arms and let him kiss her after all the cruel and bitter things which had been done and said? How could she bear to feel him deep inside her body when he'd been so eager to think badly of her?

She remembered freezing as his hands went to her expanded waist, feeling as if her body had suddenly turned to marble. 'Please, Renzo,' she'd whispered, her words a soft protest, not a plea.

But he hadn't let her go or changed his position. He'd dipped his head and spoke to her in low and rapid English, his fingers spanning the delicate fabric of the dress and increasing the points at which he'd been in contact with her.

'You are dressed to play the part of my bride and therefore you will act the part of my bride,' he'd said softly. 'Let's show the world that I have married a flesh-and-blood woman and not some pale-faced doll.'

It was then that he'd bent his head to claim her lips and it had been the weirdest kiss of her life. At first her determination had made it easy not to respond, but the sensation of his lips on hers had soon melted away her reservations and she'd sunk into that kiss with an eagerness she hadn't been able to disguise. She'd felt powerless beneath that brief but thorough exploration. She hadn't been able to hold back her gasp as she'd felt that first sweet invasion of his tongue. Heat had flooded over her. Her hands had reached up to hold on to him as the beat of her heart had become erratic but suddenly the movement had become about so much more than support. Suddenly she'd been clinging to him and revelling in the feel of all that rock-hard flesh beneath her fingertips. She'd wanted him so much that she hadn't even cared about his triumphant laugh of pleasure as he'd drawn his lips away because it had felt like for ever since he'd kissed her and it had tasted as delicious as having a drink after a dusty walk. Like the first hint of sweetness on your tongue when you badly needed the boost of sugar.

A kiss like that was the inevitable forerunner of intimacy and she must not let it happen again. She *dared* not…

'You look miles away.' Renzo's low drawl broke into Darcy's reverie and she watched his reflected body as he strolled in from the en-suite bathroom of their honeymoon suite, wearing nothing but a too-small white towel slung low over his hips. Crystalline droplets of water glittered like diamonds in his ebony hair and, despite knowing she shouldn't be affected by his near-nakedness, Darcy's brain was refusing to listen to reason and instead was sending out frantic messages to her pulse points.

It was the first time she'd seen him in a state of

undress since the night of the ball, when they'd come home and he'd made rapturous love to her. The night before Drake had visited and the necklace had disappeared and her whole world had come crashing down around her. A necklace Renzo had been prepared to write off in his eagerness to be rid of her. It all seemed like a dream now and yet suddenly all that honed silken flesh was haunting her with everything she'd been missing.

'So why,' he questioned, his voice growing sultry as he walked over and stood behind her and wound one long finger around an errant curl, 'did you let them put your hair up like that?'

Darcy swallowed because, from this position, far too much of his flesh was on show and his skin was still damp and soap-scented from the shower. 'The hairdresser said loose hair would look untidy.'

'But perhaps your husband doesn't like it to look *tidy*,' he mocked, pulling out one pearl-topped pin quickly followed by another. 'He likes it to look wild and free.'

'Which is slightly ironic given that you're the most precise and ordered man on the planet. And I don't remember giving you permission to do that,' she protested as he continued to remove them.

'I'm your husband now, Darcy. Surely I don't have to ask permission to take your hair down?'

Glad for the tumble of curls concealing the reluctant lust which was making her cheeks grow so pink, Darcy stared down at her lap. 'You're my husband in name only,' she said quietly.

'So you keep saying. But since we're sharing a room and a bed—'

'Yes, I wanted to talk to you about that. Tell me again *why* we're sharing a bed.'

'Because I need to keep an eye on you. I promised the midwife and the doctor.' His black eyes glittered. 'And that being the case—just how long do you think you can hold off from letting me make love to you when you're as jumpy as a scalded cat whenever I come near?'

'I think *making love* a rather inaccurate way to describe what we do,' she said, sighing as the last curl tumbled free and he added the final pearl pin to the neat little line he'd assembled on the dressing table. 'I wish we didn't have this wedding party tonight.'

'I know. You'd much rather be alone with me.'

'I didn't say that.'

'I know you didn't.' His dark gaze was full of mockery. 'But a wedding is a wedding and it is fitting to celebrate such a momentous occasion with friends. We don't want them thinking our union is in name only, do we?'

'Even if it is?'

'Even if it is. So why not try playing your part with enthusiasm? Who knows? Sooner or later you might find the feelings have rubbed off.' He stroked her hair. 'You won't have anything to do, if that's what's worrying you. The food, the wine and the guests have all been taken care of.'

'And in the meantime I'm to be brought down and paraded around in my white dress like a cow in the marketplace?'

He gave a soft laugh. 'Looking at you now, that's the very last image which springs to mind.'

He leaned forward, his hands on her shoulders, his mouth so close that she could feel his warm breath fanning the curls at the back of her neck. And suddenly his voice was urgent. 'Listen to me, Darcy. Neither of us wanted this to happen but it's what we've ended up with. I didn't want to get married and I certainly didn't plan to be a parent and neither, presumably, did you.'

Her lips folded in on themselves. 'No.'

In the reflection of the glass their eyes met and Renzo wondered why, even in the midst of all this unwanted emotional drama, their chemistry should be as powerful as ever. Did she feel it too? She must.

He could see her nipples pushing against the silk of her wedding gown and the darkening of her emerald eyes, but the tight set of her shoulders and her unsmiling lips were telling him quite clearly to stay away. Once he had known her body completely, but not any more. Her bulky shape was unfamiliar now, just as she was. She was spiky, different, wary. It was difficult being around her without being able to touch her and, oh, how he wanted to touch her. That had not changed, despite everything which had happened. Her skin was luminous, her eyes bright, and the rampant red curls even more lustrous than before. Didn't people say that a woman with child developed a glowing beauty all of her own? He'd never really thought about it before now— why would he?—but suddenly he knew exactly what they meant. He noticed the way she kept moving her hand to her growing bump, as if she were in possession of the world's greatest secret.

Pregnant.

His mouth dried. It was still hard for him to get his head around that. To believe that a whole new life was about to begin and he must be responsible for it. He'd meant it when he told her he never wanted a family and not just because he recognised all the potential for pain which a family could bring. He had liked his life the way it was. He liked having to answer to no one except himself. And if every female who'd fallen into his arms had thought they'd be the one to change his mind, they had been wrong. He'd managed to get to the age of thirty-five without having to make any kind of commitment.

Had Darcy done what nobody else had been able to do—and deliberately got herself pregnant? But if that had been the case then he must take his share of the blame. He'd been so blown away by discovering she was a virgin that he couldn't wait for her to go on the pill. He remembered the first time he'd entered her without wearing a condom and the indescribable pleasure he'd felt. It had been primitive, powerful and overwhelming but it hadn't been wise. He had allowed sexual hunger to blind him to reason. He'd allowed her to take sole responsibility for birth control and look what had happened. His heart clenched tightly with an emotion he didn't recognise as he stared into her green eyes.

'Did you mean to get pregnant?' he demanded.

He saw her flinch and compose herself before answering.

'No,' she answered quietly. 'I had some sort of

bug just before we went to Tuscany and I didn't realise…'

'That sickness would stop the pill from working?'

'Apparently.'

He raised his eyebrows. 'You weren't warned that could happen?'

'Probably—but with all the excitement about the holiday, I forgot all about it. It wasn't deliberate, Renzo—if that's what you're thinking.' She gave a wry smile. 'No woman in her right mind would want to tie herself to a man with ice for a heart, no matter how rich or well-connected he might be.'

And he believed her. He might wish he didn't but he did. His pale-faced bride in the floaty dress was telling the truth. 'So it seems we have a choice,' he said. 'We can go downstairs to our guests with good grace or I can take you kicking and screaming every inch of the way.'

'I won't embarrass you, if that's what you're worried about. I have no desire to make this any more difficult than it already is.'

'Good.'

Turning away, he dropped the towel and Darcy was treated to the distracting sight of his bare buttocks—each hard globe a paler colour than the dark olive of his back. She could see the hair-roughened power of those thighs and hated the way her stomach automatically turned over when she was doing everything in her power to fight her attraction.

'Tempted?' His voice was full of sensual mockery—as if he had the ability to read her expression even with his back turned. And she mustn't let him realise the accuracy of his taunt. If she wanted to protect herself, she mustn't let him get close to her—not in any way.

'Tempted by what—our wedding feast?' she questioned, sniffing at the air as if trying to detect the rich scents of cooking which had been drifting through the downstairs of the house all morning. 'Absolutely! To be honest, I do have a little of my appetite back. I could eat a horse.'

He gave a low laugh as Darcy scuttled into the bathroom where she spent a long time fiddling with her hair, and when she returned to the bed-room it was to find him dressed in that head-turning way which only Italian men seemed able to pull off. His dark suit emphasised his broad shoulders and powerful physique and he'd left his silk shirt open at the neck to reveal a sexy smattering of dark hair.

Uncertainly, she skimmed her hand down over her dress. 'Won't I look a little overdressed?'

'Undoubtedly,' he said drily. 'But probably not in the way you imagine.'

Her cheeks were still pink by the time they walked into the formal salon, which had been transformed with bridal finery by Gisella and a team of helpers from the nearby village. The cold winter weather meant they couldn't venture out into the huge grounds, but instead enormous fires were blazing and dark greenery festooned the staircases and fireplace. There were white flowers, white ribbons and sugar-dusted bon-bons heaped on little glass dishes. A tower-ing *croquembouche* wedding cake took pride of place in the dining room and on a table at the far end of the room—a pile of beautifully wrapped presents which they'd expressly stated they didn't want!

A loud burst of applause reached them as they walked in, along with cries of *'Congratulazioni!'* and *'Ben fatto, Renzo!'* The guests were all Renzo's friends, and although he'd told her he would pay for anyone she wanted to fly out to Tuscany for the celebration, Darcy hadn't taken him up on his offer. Because who could she invite when she'd lived her life a loner—terrified of forming any lasting commitments because of her past and the very real fear of rejection?

But she was pleased to see Nicoletta and not just because the glamourous Italian had helped with her trousseau. She'd realised that Renzo no longer had any lingering feelings about the woman he'd once had a 'thing' with. Darcy might have had an innate lack of self-confidence brought about by years of neglect, but even she couldn't fail to see the way her husband was looking at her tonight—a sentiment echoed by Nicoletta.

'I have never seen Renzo this way before,' she confided as Darcy sucked *limonata* through a straw. 'He can barely tear his eyes away from you.'

Darcy put her glass down. Because he was one of life's winners, that was why. He would want his marriage to succeed in the way that his business had succeeded and because his own parents' marriage had failed. That was why he was suddenly being so nice to her. And that scared her. It made her want to fight her instinctive attraction and to pull away from him. She didn't dare sink into a false state of security which would leave her raw and hurting when their marriage hit the skids. Because it would. Of course it would. How long would it take before her brilliant husband tired of her once reality kicked in? Had he even stopped to consider how a wife at the mercy of fluctuating hormones might fit into his calm and ordered life, let alone all the change which a new baby would bring?

But the evening fared better than she would have imagined. Renzo's obvious appreciation—

whether faked or not—seemed to make everyone eager to welcome her into their midst. His friends were daunting, but essentially kind. She met lawyers, bankers and an eminent heart surgeon and although each and every one of them spoke to her in perfect English, she vowed to learn Renzo's native tongue. Because suddenly, she caught a glimpse of what the future could be like if she wasn't careful. Of Renzo and their son speaking a language which the new *mamma* couldn't understand, with her inevitably being cast into the role of outsider.

And that could also be dangerous. Renzo had been reasonable before the marriage, but now she had his ring on her finger there was no longer any need for him to be. If she didn't watch her back she would become irrelevant. She looked around at the elegant room her new husband was renting for what she considered an extortionate amount of money. Could she really envisage their son willingly accompanying her back to an unknown England and an uncertain future if the marriage became unbearable, and leaving all this privilege and beauty behind?

But she ate, chatted and drank her *limonata*, waiting until the last of their guests had gone before following Renzo up to their suite, her heart rattling loudly beneath her ribcage. She undressed in the bathroom, emerging wearing a nightgown Nicoletta had insisted on gifting her. It was an exquisite piece for a new bride to wear and one designed to be removed almost as soon as it had been put on. Despite the hard curve of her baby bump, the ivory silk-satin coated her body as flatteringly as a second skin. Edged with ivory lace, the delicate fabric framed the skin above her engorged breasts and the moment she walked into the bedroom Darcy saw Renzo's eyes darken.

Her own answering tug of lust made her reconsider her decision to distance herself from him, because surely physical intimacy would provide some kind of release and lessen the unmistakable tension which had sprung up between them. But sexual intimacy could also be dangerous, especially in their situation. Something was growing inside her which was part of him and how could she bear to cheapen that by having sex which was nothing but a physical *release*?

She sat down heavily on the side of the bed, not realising that she'd given a little groan until he glanced across at her.

'You must be tired.'

She nodded, suddenly feeling as if all the stuffing had been knocked out of her. 'I am. But I need to talk to you.'

'About…?'

'Stuff.'

His smile was slow, almost wolfish. 'Be a little bit more explicit, Darcy. What kind of stuff?'

She shrugged. 'Where we're going to live. Practicalities. That kind of thing. And we need to decide soon because I won't be allowed to fly once I'm past thirty-six weeks.'

His self-assured shake of his head was tinged with the arrogant sense of certainty which was so much a part of him. 'I have my own jet, Darcy.

We can fly when the hell we like, provided we take medical support with us.'

She nodded as she pulled back the covers and got into the king-size bed, rolling over as far as possible until she had commandeered one side of it. 'Whatever,' she said. 'But we still need to discuss it.'

'Just not tonight,' he said, the bed dipping beneath his weight as he joined her. 'You're much too tired. We'll talk in the morning. And—just for the record—if you lie much closer to the edge, you're going to fall off it in the middle of the night and, apart from the obvious danger to yourself, you might just wake me up.' She heard the clatter as he removed his wristwatch and put it on the bedside table. 'Don't worry, Darcy, I'm reading your body language loud and clear and I have no intention of trying to persuade a woman to make love if she has set her mind against it.'

'Something which has never happened to you before, I suppose?' she questioned waspishly.

'As it happens, no,' he drawled. He snapped off the light. 'Usually I have to fight them off.'

Darcy's skin stung with furious heat. It was a lesson to never ask questions unless you were prepared to be stupidly hurt by the answer you might receive. Lying open-eyed in the darkness, almost immediately she heard the sounds of Renzo's deep and steady breathing and fearfully she foresaw a restless night ahead, plagued by troubled thoughts about the future. But to her surprise she felt warm and cosseted in that big bed with a brand-new wedding ring on her finger. And, yes, even a little bit *safe*.

As the keen Tuscan wind howled outside the ancient house Darcy snuggled down into her pillow and, for the first time in a long time, slept soundly.

CHAPTER EIGHT

RENZO INSISTED ON a honeymoon—cutting through Darcy's automatic protests when she went downstairs the following morning to find him in the throes of planning it. As she glanced at the road map he'd spread out on the dining-room table, she told him it would be hypocritical; he said he didn't care.

'Maybe you're just doing it to make the marriage look more authentic than it really is,' she observed, once she had selected a slice of warm bread from the basket. 'Since we haven't actually consummated it.'

'Maybe I am,' he agreed evenly. 'Or maybe it's because I want to show you a little of my country and to see you relax some more. You slept well last night, Darcy.' His black eyes gleamed but that was the only reference he made to their chaste wedding night, though she felt a little flustered as his gaze lingered on the swell of her breasts for slightly longer than was necessary. 'And we can consummate it anytime you like,' he said softly. 'You do realise that, don't you?'

She didn't trust herself to answer, though her burning cheeks must have given away the fact that the subject was very much on her mind. Sharing a bed so he could keep an eye on her was more straightforward in theory than in practice. Because a bed was a bed, no matter how big it was. And wasn't it true that at one point during the night her foot had encountered one of her new husband's shins and she'd instinctively wanted to rub her toes up and down his leg, before hastily rolling away as if her skin had been scorched?

She told herself their situation was crazy enough but at least she was in full control of her senses—and if she had sex with him, she wouldn't be. And she was afraid. Afraid that the pregnancy was making her prone to waves of vulnerability she was supposed to have left behind. Afraid he would hurt her if he saw through to the darkness at the very core of her. Because something had changed, she recognised that. He was being *gentle* with her in a way he'd never been before. She knew it was because she was carrying his baby but even so… It was intoxicating behaviour coming from such an intrinsically cold man and Darcy might have been bewitched by such a transformation, had she not instinctively mistrusted any type of kindness.

But she couldn't get out of the 'honeymoon' he was planning and perhaps that was a good thing. It would be distracting. There would be things to occupy them other than prowling around their beautiful rented villa like two wary, circling tigers, with her terrified to even meet those brilliantine black eyes for fear he would read the lust in hers and act on it…

So she packed her suitcase with the warm clothes which had also been purchased from Nicoletta's boutique and Renzo loaded it into the back of his sports car. The air was crisp as they drove through the mountains towards

Italy's capital, the hills softly green against the ice-blue sky as the powerful car swallowed up the miles. They stopped in a small, hilltop town for an early lunch of truffled pasta followed by *torta della nonna* and afterwards walked through narrow cobbled streets to the viewpoint at the very top, looking down on the landscape below, which was spread out like a chequered tablecloth of green and gold.

Darcy gave a long sigh as her elbows rested on the balustrade and Renzo turned to look at her.

'Like it?' he questioned.

'It's beautiful. So beautiful it seems almost unreal.'

'But there are many beautiful parts of England.'

She shrugged, her eyes fixed on some unseen spot in the distance. 'Not where I grew up. Oh, there were lots of lovely spaces in the surrounding countryside, but unless they're on your doorstep you need funds to access them.'

'Was it awful?' he questioned suddenly.

She didn't answer immediately. 'Yes,' she said, at last.

He heard the sadness in that single word and saw the way her teeth chewed on her bottom lip and he broke the silence which followed with a light touch to her arm. 'Come on. Let's try and get there before it gets dark.'

She fell asleep almost as soon as she got in the car and as Renzo waited in line at a toll gate, he found himself studying that pale face with its upturned freckled nose. Her red curls hung over one shoulder in the loose plait she sometimes wore and he thought that today she looked almost like a teenager, in jeans and a soft grey sweater. Only the bump reminded him that she was nearly twenty-five and soon going to have his baby.

Could they make it work? His leather-gloved fingers gripped the steering wheel as they moved forward. They *had* to make it work. There was no other choice, for he would not replicate his own bleak and fatherless childhood. He realised how little she'd actually told him about her own upbringing, yet, uncharacteristically, she had mentioned it today. And even though that haunted look had come over her face, he had found himself wanting to know more.

Wasn't that his role now, as husband and pro-spective father—to break the ingrained rules of a lifetime and find out as much about Darcy as possible? And wasn't the best way to do that to tell her something about *him*—the kind of stuff women had quizzed him about over years, to no effect. Because communication was a two-way street, wasn't it? At least, that was what that therapist had told him once. Not that he'd been seeing her professionally. To him she was just a gorgeous brunette he'd been enjoying a very physical relationship with when she'd freaked him out by telling him that she specialised in 'family therapy' and he could confide in her anytime she liked. His mouth thinned. Maybe he should have taken her up on her offer and gathered tips about how to deal with his cur-rent situation.

Darcy woke as they drove into the darkening

city whose ancient streets were deeply familiar to him from his own childhood. Taking a
circuitous route, Renzo found himself enjoying
her murmured appreciation of the Campidoglio,
the Coliseum and other famous monuments,
but he saw her jaw drop in amazement when he
stopped outside the sixteenth-century *palazzo*
on the Via Condotti, just five minutes from the
Spanish Steps.

'This isn't yours?' she questioned faintly, after
he'd parked the car and they'd travelled up to the
third floor.

'It is now. I bought it a couple of years ago,' he
replied, throwing open the double doors into the
main salon, with its high ceilings, gilded furniture and matchless views over the ancient city.
'Although the Emperor Napoleon III happened
to live here in 1830.'

'Here? Good grief, Renzo.' She stood in the
centre of the room, looking around. 'It's gorgeous. Like…well, like something you might
see in a book. Why don't you live here? I mean,
why London?'

'Because my work is international and I wanted to establish a base in London and the only way to do that properly is to be permanently on-site. I don't come back here as often as I should, but maybe some day.'

'Renzo—'

But he cut her off with a shake of his head. 'I know. You want to talk—but first you should un-pack. Get comfortable. We need to think about dinner but first I need to do a little work.'

'Of course,' she said stiffly.

'Come with me and I'll show you where the main bedroom is.'

Down a high-ceilinged corridor she followed him to yet another room which defied expecta-tion. The enormous wooden bed had a huge oil painting on the wall behind it, with elaborate silk drapes on either side, which made it seem as if you were looking out of a window onto moun-tains and trees. Darcy blinked as she stared at it. *How am I even* here? she wondered as she unwound the soft blue scarf which was knotted around her neck. She looked around the room, taking in the antique furniture, the silken rugs and the priceless artwork. Yet this staggering display of a wealth which many people would covet had little meaning for her. She didn't want *things*—no matter how exquisite they were. She wanted something which was much harder to pin down and which she suspected would always elude her.

She showered and changed into a cashmere tunic with leggings, padding barefoot into the salon to see her new husband at his computer, the familiar sight of one of his spectacular designs dominating the screen. But despite her noiseless entrance he must have heard her because he turned round, those dark-rimmed spectacles on his nose giving him that sexy, geeky look which used to make her heart turn over.

Still did, if she was being honest.

'Room to your satisfaction?' he questioned.

'Bit cramped, actually.'

He gave the glimmer of a smile. 'I know. Makes you claustrophobic. Hungry?'

'After that enormous lunch?' She wrinkled her nose. 'Funnily enough, I am.'

'Good.' His gaze roved over her, black eyes gleaming as they lingered a little too long. 'Looks like you have some catching up to do. You need to put some meat on those bones.'

She didn't reply to that. She wasn't going to tell him that she felt all breasts and bump. She wanted to tell him not to look at her body any more than was absolutely necessary.

And yet she wanted him to feast his eyes on it all day and make her glow inside.

'We could eat out,' he continued. 'I could take you to Trastevere, where you can eat some real Italian food and not something designed to try to appeal to an international palate. Or…'

She raised her eyebrows questioningly. 'Or?'

'We could order in pizza.'

'Here?'

'Why not?'

She shrugged as she stared through an arch to see a long, softly polished dining table set with tall silver candelabra. 'It seems way too grand.'

'A table is there to be used, Darcy, no matter what you're eating.'

It seemed decadent to find themselves there an hour later sitting on ormolu chairs, eating pizza with their fingers. As if they had broken into a museum and had temporarily set up home for the night.

'Good?' questioned Renzo as she popped the last piece of anchovy in her mouth and licked bright orange oil from her fingers.

'Heaven,' she sighed.

But it still seemed like a dream—as if it were happening to someone else—until they returned to the main salon and he asked her if she wanted mint tea. She didn't know what made her ask if he had hot chocolate and was surprised when he said he'd find out—and even more surprised when he returned a few minutes later with a creamy concoction in a tall mug. A potent memory squeezed at her heart as she took the drink from him—perhaps it was the sweet smell of the chocolate which made the words slip out before she could stop them.

'Wow! I haven't had this since...'

She caught herself on but it was too late.

'Since when?'

She kept her voice airy. 'Oh, nothing to interest you.'

'I'm interested,' he persisted.

She wondered if the shaky way she put the mug down gave away her sudden nerves. 'You've never been interested before.'

'True,' he agreed drily. 'But you're carrying my baby now and maybe I need to understand the mother of my child.'

And Darcy knew she couldn't keep avoiding the issue—just as she knew that to do so would probably intrigue him. Even worse—it might make him start to do his own investigative work and *then* what might he discover? Her heart sank. She knew exactly what he would discover. He would discover the reason for the deep dark shame which still festered inside her. She stared at the cooling chocolate, wishing she could turn back time and that this time he wouldn't ask. But you couldn't turn back time.

Just as you couldn't hide everything from a man who was determined to find out.

'It sounds so stupid—'

'Darcy,' he said, and his voice sounded almost *gentle*.

She shrugged. 'The chocolate reminded me of going out to a café when I was a little girl. Going to meet some prospective new foster parents.'

The image came back to her, unbearably sharp and achingly clear. She remembered strawberry-covered cakes gleaming behind glass frontage and the waitresses with their starched aprons. It had been one of those awkward but hope-ful meetings, with Darcy's social worker the referee—observing the interaction between a lit-tle girl who badly needed a home and two adults who wanted to give her one. They'd bought her hot chocolate in a glass mug, topped with a hillock of whipped cream and a shiny cherry on top. She'd stared at it for a long time before she could bear to disturb its perfection and when she'd drunk from it at last, the cream had coated her upper lip with a white moustache and made everyone laugh. The laughter was what she remembered most.

'Foster parents?' prompted Renzo, his deep voice dissolving the image.

'I didn't have the most…stable of childhoods. My mother was seventeen when she was orphaned. The roads were icy and her father took the bend too fast. They said he'd been…drinking. The police knocked at her door on Christmas Eve and said she'd better sit down. She once told me that after they'd gone she looked at the Christmas tree and all the presents underneath it. Presents which would never be opened…' Her voice trailed off. It had been a rare moment of insight and clarity from a woman whose life had been lived in pursuit of a constant chemical high. 'And it… Well, it freaked her out.'

'I'm not surprised. Did she have any relatives?'

Darcy shook her head. 'No. Well, there were some on the west coast of Ireland but it was too late for her to get there in time for the holiday. And she couldn't face intruding on someone else's Christmas. Being the spectre at the feast. Being pitied. So she spent the holiday on her own and soon after she went to Manchester with the money she'd inherited from her parents but no real idea about a career. In fact, she had nothing to commend her but her looks and her new-found ability to party.'

'Did she look like you?' he questioned suddenly.

'Yes. At least, at the beginning she did.' Darcy closed her eyes. She'd seen pictures of a feisty-looking redhead with green eyes so like her own. Seen her tentative smile as that young woman cradled the infant Darcy in her arms. She didn't want to tell Renzo what had happened to those looks—not when she couldn't bear to think about it herself. 'Before the drugs took hold. I was first taken into care at the age of two and I stayed there until I was eight, when my mother went to the courts to try to "win" me back, as she put it.'

'And did she succeed?'

'She did. She could put on a good performance when the need arose.'

'And what was that like—being back with her?'

Darcy swallowed. How much could she tell him? How much before a look of disgust crossed his face and he started to worry whether she might have inherited some of her poor mother's addictive traits—or the other, even more unpalatable ones? 'I'll leave that to your imagination,' she said, her voice faltering a little. 'She used me to interact with her dealer, or to answer the door when people she owed money to came knocking. There's nothing quite like a child in an adult's world for throwing things off balance.'

'And were you *safe*?' he demanded.

'I was lucky,' she said simply. 'Lucky that some kind social worker went over and above the call of duty and got me out of there. After that I went to the children's home—and, to be honest, I felt glad to be there.'

Not safe. Never really safe. But *safer*.

'And what did you do when you left there?'

'I came to London. Went to night school and caught up with some of the education I'd missed. It's why I ended up waitressing—nobody really cares if you've got a GCSE in Maths if you can carry a tray of drinks without spilling any.'

There was no sound in the room, other than the ticking of some beautiful freestanding clock which Darcy suspected might have been in place when Napoleon himself was living there.

'So...' His voice was thoughtful now; his black eyes hooded. 'Seeing as so much of your child-hood was spent with people making decisions for you, where would *you* like to live when our baby is born, Darcy?'

Not only was it not the reaction she'd been ex-pecting, it was also the most considerate ques-tion anyone had ever asked her and Darcy was terrified she was going to start blubbing—an over-the-top response from someone who'd ex-perienced little real kindness in her life. But she needed to keep it together. She'd been given enough false hope in life to build Renzo's offer up into something it wasn't.

'I would prefer to be in England,' she said slowly. 'Italy is very beautiful and I love it here but I feel like a foreigner.' She forced a laugh. 'Probably because I am.'

'My apartment in Belgravia, then?'

She shook her head. 'No. That won't do. I don't really want to go back there.'

He looked faintly surprised, as she supposed anyone might be if their new wife had just rejected a luxury apartment worth millions of pounds. 'Because?'

Should she tell him that she felt as if she'd lived another life there? She'd behaved like someone she no longer recognised—with her balcony bras and her tiny panties. She'd been nothing but his plaything, his always-up-for-it lover who was supposed to have been expendable before all this happened. How could she possibly reconcile that Darcy with the woman she was now and the mother she was preparing to be? How could she bear to keep reminding herself that he'd never planned for her to become a permanent fixture in his life? 'It's not a place for a baby.'

He raised his dark eyebrows. 'You're not suggesting we decamp to that tiny cottage you were renting in Norfolk?'

'Of course not,' she said stiffly. 'I think we both know that wouldn't work. But I would like to bring up the baby away from the city.' She licked her lips and her tongue came away with the salty flavour of capers. 'Somewhere with grass and flowers and a park nearby. Somewhere you can work from, so it doesn't necessarily have to be a long way out of London, just so long as it's *green*.'

He nodded and gave a small smile. 'I think we can manage that.'

'Thank you.'

Hearing her voice tremble, Renzo frowned. 'And you need to get to bed. Now. You look washed out.'

'Yes.' Awkwardly, she rose to her feet and walked across the room, feeling the soft silk of a Persian rug beneath her bare feet. But despite her initial reservations at having told him more than she'd ever told anyone, Darcy was amazed by how much *lighter* she felt. And she was grateful to him, too—stupidly relieved he'd managed to keep his shock and disgust to himself because most people weren't that diplomatic. All she wanted now was to climb into bed and have him put his arms round her and hold her very tight and tell her it was going to be all right. She closed her eyes. Actually, she wanted more than that. Could they be intimate again? Could they? Hadn't that book on pregnancy explained that sex in the latter stages was perfectly acceptable, just as long as you didn't try anything too adventurous?

For the first time in a long time, she felt the faint whisper of hope as she brushed her teeth, her hands wavering as she picked up the exquisite silk nightgown she'd worn on her wedding night, feeling the slippery fabric sliding between her fingers. It was beautiful but it made her feel like someone she wasn't. Or rather, somebody she no longer was. Wouldn't it be better to be less *obvious* if she wanted them relaxed enough to get to know one another again? Shouldn't it be a slow rediscovery rather than a sudden wham-bam, especially given the circumstances in which they found themselves?

Pulling on one of Renzo's T-shirts, which came to halfway down her thighs, she crept beneath the duvet and waited for him to come to bed.

But he didn't.

She tried to block the thoughts which were buzzing in her mind like a mosquito in a darkened room, but some thoughts just wouldn't go away. Because apart from that very public kiss when he'd claimed her as his bride, he hadn't come near her, had he? And something else occurred to her, something which perhaps *she* had been too arrogant to take into account. What if he no longer wanted her? If he no longer desired her as a man was supposed to desire a woman.

Tossing and turning in those fine cotton sheets, she watched the hand of the clock slowly moving. Soon her heart rate overtook the rhythmical ticking. Eleven o'clock. Then twelve. Shortly before one she gave in to the exhaustion which was threatening to crush her and Darcy never knew what time Renzo came to bed that night, because she didn't hear him.

CHAPTER NINE

'So... What do you think? Does it meet with your approval?' Renzo's eyes didn't leave Darcy's profile as they stood in the grounds of the imposing manor house. A seagull heading for the nearby coast gave a squawk as it flew overhead and he could definitely detect the faint tang of salt in the air. A light breeze was ruffling his wife's red curls, making them gleam brightly in the sunshine. How beautiful she looked, he thought—and how utterly unapproachable. And how ironic that the woman he'd spent more time with than anyone else should remain the most enigmatic woman of them all. 'You haven't changed your mind about living here now that it's actually yours?'

Slowly she turned her head and returned his

gaze, those glittering emerald eyes filled with emotions he couldn't begin to understand.

'Ours, you mean?' she said. 'Our first marital home.'

He shook his head. 'No. Not mine. I've spoken with my lawyers and the deeds have been made over to you. This is yours, Darcy. Completely yours.'

There was a moment of silence before she frowned and blinked at him. 'But I don't understand. We talked about it in Rome and I thought we'd agreed that a house in England was going to be the best thing for us.' She touched the ever-increasing girth of her belly. 'All of us.'

Was she being deliberately naïve, he wondered—or just exceptionally clever? Did she know she had him twisted up in knots and he didn't have a damned clue how to handle her? Because he was starting to realise that, despite his experience with women, he had no idea how to sustain a long-term relationship. He'd never had to try before. In the past he had always just walked away—usually because boredom had set in and he'd found the increasing demands tedious. But with Darcy he couldn't do that. Furthermore, he didn't want to. He wanted this baby so badly. It scared him just how badly. For a man who'd spent his life building things for other people—someone who considered himself urbane, sophisticated and cool—he hadn't reckoned on the fierce and primitive pride he felt at having created the most precious thing of all.

Life.

But Darcy remained a mystery he couldn't solve. She'd closed herself off to him since that night in Rome. She'd told him more about what he'd already known and the brutal facts had horrified him when he'd thought how tough her childhood must have been. He'd sat up for a long time that night after she'd rushed off to bed, drinking whisky until it had tasted stale in his mouth and gazing into space as he'd wondered how best to deal with the information. But he had dealt with it in the same way he dealt with anything emotional. He'd compartmentalised it. Filed it away, meaning to do something about it sometime but never getting round to it. She'd been asleep by the time he'd slid into bed beside her, her fecund body covered in one of his over-sized T-shirts, sending out a silent signal to stay the hell away from her. He remembered waking up to a beautiful Roman morning with the air all clear and blue. They'd gone out for coffee and *cornetti* and he hadn't said a word about her revelations and neither had she. She'd closed herself off from him again and he sensed that he could frighten her away if he didn't let her take this thing at her own pace.

But it hadn't worked.

Because now she looked at him so warily by day, while at night she still wore those infernal all-enveloping T-shirts and lay there quietly, holding her breath—as if daring him to come near. Had he handled it badly? If it had been any other woman he would have pulled her into his arms and kissed her until she was wet and horny—reaching for him eagerly, the way she used to.

But she was not *any other woman*. She was his

wife. His pregnant wife. How could he possibly ravish her when she was both bulky and yet impossibly fragile? Her skin looked so delicate—the blue tracery of her veins visible beneath its porcelain fragility—as if to even breathe on her might leave some kind of mark. And against her tiny frame, the baby looked huge—as if what her body had achieved was defying both gravity and logic, something which continued to amaze him. He'd even taken to working solely from home these past weeks, cancelling a trip to New York and another to Paris, terrified she was going to go into labour early even though there were still three weeks to go.

'Let's get inside,' he said abruptly. He unlocked their new front door and stood back to let her pass and their footsteps sounded loud in a house which was still largely empty, save for the few pieces of furniture which had already been delivered. But at least it wasn't cold. Despite the bite of early spring, the estate agent must have put on the heating—knowing that today was their first visit as official owners. The door swung closed behind them and he realised that she was still looking at him with confusion in her eyes.

'Why have you put the house in my name, Renzo? I don't understand.'

'Because you need to have some kind of insurance policy. Somewhere to call home if—'

'If the marriage doesn't work out?'

'That's right.'

She nodded as if she understood at last for her face had whitened, her eyes appearing darkly emerald against her pale skin.

'But you said—'

'I know what I said,' he interrupted. 'But I didn't factor in that the situation might prove more difficult than I'd anticipated.'

'You mean, my company?'

'No, not your *company*,' he negated impatiently, and then suddenly the words came bubbling out of nowhere, even though he hadn't intended to say them. 'I mean the fact that I want you so damned much and you don't seem to want me any more. The fact that you're always just out of reach.'

Shocked, Darcy stared at him. So she *hadn't* been imagining it. It *had* been lust she'd seen in his eyes and sexual hunger which made his body grow tense whenever she walked in the room. So why hadn't he touched her? Why did he keep coming to bed later and later while keeping their days ultrabusy by whisking her from property to property until at last she'd fallen in love with this East Sussex house which was only eight miles from the sea?

The truth was that he hadn't come near her since that night in Rome, when she'd told him everything about her mother. She felt her stomach clench. Actually, not quite everything— and hadn't she been thankful afterwards that she hadn't blurted out the whole truth? Imagine his reaction if she'd told him *that*, when he was already repulsed by what he knew, even though he'd done his best to hide it. And it was funny how the distance between a couple could grow almost without you realising. They'd been wary in each other's company. As the space between them had increased, she'd found the presence of her Italian husband almost...*forbidding*.

But if she had read it all wrong, then where did that leave her? If he hadn't been making value judgments about her, then why was she being so passive—always waiting for Renzo to make the first move? Yes, he was an alpha man with an instinctive need to dominate but it wasn't beyond the realms of possibility that he was simply being cautious around the baby she carried in her belly. He'd never had a pregnant lover before. He had taught her so much—wasn't this her chance to teach *him* something?

She walked over to him and, without warning, raised herself up on tiptoe to press her lips against his—feeling him jerk with surprise before sliding his arms around her waist to support her. Their tongues met as he instantly deepened the kiss but although Darcy could feel herself begin to melt, she forced herself to pull away.

'No,' she whispered. 'Not here. Not like this. Let's go upstairs. I need to lie down.'

'To bed?'

She took his hand and began to walk towards the stairs. 'Why not? It just happens to be about the only piece of furniture we have.'

An old-fashioned boat bed had been delivered to the master bedroom, her only instruction to the removal men being that the thick plastic covering the mattress should be taken away and disposed of. The wooden-framed structure dominated an otherwise empty room and on its king-size surface lay the embroidered coverlet she'd found when she and Renzo had been rooting around in one of Rome's antiques markets. She hadn't asked for it to be placed there but now it seemed like a sign that this had been meant to happen.

'Get undressed,' she whispered as she pulled off her overcoat and dropped it to the ground.

His eyes were fixed on hers as he removed his jacket, his sweater and trousers. Soon their discarded clothes were mingled in a heap beside the bed and at last Darcy stood in front of him. She was naked and heavily pregnant and feeling more than a little awkward, yet the look of desire in his eyes was melting away any last trace of shyness.

'I feel…bulky,' she said.

'Not bulky,' he corrected, his voice husky. 'Beautiful. Luscious and rounded—like the ripest of fruits about to fall from the tree.'

She shivered as he spoke and he took her into his arms.

'You're cold,' he observed.

She shook her head, still reeling from his words and the way he'd looked at her as he said them. 'No, not cold. Excited.'

'Me, too.' He gave a low laugh as he unfolded the coverlet and shook it out over the mattress.

'It almost looks as if we're planning on a picnic,' she said, her voice suddenly betraying a hint of uncertainty.

'That's exactly what I'm planning. I'm going to feast on you, *mia bella.*' But his face suddenly darkened as he pulled her into his arms and their bare flesh met for the first time in so long. 'I'm out of my depth here, Darcy,' he groaned. 'I've never made love to a pregnant woman before and I'm scared I'm going to hurt you. Tell me what you want me to do.'

'Just kiss me,' she whispered as they sank down onto the mattress. 'And we'll make it up as we go along.'

He kissed her for a long time. Tiny, brushing kisses at first and then deeper ones. And for a while, there were hard kisses which felt almost angry—as if he was punishing her for having kept him away for so long. But his anger soon passed and the kisses became exploratory as he licked his way inside her mouth and they began to play a silent and erotic game of tongues.

And then he started to touch her as Darcy had ached for him to touch her night after lonely night, waiting in vain for him to come to bed. At first he simply skated the palms of his hands down over her, as if discovering all the different contours and curves which had grown since last time they'd been intimate. No area of skin escaped the light whisper of his fingertips and she could feel every nerve ending growing acutely sensitised. Slowly, he circled each breast with his thumb, focussing his attention on each peaking nipple and putting his mouth there to lick luxuriously until she was squirming with frustrated longing. She wanted him to hurry yet she wanted him to take all day. But the rhythmical movements of his hand relaxed her completely, so that she was more than ready for his leisurely exploration of her belly when it came.

Their gazes met as his fingers splayed over the tight drum, his black eyes filled with question. 'This is okay?' he breathed.

'This is more than okay,' she managed, her voice growing unsteady as he slipped his hand down beyond to the silky triangle of hair, fingering her honeyed flesh so that she gasped with pleasure and the scent of her sex filled the air.

She reached for him, her pleasure already so intense that she could barely think straight as she tangled her fingers through his thick black hair, before hungrily reacquainting herself with the hard planes of his body. His shoulders were so broad and powerful; his pecs iron-hard. She loved the smattering of hair which roughened the rocky torso. Her fingertips skated lightly over his chest, feeling the rock-like definition of his abs. She thought his skin felt like oiled silk and she traced a lingering path over the dip of his belly before her fingers curled around the hardness of his erection, but he shook a cautionary head and pulled her hand away.

'It's been too long,' he said unevenly.

'You're telling me!'

'And I need to do it to you right now before I go out of my mind—the only question is, how?'

In answer, Darcy turned onto her side, wiggling her bottom against his groin in blatant invitation. 'Like this, I think.'

'But I can't see you.'

'Doesn't matter. And it never used to bother you. Go on.' She wiggled again and he groaned and she could feel how big he was as his moist tip positioned enticingly against her wet heat. 'You can feel me now and look at me later.'

He gave a low laugh and said something softly profound in Italian as he eased inside her. But the moan he gave was long and Darcy thought she'd never heard such an exultant sound before.

'Okay?' he bit out, holding himself perfectly still.

'More than okay,' she gasped.

'I'm not hurting you?'

'No, Renzo, but you're frustrating the hell out of me.'

His laugh sounded edgy but he began to move. In slow motion, he stroked himself in and out of her, his palms cupping her heavy breasts, his lips on her neck—kissing her through the thick curtain of curls. Darcy closed her eyes as she gave into sensation, forgetting that this was the only time they ever seemed truly equal. Forgetting everything except for the pulse points of pleasure throbbing throughout her body and the inexorable building of her orgasm as Renzo made love to her. Insistent heat pushed towards her. She could feel it coming—as inevitable as a train hurtling along the track—and part of her wanted to keep it at bay, to revel in that sweet expectation for as long as possible. But Renzo was close, as well—she could sense that, too. She'd had him come inside her too many times not to realise when he was near the edge. So she let go. Let pleasure wash over her—wave after sweet wave of it—until his movements suddenly quickened. He thrust into her with a deeper sense of urgency until at last he quivered and jerked and she felt the burst of his seed flooding into her.

Afterwards he lay exactly where he was and so did she. His skin was joined to hers, his body, too. It felt warm and sticky and intimate. Darcy just wanted to savour the moment and her deep sense of contentment as she waited for his verdict on that deeply satisfying interlude. Still remembering the dreamy things he'd murmured when they'd started to make love, part of her anticipating just what his next words might be. But when they came, it felt as if someone had ripped through that lazy contentment like a knife ripping through delicate silk.

'So... Was that my reward, I wonder, *cara mia*?' he questioned softly.

She pulled away from him, aware of the sudden pounding of her heart and the general indignity of turning to face a man when any kind of action was proving laborious. Especially when you were completely naked beneath the gaze of a pair of eyes which looked suddenly distant. She told herself not to read unnecessary stuff into his words—not to always imagine the worst. *He told you he wanted you and that he's been lusting after you...so go with that.*

'I'm afraid I'm not with you,' she said lightly.

'No?' He turned onto his back and yawned. 'You mean that wasn't your way of thanking me for buying you a home of your own? For finally getting the independence you must have craved for all these years?'

Darcy froze as the meaning of his words sank in and suddenly all that vulnerability which was never far from the surface began to rise in a dark unwanted tide. Groping down over the side of the bed, she managed to retrieve her overcoat and slung it over herself to cover her nakedness.

'Let's just get this straight.' Her voice was trembling. 'You think I had sex with you because you made me an overgenerous offer I hadn't actually asked for?'

'I don't know, Darcy.' His tone had changed. It rang out, iron-hard—like the sound of a hammer hitting against a nail. And when he turned his head to look at her, his eyes were icy. Like the black ice you sometimes saw when you were out on the roads in winter. Or didn't see until it was too late. 'I just don't get it with you. Sometimes I think I know you and other times I think I don't know you at all.'

'But aren't all relationships like that?' she questioned, swallowing down her fear. 'Didn't some songwriter say that if our thoughts could be seen, they'd probably put our heads in a guillotine?'

His eyes were narrowed as they studied her. 'And if I promised to grant you leniency, would you give me access to your thoughts right now?'

Darcy didn't react. She could tell him the rest of her story—and maybe if it had been any other man than Renzo she would have done so. But he had already insulted her by thinking she'd had sex with him just because he'd bought her this house. To him, it all boiled down to a transaction and he didn't really trust himself to believe anything different. He thought of everything in terms of barter between the sexes because he didn't really *like* women, did he? He'd told her that a long time ago. He might want her but he didn't trust her and even though she could try to gain that trust by confessing her biggest secret, surely it was too big a gamble?

'I'm just wondering why you seem determined to wreck what chance we have of happiness,' she said, in a low voice. 'We have a lovely new home and a baby on the way. We're both healthy and we fancy each other like crazy. We've just had amazing sex—can't we just enjoy that?'

Black eyes seared into her for a long moment until eventually he nodded, his hand snaking around her waist and pulling her closer so that she could feel the powerful beat of his heart.

'Okay,' he said as he stroked her hair. 'Let's do that. I'm sorry. I shouldn't have said that. It's just all very new to me and I don't do trust very easily.'

Silently, she nodded, willing the guilt and the tears to go away. All she wanted was to live a decent life with her husband and child. She wanted what she'd never had—was that really too much to ask? She relaxed a little as his hand moved from her hair to her back, his fingertips skating a light path down her spine. Couldn't she be the best kind of wife to him, to demonstrate her commitment through her actions rather than her words?

He leaned over her, black fire blazing as he bent his face close. 'Are you tired?'

She shook her head. 'Not a bit. Why?'

His thumb grazed the surface of her bottom lip and she could feel his body hardening against her as he gave a rueful smile. 'Because I want you again,' he said.

CHAPTER TEN

DARCY'S FIRST INKLING that something was wrong came on a Monday morning. At first she thought it was nothing—like looking up at the sky and thinking you'd imagined that first heavy drop of rain which heralded the storm.

Renzo was in London unveiling his design for the Tokyo art gallery at a press conference—having left the house at the crack of dawn. He'd asked if she'd wanted to accompany him but she'd opted to stay, and was in the garden pegging out washing when the call came from one of his assistants, asking if she was planning to be at home at lunchtime.

Darcy frowned. It struck her as a rather strange question. Even if she wasn't home, Renzo knew she wouldn't have strayed much further than the local village—or, at a pinch, the nearby seaside town of Brighton. All that stuff they said about pregnant women wanting to nest was completely true and she'd built a domestic idyll here while awaiting the birth of their baby. And hadn't that nesting instinct made her feel as though life was good—or as good as it could be? Even if sometimes she felt guilt clench at her heart unexpectedly, knowing that her husband remained ignorant of her biggest, darkest secret. But why rock the boat by telling him? Why spoil something which was good by making him pity her and perhaps despise her?

Placing the palm of her hand over the tight drum of her belly, she considered his assistant's question. 'Yes, I'm going to be here at lunchtime. Why?'

'Signor Sabatini just asked me to make sure.'

Darcy frowned. 'Is something wrong? Is Renzo around—can I speak to him, please?'

The assistant's voice was smooth but firm. 'I'm afraid that won't be possible. He's in a meeting. He said to tell you he'll be with you soon after noon.'

Darcy replaced the receiver, trying to lose the sudden feeling of apprehension which had crept over her, telling herself it was only because that fractured phone call felt a little like history repeating itself which had made her nervous. At least it hadn't been the same assistant who had stonewalled her attempts to get through to Renzo to tell him she was pregnant. That assistant had suddenly been offered a higher position in a rival company, something which Darcy suspected Renzo had masterminded himself. He'd seemed to want to put the past behind them as much as she did. *So stop imagining trouble where there isn't any.*

But it didn't matter how much she tried to stay positive, she couldn't seem to shake off the growing sense of dread which had taken root inside her. She went inside and put away the remaining clothes pegs—something her billionaire husband often teased her about. He told her that hanging out washing was suburban; she told him she didn't care. She knew he wanted to employ a cleaner and a housekeeper, and to keep a driver on tap instead of driving herself—in the fairly ordinary family car she'd chosen, which wasn't Renzo's usual style at all. The private midwife who lived locally and could be called upon at any time had been her only concession to being married to a billionaire.

But she wanted to keep it real, because reality was her only anchor. Despite Renzo's enormous power and wealth, she wanted theirs to be as normal a family as it was possible to be. And despite what she'd said when he'd railroaded her into the marriage, she badly wanted it to work. Not just because of their baby or because of their unhappy childhoods. She looked out the window, where her silk shirt was blowing wildly in the breeze. She wanted it to work because she had realised she loved him.

She swallowed.

She loved him.

It had dawned on her one morning when she'd woken to find him still sleeping beside her. In sleep he looked far less forbidding but no less beautiful. His shadowed features were softened;

the sensual lips relaxed. Two dark arcs of eye-lashes feathered onto his olive skin and his hair was ruffled from where she'd run her hungry fingers through it sometime during the night. She remembered the powerful feeling which had welled up inside her as the full force of her feelings had hit her and she wondered how she could have failed to recognise it before.

Of course she loved him. She'd been swept away by him from the moment she'd looked across a crowded nightclub and seen a man who had only had eyes for her. A once-in-a-lifetime man who'd made her feel a once-in-a-lifetime passion, despite the fact that he could be arrogant, tricky and, at times, downright difficult. And if fate—or rather pregnancy—had given her the opportunity to capitalise on those feelings and for passion to evolve into love, then she had to make the most of it. He might not feel the same way about her but she told herself that didn't matter because she had more than enough love to go round. She planned to make herself indispensable—not just as the mother of his child, but as his partner. To concentrate on friendship, respect and passion and reassure herself that maybe it could be enough. And if sometimes she found herself yearning for something more—well, maybe she needed to learn to appreciate what she had and stop chasing fantasy.

She spent the next hour crushing basil leaves and mashing garlic, trying to perfect a pesto sauce as good as the one they'd eaten in Rome on the last evening of their honeymoon. Then she picked a handful of daffodils and put them in a vase and had just sat down with a cup of tea to admire their yellow frilliness, when she heard the front door slam.

'I'm in here!' she called. She looked up to see Renzo framed in the doorway, her smile and words of welcome dying on her lips when she saw the darkness on his face. She put the cup down with a suddenly shaking hand. 'Is something wrong?'

He didn't answer and that only increased her fear. His hands were white-knuckled and a pulse was beating fast at his temple, just below a wayward strand of jet-black hair. She could sense an almost palpable tension about him—as if he was only just clinging on to his temper by a shred.

'Renzo! What's wrong?'

He fixed her with a gaze which was cold and hard. 'You tell me,' he said.

'Renzo, you're scaring me now. What is it? I don't understand.'

'Neither did I.' He gave a harsh and bitter laugh. 'But suddenly I do.'

From his pocket he took out an envelope and slapped it onto the table. It was creased—as if somebody had crushed it in the palm of their hand and then changed their mind and flattened it out again. On the cheap paper Renzo's name had been printed—and whoever had written it had spelt his surname wrong, she noted automatically.

His lip curved. 'It's a letter from your friend.'
'Which *friend*?'

'Shouldn't take you long to work that one out, Darcy. I mean, it isn't like you have a lot of friends, is it?' His mouth twisted. 'I never really understood why before. But suddenly I do.'

She knew then. She'd seen the look often enough in the past not to be able to recognise it. She could feel the stab of pain to her heart and the sickening certainty that her flirtation with a normal life was over.

'What does it say?'

'What do you think it says?'

'I'd like to hear it.' Was she hoping for some sort of reprieve? For someone to be writing to tell him that she'd once told a policewoman a lie—or that she'd missed school for a whole three months while her mother kept her at home? She licked her lips and looked at him. 'Please.'

With another contemptuous twist of his lips he pulled out the lined paper and began to read from it, though something told her he already knew the words by heart.

'"Did you know that Pammie Denton was a whore? Biggest hooker in all of Manchester. Ask your wife about her mam."'

He put the note down. 'It's pointless asking if you recognise the writing, since it's printed in crude capitals, but I imagine Drake Bradley must be the perpetrator and that this is the beginning of some clumsy attempt at blackmail. Don't you agree?' he added coolly.

Her normal reaction would have been to shut right down and say she didn't want to talk about it because that had been the only way she'd been able to cope with the shame in the past, but this was different. Renzo was her husband. He was the father of her unborn baby. She couldn't just brush all the dirty facts under the carpet and hope they would go away.

And maybe it was time to stop running from the truth. To have the courage to be the person she was today, rather than the person forged from the sins of yesterday. Her heart pounded and her mouth grew suddenly dry. To have the courage to tell him what maybe she should have told him a long time ago.

'I'd like to explain,' she said, drawing in a deep breath.

He gave her another unfathomable look as he opened up the refrigerator and took out a beer and Darcy blinked at him in consternation because cool and controlled Renzo Sabatini never drank during the day.

'Feel free,' he said, flipping the lid and pouring it into a glass. But he left the drink untouched, putting it down on the table and leaning against the window sill as he fixed her with that same cold and flinty stare. 'Explain away.'

In a way it would have been easier if he'd been angry. If he'd been hurling accusations at her she could have met those accusations head-on. She could have countered his rage with, not exactly *reason*—but surely some kind of heartfelt appeal, asking him to put himself in her situation. But this wasn't easy. Not when he was looking at her like that. It was like trying to hold a conversation with a piece of stone.

'My mother was a prostitute.'

'I think we've already established that fact and I think I know how prostitution works,' he said. 'So what exactly was it you wanted to *explain*, Darcy?'

It was worse than she'd thought because there *was* anger, only it was quiet and it was brooding and it was somehow terrifying. Because this was a man she scarcely recognised. It was as if his body had become encased in a thick layer of frost. As if liquid ice were running through his veins instead of blood.

She looked at him, wanting to convey a sense of what it had been like, trying to cling on to the certainty that there *was* something between her and Renzo—something which was worth fighting for. There had to be. He might take his parental responsibilities very seriously but deep down she knew he wouldn't have married her or contemplated staying with her unless they had *something* in common. 'She was an addict. Well, you know that bit. Only… Well, drugs are expensive—'

'And a woman can always sell her body?' he interposed acidly.

She nodded, knowing this time there was no

going back. That she needed to tell him the truth. The cruel, unedited version she'd never even been able to admit to herself before, let alone somebody else.

'She can,' she said. 'Until her looks start to go—and that tends to happen sooner rather than later where addicts are concerned. My mother had once been beautiful but her looks deserted her pretty quickly. Her…her hair fell out and then…'

She flushed with shame as she remembered the kids at school taunting her and she remembered that she'd once thought she would never tell him this bit, but she knew she had to. Because why was she trying to protect her mother's memory, when she had uncaringly gone out and wrecked as many lives as it took to get that hypodermic syringe plunging into her arm?

'Then her teeth,' she whispered, staring down at the fingers which were knotted together in her lap. 'And that was the beginning of the end, because she kept losing her dentures whenever she got stoned. She was still able to get clients—

only the standard of client went rapidly down-hill, as I'm sure you can imagine, and so did the amount of money she was able to charge.'

And that had been when it had got really scary. When she hadn't wanted to go home from school at night—even though she was so stressed that learning had become impossible. She'd never know what she'd find when she got there—what kind of lowlife would be leering at her mother, but, worse, leering at *her*. That had been where her mistrust of men had started and if that kindly social worker hadn't stepped in, she didn't know what would have happened. To most people, going back to the children's home would have seemed like the end of the road—but to her it had felt like salvation.

'It sounds a nightmare,' he said flatly.

Sensing a sea change in his mood, Darcy looked up but the hope in her heart withered immediately when she saw that his stony expression was unchanged. 'It was. I just want you to understand—'

'No,' he said suddenly, cutting across her

words. 'I'm not interested in understanding, Darcy. Not any more. I want you to know that something was destroyed when I received this letter.'

'I realise it was shocking—'

He shook his head. 'No. You're missing the point. I'm not talking about *shocking*. Human behaviour has always been shocking. I'm talking about trust.'

'T-trust?'

'Yes. I can see the bewilderment on your face. Is that word such an alien concept to you?' His mouth twisted. 'I guess it must be. Because I asked you, didn't I, Darcy? I asked you not once, but twice, whether you were keeping anything else from me. I thought we were supposed to be embracing a new openness—an honest environment in which to bring up our child, not one which was tainted by lies.'

She licked her lips. 'But surely you can understand why I didn't tell you?'

'No,' he snapped. 'I can't. I knew about your mother's addiction. Did you expect me to judge you when I found out how she paid for that addiction?'

'Yes,' she said helplessly. 'Of course I did. Because I've been judged by every person who ever knew about it. Being the daughter of Manchester's biggest hooker tends to saddle you with a certain reputation. People used to sneer at me. I could hear them laughing behind my back. And even though my social worker said it was because I was attractive and people would try to bring me down by exploiting my vulnerability, that didn't stop the hurt. It's why I left and came to London. It's why I never was intimate with a man before I met you.'

'Why you never accepted the gifts I tried to give you,' he said slowly.

'Yes!' she answered, desperately searching for a chink in the dark armour which made him look so impenetrable. Searching for the light of understanding in his eyes which might give her hope.

But there was none.

'You do realise, Darcy,' he questioned, 'that I can't live with secrets?'

'But there aren't any—not any more. Now you know everything about me.' Her heart was crashing wildly against her ribcage as she pleaded her case like a prisoner in the dock. 'And I need never lie to you again.'

He shook his head. 'You just don't get it, do you?' he said and his voice sounded tired. 'You knew that my childhood was tainted with secrets and lies. I told you a long time ago that I had trust issues and I meant it. How the hell can I ever trust you again? The truth is that I can't.' He gave a bitter laugh. 'And the even bigger truth is that I don't even want to.'

She was about to accuse him back. To tell him that he'd never trusted her in the first place. Look how he'd reacted when he'd discovered she was pregnant—showering her with suspicious questions when she'd lain in her hospital bed. He'd even thought she'd had wild sex with him just because he'd bought her a house. But her accusations remained unspoken because what was the point? No matter what she did or said, something in him had died—she could tell that from the emptiness in his eyes when he looked at her.

She nodded. 'So what do you want to do?'

He lifted the glass of beer now and drank it down in a draught, before slowly putting the empty glass back down on the table. 'I'm going back to London,' he said and Darcy could hear the bitterness in his tone. 'Because I can't bear to be around you right now.'

'Renzo—'

'No, please. Let's keep this dignified, shall we? Don't let's either of us say anything we might later regret, because we're still going to have to co-parent. We'll obviously need to come to some sort of formal agreement about that but it isn't something we need to discuss right now. I think you know me well enough to know that I won't be unreasonable.'

She nearly broke then—and what made it worse was the sudden crack in his voice as he said those words. As if he was hurting as much as she was. But he wasn't, was he? He couldn't be. Because nobody could possibly share this terrible pain which was searing through her heart and making it feel as if it had exploded into a million little pieces.

'You have the services of the midwife I've employed,' he continued. 'I spoke to her from the car on the way here and explained the circumstances and she has offered to move into the annex if that would make you feel more secure.'

'No, it would not make me feel more secure!' Darcy burst out. 'I don't want a total stranger living here with me.'

He gave a short, sarcastic laugh. 'No. I can't imagine you do. Living with a stranger isn't something I'd particularly recommend.'

And then he turned his back on her and walked out, closing the door with a click behind him. Darcy struggled to her feet to watch him walking down the garden path, past the washing line. The wind was blowing the sleeves of her shirt so that they flapped towards him, as if they were trying to pull him back, and how she wished they could. She considered rushing down the path after him, cumbersome in her late pregnancy, grabbing the sleeve of his handmade Italian suit and begging him to give her another chance. To stay.

But dignity was the one thing she had—maybe the only thing she had left.

So she watched him go. Watched him get into the back of the luxury car with the sunlight glinting off dark hair as blue-black as a raven's wing. His jaw set, he kept his gaze fixed straight ahead, not turning round as the powerful vehicle pulled away. There was no last, lingering look. No opportunity for her eyes to silently beseech him to stay.

The only thing she saw was his forbidding profile as Renzo Sabatini drove out of her life.

CHAPTER ELEVEN

AFTER HE'D GONE, a wave of desolation swept over Darcy—a desolation so bleak that it felt as if she were standing on the seashore in the depths of winter, being buffeted by the lashing sea. As his car disappeared from view she stumbled away from the window, trying to keep her wits about her, telling herself that her baby was her primary focus—her *only* focus—and she needed to protect the innocent life inside her. Briefly she closed her eyes as she thought about what Renzo had just found out—the shameful truth about her mother being a common prostitute. Would she be forced to tell her son about the kind of woman his grandmother had been? Yet surely if there was enough love and trust between her and her little boy, then anything was possible.

She swallowed because nothing seemed certain—not any more. She could understand her husband's anger but it had been impossible to penetrate. It had been a controlled reaction which shouldn't have surprised her—but another aspect of it had and that was what was confusing her. Because he hadn't threatened her with the full force of his wealth and power after making his sordid discovery, had he? Wouldn't another man—a more ruthless man—have pressured her with exposure if she didn't relinquish her role as primary carer to their baby?

Brushing away the sweat which was beading her brow, she knew she ought to sit down but she couldn't stop pacing the room as her jumbled thoughts tried to assemble themselves into something approaching clarity. His voice had been bitter when he'd spoken to her—almost as if he'd been hurt. But Renzo didn't *do* hurt, did he? Just as he didn't do emotion.

Surely he must recognise why she'd kept her terrible secret to herself—why the shame of the past had left her unable to trust anyone, just as *he* had been unable to trust anyone.

But Renzo had trusted *her*, hadn't he?

The thought hit her hard.

How many times had he trusted her?

He'd trusted her to take the pill and, even though that method of birth control had failed, he'd trusted her enough to believe her explanation.

He'd trusted her enough to confide in her when he first took her out to Tuscany and told her things he need never have said. And then, when they'd got back to England, he'd trusted her enough to give her the key to his apartment. He might not have wooed her with words but words were cheap, weren't they? Anyone could say stuff to please a woman and not mean it. But Renzo's actions had demonstrated trust and regard and that was pretty amazing. It might not have been love but it came a pretty close second. And she had blown it.

Tears welled up in her eyes as she stared at the yellow blur of daffodils in the vase. She had blown it by refusing to trust *him*—by not lowering the defences she'd erected all those years ago, when the police had asked her questions and she'd been too frightened to tell the truth, for fear her mother would go to jail. Renzo hadn't judged her because her mother had been an addict and he wouldn't have judged her because she'd been a prostitute—what had made him turn away with that tight-lipped face was the fact that she'd lied to him. Again and again, she'd kept her secrets to herself.

So what was she going to do about it? She looked at the bright blue sky outside, which seemed to mock her. Stay here with the midwife on standby, while she waited for the baby to arrive? Day following day with remorse and regret and the feeling that she'd just thrown away the best thing which had ever happened to her? Or have the courage to go to Renzo. Not to plead or beg but to put her feelings on the line and tell him what she should have told him a long time ago. It might be too late for him to take her back, but surely he could find it in his heart to forgive her?

Picking up the car keys, she went to the garage and manoeuvred the car out on the lane, sucking in lots of deep and calming breaths just as they'd taught her in the prenatal relaxation classes. Because she had a very precious passenger on board and there was no way she should attempt to drive to London if she was going to drive badly.

She let out the clutch and pulled away, thinking that she should have been scared but she'd never felt so strong or so focussed. She kept her mind fixed firmly on the traffic as the country roads gave way to the city and she entered the busy streets of London, glad she was able to follow the robotic instructions of the satnav. But her hands were shaking as eventually she drew up outside the towering skyscraper headquarters of Sabatini International. She left the car by the kerb and walked into the foyer, where a security guard bustled up importantly, barring her way.

'I'm afraid you can't park there, miss.'

'Oh, yes, I can. And it's Mrs, actually—or Signora, if you prefer. My husband owns this building. So if you wouldn't mind?' Giving a tight smile at his goggle-eyed expression, she handed him her car keys. 'Doing something with my car? I'd hate Renzo to get a ticket.'

She was aware of people staring at her as she headed for the penthouse lift but maybe that wasn't surprising. Among the cool and geeky workers milling around, she guessed a heavily pregnant woman with untidy hair would be a bit of a talking point. The elevator zoomed her straight up to the thirty-second floor, where one of Renzo's assistants must have been forewarned because she stood directly in Darcy's path, her fixed smile not quite meeting her eyes.

'Mrs Sabatini.' She inclined her head. 'I can't let you disturb him. I'm afraid your husband is tied up right now.'

Suddenly tempted by a wild impulse to ask whether Renzo had suddenly been converted to the pleasures of bondage, Darcy looked at her and nodded, but she didn't feel anger or irritation. The woman was only doing her job, after all. In the past she might have crumbled—gone scuttling back downstairs with a request that Renzo contact her when he had a free moment. But that was then and this was now. She'd overcome so much in her life. Seen stuff no child should ever see. She'd come through the other side of all that and yet...

Yet she had still let it define her, hadn't she? Instead of shutting the door on the past and walking away from it, she had let it influence her life.

Well, not any more.

'Watch me,' Darcy said as she walked across the carpeted office towards Renzo's office, ignoring the woman's raised voice of protest.

She pushed open the door to see Renzo seated at the top of a long boardroom table with six other people listening to what he was saying, but his words died away the moment he glanced up and saw her. Comically, every head swivelled in her direction but Darcy didn't pay them any attention; she was too busy gazing into the eyes of her husband and finding nothing in their ebony depths but ice. But she was going to be strong. As strong as she knew she could be.

'Darcy,' he said, his eyes narrowing.

'I know this isn't a convenient time,' she said, pre-empting his dismissal and drawing herself up as tall as she could. 'But I really do need to speak to you, Renzo. So if you people wouldn't mind giving us five, we'll make sure this meeting is rescheduled.'

Almost as if they were being controlled by some unseen puppet master, six heads turned to Renzo for affirmation.

He shrugged. 'You heard what the lady said.'

Darcy's heart was pounding as they all trooped out, shooting her curious looks on their way, but Renzo still hadn't moved. His expression remained completely impassive and only the sudden movement of his fingers as he slammed his pen onto the table gave any indication that he might be angry at her interruption.

'So what are you doing here?' he questioned

coolly. 'I thought we'd said everything there is to say.'

She shook her head. 'But we haven't. Or rather, I haven't. You did a lot of talking earlier only I was too shocked and upset to answer.'

'Don't bother,' he said, sounding almost... *bored*. 'I don't want to hear any more of your lies. You want to hold on to your precious secrets, Darcy? Then go right ahead! Or maybe find a man you trust enough to tell the truth.'

She let out a shuddered breath, struggling to get out the words she knew she needed to say. 'I trust you, Renzo. It's taken me this long to dare admit it, but I do. I trust you enough to tell you that I've been scared...and I've been stupid. You see, I couldn't believe someone as good as you could ever be part of my life and I thought...' Her voice stumbled but somehow she kept the tears at bay. 'I thought the only way I could hold on to it was to be the person I thought you'd want me to be. I was terrified that if you knew who I really was, that you would send me away—baby or no baby—'

'You can't—'

'No,' she said fiercely, and now the tears *had* started and she scrubbed them away furiously with the back of her fist. 'Let me finish. I should have celebrated my freedom from the kind of life I'd grown up in. I should have rejoiced that I had found a man who was prepared to care for me, and to care for our baby. I should have realised that it was a pretty big deal for you to tell me stuff about your past and give me a key to your apartment. I should have looked for the meaning behind those gestures instead of being too blind and too scared to dare. And rather than keeping my feelings locked away, I should have told you the biggest secret of all.'

He froze. 'Not another one?'

'Yes,' she whispered. 'The final one—and I'm about to let you in on it. Not because I want something in return or because I'm expecting something back, but because you need to know.' Her voice trembled but she didn't care. This was her chance to put something right but it was also the truth—shining, bold and very certain, no matter the consequences. 'I love you, Renzo. I've loved you from the first moment I saw you, when the thunderbolt hit me, too. Because that feeling never went away. It just grew and grew. When we made love that first time, it was so powerful—it blew me away. I've never wanted to be intimate with a man before you and I know that, if you don't want me, I won't ever find somebody who makes me feel the way you do.'

There was a silence when all Darcy could hear was the fierce pounding of her heart and she could hardly bear to look at him for fear that she might read rejection in his face. But she had to look at him. If she had learned anything it was that she had to face up to the truth, no matter how painful that might be.

'How did you get here?' he demanded.

She blinked at him in confusion. 'I…drove.'

He nodded. 'You parked your car in the middle of the city when you've only recently passed your test?'

'I gave the keys to the security guard.' She licked her lips. 'I told him I was your wife.'

'So you thought you'd just drive up here and burst into my building and disrupt my meeting with a few pretty words and make it all better?'

'I did...' She drew in a deep breath. 'I did what I thought was best.'

'Best for you, you mean?'

'Renzo—'

'No!' he interrupted savagely and now all the coldness had gone—to be replaced with a flickering fire and fury which burned in the depths of his black eyes. 'I don't want this. *Capisci?* I meant what I said, Darcy. I don't want to live this way, wondering what the hell I'm going to find out about you next. Never knowing what you're hiding from me, what secrets you're concealing behind those witchy green eyes.'

She searched his face for some kind of softening but there was none. And who could blame him? She'd known about his trust issues and she'd tested those issues to the limit. Broken them beyond repair so that they lay in shattered ruins between them. The hope which had been building inside her withered and died. Her lips pressed in on themselves but she would not cry. *She would not cry.*

She nodded. 'Then there's nothing more to be said, is there? I'll leave you so that you can get on with your meeting. You're right. I should have rung ahead beforehand, but I was afraid you wouldn't see me. I guess I would have been right.' She swallowed. 'Still, I'm sure we can work something out. The best and most amicable deal for our baby. I'm sure we both want that.' There was a pause as she took one long last look at him, drinking in the carved olive features, the sensual lips and the gleam of his black eyes. 'Goodbye, Renzo. Take…take good care of yourself.'

And then, with her head held very high, she walked out of his office.

Renzo stared at her retreating form, his mind spinning, aware of the door closing before opening again and his assistant rushing in.

'I'm sorry about that, Renzo—'

But he waved an impatient hand of dismissal until the woman left him alone again. He paced the floor space of his vast office, trying to concentrate on his latest project, but all he could think about was the luminous light of Darcy's green eyes and the brimming suggestion of unshed tears. And suddenly he found himself imagining what her life must have been like. How unbearable it must have been. All the sordid things she must have witnessed—and yet she had come through it all, hadn't she? He thought how she'd overcome her humble circumstances and what she had achieved. Not in some majorly high-powered capacity—she'd ended up waitressing rather than sitting on the board of some big company. But she'd done it with integrity. She'd financed her studies and read lots of novels while working two jobs—yet even when she'd been poured into that tight satin cocktail dress she had demonstrated a fierce kind of pride and independence. She'd never wanted to take a single thing from him, had she? She'd refused much more than she'd accepted and it hadn't been an act, had it? It had been genuine. From the heart. A big heart, which she'd been scared to expose for fear that she'd be knocked back, just as she must have been knocked back so many times before.

And he had done that to her. Knocked her back and let her go, right after she'd fiercely declared her love for him.

Her *love* for him.

He was prepared to give up that, along with her beauty and her energy, and for what?

For *what*?

A cold dread iced his skin as swiftly he left his office, passing his assistant's desk without saying a word as he urgently punched the button of the elevator. But the journey down to the basement seemed to take for ever, and Renzo's fist clenched as he glanced at his watch, because surely she would have left by now.

It took a moment for his eyes to focus in the gloomy light of the subterranean car park but he couldn't see her. Only now it wasn't his fist which clenched but his heart—a tight spear of pain which made him feel momentarily winded. What if she'd driven off after his callous rejection and was negotiating the busy roads to Brighton as she made her way back towards an empty house?

Pain and guilt washed over him as his eyes continued to scan the rows of cars and hope withered away inside him. And then he saw her on the other side of the car park in the ridiculously modest vehicle she'd insisted she wanted, in that stubborn way which often infuriated him but more often made his blood sing. He weaved his way through the cars, seeing her white face looking up at him as he placed the palm of his hand against the glass of the windscreen.

'I'm sorry,' he mouthed, but she shook her head.

'Let me in,' he said, but she shook her head again and began putting the key in the ignition with shaking fingers.

He didn't move, but placed his face closer to the window, barely noticing that someone from the IT department had just got out of the lift and was staring at him in open-mouthed disbelief.

'Open the door,' he said loudly. 'Or I'll rip the damned thing off its hinges.'

She must have believed him because the lock clicked and he opened the door and sat in the passenger seat before she could change her mind. 'Darcy,' he said.

'Whatever it is you want to say,' she declared fiercely, 'I don't want to hear it. Not right now.'

She'd been crying. Her face was blotchy and her eyes red-rimmed and he realised that he'd never seen her cry—not once—she, who probably had more reason to cry than any other woman he'd known.

He wanted to take her in his arms. To feel her warmth and her connection. To kiss away those drying tears as their flesh melted against each other as it had done so many times in the past. But touching was cheating—it was avoiding the main issue and he needed to address that. To face up to what else was wrong. Not in her, but in him. Because how could she have ever trusted him completely when he kept so much of himself locked away?

'Just hear me out,' he said, in a low voice. 'And let me tell you what I should have told you a long time ago. Which is that you've transformed my life in every which way. You've made me feel stuff I never thought I'd feel. Stuff I didn't want to feel, because I was scared of what it might do to me, because I'd seen hurt and I'd seen pain in relationships and I didn't want any part of that. Only I've just realised...' He drew in a deep breath and maybe she thought he wasn't going to continue, because her eyes had narrowed.

'Realised what?' she questioned cautiously.

'That the worst pain of all is the pain of not having you in my life. When you walked out of my office just now I got a glimpse of just what that could be like—and it felt like the sun had been blotted from the sky.'

'Very poetic,' she said sarcastically. 'Maybe your next girlfriend will hear it before it's too late.'

She wasn't budging an inch but he respected her for that, too. If it had been anyone else he wouldn't have stayed or persisted or cared. But he was fighting for something here. Something he'd never really thought about in concrete terms before.

His future.

'And there's something else you need to know,' he said softly. 'And before you look at me in that stubborn way, just listen. All those things I did for you, things I've never done for anyone else— why do you think they happened? Because those thunderbolt feelings never left me either, no matter how much I sometimes wished they would. Because I wanted our baby and I wanted you. I like being with you. Being married to you. Waking up to you each morning and kissing you to sleep every night. And I love you,' he finished simply. 'I love you so much, Darcy. Choose what you do or don't believe, but please believe that.'

As she listened to his low declaration of love, Darcy started to cry. At first it was the trickle of a solitary tear which streaked down her cheek and ended up in a salty drip at the corner of her mouth. She licked it away but then more came, until suddenly they were streaming her face but the crazy thing was that she didn't care.

In the close confines of the car she stared at him through blurry vision and as that vision cleared the dark beauty of his face no longer seemed shuttered. It seemed open and alight with a look she'd always longed to see there, but never thought she would. It was shining from his eyes as a lighthouse shone out to all the nearby ships on the darkest of nights. 'Yes, I believe you,' she whispered. 'And now you need to hold me very tightly—just to convince me I'm not dreaming.'

With a soft and exultant laugh Renzo pulled her into his arms, smoothing away the tangle of curls before bending his head to kiss away the tears which had made her cheeks so wet. She clung to him as their mouths groped blindly together and kissed as they'd never really kissed before. It was passionate and it was emotional—but it was superseded by a feeling so powerful that Darcy's heart felt as if it were going to spill over with joy, until she suddenly jerked away—tossing her head back like a startled horse.

'Oh, I love you, my beautiful little firecracker,' he murmured as she dug her fingers into his arms.

'The feeling is mutual,' she said urgently. 'Only we have to get out of here.'

He frowned. 'You want to go back to Sussex?'

She flinched and closed her eyes as another fierce contraction gripped her and she shook her head. 'I don't think we're going to make it as far as Sussex. I know it's another two weeks away, but I think I'm going into labour.'

It was a quick and easy birth—well, that was what the cooing midwives told her, though Darcy would never have described such a seismic experience as *easy*. But she had Renzo beside her every step along the way. Renzo holding her hand and mopping her brow and whispering things to her in Italian which— in her more lucid moments—she knew she shouldn't understand, but somehow she did. Because the words of love were universal. People could say them and not mean them. But they could also say them in a foreign language and you knew—you just *knew*—what they meant and that they were true.

It was an emotional moment when they put Luca Lorenzo Sabatini to her breast and he began to suckle eagerly, gazing up at her with black eyes so like his daddy's. And when the midwives and the doctor had all left them, she glanced up into Renzo's face and saw that his own eyes were unusually bright. She lifted her hand to the dark shadow of growth at his un-shaven jaw and he met her wondering gaze with a shrug of his powerful shoulders. Was he *crying*?

'Scusi,' he murmured, bending down to drop a kiss on his son's downy black head before briefly brushing his lips over Darcy's. 'I'm not going to be a lot of use to you, am I—if I start letting emotion get the better of me?'

And Darcy smiled as she shook her head. 'Bring it on,' she said softly. 'I like seeing my strong and powerful man reduced to putty by the sight of his newborn baby.'

'It seems as if my son has the same power over me as his mother,' Renzo responded drily. He smoothed back her wild red curls. 'Now. Do you want me to leave and let you get some rest?'

'No way,' she said firmly, shifting across to make space for him, her heart thudding as he manoeuvred his powerful frame onto the narrow hospital bed. And Darcy felt as if she'd never known such joy as when Renzo put his arm around her and hugged her and Luca close. As if she'd spent her life walking along a path— much of the time in darkness—only to emerge into a place full of beautiful light.

'It's not the most comfortable bed in the world, but there's room on it for the three of us. And I want you beside me, Renzo. Here with me and here with Luca.' And that was when her voice cracked with the emotion which had been building up inside her since he'd told her he loved her. 'In fact, we're never going to let you go.'

EPILOGUE

KICKING OFF HER shoes and flopping onto the sofa with a grateful sigh, Darcy frowned as Renzo handed her a slim leather box. 'What's this?' she questioned.

He raised his brows. 'Isn't the whole point of presents that they're supposed to be a surprise?'

'But it isn't my birthday.'

'No,' he said steadily. 'But it's Luca's.'

'Yes.' The box momentarily forgotten, Darcy looked into her husband's ebony eyes and beamed. Hard to believe that their beautiful son had just celebrated his first birthday. A year during which he'd captivated everyone around him with his bright and inquisitive nature, which at times showed more than a glimpse of his mother's natural stubbornness.

Today, with streamers and balloons and a bit

too much cake, they'd held a party for all his little friends in Sussex—while the mothers had each sipped a glass of pink champagne. Confident in her husband's love, and freed from the shame of the past, Darcy had started to get to know people—both here in Sussex and in their London house, as well as the beautiful Tuscan villa where they spent as many holidays as they could. Invitations had started to arrive as, for the first time in her life, she'd begun to make friends. Real friends—though her best friend was and always would be her husband. She looked at him now with bemusement.

'Open it,' he said softly.

She unclipped the clasp and stared down at the necklace. A triple row of square-cut emeralds gleamed greenly against the dark velvet and there was a moment of confusion before she lifted her eyes to his. She remembered how, just after Luca's birth, he'd gone to see Drake Bradley and persuaded the blackmailer to tell him where he'd pawned the diamond necklace. He'd got Drake's confession on tape of course and, with the threat of prosecution and prison very real, Renzo had surprised everyone by refusing to turn him in to the police. Instead, he'd given Drake a chance—offering him a job working on the site clearance of one of his new projects in England. Employment Drake had eagerly accepted—possibly his first ever legitimate job and one which, against all the odds, he excelled at. For ever after, he treated Renzo with the dedication and loyalty a badly beaten dog might display towards the man who had rescued him.

Keep your friends close... Renzo had whispered to her on the night when the diamond necklace was back in his possession, after she'd finished remonstrating with him for putting himself in possible danger. But his expression had been rueful as she had held the dazzling diamond neckpiece as if it were an unexploded bomb.

'I guess you wouldn't get a lot of pleasure out of wearing this now?'

Darcy had shaken her head. 'Nope. Too much

bad history. And I'm no big fan of diamonds, you know that.'

The next day Renzo had returned the piece to the charity, telling them to auction it again. And he hadn't mentioned jewellery since.

Until now.

'Renzo,' Darcy whispered, her gaze dazzled by the vivid green fire of the emeralds. 'This is too much.'

'No,' he said fiercely. 'It isn't. Not nearly enough. If I bought up the contents of every jewellery shop in the world, it still wouldn't be enough. Because I love you, Darcy. I love what you've given and shown me. How you've made me the man I am today, and I like that man much better than the one I was before.' His voice dipped, his gaze dark as the night as it blazed over her. 'And didn't I always say you should have emeralds to match your eyes?'

Very wet eyes now, she thought, but she nodded as he kissed away her tears. And the jewels were suddenly forgotten because, when it boiled down to it, they were just pretty pieces of stone. The most precious thing Darcy had was her love—for her son and for her husband. And the chance to live her life without shame and without secrets.

'Come here, *mia caro*,' she whispered, practising her ever-increasing Italian vocabulary as she pulled him down onto the sofa next to her.

'What did you have in mind?'

'I just want to show you…' she smiled as her fingertip stroked his cheek until she reached the outline of his sensual mouth, which softened as she edged her own lips towards it '…how very much I love you.'

* * * * *

MILLS & BOON®
Large Print – July 2017

Secrets of a Billionaire's Mistress
Sharon Kendrick

Claimed for the De Carrillo Twins
Abby Green

The Innocent's Secret Baby
Carol Marinelli

The Temporary Mrs Marchetti
Melanie Milburne

A Debt Paid in the Marriage Bed
Jennifer Hayward

The Sicilian's Defiant Virgin
Susan Stephens

Pursued by the Desert Prince
Dani Collins

Return of Her Italian Duke
Rebecca Winters

The Millionaire's Royal Rescue
Jennifer Faye

Proposal for the Wedding Planner
Sophie Pembroke

A Bride for the Brooding Boss
Bella Bucannon

0617 Rom LP

MILLS & BOON®
Large Print – August 2017

The Italian's One-Night Baby
Lynne Graham

The Desert King's Captive Bride
Annie West

Once a Moretti Wife
Michelle Smart

The Boss's Nine-Month Negotiation
Maya Blake

The Secret Heir of Alazar
Kate Hewitt

Crowned for the Drakon Legacy
Tara Pammi

His Mistress with Two Secrets
Dani Collins

Stranded with the Secret Billionaire
Marion Lennox

Reunited by a Baby Bombshell
Barbara Hannay

The Spanish Tycoon's Takeover
Michelle Douglas

Miss Prim and the Maverick Millionaire
Nina Singh